W. (Wilhelm) Ihne

The history of Rome

Vol. III.

W. (Wilhelm) Ihne

The history of Rome
Vol. III.

ISBN/EAN: 9783742865854

Manufactured in Europe, USA, Canada, Australia, Japa

Cover: Foto ©ninafisch / pixelio.de

Manufactured and distributed by brebook publishing software (www.brebook.com)

W. (Wilhelm) Ihne

The history of Rome

THE HISTORY OF ROME.

VOL. III.

LONDON: PRINTED BY
SPOTTISWOODE AND CO., NEW-STREET SQUARE
AND PARLIAMENT STREET

THE HISTORY OF ROME.

BY

WILHELM IHNE.

ENGLISH EDITION.

VOL. III.

LONDON:
LONGMANS, GREEN, AND CO.
1877.

CONTENTS

OF

THE THIRD VOLUME.

FIFTH BOOK.

THE WARS FOR SUPREMACY IN THE EAST.

CHAPTER I.

THE SECOND MACEDONIAN WAR, 200-196 B.C.

	PAGE
Immediate results of the peace	3
Rome after the peace of Carthage	3
Motives for a new war with Macedonia	3
Condition of Macedonia	5
Condition of the Greek states	6
Philip, king of Macedonia	6
Extent of the kingdom of Egypt	7
The Syrian kingdom of the Seleucidæ	8
Character of the Seleucidæ	10
Antiochus the Great	10
Alliance between Antiochus and Philip	10
Philip's expedition into Asia Minor	11
Dicæarchus	11
The islands of Crete and Rhodes	11
Wanton attacks of Philip on independent Greek cities	12
Coalition of Greek cities against Philip	13
Capture of Samos by Philip	13
Sea-fights of Chios and Lade	14
Ravaging of Caria by Philip	15
Philip's campaign on the Hellespont	16

Dispute between Athens and the Acarnanians	17
Interference of Rome	18
Attalus at Athens	18
Declaration of war against Philip	19
Siege of Abydos by Philip	19
Policy of the Romans	19
Successful efforts of the Romans to secure the neutrality of Antiochus	20
Roman embassy to Philip ending in a declaration of war	20
Taking of Abydos	22
Operations of Attalus	23
Attitude of Ætolians	24
Attitude and policy of the Greek states	24
Ineffectual efforts of the Romans to secure the active aid of the Achaeans	24
Sulpicius Galba sent to Macedonia	25
Capture of Chalcis by the Roman fleet	26
Philip's invasion of Attica	27
Sparta and the Achaean league	28
Neutrality of the Achaeans	28
Renewed devastation of Attica	29
First military operations of the Romans	29
Alliance of Dardanians, Illyrians, and Athamanians with Rome	30
Neutrality of the Ætolians	31
Defensive measures of Philip	31
First campaign of Romans and their allies	32
Ætolians, allied with Rome, invade Thessaly	33
Operations of the allied fleet	33
Demonstrations at Athens hostile to Philip	35
Result of the first campaign	36
Mutiny in the Roman army	36
Neutrality of Antiochus	37
Continued neutrality of the Achaeans	38
Opening of the third campaign	38
T. Quinctius Flamininus	39
Abortive negotiations of peace	41
Forcing of the pass of the Aous	42
Ætolian devastation of Thessaly	43
Flamininus in Thessaly	43
Last operations of Flamininus in the campaign	43
Naval operations	44

	PAGE
Congress at Sicyon	44
Alliance between Rome and the Achaeans	45
Philocles at Corinth	46
Argos captured by Philocles	47
Second peace negotiations	47
Terms offered and refused	48
Armistice of two months	49
Flamininus continued in the command as proconsul	50
Device of Philip for the alliance of Nabis	51
Argos handed over to Nabis	51
Bœotia joins the Roman alliance	·52
Strength of the Roman army	53
Strength of the Macedonian army	54
Battle of Cynoscephalæ	54
Victory of the Romans	57
The phalanx and the maniple	58
Share of the Ætolians in the battle	59
Taking of Leucas	59
Loss of Caria	60
Defeat of Macedonians in Peloponnesus	60
Philip's wish for peace	60
Motives of Flamininus for granting favourable terms	61
Peace negotiations	61
Pretensions of the Ætolians	62
Truce	62
Disturbances in Bœotia	63
Assassination of Brachyllas	63
The senate as umpire in Greek affairs	64
Conditions of peace	65
Difficulties of a new settlement of Greek affairs	66
The three great fortresses	67
Solemn declaration of the independence of Greece	68
Discontent of the Ætolians	69
The affairs of the Peloponnesus	70
Character and practices of Nabis	71
War against Nabis	71
Attack upon Sparta	72
Capture of Gythium	73
Assault on Sparta	73
Peace with Nabis	74
The Spartan exiles not reinstated	75
Unsatisfactory character of the new settlement	75

	PAGE
The Greek fortresses evacuated by the Roman garrisons	76
Restriction of Greek democracy	77
The war in a military point of view	77
Auxiliary troops in the Roman army	78
The naval war	78
Political object of the war	79
Roman estimation of the Greek character	79

CHAPTER II.

THE SYRO-ÆTOLIAN WAR, 192-189 B.C.

The success of Roman diplomacy in isolating Macedonia	81
Ambitious schemes of Antiochus	81
The Rhodians opposed to the encroachments of Antiochus	83
Change in the policy of Rome with regard to Antiochus	84
Conquests of Antiochus in Asia and Thrace	85
Roman embassy to Antiochus	85
Negotiations broken off and resumed	86
Hannibal's flight from Carthage	87
Renewed negotiations	89
Antiochus attempts to secure allies	89
Diplomatic congress in Rome	90
Final rupture delayed	91
The frequency of embassies	92
Last Roman embassy in Asia	93
Hannibal's intrigues in Carthage	93
Suspicions cast on Hannibal	94
Difficulties of the Roman ambassadors	95
Antiochus urged by the Ætolians to declare war	95
His determination to reject the Roman demands	95
Negotiations broken off	97
Plans for the war	97
Discontent in Greece	98
Gythium attacked by Nabis	99
Roman delay and indecision	100
Philopœmen's campaign against Nabis	101
Discontent in Greece	102
Macedonian alliance secured by Rome	102
The Achaeans leagued with Rome	103
Resentment of the Ætolians	104
Resolution to invite Antiochus	104

	PAGE
Slowness of Roman preparations	105
Federal institutions in Greece	105
Demetrius seized by the Ætolians	107
Ætolian force sent to Sparta	108
Assassination of Nabis	109
Sparta incorporated in the Achaean league	109
Landing of Antiochus in Greece	110
Hannibal in a secondary station	111
Antiochus declared commander of the Ætolians	111
Attempt to gain Chalcis	112
Disappointment of the king	112
His proposals rejected by Philip	113
The Achaeans declare for Rome	113
Capture of Chalcis	115
Antiochus invades Thessaly	116
Antiochus at Chalcis	117
Roman military movements	117
Proportion of Romans and allies in the legions	118
Commencement of the war by the Romans	119
Formal declaration of war	119
Roman armaments	121
Departure of Acilius Glabrio	122
Advance of the Romans and Macedonians into Thessaly	123
Position of Antiochus at the pass of Thermopylæ	124
Forcing of the pass	125
Return of Antiochus to Asia	126
Continued resistance of the Ætolians	126
Offence given to Philip	127
Submission of the Ætolians given in and retracted	128
Pacification of the Peloponnesus	129
Policy of Rome with regard to acquisitions in Greece	130
Co-operation of Philip secured	131
Armistice granted to the Ætolians	132
Character of the campaign	132
Operations of the fleet	133
Battle of Corycus	134
Roman reply to the Ætolian embassy	135
L. Cornelius Scipio elected consul	136
New armaments	136
Third armistice granted to the Ætolians	137
March of Scipio to the Hellespont	138
Loyalty of Philip	139
Antiochus' preparations to meet the Romans	139

	PAGE
The Greek towns in Asia Minor	139
Sestos and Abydos	140
Defeat of the Rhodian fleet	140
Operations of the Roman fleet	140
Difficulty of provisioning the fleets	142
Measures of Antiochus on the approach of the Roman army	143
Fruitless attack on Pergamum	144
Ineffectual attempts at peace negotiations	144
Battle of Sida or Aspendus	145
Battle of Myonnesus	147
Effect of the victory of Myonnesus	148
Sack of Phocæa	149
Second attempts at peace negotiations	149
Conditions of peace rejected by Antiochus	151
P. Scipio's sickness and transactions with Antiochus	151
The Roman army at Ilium	152
Battle of Magnesia	153
Effect of the battle of Magnesia	157
Antiochus sues for peace	157
Political congress in Rome for the settlement of the affairs of the East	158
Conflicting interests of Pergamum and Rhodes	159
Senatorial commission to decide disputed claims	160
Settlement of the affairs of Asia	160
Enlargement of Pergamum	162
Prolonged stay of the Roman army in Asia	162
Expedition to Crete	163
Manlius Vulso's plans of a campaign, irrespective of orders from Rome	163
Expedition against the Galatians	164
The Galatians	165
Return of the Roman army	167
New rising of the Ætolians	168
Siege of Ambracia	170
Peace with the Ætolians	171
The condition of Greece	173
Constant interference of Rome	174
Seeds of discord at Sparta	175
Disturbances at Sparta put down by the Achaeans	177
Roman interference	179
Secession of Messenia from the Achaean league	183
Death of Philopoemen	183
Vigorous policy of Lycortas	184

CHAPTER III.

THE THIRD MACEDONIAN WAR, 171–168 B.C.

	PAGE
Hannibal's death	186
Unsettled state of affairs	188
Ungenerous policy towards Macedonia	188
Charges brought against Philip	190
Philip's preparations for war	191
Murder of Demetrius	193
Character and policy of Perseus	195
Anti-Roman feeling in Greece	197
Frightful condition of Greece	198
Eumenes in Rome as accuser of Perseus	199
Alleged attempt to murder Eumenes	200
Dispute between the senate and the consul Popillius Laenas	202
Moderation shown by the senate	205
Condition of Macedonia and Greece	206
The war voted by the centuries	207
Roman preparations	208
Perseus endeavours to preserve peace	209
Perseus isolated and outwitted	210
Armistice concluded	212
Permanent character of Roman policy	213
Weakness of Macedonia and Perseus	214
Defensive measures of Perseus	215
Roman invasion of Thessaly	215
Pass of Tempe fortified by Perseus	216
Combat of Callicinus	217
Combat of Phalanna	218
Destruction of Haliartus	219
Treatment of Thebes, Coronea, and Chalcis	220
Ætolians charged with cowardice	220
Revolt of Epirus	221
Campaign of 170 B.C.	222
Plundering of Abdera	223
Gentius of Scodra	224
Appius Claudius in Illyria	225
Perseus' operations in Illyria and Ætolia	226
Q. Marcius Philippus	228
Marcius invades Macedonia	230
Retreat of Perseus	231

xii   CONTENTS OF

	PAGE
Roman advance delayed	233
Operations of the fleet	234
Attempt to form a coalition against Rome	236
Negotiations of Perseus with Eumenes	237
Continued neutrality of Syria	238
Rhodian policy	239
Gallic mercenaries refused by Perseus	242
Alliance of Gentius with Perseus	242
Condition of the Roman land forces	243
Condition of the Roman fleet	244
L. Æmilius Paullus	244
Roman armaments	246
Defeat of Gentius	247
Rhodian mediation	248
Battle of Pydna	249
Conduct of Perseus	251
Perseus' flight	252
Collapse of the Macedonian monarchy	253
Capture of Perseus	254
Macedonia left in nominal independence	256
Congress at Amphipolis	258
Settlement of Macedonia	258
Settlement of Illyria	260
Greece after the war	261
Relations of Achaia to Rome	262
Achaeans exiled to Italy	265
Distress of Rhodes	266
Fate of Polyaratus	267
Rhodes admitted into the Roman alliance	270
Humiliation of Eumenes of Pergamum	272
Roman intrigues to cause disunion in the family of the Attalidæ	274
Galatian inroads encouraged	275
Eumenes refused admittance to the senate	276
Servility of Prusias	277
War between Syria and Egypt	278
Interference of Rome	279
Results of the battle of Pydna	280
Æmilius Paullus' journey through Greece	281
Congress of Amphipolis	282
Devastation of Epirus	283
News of the battle of Pydna brought to Rome	284

	PAGE
Æmilius Paullus' return	285
Opposition to his triumph	285
His domestic affliction	287
Triumph of Æmilius Paullus	287
Character of Æmilius Paullus	289

CHAPTER IV.

THE FALL OF MACEDONIA AND GREECE, 148-146 B.C.

Condition of Macedonia after the war	291
Treatment of Perseus	292
Andriscus a pretender to the Macedonian crown	292
Defeated by Cæcilius Metellus	293
Macedonia a Roman province	294
Last period of Greek independence	295
Athenian quarrel with Oropus	296
Achaia after the war	298
Return of the exiles delayed	299
Polybius one of the exiles	300
Condition of Peloponnesus on the return of the Achaean exiles	301
Political unfitness of the returned exiles	302
New rupture between Achaia and Sparta	303
Roman decree to break up the Achaean league	305
Outburst at Corinth against Rome	306
Critolaus captain of the Achaean league	307
Agitation against Rome	308
Meeting of the Achaeans at Corinth	308
War declared	309
Battle of Scarphea	310
Lucius Mummius	311
Defeat of the Achaeans	312
Destruction of Corinth	313
Acts of punishment	314
Good services of Polybius	315
Roman settlement of Greece	316
Changed condition of Greece	317
Causes of the downfall of Greece	318

CHAPTER V.

THE THIRD WAR WITH CARTHAGE, 149–146 B.C.

	PAGE
Roman feelings towards Carthage	320
Hostility of Masinissa to Carthage	321
Roman unfairness	323
Continued aggression of Masinissa restrained by Rome	324–327
New aggression of Masinissa	327
Cato as ambassador in Carthage	327
Cato's views with regard to Carthage	328
Cato's views adopted	329
Internal strife at Carthage	330
War with Masinissa	330
Roman interference	332
Carthaginian endeavours to deprecate the hostility of Rome	333
War decreed	333
Submission of Carthage tendered	334
The Carthaginians disarmed	336
Carthaginians refuse to give up their town to destruction	337
Resolve to defend the town	339
Postponement of the siege	340
Difficulty of ascertaining the topography of Carthage	341
Site of Carthage	343
The ports of Carthage	346
Siege of Carthage begun	347
Result of the first campaign	348
Death of Masinissa	349
Settlement of the succession in Numidia	349
The second campaign	351
Scipio Æmilianus elected consul	352
Perilous situation of Mancinus	353
Scipio takes the command	354
Abandonment of the suburb	356
Entrance to harbour blocked up	357
New entrance to harbour made	357
Sea fight	358
Attack on the dock quay	359
Terms of surrender rejected by Hasdrubal	360
Capture of Nepheris	361

	PAGE
Capture of Carthage	361
The Roman deserters	363
Destruction of Carthage	363

CHAPTER VI.

THE WARS IN SPAIN UP TO THE FALL OF NUMANTIA, 200–133 B.C.

Geographical condition of political power	367
Geographical seclusion of Spain	368
Character of the native Spaniards	369
First Roman possessions in Spain	370
Wars in Spain imperfectly known	371
Distance of Spain	372
No Roman colonisation in Spain	373
Character of the wars in Spain	374
Numerous reverses of the Romans in Spain	376
Roman victories	377
Oppression of Roman magistrates in Spain	378
Treaty of Gracchus with Spanish towns	380
War with the Bellians	381
Disastrous campaign of Fulvius Nobilior	382
Treaty of Marcellus	383
Lusitania in arms	384
Campaign of Lucullus	384
Treachery of Lucullus	385
Atrocities of Sulpicius Galba	386
Trial and acquittal of Galba	388
Viriathus	389
Murder of Viriathus	393
Subjection of the Lusitanians	394
War with Numantia	395
Treaty of Pompeius	396
Defeat of Mancinus	399
Treaty of Mancinus rejected by the Senate	400
Lepidus routed by the Vaccæans	402
Scipio elected consul	403
Discipline restored in the Roman army	404
Siege of Numantia	405
Capture of Numantia	406
Pacification of Spain	406

CHAPTER VII.

THE CONQUEST OF NORTHERN ITALY. THE WARS WITH THE GAULS, LIGURIANS, AND ISTRIANS.

	PAGE
Annalistic method of history not applicable	408
Our knowledge of the Italian wars	409
The Gauls during the Hannibalic war	409
Gauls continue the war under Hamilcar	410
Capture of Placentia	411
Reverses of the Romans	411
Campaign of Cethegus and Minucius, consuls of 197 B.C.	412
Campaign of Marcellus and Furius, consuls of 196 B.C.	413
Campaign of Cornelius Merula, consul of 193 B.C.	414
The Boians exhausted and subdued	415
Colonisation of conquered districts	415
War in Istria	417
The Ligurians	417
The frequent wars with the Ligurians	418
Defeat of Marcius Philippus	420
Campaign of Æmilius Paullus	420
Transference of Ligurians to Southern Italy	421
Pisæ reinforced	421
Colony of Luna founded	422
Popillius Lænas' war with the Statellates	422
Appius Claudius' war with the Salassians	423
Conquest of Illyria and Dalmatia	425
Wars in Sardinia and Corsica	425
The formation of the Roman empire facilitated by the geographical position of Rome and Italy, and by the submission of the Romans to the government of laws	426–427–428

FIFTH BOOK.

THE WARS FOR SUPREMACY IN THE EAST.

CHAPTER I.

THE SECOND MACEDONIAN WAR, 200–196 B.C.

THE peace of the year 201 B.C. between Rome and Carthage had not put an end to hostilities in all the countries which had been the theatre of the Hannibalic war. The Gauls were not included in its provisions, and were now carrying on the war on their own account with a degree of determination and energy which they had failed to display for a long time. Nor could Spain be transferred without much difficulty from the dominion of Carthage to that of Rome. The Spaniards had hoped to find in the Romans their deliverers from a hateful oppression, not new and more exacting masters. The proud and warlike nation, impatient of control, struggled hard, before it would submit. At the same time the periodical insurrections in Corsica and Sardinia continued as before, and in Italy the long war had brought about a state of things which imperatively demanded permanent peace, if order and national wealth were to be restored. In spite of all these considerations, the peace with Carthage was scarcely concluded, when the Roman senate decided on commencing a new war, a war not like those of Cisalpine Gaul, Liguria, and Spain, which were only continuations of the Punic war, but one coolly planned for a political purpose and forced upon an enemy who wished nothing more than to live in peace with Rome.

Four years before the end of the Hannibalic war, in the year 205 B.C., Rome had come to terms with king Philip of Macedonia. This step had become necessary, because Rome's allies, the Ætolians, had already given up the unequal struggle with Philip, in which they had

BOOK V.
200-196 B.C.

not been strenuously supported by Rome.¹ The exhaustion of Italy in the latter part of the Hannibalic war, which had been the cause of this neglect of the Ætolians, made it imperative for the senate to purchase the peace with Philip even at the sacrifice of some Roman possessions in Illyria.² That a peace concluded under such circumstances and such conditions could not be a sincere and lasting one is very clear. The Romans looked upon it only as a suspension of hostilities,³ and resolved to use the first opportunity to make Philip suffer for the troubles which he had caused them by interfering in the Hannibalic war. Yet it was not solely a feeling of revenge by which the cool and far-seeing statesmen in the Roman senate were determined in their policy. It was the well-founded apprehension which the alliance between Philip and Hannibal in the course of the second Punic war had called forth. It seemed at that dark period that the power of Rome would soon be at an end, if Philip acted as boldly as his ally, and carried the war into Italy. After the humiliation of Carthage, a similar danger, it is true, was not to be feared, at least for some time to come; but who would undertake to answer for the future? Once already Carthage had recovered with wonderful rapidity after a great fall, and had become more formidable to Rome in the second war than she had been in the first. Though Masinissa, the king of Numidia, was now a troublesome neighbour and relentless foe of the Carthaginians, yet he afforded the Romans no absolute security. No reliance could be placed on the permanence of a Numidian kingdom. The condition of the unsteady barbarian communities in the north of Africa changed as easily as

---

[1] See vol. ii. p. 414. Livy, xxix. 12: Neglectæ eo biennio res in Græcia erant. Itaque Philippus Ætolos, desertos ab Romanis, cui uni fidebant auxilio, quibus voluit conditionibus, ad petendam et paciscendam subegit pacem.

[2] Livy, xxix. 12: Iusserunt (pacem) omnes tribus, quia verso in Africam bello omnibus aliis in præsentia levari volebant bellis.

[3] Appian, ix. 3: Καὶ τὰς συνθήκας οὐδέτεροι βεβαίους οὐδ' ἀπ' εὐνοίας ἐδόκουν πεποιῆσθαι. Justin, xxx. 3: Grata legatio Romanis fuit, causam belli adversus Philippum quærentibus, quia insidiatus eis temporibus Punici belli erat.

the sand of their native desert. The very existence of these states depended mostly on the life and prosperity of a chief, and their policy was equally shifting and uncontrollable. Syphax had once been the great enemy of Carthage. He became afterwards her useful ally. Who could vouch for Masinissa's fidelity, if the crafty Punians should offer a sufficient temptation to gain him over to their side? Above all, Hannibal was yet living, and was actually guiding the policy of the Carthaginian states. His name, even after the defeat at Zama, had hardly lost anything of the terror with which during a seventeen years' war it had fascinated all Italy. It was, therefore, a natural and well-considered plan of the men who ruled the Roman state, to make use of the first leisure which the peace with Carthage afforded for the purpose of humbling Macedonia. The actual conquest of the lands on the east side of the Adriatic was not yet aimed at; at most, a moderate extension of the possessions in Illyria was contemplated as the prize of victory.[1]

Macedonia alone, as things then stood, was not dangerous to the Roman republic. It was no longer the Macedonia of the second Philip and of the great Alexander. The endless wars and the inroads of the Northern barbarians had depopulated and impoverished the country. But it was still the first power on the eastern peninsula, and king Philip, who had ruled it since the year 221 B.C. had displayed unusual military abilities which had procured for him an undisputed pre-eminence in Greece. He had humbled the Ætolian confederation, the most powerful of his enemies, notwithstanding its alliance with the Romans. The Achaean League, which was second in

---

[1] This may be inferred from the policy adopted after the successful termination of the war, and from the auguries which the priests announced before it was undertaken. A solemn sacrifice and prayers having been ordered, the consuls reported to the senate (Livy, xxxi. 5, 7): Rem divinam rite peractam esse et precationi annuisse deos haruspices respondere, lætaque exta fuisse et prolationem finium, victoriamque, et triumphum portendi. Some extension of territory was therefore expected, though the war was not simply undertaken for conquest.

BOOK V.
200-196 B.C.

importance among the Greek states, had ever since the time of Aratus been entirely subject to Macedonian influence. The Acarnanians, Bœotians, Locrians, Dorians, Phocians, Eubœans were intimately connected with Macedonia as friends and allies. Besides these states, which were more or less independent, the kings of Macedonia possessed, as direct dependencies, the whole of Thessaly, and several places in different parts of Greece, the most valuable of which were the three great fortresses, Demetrias on the Pagasæan Gulf, Chalcis on the Euripus, and Corinth. Holding these towns with strong garrisons, they commanded the most important military positions in Greece.

Condition of the Greek states.

After the reverses sustained by the Ætolians, no single state on the whole of the Greek continent was in a position to counterbalance the preponderance of Macedonia. The Athenians were anti-Macedonian in their politics, and did their utmost to counteract the supremacy of the leading state; but their power was small, and it was only the memory of the days of past greatness that secured for this degenerate people any consideration or respect. In the Peloponnesus the anti-Macedonian party was headed by Sparta, more from old enmity to the Achaeans than for any other reason; and the insignificant states of Messenia and Elis were united with Sparta in like opposition to Achaia. It was only on the islands and in different commercial towns on the coasts of Asia Minor and of Thrace that the old Greek spirit of restless activity survived together with the pride of local independence. Before all others, it was the island of Rhodes which, as champion for the ancient republican and city freedom, stoutly opposed the encroachments of the military monarchies.

Philip, king of Macedonia.

Philip was a thorough soldier-king, like the first successors of Alexander the Great. He knew nothing of any duties of a king but the extension of his territory. Always on the watch for the chance of new conquests, he led a restless life, full of excitement and vicissitudes.

Personally courageous, active, and skilful in war, he had made himself the terror of all those states which seemed to offer a tempting spoil. He delighted in destroying works of art, in devastating towns and lands, in torturing and murdering conquered enemies. From year to year he became more reckless, more grasping, and more savage. At last he ceased to be a Greek king, and assumed the character of an Eastern despot, self-willed and tyrannical, jealous, and cruel. His most intimate friends and counsellors were no longer safe from a sudden outbreak of suspicion, which was equivalent to a sentence of death.[1] Thus he gradually alienated most of his friends, and created for himself throughout Greece well-founded distrust and bitter enmity. Not content with the success which he had had in his war with the Ætolians and the Romans, he contemplated extending his territory on the east after the conclusion of the treaty of peace with Rome, and he flattered himself with the deceitful hope that, even after the overthrow of Carthage, the Romans would stand by as quiet spectators of his aggrandisement. By this shortsightedness and love of conquest he brought about complications and difficulties which enabled and even invited the Romans to turn their arms against him.

The king of Egypt, Ptolemæus Philopator, had died in 205 B.C. leaving a son only five years old. Under the first three Ptolemies, from 321 to 220 B.C. Egypt had enjoyed a century of great prosperity, and had grown to power and opulence. The kingdom comprehended not only the valley of the Nile properly so called, but had been extended under these warlike and victorious rulers far into Asia, Africa, and Europe, thus relinquishing the secure and defensive position of Egypt proper, and offering tempting objects of attack to the ambition and cupidity of its neighbours. It had acquired in Africa the important Greek city of Cyrene, in Asia the provinces of Palestine and Phœnicia together with Cœlesyria; besides the island of Cyprus and many

[1] Diodorus, xxviii. ffr. 2 and 3.

towns on the coast of Asia Minor, a number of islands in the Ægean Sea, and even in Europe some districts on the Thracian coast. By these conquests Egypt was completely brought out of its former isolation; and by her possessions on the opposite coasts, and by the importance of her commercial towns, she had risen to be a great maritime power. Such a kingdom could be protected and kept together only by able and vigorous rulers; the distant possessions especially were not easily defended. The kings of Macedonia and Syria saw their advantage, and without any other pretext or excuse than the desire to make use of so good an opportunity, they formed an alliance in 205 B.C. for the purpose of robbing the youthful Ptolemæus Epiphanes.[1]

The Syrian kingdom of the Seleucidæ.

The ally of Philip in this project for robbing or eventually dismembering Egypt was Antiochus III. of Syria, the fourth successor of Seleucus, the founder of the Syrian monarchy and of the royal house of the Seleucidæ.[2] Of the three great states into which the vast Macedonian empire was broken up, the kingdom of Syria was in size the largest, and her rulers arrogated to themselves the first rank among the so-called Successors of Alexander the Great. It extended from the coasts of the Mediterranean, beyond the two great rivers Euphrates and Tigris, over the high lands of Persia, as far as the Indus and the Jaxartes (the modern Sir Daria), thus including the empire of Persia proper with the renowned old capitals of Babylon, Susa, Persepolis, and Ecbatana. But, notwithstanding its enormous size, and the claim derived therefrom, the empire of Syria was in point of fact weaker than either Egypt or Macedonia. It was a helpless Colossus,

---

[1] Polybius (xv. 20) severely censures this policy: οὐδ' οὖν καθάπερ οἱ τύραννοι βραχεῖαν δή τινα προβαλλόμενοι τῆς αἰσχύνης πρόφασιν ἀλλ' ἐξαυτῆς ἀνέδην καὶ θυμωδῶς οὕτως ὥστε προσόφλειν τὸν λεγόμενον τῶν ἰχθύων βίον, ἐν οἷς φάσιν ὁμοφύλοις οὖσι τὴν τοῦ μείονος ἀπώλειαν τῷ μείζονι τροφὴν γίγνεσθαι καὶ βίον.

[2] Polybius, iii. 2, 8; xv. 20, 2. Appian, ix. 3. Polybius speaks of a compact between Philip and Antiochus for the division (διαίρεσις) of the Egyptian monarchy, and says that Antiochus was to have Cœlesyria and Phœnicia, whilst Philip's share was to be Egypt, Caria, and the island of Samos. Comp. Nissen, *Untersuchungen über die Quellen des Livius*, p. 120.

the members of which were no longer moved and governed by one spirit; it was in a state of progressing decomposition, and new life was already springing up in the elements which composed it. Even before the conquest of Alexander the Great, when the vast territories between India and Europe were yet parts of the Persian empire, many indigenous races had opposed a stubborn resistance to the invading Persians, and had succeeded in maintaining a more or less complete independence. The rapid march of Alexander's victorious army left but few traces among these tribes. That which could be accomplished neither by the Persian kings in the prolonged period of their mighty sway nor by the genius of Alexander, was still more beyond the power of the degenerate successors of the brave Seleucus. Upper Asia, the old empire of Persia, on the eastern side of the Tigris, cast off the Macedonian yoke soon after Alexander's death, and notwithstanding some expeditions undertaken by the third Antiochus, fell under the dominion of the Parthians, who, under their native kings of the house of Arsaces, successfully maintained their independence against Syria as afterwards against Rome. The rule of the Seleucidæ and the influence of Greek culture extended only as far as the Tigris.[1] But on the western side of that boundary independent states had also been formed in the east and north of Asia Minor,[2] whilst in the south of this peninsula many different nations, for instance, the wild Isaurians, lived in a state of independence, which was never seriously interfered with. The Greek commercial towns on the sea coast were more or less autonomous. The Galatians had established themselves in the centre of Asia Minor and had formed a free Gallic community. Even in the immediate vicinity of Syria itself and of the chief town of Antiochia the provinces of Cœlesyria, Phœnicia, and Palestine had been

---

[1] Too little is known of the Bactrian kingdom to enable us to reckon it as one of the states which carried Greek culture into the barbarous East.

[2] Such were the kingdoms of Armenia, Cappadocia, Pontus, Bithynia, and Pergamum.

annexed by Egypt, which had moreover seized Cyprus and many other islands, as well as a strip of land on the coast of Caria and Cilicia in Asia Minor.

Character of the Seleucidæ.

Thus the king of Asia was in truth nothing but the shadow of a great name, and the Seleucidæ did not supply by personal qualifications the want of material power. In no part of the old Persian empire had the spirit of Greek self-respect, moderation, and the love of liberty so completely died out after the Macedonian conquest as in Syria. Nowhere else had the brave leaders of the Macedonian army so quickly degenerated into Asiatic despots. Nowhere had Eastern voluptuousness, immorality, servility, and an effeminate spirit become so general as at the court of Antioch, where in the family of the royal house poison and the dagger became more familiar instruments of policy than they ever had been in the house of the Persian Achæmenidæ.

Antiochus the Great.

Antiochus III. had been on the throne since the year 224 B.C. After an unhappy war, which he carried on with Egypt for the possession of Phœnicia and Cœlesyria, and which terminated in his complete overthrow in the decisive battle of Raphia (217 B.C.), he succeeded in vanquishing his rebellious uncle, Achæus, whom he put to a cruel and ignominious death. Elated by this success, Antiochus aspired to greater things. He endeavoured to re-unite with his empire that great extent of territory in which the kings of Parthia and Bactria had asserted their independence. But the result of a war of several years did not answer his expectations. He was finally compelled to recognise the independence of these states; and though he actually penetrated into India and returned home with a large number of elephants and other trophies, he had really gained nothing except the barren title of 'the Great,' which he allowed his flatterers to bestow upon him.

Alliance between Antiochus and Philip.

When in 205 B.C. Ptolemæus Philopator, the king of Egypt had died, Antiochus formed an alliance with Philip of Macedonia for the purpose of despoiling Ptolemy's successor, a child of five years, of his kingdom.[1] He overran

---

[1] Above, p. 8.

and conquered Cœlesyria, Phœnicia, and Palestine, the long-disputed territory between Syria and Egypt—a conquest, which in the sequel led to the heroic opposition of the Maccabees against Syrian oppression, and to the independence of the Jewish nation.

200–196 B.C.

While Antiochus was taking that portion of the Egyptian spoil which he had bargained for in his contract with Philip, his ally was anxious on his side to secure the advantages which he had hoped to gain from the plunder of Egypt. Instead of attacking with combined forces the seat and centre of the Egyptian power, each of the allies tried to obtain those countries which were most conveniently situated for him, just as in his alliance with Hannibal against Rome the shortsighted Philip only thought of extending his territory on the side of Illyria, instead of supporting Hannibal in Italy with all his strength. Philip had in his service, as commander of the fleet, the Ætolian Dicæarchus, a pattern of a reckless, insolent mercenary, who, in his contempt of the old Greek veneration for the gods, went so far as to put up altars for 'Godlessness' (Asebeia) and 'Lawlessness' (Paranomia). This worthy servant of Philip sailed about in the Ægean Sea with a fleet of twenty Macedonian ships, practised piracy, laid the smaller islands under contribution, and subjected without difficulty those of the Cyclades which were under Egyptian rule, and which were for the most part utterly defenceless. Every independent Greek state seemed now exposed to be plundered and violated by the two great allied powers of Syria and Macedonia.

Philip's expedition into Asia Minor.

Dicæarchus.

No Greek community felt this danger more than the island and republic of Rhodes, which had for a long time been closely connected with Egypt by commerce and mutually profitable intercourse. A great contrast to the industrious and thrifty Rhodians was presented by the rude and half-barbarised communities of Crete. No Greek island was so completely estranged from peaceful pursuits and the habits of order. In Crete every man grew up a soldier and pursued war as his profession. Whoever was

The islands of Crete and Rhodes.

BOOK V.
200–196 B.C.

not engaged in the eternal feuds within the island, enlisted as mercenary in some foreign service, or practised piracy on his own account. Rich trading towns like Rhodes had to suffer the greatest annoyances from these lawless robbers, and the encouragement and support of Philip and his admiral Dicæarchus were hardly necessary to excite the Cretans against Rhodes.[1]

Wanton attacks of Philip on independent Greek cities.

Philip, like the captain of a band of robbers, revelled in the delights of pouncing upon innocent towns, burning them to the ground, and murdering the inhabitants or selling them as slaves. He troubled himself with no scruples and asked for no pretext, for he thought himself secure and far above all such consideration of the weak. The towns of Lysimachia on the Thracian Chersonesus, Perinthus on the European, Cios on the Asiatic coast of the Propontis, Chalcedon opposite Byzantium, and the island of Thasos on the Thracian coast, experienced one after another his treachery, violence, and savage cruelty. Those which did not submit voluntarily, or, like Thasos, were entrapped into submission by false promises, were conquered by force, and had to suffer the dreadful consequences of such a fate. The unhappy city of Cios suffered all the terrors of a siege; and, notwithstanding the intercession of the Rhodians, was utterly destroyed, the inhabitants being sold into slavery. This ruthless abuse of power roused the discontent even of Prusias, king of Bithynia, Philip's ally, who had hoped to acquire the town of Cios uninjured. The Ætolians, Philip's old enemies, resented his proceedings as an act of hostility against themselves, for some of the towns thus shamefully treated (like Lysimachia, Chalcedon and Cios) were old members of the Ætolian league. For the same reason the important city of Byzantium, the close ally of Perinthus, was forced into opposition to Philip as the common enemy of independent city communities. Indeed, Philip earned in the whole of Greece nothing but hatred and distrust.

[1] Diodorus, xxviii. fr. 1.

For, notwithstanding many internal wars and outrages committed by Greeks against Greeks, a generous Hellenic feeling had not yet died out entirely, and the cruel treatment of a Greek town by a foreign conqueror deeply wounded the whole people. Those states especially which were more directly exposed to similar attacks saw the necessity of strenuously opposing the rapacity of Philip for the sake of their own security.

Thus a league was formed against him, at the head of which were the enterprising Rhodians, united with Attalus, the king of Pergamum, in Asia Minor, who even in the first Macedonian war had fought on the side of Philip's foes. Byzantium, Chios, and other Greek towns joined this league, and had the courage to undertake a contest with the powerful and defiant king of Macedonia, even before they had the prospect that Rome would join in the struggle for the independence of the smaller Greek states. Yet the hopes of all the enemies of Philip were fixed on the great Western power, and embassies were being continually sent to Rome to warn the senate of the danger with which the increasing strength of Macedonia threatened not only her weaker neighbours and Egypt, which had stood so long in friendly relations with Rome, but also the security of Rome herself.[1]

In the meantime, before Rome was able to interfere in Eastern affairs—that is, before the peace with Carthage had been concluded, the war between Philip and the allied cities broke out with great fury. Philip advanced quickly to the attack. He sailed with his fleet and army against the Egyptian island of Samos, and took possession of it. Whilst he was proceeding to lay siege to Chios, he encountered, between the island and the continent, a fleet of Pergamenian and Byzantian ships, under the command of old king Attalus, of Pergamum, and of the enterprising Rhodian admiral Theophiliscus, the man who had decided his countrymen to enter on the war, and had even induced king Attalus to take part in it.

[1] Appian, ix. 8; Justin, xxx. 2.

BOOK V.
200–196 B.C.
Sea fights of Chios and Lade.

It was the object of the allies not only to prevent the conquest of Chios, but also to cut off Philip's retreat to Samos. They had sixty-five decked vessels at their disposal against fifty-three of the Macedonians; but Philip had a larger number of smaller craft, and thus the two fleets may have been about equally matched. Philip had the advantage of not being obliged to consult an ally. He was consequently enabled to act quickly, and he surprised the hostile fleets before they had quite effected a junction. The battle is one of the most interesting of the ancient sea fights, for Polybius[1] has handed down to us a full and detailed account, which enables us to form a tolerably clear notion of the naval tactics of that period, of which, comparatively speaking, we know so little. Philip had several large vessels with from six to ten rows of oars, which must have been very unwieldy, and probably served more for royal pomp than for real war, or, like the elephants on land, caused more consternation than harm in the hostile ranks. Some of these ships were pierced by the enemy's beaks below the water-line and sunk; others, being entangled in collisions with hostile vessels, were too slow of movement to clear off, and were boarded. Others, again, had whole rows of oars brushed off by fast-sailing small craft. Thus were destroyed a Macedonian ship of ten rows of oars, one of nine, one of seven and one of six, besides twenty other decked vessels and sixty-eight smaller ones, while only nine were captured. It is reported that the allies lost in all only seven ships.[2] Not-

[1] Polybius, xvi. 2–9.

[2] The reports of the losses on both sides (Polyb. xvi. 7) represent the issue of the battle as so favourable to the Rhodians and Attalus, and so pernicious to Philip, that we are at a loss to understand how, under such circumstances, Philip could claim the victory at all, and how his enemies did not reap the benefit of the battle. For it is stated that, besides the great number of ships mentioned in the text, Philip lost nine thousand dead, whereas the allies lost only one hundred and twenty. It seems almost certain that the materials for the description of the sea fight at Chios were furnished by Zenon and Antisthenes, the Rhodian historians, whom Polybius (xvi. 14) charges with the perversion of the truth in the interest of their native city, and who did not scruple to represent the defeat of their countrymen at Lade soon after as a victory. It is always a great temptation for a beaten general to palliate his

withstanding this, however, the result of the battle was by no means favourable to them. Attalus had narrowly escaped being captured in the fight by running his flagship aground, and sacrificing it to the enemies who plundered it. And, moreover, whilst the Rhodians suffered an irreparable loss through the mortal wound of their brave admiral Theophiliscus, Philip actually kept possession of the ground, collected the wrecks of the vessels, buried the slain, and openly boasted of a triumph, though the allies offered battle again on the following day. Yet the continuance of the siege of Chios was not possible on account of the great losses which Philip had sustained, and he had to be content with being able to return unmolested to Samos. The Pergamenian fleet sailed home. The Rhodians, perhaps reinforced by other Greek ships, ventured soon after to encounter the Macedonians again; but they were defeated at Lade,[1] and thus prevented from opposing the further operations of Philip, who soon afterwards conquered Chios,[2] landed with his army in Asia Minor, entered Miletus in triumph, and ravaged the territories of king Attalus, of the Rhodians, and of Egypt.

It appears that he no longer encountered any opposition on the part of his enemies, and he took a number of fortified places. An attempt to take Pergamum failed.[3]

Ravaging of Caria by Philip.

discomfiture by representing the loss of his opponents as enormous, and as larger, if possible, than his own. In such false statements patriotic historians can easily find arguments to show that a battle in which the enemy lost so much was a victory; at least, they will easily persuade themselves and their own countrymen of it. The only things which cannot well be concealed or perverted are the results and consequences of a battle; and though a victory is not always followed by an advance of the victors, yet it is not difficult, on the whole, to infer the issue of a battle from the subsequent movements of the belligerents. With regard to the sea fight at Chios, we are inclined to think that the advantage was on the side of Philip, as Attalus returned home with his fleet, and the Rhodians could not effectually stop Philip's advance.

[1] Polybius, xvi. 14.
[2] Appian, ix. 3.
[3] It seems to follow, from the statements of Polybius (xvi. 1 and 24) and Diodorus (xxviii. fr. 5), that the attack upon Pergamum took place not before but after the battles of Chios and Lade. Yet it is very difficult to fix the chronology, owing to the fragmentary condition of the evidence.

BOOK V.
200-196 B.C.

But he so effectually laid waste Caria, in the south of Asia Minor, that at last he began to suffer want in the hostile and desolated country, and was in danger of losing his whole army by famine. When the summer and autumn of 201 B.C. were past and the inclement season had set in, it became absolutely necessary for him to return to Macedonia. The return was now rendered dangerous, partly by the tempestuous state of the weather and partly by the hostile fleets which had been gathering in the interval. Still Philip, against all expectation, did succeed in avoiding both these dangers, and in bringing his army back to Macedonia after a campaign which proved utterly fruitless in results.

Philip's campaign on the Hellespont.

It might have been expected that Philip would soon give up the task of making conquests in Asia, and prepare to meet the danger which he could not fail to see approaching from the West. In the course of the year just expired, 201 B.C., the peace between Rome and Carthage had been concluded; nor did it need a keen vision to foresee that Rome would soon call Philip to account for his support of Hannibal, and join the alliance against him which had been called forth by his aggressive policy in Greece. But whether Philip, after the manner of despots, obstinately closed his eyes to an unpleasant fact, or whether he allowed himself to be deceived by his wretched counsellors, a band of adventurers from all nations, who encouraged his worst vices and passions (for no one ventured to tell him the truth),[1] certain it is that in the beginning of the year 200 B.C. he engaged with blind recklessness in new enterprises, which, even in case of complete success, must have weakened him for a contest with Rome. It is plain that he and his captains of mer-

[1] Diodorus, xxviii. fr. 2: Φίλιππος Ἡρακλείδην τινὰ Ταραντῖνον εἶχε μεθ' ἑαυτοῦ πονηρὸν ἄνθρωπον, ὃς κατ' ἰδίαν αὐτῷ λαλῶν . . . . ἐπὶ τὸ χεῖρον αὐτῷ τὰ πράγματα προηγάγετο· Πολέμους γὰρ οὐκ ἀναγκαίους ἐπαναιρούμενος ἐκινδύνευσεν ἀποβαλεῖν τὴν βασιλείαν ὑπὸ Ῥωμαίων· οὐκέτι γὰρ οὐδεὶς ἐτόλμα τῶν φίλων ἔχειν παρρησίαν, οὐδὲ ἐπιπλήττειν τῇ τοῦ βασιλέως ἀνοίᾳ πεφρικὼς αὐτοῦ τὴν προπέτειαν· How Philip had allowed himself to be swayed by the adventurer Demetrius of Pharos has been related, vol. ii. p. 276 ff.

THE SECOND MACEDONIAN WAR.

CHAP. I.
200–196 B.C.

cenaries had begun to take great pleasure in the capturing and plundering of Greek towns, without carefully discriminating between such as were independent and those that were Egyptian dependencies. But his campaign in Caria had almost terminated fatally, because during the winter season he had been very nearly prevented by the enemy's fleet from returning home. He marched now towards the Hellespont, where the towns of Sestos and Abydos commanded the narrow arm of the sea between Europe and Asia, the spot where Xerxes had constructed his celebrated bridge of boats. If he possessed these towns, his communication with Asia could not be interrupted. Therefore, after taking some of the Thracian coast towns and castles in the neighbourhood,[1] which belonged to the kingdom of the Ptolemies, he marched to the Hellespont, and laid siege to Abydos. This undertaking occupied a considerable time, for Abydos offered a determined resistance. During the progress of the siege, his enemies, especially the Rhodians and Athenians, had full leisure, with the assistance of their fleet, not only to expel the Macedonian garrisons from most of the islands which he had conquered, but to form an alliance against him, to which he was soon doomed to succumb.

Dispute between Athens and the Acarnanians.

Whilst Philip was pursuing his ambitious policy beyond the Ægean, serious disagreements had broken out between Athens and Macedonia, which, in the end, furnished the ostensible grounds for the Roman declaration of war. At a festive celebration of the Eleusinian mysteries two Acarnanian youths, who happened to be on a visit in Attica, mingled with a crowd of mystics, and thus found their way into the sacred precincts of the temple of Demeter. They intended no harm, and were unconscious of the enormity of the offence which they had committed. Betrayed by their incautious questions, they were discovered as intruders, brought up before the high priest of the temple to

---

[1] The towns of Maronea and Ænus, and the castles of Cypsola, Doriscus, Serrhius, Elæus, Alopeconuesus, Callipolis, Madytus, and others. Livy, xxxi. 16.

VOL. III.   C

answer for their conduct, condemned to death and executed.¹

BOOK V.
200-196 B.C.

This fanatical outrage produced a violent outburst of rage among the Acarnanians. They addressed their complaints to their ally and protector, the king of Macedonia, and were encouraged and supported by him to invade Attica, to lay waste the level country with fire and sword, and to gratify not only their revenge but their love of spoil.

Interference of Rome.

All this happened in the autumn of the year 201 B.C., when Philip had not yet returned from his campaign against the possessions of the Rhodians, of Egypt, and of Attalus in Asia Minor.² The Athenians in their distress immediately sent an embassy to Rome, asking for help against the Acarnanians and Philip,³ and thus affording the Romans the best excuse they could desire for interfering in the internal affairs of Greece, and for a formal declaration of war. The senate had already foreseen the necessity of such a war so clearly that they had ordered a part of the fleet on its return from Africa to set sail from Vibo in southern Italy for Macedonia, and to hold itself in readiness for any emergency.⁴ The Athenian ambassadors found therefore an attentive hearing in Rome. The senate, notwithstanding the remonstrances of two tribunes of the people, and in spite of the unpopularity of a new war, obtained the consent of the people to their proposed warlike policy, and immediately despatched an embassy commissioned to visit the several Greek states, for the purpose of enlisting allies, and of eventually delivering to the king of Macedonia the final demands of the Roman republic. This embassy arrived at Athens at the time when the fleet of the allied Greek states,⁵ which had endeavoured to cut off the retreat of the Macedonian king from Caria, had returned from its fruitless expedition, and had

Attalus at Athens.

―――――――

¹ Livy, xxxi. 14. 6.   ² See p. 16.
³ As early as the year 228 B.C. the Athenians had become the friends of Rome (see vol. ii. p. 110) In the peace between Rome and Macedonia (205 B.C.) they were referred to as Roman allies (Livy, xxix. 12, 14). They were therefore entitled in some manner to claim the protection of Rome.
⁴ Livy, xxxi. 3.   ⁵ See p. 16.

just cast anchor at the island of Ægina. Attalus was received by the Athenians as their deliverer, and was overwhelmed with extravagant honours, in conformity with a practice which unfortunately had, by this time, ceased to be novel at Athens. The whole people came out from Athens to meet him in the Piræus; the priests awaited him in their festive robes; the temples were opened, and solemn offerings prepared; even the gods themselves were to receive the honoured guest of the republic. Amidst universal acclamations, Attalus was enrolled among the national heroes, and a phyle, or tribe, of the Attic land was named after him.

Similar honours sealed the fraternal bond between the Athenians and the Rhodians, and a formal declaration of war against Macedonia followed immediately. The first fruit of the alliance with Rome was the retreat of the Macedonian general, Nicanor, who, in the meantime, had marched into Attica, but did not like the risk of provoking the anger of the Roman ambassadors by harassing the new allies of the great republic.

Meanwhile Philip, as we have seen,[1] had opened the campaign of the year 200 B.C. on the Hellespont, and was now besieging Abydos, leaving the Rhodians in undisturbed possession of the Ægean sea. These accordingly retook all the Cyclades, with the exception of Andros, Paros, and Cythnos, but they accomplished nothing more, neither attacking Macedonia, which was destitute of troops, nor coming to the assistance of Abydos, perhaps, because they expected everything from the Romans.

But the latter had not yet completed the preliminary diplomatic arrangements which they deemed indispensable before the commencement of hostilities. Their object was to unite, if possible, all the Greek states in one great offensive and defensive alliance, in order to carry on the war against Philip (just as they had done in the first Macedonian war), chiefly with the arms of their allies, and with the smallest possible addition of Italian

[1] See p. 17.

troops. The Roman embassy had already visited Epirus, Acarnania, Ætolia, Achaia,[1] and lastly Attica. They had not everywhere found a hearty readiness to join the alliance. But, on the other hand, they discovered no decided sympathy for Philip.

From Greece the ambassadors proceeded to Egypt, where they had a most delicate commission to execute.

The Egyptian government had asked the Roman people to act as guardians of the infant king, Ptolemæus Epiphanes, in other words, to protect him from the spoliation which his two powerful enemies, Philip of Macedonia and Antiochus of Syria, had planned.[2] The Romans had not the slightest wish to commit themselves to a contest with these two powers at once. But how could they proceed against Philip without giving such offence to his ally as would make him take an active part in the war? This object was nevertheless attained. Rome made her client, the king of Egypt, pay the cost of securing the neutrality of Antiochus. No obstacle was placed in the way of the conquest of the whole of Phœnicia by that monarch.[3] Whether his claims to it were formally recognised by Rome we do not know; at any rate, they were recognised *de facto*, and Antiochus, who wisely gave up all thoughts of conquering Egypt proper, found in the unchallenged acquisition of Phœnicia a sufficient inducement to leave his ally, the king of Macedonia, to his fate, and to avoid the hostility of Rome. The government of Egypt were not in a position to compel their Roman friends and protectors to render direct assistance for the defence of Phœnicia. Perhaps they hoped for or received assurances that after the overthrow of Philip the Egyptian possessions in Asia Minor, Thrace, and in the Ægean sea would be restored to Egypt.

Before the termination of their mission in Egypt and Syria, the Roman ambassadors despatched Marcus Æmilius, the youngest of their number, from Rhodes to Philip, who

---

[1] Polybius, xvi. 27.   [2] See p. 10.
[3] Livy, xxxiii. 19. From Justin (xxxi. 1) it would appear that Antiochus had conquered Cœlesyria as early as 201 B.C.

was still occupied with the siege of the dauntless town of Abydos. The task of Æmilius was only to comply with an empty formality. He had to declare war on the part of Rome; for it was easy to foresee that Philip would reject the terms on which peace might yet be preserved. These terms contained a demand that the king of Macedonia should make war upon no Greek city, that he should give up the possessions of Ptolemy which he had seized, and submit to a court of arbitration, which would settle the damages to be paid by him to king Attalus and the Rhodians.[1] There is no mention made of a demand in the interest of the Athenians; probably because the Macedonian general Nicanor had, at the request of the Roman ambassadors during their stay in Athens, evacuated Attica.[2] The ostensible pretext under which the senate had obtained the sanction of the Roman people for a declaration of war, viz., Philip's attack upon a Roman ally, had under these circumstances become untenable. The Romans were constrained to speak for Attalus and the Rhodians, although, as Philip justly observed, the Rhodians were the aggressors and not the attacked. Moreover, in assuming the attitude of a protecting power with regard to Egypt and Greek towns in general, and in requiring of Philip that he should refrain from all attacks upon them, the Romans claimed a right which was founded neither on special treaties nor on international law, but merely on the consciousness of their superior power and on the calculation of what their own interest demanded. Philip's answer, therefore, contained a sharp and deserved rebuke. The Romans, he said, should strictly observe the sworn treaty and not break the peace. But if they were bent on war, the Macedonians would call

---

[1] Polybius, xvi. 27 and 34.

[2] See p. 19. Philip, it is true, had not approved of Nicanor's retreat, and had afterwards ordered Philocles to invade Attica a second time (Livy, xxxi. 16, 1), but either this invasion had not yet taken place, or Æmilius had not yet any knowledge of it at the time when he delivered the Roman ultimatum to Philip during the siege of Abydos.

upon the gods as witnesses, and resist force by force.[1] With these words, which breathe a truly royal pride, and with the feeling that he was resisting an unjustifiable interference, Philip broke off the negotiations. But, with some approach to the courteous diplomacy of our own days, he seized the opportunity of assuring the representative of the Roman people personally of his distinguished respect and regard. He told him he would pardon the frankness of his speech for three reasons, first, because he was young and inexperienced; secondly, because he was a handsome man; and, thirdly, because he was a Roman.

Taking of Abydos.

Soon after the failure of the Roman negotiations, the fate of the unhappy town of Abydos was decided. Up to the present time it had been defended with the courage of despair. The town wall had already been thrown down by a mine in one place, and a second wall, which had been built behind the first, had been undermined, when at length, despairing of all assistance from without, the besieged offered to surrender the town to Philip on condition of being permitted to leave it unmolested. But Philip required unconditional submission; and the inhabitants of Abydos, knowing full well that this meant death, slavery, and dishonour, prepared to die as free men on their native soil. They collected the women in the temple of Artemis, the children in the gymnasium, and commissioned a number of older men to kill them all, and then to cast into the sea or to burn all the gold and silver and other treasures as soon as they should see the enemy penetrate into the town over the corpses of the defenders. Thereupon they took up their post in the breach of the inner wall, and fought as men determined to conquer or die. In the evening, after most of them had fallen, the Macedonians desisted from the attack. The courage of some of the survivors then gave way, and they resolved to send the priests to supplicate Philip for

---

[1] Polybius, xvi. 34, 7; Livy, xxxi. 18.

mercy. This weakness the patriotic fanatics abominated as treason to the cause of the fatherland and as a crime against the gods whom they had called upon to witness their voluntary death. On the following day, therefore, while the Macedonian troops were taking possession of the treasures heaped up in the market-place, the remnant of the people of Abydos carried out their terrible resolution. Philip gave them three days' time to murder the women and children, and finally themselves, and then he took possession of the depopulated town.[1]

The terrible end of Abydos reminds us of the similar catastrophe of Saguntum in 218 B.C. But it is not subject to historical doubts, like the narrative of the fall of the Spanish town.[2] It is authenticated by the testimony of Polybius. There are other points of likeness in the fate of the two towns. The siege and conquest of each of them mark the commencement of a great war of the Romans; and both towns were left to their fate by their allies, while greater decision and promptness might have been the means of saving them. And as during the siege of Saguntum Roman ambassadors appeared before Hannibal in the camp, begging him to desist,[3] so Æmilius came to Philip while he was blockading Abydos, without being able to stop the impending war by a mere diplomatic interference.

Attalus meanwhile had sailed with his fleet from Ægina, where he had passed the winter, and proceeded as far as the coast of the Troad, near Tenedos; but he had not courage enough to avert the fall of Abydos. In spite of the threats of Rome and the hostile demonstrations of his Greek enemies, Philip had attained his object. He had won bloody laurels, and returned to Macedonia towards the autumn of the year 200 B.C. to prepare for the attack of the Romans, which now he could expect with positive certainty.

We have seen with what decision the Roman senate

---

[1] Polybius, xvi. 29–34; Livy, xxxi. 18.   [2] Vol. ii. p. 157.
[3] According to the narrative of Livius, xxi. 9.

determined upon the struggle with Macedonia immediately after the conclusion of peace with Carthage, and how skilfully they made use of the complications in the east for carrying on that war, more with the arts of diplomacy and the military strength of allied towns than with Roman legions. Yet the Roman negotiators had not succeeded in uniting all the Greeks in an alliance against Philip. The Acarnanians, the Bœotians, Phocians, Locrians, Dorians, and Eubœans were too dependent on Macedonia, because Macedonian power protected them from their nearest enemies, especially the Ætolians.[1] But the Ætolians were slow to declare themselves. During the preceding winter Attalus had in vain urged them to a war against Philip.[2] Between them and Rome a marked coolness, almost amounting to enmity, had been apparent from the time when, in the first Macedonian war, they had been insufficiently supported by Rome, and had in consequence concluded a separate peace with Philip. Since then the former allies accused one another mutually of a breach of contract. But the Romans were quite right in thinking that the force of circumstances would after all draw the Ætolians into the war with Macedonia, especially as the domineering spirit of Philip had during the last few years become very troublesome to the Ætolians, and as they had not been able to repel or to punish his attacks on their allies, the towns of the Propontis.[3]

If it was not quite easy for the Romans to gain the hearty alliance of the Ætolians in a war with Macedonia, it seemed utterly hopeless to determine the Achaeans to the same line of policy. Ever since the time of Aratus

---

[1] There is a striking resemblance between the policy of the petty Greek states and the Highland clans in the time of William III. Both were determined in their alliances and hostilities, not by the principles and general views which swayed the contest of the great powers, but by their relations to their immediate neighbours. Because the Campbells were Whigs and Presbyterians, their neighbours espoused the cause of the Stuarts. Had the Campbells been royalists, their neighbours would have been ranged on the opposite side. See Macaulay's *History of England*, vol. i. chap. 13.

[2] Livy, xxx. 15. [3] See p. 12.

the Achaeans had been closely allied with Macedonia, because they had found in the Macedonian kings their natural allies in their continual struggles with their neighbours the Ætolians and Sparta. Yet when the Achaean league, under the able direction of Philopœmen, had become a great military power, a party of the Achaean people was no longer opposed to a line of policy which seemed likely to make them independent of Macedonian protection. Moreover, Philip had alienated his best friends, and given just cause of apprehension, by attempting the assassination of Philopœmen,[1] because he could not look upon him on all occasions as a ready tool.

Under such circumstances the Roman envoys could hope to organize a party hostile to Philip. Their watchword was 'the liberation of Greece,' a phrase which had always exercised a magic influence on the easily deluded Greeks. Nevertheless, the Achaeans could not be brought at once to act a decided part. Whether from fear of Philip or from distrust of the Romans, most of the Greek states could not summon resolution enough to side with one or the other party. When the war actually broke out, Rome had for acknowledged allies only those who were already at war with the Macedonians, namely, Egypt, Rhodes, Pergamum, Byzantium, and lastly, Athens.

Immediately after the consuls for the year 200 B.C., Publius Sulpicius Galba and Caius Aurelius Cotta, had entered on their office, the war against Macedonia was formally determined on. Nevertheless, the greater part of the year passed away in the negotiations just related and in military preparations. The chief cause, however, for the delay in the operations was an alarming rebellion among the Gauls, who, under the command of an able Punic general named Hamilcar, in the year of the conclusion of peace with Carthage, attacked and utterly destroyed a Roman army of seven thousand men.[2] Thus it happened that the autumn of the year 200 B.C. was

---

[1] Plutarch, *Philopœmen*, 12.　　[2] Livy, xxxi. 2.

almost past before the consul P. Sulpicius Galba[1] set out with his army for Macedonia. Two legions only were destined for this campaign,[2] and with a view of taxing Italy with no more new levies of troops than was absolutely necessary, the senate ordered that Sulpicius should collect as many volunteers as possible from Scipio's army just then returned from Africa.[3] He received, moreover, a reinforcement of one thousand Numidian horse, and a number of elephants. Having landed in Apollonia, the Roman consul was prevented from commencing operations by the advanced season of the year; for between the western coast of the Græco-Macedonian peninsula and the kingdom of Philip lay a broad, wild, impracticable mountain tract, which, extending from north to south, formed an almost impassable barrier. The navigation, however, was not yet closed. The fleet, therefore, had time to inflict a quick and unexpectd blow.

Capture of Chalcis by the Roman fleet.

Attica, as we have seen,[4] was freed by the protest of the Roman ambassadors[5] from the Acarnanian and Macedonian bands, which under the command of Nicanor had advanced so far in order to take revenge for the two murdered Acarnanians.[6] But Philip in his hatred of Athens had disapproved of Nicanor's retreat, and had commissioned another general Philocles, who then commanded the Macedonian troops in Eubœa, to attack Attica with renewed vigour. In their trouble the Athenians had received but little help from Attalus, and now turned to the Romans.

---

[1] This Sulpicius Galba was now consul for the second time. In his first consulate, 211 B.C., he had been opposed to Hannibal, and helped to protect the city of Rome from the sudden attack of the latter. He was after that time employed in Apulia, and when Valerius Lævinus had concluded a treaty of alliance with the Ætolians, he had crossed over into Greece, where he remained in command for five years. He was thus familiar with the affairs of the countries east of the Adriatic, and when the war with Macedonia was resolved upon, he was selected for the consulship of 200 B.C. Accordingly, we find that he was most zealous in procuring the consent of the people for the war. Livy, xxxi. 5 8

[2] Livy, xxxi. 8. [3] Livy, xxxi. 8.
[4] See p. 19. [5] In the spring of 200 B.C.
[6] See p. 17.

Sulpicius had crossed the Ionian sea, and by this time had selected Corcyra as the winter station for the Roman fleet. From this island he sent a number of ships and one thousand men to the Piræus under the command of Caius Claudius.

On reaching Athens, Claudius was informed by exiles from Chalcis in Eubœa that this chief fortress of the Macedonians was left with an insufficient garrison and was badly guarded; that it might, therefore, be easily surprised and taken. He seized the opportunity without delay, sailed to Sunium the southern cape of Attica, and from thence in the night to Chalcis, which he reached before break of day. The walls were scaled, all men capable of bearing arms cut down, the magazines and arsenals, which were full of provisions and stores, were set on fire, the statues of the king thrown down and mutilated, and a quantity of rich spoil carried away to the ships. Unfortunately, the Roman force, too weak to hold the important town, was compelled, after inflicting as much damage as they could, to return in all haste to the Piræus.[1]

The report of this disaster reached Philip at Demetrias on the northern extremity of the Pagasæan gulf, not far from the venerable old town of Iolkos, from whence, according to the legend, the Argonauts had sailed to the land of Colchis in quest of the Golden Fleece. Beside himself with rage, he determined to take summary vengeance, hoping to be able by great expedition still to overtake the Romans in Chalcis. In a run rather than a march, he proceeded to Chalcis with five thousand light armed troops and three hundred horse. When he found, instead of the Romans, only the smoking ruins of the destroyed houses and the unburied bodies of the slain, he hurried across the Euripus, and through Bœotia straight to Athens, in the hope of taking it by surprise. His plan almost succeeded, for the Athenians were far from expecting an attack of the Macedonians. But a spy, on the

---

[1] Livy, xxxi. 23.

look-out, had observed the advance of the enemy, had traversed the space from the Euripus to Athens in one day, and arriving in the middle of the night alarmed the town.¹ When Philip appeared before the walls a few hours later, he found his plan frustrated, and the Athenians not only prepared to receive him, but bold enough actually to sally out and attack him. Philip having driven them into the town without difficulty, applied himself deliberately and systematically to lay waste the immediate neighbourhood. In true barbaric fashion he desecrated, destroyed, or defaced all the temples, sacred groves, and even the burial places of the dead. After an attempt to carry by assault the fortified temple of Demeter in Eleusis, he marched off to Megara, and from thence to Corinth, the Macedonian fortress of the Peloponnesus.²

Sparta and the Achaean league.

It so happened, that at that very time the federal council of the Achaean league was assembled at Argos, for the purpose of devising ways and means for a war against Nabis, the tyrant of Sparta. Sparta, of old the enemy of the Achaeans, and the chief obstacle to the extension of the Achaean league over the whole of the Peloponnesus, had been humbled seven years before, in the year 207 B.C. at Mantinea by Philopœmen, the re-organizer of the Achaean army, and had since then been obliged to submit and keep the peace. But when Philopœmen in 200 B.C., annoyed at not being re-elected to the place of federal chief magistrate (strategos), left the Peloponnesus to take part in the domestic quarrels of Crete, Nabis watched his time, and harassed the Achaeans again.

Neutrality of the Achaeans.

The Achaeans found themselves now in a very difficult position. Having already been called upon by the Romans to join the alliance against Philip, a demand which they had not without some misgivings declined, on the plea that

---

¹ Livy, xxxi. 24, 4: Speculator, hemerodromos vocant Graeci. The spies, who kept watch on some look-out (specula) were at the same time trained to run fast. Comp. Æneas Poliorcet. 6: Χρὴ δὲ καὶ ἡμεροσκόπους πρὸ τῆς πόλεως καθιστάναι--εἶναι δὲ τοὺς ἡμεροσκόπους καὶ ποδώκεις. Cornel. Nepos, *Miltiades*, 4: Cursorem ejus generis, qui hemerodromi vocantur.

² Livy, xxxi. 24, 25.

they wished conscientiously to preserve their neutrality, they were now importuned by Philip in person, who pressed them, in conformity with their ancient connexion with Macedonia, to place their military force at his disposal against the Romans. He promised on his part to protect them against Sparta, desiring only that the Achaean troops should be used for garrisoning Corinth, Chalcis, and Oreus. But the Achaeans neither trusted Philip's words nor did they place confidence in his power. They were afraid that he would use their troops as hostages to compel the league to engage in the war against the overwhelming power of Rome, and that after all he would give them no security from the attacks of Nabis. Hence, although Philip had some sincere friends and partisans in the Achaean towns, and though the chief magistrate of the year was personally devoted to him, the assembly refused to depart from their neutrality, and declined even to submit Philip's proposal to a formal vote, under the pretext that it was irregular to pass a resolution on any but those subjects for which the assembly had been called together.

Full of resentment, Philip, on his return from the Peloponnesus, attempted another attack upon Athens, the Piræus, and Eleusis, and avenged himself for his failure by a second and more systematic devastation of the open country. In the course of these ravages he caused the pillars and sculptured stones of the temples and public buildings, not only to be thrown down, but to be defaced and broken, in order to render the injury irreparable.[1] He then left Attica, and retreated with his troops through Bœotia to Macedonia, where he passed the winter, and where he planned the campaign for the following year.[2]

The Roman consul, Publius Sulpicius Galba, had[3] landed in Apollonia in the autumn of the year 200 B.C., after the season for advancing into the mountains on the frontier of Macedonia had long passed; he was moreover incapacitated for a time from military action by illness. He therefore sent for his legate, Lucius Apustius, who was

---
[1] Livy, xxxi. 25, 26.   [2] Livy, xxxi. 28.   [3] See p. 26.

BOOK V.
200–196 B.C.

with the fleet then wintering near Corcyra, and commissioned him to make a series of short expeditions into the country near the Apsus, a large river on the coast, flowing from the watershed in the middle of the peninsula through the territory of Dassaretia, and falling into the Adriatic between Apollonia and Dyrrhachium. Here were some inconsiderable towns and fortresses, protecting the extreme frontier of Macedonia on the west, of which the most important seems to have been the town of Antipatrea. Apustius passed through the district, took Antipatrea and other places, and returned to Apollonia almost unmolested and laden with spoil.

Alliance of Dardanians, Illyrians, and Athamanians with Rome.

If, in a military point of view, but little had been accomplished by this march, still the neighbouring tribes were now convinced that the Romans meant to carry on the war in earnest, and it induced the petty chiefs of the Dardanians, Illyrians, and Athamanians to make common cause with the Romans, and to agree with them on a combined attack upon Macedonia in the following year. The Dardanians, a powerful tribe of mountaineers in the north of Macedonia, on the other side of the Scardus chain, were bitter enemies to the Macedonian kingdom, and nothing could be more welcome to their king or chief, Bato, than to unite with the Romans for an invasion of Macedonia. Not less ready in his friendship was Pleuratus, the prince of Illyria, who threatened Macedonia on the west. Amynander, the chief of the Athamanians, one of the tribes of Epirus, had some time previously been visited by the Roman ambassadors, but had hesitated to relinquish his neutral position. His scruples were now overcome; he not only joined the Roman alliance, but undertook at the same time to secure the co-operation of the Ætolians, who had always been on friendly terms with him, for the purpose of securing a road from the south through Thessaly into Macedonia. It was also arranged with Attalus and the Rhodians that the allied fleet should meet at Ægina, to open the attack on Macedonia from the sea.[1]

[1] Livy, xxxi. 28.

It was not, however, quite certain that the Ætolians would enter into the Roman alliance. Considering their adhesion to be of the greatest importance, the consul, Sulpicius Galba, resolved formally to solicit their alliance, though such a step could not fail to be somewhat humiliating to Roman pride; for it showed that Rome could not dispense with the aid of these unruly and wayward allies. The consul's legate, Lucius Furius Purpureo, accordingly appeared at a congress of the Ætolian league, which was held at Naupactus in the course of the winter. His request was vigorously supported by the loud declamations of the Athenians, who, with just and pardonable bitterness, declared that Philip's treatment of them was that of a savage barbarian, while the representatives of the Macedonian king did all they could to justify their master's proceedings. The Ætolian congress, before which the most powerful states of the time thus presented themselves as petitioners for aid, must have felt not a little flattered; and the arrogance with which this small mountain tribe behaved is as easy to comprehend as the cool contempt with which Rome treated it after the overthrow of the Macedonian power. The Romans were already sufficiently disgusted with the Ætolians. But their anger was greatly increased, when, even after their urgent entreaties, the Ætolians, like the Achaeans, declined to give a final decision, but persisted in remaining neutral, evidently from distrust of the Romans, who had once already left them without support in a quarrel with Macedonia, which they had undertaken in the Roman interest.[1]

In the meantime the season for opening the campaign of the year 199 B.C. had become favourable. For the purpose of protecting the Thessalian coast from an attack on the sea side, Philip had already destroyed the towns of Sciathos and Peparethos on the islands of the same name, and had thus rendered these places useless as a basis for the operations of the enemy's vessels.[2] He then ordered

[1] Livy, xxxi. 29, ffr. [2] Livy, xxxi. 28, 6.

his fleet, under the command of the Tarentine Heraclides, to take shelter in Demetrias, as it was decidedly too weak to keep the open sea against the combined squadrons of the Romans, the Rhodians, and king Attalus.[1] Against a threatened invasion of the Dardanians and Illyrians he sent his son Perseus to occupy the mountain passes of Pelagonia, on the north-west boundary of Macedonia, while with the principal part of his troops he marched westward to the neighbourhood of Lyncestis, where he expected the approach of the Romans.

First campaign of Romans and their allies.

About the same time Sulpicius also had started from Apollonia, and the two hostile armies, after marching about apparently lost in the wild uncultivated mountain districts, formed by the watershed between the Ægean and Adriatic seas, at length encountered each other. A few cavalry engagements took place without any decisive result. Philip seems to have intended to draw the Roman army into the barren mountain regions, where it was difficult for the troops to obtain the necessary supplies.[2] In vain Sulpicius tried to bring about a decisive battle. While he had been marching forwards and backwards, through the border countries of Dassaretia, Lyncestis, Eordæa, and Elimia without accomplishing anything, and finally had commenced his retreat to Apollonia,[3] Philip was able to send a body of troops under Athenagoras against the united forces of the Dardanians and the Illyrians, who endeavoured to penetrate through Pelagonia into Macedonia, intending to effect a junction with the Roman army.[4] They were easily repulsed; and now there remained

---

[1] Livy, xxxi. 33, 1.

[2] Dio Cassius, fragm. 58, 2: ὁ δὲ δὴ Φίλιππος τοῖς μὲν ὅπλοις ἀσθενέστερος ὤν, τῇ δὲ παρασκευῇ τῶν ἐπιτηδείων διὰ τὸ τὴν οἰκείαν οἱ ἐγγὺς εἶναι προφέρων ἀνεῖχεν, ἐκτρυχοῦσθαι αὐτοὺς ἀμαχὶ προσδοκήσας.

[3] Dio Cassius, fragm. 58, 2: οὐ μέντοι ὁ Γάλβας (after an alleged victory) ἐπεδίωξεν αὐτὸν (Philip)· τῇ τε γὰρ ἀπορίᾳ τῶν τροφῶν καὶ τῇ ἀπειρίᾳ τῶν χωρίων, τὸ δὲ δὴ πλεῖστον καὶ τῇ ἀγνωσίᾳ τῆς παρασκευῆς αὐτοῦ καὶ δέει μὴ ἀπερισκέπτως ποι προχωρῶν σφαλῇ, οὐκ ἠθέλησεν περαιτέρω προχωρῆσαι ἀλλ' ἐς τὴν Ἀπολλωνίαν ἀνεκομίσθη.

[4] The narrative of the campaign of Sulpicius Galba, in the year 199 B.C., bears the usual characteristics of the Roman annals, which are full of fictitious

THE SECOND MACEDONIAN WAR.

only a third enemy, but one who for the moment was more dangerous than the northern barbarians. For when Sulpicius had begun the campaign in good earnest, the Ætolians had at last resolved to take the side of Rome, and early in the summer of 199 B.C. had invaded Thessaly in conjunction with Amynander, the chief of the Athamanians.[1] Without meeting with any opposition, they marched through that fertile land, ravaging everywhere without mercy, till at last Philip, after the retreat of the Roman army, was at liberty to turn towards Thessaly. He surprised the undisciplined bands of plunderers, and drove them back to their own country with great loss.

In this manner the three attacks which the Romans and their allies had made on Macedonia by land on the north, west, and south, utterly failed. Not much more satisfactory was the result of the attacks of the allied fleet, although the Macedonian ships did not venture to issue

CHAP. I.
200 199 B.C.
Ætolians, allied with Rome, invade Thessaly.

Operations of the allied fleet.

---

victories gained far away in countries imperfectly known. If we pay no attention to the details of battles, which are as entirely the product of imagination as the pictorial battle scenes of 'our own artist' in the illustrated papers of our own time, and if we judge of the course of the campaign from the result, we cannot fail to come to the conclusion, that it was a miserable failure. Sulpicius Galba neither succeeded in reaching Macedonia proper, nor effected that junction with his allies which, according to Livy (xxxi. 28, 2), he was especially anxious to accomplish. Without having gained the least military advantage, he was compelled to return to Apollonia. If Philip had suffered a reverse ever so insignificant, he would not have been able to detach any portion of his army, to march first against the Dardanians and Illyrians, and then against the Ætolians and Athamanians. We therefore come to the conclusion, that the Romans were defeated by Philip, and that this was the reason for their retreat. This conjecture is indirectly confirmed by the circumstance that the Romans never repeated subsequently the attempt to penetrate into Macedonia by the route which the consul Sulpicius Galba had followed. But as we have no direct testimony for our conjecture, we will let the text stand as it is, adding only that Plutarch, in the life of Flamininus (chap. 4), confirms the views we have expressed. The Roman historians have less hesitation in speaking without reserve of the defeat of their allies. Livy (xxxi. 41, 14) says: Itaque primo impetu fusi (Ætoli), vix temptato certamine, *turpi fuga reptiunt castra*; and ib. chap. 42, 6: Postquam mota signa Macedonum sunt, et succedere ad vallum parati atque instructi cœpere, repente omnes, relictis stationibus, per aversam partem castrorum ad tumulum, ad castra Athamanum perfugiunt. Multi in hac quoque *tam trepida fuga* capti caesique sunt. Ætolorum. It appears that Livy took pleasure in dwelling on the shortcomings of the Ætolians.

[1] Livy, xxxi. 40. See p. 30.

VOL. III.   D

from their safe refuge in the port of Demetrias to thwart the operations of the enemy. The Roman fleet, from its winter station at Corcyra, had sailed round the Peloponnesus in the beginning of the summer, and had in the Saronic gulf joined the Pergamenian fleet, which came from Ægina. Later on in the season this squadron was reinforced by twenty large ships of the Rhodians, and the same number of smaller undecked vessels from the Illyrian island of Issa. The chief object of this naval force seemed to be plunder, as may be seen by the readiness with which the Illyrians of Issa took part in the expedition. They evidently hoped to carry on their favourite occupation of piracy, under the plea that for belligerents it was legitimate.[1] First of all, the island of Andros, close to the southern extremity of Euboea, was taken. The Romans carried off all the moveable spoil, especially the works of art, and handed over the island to Attalus as a permanent possession, although by right it should have been restored to the king of Egypt, from whom it had been taken by Philip. The southern port of Euboea was plundered next. Sciathus would have suffered a similar fate, if Philip had not devastated it before the campaign, and thus deprived his enemies of this pleasure. The fleet sailed afterwards further northwards, and visited the Chalcidian peninsula. Here it suffered from storms, and being repulsed from Cassandrea, found a compensation in the capture of Acanthus. Having returned to Euboea, the expedition finished the year's operations by achieving a great success in the capture of the fortress of Oreus on the north of the island, after a long and obstinate resistance. Here, also, the Romans and their allies divided the spoil, according to their custom.[2] The town was given over to

[1] The modern practice of privateering is, in truth, nothing else but piracy legitimized by the law of war. As long as this remnant of barbarism is not swept away by the unanimous consent of the civilized world, we have no right to censure the ancients, whose wars had all more or less the stamp of robbery on a large scale.

[2] This was on the part of the Romans a political blunder, which produced a great deal of bad blood. Instead of plundering Oreus, and then handing it

Attalus, the Romans took the prisoners with the rest of the booty.

With this final stroke the naval operations terminated for the year. Philip had not suffered any material loss. The Rhodians and the Pergamenians returned home; the Romans sailed to Corcyra, leaving thirty ships in the Piræus for the protection of the Athenians.[1] The Athenians alone, who had carried on the war with brave slashing words and patriotic demonstrations, could boast of complete success. They destroyed all the monuments erected in honour of Philip and his ancestors, whether male or female, desecrated the altars which had been erected to him, and commanded the priests of the state to add to the prayer for the prosperity of Athens a curse on Philip, on his children, his empire, his army, his fleet, nay, on the whole Macedonian people and name. It was further resolved that, if any one in future should make a proposal for putting some fresh insult or dishonour on Philip, the Athenian people should be bound to sanction such a proposal; on the other hand, whoever should be found guilty, either in words or in deed, of honouring or respecting the memory of Philip, should be declared an outlaw. Finally, all the old decrees against the tyrannical house of Pisistratus should be applied to Philip. In order to give these resolutions the proper relief, king Attalus and the Romans were loaded with extravagant and boundless honours.[2]

---

over to Attalus, they ought to have made it a free town. This is what Appian (xi. 5) refers to: καὶ οἱ πλείονες (τῶν Ἀχαιῶν) ἡροῦντο τὰ Φιλίππου καὶ ἀπεστρέφοντο Ῥωμαίους διά τινα ἐς τὴν Ἑλλάδα Σουλπικίου τοῦ στρατηγοῦ παρανομήματα. That these παρανομήματα consisted in the hostile treatment of Oreus may be inferred from Pausanias (vii. 7, 9). This writer, speaking of the capture of Oreus, which he calls by its former name Histiæa, and of that of Anticyra, which is not mentioned by any other source, characterises the cruel treatment which these two towns received at the hands of the Romans, as an act of hostility to the Greek nation, because they were only ὑπήκοοι κατ' ἀνάγκην Φιλίππου.

[1] Livy, xxxi. 44–47.
[2] Livy, xxxi. 44: Rogationem tulerunt, plebesque scivit, ut Philippi statuæ imaginesque omnes, nominaque earum, item maiorum eius virile ac muliebre secus omnium tollerentur, delerenturque, diesque festi, sacra, sacerdotes, quæ ipsius maiorumque eius honoris causa instituta essent, omnia profanarentur; loca

The result of the campaign of 199 B.C. was, that Philip had repulsed the attacks of his opponents on all sides, and was now the master of the theatre of war. He employed the remainder of the favourable season of the year to make an attack on the fortified town of Thaumaci, which was held by an Ætolian garrison, and commanded the road from Macedonia into Thessaly. But a body of Ætolians succeeded in passing into the town through the midst of the besieging army of Macedonians, and thus frustrated all Philip's attacks, so that at last, as the winter was approaching, he desisted from the undertaking.[1]

Publius Villius Tappulus, the consul of the year 199 B.C., had waited until the autumn, before he proceeded to Greece to relieve his predecessor, Publius Sulpicius Galba. He arrived at Apollonia just when Sulpicius Galba returned from his fruitless campaign in the mountainous border country of western Macedonia. Military operations were out of the question at that late season of the year, particularly as discontent, amounting to mutiny,[2] had broken out in the Roman army. The volunteers, who in the beginning of the war had been selected from Scipio's African legions,[3] now declared that they were sent to Macedonia against their will, and insisted on being discharged. The men had probably hoped to amass rich and easy spoil in Greece, and were tired of marching to and fro in the barren and thinly populated mountains of Macedonia, where they found no reward for endless toils. Perhaps we may even infer that the discontent of the soldiers had something to do with the failure of the consul's campaign, and contributed to determine him to an early retreat. How the mutiny of the soldiers was put down, we are not informed. It may have been that the Roman government yielded, and allowed the malcontents to go home, for we hear that in the following year, 198 B.C.,

---

quoque in quibus positum aliquid inscriptumve honoris eius causa fuisset, detestabilia esse, neque in iis quicquam postea poni dedicarique placere eorum, quae in loco puro poni dedicarique fas esset.

[1] Livy, xxxii. 4, 1.   [2] Livy, xxxii. 3.   [3] See p. 26.

Flamininus brought eight thousand eight hundred fresh troops with him to Macedonia, who served to replace those who had been discharged.

In the course of the winter Philip displayed great activity. Indefatigable in his military preparations, he was at the same time intent on strengthening his political position. The commander of the fleet, Heraclides of Tarentum, had by his injudicious conduct and his cruelty made the king's government generally detested. To gain popularity Philip now sacrificed this man to the vengeance of his subjects by dismissing him and throwing him into prison.[1] Above all things, it was his great desire to gain allies. The king of Syria had been detached from his alliance. In truth, Antiochus could offer him no help. Though he made common cause with Philip for the purpose of attacking Egypt, he had so far been influenced by Roman diplomacy as to preserve friendly relations with Rome. Probably, as we have surmised,[2] the Romans had promised him to acquiesce in his obtaining permanently the province of Cœlesyria, which he had conquered from Egypt. He was therefore prevented from supporting Philip in his war with Rome, even if he had been willing to do so, which is very doubtful. He could not hope to gain anything by such a policy. But as he had succeeded, with the consent of Rome, in despoiling their client Ptolemæus, he thought he might possibly meet with equal success on the northern frontier of his kingdom. He calculated that the Romans were too busy in Macedonia to trouble themselves much about the affairs of Asia. But here he found himself mistaken. Upon the complaint of Attalus, the Romans gave Antiochus to understand that he had better desist from hostilities[3] against their friend.

CHAP. I.
200-196 B.C.

Neutrality of Antiochus.

---

[1] Diodorus, xxviii.; Livy, xxxii. 5, 7: Multis criminibus oneratum (Heracliden) in vincla coniecit, ingenti popularium gaudio. Polybius (xiii. 4, 8) says of this unprincipled adventurer that, through the influence he had over Philip, and the undeserved confidence placed in him by the king, he became almost the chief instrument of the downfall of the Macedonian kingdom.

[2] See p. 15.   [3] Livy, xxxii. 8 and 27.

Thus Attalus was free to continue in conjunction with Rome his operations against Macedonia.

Philip had now only one faint hope left, that, namely, of persuading the Achaeans to take part with him in the war with Rome. He delivered over to them several towns in Peloponnesus, which he had seized at a former time, and had kept in his possession. But he failed to conciliate the Achaeans by this tardy restitution. When the election of a new chief magistrate of the league came on, Cycliades, who favoured the Macedonian party, succumbed to Aristaenus, the Roman candidate.

Significant as this decision was, it was by no means final, and the Achaeans persevered for the present in their neutrality, which did them but little honour, and prejudiced their vital interests.

After the expiration of the winter (199-198 B.C.), when the mountain passes became practicable, Philip, without waiting for the attack of the Romans, went to meet them in the direction of Corcyra, more to the southward than in the previous year. He crossed the watershed, and took up a position in the narrow valley of the Aous, near Antigonea, which he strongly fortified by intrenchments. Thus the consul Publius Villius, who, on the arrival of spring, had set himself likewise in motion, and was advancing up the same valley, was forced to remain stationary for some time in front of the Macedonian position, unable to commence an attack. During this inaction the summer approached, and the newly elected consul for the year 198 B.C., Titus Quinctius Flamininus, who had started for the scene of action earlier in the year than his predecessor,[1] landed in Corcyra with reinforcements of eight thousand foot and eight hundred horse,[2] crossed from thence to the continent, and assumed the

---

[1] Livy, xxxii. 9, 6: Et T. Quinctius alter consul maturius, quam priores soliti erant consules, a Brundusio cum tramisisset Corcyram tenuit cum octo militibus peditum, equitibus octingentis.

[2] Of this force only three thousand foot and three hundred horse were Roman citizens, the rest were allies. Livy, xxxii. 8, 2.

command of the Roman army and the allied contingents.[1]

The family of the Quinctii belonged to the noblest and most prominent of the Roman people. Though they did not boast, like the Julii, that they were descended directly from the Trojans, yet they pretended to trace their family traditions back to the time of the earlier kings, and derived their descent from one of those families, which, after the destruction of Alba Longa under Tullus Hostilius, the third king, were transplanted to Rome, and received among the patrician houses.[2] One branch of the *gens* was the family of the Cincinnati, highly respected in the time of the older republic.[3] The family of the Fla-

---

[1] It appears from the above narrative that the consul Publius Villius accomplished, in a military point of view, nothing at all. Nevertheless, the annalist Valerius Antias related of his campaign a series of glorious exploits. According to this veracious historian (quoted by Livy, xxxii. 6, 5), Villius defeated the king of Macedonia in a pitched battle, took his camp, killed twelve thousand enemies, made two thousand two hundred prisoners, captured one hundred and thirty-two military standards and two hundred and thirty horses, having in the tumult of battle vowed a temple to Jupiter if he should be victorious. 'The other Greek and Latin authors,' continues Livy (xxxii. 6, 8), 'whose annals I have consulted, report that Villius did nothing worth mentioning, and that his successor, Titus Quinctius Flamininus had to begin the war afresh.' This sample of the mendacity of a Roman annalist is very instructive, as we have fortunately the means of exposing it. We find here the lie circumstantial in all perfection. What can look more authentic than the precise numbers given of the slain and captured? And what seems most convincing is the story about the vowing of a temple. Could such a statement have been ventured, unless there really existed a temple of Jupiter that would answer the description? And if so, would not the existence of such a temple be satisfactory evidence of the event, to which it owed its origin? Such reasoning seems natural, and would be justified, if the contradictory evidence were not so strong. In the present case we cannot doubt, even if Publius Villius or one of his family was impudent enough to erect a temple to Jupiter in commemoration of an alleged victory, that this victory nevertheless is fictitious. But as a temple of Jupiter is not a thing that can be put up in a hurry and in a corner, and as we know nothing from other sources of such a temple erected by Villius, we may infer that Valerius Antias was, as usual, not very scrupulous in verifying the fact which he relates on the authority perhaps of some family chronicler of the Villian house. The whole story falls to the ground, and we derive from it the valuable lesson that, if even the events of this Macedonian war, in the second century before Christ, are exposed to such barefaced falsifications, we must be very careful in sifting the reports of Roman victories in the earlier periods. Compare above, p. 32, note 4, and vol. i. p. 408, note 3.

[2] Livy, i. 30.   [3] See vol. i. p. 166.

minini was a younger branch of the Quinctian *gens*. At any rate, they first appear in the ranks of the high official nobility after the war with Hannibal. Immediately after this period, however, they seem to have been distinguished by great wealth; for in the year 200 B.C. the dramatic games of the Aediles, of whom Lucius Quinctius Flamininus was one, were represented with unusual splendour.[1] This liberality may have had some influence on the Comitia Centuriata, by which Titus Quinctius Flamininus, the brother of the ædile, was chosen as consul for the year 198 B.C., though he was scarcely thirty years old, and had never filled the office either of ædile or of prætor. It is true he had served in the war with Hannibal as legionary tribune, but he had had no opportunity of distinguishing himself in an independent command, and he belonged, therefore, to that large number of Roman generals who owed their election to party influence among the citizens, and not to any proved personal merit. Nothing justified the expectation of great military success from the young man, nor did he at the head of the legions show himself superior to the common run of Roman citizen-generals. It appears, however, that he was a skilful diplomatist, and particularly qualified to sift and settle the affairs of Greece; for he understood the Greek character, and was not inaccessible, like so many other Romans, to Greek views and opinions. But it is a great error to attribute to him, as is often done, a predilection or partiality for the Greeks; a partiality which overruled the calculations of interested statesmanship, and made political considerations to depend on sentiment. It is a great error to suppose that he was induced by mere generosity and good will for the Greeks to make concessions which were not entirely in harmony with the interests of Rome. He proved himself throughout to be a cool, clear-headed statesman, keeping always in view the solid advantage of his own country. If he acted the part of friend and liberator of the Greeks, he adhered closely

---

[1] Livy. xxxi, 4, 5.

to his instructions; for the Roman senate desired by means of the Greeks to keep the king of Macedonia in check, and thus to use the Greeks for the interests of Rome; while the freedom of Greece itself was as much a matter of utter indifference to all true Romans as in recent times the so-called Germanic liberties were to the statesmen of France. Flamininus was just the man to undertake the part of protector of the Greeks, and if he was to a certain extent a Philhellene, that sentiment did not interfere with his main duty. In one point only he showed himself weak. He was most sensitive to praise and blame, and easily wounded by the sharp tongue of the Greeks. Many actions which he may have wished to see attributed to his high admiration of the Greeks may really have been prompted by considerations such as these. He was, however, never misled into forgetting that he was a Roman, and responsible for all his acts to an inexorable judge, the Roman senate.[1]

His first operations against Philip promised no better result than those of his predecessors. During the whole of forty days he lay before the strongly fortified position of the king in the narrow valley of the Aous, making plans for the attack. During this period of inactivity an attempt was made, through the Epirots, who had always been well inclined to Philip, to settle the quarrel amicably. But as Flamininus insisted on the original demands of Rome, and required that Philip should set free all the Greek towns which he held in his possession, and that he should give, moreover, full compensation to those whom he had injured, Philip indignantly broke off the negotiations.

Flamininus was now in doubt, whether he should force

---

[1] Let the reader make his choice between this view of Flamininus' character and that of Mommsen (*Röm. Gesch.* i. p. 718). According to Mommsen, Flamininus belonged to that younger generation of Roman statesmen who had put off the old-fashioned notions and the old-fashioned patriotism of their fathers, and had begun to think more of Hellenism than of their own country ("die jüngere generation, welche zwar auch an das Vaterland, aber mehr an sich und an das Hellenenthum dachte").

the pass of the Aous or, retreating to the coast, should try to penetrate into Macedonia by the road which Sulpicius had followed through the more northerly passes. The failure of Sulpicius was no recommendation of this plan; and, on the other hand, an attack on the Macedonians in their very strong position would have been too great a risk, and would even, in case of success, have considerably weakened his army. It happened, therefore, very opportunely for the Roman general that with the help of an Epirote chief named Charops[1] a shepherd, acquainted with the country, was found[2] who promised to show the Romans a path over the mountains by which they could get into the rear of the enemy's position. This plan was carried out. After a difficult march of three days, a few thousand men arrived in the rear of the Macedonian camp, and announced the success of their march by fire signals, upon which the king, attacked on two sides at the same time, was forced to abandon his position with a loss of two thousand men, and to retire into Thessaly. In order to retard the expected pursuit of the Romans, Philip devastated the whole country which he traversed on his march to Macedonia. He burnt down towns and villages, and carried the inhabitants away with him.[3] The province so barbarously treated was not, as one might think, a hostile country; it was part of the Macedonian kingdom, and the Thessalians were no rebels, but faithful subjects. No wonder if the inhabitants of Pheræ closed the gates of their town, thinking that if they must perish, it was preferable to be ruined by the enemies of their country rather than by their own sovereign.

---

[1] To this Charops (according to Polybius, xxvii. 13, 2) belongs the chief merit of the success of Flamininus' campaign. Polybius, xxvii. 13, 2: Χάροψ ἦν Ἠπειρώτης ἀνὴρ τἆλλα μὲν καλὸς κἀγαθὸς καὶ φίλος Ῥωμαίων· ὃς Φιλίππου τὰ κατὰ τὴν Ἤπειρον στενὰ κατέχοντος αἴτιος ἐγένετο τοῦ Φίλιππον μὲν ἐκπεσεῖν ἐκ τῆς Ἠπείρου, Τίτον δὲ καὶ τῆς Ἠπείρου κρατῆσαι καὶ τῶν Μακεδόνων. Compare Diodorus, xxx. 5.

[2] Livy, xxxii. 11, 1: Pastor quidam, a Charopo, principe Epirotarum missus, deducitur ad consulem. According to Plutarch, *Flamin.* 4, the road was shown by several shepherds of the neighbourhood (ἄνθρωποι τῶν αὐτόθι νεμόντων).

[3] Livy, xxxii. 13. Plutarch, *Flamininus*, 5.

On the news of Philip's retreat the Ætolians again invaded unhappy Thessaly, and their worthy ally, Amynander of Athamania, vied with them in their work of devastation. The open towns were plundered and reduced to ashes, the inhabitants cut down or made prisoners, and the land transformed into a desert.

This dreadful devastation of Thessaly stopped the advance of the allied armies. Flamininus, instead of marching after the king of Macedonia, turned back towards Epirus, and secured for himself by mild treatment the neutrality and even support of a portion of the Epirote population, who till now had remained true to Philip. He then ordered the fleet at Corcyra to bring provisions for his troops to the eastern end of the Ambracian gulf;[1] and having from thence supplied his army, he advanced to attack the fortified town of Atrax, on the Peneus, westwards from Larissa, in the heart of the Thessalian plain. The town was defended by the Macedonian garrison with persevering bravery; and, after an assault had been repelled, Flamininus found himself obliged to retreat from a land which had been totally devastated by four armies, and was utterly destitute of means for the maintenance of the troops.[2]

Thus Philip's desperate method of resisting the advance of his enemies had answered his purpose, and this campaign also ended in the evacuation of Thessaly by the combined allied forces. Flamininus returned southwards before the fine season of the year was quite gone, and took up his winter quarters in the Phocean town of Anticyra, on the Corinthian gulf. He had previously taken some small places in the neighbourhood necessary to cover his position, but had been repulsed from the fortified town of Elatea. In Anticyra he was able to procure during the winter provisions for his army by sea, and at the same time he was in close vicinity to the Peloponnesus, so that he had an opportunity during the cessa-

---

[1] Livy, xxxii. 14, 7.   [2] Livy, xxxii. 17, 4.

tion of hostilities of treating with the Achaean league, and of inducing them at last to take part in the war.¹

The operations of Flamininus by land were to some extent supported by those of the allied fleet. This was commanded by Lucius Quinctius Flamininus, the consul's brother, a man who several years later (184 B.C.) was ignominiously expelled from the senate by Marcus Porcius Cato for wantonly murdering a prisoner of war. When the Roman ships had joined, near the island of Andros, the ships of the Rhodians and of Attalus, the combined naval force took two Euboean towns, Eretria and Carystus, pillaged them in the usual manner, and left them.² After this feat the allied vessels sailed to Cenchreae, the eastern harbour of Corinth, in order to be in readiness to support the consul's policy in the Peloponnesus. The allies were making preparations to besiege the town of Corinth, the chief fortress of the Macedonians in all Greece; but before they commenced their operations, the consul, Titus Flamininus, commissioned his brother Lucius, the commander of the fleet, to offer to the Achaeans this important and long desired town as the price for their participation in the league against Philip. To decide this important question, Aristaenus, the chief magistrate of the Achaean league, and a partisan of Rome, called together a federal congress at Sicyon. Here the representative of the several Achaean towns, and the ambassadors of the Romans, of the Rhodians, of Attalus, and of the Athenians met together. An embassy of Philip was also admitted, and demanded nothing more than the continued neutrality of the Achaeans.

The Achaeans were in a state of deplorable difference of opinion, fear, and indecision; and the earnest appeals of

---

¹ Livy, xxxii. 18.

² Livy (xxxii. 16, 11), in relating these proceedings, makes a remark characteristic of the avidity of the Romans for works of art, which had recently become a mania, and at the same time of the rich stores of art-works in Greece: Pecuniae aurique haud sane multum fuit; signa et tabulae priscae artis, ornamentaque eius generis plura, quam pro urbis magnitudine et opibus ceteris, inventa.

the various negotiators contributed still more to confuse them. The Macedonians could plead the ancient alliance and the essential services rendered by their king to the league in the war with Sparta. Then there was Philip's promise to continue to defend the league against this ever dangerous hereditary enemy. Lastly, he had quite recently given them possession of several places in the Peloponnesus as a proof of his goodwill.[1] But all these reasons in his favour were counterbalanced by his notorious dishonesty, and by his tyrannical and cruel temper, by which he had long made himself detested. On the other side, the Romans could allege neither old friendly relations with the Achaean league, nor especial services rendered. Nay, their amicable relations with Nabis, the detestable tyrant of Sparta, were calculated to call forth serious apprehensions. Nor had the success of the Roman arms up to this time been such that it could weigh heavily in their favour. On the contrary, the eagerness with which they sought the alliance of the Achaeans showed clearly that they did not feel themselves strong enough to carry on the war alone.

Thus the opinions wavered from side to side, and none of the assembled Achaeans ventured to make a clear and distinct proposal. This indecision, so unworthy of a proud and independent nation, was at length put an end to by Aristænus, the strategos of the league. He gave his vote in favour of the Romans, declaring that the neutrality of the Achaean league was no longer to be maintained, and that an alliance with Rome was their only true policy, partly on account of the geographical situation of the Achaean towns, partly on account of the superior power of the Romans. He went so far as to urge that it was also in the interest of Greece, which, under the protection of such powerful allies, might at length regain her freedom, and her independence from Macedonia. Notwithstanding these weighty reasons, the ten representatives of the Achaean towns were split up into two equal parts; and it was not till one of the members of the congress was threatened

[1] See p. 38.

with death by his own father, and consequently changed his opinion, that a majority in favour of the Romans was formed on the following day. But even now the men of Argos, Megalopolis, and Dyme could not make up their minds to renounce the Macedonian alliance, and they resentfully left the assembly. The remainder agreed upon a formal resolution to take the Roman side, and a part of the Achaean army was at once despatched to join the allied forces destined for the siege of Corinth. To calm the apprehensions of the Achaeans with respect to the designs of Nabis, Flamininus brought about the conclusion of an armistice between the two.[1]

Thus the anti-Macedonian alliance had grown very considerably in strength and numbers. It now embraced all Greek towns with but few exceptions, and gave the war more and more the character of a national contest against the king of that country, which, under a former Philip, had destroyed the independence of Greece. There were now on the side of Macedonia only the Acarnanians, who did not count for much; Boeotia which, except in the days of Epaminondas, had always systematically opposed the rest of Greece; and a few isolated towns, such as the three members of the Achaean league, which could not be induced to make common cause with the rest.[2]

Philocles at Corinth.

Notwithstanding all this, the cause of Philip was by no means lost. The Romans, indeed, succeeded in taking Elatea in Phocis by storm; but the attacks of the allies on Corinth were all beaten off by the citizens and the brave Macedonian garrison, which had been reinforced in good time by a detachment of one thousand five hundred men, under the command of Philocles,[3] sent from Chalcis, the Macedonian stronghold in Euboea. After the allied fleets had separated and returned to their winter stations in the Piraeus and Corcyra, the enterprising Philocles, not satis-

---

[1] Livy, xxxii. 19-23. Plutarch, *Flamin.* 5. Appian, ix. 5. Zonaras, ix. 16.
[2] Argos, Megalopolis, and Dyme.
[3] Livy, xxxii. 23, 11. This was the same officer who made the second invasion into Attica. See p. 26.

fied with the successful defence of Corinth, made an attempt to gain the important city of Argos for Philip. He appeared suddenly before this town, into which the Achaeans, immediately after embracing the Roman alliance, had thrown a garrison of five hundred chosen warriors. The sympathy of the citizens was entirely on the Macedonian side, and they had not by any means accommodated themselves to the resolution of the Achaean league. When, therefore, Philocles advanced to the town, and the five hundred Achaeans of the garrison made preparations to repel him, they were attacked in the rear by the armed citizens. The valiant Achaean captain, Ænesidemus, saw the fruitlessness of resistance, and instead of uselessly sacrificing the troops which had been entrusted to him, he surrendered the town on condition that he might send away his men unmolested. But, resolved to save his military honour, he himself remained with a few faithful men at his post, threw away his shield, and allowed himself to be pierced to death by Thracian archers.[1]

The two principal towns of the Peloponnesus, Corinth and Argos, were, therefore, at the end of the year 198 B.C., in the hands of Philip, and he hoped by this means to keep the Achaeans in check, the more so, as he finally reckoned on securing the alliance of their irreconcilable enemy, the tyrant Nabis of Sparta, although Nabis had concluded an armistice with the Achaeans under Roman mediation.

Although winter had now put an end to the operations in the field, hostilities did not altogether cease. The Romans occupied Phocis and Locris, and the town of Opus opened her gates voluntarily to them, after the Macedonian garrison had retired into the fortress. Flamininus had not had time in his year of office to bring the war to a close, and he much feared that he would be called upon to resign the command to his successor in the consulship. He did all he could, and exercised all his influence in

[1] Livy, xxxii. 25.

BOOK V.
200–196 B.C.

Rome, to be allowed to remain in Greece with the power of pro-consul; but as he could not calculate with certainty upon a prolongation of his command, he was not disinclined to meet the wishes of Philip, who now for the second time offered to enter into negotiations for the settlement of disputes. An interview was, therefore, agreed upon on the coast of the Malian gulf, not far from the town of Nicaea. Flamininus appeared accompanied by prince Amynander of Athamania, by Dionysodorus the Pergamenian ambassador, by Agesimbrotus the commander of the Rhodian fleet, by Phaeneas the strategos of the league of the Aetolians, and by the two Achaeans Aristaenus and Xenophon. The king of Macedonia, standing on the prow of a ship, approached the shore, where the Roman consul and the allied chiefs were waiting for him. Flamininus and his suit advanced to the margin of the water to meet the king. The ship cast anchor; but the king remained standing on the deck, hesitating to go on land at the invitation of the consul. Being asked of whom he was afraid, he said he feared none but the gods, but he could not place confidence in all those who accompanied the consul, and least of all in the Aetolians. With such distrust on both sides the negotiations were commenced, and as was to be expected they led to no satisfactory result.[1]

Terms offered and refused.

Philip, more and more conscious of the difficulty of his situation, was resolved to make great concessions. He declared himself prepared to restore the districts on the Illyrian coast which he had taken from the Romans, to give up the deserters and prisoners, to send back to Attalus the ships taken in the battle near Chios with the captured sailors, to resign the possessions of the Rhodians called Peraea on the continent of Asia Minor, to give to the Aetolians Pharsalus and Larissa, and to the Achaeans Argos, and even Corinth, the most important town of all.[2] But

[1] Livy, xxxii. 32; Polybius, xvii. 1.

[2] Probably the rock and castle of Acrocorinthus were not included. This important position was not handed over to the Corinthians even when they obtained their liberty and independence from Flamininus. Livy, xxxiii. 31. 11 Postremo ita decretum: Corinthus redderetur Achaeis, ut in Acrocorintho tamen praesidium esset.

these concessions satisfied neither the Romans nor their allies. The Romans insisted on the evacuation of all Greek towns, and the restoration of the Egyptian possessions which Philip had conquered after the death of Ptolemæus Philopator. Attalus wanted compensation for the ravages committed in his kingdom; the Rhodians demanded that all the towns conquered by Philip in Asia and on the Hellespont should be declared free. But the highest demands were made by the Ætolians, who wished to make use of this opportunity thoroughly to weaken Macedonia, and to recover all the places which at one time or another had been members of the Ætolian confederation. The animosity and personal rancour between Philip and the representatives of the Ætolians were so great that they threatened to break off the negotiations. Flamininus felt obliged on the second day of the conference to agree to Philip's wish and to negotiate with him alone, without admitting the allies, although their exclusion could not fail to offend them. Finally, contrary to the advice of the Greeks, he granted an armistice of two months to the king of Macedonia, the price of which was the evacuation of all the places in Locris and Phocis which were still occupied by Macedonian troops. Thus time was gained to send an embassy to Rome, and to ascertain the final decision of the senate respecting the conditions of peace.[1] It was not difficult to foresee that in the present state of things a peaceful settlement of the dispute was impossible. The demands of the Romans went a great way beyond the concessions which Philip was prepared to make, and yet up to this time no single military event had taken place during the war of decided importance. Philip's power was as yet untouched. Nei-

CHAP. I.

200-196 B.C.

Armistice of two months.

---

[1] On this occasion we see again how carefully we must distinguish between the conditions of peace and those of an armistice. The latter are temporary advantages of a military character for the party which grants the armistice. As Flamininus stipulated for the evacuation of Locris and Phocis by the Macedonians, so the evacuation of Italy by Hannibal and Mago had no doubt been a condition for the armistice granted by Scipio to the Carthaginians. See vol. ii. p. 439.

ther his army nor his fleet had suffered a defeat. The devastations which the Romans, and still more their allies, had committed in Thessaly had no other result than that of hindering the military operations against Macedonia, for they made it difficult to feed an army in that country, which was the only direct road for an army bent on invading Macedonia. If the Romans and their allies had conquered a number of fortified places, they, were on the other hand, baffled in their attacks on others, or they had been compelled to give up again places which they had taken. The alliance between Achaia and the Romans was almost outweighed by the acquisition of Argos by Philip, who moreover retained in his hands the chief fortresses of Greece. It was therefore, as we have already remarked, not to be expected that he should comply with the demands of the Romans before he should have suffered a decided defeat. When his ambassadors were roundly asked in Rome whether they were authorised to promise the evacuation of Corinth, Chalcis, and Demetrias, they had to reply by a negative, and were requested to leave Rome immediately.

Flamininus continued in the command as proconsul.

The war accordingly continued. The chief command was prorogued to Flamininus, as proconsul for the year 197 B.C., through the intercession of his friends in Rome,[1] and a reinforcement of six thousand infantry, three hundred horse, and three thousand sailors was sent out to him.[2] Flamininus, more intent, as Livy remarks,[3] on victory than on peace, declined all further negotiations

---

[1] Livy, xxxii. 32, 7: needum enim sciebat (Flamininus) utrum successor sibi alter ex novis consulibus mitteretur, an, quod summa vi ut tenderent amicis et propinquis mandaverat, imperium prorogaretur. Hence it appears that the two tribunes of the people, Lucius Oppius and Quintus Fulvius, who opposed the assignation of the command in Macedonia to one of the consuls of the year 197 B.C. (Livy, xxxii. 28, 3) belonged to these "friends and relatives" who agitated for Flamininus. The arguments of these men were not unreasonable: "quod longinqua provincia Macedonia esset, neque ulla alia res magis bello impedimento ad eam diem fuisset quam quod vixdum inchoatis rebus in ipso conatu gerendi belli prior consul revocaretur, etc.," xxxii. 28.

[2] Livy, xxxii. 28.

[3] Livy, xxxii. 37, 6: victoriae quam pacis avidior.

with Philip, which should not have for their basis the acceptance of all the demands of the senate, and prepared himself to strike a decisive blow.

From that moment when the Achaeans had joined the Roman alliance, the prospect was opened to Philip of securing the co-operation of Nabis in their place. It seemed natural that, of the two hostile neighbours in the Peloponnesus, the one should make common cause with that party with which the other was at war.[1] Up to this time Macedonia had been always allied with Achaia against Sparta. Now, after this alliance had been broken, Philip hoped to be able to draw Nabis over to his side, and he determined to do this in a manner which was calculated to brand him throughout all Greece as an infamous traitor to his best friends, and to deprive him of the small remnant of confidence and attachment still felt for him.

The citizens of Argos had given proofs of their loyalty to Macedonia by seceding from the Achaean league, and by surrendering their town to the Macedonian general Philocles.[2] As a reward for this service, Philip now gave over the town of Argos to the detestable Nabis, who had most deservedly drawn upon himself the loathing of all the Greeks. Some of the most respectable citizens, knowing well what fate awaited them, made a timely escape out of the betrayed town, and thus sacrificed only the property which they had to leave behind. The others found themselves exposed not only to plunder, but also to ill-treatment, and even the women were robbed by Apega, the worthy spouse of Nabis, of their costly garments and their jewels.[3] A general cancelling of debts, and an

---

[1] Just so the two Numidian kings, Syphax and Masinissa, were by the necessities of their position always ranged on two opposite sides. They could not both be at the same time the friends of either Carthago or Rome. See vol. ii. pp. 402, 425.

[2] See p. 47.

[3] Polybius, xiii. 7, describes an ingenious instrument of torture which Nabis is said to have employed for the purpose of obtaining money. It was the shape of a woman, and represented his wife Apega. The arms and the bosom were covered with sharp nails hidden under the dress. When Nabis found that arguments and persuasion failed in convincing any one of his new subjects of

assignation of land to the poor, secured for the tyrant a numerous party of warm adherents and admirers, and thus he obtained secure possession of Argos, just as similar measures had established his dominion over Sparta.[1]

When we read of these revolting proceedings we feel a kind of satisfaction in learning that one villain cheated the other. Nabis accepted the town of Argos from Philip. But instead of joining his party, he entered into negotiations with the Romans, by whose mediation an armistice was concluded between him and the Achaeans for the duration of the war.[2] He even sent them an auxiliary force of six hundred Cretan mercenaries for the war against Philip; and thus the tyrant loaded with the curses of half Greece, the man who had made a robber's den of the proud commonwealth of Sparta, could boast of taking part under the chief leadership of Rome in the great war of liberation of the Greek people.

Bœotia joins the Roman alliance.

The whole of the Peloponnesus had now joined the league against Philip. In central Greece the Bœotians alone still held aloof. These, too, Flamininus managed now to gain for his side. Their good will was of the greatest importance to him, as they might have interrupted his line of operations, which extended from the south of Greece through Thessaly. Determined to secure it, he entered Bœotia in the spring of 197 B.C., gained possession of Thebes by a stratagem, and by displaying the overwhelming force at his command, frightened the

---

the necessity of giving up what he demanded, this figure was brought in, and Nabis, saying that he must try his wife's eloquence, drew the arms of the figure round the person's body, and pressed it by means of machinery so close that the nails penetrated to the flesh. Some people were said to have been thus tortured to death. It appears from this that the plan of drawing the teeth of a man for the purpose of inducing him to lend money was a novelty in England only in so far as it was less refined than the ingenious combination of humour and cruelty invented by the worthy old tyrant.

[1] Livy, xxxii. 38, 9: contione inde advocata rogationes promulgavit, unam de tabulis novis, alteram de agro viritim dividendo, duas faces novantibus res ad plebem in optimates accendendam.

[2] Livy, xxxii. 39. See p. 46.

Bœotians, though most reluctant to abandon the Macedonian side, to declare for the Roman alliance. There was nothing now to threaten the rear of the advancing army, except the two Macedonian fortresses of Chalcis and Corinth, the latter of which alone contained a garrison of no less than six thousand men. However, as all the Greek states had now declared themselves in favour of Rome, and were united in a common war against Macedonia, these two strongholds could easily be kept in check, and they could benefit Philip only so far as they detained before them a portion of the auxiliary forces which otherwise would have joined the invading army in its advance northwards. Flamininus, therefore, as soon as he had secured the co-operation of Bœotia, advanced at once towards Thessaly, determined, if possible, to bring the war to a close in this the fourth campaign. He commanded, in addition to his two legions, a heterogeneous mass of Greek and African soldiers, an army such as no Roman general had ever before led into the field. Besides the Roman legions, he had Numidian and Ætolian horsemen, African elephants, Cretan archers, Epirots, Illyrians, and Greek Hoplites and Peltasts.[1] The whole force seems to have amounted to no more than twenty-four thousand men, if we can rely on the accuracy of Livy's statements.[2] But the numbers appear very small, and, as usual with Roman annalists, the contingents of the allies seem to have been unduly understated.[3]

Strength of the Roman army.

---

[1] Livy, xxxiii. 3.

[2] Livy (xxxiii. 4), after enumerating the component parts of the Macedonian army, which he brings to twenty-three thousand five hundred men, adds that the Roman force was about equal, but that owing to the Ætolian contingent they were stronger in cavalry. This expression is sufficiently vague to suggest a suppression of the truth.

[3] This statement seems to have been especially unfair to the Ætolians, for whom not only the Roman annalists, but also Polybius, invariably show evident ill-will. It is uncertain whether Livy's statement includes the whole strength of the Ætolian contingent. He says (xxxiii. 3, 9) that, under the command of Phænens, six hundred Ætolian foot and four hundred horse joined the Roman army at Xyniæ. He does not say in express words that this was the whole Ætolian force. We need not therefore hesitate in accepting a statement of Plutarch (*Flamininus*, 7) that the Ætolian contingent amounted to six thousand men. This number cor-

BOOK V.
200-196 B.C.

Strength of the Macedonian army.

Philip in the preceding autumn could hardly have entertained any hope of successful negotiations for peace. He, therefore, made use of the winter to replenish his army and to train his new soldiers. Macedonia was so exhausted that Philip had to press boys and old men into his service to raise in all about twenty-three thousand five hundred men. Sixteen thousand of these were Phalangites or heavy-armed men. The rest were light-armed, and among them were Thracians, Illyrians, mercenaries from different countries, Thessalian horse, and some Greek auxiliaries, notably the Bœotians, who had remained faithful to him, when the rest of their countrymen had joined the Romans. The strength of this army consisted in the dreaded Phalanx, which was still regarded as invincible, but the charm of which was soon to be broken. Notwithstanding the efficient Thessalian cavalry in Philip's army, the allies were superior to Philip in this respect, thanks to the excellent Ætolian horse.

Battle of Cynoscephalae.

It was the summer of the year 198 B.C., and the yellow corn was waving in the fields of Thessaly,[1] when Philip, marching southwards from Larissa, on the Peneus, looked

---

responds with the military strength and importance of the Ætolian confederacy, which was of the first rank among all the Greek states, and a match for the Achaeans. It would probably have been still greater if, shortly before the Macedonian campaign, six thousand Ætolian mercenaries had not entered the service of Egypt. As we shall see by-and-by, the Ætolians claimed the chief merit for the victory gained over Philip at Cynoscephalae (Livy, xxxiii. 11, 8; Plutarch, *Flamininus*, 9). This would have been a ridiculous presumption and conceit if they had furnished no more than a thousand men for the decisive battle. But Dio Cassius (frgm. 60 Dindorf, 157 Tauchnitz) speaks of the assertion of the Ætolians as if it were well founded (Καὶ οἱ Αἰτωλοὶ ἐν μεγάλῳ καὶ τότε αὐχήματι, ὅτι τὸ πλεῖστον τῆς νίκης κατειργάσαντο ὄντες, κ.τ.λ.). The Achaeans, even after the loss of Argos and Corinth, their two most important towns, furnished a contingent of five thousand three hundred men for the blockade of Corinth, whilst Achaean mercenaries, no less than Ætolian, were serving abroad (Livy, xxxiii. 18, 2). Nabis, the tyrant of Sparta, raised in the following year an army of fifteen thousand men. It is therefore not likely that the contingent of the Ætolians was so insignificant as has been taken for granted from Livy's imperfect statement. We cannot imagine that the Romans would have been so very anxious to secure the alliance of the Ætolians (see page 24) if they had not just grounds to expect from them a considerable reinforcement. Therefore, if we have to choose between the thousand men of Livy and the six thousand of Plutarch, we do not hesitate to decide in favour of the latter.   [1] Polybius, xviii. 3, 3, 4.

out for the Roman army, which was moving northwards, near the coast of the Pagasæan Gulf. The intention of Flamininus may have been to attack the fortress of Demetrias, and perhaps Philip came to protect it. But our informants are silent on the cause which brought the two armies into this corner of Thessaly. The light-armed advanced guards of both encountered each other in the neighbourhood of Pheræ. As, on account of numerous fences and garden walls, this locality was very unfavourable for the evolutions of large bodies of troops, Philip retired in the direction of Scotussa. A low chain of hills called Cynoscephalæ (the hound's heads) stretched in the direction from Pheræ towards Scotussa. Separated by these hills from one another, the Macedonians and the Romans marched for two whole days side by side in the same direction, without seeing one another or having the remotest idea that a collision was all but unavoidable. If there had been a Hannibal opposed to the Romans, it would have been difficult for them to escape the fate of the unhappy Flaminius at the Thrasymenian lake. But Philip knew neither how to make use of the ground nor to avail himself of the negligence of the Roman general, who, although he had a numerous and excellent cavalry, familiar with the country, had entirely lost sight of the enemy, and was groping about like a blind man. On the third day, while mist and heavy showers of rain almost enveloped the country in darkness, Philip halted, pitched a camp, and sent out a detachment to take possession of the ridge of the hills. By chance a troop of Roman horse and light-armed foot met the Macedonians, who were coming from the other side. Thus a skirmish took place, without object or plan, in which alternately one and the other side had the advantage, according as each received reinforcements. Philip did not wish to bring on a battle, especially as one half of his phalanx had been sent out to forage. But when the fight of the advanced guard seemed to grow more and more favourable for the Macedonians, and the Romans were repulsed, in spite of the devoted bravery of the Ætolian horse, Flamininus found himself obliged, for the protection of his fleeing troops, to draw up his whole army in order of battle. Philip now complied with the solicitations of his chief officers, and gave orders for a general advance. He marched himself at the head of the right wing of the phalanx towards the hills, and having reached the top saw his advanced troops engaged with the whole left wing of the Romans. The light-armed Macedonians, unable to withstand the onslaught of the legions, sought protection behind and near the approaching phalanx, which now commenced the attack, and by the weight of its closed ranks, increased by the sloping ground, drove back the Romans, and compelled them to retire fighting towards their camp.

The chances of the battle seemed to turn in favour of the Macedonians. But as yet only one wing had been engaged as well on the Roman as on the Macedonian side. The right wing of the Romans was yet unbroken, and now moved, with the elephants at its head, towards the heights where the remainder of the Macedonian phalanx, which had only just returned from their foraging expedition,[1] were in the act of forming into line, an operation which the broken and irregular ground rendered peculiarly difficult. Nicanor, who commanded here, did not wait until the phalanx had completed its order of battle. He rushed, without order, with the foremost ranks against the advancing Romans; but the feeble line was in a moment broken and routed by the elephants. Disorder soon spread over the whole wing, and the phalanx turned to flight without even waiting for the arrival of the Roman infantry.

At this momentous juncture a legionary tribune, whose name is unfortunately not recorded, seized the favourable opportunity to shape the battle which had been begun without plan into a brilliant victory for Rome. He desisted from pursuing the routed wing of the Mace-

[1] This was probably the reason why the left wing of the Macedonians was so very late.

donians, and wheeling round to the left with a small detachment against the victorious wing of the enemy's right, which was advancing upon the Roman camp, fell upon their rear. The phalanx, firm as a wall against an attack in front, was too unwieldy to turn quickly and meet an attack coming from behind. It was at once broken. The Macedonians threw away their long spears, which were only impediments in a hand-to-hand combat. At the same moment the Romans on the left wing, which was in full retreat towards the camp, had no sooner perceived what was going on in the rear of the phalanx, than they turned round and resumed the attack. The Macedonians, thus assaulted in front and rear, were utterly routed and turned to flight.

The battle was soon decided. Five thousand Macedonians were made prisoners, eight thousand were killed,[1] partly in consequence of a mistake, because the Roman soldiers, not knowing that the Macedonians placed their lances upright as a token of surrender, cut down many who asked for quarter. The Romans lost altogether only seven hundred men. That was the price paid for a victory which laid the monarchy of Alexander the Great in the dust.

The detailed account of Polybius,[2] which we have

[1] According to Livy (xxxiii. 10, 8) Valerius of Antium, whose besetting sin, as we know, was exaggeration (omnium rerum immodice numerum augens), the number of slain Macedonians was forty thousand. Another Roman annalist, Claudius Quadrigarius, whose reputation is not quite so bad, is satisfied with thirty-two thousand. Who knows what the statement of Livy himself would have been, if he had not had the good luck and the good sense to consult Polybius? In cases where there was no Polybius to check the vainglorious mendacity of Roman annalists, it is allowed, as we see from the present illustration, to be a little incredulous.

[2] Polybius, xviii. 2-10. Livy's report (xxxiii. 7-10), which is based on Polybius, contains some rhetorical embellishments and some curious blunders. Instances of the former are the following. xxxiii. 7, 2 ; sed tam densa caligo occoecaverat diem, ut neque signiferi viam, nec signa milites cernerent, agmen ad incertos clamores vagum velut errore nocturno turbaretur. These fine words are Livy's version of part of the dry narrative of Polybius, xviii. 3, 9: δυσχρηστούμενος δὲ κατὰ τὴν πορείαν διὰ τὴν ὁμίχλην βραχὺν τόπον διανύσας τὴν μὲν δύναμιν εἰς χάρακα παρενέβαλε. The latter portion of this statement of Polybius Livy gratuitously misrepresents by adding " supergressi tumulos qui Cynoscephalae vocantur . . . . posuerunt castra," though even Livy's own description of the battle places the Macedonian

BOOK V.
200–196 B.C.
The phalanx and the maniple.

followed in our narrative, leaves no room for a doubt as to the character of the battle. It was won, not by the superior generalship of Flamininus, but by the superiority of the Roman manipular tactics over the cumbrous and unwieldy Macedonian phalanx. In a narrow breach, or wherever the flanks and rear were covered, the phalanx, it is true, formed an impenetrable living wall; but where it could be attacked in flank or rear it was helpless. It was scarcely possible to move round quickly or to change the front of a solid body of men of sixteen ranks, drawn up behind one another and armed with spears twenty feet long,[1] which projecting from the second, third, fourth and fifth rank to a distance of eight, six, four and two cubits beyond the front, bound them all together into a compact mass. Every inequality in the ground, every ditch, bush, or stone that hindered the closing of ranks, every quick and sudden movement, necessarily broke up this solid mass, in which the single soldier counted for nothing unless he remained closely united to the whole. One gap

camp on the opposite side of the hills, not on that where the battle took place. Further on (chap. 7, 5) Livy relates that the reconnoitring party of the Romans fell in with the Macedonian outposts: "pavore mutuo inicto velut torpentes quieverunt, dein nuntiis retro in castra ad duces missis, ubi primus terror ab necopinato visu consedit, non diutius certamine abstinuere. Principio a paucis procurrentibus lacessita pugna est, deinde subsidiis tuentium pulsos aucta." This corresponds with the far simpler words of Polybius (chap. 4, 3) : οὗτοι μὲν οὖν ἐν ταῖς ἀρχαῖς ἐπὶ βραχὺ διαταραχθέντες ἀμφότεροι μετ' ὀλίγον ἤρξαντο καταπειράζειν ἀλλήλων. So far Livy is only guilty of inaccuracies arising from a desire to paint an effective scene. But his imperfect knowledge of Greek, and his carelessness, exposed him to far greater faults. He tells us (chap. 8, 13) that Philip gave the order: "Macedonum phalangem, hastis positis quarum longitudo impedimento erat, gladiis rem gerere." The words of Polybius are (chap. 7, 9): τοῖς μὲν φαλαγγίταις ἐδόθη παράγγελμα, καταβαλοῦσι τὰς σαρίσσας ἐπάγειν. Livy mistook the expression καταβάλλειν τὰς σαρίσσας, which means "to lower the spears for attack," for "hastas ponere," to throw the spears down, although in other passages (xxxii. 17, 13; xxxiv. 18, 6) he correctly renders it by "hastas prae se obiicere." See Nissen, *Untersuchungen über die Quellen des Livius*, pp. 24, 32, and Weissenborn's notes to Livy, xxxiii. 7, 3; 8, 13.

[2] According to Polybius, xviii. 12, the Macedonian *sarissa* was fourteen cubits (πήχεις) long, of which ten cubits projected in front of the man who held it, and four were between and behind his hands. Reckoning a cubit (πῆχυς) at 0·4434 mètre, the sarissa would be 6·2076 mètres long, or nearly twenty feet and a half.

in the forest of lances was sufficient to split up the whole phalanx, and once broken it could not easily form again. Thus it happened that in the first serious encounter after the commencement of the war the rapidly moving maniples of the Roman legions, without any direction from an able leader, found out almost by instinct the weak part of the phalanx and broke into it, as water finds its way into the chinks of an old ship. This result was perhaps materially facilitated by the circumstance that a portion of Philip's soldiers consisted of newly levied and almost useless recruits. At least it is probable that the discreditable conduct of the left wing may be attributed to the inferior quality of the troops composing it.

What share the Greek auxiliaries had in the victory at Cynoscephalae is not reported by our authorities. We hear only that in the beginning of the combat the Ætolian horse conducted themselves well and delayed the Macedonian advance. But after the victory an outcry was raised among the legions against the Ætolians for having immediately broken into the enemy's camp to plunder it, while the Romans were still occupied with the pursuit. The jealousy and envy among the allies therefore broke out immediately after the first great success which they had gained by their united efforts, and this feeling could not fail to lead more and more to mutual estrangement.

At about the same time when Philip's principal army succumbed in Thessaly to the Roman legions and to the allied Greeks, he experienced in three different places unexpected and heavy blows which, in connexion with his own defeat, impressed upon him the absolute necessity of a speedy reconciliation with Rome.

After the successive defection of the Epirots, the Achaeans and Boeotians, and after the loss of Phocis, Locris and Thessaly, the only allies which Philip had yet in Greece were the Acarnanians. Their chief town, Leucas, on the island of the same name, was at that time besieged by a Roman fleet under the proconsul's brother,

BOOK V.
200-196 B.C.

Loss of Caria.

Defeat of Macedonians in Peloponnesus.

Philip's wish for peace.

Lucius Quinctius Flamininus,[1] and after an heroic resistance was taken. When after this loss the news arrived of the battle of Cynoscephalae the brave and faithful Acarnanians resigned themselves to their fate, and submitted to the Romans.[2]

The second mishap was announced from Peraea, an ancient possession of the Rhodians, on that part of Caria which was opposite the island of Rhodes. It had lately been conquered by Philip on his expedition into Asia Minor in 201 B.C., of which we have spoken above.[3] The Rhodians had formed an army of Greek, Gallic, Asiatic, and African mercenaries, and defeated so completely the Macedonian general Dinocrates, who commanded a no less heterogeneous army, that he had to give up all the fortified towns in the land, except Stratonicea.[4]

The third and heaviest reverse of the Macedonian arms was reported from the Peloponnesus. Though the strong Macedonian garrison of Corinth, of six thousand men, had not been able to stop the advance of the Romans towards Thessaly, nor to threaten them in the rear, they had occupied the forces of the Achaeans, and the Macedonian commander, Androsthenes, considered himself strong enough to lay the surrounding lands under contribution, while Nicostratus, the strategos of the Achaean league, for a long time did not venture to leave the shelter of the walls of Sicyon. But at last Nicostratus made a well-planned attack on the plundering bands, routed them completely, and drove them back to Corinth, with the loss of eighteen hundred men.[5]

Even before Philip could have heard of these disasters, he had lost the courage to continue the contest any longer. Straight from the field of battle, he hurried into his own country, where he collected the flying remnants of his army. He sent heralds to ask for the permission to bury the dead, and at the same time to ascertain

---

[1] See p. 44.
[2] Livy, xxxiii. 17, 18.
[3] See p. 16.
[4] Livy, xxxiii. 18.
[5] Livy, xxxiii. 14, 15.

whether Flamininus was inclined or not to receive ambassadors.[1] The Roman general showed so much readiness to enter into negotiations, and such a generous disposition towards the king of Macedonia, that his allies, the Ætolians, were baffled in their eagerness for revenge, and at once accused him of neglecting their wishes and interests, inasmuch as he was about to negotiate with the enemy without consulting those "who had contributed most towards the victory."

Such presumption had only the effect of confirming the Roman statesman in his determination to grant the king of Macedonia at once favourable terms of peace. He was, moreover, anxious to bring the Macedonian war to a close before the king of Syria should be tempted to make common cause with his old ally. It was enough for the present, if Macedonia was humbled and weakened. By a show of moderation it might be expected that king Philip would be reconciled to the position of a Roman ally. It was desirable to establish a kind of political equilibrium in the East, so that no single state might grow powerful enough to pursue an independent policy, to withdraw itself from Roman influence, and possibly become dangerous in the end. Flamininus had, moreover, a personal interest in his conciliatory policy, as was so often the case with Roman statesmen. He wished to put an end to the war before the arrival of a successor in the command could deprive him of the glory of triumphing in Rome as the conqueror of Macedonia. He explained, therefore, to his allies that Rome had determined to let Macedonia remain intact within her old boundaries. She would thus, he said, serve to protect Greece from the Northern barbarians without being able further to threaten the liberty of the Greek states. He then arranged a conference with Philip at the opening of the pass of Tempe, which leads from Thessaly to Macedonia along the foot of Mount Olympus. Here Philip declared himself ready to comply

[1] Polybius, xviii. 17.

with all the demands formerly made by Rome, and to let the Roman senate draw out the final and detailed conditions of peace.[1] When the Ætolians saw that in these negotiations between Macedonia and Rome they were being disregarded, Phæneas, the strategos of their league, tried to establish the claim of the Ætolians to those towns in Thessaly which Philip had taken from them. He thought himself at liberty to base his claim on the treaty which was concluded in the year 211 B.C. between the Ætolians and the Romans, and according to which the spoil gained in the war was to be divided, so that Rome should have all that was movable, and Ætolia all the conquered countries and towns.[2] But he was severely rebuked by Flamininus, and reminded that that treaty could no longer be considered as binding, since the Ætolians had violated it by their separate peace with Philip.[3] This act the Romans could never forget or forgive, and it made it impossible for them to entertain perfect confidence and hearty goodwill towards the Ætolians in the second alliance against Macedonia, an alliance which nothing but the necessities of the war had compelled them to seek.

In order to give time to the Roman senate to settle the questions of peace and war, a truce of four months was concluded. As a security for its rigid observance, Philip gave up his son Demetrius and several men of high rank as hostages, besides the sum of two hundred talents, on condition that the money and the hostages should be returned if the peace were not concluded.[4] During this time of truce Philip was at liberty to drive back the Dardanians, who in the meantime had invaded Macedonia. Why the Romans abandoned those barbarians, who till now had been their allies, we cannot tell. Perhaps the Dardanians had neglected to make the diversion in favour of the Romans at the right time, according to the agreement. At all events, the proceeding of both allies shows

---

[1] Polybius, xviii. 21, 1.
[2] Vol. ii. p. 411.
[3] In the year 205 B.C. See vol. ii. p. 441.
[4] Livy, xxxiii. 13.

that they did not consider themselves much bound by their mutual obligations. The Dardanians, being left to themselves, could not resist the Macedonian army, and were driven back to their own country with great loss.[1]

As hostilities were now at an end, the troops out of the different Greek towns, which till now had served in the Macedonian army, returned to their homes at the suggestion of Flamininus. This measure was indispensable, because the connexion was dissolved which up to this time had united so many Greek towns to Macedonia. The Macedonian army—the strength of which was to be reduced to a lower standard—could for the future no longer contain any Greek contingents; and, on the other hand, the Greeks, if they wished to preserve their independence, were obliged to keep their fighting men at home.[2]

The return, however, of so many men from the Macedonian service could not fail to give a new impulse to party hatred, and to impart new strength to the adherents of Macedonia, who had temporarily given way to the superiority of Rome. In Bœotia they felt themselves so encouraged, that they chose for the coming year as head of the Bœotian league one Brachyllas, the late commander of the contingents just returned from Macedonia, the most zealous friend of Philip, and, of course, leader of the opposition to Rome.

That the beaten party could summon up courage to take such a bold step before the eyes and under the pressure of the Roman army was a warning to their opponents, and caused them to fear the worst after the Romans should have left the country. In order to secure the power for themselves betimes, they determined to get rid of the head of the Macedonian party. Flamininus knew of the plan, and neither disapproved nor prevented

---

[1] Livy, xxxiii. 19, 1. In the peace which was afterwards concluded the Dardanians are not even mentioned.

[2] Livy, xxxiii. 27, gives a different reason for this measure, which seems to be incorrect. He represents it as resulting merely from the kind disposition of the Romans towards the Bœotians.

its execution.¹ He confined himself to allowing the Bœotians to do as they pleased, and this alone was encouragement enough for the hot-headed faction. Two of the Roman sympathisers, Zeuxippus and Pisistratus, hired assassins to kill Brachyllas in the street by night, as he was returning, full of wine, with some boon companions from a public banquet. This criminal as well as foolish deed, for which the authors immediately suffered death, produced in the whole of Bœotia such a violent rage against the Romans, that no isolated Roman soldier was safe anywhere, and some hundreds of them were surprised and murdered. Flamininus saw himself compelled to adopt most rigorous measures of repression. He imposed a heavy fine on the Bœotians; and when they were unable to pay it, and endeavoured to excuse or even to justify themselves, he sent troops to lay waste the neighbourhood of Coronea and Acræphia, in the vicinity of the lake Copais, where most of the murders had taken place. At length, through the mediation of the Athenians and Achaeans, a compromise was agreed upon. The Bœotians consented to give up the chief malefactors, and to pay a penalty of thirty talents.² This whole episode shows how little prospect there was that, if the Greeks gained their independence and freedom with Roman help, they would ever put off their old sins, and establish order and peace under any form of national self-government.

The senate as umpire

Towards the end of the year 197 B.C.³ Philip's ambassadors appeared in Rome, and tried to obtain the con-

---

¹ Livy (xxxiii. 28) is disingenuous enough to conceal this, evidently because he was ashamed to report such a dishonourable act of a Roman general. But Polybius, whom Livy follows in the narrative in other respects, has preserved this characteristic fact. Polybius, xviii. 26. 10 : ὁ δὲ Τίτος ταῦτα διακούσας αὐτὸς μὲν οὐκ ἔφη κοινωνεῖν τῆς πράξεως ταύτης τοὺς δὲ βουλομένους πράττειν οὐ κωλύειν.

² Livy, xxxiii. 29.

³ It is surprising that so much time was lost. Even the consul's report of the battle of Cynoscephalae only arrived in Rome towards the end of the year. Livy, xxxiii. 24. 3: Exitu ferme anni literae a T. Quinctio venerunt se signis collatis cum rege Philippo in Thessalia pugnasse, hostium exercitum fusum fugatumque.

sent of the Roman people to the treaty of peace. At the same time the allies of the Romans made use of the opportunity to lay their especial wishes, demands, and complaints before the senate. No doubt the worthy senators must have felt confused and worried when they were called upon by the glib-tongued Greeks to decide whether Triphylia belonged in justice to the Eleans or to the Achaeans, whether the Messenians had a well-grounded claim upon Asine and Pylos, or the Ætolians on Heraea, and to determine other like questions of detail.¹ The difficulty was increased by the circumstance that Marcus Claudius Marcellus, one of the consuls elected for the ensuing year, did all he could to frustrate the peace, in hopes that the glory of bringing the Macedonian war to a close might devolve upon him.² Fortunately these machinations utterly failed. The senate and the people approved the proceedings of Flamininus, and it was determined to send a commission of ten senators to Greece for the final settlement of the conditions of peace, and for the regulation of all matters of detail. The ten deputies arrived a few days after the disturbances in Boeotia had been put down, and now the conditions under which the Roman people were inclined to conclude peace were communicated to the king of Macedonia.

These conditions were so hard that only the consciousness of thorough exhaustion could make them appear acceptable. Macedonia was, indeed, allowed to continue as an independent state, but like Carthage a few years before, she was to lose all foreign possessions; even the old dependency of Orestis was to be detached and declared free. This district of Orestis was of special importance, because it was an easily defended mountain region, and lay on the line of communication with Illyria, the line by which the Romans, in a future war, were likely to advance, provided the kings of Macedonia were no longer able, as hitherto, to close the road against a hostile army. Moreover, the so-called independence of Macedonia was

Conditions of peace.

¹ Polybius, xviii. 25.   ² Livy, xxxiii. 25.

very materially modified by restrictions, whereby it was placed under the suzerainty of Rome, and in fact sunk to the level of a vassal state. Philip was obliged to reduce his army to five thousand men, his fleet to five ships, to keep no war elephants, and to pledge himself to carry on no foreign war without the consent of the senate. The last of these conditions alone sufficed to take away the semblance of independence, and to range Macedonia among those states which, though honoured by the name of allies and friends, were really subject to Rome. A last condition which followed, as a matter of course, was the delivering up of all the prisoners of war, of the deserters, and of those ships which were over and above the stipulated number of five. Finally, a war indemnity was imposed of a thousand talents, or about two hundred and fifty thousand pounds sterling.[1]

Difficulties of a new settlement of Greek affairs.

The conclusion of a treaty of peace with Philip offered no very great difficulty to the ingenuity of the Roman negotiators, as Philip was bent upon peace at any price. But a task much more complicated and delicate was the new order to be established in all those towns which had been delivered from the Macedonian dominion, and the settlement of their mutual relations to one another. It

---

[1] An attempt has been made (by Nissen, *Untersuchungen über die Quellen des Livius*, p. 144 f.) to show that it was an exaggeration of the Roman annalists if they stated that the full sovereignty of Macedonia was limited by a condition of peace which took away the right of making peace and war, and which reduced the Macedonian army and fleet to a stipulated maximum. It has been affirmed that in reality Philip only bound himself not to attack Roman allies, nor to conclude with them any sort of alliance. The proof of this assertion is supposed to lie in the silence of Polybius, who (xviii. 27) indeed does not mention those conditions of peace which are incompatible with the full sovereignty and independence of Macedonia. But we must bear in mind that Polybius himself professes to give only the principal conditions (τὰ συνέχοντα τοῦ δόγματος τῆς συγκλήτου). Moreover, we know that such restrictions as those to which the king of Macedonia was subjected were generally applied by Rome in similar treaties of peace. It is true that Philip's army after the peace amounted to more than five thousand men. But it was surely not in the interest of the Romans to insist upon a reduction of the Macedonian army, when they were making use of it themselves in their war with Antiochus. Conditions and stipulations of all sorts are easily forgotten and neglected if it suits both parties to do so. (Compare p. 74, note 1.)

was in no way sufficient to leave each separate community to itself. All were not in a position to maintain such independent existence. Many of them were, of old, either subject to a more powerful neighbouring state, or they were members of confederacies more or less extensive. Some were claimed by jealous neighbours on all sorts of pleas. It was impossible to fulfil all hopes. The general declaration that the war had been undertaken for the liberation of Greece, could not, except under many limitations and reserves, be carried out without giving mortal offence to deserving allies. The Ætolians hoped to rule in Thessaly in Philip's place; the Rhodians insisted on recovering their possessions on the continent of Asia Minor; nor could it be expected of the king of Pergamum that he should lose the Greek towns lying within the boundaries of his kingdom, which had always been subject to him, or that he should resign Ægina which Attalus had purchased from the Ætolians in the first Macedonian war for the sum of thirty talents.[1]

But the most difficult question of all seemed to be what should be done with the three great Macedonian fortresses of Corinth, Chalcis, and Demetrias. Whatever might be thought of Corinth, which had always been a great autonomous state, and was safe as a member of the Achaean league, the condition of Chalcis and Demetrias was very different. It was not to be expected that, if left to themselves, they would be able to remain neutral or independent, because they had not sufficient resources to resist a vigorous attack from one of the greater powers. The king of Syria assumed from day to day a more hostile position. If he, or any other power, were to get possession of them, they would again become what they had been in the hands of Macedonia—the means for enslaving Greece.

The three great fortresses.

---

[1] Polybius, xxiii. 8, 10. The Ætolians had a perfect right to sell the island. At least the Romans could not dispute it; for, according to the treaty of alliance between Rome and the Ætolians, the latter were to retain, as their portion of the booty gained in common, all the conquered land, whereas the Romans obtained the movable property. See vol. ii. p. 411.

Across all these difficulties Flamininus, with the senatorial committee deputed to assist him, at length found a way which promised to satisfy, if not all, at least the great majority of the Greeks, and he resolved to declare his resolutions with such solemnity that their new liberty might appear to the Greeks in the light of a free gift of Roman magnanimity. The grand festival of the Isthmian games was about to be celebrated. A rumour had already prepared the Greeks for the important message which was to be delivered to them by their powerful protectors at this national meeting of the whole race. Full of expectation and delight, like children who are promised an unusual pleasure, they assembled in large numbers on the isthmus of Corinth, and filled the race-course with an impatient crowd, expressing their wishes, doubts, and hopes with the liveliness and excitement characteristic of the Greek race. At length a herald stepped forth into their midst. A blast of the trumpet commanded silence, and with a loud voice the herald read the following decree: "The Roman senate and Titus Quinctius the consul, having conquered king Philip and the Macedonians, accord their liberty to the Corinthians, Phocians, Locrians, Eubœans, Phthiotians, Magnesians, Thessalians, Perrhæbeans, that they may live according to their own laws without foreign garrisons, and without paying tribute." The herald was obliged to read the resolution a second time, for many thought they were dreaming, or could not trust their own ears, so overjoyed were they when the news reached them. There were no bounds to the rejoicings,[1] and Flamininus was overwhelmed with the demonstrations of thanks from the intoxicated crowd. The sanguine people gave themselves up without reserve to the hope that now at last, purchased almost without a sacrifice of their own, the long-desired day of freedom and independence was breaking, and that all the long trials and calamities of evil days would be forgotten in the new

---

[1] Plutarch, *Flamininus*, 10.

prosperity of the people. They believed with child-like simplicity that the Romans really cared for their freedom, and that they had crossed the sea with no other object than to deliver Greece from a foreign yoke. They seriously considered it a gain that they had exchanged the dominion of a neighbour, arrogant indeed, but of kindred blood, for that of a foreign people, because this people, conscious of superior strength, left them for the present undisturbed to the play of their national passions, their everlasting jealousies, their mutual encroachments, waiting patiently for the time when it might be opportune to make them feel that they had only placed a heavier yoke about their necks. A close observer might indeed, even now, have had a foretaste of the Roman mode of treating their friends. For in the solemn proclamation of independence the co-operation of the Greeks in the war against Macedonia was passed over with significant silence, and Greece was treated as if she were the private property of the Roman people. Was it possible not to feel the humiliation which lay in the whole proceeding, or to hope that Greece would be able to guard a possession which she had received as a free gift of generosity?

Though such considerations were swallowed up in the first gush of excitement and in the general rejoicings, it was unavoidable that here and there, where private interests had been injured, discontent should show itself. Perhaps after the first frenzy of delight had abated, few were perfectly satisfied, when they compared what had been granted by Flamininus with that to which, by their own services, they thought they could lay just claim. Above all others, the Ætolians were deeply hurt. They had reckoned on new acquisitions in Thessaly and Acarnania. But Thessaly, according to the intentions of Rome, was to form a neutral ground between Macedonia and Ætolia to keep the ambition of both states within bounds. It was, therefore, divided into four free and autonomous cantons, called Phthiotis, Magnesia, Thessaly, and Perrhæbia, and every kind of dependence on Macedonia as well as on

BOOK V.
200–196 B.C.

Ætolia which had formerly existed was removed. Moreover, the Ætolians received neither Acarnania, nor the towns in the Peloponnesus which formerly belonged to them; they were allowed to extend their confederacy only in the direction of Locris and Phocis, and besides this they received Ambracia and Œniadæ in Epirus.[1]

The affairs of the Peloponnesus.

The year 196 B.C. was spent in adjusting the internal affairs of Greece. The most difficult task, however, of all yet remained to be done, the final establishment of peace in the Peloponnesus. The Romans found themselves here in a very awkward position, in so far as they had for their allies both Sparta and Achaia, two states at war with one another. Each of these had rendered important services in the last campaign, and each expected now to be rewarded by Rome at the expense of the other. The Achaeans had joined the Roman alliance not readily, but with great reluctance, while Sparta could boast of her old

---

[1] The detail of the territorial arrangements cannot be ascertained with certainty; for the full text of the treaty of peace is not preserved in the fragments of Polybius, and the Roman annalists are not entirely trustworthy. See Nissen, *Untersuchungen über die Quellen des Livius*, p. 144. But it is not likely that these writers simply invented the statements which they give. How came Valerius Antias to tell us (Livy, xxxiii. 30) that Ægina was to be given to Attalus, Stratonicea and the other Carian towns to the Rhodians, the islands of Lemnos or Paros, Imbros, Delos, and Scyros to the Athenians? Such statements are not invented even by habitual liars. It is no contradiction of the narrative with regard to Ægina to say that it could not have been given to Attalus, because Attalus had died a year before. Attalus stands here simply for the kingdom of Pergamum, and it would be nothing but a pardonable inaccuracy if the Roman annalist had for reasons of style put the name of the king instead of that of the kingdom. Nor is the statement invalidated by the fact that Attalus had purchased the island of Ægina from the Ætolians, and that his successor was therefore in possession before the disposition made by Flamininus at the Isthmian festival. The Romans were not obliged to recognise the sale of the Ætolians as a perfect title, and by solemnly assigning the island to the king of Pergamum they were enabled to put a slight on the Ætolians, whilst at the same time they impressed the king of Pergamum with the fact of their suzerainty. It is therefore probable that they formally acknowledged the right of Pergamum to Ægina, and that Valerius found in his sources a statement to this effect. The gifts made to the Athenians and Rhodians were probably also referred to in the treaty of peace. Delays and obstacles may have been interposed between the formal promise and the actual delivery; but this throws no doubt on the original intention as contained in the formal instrument of peace.

friendly relation to Rome.[1] Still Rome could hardly side with a tyrant like Nabis, while ostensibly fighting for the liberty of the Greeks. Nabis had not only laid his neighbours in the Peloponnesus under contributions in a shameless manner, but had also practised piracy on a large scale in connexion with notorious pirates from the island of Crete where he had possessions. He had not even spared Italian vessels. He paid not the slightest respect to sworn obligations, or to international rights and duties; and as till now he had acted with impunity, his presumption passed all bounds. All principles of political honour would, therefore, justify the Romans in delivering Greece and the world from such a monster, if only they could release themselves from the obligation which they had incurred towards the tyrant by the acceptance of Spartan aid.

CHAP. I.

200–196 B.C.

Character and practices of Nabis.

A cause of war with Nabis was easily found in his refusal to give up Argos, which he had acquired by treachery, and oppressed with heartless cruelty.[2] He thus compelled the Romans to take part openly against him. Flamininus was authorised, or rather commissioned, by the Roman senate to compel the tyrant by force to submit to the Roman demands,[3] and he summoned at Corinth an assembly of the great states, in which the war with Sparta was determined upon. The most eager of all the enemies of Nabis were of course the Achaeans, who, having suffered most from his hostility, now hoped to have their long-cherished desire fulfilled, and to receive Sparta as a member into their confederation.[4] Their strategos, Aristænus, with no less than ten thousand foot and a thousand horse, joined the Roman army, which Flamininus at the commencement of the mild season of 195 B.C. led from Elatea into the Peloponnesus. The Ætolians took no part in this expedition. They were dissatisfied with the whole turn which affairs had taken, and looked with great displeasure

War against Nabis.

---

[1] Livy, xxxiii. 31, 5.   [2] See p. 51.   [3] Livy, xxxiv. 22.
[4] The armistice between Sparta and Achaia which had been concluded in 197 B.C., under the mediation of Flamininus (see p. 46), for the duration of four months, must be supposed to have been prolonged by tacit agreement, but as yet no peace had been concluded.

and jealousy on the possible increase of power which their old rivals, the Achaeans, might derive from the subjection of Sparta. But king Philip of Macedonia, the most recent ally of Rome, sent a detachment of one thousand five hundred men. In addition to these military contingents, the allied forces were joined by a number of Spartan citizens, who had been robbed and exiled by the tyrant, with Agesipolis the legitimate heir to the throne of Sparta at their head.

Attack upon Sparta.

The first point of attack was the important town of Argos, which was besides the foremost object of contention. But Pythagoras, the son-in-law of Nabis, a determined and able soldier, who had the command in the town, frustrated a conspiracy among the citizens, and foiled an attempt of the besiegers to carry the place by a sudden onset. Flamininus, on the advice of the Achaeans, now determined not to allow himself to be detained by the siege of Argos, but to march straight against Sparta, in the hope that Nabis would submit, as soon as he saw himself seriously threatened in the very centre of his dominions. But the petty tyrant's power was by no means contemptible. Being determined to resist to the utmost, he had collected a force of no less than fifteen thousand men. To guard against internal treason, he had caused eighty of the chief men in Sparta, and a number of Helots whom he looked upon as suspicious, to be seized and murdered in prison. The town of Sparta, which in the old time was not fortified, had been protected since the Macedonian period in many places by walls and trenches wherever the approach was open and easy.[1] Nabis had strengthened these defences, and so had made the town secure against a surprise. The Romans, however, attempted no serious attack. After some slight skirmishes they marched round the town to

---

[1] Livy, xxxiv. 38, 2: Fuerat quondam sine muro Sparta; tyranni nuper locis patentibus planisque obiecerant murum; altiora loca et difficilia aditu stationibus armatorum pro munimento obiectis tutabantur. This is not quite correct, for, according to Plutarch (*Pyrrhus*, 29), the town was hastily fortified to resist the attack of Pyrrhus. But even before this period similar measures had been taken occasionally. Compare Pausanias, vii. 8, 3; Justin. xiv. 5.

Amyclæ, in order to reach the important town of Gythium on the coast, by which Nabis had access to the sea, and which was his starting point and place of refuge on his piratical excursions. Before this port appeared now the united fleets of the Romans, the Rhodians, and Eumenes, who two years before had succeeded his deceased father, Attalus, in the kingdom of Pergamum. The surrender of the town of Gythium, after a valiant defence, enabled the allies, whose numbers had grown to fifty thousand, to march leisurely against Sparta.

Nabis had, in the meantime, been reinforced by the brave Pythagoras and a portion of the garrison of Argos; but in spite of this he had not the least chance of being able to resist such an overwhelming force as was now brought against him. He would, perhaps, at once have submitted, if he had not felt convinced that it was not the intention of the Romans to put an end to the independence of Sparta. He knew that they were jealous of the Achaeans; that they desired to see the influence of the league in the Peloponnesus checked by another power; and that, therefore, the existence of Sparta was indispensable to Rome. Thus he was encouraged to resist, as long as possible, the feeble attack, and even to propose a peaceful arrangement. Flamininus seemed indeed disposed to negotiate. He offered conditions which must have appeared most favourable to Nabis in his desperate situation. Nabis, however, was aware of the dilemma in which the Romans found themselves, and knowing how unwilling they were to take extreme steps against him, he hoped to satisfy them by promising to restore Argos. At the same same he stimulated his soldiers to the most desperate resistance by spreading reports of the fearful treatment to be expected from Flamininus. The wild beast was fairly at bay, and it was absolutely necessary to use force against him. The allies made an assault, forced the weak defences of the town, and drove the enemy into the interior. Sparta was taken, and it might have been thought that the conquerors had only to follow up their advantage in order to crush the tyrant completely with their immensely superior forces, when, at the command of Pythagoras, the streets, already crowded by the assailants, were set on fire. Flamininus immediately gave the signal for retreat. But it soon became evident that the retreat had not been caused only by a sudden alarm. There was nothing to prevent the repetition of the attack. Nevertheless, when, after a few days, the tyrant declared himself ready to accept the conditions offered before, to give hostages, and to pay an indemnity, Flamininus granted him an armistice, and at length concluded peace under conditions similar to those which he had imposed on the king of Macedonia. The first condition was of course the restoration of Argos. But this had in the meantime become superfluous, for the citizens of Argos had themselves recovered their freedom, after the withdrawal of Pythagoras and the Spartan garrison. The second demand of Flamininus was the surrender of all the country along the sea coast of Laconia, and of the Spartan possessions in Crete. Nabis was thus completely cut off from the sea, was obliged to sacrifice his fleet, and to discontinue the practice of piracy, which had been such a source of profit to him. As a matter of course, he was called upon to give up the deserters and prisoners of war, and to restore all the plunder that was not yet destroyed or consumed, and which could be identified. He was, moreover, compelled to discharge those mercenaries who had left his service, or in other words, had deserted to the allies, and to give up to them their private property. As a mark of his lasting dependence on Rome, Nabis had to resign the right of carrying on war or making alliances with foreign powers,[1] and he was forbidden to establish anywhere fortified castles or towns. As a war indemnity one hundred talents were to be paid at once, and four hundred talents in eight years.[2]

---

[1] Livy, xxxiv. 3, 5, 9. This condition is the same which was inserted in the peace with Philip of Macedonia (see page 66) and in the peace with Carthage. Vol. ii. p. 445.

[2] Livy, xxxiv. 30-40.

The one condition which Nabis personally must have dreaded most he was spared. He was not compelled to allow the Spartan exiles to return, and to restore to them their right of citizenship and the property which had been divided among the mercenaries and the freed slaves. Such a measure would naturally have called forth without delay a political and social revolution in Sparta, the consequence of which, in case of success, would have been the downfall of the tyrant. The exiles who, with Agesipolis, the legitimate claimant of the Spartan throne, at their head, had joined the Roman army, could not obtain the full acknowledgment of their rights. The only condition made in their favour was, that Nabis was compelled to deliver up to them their wives and children, if these should wish to leave Sparta. The fate of these women seems not to have been enviable. Nabis had given them in marriage to his new citizens, who were either the emancipated slaves of the exiles, or adventurers and criminals from abroad.[1] These conditions of peace exhibit a mournful picture of the terrible disruption of family ties, of property, and of all domestic life, which the infamous reign of terror had caused in Sparta. The exiles, instead of returning to their old possessions, were settled in the coast district which had been detached from the Spartan territory, and entered into the Achaean confederation under the name of free Laconians.[2]

Thus were the affairs of the Peloponnesus settled at last, but settled in a way which fulfilled neither the promises of the Romans nor the wishes of the best men in Greece. The root of the most destructive dissensions was left in the ground in the person of the tyrant Nabis, and the Roman politicians could not justify themselves by

---

[1] Livy, xxxiv. 35, 7 : Exulibus quoque Lacedæmoniis liberos et coniuges restitueret, quæ earum viros sequi voluissent ; invita ne qua exulis comes esset. The legend of Romulus and his asylum was realised in that model state which Nabis established on the ruins of the old Spartan institution. Polybius, xvi. 13 : ἀναδείξας τὴν ἑαυτοῦ δύναμιν οἷον ἄσυλον ἱερὸν τοῖς ἢ δι' ἀσέβειαν ἢ πονηρίαν φεύγουσι τὰς ἑαυτῶν πατρίδας ἤθροισε πλῆθος ἀνθρώπων ἀνοσίων εἰς τὴν Σπάρτην.

[2] Livy, xxxv. 12, 8 ; xxxviii. 30, 6 ; 31, 2. Strabo, viii. 5.

saying that their power was insufficient for the liberation of Sparta. Evidently they had not desired the downfall of Nabis and the reception of Sparta in the Achaean league. As in the north of Greece they had only humiliated and weakened Philip, and had prevented the Ætolians from extending their power, so they tried to establish a political equilibrium in the Peloponnesus, and they allowed Sparta to continue within moderate bounds as an independent state, in order to teach the Achaeans that the protection of Rome was indispensable to them. This was deeply felt as a great disappointment, and no real joy was possible in Greece,[1] especially as Roman garrisons continued to hold the strongest fortresses, the most important of which were Acrocorinthus, Chalcis, and Demetrias. Flamininus, who personally coveted the fame of being known as the deliverer of Greece, was very sensitive to the censure directed against him as the most prominent expounder of the Roman policy; but he had no choice in his actions, and he could not help seeing that in view of the threatening attitude of Antiochus the withdrawal of all Roman troops from Greece might be attended with danger. At last, however, the Roman senate yielded to the entreaties of the Greeks and their friends. Perhaps they hoped that the moral conquest of Greece might outweigh the material possession of it, and that in a war with Antiochus, who threatened the freedom of Greek towns in Asia and Thrace, the Greeks, completely freed from foreign rule, would, from gratitude and self-interest, support the Roman cause as their own. In the spring of the year 194 B.C. Flamininus was able, in a large assembly of deputies from all the Greek states at Corinth, and amid the joyful acclamations of the crowd, to communicate the resolution of the senate that all the towns still occupied by the Roman troops should now

[1] What the sentiments of the Greeks, especially the Achaeans, were at that time we learn from the following words of Plutarch, which are probably taken from Polybius, *Flamininus*, 13: ὁ δὲ Τίτος τότε καλλίστου καὶ δικαιοτάτου τοῦ πρὸς Νάβιν ἀρξάμενος πολέμου τῶν Λακεδαιμονίων ἐξωλέστατον καὶ παρανομώτατον τύραννον ἐν τῷ τέλει διεψεύσατο τὰς τῆς Ἑλλάδος ἐλπίδας ἑλεῖν παρασχὸν οὐκ ἐθελήσας, ἀλλὰ σπεισάμενος καὶ προέμενος τὴν Σπάρτην ἀναξίως δουλεύουσαν.

be evacuated. The promise was no sooner made than fulfilled. Under the eyes of the assembly the Roman garrison marched off from Acrocorinthus. The same scene was witnessed soon afterwards in Chalcis and in other Euboean towns, Oreus, and Eretria, as also in the Thessalian town of Demetrias.[1]

Flamininus was occupied for some months longer with settling the internal affairs of many towns, being especially anxious to set limits to the extravagance of democracy, and to secure to the owners of property the influence which was their right. The deliverer of Greece had at the conclusion of his successful work the satisfaction of setting free from slavery some thousands of his own countrymen. At his desire the different states purchased the freedom of all the Italians who in the war with Hannibal had been sold as slaves in great numbers throughout Greece.[2] The Roman legions then marched to Oricum in Epirus, and embarked for Italy, where celebrations of victory and a brilliant triumph awaited them.

On reviewing the course of the second Macedonian war from a military point of view, we are struck by a fact which we have already remarked on former occasions, and which we can easily explain from the Roman military organization and the frequent change of commanders. The first operations were not favourable to the Roman arms. More than two years passed in fruitless marches and counter-marches in the frontier lands of Macedonia, and when at length a more skilful general than the first two consuls was sent to the theatre of war, it was not by calculation, but by accident, that the decisive encounter took place; and the victory was attributable, not to the genius of the leader, but to the greater ease and rapidity with which the Roman legions could outmanœuvre the unwieldy Macedonian phalanx, and to the skill and promptitude of a nameless inferior officer. If the manner in which the war against Nabis was conducted had to be judged from

---

[1] Livy xxxiv. 48, 2; Plutarch, *Flamininus*, 12.   [2] Livy, xxxiv. 50.

BOOK V.
200-196 B.C.

military grounds alone, the Roman commander would appear in a still more unfavourable light. It cannot, however, be doubted that Flamininus had orders to spare Nabis, and that for this reason he displayed no more military force than was necessary to bring him to subjection.

Auxiliary troops in the Roman armies.

More than in former wars we observe that the Romans availed themselves of auxiliary troops. By the side of the legions we find Numidians with elephants, Illyrians, Epirots, and Greeks from all parts, towards the end even Macedonians. For wars beyond the sea it was evidently difficult to make use of the Italian militia. At the beginning of the war, therefore, volunteers were enlisted; but soon these also began to create difficulties, and clamoured to be discharged and sent home as soon as they had experienced the fatigues and dangers of the campaign. The senate sent no more than one consular army to the East, and yet it was with much trouble that its numbers were kept up, and that supplies were provided. We discover here the traces of the exhaustion of Italy by the war with Hannibal, which was more keenly felt when the unnatural strain on the national strength was relaxed by the treaty of peace in 201 B.C.

The naval war.

If the war by land was not carried out with vigour, nor on a grand scale, the naval war showed even less enterprise and consequently contributed, but in a small degree to secure the final result. The Roman fleet, in conjunction with the Rhodian and the Pergamenian, dealt some successful blows against hostile ports; but they had no chance of a conflict with the Macedonian fleet, which, during the whole war, did not venture out of Demetrias, nor did they make an attack on Macedonia itself. It seems never to have occurred to either of the belligerents that under the protection of their fleets the allied army could effect a landing in Macedonia, instead of advancing with difficulty through inhospitable or impoverished frontier lands. Lastly, it must have been humiliating to Roman pride that, while the allied fleets were scouring the sea without encountering an antagonist, they could not suppress the outrageous proceedings of the Lacedæmonian and Cretan pirates.

The political object of the war was completely gained at a small expense. It was undertaken to restore the liberty of Greece, or rather to destroy the predominance of Macedonia, and to establish a sort of balance of power among the second-rate states, which would compel them to keep one another in check, and to remain dependent on the protecting power of Rome. It is certain that the Romans in general were perfectly innocent of anything like enthusiasm for the Greeks as a race. They saw no reason for dealing with them in a way different from that pursued towards other states. Even Flamininus was not guilty of such weakness; at any rate, he would never have dreamt of carrying his admiration of Greek art and literature so far as to sacrifice Roman interests.[1] The influence of the Greek mind, it is true, had been growing in Rome for some time, and was still on the increase. But there was a great deal of mere fashion in all this, and even the admiration which the great Grecian works of art called forth suffered by the low estimation in which the Romans were taught to hold the character of the Greeks, the more they came in contact with them politically and socially. The Romans were disgusted by the servility, the dishonesty and cunning, the mean and revengeful spirit, which characterised the degenerate Greeks, as well as by the impotence and rottenness of their political life. They considered themselves superior men, though they admitted that in painting, carving and writing verses they possessed less skill. That a Roman like Flamininus, though holding such opinions, should feel gratified by the eulogiums of Greek orators and poets, that he should be pleased when the crowd applauded him, when statues and chaplets were dedicated to him, can scarcely seem strange to those who know that such human weakness is by no means unusual or unnatural.

[1] See p. 41.

BOOK V.
200-196 B.C.

But if a Frederick, with all his partiality for the French language and literature, remained yet in heart and action a German, and as a politician never made the smallest sacrifice to his literary predilections, we are justified in thinking that the statesmen of antiquity were still less influenced by sentiments of this sort, as all human virtues and duties were in those times confined to the narrow circle of fellowship in civil rights and national worship.[1]

---

[1] The readers of Mommsen's *History of Rome* will have perceived that his views differ materially from those expressed above. Mommsen says (Vol. i. 729, Germ. ed.): "Nothing but contemptible dishonesty and feeble sentimentalism can fail to see that the Romans acted with perfect honesty in the liberation of Greece . . . . . It is only meanness (*Jämmerlichkeit*) which discovers nothing but political calculation in the liberation of Greece." These are hard words. But I am not afraid of being charged with "contemptible dishonesty" or "feeble sentimentalism" if I persist in thinking that the Roman senate was guided by "political calculations" alone. I even venture to think that the senate in deciding thus was doing its duty, and that no healthy and strong state can act otherwise. Had the senate acted as Mommsen suggests, it would have been guilty of that very "sentimentalism" with which Mommsen, strangely enough, taunts those who are unwilling to ascribe it to the Romans.

CHAPTER II.

THE SYRO-ÆTOLIAN WAR, 192–189 B.C.

The Roman policy had succeeded in completely isolating Philip of Macedonia, and in forming against him a powerful coalition. The whole of the Greek states, usually so divided against each other, had merged their private quarrels in one common cause. The Ætolians and their hereditary foes, the Achaeans, the Spartan tyrant Nabis and degenerate Athens, the spirited merchants and enterprising mariners of Rhodes, and the cautious scheming king of Pergamum, nay, even Illyrian and Dardanian barbarians, had been acting for one common plan under one general direction. This was a great triumph of Roman diplomacy. But a still greater and more difficult task than that of uniting all those states in common opposition to Macedonia was that of keeping in a condition of neutrality the powerful kingdom of Syria—a kingdom, which if it had been ranged on the side of Philip, would in all probability have turned the scale against the Roman alliance, or at least would have compelled Rome to make efforts on a very much larger scale.

CHAP. II.
192–189 B.C.
The success of Roman diplomacy in isolating Macedonia.

Antiochus the Great, of Syria, was, at the beginning of the war between Rome and Philip, allied with the latter for the common spoliation of Egypt.[1] It was his ambition to recover for the kingdom of Syria all those provinces which it had lost after the death of its founder, Seleucus. He had in a bold and not wholly unsuccessful expedition to the far East made good his claims to the heritage of his ancestors, and was now planning the exten-

Ambitious schemes of Antiochus.

---

[1] See pp. 8, 10.

sion of the Syrian dominions beyond Asia Minor to Thrace, and the recovery of all the towns and countries which in the course of time had gained their independence, or had become Egyptian possessions. But Rome had assumed the part of protector of Egypt, as well as of the Greek towns in Asia Minor. Antiochus had therefore good reason to make common cause with his ally, the king of Macedonia, against the common enemies, in order to prevent their interference in the affairs of the East. However wise and natural, this policy was frustrated by the shortsighted covetousness of both princes, each of whom had secretly the intention of keeping for himself his own part of the common spoil, if this were possible by the sacrifice of his rival. The consummate diplomacy of the Roman senate turned this rivalry to the best advantage, and succeeded in preventing king Antiochus from interfering directly in Greek affairs, not only during the continuance of the war with Macedonia, but also after the subjection of Nabis, and down to the final settlement of affairs in Greece, in 194 B.C.

We have already seen[1] that while Philip was attacking the Egyptian possessions in the islands and in Asia Minor, Antiochus succeeded in establishing the old claims of Syria, which he had never fully relinquished, to the lands on the coast of Phœnicia. The attention of Rome was at that time so much taken up with Macedonia and Greece, that she could not venture to interfere in favour of the king of Egypt. Thus Antiochus, without caring about any protests that might be raised by Rome, conquered Cœlesyria, Phœnicia, and Palestine, in the year 201 or 200 B.C.[2] He desisted from attacking the Pergamenian kingdom 199 B.C., at the intercession of the Romans;[3] but after he had completely routed an Egyptian army, commanded by Scopas, an Ætolian leader of mercenaries, near Mount Panion, by the river Jordan, he thought that he had frustrated the chance which Egypt had of

---

[1] See p. 11.   [2] Justin. xxxi. 1. See p. 20.   [3] See p. 37.

ever regaining the coast lands of Syria,[1] and now directed his attacks against the Egyptian possessions in Asia Minor, where, in the year 201 B.C., Philip of Macedon had been thwarted in his attempt at conquest by the interference of the allied Romans, Rhodians, and Pergamenians. Antiochus hoped to gain these countries for himself while Philip engaged the forces of the allies in Greece, and he actually took several fortified places in Cilicia and Caria.

The Rhodians opposed to the encroachments of Antiochus.

This policy of the king of Syria was not less menacing to the republic of Rhodes than Philip's love of conquest had been before. As on the former occasion the Rhodians had not hesitated to declare and to commence war against Philip, without waiting for the Roman alliance, so they now took it upon themselves, before Rome had signified her consent or promised her assistance, to warn the king of Syria that they should consider it an act of hostility if his fleet should sail westward beyond the Chelidonian promontory on the Cilician coast.[2] Antiochus gave the pacific but evasive answer that he did not intend to mix himself up in the quarrel between the king of Macedonia and Rhodes; and soon after, when the news of the battle of Cynoscephalæ arrived, the Rhodians, in anticipation of speedy help from the Romans, did not consider it advisable to wage open war against Antiochus on their own account. They contented themselves with warning, or with reinforcing, those towns which were threatened by him, and thus, without a formal rupture,[3] opposing the

---

[1] Polybius, xvi. 18; Livy, xxxi. 43, 5.

[2] Livy, xxxiii. 20: Non territi tanta mole imminentis belli, legatos ad regem miserunt, ne Chelidonias . . . superaret; si eo fine non contineret classem copiasque suas, se obviam ituros.

[3] It would at first sight appear strange that the Rhodians should continue to be at peace with Antiochus, and yet give aid to his enemies. But the law of nations was lax in this respect. It was possible for two independent powers to remain ostensibly on terms of peace whilst they were indirectly making war on each other. A good illustration is offered by an incident which occurred in Greece after the conclusion of the fifty years' peace in 421 B.C. In spite of this peace between the Athenians and Lacedæmonians, the former fought as allies of the Argives in the battle of Mantinea, 418 B.C., against the latter. And this act of hostility was not considered a rupture of the peace. Even in modern

BOOK V.
192-189 B.C.

aggressive policy of the king in Asia Minor. But they could not boast of much success. The power and the arrogance of Antiochus grew from day to day. He advanced victoriously in Asia Minor. A number of Greek towns were taken by force, others submitted voluntarily to him. The important town of Ephesus, which he wished to make his starting-point for further conquests,[1] fell into his hands; and here, in 196 B.C., he took up his winter quarters, intent on the complete conquest of the remaining part of Asia Minor, and even on regaining Thrace.

Change in the policy of Rome with regard to Antiochus.

So far the king of Syria had pursued his schemes of aggrandisement without any serious check or interference on the part of the Romans. But after the victory over Philip a change took place in the policy of the great republic. It was no longer necessary to keep a watchful eye on Macedonia. Rome could hope henceforth to keep the ambition of the king of Syria within due bounds, and to establish a political equilibrium in Asia in which the Roman allies, especially the republic of Rhodes and the king of Pergamum, would be enabled to maintain their independent position. At the festival of the Isthmian games in 196 B.C., where Flamininus solemnly proclaimed the freedom of the Greeks, he found ambassadors from king Antiochus who had been in Rome, and had been directed by the senate to confer with Flamininus and the committee of ten senators specially sent out to act as his council. The Romans now spoke out boldly, and without any reserve,[2] declaring that Antiochus must

times similar irregularities have occurred. Whilst France and England were at peace in Europe, India was the scene of severe conflicts between Frenchmen and Englishmen as the respective allies of native Indian princes.

[1] Polybius, xviii. 32: 'Αντίοχος ὁ βασιλεὺς πάνυ ὠρέγετο τῆς 'Εφέσου διὰ τὴν εὐκαιρίαν τῷ δοκεῖν μὲν κατὰ 'Ιωνίας καὶ τῶν ἐφ' 'Ελλησπόντου πόλεων καὶ κατὰ γῆν καὶ κατὰ θάλασσαν ἀκροπόλεως ἔχειν θέσιν, κατὰ δὲ τῆς Εὐρώπης ἀμυντήριον ὑπάρχειν ἀεὶ τοῖς 'Ασίας βασιλεῦσιν εὐκαιρότατον.

[2] Livy, xxxiii. 34, 3: Legatis regis Antiochi nihil iam perplexe, ut ante, cum dubiae res incolumi Philippo erant, sed aperto denunciatum, ut excederet Asiae urbibus, quae Philippi et Ptolemaei regum fuissent, abstineret liberis civitatibus, neu quam lacesseret armis: et in pace et in libertate esse debere omnes ubique Graecas urbes: ante omnia denunciatum, ne in Europam aut ipse transiret, aut copias traiiceret.

surrender all the towns in Asia Minor which had formerly belonged to the Egyptian kingdom, and which had been partly conquered by Philip, and had then at the command of Rome been evacuated by him; that he must not touch any of the independent towns, for that Rome intended all the Greek towns to remain free; finally, he must not send any troops into Europe.

This warning, as it appeared, made no impression on Antiochus, who, surrounded by flatterers and blinded by vanity, really considered himself a "Great King," and was now, by the success which he had hitherto met with, confirmed in the notion that he was destined to restore the Syrian empire of Seleucus, or even the great monarchy of Alexander.

For the present the Romans were too much occupied in Greece to insist upon his obeying their haughty command; and accordingly Antiochus continued his schemes of conquest unmolested. The most important among the towns which refused to submit to him were Smyrna and Lampsacus. He now laid siege to them, troubling himself but little about their appeal to the protection of Flamininus.[1] Nay, in spite of the protest of the Romans, he even crossed over to Europe to conquer Thrace, which his ancestor Seleucus, after the overthrow of Lysimachus, had had in his possession for some time. He took several towns on the Hellespont, and restored Lysimachia, which shortly before had been destroyed by the barbarians of Thrace.[2] Here a Roman embassy appeared before him,[3] under the pretext of adjusting the dispute between him and the king of Egypt, the client of Rome. The ambassadors repeated the same demands which Flamininus had made a few months before to the Syrian ambassadors at Corinth.[4] Antiochus replied with firmness and dignity. He denied the right of the Romans to mix themselves up in his dispute with Egypt, adding that he was not only on

---

[1] Appian, *Syr.* 1.   [2] Livy, xxxiii. 38.
[3] It was still the year 196 B.C.
[4] Polybius, xviii. 33; Livy, xxxiii. 39; Appian, *Syr.* 3. See p. 84.

good terms with Ptolemæus, but would soon be able to reckon him among his relations. He had a just claim to Thrace; and as to the Greek towns in Asia, he would grant them their freedom, not at the bidding of Rome, but by his own free will.[1] Lastly, he said he could see no reason why Rome assumed the right to interfere in the affairs of Asia, considering that he had left her unmolested in Italy.

Negotiations broken off and resumed.

The negotiations assumed a threatening aspect, when suddenly they were interrupted by the rumour that the young king of Egypt was dead. The Romans as well as Antiochus now thought there were more important things to attend to than carrying on a dispute of words far away in Thrace. Without coming to a conclusion, both parties dropped the discussion, and hurried off to Egypt. But on the way they found that the rumour of the death of the king of Egypt was false. Antiochus now went to his capital to pass the winter. But previously he despatched a new embassy to Flamininus in Greece, in order, if possible, to preserve the hitherto untroubled relations with Rome, and to give the assurance that he had no hostile intentions.

Till now the negotiations between the two powers had brought to light no dissensions that might not have been peaceably smoothed over. There was nothing to show that either Rome or Antiochus was from the first determined to push the difference to a rupture. Rome, it is true, had assumed a haughty and offensive attitude. She had presumed to dictate laws to a power independent and equal with herself, and to control its action within its own proper sphere. But an arrogant and defiant tone was a peculiarity of the Roman diplomatic style, which was scarcely so dangerous as we might think, if we judge from the cautious, polite and respectful phrases of modern diplomacy. The real object of the Romans was to keep

---

[1] This is the meaning of the words of Appian (*Syr.* 3): τὰς δ' ἐν Ἀσίᾳ πόλεις αὐτονόμους ἐάσειν, εἰ χάριν οὐ Ῥωμαίοις ἀλλ' ἑαυτῷ μέλλοιεν ἕξειν. Compare Livy, xxxiii. 38, 5.

Antiochus at a distance during the Græco-Macedonian complications, and this object they attained completely, by alternately quieting, entreating, and then again advising and threatening him through their ambassadors. Antiochus understood this completely; and as he too desired no rupture with Rome, he avoided everything which might have rendered it unavoidable, occasionally yielding and flattering the Roman pride, but never allowing himself to be thwarted in the pursuit of his own advantage.

CHAP. II.

192–189 B.C.

This state of things, which, if it did not show hearty good feeling, was yet compatible with friendly relations, underwent a great change in the year 195 B.C. In that year Hannibal and king Antiochus met in Ephesus, and thenceforth the preservation of peace was only a question of time and expediency.

A few years only had been granted to the greatest of all Carthaginians, in which to devote himself to the peaceful duties of a statesman. According to the traditions of his house, he exerted himself after the conclusion of peace to restore the strength of the exhausted state by means of democratic reform. Being elected a suffete,[1] he proposed a law to change the office of judges, which had become an office for life,[2] into an annual office, and he completely reformed the financial administration. Thus he had made himself so hated by the Conservative party, that, to get rid of him, they did not hesitate to denounce him in Rome as making plans for a new war. Hannibal's name was still a terror to the Romans, and the senate considered it not beneath the dignity of Rome to send an embassy to Carthage to overthrow him by assisting the opposite party, in spite of the dissuasions of the proud and noble-

Hannibal's flight from Carthage.

---

[1] Livy (xxxiii. 46, 3) and Cornelius Nepos (*Hannib.* 7) call the office with which Hannibal was invested "prætura;" Justin (xxxi. 2) calls him "consul"; Zonaras (ix. 18, p. 1449) says he administered the highest office. We cannot doubt therefore that the office of the suffetes was meant. See vol. ii. page 15.

[2] Vol. ii. page 18.

minded Scipio Africanus.[1] Hannibal did not venture to brave the threatening storm. The times were past when the Carthaginian senate could reply to the Roman demand of the surrender of Hannibal by a declaration of war. Like a convicted criminal, the greatest citizen and chief magistrate escaped from his native town, and took refuge in the far East, to nourish his hatred, and to continue that hostility to Rome to which he had pledged himself as a child. His eye had, of course, long been directed to the complications in Greece and Asia,[2] and he had probably been retained in his home wholly by the conviction that Carthage beyond anything required internal reform before she could free herself from the humiliating bondage to which the exasperated victors had doomed her. The Romans might well ask themselves whether it was advisable to banish just that man, who alone was equal to an army, from a place where he was bound to pursue a peaceful policy, and where he was within the range of Roman ascendancy. Once in the enemy's council of war Hannibal could no longer feel himself restrained by any secondary considerations. On the contrary, he could now have only one object in view, to implicate Rome in a great war, and to give his services to her enemies.

In the year 195 B.C. Hannibal visited Antiochus in Ephesus, and was received with great honour and respect. He took at once a prominent part in the councils of the king, who now, without paying any further regard to diplomatic intervention, was determined to pursue his conquests in Thrace. Flamininus was still fully occupied in Greece with the war against Nabis, and the arrogant language of the Romans had, up to this time, been supported

---

[1] Livy, xxxiii. 47, 4 : Ita diu repugnante P. Scipione Africano, qui parum ex dignitate populi Romani esse ducebat subscribere odiis accusatorum Hannibalis et factionibus Carthaginiensium inserere publicam auctoritatem, nec satis habere bello vicisse Hannibalem, nisi velut accusatores calumniam in eum iurarent ac nomen deferrent, tandem pervicerunt ut legati Carthaginem mitterentur, qui ad senatum eorum arguerent Hannibalem cum Antiocho rege consilia belli faciendi inire. Valer. Maxim. iv. 1, 6.

[2] Livy, xxxiii. 49, 1.

by no measures likely to convince the king of the risks to which his policy exposed him. He felt himself to be completely a match for Rome, and he hoped also to bring the Romans to recognize him as their equal. At once, then, without paying any attention to the further demands of the Romans, he despatched ambassadors to Flamininus in Greece, after the breaking off of negotiations in Lysimachia,[1] offering to conclude an alliance with Rome on the footing of equality.[2] Flamininus referred them to Rome; and a long time seems to have passed in slow and tedious negotiations, which were made use of on both sides to gain time, to put off the final decision, and meanwhile to improve every opportunity for gaining some new ground of vantage.[3]

While the Romans were occupied in the pacification of Greece, and concluded a formal alliance with king Philip of Macedonia, thus depriving Antiochus of the prospect of a most powerful confederate on whom Hannibal had especially calculated, Antiochus fortified and extended his possessions in Asia Minor and Thrace, and endeavoured to gain allies for the coming war. The town of Byzantium, important through its commerce and its position on the Thracian Bosporus, was drawn to his side by the promise of some advantages of trade; the Galatians were secured by presents and threats; one of the king's daughters was betrothed to the youthful Ptolemæus of Egypt, and the conquered Syro-Phœnician coast lands were promised her as a dowry. By this promise the king of Egypt, who had been neglected by Rome, was induced to remain neutral. Antiochus married his second daughter to Ariarathes, king of Cappadocia. In the same way he tried to gain over to

---

[1] See page 86.   [2] Livy, xxxiii. 41, 5.
[3] The fragmentary state of the work of Polybius, the only trustworthy witness, makes it impossible for us to trace the detail of the numerous embassies with regard to time and matter. We lose sight of them especially in the year 194 B.C. It is by no means certain, as Nissen concludes (*Untersuchungen über die Quellen des Livius*, p. 162), that the embassy of Publius Sulpicius, Publius Villius, and Publius Ælius, to which Livy (xxxiv. 59, 8) refers, negotiated with Antiochus in Lysimachia.

his side Eumenes, king of Pergamum; but this keen-sighted prince declined to accede to his proposals. It was clear to him that if Antiochus succeeded in restoring the great Syrian empire, his own kingdom of Pergamum was exposed to a most ambitious and grasping neighbour. He therefore held firmly to the Roman alliance, the more so, as he felt assured that Roman valour and perseverance would in the end prevail. He now set himself to work to keep alive with the Romans the suspicion against Antiochus, and to urge them to a war.[1] Thus Eumenes on the one side and Hannibal on the other acted as instigators to urge the powerful adversaries to the conflict.

Diplomatic congress in Rome.

In the year 194 B.C., after the complete pacification and settlement of affairs in Macedonia and Greece, Titus Quinctius Flamininus returned to Italy, and celebrated a three days' triumph.[2] When the consuls had been elected for the following year, Flamininus and the senatorial commission which had acted as his council, gave their report of the regulations made in Greece, and asked for the final approval of the senate.[3] On this occasion ambassadors from all parts of Greece and from Asia were collected in Rome. A great diplomatic congress took place, in which the preliminaries of peace were finally settled, and each of the new client states was anxious to obtain from the protecting power the most favourable conditions. With the rest had come to Rome a Syrian embassy, at the head of which was Menippus, an accomplished orator and good soldier.[4] The senate did not enter into direct negotiations

---

[1] Appian, *Syr.* 5, 6; Polybius, xxii. 1, 3, 8; Livy, xxxv. 13, 10: Eumenes, quantum auctoritate, quantum consilio valebat, incitabat Romanos ad bellum.
[2] Livy, xxiv. 52.   [3] Livy, xxxiv. 57, 1.
[4] Nothing prevents us from supposing that this was the same embassy which conferred with Flamininus in Greece in the year before (in 195 B.C.), and which had been directed by him to proceed to Rome (Livy, xxxiv. 25, 2). In that case it is improbable that a Roman embassy, crossing that of Menippus, was sent to Antiochus in the year 194 B.C. (See above, p. 89, note 3.) Moreover, the time which the embassy of Menippus would have taken for delivering the king's message appears rather long. But neither of the two objections is of much weight. More particularly, we need not wonder at delays which were often intentionally thrown in the way for the purpose of gaining time. See below, p. 92.

with these ambassadors, but referred them to the diplomatic committee, at the head of which was Flamininus, the man whose voice was now decisive in Greek affairs. It soon became evident that the disputes between Rome and Syria could not be settled amicably in a way satisfactory to both parties, because both obstinately maintained the position which they had occupied from the first. The Syrian ambassadors disputed the right of the Romans to mix themselves up in the affairs of Asia, and to dictate to their master how he should treat the several towns, just as if he, like Philip, had been conquered by them in war, and was not an independent sovereign, only animated by the desire to live with them in peace and friendship, without sacrificing either his dignity or his rights. Upon this, the Romans gave him his choice, either to relinquish Europe, which meant that he should resign his newly-acquired possessions in Thrace, or to recognise their right to interfere in favour of their friends in Asia.

Thus the dispute was brought to an issue, and an immediate rupture seemed unavoidable. Both parties, however, hesitated to speak the last and decisive word. Neither the one nor the other had really a decided wish for war, and they probably thought that they would gain their ends by negotiation. The Romans were interested only in playing to the end their part as protectors of the Greeks, to maintain the order of things which they had established in Greece, and, by protecting the minor states also in Asia, to establish a balance of power in the East. They could not speculate on acquisitions in Asia as long as they had no possessions in Greece. If, then, Antiochus yielded, they would have won a bloodless but important victory, which could not fail to strengthen their commanding position in the whole of the Eastern world. Antiochus, on the other side, found himself opposed by a coalition of the Romans and all the Greeks, including Macedonia, and his representatives thought it better, therefore, to ask for a delay, that the king might himself decide whether he would accept or reject the terms proposed. This delay was wil-

Final rupture delayed.

BOOK V.
192-189 B.C.

The frequency of embassies.

lingly granted them by the senate, and again a Roman embassy was sent to the East, to endeavour, by diplomatic skill, to avoid a great and dangerous war, and yet to gain the essential advantages of a victory.[1]

The numerous embassies which we meet in these negotiations, and which play such a prominent part, appear strange at the first glance. We are accustomed to consider the political questions of antiquity more simple, and especially to assume that the diplomacy of Rome proceeded boldly and straightforwardly to its destined end, avoiding the crooked ways by which modern diplomatists try to edge their way through the endless complications and conflicting interests of our present commonwealth of states. Nor is such a view quite incorrect. But the international relations between state and state were at that time not so exactly regulated that an understanding about even a simple matter was quite easy. The mode of business and the language of business were not sufficiently established upon universally recognised principles. There was a great deal of palavering and haggling, as in an Eastern bazaar, whereas our modern statesmen cannot easily retreat from a position which they have once taken. Still more important is the fact, that the states of antiquity did not know the institution of resident ambassadors, and in case of difficulties arising from conflicting interests, had to avail themselves of special envoys, who not only made and received communications, but who also, like modern plenipotentiaries and representatives at foreign courts, acted as informants, and sent home all the news which they could pick up regarding the war-preparations, the views, plans, alliances, and political parties in the countries to which they were sent. This required time, a repetition of coming and going, and a large staff of envoys. It cannot, therefore, be wondered at, if after a war had been as good as determined on, messengers still used to come and go, and that they sometimes acted as spies, and were treated as such.

[1] Livy, xxxiv. 39.

Such were the objects for which a Roman embassy was sent to Asia under Publius Sulpicius and Publius Villius in the year 194 B.C., after the negotiations in Rome had led to no result. They endeavoured only to gain time, and to urge the Roman allies in Asia to make preparations for war. They went first to Pergamum, to king Eumenes.[1] This ambitious potentate eagerly desired a war against Antiochus, in the hope of obtaining from the Romans an extension of power, which would enable him in future to maintain his position without foreign assistance against his powerful and encroaching neighbour. The Romans could with certainty reckon on him in case of need. The ambassadors next[2] repaired to Ephesus, which town Antiochus had conquered a few years before, and since then had made his capital in Asia Minor. The king of Syria happened not to be there at that time, having just undertaken an expedition against the rebellious Pisidians in the south of the peninsula. But in Ephesus the Roman diplomatists found Hannibal, who for two years had been trying in vain to foment the differences between Rome and Antiochus, and to urge on a war. In case of such a war with Rome, he reckoned on the vigorous co-operation of Carthage, and he had sent a Tyrian merchant named Aristo to Carthage, with the knowledge and consent of the king, to sound the views of his countrymen, and especially of his own party, and to concert measures for united action.[3] But Carthage lived at that period under the spell of a well-grounded fear of the power of Rome and of Rome's readiness to embrace every opportunity of still further humbling and weakening her old rival. This fear had been the cause of Hannibal's undignified flight, and it now compelled Aristo to leave his mission

---

[1] Livy xxxv. 13, 6. Eumenes II. had succeeded Attalus in 197 B.C.

[2] According to Livy, Publius Villius and Publius Sulpicius proceeded to Pergamum, where the latter remained, on account, as was alleged, of sickness. It is, however, not unlikely that his real object was to watch Eumenes. Livy, xxxv. 14, 1. Afterwards he accompanied Publius Villius to Ephesus. Livy, xxxv. 16, 1.

[3] Livy, xxxiv. 60-62.

unaccomplished, and to flee by night from the dangerous place where abject fear had changed even good patriots into Roman spies and satellites.

Of course Villius knew of these intrigues; but when he met Hannibal in Ephesus, he expressed his surprise to him that he should have left his country, though peace was established between Rome and Carthage, and he had nothing to fear at home. These fine words and the many meetings which Villius arranged with Hannibal, were not designed to deceive Hannibal as to the intentions of the Romans, still less to reconcile him with Rome; for no Roman could think so meanly of the Punic general's understanding or honour to hope to catch him by such talk. They were designed to throw suspicions of Hannibal's honesty into the weak mind of king Antiochus, and thus to deprive him of so useful a servant.[1] Nor did Villius fail in his deep-laid scheme. The jealous king, to whom faith and patriotism were incomprehensible feelings, or mere empty words, conceived a suspicion against Hannibal, and excluded him henceforth from the circle of his confidential councillors.[2]

On the whole the position of the Roman ambassadors

---

[1] Polybius, iii. 11. 2: οἱ πρέσβεις (the Roman ambassadors) ὁρῶντες τὸν Ἀντίοχον προσέχοντα τοῖς Αἰτωλοῖς καὶ πρόθυμον ὄντα πολεμεῖν Ῥωμαίοις, ἐθεράπευον τὸν Ἀννίβαν σπουδάζοντες εἰς ὑποψίαν ἐμβαλεῖν πρὸς τὸν Ἀντίοχον, ὃ καὶ συνέβη γενέσθαι. Appian, *Syr.* 9. Livy, xxxv. 14, tries to produce the impression that the Roman ambassador had not the intention to discredit Hannibal with Antiochus, and that the suspicion of the king was not produced by him.

[2] On this occasion, according to a statement of Caius Acilius, a Roman annalist who wrote in Greek (Livy, xxxv. 14, 5), Publius Cornelius Scipio, the conqueror of Zama, was said to have been at Ephesus, and in an interview with Hannibal to have asked him the celebrated question, who was the greatest general. Hannibal, it is further reported, mentioned, first of all, Alexander the Great, then Pyrrhus, and at last himself; upon which Scipio, disappointed in his expectation, enquired what he would think of himself if he had been victorious at Zama. "In that case," Hannibal is reported to have replied, "I should consider myself the greatest of all." This anecdote, which is related by Appian (*Syr.* 10) and by Plutarch (*Flamin.* 21), belongs to that class of fictions of which we have already had occasion to speak. (Vol. ii. pp. 403, 449, note 1.) It was evidently not told by Polybius. Otherwise Livy, who made ample use of Polybius in his narrative of these events, would have quoted him as his authority instead of Acilius.

in Asia was one of great difficulty at the present juncture. Had they been charged to make a peremptory demand, and in case of refusal, to declare war without delay, their task would have been easy enough. But, it appears, they were commissioned to temporise, and, if possible, to obtain the advantages of Roman intervention by diplomatic means without the necessity of resorting to war. Unfortunately the time was less favourable for this now than in the previous year (194 B.C.), before the withdrawal of the Roman troops from Greece, and the evacuation of the three great fortresses of Demetrias, Chalcis, and Corinth. Antiochus was well acquainted with the state of things in Greece, with the universal agitation and discontent, and the utter weakness and insufficiency of the arrangements made there by the Romans. He was already importuned by Ætolian envoys to come to Greece.[1] The Ætolians, who, it is true, had been treated contemptuously and unjustly by the Romans, thirsted for revenge. They possessed a boundless confidence in their own strength, as is usual with ignorant and rude peoples who, having no idea of the relative power and resources of other states, always over-estimate their own importance. They assured Antiochus that Philip of Macedonia and Nabis of Sparta were prepared to unite with him against the Romans, and that Amynander also, the chief of Athamania, disappointed in his hopes of spoil after the victory over Philip, had joined the conspiracy against the Romans.[2]

Thus the affairs of Greece were sufficiently complicated, and appeared highly favourable to Antiochus. At the same time his position in Asia seemed secure by his affinity with the kings of Egypt and Cappadocia, by the friendly disposition of the Galatians, and by the success which had hitherto accompanied his military enterprises. No wonder that he exhibited less readiness than before to accede to the Roman demands. In truly Oriental style he showed this immediately by a marked want of politeness to the

[1] Livy, xxxv. 12.   [2] Livy, xxxv. 18.

Roman ambassadors. At first he caused Villius to wait for a long time at Ephesus, while he was occupied with his campaign against the Pisidians. Villius was then allowed to follow the king to the source of the river Mæander; but the negotiations were soon interrupted, under the pretext that the court was in mourning for a royal prince. Villius had to return to Pergamum, leaving his mission unaccomplished. At a later period, when Antiochus was residing at Ephesus, the Roman ambassadors returned; but they were no longer admitted to the presence of the king, and were referred to a royal officer called Minnio. The question was no longer discussed whether the Thracian conquests of Antiochus should be given up. Nor did Antiochus repeat his promise to grant the Asiatic towns their freedom on the condition that they should acknowledge him as their deliverer and protector, instead of the Romans. On the contrary, Minnio maintained his master's right to all the states in Æolia and Ionia, and especially to Smyrna, Lampsacus, and Alexandria Troas, which alone had not submitted to him, because all these towns had always been subject to the sovereigns of Asia, and latterly also to the predecessors of Antiochus. It looked like an intentional affront when Antiochus declared himself willing to leave their ancient independence to Rhodes, Cyzicus, and Byzantium,[1] if the Romans would enter into an alliance with him, that is, if they would acknowledge and guarantee all those claims which hitherto they had uniformly disputed. The independence of Rhodes had never been questioned or attacked by any one, and a short time before even Antiochus himself had eagerly wished to obtain the friendship of the important town of Byzantium.[2] It was, therefore, clear that on the basis now proposed by Antiochus an understanding with Rome was not possible. The Roman ambassadors returned home without having accomplished their object, and with the conviction that all the arts of

---

[1] Appian (*Syr.* 12) says: 'Ροδίους μὲν καὶ Βυζαντίους καὶ Κυζικηνοὺς καὶ ὅσοι ἄλλοι περὶ τὴν 'Ασίαν "Ελληνες αὐτονόμους ἐπηγγείλατο ἐάσειν κ.τ.λ.; it is not clear which towns can be meant by the "others." [2] Appian, *Syr.* 6.

diplomacy were now exhausted, and an appeal to arms had become indispensable.[1]

At the court of Antiochus likewise a peaceful settlement with Rome was no longer thought of. The king and his councillors saw that war was now unavoidable. Antiochus could say with perfect truth that he had never sought a war with Rome, and would eventually carry it on only to defend himself against an uncalled-for and unjust interference in his affairs. Nothing was further from his intentions than an attack on the independence or on the dignity of the Roman republic. The Romans had pursued their usual insidious policy with regard to him. They had formed a friendship with his natural rivals and enemies; they had made Rhodes and the king of Pergamum their allies, while Antiochus, to avoid a rupture with Rome, had scrupulously refrained from making any attack on them, and had indeed avoided all open hostilities. But, not satisfied with setting limits to his free action so far, the Romans had assumed to be the protectors of all the Greek towns in Asia, as if the part which they had just played as liberators in European Greece gave them, as a natural consequence, the right to do the same everywhere. Antiochus was resolved to oppose this presumption with all his power, and from this time resolved to meet the inevitable war.

The question was now, whether he should await an attack of the Romans in Asia, or anticipate them by an invasion of Italy or Greece. The plan of the war was carefully discussed in Ephesus. Hannibal was at first excluded from the secret councils of the king in consequence of the suspicion of which he had recently become the object. As soon as he remarked this, he had no difficulty in convincing the king of his real sentiments. Then it was that he related the story of the oath by which, as a boy, he had sworn to his father, Hamilcar, to remain all his life long an enemy of Rome.[2] Antiochus seemed inclined to avail himself of Hannibal's services for a diversion to be directed from Carthage upon Italy; but he was wise enough to give up

CHAP. II.

192–189 B.C.

Negotiations broken off.

Plans for the war.

---

[1] Livy, xxxv. 15–17; Appian, *Syr.* 12.   [2] Vol. ii. p. 152.

the idea of a serious invasion with his main force. After the experience which Hannibal had had, an offensive war in Italy seemed too dangerous an undertaking. If, however, giving up the plan of offensive warfare, Antiochus resolved to remain on the defensive, it seemed that Greece was the most favourable ground on which he could await the Roman assault. A faint hope yet remained that Rome might abate her demands, and in this case Antiochus would have preferred to avoid the war altogether. He therefore took no steps which might precipitate events; nor did he even get together the armaments which his critical situation urgently demanded.

Discontent in Greece. The actual conflict of the two great powers was at length made unavoidable through the impatience of the minor Greek communities, which found the state of things created by Flamininus unbearable. In point of fact, all the Greeks were discontented after their first intoxication of joy had passed off. The time of universal happiness which they had expected had not come. The disappointment which must follow every extravagant hope was so much the greater, as, in truth, the Romans had not wished a single Greek state to enjoy so much of vitality and strength as would make it really independent, and consequently had only fostered aspirations which could not be gratified, and which led to just complaints. It is true, no settlement of Greek affairs could have been imagined which could satisfy every part of this restless and impatient people, and which would have remained undisturbed without the use of external force. The small Greek commonwealths were by their very nature and the temper of the race incapable of exercising sovereign rights with moderation. They could not bring themselves to respect the rights of others, nor make any sacrifices for the common good. Even the establishment of the Achaean league, the most hopeful creation of the Greeks in the field of internal politics, sowed the seeds of new discord. The natural and reasonable aspirations of this league to unite all the scattered fragments of the whole people into one body politic were frustrated by the obstinate exclusiveness of some, which at last paved the way for the interference of foreign powers. The best thing for Greece would have been the extension of the Achaean league to an organization embracing the whole Greek race. As this was not possible, a union with Macedonia, allowing a moderate degree of local self-government, might possibly have secured peace and prosperity to the great number of separate states; but monarchy was in the whole of antiquity a form of government which never could give any security for the permanence of political rights: besides, every union with a stronger power was apt at any time to lead to the oppression of the weaker. Philip of Macedonia might perhaps have made himself the Protector of the Greeks; instead of this, however, he degenerated soon into a despot, and made himself hateful to the noblest and best of his former friends. Nevertheless, some parts of Greece were so accustomed to Macedonian rule, that in all probability this rule would have been more widely extended, had not Rome interfered. Thessaly, Bœotia, Locris, Phocis, and Eubœa were, to a certain extent, parts of the Macedonian empire. Even the Achaean league was only alienated from Philip for a time; Epirus and Acarnania were his warm adherents. All these bonds of union were broken by the interference of the Romans. A new order of things was forcibly introduced; but it was not likely that, at the dictation of a foreign power, the peoples who had suffered so much, and been so disturbed in their old customs and habits, would feel satisfied and quietly submit. Even under the eyes of the Roman army the Macedonian party had raised its head in Bœotia;[1] what could be expected after the legions had evacuated the country, and left free scope to all the passions and the savage party spirit of the Greeks?

The first who tried to upset by force of arms the universal peace and liberty established in Greece by Roman arms was Nabis, the tyrant of Sparta, the same man whom, in spite of the general wish of the Achaeans,

[1] See p. 63.

BOOK V.
192–189 B.C.

Flamininus had only weakened but not crushed, lest the Achaeans should grow too powerful in the Peloponnesus, and thus become independent of Rome. After the maritime districts of Laconia, with the important seaport of Gythium, had been taken from him, he behaved like a wild beast which, being confined in a cage, becomes conscious for the first time of the limits to its freedom. He was unable or unwilling to estimate correctly his own power, and that which was opposed to him. Seeing that the Romans had left the country, he determined in the year 192 B.C. to attack Gythium, without which he could not carry on his accustomed trade of piracy. The Achaean league, to which Gythium had been assigned by Flamininus in 195 B.C., promptly sent a garrison into the place. They also informed the Romans of the outbreak of hostilities, and made preparations to resist the plundering of Achaean territory. But, fearing to offend Rome, they did not openly declare war, for as a Roman vassal state Achaia had lost the right of independent warfare.[1]

Roman delay and indecision.

The Romans were now fully aware that the time for immediate action had come. But in spite of this, they delayed, with their accustomed slowness, not only to declare themselves, but even to make the necessary preparations.[2] It is true, one of the consuls of the year 192 B.C. was instructed to levy two new legions, with twenty thousand infantry and eight hundred cavalry of the allies; but only an insignificant fleet was sent to the Peloponnesus under the prætor, Atilius Serranus, while the prætor, Bæbius Tamphilus, received only three thousand men (one thousand Romans and two thousand allies), with whom, after a time, he crossed over to Apollonia. In the meantime Flamininus was sent once more to

---

[1] In a similar manner the Rhodians, without formally declaring war against Antiochus, and without being looked upon as belligerents, had come to the assistance of the towns threatened by him. See above, p. 83. The international code of peace and war was less stringent and logical in a question of this sort than that of modern times, when even the furnishing of arms to either belligerents by neutrals is not allowed.

[2] Livy, xxxv. 20, 1 : Romæ destinabant quidem sermonibus hostem Antiochum, sed nihildum ad id bellum præter animos parabant.

Greece, in order, if possible, to compose the quarrel in the Peloponnesus, to prevent the spreading of the war, and, above all, to warn the Ætolians. Flamininus sent instructions to the Achaeans to abstain from hostilities against Nabis until the arrival of the Roman fleet. The able Philopœmen, who was now strategos of the Achaean league, saw that the chief object of the Romans was to prevent the overthrow of Nabis. He therefore resolved to put him down before the arrival of the Roman force, though he was well aware that Achaia would incur the displeasure of Rome by trying to assert her own right without waiting for the approval of the protecting power.

Unfortunately, the precipitation with which this plan was carried out led to a sad failure. Philopœmen, who did not shine as a naval commander, nevertheless tried an attack by sea. He sailed from Ægium on the Corinthian Gulf to Gythium with a squadron of a few ships, one of which had four tiers of oars and served as a flag-ship, though it was more than eighty years old, and of course rotten and unseaworthy. He was completely defeated by the small fleet of Nabis, consisting of only three decked vessels and a few smaller boats, so that he himself escaped with difficulty. A second naval expedition, starting from Argolis, landed Philopœmen in the neighbourhood of the besieged town, where he annihilated a part of the hostile troops by a night surprise, and hoped by devastating the Spartan territory and threatening Sparta to draw the besiegers off from Gythium. But this hope was disappointed. Gythium, which might easily have been relieved by the Romans, fell into the hands of Nabis, who now turned with all his forces against Philopœmen. Meanwhile the latter had collected a sufficient number of troops out of the Achaean towns, and so completely defeated Nabis in the mountainous region (called Barbosthenes), north of Sparta, that only the fourth part of the beaten army escaped to Sparta.[1] Nabis was again in a desperate position, and this time he had been put down by the Achaeans

[1] Livy, xxxv. 25-30.

BOOK V.
192–189 B.C.

alone, without the aid of the Romans. No wonder they were elated, and with pardonable vanity extolled the merits of their own general Philopœmen high above those of Flamininus.[1] In this however they acted very unwisely; for the Roman held their fate in his hands. He wished naturally to uphold his former policy, and the bold and independent attitude which the Achaeans had assumed under the enterprising Philopœmen was calculated, even if his vanity had not been hurt,[2] to induce Flamininus to put a stop to the military action of the Achaeans, and once more to take the wretched Nabis under his protection. At his bidding an armistice was concluded, and Philopœmen was obliged to evacuate Laconia with the Achaean troops.[3]

Discontent in Greece.

Flamininus had now a difficult task to perform. It had been easier to "liberate" the Greek states than it was now to keep alive the persuasion that real liberty had been gained. A cry went through the whole of Greece that a new and a real liberation was needed, a liberation from the unbearable dominion of Rome. In all places the old enemies of Rome and the new malcontents rallied under this watchword. There was almost everywhere an active anti-Roman party, even in Athens, which had been so tenderly patronised by Rome, and where but a short time before the admiration for the Romans was without bounds.[4]

Macedonian alliance secured by Rome.

The discontent of most of the Greek states counted for very little, for only three states in Greece were of any weight at that time. These were Macedonia, and the Achaean and Ætolian leagues. Before all, the Romans were bent on securing the alliance of the king of Macedonia, the more so as Antiochus was bidding for his friendship. Various promises, of the nature of which we are unfortunately not informed, were made to him by Rome. So much, however, is known for certain, that he was assured that

---

[1] Livy, xxxv. 30, 13.
[2] Livy is too partial to mention this foible of his countryman. But Plutarch (*Philip*, 15) on the authority probably of Polybius, has preserved this trait.
[3] Pausanias, viii. 50, 10.   [4] Livy, xxxv. 50, 4.

if he remained true to the Roman alliance, his son Demetrius, who was then a hostage in Rome, would be sent back to him, and that the remainder of the contributions of war should be remitted.¹ It is probable that the prospect was opened to him of recovering several of the lost possessions in Thessaly, especially the important fortress of Demetrias, as well as parts of Thrace, for instance, those towns which had been taken by Antiochus. The equivocal attitude of Amynander of Athamania probably induced Philip to reckon, in case of victory, on the acquisition of the district possessed by that chief. But what most decided Philip to take the part of the Romans was in all probability not so much the promises of the Romans as resentment against Antiochus, who had not only forsaken him in the late war, but had enriched himself at his expense, and was now short-sighted enough to favour a relative of the prince of Athamania, who put forward claims to the Macedonian throne. At a later period, as we shall see,² Antiochus made other mistakes, which played into the hands of Flamininus and retained Philip in the Roman alliance. The consequence of Philip's policy was that, in the end, he gained hardly any of the advantages on which he had reckoned, that he became still more dependent on Roman supremacy, and that he had to suffer the most unworthy and humiliating treatment.

The part to be taken by the Achaeans was determined by that of the Ætolians. If the latter ranged themselves on the side of Antiochus, the Achaeans were of necessity compelled to join the Roman alliance.³ The opposition between the two confederations was so great that there was something unnatural even in their common alliance with Rome. The hereditary animosity between the two

---

¹ Diodorus, xxxviii. 15, *Dindorf*; Livy, xxxv. 31, 5.   ² See below, p. 116.
³ Livy, xxxv. 31, 2: Minimum operæ legati Romanorum in Achæis adeundis consumpserunt, quos quia Nabidi infesti erant ad cetera quoque satis fidos censebant esse. Here Livy lets out the fact, that the continuance of the power of Nabis was looked upon by the Romans as a guarantee of the fidelity of the Achaeans. This is a confirmation of our views expressed above, page 76.

BOOK V.
192–189 B.C.

nations contributed to a general discontent with the settlement of Flamininus: and as it was chiefly the Ætolians who fanned the flame of this discontent, the Achaean confederation was necessarily ranged on the side of the Romans. Flamininus reckoned so firmly upon it, that he ventured, plainly against the wishes and interests of the Achaeans, again to take the Spartan tyrant under his protection.

Resentment of the Ætolians.

The Ætolians, from the very first, openly proclaimed that they were dissatisfied with the Roman settlement. They claimed for themselves, whether with justice or unjustly, the largest share in the victory over Macedonia; and in all the numerous negotiations they thought that they were entitled to have a weighty voice. They had advocated the complete annihilation of Philip's power, hoping that in the place of Macedonia they would become a leading power in Greece. It had been a bitter disappointment for them that the Romans rejected their proposals, affronted them intentionally, neglected them on every occasion, and finally threw to them only small fragments of the spoil which they greedily demanded.

Resolution to invite Antiochus.

As long as the Roman army was stationed in Greece, the Ætolians gave vent to their resentment only in abusive language; but in the year 194 B.C., as soon as Demetrias, Chalcis, and Acrocorinthus were evacuated, and the Roman legions had returned to Italy, they began a busy agitation which tended to nothing less than the total overthrow of the new order of things. They had already entered into a correspondence with Antiochus, and held out the hope to him that he would find numerous and zealous adherents in Greece, if he would now undertake its real deliverance. It was at their advice that Nabis had commenced hostilities,[1] and when the conflict had been thus begun by

---

[1] Livy, xxxv. 12, 7: Tyranno Lacedaemonio Damocritus—ademptis maritimis civitatibus enervatam tyrannidem, dicere; inde militem, inde naves navalesque socios habuisse; inclusum suis prope muris Achaeos videre dominantes in Peloponneso; nunquam habiturum recuperandi sua occasionem, si eam quae tum esset praetermisisset; nullum exercitum Romanum in Graecia esse, nec propter Gythium aut maritimos alios Laconas dignam causam existimaturos Romanos, cur legiones rursus in Graeciam transmittant.

the advanced guard, they hoped to be able to make it soon general. They assumed now a decided position. A congress of the league was called, and here, in the presence of Flamininus, who even to the last exerted himself to bring the excited nation to their senses, a resolution was adopted to call upon king Antiochus to liberate Greece, and to settle disputes between the Ætolians and the Romans. When Flamininus asked for a copy of this resolution, Democritus, the captain of the league for the time, had the impudence to say that he was too busy then, but that he would send the Romans a copy, when the Ætolian army should be encamped by the Tiber.[1]

Were we not from former times acquainted with the slowness of the Romans in such matters, it would strike us as strange that with the sure prospect of such a course of events an adequate military force had not even before this been sent to Greece. Nothing, it appears, hindered the senate from ordering, even in the beginning of the year 192 B.C., a fleet and troops to those important places which were most exposed to attack in the first line, particularly to Chalcis and Demetrias. But nothing was done, and the consequence was that first Demetrias and afterwards Chalcis were lost, and that the war against Antiochus, instead of being at once begun in Asia, had to be carried on in Greece for a long time, and there assumed a tedious and obstinate character.

The two leagues of the Achaeans and the Ætolians were not the only federal forms of government in Greece in this period of her decline. The germ of federal institutions can be discovered in the oldest times. Scattered about in many places we find towns which, under the significant names of Tripolis or Tetrapolis,[2] make themselves known as federal communities. Triphylia, the southern part of Elis, was evidently a union of three phylæ. Such phylæ are met with not only in the early period of Attica,

---

[1] Livy, xxxv. 33, 9.
[2] A tetrapolis in Cephallenia is mentioned by Thucydides, ii. 30. Strabo, x. 2. 13: a tetraphylia in Athamania, by Livy, xxxviii. 1.

BOOK V.
192-189 B.C.

but in numerous localities inhabited by Ionians, as well well as by Dorians and other Greeks. The ancient Amphictyonies rested on the same foundation, though they were rather religious than political associations. The leagues of Ionian, Æolian, and Dorian towns in Asia Minor, as also the numerous Symmachiæ and Sympolitiæ (alliances for mutual support and common government) of the earlier and the later time, were so many attempts at permanent confederations. In Thessaly, Bœotia, and Arcadia, several attempts were made of the same kind; but they were all thwarted by the deep-rooted spirit of local independence. It was found impossible to form a powerful executive, and to assemble together in one locality the various bodies of sovereign citizens for periodical legislative action. Some of the larger communities, like Athens, Corinth, Argos, and Thebes, succeeded at different times in rising to comparative importance, by concentrating in a dominant capital the material strength of a number of dependent townships and villages. Each of these states aspired in turn to be the head and ruler of more or less extensive dependencies. Their efforts were not directed towards federal constitutions, but towards the establishment of centralised states on a larger scale. But they were too weak or too deficient in political qualities to succeed like Rome in establishing the permanent government of one town over a larger territory. Thus the best period of Greek history was not favourable to the development of federal governments. In the decline of national prosperity, when the greatness of Athens and Sparta had dwindled to a shadow, the old principle of confederation was revived, and became more vigorous than it had ever been before. Besides the Ætolian and the Achaean leagues, we find now the federal communities of the Acarnanians, the Epirots, the Magnesians, the Bœotians, the Eubœans. In Phocis, Doris, and Locris, the same political combinations appear to have sprung up spontaneously, or to have still continued from old habit. Everywhere each separate community or town had an independent local government, but it was united with others for common objects, political as well as religious. A chief magistrate, called captain (strategos), and a second in command (hipparchos), changing every year, commanded the forces. A public secretary (grammateus), and a committee of chosen councillors (apokletoi), conducted the internal government and the foreign policy; but only the people themselves had a voice in the periodical or extraordinary great assemblies, when they elected public officers, determined questions of war or peace, and passed general laws.[1]

Such were the states which had received their independence as a gift of the Roman people, after they had been for a long time more or less dependent on Macedonia. It was, therefore, quite natural that states which had such a loose and weak constitution, should speedily relapse into disorder, and be agitated by the two opposing parties—the adherents of the old sovereign and those of the new protecting power.[2] Unfortunately the possession of these states was the price for which alone the Romans could hope to purchase the co-operation of Philip. It was, therefore, easy for the Ætolians, whether they spoke the truth or not, to make the Magnesians believe that Demetrias had been promised to the king of Macedonia; and before the Romans had secured this place by a garrison, as they might have done, had they been less slow, it was betrayed to the Ætolians by the partisans.[3] Thereupon the indefatigable Ætolian captain, Thoas, made an

Demetrias seized by the Ætolians.

---

[1] The voting took place not by counting the heads of the whole federal community assembled at any particular place, but each separate community of the confederation had one aggregate vote. Heads were counted only within each separate community to determine the majority in each. If this arrangement had not been adopted, the votes of the more distant communities would have been swamped by the great mass of voters of that community where the assembly was held. It was by a similar arrangement in Rome that the population of the city, which was contained in the four *tribus urbanæ*, was prevented from acquiring an undue influence. The distant country tribes were of equal weight with the town tribes, and they were looked upon as more select and aristocratic.

[2] Regarding the Roman and the anti-Roman parties in Chalcis, see Livy, xxxv. 37, 7; in Bœotia, Livy, xxxv. 47, 2. As usual, the Roman party was that of the aristocracy, which Flamininus, after the pacification of Greece, had endeavoured to establish in all places. [3] Livy, xxxv. 34.

attempt on Chalcis; but the Roman party received information of the design in due time. Reinforcements, sent from Eretria and Carystus, placed the town in such a state of defence, that Thoas gave up his intended attack.[1] In order still more to secure this important place, Eumenes soon afterwards, at the request of Flamininus, placed there a Pergamenian garrison of five hundred men.[2]

Ætolian force sent to Sparta.

It was a matter of great importance to the Ætolians to begin the war, on which they were bent, by some decided military success, and to spread in Greece the insurrectionary movement against Rome, in order to inspire Antiochus with confidence and to engage him to co-operate. The acquisition of Demetrias was, therefore, of great value to them; nor did they give up the hope of gaining Chalcis after the failure of their first attempt. But Sparta was almost of still greater importance, because by it the whole of the Achaean league could be kept employed during the war. When Nabis had been defeated by Philopœmen,[3] he had, by the intercession of the Romans, obtained an armistice, and had applied to the Ætolians to send him a reinforcement. The Ætolian confederation readily acceded to this request, and sent Nabis about one thousand men, under the command of a certain Alexamenos.[4] This was a step of very doubtful policy. The intimacy existing between Nabis and Flamininus could not be otherwise than suspicious to the Ætolians. If Flamininus allowed Nabis to keep possession of Gythium, which he had just taken in defiance of the Roman settlement, might he not easily be induced by this or any other promise to make peace with the Achaeans? In that case the

---

[1] Livy, xxxv, 37, 38.

[2] Livy, xxxv, 39, 2. Livy omits altogether to relate when Eumenes had come to Greece, and what force he had brought with him. This is an instance of the usual negligence, or intentional concealment of facts, of which the Roman annalists are guilty, when the co-operation of their allies ought to have been honestly stated. Compare vol. i. p. 276.

[3] See p. 101.

[4] This is another instance of the looseness of international law in antiquity. The Ætolians were still at peace with the Achaeans, but they had no hesitation in sending auxiliaries to Sparta, which was at open war with them. Compare note, p. 100.

latter had all their forces at their disposal against the Ætolians and the king of Syria. A precedent for such a combination had occurred in the war with Philip of Macedonia only a few years before. At that time the Romans had brought about an armistice between Nabis and the Achaean league, and had thus disengaged the Achaean contingents.[1] The Ætolians determined to gain Sparta at all price, and gave secret instructions to Alexamenus, in case Nabis should be inclined to come to an understanding with the Romans and Achaeans. This contingency, it appears, really occurred. Alexamenos decided to act promptly. At a review of the combined Lacedæmonian and Ætolian troops, he watched a moment when Nabis had approached the body of one thousand horse under his command, suddenly attacked the unsuspecting tyrant, cut him down from his horse, and had him despatched by a few of his own trusty followers, before the amazed Spartans could hasten to the rescue. But the great body of the Ætolians, not initiated into the plot, and entirely ignorant of its political bearing, thought that it was a signal for falling upon the town and plundering it. While they were ransacking the houses, and revelling in their natural love of spoil, the Spartans recovered from their surprise, rushed upon the plunderers, and killed them to the last man. At the invitation of Philopœmen, Sparta shortly after joined the Achaean confederation. Thus the bold undertaking of the Ætolians failed, and the deep scheme of Flamininus was crossed, whilst the Achaean league, after long and fruitless endeavours, at length succeeded, suddenly and unexpectedly, in making Sparta one of its members.[2]

Assassination of Nabis.

Sparta incorporated in the Achaean league.

---

[1] See p. 46.

[2] Livy, xxxv. 35, 37. The narrative given in the text is an attempt to combine the facts narrated by Livy in such a manner as to assign reasonable motives of action to the Ætolians. Perhaps no conjectures would be necessary if we had the narrative of Polybius. Livy, as we know, has often purposely suppressed circumstances which, in his opinion, cast an unfavourable light upon his countrymen. It may, therefore, not be going too far to suppose, as we have done in the text, that the murder of Nabis was provoked by intrigues of the Romans, tending to keep up the power of Nabis as a check upon the Ætolians.

Although this result was not what the Romans had intended, they yet accepted the situation such as it was, fully assured that if the Achaean league should at any time become too powerful, they would find means to confine it within due bounds, a calculation which, in the sequel, was proved to be correct. Hence, after their fleet had at last appeared before Gythium, they approved of the union of Sparta and Achaia, being determined, in the first place, to make full use of it in the war which was in prospect.

Landing of Antiochus in Greece.

Of the three attacks which the Ætolians had planned, on Demetrias, Chalcis, and Sparta, the first only had been successful. In order to make the most of this first success, Thoas proceeded again to Asia to king Antiochus, and tried to convince him that the time had now come for him to take the field in Greece. He assured him that he would be received with open arms by the Greeks, to whom Roman tyranny had become unbearable, and who had already commenced so vigorously the work of deliverance with their own hands. Though Antiochus had not yet settled matters in Asia according to his desire, and especially had not broken the resistance of the three towns, Smyrna, Lampsacus, and Alexandria Troas, and though he had not nearly completed his preparations for war, he was yet so dazzled by the brilliant prospects which Thoas opened to him, that he actually resolved to start with the insufficient forces which he had at his disposal. Sailing with forty decked and sixty open ships of war, and two hundred transports from the Hellespont to Thessaly, he landed at Demetrias with ten thousand infantry, five hundred horse, and six elephants.—It is surprising that Antiochus ventured to commence war with Rome with such a paltry force. Evidently he calculated on the Greeks collecting around him, and he was blind enough not only to trust to the support of the Ætolians and the smaller states, but also to reckon on the assistance of Philip of Macedonia. The Achaeans, he hoped, would at least remain neutral. But even when he learnt how deceitful the promises of the Ætolians were, he was unable to draw sufficient reinforcements from Asia, and he succumbed in the following year to the superior power of his opponents. So great was the difference between the pretensions of the Great King and his actual power.

Under such circumstances an expedition led by Hannibal to Italy was not to be thought of, even if Antiochus had entertained neither distrust nor jealousy, as Livy says,[1] towards the great Punian commander. The conqueror of Cannae was condemned to play an undignified part among the courtiers and flatterers of an Asiatic despot. In endeavouring to secure the favour of the great potentate he had to encounter the ill-will, envy, and malevolence of obscure men, who shuddered at the thought that he might by some great exploit outshine the renown of the king, or be wanting in submission after the complete overthrow of the Romans.[2] He was, therefore, not entrusted with an independent command, but remained as counsellor in the train of the king, until later on, in the course of the war, he obtained a post as commander of a fleet, for which, by his genius and his experience, he was least of all adapted.

After the Syrian army had landed in Demetrias in the autumn of the year 192 B.C., the Ætolians held a congress in Lamia, near to the Malian gulf. Here Antiochus appeared on a formal invitation, was received with boundless rejoicings, and declared commander of the Ætolian confederation, after the failure of a feeble and unpractical attempt of the moderate party to settle the dispute with Rome by a compromise under his mediation. A committee of thirty members of the Ætolian federal council was appointed as a permanent addition to the royal council of war.[3]

Things had gone now so far that neither party could retire from the contest without sustaining a moral defeat, and yet, curiously enough, war had not yet been formally declared. Nay, Antiochus acted and talked

---

[1] Livy, xxxv. 42.

[2] Livy, xxxv. 42, 9: Ipsam gloriam belli, qua velut dote Hannibal concilietur, nimiam in præfecto regis esse; regem conspici, regem unum ducem, unum imperatorem videri debere, etc.

[3] Livy, xxxv. 45.

as if he were the friend and protector of the Greeks without necessarily becoming thereby the enemy of the Romans.[1] Under this pretext he hoped to gain those who did not venture to desert Rome. Above all, he hoped to obtain possession of Chalcis. Thinking that by a personal appeal to the citizens he could induce them to embrace his cause, he hurried with a small force straight from Lamia to Salganeus, crossed the Euripus with but a few companions, and had an interview with the principal citizens of Chalcis. He requested them to regard him as a friend and ally without prejudice to their friendship for Rome; for he was come to Europe with no hostile intention, but to liberate the Greeks, really and truly, not in form and in words, as the Romans had done. Nothing, he said, could be more useful to the Greeks than that they should be friends with the two powers, for in this manner they would be protected by the one against the encroachments of the other. The people of Chalcis were too shrewd to allow themselves to be deceived by such words. They disclaimed a wish to reject the friendship of the king and of the Ætolians, but they would conclude an alliance only with the consent of the Romans. Thus the second attempt to gain Chalcis failed through the firmness of the Roman party of that place, and Antiochus was obliged to return to Demetrias, in order to determine with the council of thirty members of the Ætolian confederation, which had been deputed to assist him, what further steps should now be taken.[2]

By this time it must have been evident to the king, that what Thoas had said about the universal readiness of the Greeks to join him was an empty boast and a deception, intended only to stimulate him to the enterprise. At the same time the Ætolians became aware how inconsiderable was the power of the king, who boasted that he would fill all Greece with arms, troops, and horses, and line its

---

[1] Another instance of the vague state of international law at the time. See p. 108, note 5.
[2] Livy, xxxv. 46. Compare above, p. 100, note 1.

coasts with ships.¹ Both parties had mutually encouraged each other by specious representations, and now, in the time for action, both found themselves deceived, when it was too late to retrieve the mistakes which had been made. It was not of much consequence that the Bœotians were the declared enemies of Rome,² and that Amynander, the prince of the Athamanians, might be induced to join them.³ The only states which were of real weight and importance were Macedonia and Achaia. It was especially Hannibal who, in the council of Antiochus, pointed out the importance of the alliance of Macedonia; and it seems that Antiochus actually made one more attempt to gain Philip, although by his policy hitherto he must entirely have forfeited the confidence of his old ally. He calculated that Philip could never give up the hope of regaining his former position, and made proposals to him which opened prospects of this kind. But Philip had no confidence in him, and determined to remain true to the Romans, whose power he had learnt to dread, but of whose perfidious policy he knew so little that he hoped after a common victory to obtain for himself a valuable prize for his services.⁴

His proposals rejected by Philip.

As there was no prospect of gaining the alliance of Macedonia, it was the more important for Antiochus to insure at least the neutrality of the Achaean confederation, the second greatest power in Greece, especially as since the death of Nabis, and after the annexation of Sparta to the league, it had the whole military strength of that city at its disposal. Antiochus cherished some hopes of being able to attain this object, as he had heard of a misunder-

The Achaeans declare for Rome.

---

¹ Livy, xxxv. 44, 5: Nam simul primum anni tempus navigabile præbuisset mare, omnem so Græciam armis, viris, equis, omnem oram maritimam classibus comploturum etc.
² Livy, xxxv. 47, 3.
³ Livy, xxxv. 47, 5.
⁴ No distinct stipulations between king Philip and the Romans are known, except the remission of the war contribution and the restoration of the king's son, Demetrius. See above, p. 103. Livy, xxxv. 31, 5; xxxvi. 35, 13; Polybius, xx. 13.

BOOK V.
192–189 B.C.

standing between Flamininus and Philopœmen;[1] and the Achaeans actually admitted the ambassadors of Antiochus and of the Ætolians to a council held at Ægium in the presence of Flamininus. The result was that they found themselves placed in the proud position of seeing the greatest powers of the time sue, as it were, for their favour, and they seemed to hold the fate of Greece in their hands. On such a height of momentary power many an Achaean patriot was apt to turn giddy. Self-knowledge, self-control, and moderation were not exactly Greek virtues. But the Achaean confederation was at that time headed by a man who belongs to the wisest and best whom that highly gifted people ever produced. Philopœmen saw that neutrality would lead to nothing but unconditional subjection to the conqueror, and that steady fidelity to the Roman alliance was not less honourable than advantageous for the Achaean confederation. Rome had only just consented to the annexation of Sparta, and Rome alone could either secure or endanger that of the remaining communities in the Peloponnesus, such as Messenia and Elis, which were yet outside the league. The congress accordingly decided without hesitation to conclude a formal alliance with Rome, and it declared war at the same time against Antiochus and the Ætolians.[2] This resolution was carried out immediately. At the request of Flamininus a body of five hundred Achaeans was sent to garrison Chalcis, which was most exposed, and an equal number was despatched to the Piræus, because in the vacillating community of Athens a Syrian party was active, and threatened to deliver this important harbour into the hands of Antiochus.[3]

---

[1] Livy, xxxv. 47, 4 : Achæorum Philopœmenem principem, æmulatione gloriæ in bello Laconum, infestum invisumque esse Quinctio credebant. We must be satisfied with this slight hint, as we have no further evidence. But it does not seem unlikely that, apart from personal rivalry between the two leading men, which cannot have had a great influence, Antiochus founded his expectations on a conflict of interests which seemed to divide Rome and the Achaean league.

[2] Livy, xxxv. 50, 2 : Nulla nec disceptatio, nec dubitatio fuit, quin omnes, eosdem genti Achæorum hostes et amicos, quos populus Romanus censuisset, indicarent bellumque et Antiocho et Ætolis nuntiari juberent.

[3] Livy, xxxv. 50, 4.

Thus, at length, the war was formally declared, at least by one of the belligerents, and all the tedious discussions and deliberations were abandoned. Antiochus who, in order to maintain his position in Greece, was absolutely compelled to gain Chalcis, advanced now with his whole land and sea force against that town, which, though it had been twice threatened, still had no Roman garrison, and was defended only by the citizens, who were divided among themselves, and by a garrison of five hundred Pergamenians[1] and five hundred Achaeans. At last a small Roman detachment of five hundred men was sent by Flamininus to assist in defending the town.[2] Even this tardy and, as the event proved, too tardy step was taken only at the urgent entreaties of the party of Chalcidian citizens, faithful to Rome. But the Roman detachment never reached its destination. They found the passes already blocked up, and being attacked by superior forces at Delium, perished almost to a man. The first blood was thus shed, and the war, although not yet formally declared by either of the principal powers, had actually begun.

The destruction of the Roman detachment sent to the relief of Chalcis decided its fall. The courage of the Roman party sunk, and they made their escape from the town. The foreign garrison, too weak to confront enemies within and without, marched out, reached Salganeus on the continent, was here attacked by Syrian troops, and capitulated on condition of being allowed to retreat unmolested. The example of Chalcis, the capital of Euboea, was followed by the other towns in the island, and thus a short time after his arrival in Greece, Antiochus found

---

[1] Livy, xxxv. 39, 2, and above, p. 108.

[2] Livy, xxxv. 50. 9. We are not informed whether this detachment was sent from the Roman fleet under Atilius, which had been long stationed on the coasts of the Peloponnesus (Livy, xxxv. 37, 3) or from the land force which Bæbius commanded in Epirus (Livy, xxxv. 24, 7). The former alternative is the more likely. The narrative of Livy (xxxv. 50, 51) does not give a favourable impression of the way in which the Roman troops conducted themselves in the presence of the enemy. But it is possible that the historian exaggerates the carelessness and negligence of the troops in order to give proper relief to their bravery.

himself in possession of a strong and secure basis of operations against northern and central Greece. This success did not fail to make such an impression on some of the smaller states, which were incapable of an independent line of policy, that they were induced at once to join the Syro-Ætolian alliance. Such were the Eleans in the Peloponnesus, who had of old been the neighbours and enemies of the Achaeans. Antiochus sent them an auxiliary corps of one thousand[1] men to enable them to play the part originally assigned to the Spartans, and to give sufficient occupation to the Achaeans in the Peloponnesus. In central Greece, the weak and degenerate Bœotians now summoned up courage to express, at least in words and demonstrations, their hatred of the Romans.[2] The Epirots, also, who, owing to their geographical position, had to expect the first attack from the Romans, tried to engage Antiochus to send a force for their protection, promising in that case to join him unreservedly. In the event of his being unable to do this, they begged him to excuse them if they should be compelled to avoid a rupture with the Romans. It was clear that Antiochus needed only to throw into Greece a powerful military force, in order to gain over all those who were still wavering and hesitating. He sent accordingly to Asia for more troops;[3] but feeling now assured that he could no longer expect any aid from Philip, he resolved, even before the reinforcements could arrive, to make a sudden invasion into Thessaly.

Antiochus invades Thessaly.

Towards the end of the year 192 B.C., when the winter had already set in, Antiochus, in conjunction with an Ætolian and Athamanian army, invaded Thessaly, and, after an obstinate resistance, took Pheræ, Scotussa, and several other Thessalian towns. Having reached the neighbourhood of the battle-field of Cynoscephalæ, he collected together the unburied remains of the slain Macedonians, and caused them solemnly to be interred, an act by which he mortally offended the pride of king Philip,

---

[1] Livy, xxxvi. 5 and 31; Polybius, xx. 3.   [2] Livy, xxxvi. 6.
[3] Livy, xxxvi. 8, 1.

and made him his personal enemy. But he found in Thessaly no disposition to join him; and after long and fruitless efforts he had to give up the siege of Larissa, on receiving tidings that a Roman army, in union with a Macedonian force, was advancing to relieve the place. As the winter was already advanced, Antiochus discontinued his operations, and returned to Chalcis, there to await the season for the opening of the next campaign and the arrival of the reinforcements which were expected from Asia.

The winter of 192–191 B.C. was spent by Antiochus in Chalcis in a series of festivities. The king, although upwards of fifty years, fell in love with a handsome Chalcidian girl, and celebrated his marriage with great pomp in true Oriental style, as if he had abundance of leisure, and as if the war with the Romans and the deliverance of Greece caused him no longer any anxiety. The army followed his example, and the Asiatic troops, whose discipline at all times was of no high order, indemnified themselves for the toils and fatigues of the prolonged campaign by indulging in luxuries and licentiousness, in which they found in the Bœotians no unworthy rivals.

Although in the year 192 B.C. the war was evidently impending, the Romans had made neither a formal declaration of war, nor such military preparations as might enable them in case of necessity to act at once with vigour. It appears that since Hannibal's flight from Carthage they expected an attack on Italy or Sicily, and that on this account they delayed sending to Greece the forces at their disposal. It is easy to recognise in their entire policy and military proceedings at this time the influence of the Hannibalic invasion.[1] Only the prætor, Atilius Serranus, was sent to the Peloponnesus with a small fleet of thirty quinqueremes (vessels with five tiers of oars), at the time when Nabis commenced hostilities.[2] The prætor, Bæbius Tamphilus, with two Roman legions and fifteen thousand

---

[1] Livy, xxxvii. 51. 9: Ineuntibus id bellum gravis hostis et suis viribus, et quod Hannibalem rectorem militiæ habebat, visus fuerat.

[2] Above, page 100.

five hundred Italian allies, that is, with an army of about twenty-five thousand or twenty-six thousand men, marched into Bruttium, that extreme corner of Italy, which had become celebrated by Hannibal's long-continued defence, and which seemed to be the most natural basis of operations for an enemy landing in Italy from Greece.[1] Besides these forces, armies of about equal strength were levied, one of which the consul, Domitius Ahenobarbus, was ordered to keep in readiness for the defence of Italy, or for operations abroad. The other consul, Lucius Flamininus, the brother of Titus, was instructed to watch the Gauls. A third army under Minucius was required to keep the Ligurians in check. Oppius Salinator was sent with twenty ships to Sicily, and the prætor of that province, Valerius Tappo, was ordered to organize an army of twelve thousand four hundred men, and to place the towns on the east coast of Sicily in a state of defence, because that island too appeared to be threatened with invasion.[2] As, moreover, Sardinia, Corsica, and the two Spanish provinces required troops, Rome was forced to make greater exertions at this period than had ever been necessary since the end of the war with Hannibal.

Proportion of Romans and allies in the legions.

In the levies now effected the Italian allies were called upon to furnish a larger proportion of men than formerly. Their contingents had been usually about equal to those of the Romans, and every Roman legion, combined with an equal number of Italian allies, formed what might be called in modern phrase a division. This equality was now no longer observed. One legion of Roman citizens now received an addition of as many allies as seemed necessary, often as much as double its own number. In the cavalry service the contingents of the allies had always been stronger than the Roman. Thus in the recent wars the burdens which the Roman subjects had to bear grew

---

[1] It appears, moreover, that the Romans were not free from the fear of another insurrection in Italy. Appian, *Syr.* 15 : ὡς δ' ἐν μεγάλῳ φόβῳ, καὶ περὶ τῆς Ἰταλίας ἐδείμαινον, μὴ οὐδ' αὐτὴ σφίσιν ᾖ πιστὴ ἢ βέβαιος ἐπ' Ἀντιόχῳ. [2] Livy, xxxv. 23.

heavier and heavier, and yet they were not admitted to a larger share of the privileges of Roman citizens. It is well to bear this in mind in order to understand that the extension of the Roman power was in itself one of the causes which brought about the internal change in the constitution. The inequality between Roman citizens and allies was at the bottom of the disturbances of the period of the Gracchi; the inequality between Romans and provincials was the cause which changed the republic into an empire.

At length, when the news of the landing of Antiochus in Greece had arrived[1] and an invasion in Italy was no longer to be feared, Bæbius received orders to cross over to Epirus with all his troops (about twenty-five thousand five hundred men), towards the end of the year 192 B.C.[2] It was then already too late to prevent the capture of Chalcis.

Bæbius remained stationary even after his landing with the principal force at Apollonia, and sent only a small detachment of two thousand men, under Appius Claudius, to Thessaly. But even this sufficed, as we have seen,[3] in conjunction with a Macedonian corps, to decide Antiochus to abandon the siege of Larissa, and to retreat from Thessaly. The winter then put an end to further operations on both sides.

The consuls for the year 191 B.C. were Publius Cornelius Scipio Nasica, a cousin of the conqueror of Zama, and the plebeian, Marcus Acilius Glabrio. They entered on their office on the Ides of March, which month, owing to the confusion in the calendar at that time, coincided with our January; and now that the war had actually begun, Scipio Nasica, upon a resolution of the senate, brought before the people the proposal to authorise the government to declare and carry on war with king Antiochus

---

[1] Livy, xxxv. 23, 10. It is worthy of notice that this news was brought to Rome by Attalus, the brother of king Eumenes of Pergamum.
[2] Livy, xxxv. 24, 7.
[3] Above, page 117.

and his allies.¹ The vote of the people was by the constitution of the Roman republic indispensable, nay, it was that public act which alone could decide the question of peace or war. But Livy barely takes the trouble to mention it in four words,² showing thereby that it had by this time become a mere form, and that the people of Rome and the thirty-one country tribes had ceased, at least in matters of foreign policy, to have a judgment and a will of their own, and were in a state of complete dependence on the senate. In truth, the Roman popular assembly had for a long time been unable to understand the complicated diplomatic questions, or to follow the negotiations with a great number of foreign states. They were absolutely obliged to trust to the skill and experience of professional politicians. If, by a capricious exercise of their sovereign rights, they had disapproved of the measures which the senate from time to time had taken, and if they had refused to accept a war which was the necessary consequence of such steps, the constitution of the republic would have broken down. The people as such, that is the popular assembly, could not dream of thwarting the deliberate policy of the senate. The majority of the senators formed what we should call the 'government' of the republic: the minority formed the 'opposition.' Whatever contests took place between these two parties were confined to internal discussions within the senate. The people, as such, could take no part in these contests, unless a question was laid before it by one of the tribunes or other magistrates, who, being unable to secure a majority in the senate, might appeal to the people as the sovereign power in all matters. Such an appeal was made in the beginning of the second war with Macedonia.³ But the opposition was powerless when the majority of the senate were firm, and thus it was, that in spite of the

---

¹ Livy, xxxvi. 1, 4: Patres rogationem ad populum ferri iusserunt, vellent iuberentne, cum Antiocho rege, quique eius sectam secuti essent, bellum iniri.
² Livy, xxxvi. 1, 5: Cornelius eam rogationem pertulit.
³ Above, p. 18.

formal law of the constitution, the senate and not the people actually enjoyed the right of declaring war.[1]

The preparations were at last complete, and the troops were on the march. The army of twenty-five thousand men which was already stationed in Greece under Bœbius was reinforced by a double legion, ten thousand seven hundred men strong, with twenty elephants, and five hundred Numidian horsemen furnished by Masinissa.[2] The commander of this army, the strength of which was thus raised to upwards of thirty-six thousand men, was, moreover, directed to enlist five thousand men of the non-Italian allied peoples,[3] and thus the actual forces with which the Romans took the field against Antiochus were increased to the number of forty thousand. The fleet of Atilius, consisting of thirty quinqueremes,[4] was already stationed in the Greek seas. It was now raised to double the number of ships, and a reserve of twenty ships was kept ready in Sicily. As a reserve for the land forces, a consular army remained in the town of Rome, one army in Bruttium, and a third in Sicily, destined especially for the protection of the island.[5] As apart from these various

---

[1] A decision of the people approving of war was not equivalent to a declaration of war, nor was actual war an absolutely necessary consequence. It only empowered the government to take the necessary preliminary measures, and to declare and wage war. It resembled, therefore, a grant of supplies for war by a modern parliament. As a citizen elected for a public office by the people acquired only the right of entering on his office by the act of 'renunciation,' i.e., the publication of his election, so actual war was preceded by the solemn declaration of the 'fetialis.' Both acts, the renunciation of a magistrate, and the despatch of a fetialis, though authorised by a popular vote, required the additional sanction of a 'patrum auctoritas' (See vol. i. p. 135). Thus the formal law was brought into harmony with the actual practice.

[2] Livy, xxxvi. 4, 8.

[3] Livy, xxxvi. 1, 8: Et extra Italiam permissum, ut, si res postulasset, auxilia ab sociis ne supra quinque milium numerum acciperet. These five thousand socii are of course not included in the troops furnished by Philip and by the Achaeans. The latter were auxiliaries, commanded respectively by Macedonian and Achaean officers. The five thousand now to be enlisted, or, as Livy expresses it, 'accepted,' by the Romans were either volunteers or troops lent to the Romans by their allies, and they formed an integral part of the Roman army.   [4] Above, p. 117.

[5] The naval armaments cannot be ascertained with accuracy. In the preceding year orders had been given to fit out one hundred quinqueremes

corps, considerable forces were necessary in the north of Italy, in Sardinia, Corsica, and Spain, it is apparent that the military preparations occasioned by the war with Antiochus were on a scale which recalled the memory of the stupendous efforts made during the war with Hannibal.[1]

Departure of Acilius Glabrio.

The question which of the consuls of the year was to have the command in the war against Antiochus being decided by lot in favour of Acilius Glabrio, the senate, as usual on such momentous occasions, appointed several days for prayer and sacrifice. Acilius Glabrio pronounced, after the chief pontiff, the solemn words of a vow: 'If the war which the people have resolved to wage against king Antiochus shall have been carried on to the end, according to the wish of the senate and of the Roman people, then shall the Roman people for ten days celebrate to thee, oh Jupiter, great games! and at all the shrines of the gods gifts shall be offered out of the sum which the senate shall have appointed; and whatever magistrate shall celebrate these games, whenever and wherever he may celebrate them, they shall be reputed as celebrated according to divine law, and the gifts shall be considered to be duly offered.'[2]

(Livy, xxxv. 21, 1), and after that fifty new ships were to be laid on the stocks (Livy, xxxv. 24 8): M. Fulvio prætori urbano negotium datum est, ut quinqueremes novas quinquaginta faceret. From this it would appear that the former hundred vessels were old. If from this number of one hundred and fifty ships those are deducted which were sent to Greece and Sicily (chap. 23), there remains still a reserve of fifty ships. As in the course of the war a descent of the enemies on Italy was no longer apprehended, it was resolved to send fifty ships to Greece instead of thirty. Livy, xxxv. 42, 1. These were probably the fifty new built ships mentioned by Livy, xxxv. 24, 8.

See p. 118. One proof of this is, that the maritime colonies, in spite of their protest, were called upon to furnish troops for the naval service (Livy, xxxvi. 3), just as in the general calamity of the Hannibalic war they had been obliged to do. Livy, xxvii. 36. See vol. ii. p. 383.

[2] Livy, xxxvi. 2, 3: Si duellum, quod cum rege Antiocho sumi populus jussit, id ex sententia senatus populique Romani confectum erit, tum tibi, Jupiter, populus Romanus ludos magnos dies decem continuos faciet, donaque ad omnia pulvinaria dabuntur de pecunia, quantam senatus decreverit, etc. This vow is a good illustration of the narrow and strictly legal character of the Roman religion. It reads like a formal contract between the parties, and

The sacrifices proved favourable.[1] The haruspices announced victory and triumph, and an extension of the Roman frontier.[2] The Fetiales being consulted as to the manner in which the war ought to be declared, gave the same opinion on the subject as in the case of the Macedonian war against Philip. The formal announcement, they said, could be made either to Antiochus himself or to any hostile post. Thereupon Acilius crossed over from Dyrrachium to Apollonia, about the middle of May.[3]

Antiochus had already opened the campaign. Early in the year 191 B.C. he had proceeded from Chalcis to Acarnania, and had, in concert with the party hostile to the Romans, seized the town of Medeon, when he heard of the landing of the consul at Apollonia, and of the simultaneous attack of the united Roman and Macedonian army under Bæbius and king Philip on Thessaly. He returned immediately to Chalcis, in order to complete his army with the reinforcements which he expected from Asia. In a very short space of time the Thessalian towns which he had conquered at the beginning of the past winter were lost again. The Romans and Macedonians steadily advanced with superior forces. One town after another fell into their hands, with many thousand men of the Syrian garrisons, part of whom, being mercenaries, readily entered Philip's service. Among the prisoners was the brother-in-law of Amynander, the king or chief of Athamania.

is very particular in not leaving to the gods any plea for exacting more than the senate and the Roman people solemnly bound themselves to perform.

[1] Livy, xxxvi. 1, 3: Omnia sacrificia læta fuerunt, primisque hostiis perlitatum est.

[2] Livy, xxxvi. 1, 3: et ita haruspices responderunt, eo bello terminos populi Romani propagari, victoriam et triumphum ostendi. In Livy's narrative this prediction and the favourable sacrifice (note 1) preceded the formal vote of the people which sanctioned the war. The chronological deviation which we have ventured upon for reasons of style in our abridged account is, on the whole, immaterial, and does not misrepresent the events. But it is worth while remarking that the vote of the people appears still more a mere matter of form if it was taken after the decision of the gods had been given. See p. 120.

[3] What was nominally the middle of May at that time was, in reality, the middle of March. The Roman calendar, owing to the slovenly practice of the Pontifices, the state astronomers, was no longer in agreement with the seasons

BOOK V.
192–189 B.C.

He was a citizen of Megalopolis, named Philip, and gave himself out for a descendant of the royal house of Macedonia. His absurd pretensions to the Macedonian throne had been supported by Antiochus.[1] When the wretched pretender was brought in chains before king Philip, previously to being sent to Rome, Philip could not deny himself the satisfaction of greeting him ironically as king and brother. The king of Athamania saw his whole land overrun by the enemy, and fled to Ambracia. He was sadly disappointed. Dissatisfied with the Romans, because after the common victory over Philip they had not consented to his acquiring the land on which he calculated, he had deserted them, hoping for better success if he joined the Ætolians and Antiochus. He was now left to his fate by his allies at the very beginning of the war, and lost even his old hereditary possessions. These countries king Philip hoped to obtain as his share of the spoil. He therefore treated the Athamanian captives with humanity and kindness, and even gave them back their freedom, expecting that they would influence their countrymen favourably for him, as their future sovereign.

Position of Antiochus at the pass of Thermopylæ.

Antiochus now saw plainly the dangers of his position. His reinforcements from Asia arrived very slowly. He had only ten thousand foot soldiers and five hundred horsemen, to oppose to the united armies of the Romans and Macedonians, which amounted at least to fifty thousand men. The Ætolians were so lukewarm or so exhausted, that they could only furnish an auxiliary corps of four thousand men. It was not possible to keep the open plains of Thessaly with such insufficient forces. Antiochus therefore abandoned Thessaly, and retired behind Thermopylæ. He fortified this celebrated pass by a double wall and trenches, and here he hoped, in a safe defensive position, to be able to detain the enemy till sufficient reinforcements from Asia should place him in a condition again to take the offensive. The Ætolians held Hypata and Heraclea, two towns belonging to the Ætolian confederation, and lying

[1] See p. 103.

to the north of the pass. They were, moreover, intrusted by Antiochus with the task of guarding the mountain paths, by which the defensive position in the pass could be turned, and which, in the memorable defence of Thermopylæ against Xerxes, the Persians had followed under the guidance of Ephialtes, in order to come upon the rear of the Spartans. It augured badly for the issue of the struggle that only one-half of the Ætolians deemed it necessary to obey the king's command. Two thousand men remained in Heraclea, where they could be of no manner of use for keeping off the hostile attack. The remaining two thousand occupied, in three separate detachments, three different heights of mount Œta, the most important of which was called Callidromus.

The consul Acilius Glabrio attacked the pass in front with his chief force, after having despatched two detachments of two thousand men the night before to cross the mountain by a devious path, and to attack the Syrians in the rear. One of these detachments was led by the famous Marcus Porcius Cato, the consul of 195 B.C., who was serving as legate in the army of Glabrio. He arrived safely on the summit of Callidromus, surprised the careless Ætolians in the early morning, and drove them down the mountain with very little trouble. As soon as the troops of the king perceived the fugitive Ætolians and the Romans pursuing them, they gave up all resistance, and sought their safety in flight. The narrowness of the pass prevented a hot pursuit; but in the further retreat through Bœotia, where the defeated and disorganized army roamed about without plan or order, the greater number were overtaken, and either slain or captured.[1] The king succeeded with only

---

[1] According to the trustworthy statement of Polybius, the army of Antiochus could have numbered little, if at all, more than ten thousand men. Nevertheless, the veracious annalist, Valerius Antias, related that in the battle of Thermopylæ forty thousand of the enemy were killed, and more than five thousand captured. The whole Syrian army, according to him, amounted to sixty thousand. (Livy, xxxvi. 19, 11.) It is satisfactory to see that Livy prefers the smaller numbers given by Polybius to the impudent exaggerations of the braggart Valerius. But what, we may ask again, is our chance of discovering

BOOK V.
192–189 B.C.

Return of Antiochus to Asia.

about five hundred men in crossing the straits to Chalcis, from whence, without further delay, he hurried back to Ephesus.

The victory at Thermopylæ cost the Romans only two hundred men. In the first outset they had succeeded in driving the king of Syria out of Greece. All the towns in Phocis and Bœotia, which during the presence of Antiochus had declared themselves in his favour, now opened their gates to the victorious Roman army, praying for indulgence and forgiveness, which was readily granted by the Romans. In Coronea alone the conquerors lost patience, when they saw in a temple of Athene a statue of king Antiochus, which had been erected by command of the Bœotian confederation. The Coroneans had to suffer for this premature adulation. The exasperated Romans devastated their territory, until an order of the consul called back the soldiers.[1] Chalcis, like the remaining towns in Eubœa, out of which the men of the Ætolian party quickly withdrew, submitted with equal promptness. At the request of Flamininus, Acilius Glabrio remitted the punishment which he had intended to inflict.[2]

Continued resistance of the Ætolians.

By the defeat of Antiochus, and his return to Asia, the war in Greece would have been ended, if the Ætolians also had submitted. They were now isolated and exposed to the overwhelming force of the Romans. If they had been wise, they would simply have accepted any terms which Rome might impose. But this rude and ignorant people was not capable of a reasonable policy. Self-deceived with respect to their own and their enemy's strength, they ventured to continue the resistance to Rome single-handed, and did so with a degree of courage and perseverance which almost inspires admiration. The garrison of Heraclea, which during the battle of Thermopylæ had made an attempt to storm the Roman camp, resolutely declined to surrender, and the town was only taken after a regular siege

the truth in those numerous cases where the statements of such writers as Valerius alone are preserved, and where we have no Polybius to control them?

[1] Livy, xxxvi. 20.   [2] Plutarch, *Flamin.* 16.

and a desperate defence. Among the prisoners was Democritus, the officer who the year before had spoken the defiant words that he would make known to Flamininus the decision of the Ætolian people when he should be encamped with his own army by the side of the Tiber.¹

While the consul was besieging Heraclea, Philip of Macedonia was occupied with the siege of the Ætolian town of Lamia, about seven miles north of Heraclea. Probably he had detained a portion of the Ætolian troops stationed in this locality, so that though he took no direct part in the fight at Thermopylæ, he rendered important help towards securing that victory.² But he had not succeeded in taking the strong city of Lamia in due time, i.e. before Heraclea was reduced by the Romans. Acilius summarily commanded Philip to abandon the siege. Thus the king of Macedonia lost not only the booty of the conquered town, but also the prospect of obtaining Lamia as a lasting possession.³ His mortification was the greater, as the Romans did not continue the siege of Lamia, and thereby showed that they had interfered not from military considerations, but from mere jealousy.

Philip, although greatly offended, was not in a position to resent this scornful treatment. The time was past when he could choose between the Roman and the Syrian alliance. He was compelled to fight the Roman battles, and as he had neglected to insist on clear and definite stipulations at the beginning of the war,⁴ his only chance of obtaining any profit for himself was to yield to all the caprices of the Roman generals, to be ready at all times with his services, and finally to throw himself upon the

CHAP. II.
192-189 B.C.

Offence given to Philip.

---

¹ Livy, xxxvi. 22-24. Above, p. 105.
² The Roman narrative, in its usual unfairness to the allies of Rome, has altogether omitted this. More than this, in the speeches attributed to the consul, king Philip is taunted with the offensive remark that he had taken no part in the contest with Antiochus. According to Livy (xxxvi. 25, 1), he was ill at the time, and thus prevented from co-operating with the Romans. But even if that were true, the king's illness would surely not have prevented the Macedonian troops from doing their duty, nor would any Roman general have excused an ally on such a flimsy pretext. ³ Livy, xxxvi. 25.
⁴ See p. 113, note 4.

generosity of the Romans for his share in the prize of victory. How he was deceived in these hopes we shall see in the sequel.

The fall of Heraclea seemed at last to have broken the courage of the Ætolians. Having, only a short time before, sent a message to Antiochus to intimate their intention of carrying on the war, and to beg for assistance either in troops or money, they now asked the consul for peace. Acilius Glabrio granted them an armistice of ten days, and sent Valerius Flaccus to the neighbouring town of Hypata to enter into negotiations with the deputies of the Ætolian government. At the advice of Flaccus a resolution was come to by which the Ætolians formally submitted themselves to the Romans.[1] They naturally hoped for the considerate and merciful treatment, which, in truth, was demanded by the interests of Rome; for in the first place their national strength was by no means broken, and secondly the Romans were obliged to keep a power in Greece, which might serve to counterbalance Macedonia as well as the Achaean confederation. This was the policy observed throughout by the able and experienced Flamininus. But Acilius Glabrio was a rough warrior, who felt a pleasure in acting with brutality, and in tearing open a wound which had begun to heal. He required, therefore, from the Ætolians, by virtue of the right which their unconditional submission had given him, that they should immediately deliver up two of their principal men, and even king Amynander and the noblest Athamanians who had plotted the desertion of that people from Rome. The Ætolians had no notion that their formal submission was to be construed in this way. Phœneas, their envoy, protested that the demand of the Romans was neither fair nor justified by any principle of right in the common practice of the Greeks.[2] Thereupon Acilius Glabrio

---

[1] Livy, xxxvi. 28, 1: Ætolos se suaque omnia fidei populi Romani permittere. Polybius, xx. 9, 10: οἱ δὲ Αἰτωλοὶ . . . . . . ἔκριναν ἐπιτρέπειν τὰ ὅπλα Μανίῳ, δόντες αὐτοὺς εἰς τὴν Ῥωμαίων πίστιν, οὐκ εἰδότες, τίνα δύναμιν ἔχει τοῦτο. [2] Polybius, xx. 10.

coolly observed, 'It mattered little to him what the Ætolians considered to be the Greek custom, while he gave his orders according to Roman custom to the subjects of Rome.' Saying this, he bade his lictors fetch chains in order, in case of necessity, to bring the refractory to their senses. Phæneas stood aghast and condescended to ask for mercy; at the same time Flaccus, as well as the tribunes who were present, begged that the sanctity of the ambassadors should be respected. Glabrio then granted a delay of ten days, during which time Phæneas might ascertain the will of the Ætolian people.[1] But the pride of the haughty mountaineers recoiled from the dishonourable demand, and they roundly refused to obey, the more decidedly as just then Nicander, the envoy of Antiochus, had returned from Asia with money and promises.[2]

The war now broke out into a new flame. The Ætolians sent their choicest troops to Naupactus on the Corinthian Gulf, which was strongly fortified, and here they stood at bay with the courage of despair. Had Flamininus been present when the negotiations with the Ætolians were going on, they would hardly have been driven to such an extremity. But Flamininus was occupied at that time in the Peloponnesus, where he had to perform the delicate task of disarming the Messenians and Eleans, who had always sided with the Ætolians, without thereby increasing too much the strength of the Achaean league. The Eleans bowed to the adverse circumstances, and submitted to the Achaeans. But the Messenians, who were already hard pressed by the Achaeans turned to Flamininus, hoping to gain more favourable conditions from him than from his Achaean allies. At the direction of Flamininus, Diophanes, who had succeeded Philopœmen as captain of the Achaeans, recalled his army

---

[1] According to Polybius (xx. 11), Glabrio only intended to frighten Phæneas. But it is hardly likely that the brutal Roman would condescend to such a questionable piece of acting. He was, no doubt, in full earnest; otherwise the intercession of his inferiors, unless it was concerted beforehand, would have been quite out of place.

[2] Livy, xxxvi. 29.

from Messenia, and the Messenians now joined the Achaean league, under conditions which the Romans dictated.¹ Thus was fulfilled the long-cherished wish of the Achaeans, and the whole of the Peloponnesus was united in the league. It is true that the manifold difficulties produced by internal revolutions in the various states, and by long-continued border feuds, were not removed by this union. But provided that foreign interference did not fan the flame of discord, there was room for hope that a happy time was coming, at least for the Peloponnesian Greeks. Under the protection of Rome, if she honourably and conscientiously fostered the elements of order and progress, Greece might again enjoy peace, opulence and prosperity, and a second season of intellectual greatness, though, perhaps, not of national independence. We shall see how the Romans, by an ungenerous, stern and perfidious policy, disappointed those hopes, drove the Greeks to despair by humiliating and cruel treatment, and almost forced them into a struggle which was utterly hopeless and ruinous.

Policy of Rome with regard to acquisitions in Greece.

As yet the Roman senate acted upon the principle that direct possessions on the Greek continent were not desirable for the republic; and this was the reason why the Epirots were not punished for their equivocal atti-

---

¹ Livy, xxxvi. 31, 9: Messeniis imperavit, ut exules reducerent et Achæorum concilii essent; si qua haberent de quibus aut recusare aut in posterum caveri sibi vellent, Corinthum ad se venirent. These words sufficiently indicate that the Messenians had to consider themselves as the special clients of Rome, and thus care was taken that there should not be wanting sufficient grounds for Roman interference in the internal affairs of the Achaean league even after the whole Peloponnesus was included in it. When the Romans, at a somewhat later period, wished to patronise the Eleans in the same way as they now did the Messenians, the Eleans were proud enough to prefer acting for themselves; Livy, xxxvi. 35, 7: Elei per se ipsi quam per Romanos maluerunt Achaico contribui auxilio. A similar spirit was shown by the Achaeans, when they deprecated Roman interference in the matter of the return of the Lacedaemonian exiles. (Plutarch, *Philopœmen*, 17.) It is therefore incorrect to say that the Romans were unwilling to trouble themselves with the internal affairs and quarrels of the Greeks. On the contrary, it is quite evident that they took particular pleasure in it, and that they fanned the flames of discord among the Greeks with insidious zeal and consummate perfidy.

tude. Though they had had transactions with Antiochus, they obtained a full pardon upon their promise of faithful attachment to Rome for the future.¹ The Ionian islands, however, were not included in this policy of abstinence. They were not unfavourably situated between Greece and Italy, and promised to be of great importance to Rome as well for military as also for commercial intercourse with Greece. Corcyra, indeed, was already in possession of the Romans since the first Illyrian war. Now they took also Zacynthus, which the Achaeans were anxious to acquire. Flamininus gave the Achaeans to understand that it would be better for the league if it did not extend beyond the Peloponnesus; it would thus be less exposed to attack, just as a tortoise was quite safe as long as its head and legs did not protrude beyond the sheltering cover.²

The Peloponnesus was now at peace, while the Achaeans, whose aid was most desirable for the prosecution of the war, were so far humoured, that they placed their forces at the disposal of the Romans as well in Asia as also against the Ætolians. Flamininus repaired to the army of the consul Acilius Glabrio, which had for two months been engaged in the siege of Naupactus, and was pressing the town very hard. The situation of affairs was similar to that in the year 196 B.C., when Nabis was reduced to the last distress.³ It was not difficult to crush the Ætolians altogether. But, as at the earlier period Flamininus, contrary to all expectation, had granted peace to the conquered tyrant in order to leave a counterpoise to the Achaeans, so now he gave his advice to the effect that the Ætolians should be treated leniently, because, in the meantime, king Philip had made use of the opportunity to strengthen his position in Thessaly and in the Ætolo-Athamanian frontier lands. He had conquered some fortified towns, among which was the important fortress of Demetrias, and had thus given uneasiness to the Roman diplomatists. As Philip's help

¹ Livy, xxxvi. 35, 8. ² Livy, xxxvi. 32. ³ See, p. 74.

could not be dispensed with any more than that of the Achaeans until the war with Antiochus had been brought to a close, the Romans sanctioned his conquests, or at least seemed to sanction them, by leaving them unnoticed, and this inspired him with the hope that he would eventually be able to retain them. They then not only made up for the offence given him at the siege of Lamia, but fulfilled their former promise by restoring to him his son Demetrius, who had been kept till now as a hostage at Rome, and by remitting the payment of the war contribution still outstanding. The complete overthrow of the Ætolian power was not, however, in the interest of Rome. It sufficed so to humiliate them that they became willing and serviceable clients of the Roman republic, who might be used against Philip in case of necessity. For this reason the siege of the almost conquered Naupactus was relinquished on the advice of Flamininus; an armistice was granted to the Ætolians, and they were directed to send an embassy to Rome to negotiate the conditions of peace.[1] Meanwhile the summer was spent, and Acilius Glabrio conducted his army back to Phocis into winter quarters.

The result of the campaign of the year, 191 B.C., if not, in a military point of view, very brilliant, had a decided influence on the course of the war. The only great feats of arms were the victory at Thermopylæ and the taking of Heraclea, both due to a crushing superiority of numbers, and not in the least to great strategic ability

---

[1] Livy, xxxvi. 34 and 35. The raising of the siege of Naupactus was a voluntary act on the part of the Romans. Like the order given to king Philip (page 127) to raise the siege of Lamia, it was an act of political calculation, not of military expedience. Its object could be no other than that indicated in the text, viz., to spare the Ætolians from political considerations. It had nothing whatever to do with any generosity or philhellenism attributed to Flamininus. Its motive is not to be sought in the reflexion of Flamininus, that he felt himself called to suffer no Greek nation to be utterly destroyed: sui maxime operis esse nullam gentem liberatæ a se Græciæ funditus everti: Livy, xxxvi. 34, 4; but rather in the consideration 'that the interest of Rome demanded that the Ætolians should not be too much weakened, and that Philip should not grow too powerful': non tantum interest nostra Ætolorum opes ac vires minui, quantum non supra modum Philippum crescere. Livy, xxxvi. 34, 10.

on the part of the Roman general. But Antiochus was forced to abandon Greece, and the resistance of the Ætolians was so effectually checked, that if it seemed desirable it might easily be put an end to altogether.

The operations of the Romans by sea were even less brilliant, being characterised not only by slowness and caution, but by timidity, and total want of enterprise. The small fleet of thirty larger and some smaller vessels, with which Atilius had been stationed as early as the preceding year on the coast of the Peloponnesus, had neither assisted in the siege of Gythium, nor had it protected Chalcis from the attack of Antiochus.[1] It was only after the battle of Thermopylæ that it ventured out into the waters east of Eubœa, where it succeeded in dispersing a fleet of transports, and in capturing some of the ships sent with provisions to king Antiochus. After this performance the Roman fleet returned to the Piræus, and awaited reinforcements from home.[2] These reinforcements were long in coming. It seems that even in the year 191 B.C., the Romans were apprehensive of an attack by Antiochus on Italy and Sicily, and that they hesitated to withdraw the fleets, and to leave the coasts unprotected. Possibly they doubted that Antiochus would, with so small a force as ten or fifteen thousand men, restrict himself to the invasion of Greece. This small number seemed to indicate that a larger army was in reserve to be directed against Italy under the command of Hannibal. It was only when this danger had entirely vanished in consequence of the events in Greece, that the prætor, Caius Livius,[3] advanced with the principal fleet to

---

[1] See pp. 99, 115. [2] Livy, xxxvi. 20.

[3] Appian (*Syr.* 22) significantly calls Caius Livius the guardian of Italy (φύλαξ τῆς Ἰταλίας). It is Appian in particular who, following probably Polybius, dwells on the fear inspired by Antiochus. The Roman annalists were too proud to own this. Livy, therefore, has carefully obliterated this interesting feature, which, as we have tried to show in the text, explains so much of the movements of the Roman fleets and armies. However, in a later passage (xxxvii. 51, 9) Livy confesses the fact that the Romans were not without serious fears in the beginning of the war: Ineuntibus id bellum gravis hostis et suis viribus, et quod Hannibalem rectorem militiæ haberet, visus fuerat.

undertake offensive operations in the eastern seas. With fifty Roman decked vessels, which were joined by contingents from Naples, Locri, Rhegium, and the other Greek towns in Italy, and by six Carthaginian ships, he sailed across the Ionian Sea[1] to Corcyra; but he gave himself time to plunder the islands of Cephallenia and Zacynthus on the pretext of punishing them for their attitude, and used the opportunity for enriching himself and his soldiers. Having arrived in the Piræus, he detached five-and-twenty ships from the squadron of Atilius, and about the time when Glabrio was besieging Naupactus, sailed across the Ægean Sea straight to Chios. After he had been joined by a Pergamenian fleet of twenty-four large and as many small vessels,[2] he had under his command a fleet of a hundred and five decked ships, and about fifty smaller ones. Thinking himself sufficiently strong, he determined, without waiting for the arrival of the Rhodian contingent, at once to strike a blow at the hostile fleet which Polyxenidas, a Rhodian exile, had assembled in the neighbourhood of Chios, to the number of about seventy large and thirty smaller vessels. Polyxenidas had hoped to attack the Roman fleet before its union with its Asiatic allies. He saw himself now opposed by a greatly superior force, and was easily defeated near the small bay of Corycus between Chios and Ephesus. The allies lost only one vessel, a Carthaginian trireme which, with too much zeal, had pressed forward, and got in between two hostile ships. The Syrians retreated with a loss of twenty-three ships, and took shelter in the harbour of Ephesus. On the following day five-and-twenty Rhodian decked vessels joined the Roman and Pergamenian squadrons. This united naval force of the allies now appeared before Ephesus to challenge the Syrian fleet to renew the battle. But Polyxenidas of course refused to accept

---

[1] Livy, xxxvi. 42, 3: This was after the battle of Thermopylæ: postquam audivit circa Thermopylarum saltum in statione consulem ac regem esse. The king here referred to was evidently Philip, not Antiochus, as Weissenborn says in his note to Livy.   [2] Appian, *Syr.* 22.

THE SYRO-ÆTOLIAN WAR.

CHAP. II.
192–189 B.C.

battle, and remained within the safe port.¹ As the season was now far advanced, the allied fleets separated again and went into their winter quarters, the Rhodians and the Pergamenians to their respective homes, the Romans to Phocæa and Canæ on the Æolian coast, opposite the island of Lesbos.

The news of the brilliant victory at Corycus was received in Rome with great rejoicings and celebrated by a nine days' festival.² The anxiety with which the movements of the powerful king of Syria had been watched up to this time now disappeared. The decided superiority of the Roman naval force was clearly demonstrated, and there was no longer any occasion to apprehend an attack on Italy by king Antiochus. This feeling of security was fatal to the Ætolians, whose ambassadors shortly afterwards appeared in Rome to learn the conditions under which Rome would grant them peace.³ They were very ungraciously received, and were hardly allowed to speak in the senate. Denounced on all sides, and urged to confess their guilt, they endeavoured to plead their former services in mitigation of their punishment; but they were told they must either submit unconditionally to the decision of the senate, or pay at once a thousand talents, and enter into an offensive and defensive alliance with Rome. On their begging to be informed how the first alternative was to be understood, they received no decisive answer, and were ordered to leave the city of Rome on that very day, and Italy within a fortnight.⁴

Roman reply to the Ætolian embassy.

---

¹ The port of Ephesus was a land-locked basin, and seems to have been more a dock than a natural harbour. Its locality can be distinctly recognised within the area of the ruins covered by the town. In its dock-like character it resembled the celebrated Kothon of Carthage. See plan of Carthage at the end of this volume.

² Polybius, xxi. 1. Livy has omitted to mention this fact, which is so characteristic of the fear inspired by the naval armaments of Antiochus. See p. 133, note 3.

³ Polybius, xxi. 1. See p. 132.

⁴ Polybius, xxi. 1; Livy, xxxvii. 1. The harshness of this answer was, as we have represented it in the text, a direct result of the recent victory of the Roman fleet in Asia. On no other ground is the proceeding of the Romans intelligible. At the siege of Naupactus they hesitated to deal the last blow

BOOK V.

192–189 B.C.

L. Cornelius Scipio elected consul.

The decisive campaign against Antiochus was now in prospect. At the consular comitia the influence of the house of Scipio preponderated and secured the election of Lucius Cornelius Scipio, and of Caius Laelius, the faithful adherent of the Scipios, for the consulship for the ensuing year 190 B.C. Lucius Scipio had nothing to recommend him, but that he was the brother of Publius Scipio, the conqueror of Zama. He was distinguished neither as a statesman nor as a soldier. In order, therefore, to secure for the house of Scipio the glory and the profit which were to be expected from the victorious termination of the war against Antiochus, the conqueror of Hannibal offered to accompany his brother as legate, and Laelius, the client of the house of Scipio, voluntarily resigned the chance of obtaining the command of the war in the east. The senate, without resorting to a decision by casting lots, conferred the command on Lucius Scipio. When it became known that Publius Cornelius Scipio would accompany his brother's army as legate, five thousand old soldiers who had served under him in Spain and Africa came forward to offer themselves as volunteers. The arrangements for carrying on the war were as usual made in the senate. Scipio received, beside the volunteers just mentioned, a reinforcement of eight thousand three hundred men for the army which was in Greece under the command of Acilius Glabrio, and he was instructed, if circumstances permitted, to transfer the war into Asia.[1] In order that Greece might not be left entirely without a military force, ten thousand seven hundred men were sent thither from Bruttium.[2] The troops in

New armaments.

---

which would have crushed the resistance of the Ætolians, and now, after giving them time to recover, they forced them to renew their resistance. They were clearly actuated by different motives at Naupactus and at Rome. At Naupactus they wished to spare the Ætolians, in order to reserve them as a counterpoise to Philip of Macedonia. After the battle of Corycus they no longer thought this necessary, and therefore they determined to compel the Ætolians to unconditional submission.

[1] Compare the similar permission given to Publius Scipio. Permissum ut in Africam, si id e re publica esse censeret, traiiceret: Livy, xxviii. 45; vol. ii. p. 418.

[2] Livy, xxxvii. 2, 7. Compare xxxvi. 2, 6, and xxxv. 41, 4. That these

Sicily were reinforced by two thousand one hundred soldiers levied in the island. Twenty ships and two thousand marines were sent to the fleet in Asia under Æmilius Regillus, fifty new decked vessels were built as a reserve, and provisions were sent in sufficient quantities from Sicily and Sardinia.

Before the consul had arrived in Greece with the reinforcements, hostilities had again commenced. The Ætolians, driven to despair, fortified the passes of their mountains, and awaited the enemy in their fortresses. The first to be attacked was Lamia, which, immediately after the battle of Thermopylæ, Philip of Macedonia had besieged and almost taken, when, by the intercession of the Roman consul, he was compelled to raise the siege.[1] Acilius Glabrio now resumed the attack, and succeeded in taking the town by storm after an obstinate resistance.[2] The second operation ought to have been directed against Naupactus, which in the preceding year had been so hardly pressed and all but forced to surrender. But the mountain pass which led to that place was this time strongly defended, and Glabrio preferred besieging the town of Amphissa. In the meantime his successor, Lucius Scipio, had arrived in Greece with his reinforcements and assumed the command. But not liking to waste his time in Greece, and to expose his troops to an obstinate struggle with the Ætolians, he offered them a truce of six months, through the intercession of the Athenians, so that he might be at liberty to prosecute the war in Asia. Thus the final overthrow of the Ætolians was again postponed for another time. They had no choice, and in their distress they accepted joyfully the short respite, hoping perhaps, though hardly entitled to hope, that owing to some military success of Antiochus, or to the generosity of the Romans, they would finally obtain more favourable

---

troops did really proceed to Greece, and remained there, is clear from Livy, xxxvii. 4. 1, and xxxvii. 48. In the year 189 B.C. they were reinforced by twelve thousand men on foot and six hundred horse. Livy, xxxvii. 50, 4.

[1] See p. 127.   [2] Livy, xxxvii. 4 and 5.

BOOK V.
192–189 B.C.
March of Scipio to the Hellespont.

terms than unconditional surrender, and the total loss of their independence.[1]

Scipio now took the long and circuitous road leading through Thessaly, Macedonia, and Thrace, towards the Hellespont, where he proposed to cross into Asia. It is surprising that, notwithstanding the immense superiority of the Romans at sea, they do not appear to have thought of avoiding this long march, on which they were exposed to the difficulty of procuring supplies, to the attack of the warlike Thracian tribes, to the fatigue and sickness of the troops,[2] and, finally, to the impediments placed in their way by the towns on the Hellespont, which were strongly fortified by Antiochus. One would have thought the way across the Ægean Sea would have been preferred, even from the motive of gaining time. The long march of Scipio to the Hellespont and Asia Minor could not take less than six months.[3] It reminds us almost of the march of Hannibal from Spain across the Pyrenees and the Alps; and so little do we really understand of the conditions of life in the ancient world, that we cannot say with any degree of certainty why this route was taken. Was it the want of transport ships, or the fear of the voyage, or was it simply custom which caused a land route to be preferred in all cases, except where a route by sea was absolutely unavoidable? We are not able to decide this, and must simply relate the fact, without attempting to explain it.[4]

[1] The Athenian Echedemus told them: τοῖς καιροῖς ἐφεδρεύειν· χείρω μὲν γὰρ ἀδύνατον γενέσθαι τῶν ὑποκειμένων τὰ περὶ σφᾶς, βελτίω γε μὴν οὐκ ἀδύνατον διὰ πολλὰς αἰτίας. Polybius, xxi. 3, 9.

[2] Livy, xxxvii. 33, 3.

[3] From the departure of the army to its arrival on the Hellespont about eight months passed. Livy, xxxvii. 33, 7, with Weissenborn's note.

[4] Mommsen (Röm. Gesch. i. 747) is of opinion that the reason why Scipio took the land route was fear of the fleet which Hannibal was charged to bring from Phoenicia. Such a fear, to say the least, would have been very unnecessary, as is shown by the course of the naval war; for the Phoenician fleet was kept in check by the Rhodians alone. But even if it had been formidable, surely Livius, the admiral of the Roman fleet, could have been employed to convoy and protect the transports, instead of being sent to the Hellespont, and there assisting the Roman army in crossing from Europe into Asia. But the

The march to the Hellespont would not have been safe, if the Roman general had not been able to trust to the loyalty, and to rely on the support of the Macedonians. Scipio may have been conscious that Philip had not been treated quite fairly by his predecessor, and he was not without anxiety with regard to the king's present conduct. But Philip was throughout loyal, and even zealous in the service of the Romans. On the march through his territory, and further on through Thrace, he opened the road for the legions, built bridges for them, and supplied them with provisions and necessaries of all kinds, so that they reached the Hellespont without meeting with any considerable obstructions.[1]

Antiochus had spent the winter in collecting troops, and preparing himself for the prosecution of the war. If at the commencement he had cherished the hope that the Romans would be satisfied with having driven him out of Europe, and that they would give up the idea of attacking him in Asia, he soon found that he was deceived. He was now inclined to adopt Hannibal's opinion, that the war ought to have been carried on in Italy. But it was too late to think of that now, when the Roman navy was blockading his ports, and the Roman army was on its march towards the Hellespont. He sent Hannibal to Phœnicia to urge his Punic countrymen to fit out new ships. At the same time he assembled reinforcements from all sides, and attacked the king of Pergamum, in order, if possible, to crush him before the arrival of the Romans.

The Greek towns in Asia Minor were now all in a state of fermentation. The aristocratic party in them set their hopes on the Romans, who were advancing as the deliverers of the Greeks. The common people were attached to the king of Syria. Even in Phocæa, where a portion of the Roman fleet wintered, the two hostile parties were in arms

circumstance which most effectually refutes Mommsen's opinion is this, that when the war was over and peace concluded, the Roman army took the same land route on its return from Asia.

[1] Livy, xxxvii. 7; Appian, *Syr.* 23.

against each other, and when the Romans left the port of the town, which they had completely drained, the populace gained the upper hand.¹ Smyrna, however, which had so long defied Antiochus, with Mitylene, Erythræ, Cyme, and other towns, received the Romans as friends.²

In the early spring a portion of the Roman and Pergamenian fleets sailed northwards towards the Hellespont, to remove the obstacles which prevented the legions from crossing. Antiochus had possession of the two fortified towns of Sestos and Abydos, on the narrowest part of the Hellespont, the usual and most convenient place of crossing. It does not seem that these two towns were furnished with more than the ordinary means of defence. Sestos surrendered at once to the Romans. Abydos, however, offered a stout resistance, and had to be besieged in due form.

While the Roman and Pergamenian fleets were thus occupied in the north of the Ægean Sea, the naval contingent of the Rhodians, under the command of Pausistratus, was watching the Syrian fleet, which had retired to the harbour of Ephesus after its defeat at Corycus in the preceding autumn.³ Pausistratus, with his thirty-six ships, was not a match for the hostile fleet which had been strengthened during the winter; but he was expecting no attack, especially as Polyxenidas, the Syrian admiral, who was his countryman and had been banished from Rhodes, had made him believe that, in order to facilitate his return to his beloved country, he would sacrifice the Syrian fleet. Thus deluded, and feeling quite secure, Pausistratus allowed himself to be surprised and suffered a disastrous defeat. Only five ships escaped, twenty were taken, and Pausistratus himself perished. Upon this news Samos, Phocæa, Cyme, Teos, and other towns again abandoned the Roman side.⁴

The Romans might easily have averted this disaster, if they had only strengthened the Rhodian contingent by

---

¹ Polybius, xxi. 4; Livy, xxxvii. 9.
² Compare Livy, xxxvii. 17.   ³ See p. 134.
⁴ Livy, xxxvii. 11, 15; xxxvii. 27, 3. Appian, *Syr.* 24, 25.

that portion of their fleet which lay on the coast at Canæ, unemployed as if it were midwinter.¹ Livius now raised the siege of Abydos, though the garrison was already negotiating about the conditions of a capitulation, proceeded in all haste from the Hellespont to Canæ, ordered the ships immediately out to sea, and took up a position at Samos. Here, joined by a new Rhodian squadron of twenty ships, he vainly offered battle to the Syrian admiral. Polyxenidas prudently kept within the safe harbour of Ephesus, and when a portion of the Roman fleet tried to effect a landing, drove them back to their ships with great loss. There was nothing left for Livius but to return with his fleet to Samos, and there to keep himself in readiness for action. His position was embarrassed by the difficulty of procuring provisions.² The

CHAP. II.

192–189 B.C.

Roman fleet.

---

¹ It appears, from Appian (*Syr.* 23), that Livius had destined that portion of his fleet which was stationed at Canæ to operate, in conjunction with the Rhodian fleet, against Polyxenidas, but that the Rhodians were too soon at the place of meeting and the Romans too late. In the preceding year the Rhodians had only arrived after the battle of Corycus. This time they probably intended to make up for their backwardness by appearing on the scene of action before their allies.

² The difficulties of the commissariat were often so great at this time, that they seriously interfered with the warlike operations in Greece as well as in Asia Minor. Both countries were drained to such an extent, that large armies had to draw their supplies from abroad. (Compare Polybius, xxi. 4; Livy, xxxvii. 19, 4). Even as early as the year 201 B.C. the army of Philip nearly perished from hunger in Asia Minor. (See p. 16.) The Romans organised regular dépôts of provisions (for instance, in the island of Chios, Livy, xxxvii. 27, 1), which were kept supplied by the provinces of Sicily, Sardinia, Spain, and by Africa. For this purpose they imposed double contributions of corn on the provinces. (Livy, xxxvii. 2, 12). If even the wretched pirates succeeded in capturing corn ships, and thus prevented the regular feeding of the troops, it is evident that the Roman navy was in a deplorable state, in spite of the extraordinary efforts made at this very time. The audacious pirates scoured the seas in every direction, and ventured into the close vicinity of the armed ships, plundering and devastating the maritime districts which had already suffered severely from the calamities of war. (Livy, xxxvii. 27, 4.) Occasionally they found it profitable to lend their services to one party or the other, and thus rose to the dignity of belligerents. The 'archipirata' Nicander, for instance, fought under the command of Polyxenidas against the Rhodians (Livy, xxxvii. 11, 6). Thus, independently of the legitimate war of the great powers, a kind of private war went on. Robber states were regularly organized for this purpose, not only in Crete, but in other places also. Nabis was not only the ruler of Sparta, but a pirate chief. Greece had almost returned to the

maritime police, exercised by the Romans, appears in a most unfavourable light, when we hear that a Lacedæmonian pirate, named Hybristas, seized the ships which were carrying provisions to the Roman magazine at Chios. Livius was compelled to send out a small squadron under the Rhodian Epicrates, to clear the sea of these pirates near the island of Cephallenia. Epicrates met in the Piræus the prætor, Æmilius Regillus, who, on receiving the news of the defeat of the Rhodians, had hurried to the theatre of war to take the command of the fleet.[1] Instead of sanctioning the operations against the pirates the new admiral took the Rhodian squadron with him back to Samos, and having assumed the command of the combined fleets, held a general council of war to decide what was to be done under the present circumstances.

The task of the allied fleet was threefold. The first and foremost was to watch, or, if possible, to beat the principal Syrian armament, now safe in the harbour of Ephesus under the command of Polyxenidas; for if this fleet forced its way out, the communication of the Romans with Greece and Italy was endangered. The second object to be secured was to make preparations for the crossing of the Roman land army over the Hellespont, and to support it. Lastly, it was necessary to adopt measures to detain the new Syrian squadron, which Hannibal was ordered to bring from Phœnicia, and to prevent its union with the main fleet. In the last operation nobody was so much interested as the Rhodians, whose possessions on their own island and on the opposite coast of Asia Minor,

condition of the heroic age in which piracy and war were not quite distinguished from one another, and both were almost equally honourable.

[1] According to Livy (xxxvii. 14, 1), he had no more than two quinqueremes with him, whilst, according to another passage of the same author (xxxvii. 2, 10), the squadron which he was ordered to take with him was to consist of twenty sail. If nothing was altered in these arrangements, we must presume that he preceded the bulk of his squadron with two ships. But it is possible that the rest of his force was directed against the pirates. At least, it is not perceptible in the later operations of the Romans on the Asiatic coast, that they received a reinforcement of twenty ships of war.

were most exposed to an attack coming from the south.[1] Hence, on the advice of Epicrates, a squadron of eight vessels under Caius Livius, who had just retired from the supreme command, was sent to Patara, a town on the coast of Lycia, opposite Rhodes, in order, if possible, to take that place, and thus to bar the passage of the Phœnician fleet.

The plan of taking Patara failed, and Livius, who had disapproved of the whole expedition, returned straight to Italy. Vexed with the failure of this his first enterprise, Æmilius now set sail with his whole fleet for Patara. But the discontent among his officers soon convinced him that this mode of carrying on the war more under the influence of passion than of reason was not likely to lead to success. He therefore stopped half-way, and returned to Samos, in order not to lose sight of the principal object of the campaign. The task of keeping in check the Phœnician fleet was left to the Rhodians, who, as experience showed, were fully equal to it.

With the advance of summer the Roman land army proceeded slowly, but without interruptions, from Greece to Thessaly, from Thessaly to Macedonia, in the direction of Thrace and the Hellespont. The danger, the possibility of which Antiochus at first refused to acknowledge, was thus approaching nearer and nearer.

He now made preparations for defence on a larger scale, and hurried about in Asia Minor from place to place with aimless impatience, attacking one ally of the Romans after another in the hope of overthrowing them before the arrival of the legions. The various maritime towns, which, as we have seen, wavered in their sympathies between Antiochus and the Romans, were all exposed to the attacks of the king; but nowhere did he act with any vigour or perseverance; nowhere did he undertake a regular siege. He indulged in the vain hope that by devastating the open country he could enforce the submission of the harassed towns.

[1] Compare Livy, xxxvii. 24, 13.

His chief object was to capture Pergamum, the king of which had always been a most zealous and faithful friend of the Romans. Antiochus and his son Seleucus appeared before the town with a body of four thousand Galatian mercenaries, who, although good hands at plundering, were ill adapted for a regular attack upon a well-fortified city, and, of course, accomplished nothing but what might have been expected from the irregular warfare of barbarians. Pergamum was not even completely blockaded. Day after day a band of undisciplined Asiatic mercenaries advanced up to the town to keep the defenders on the alert within the walls, whilst the rest of the investing army was occupied in plundering and laying waste the surrounding country. At length a reinforcement of one thousand foot and one hundred horse, which the Achaean league had sent to Eumenes, succeeded in slipping into the hard-pressed town. Under their commander Diophanes, a soldier from the school of Philopœmon, they soon changed the aspect of affairs. Making two sallies, they defeated the undisciplined hordes of the Galatians under the very walls of the town, pursued them a great distance, and thus convinced Antiochus that he had not the slightest prospect of reducing Pergamum except by a regular siege.[1]

Whilst these skirmishes were going on under the walls of Pergamum, the Roman fleet had sailed from Samos to Elæa, the port of Pergamum. The near approach of the Roman armament, in conjunction with the failure of the attack directed against the Pergamenian capital, induced Antiochus to entertain ideas of peace. He tried to commence negotiations with Æmilius, but found that in the absence of the consul he neither could nor would receive any overtures. Moreover, Eumenes was opposed to any reconciliation between Rome and Antiochus, being persuaded that no peace would be really advantageous to himself which was concluded before the total overthrow of

[1] Livy, xxxvii. 18-21.

the king of Syria. The negotiations, therefore, led to nothing. Antiochus continued as before to attack one town or to defend another from Roman attacks.[1] He also strengthened Lysimachia and other places near the Hellespont, in order to detain the Roman land army in that neighbourhood. On the other side, Eumenes also directed his attention to this spot, and sailed with a Pergamenian fleet to the Hellespont, in order to assist the Romans in crossing into Asia. Æmilius returned to his station near Samos, to watch the Syrian fleet, which still kept within the harbour of Ephesus; but he sent a squadron of fifteen ships, most of them Rhodian, southwards, to be joined by twenty-three more Rhodian ships, for the purpose of opposing the Phœnician fleet, which was now advancing, under the command of Hannibal and Apollonius. The battle took place at Sida, on the coast of Pamphylia, to the east of the mouth of the river Eurymedon, which falls into the sea below the town of Aspendus.[2] The Rhodians had thirty-two quadriremes and four triremes. The fleet of the king of Syria had about the same number of ships, but the ships were of larger size. There were among them three of seven tiers of oars and four of six tiers. The total number of ships amounted to thirty-seven; but the Phœnician ships were not a match for the Rhodian, which were better built and better manned. This superiority at once decided the battle.[3] The Phœnician line was broken, and their unwieldy vessels, attacked on all sides by the agile Rhodians, took to flight without offering an obstinate resistance. Their loss was slight, because the Rhodians did not follow up their advantage. Only one Phœnician vessel, of seven tiers of oars, fell into the hands of the victors, who returned to Rhodes less elated by their victory than disappointed by its smallness. The cause of this want of energy on their part was never fully ascertained,

CHAP. II.

192-189 B.C.

Battle of Sida or Aspendus.

---

[1] Livy, xxxvii. 21.

[2] It is difficult to see why the battle has been called not the battle of Sida, but the battle of Aspendus, a town not even situated on the sea.

[3] Livy, xxxvii. 24, 1: Momento temporis et navium virtus et usus rei maritimae terrorem omnem Rhodiis dempsit.

though the question was angrily debated, and gave rise to much irritation. Whether it was that the ship of the admiral, Eudamus, had been disabled in the battle, and was compelled to stay behind, or whether the captains commanding under him did not do their duty, or whether the sailors were suffering from sickness and unequal to their work, we know not. Perhaps we may suppose that Hannibal, who here fought a naval battle for the first time, is entitled to the credit of having directed the retreat towards the coast, whither the Rhodian ships did not venture to follow.[1] Though the great Punic captain may have done much to avoid complete disaster, we cannot without painful sympathy witness a spectacle in which the conqueror of Cannae acted the part of an inferior officer in the service of a foreign potentate, and was reduced to be the colleague of an Apollonius. It is true he was only compelled to retreat, not entirely defeated; but he felt that he was not strong enough to attack the Rhodian fleet a second time. The passage was blocked up, and the two Syrian squadrons were prevented from joining.

During the whole of the summer the principal Syrian fleet had remained inactive in the port of Ephesus, because Polyxenidas, the admiral, had not felt confident enough in his strength to meet the combined naval forces of the Romans, Pergamenians, and Rhodians. But when towards the end of August the Pergamenian squadron had sailed to the Hellespont, and that of Rhodes to Lycia, he thought the time had come when he might venture to attack the Roman fleet, which alone was left behind. King Antiochus himself proceeded to Ephesus to concert plans for the operation with Polyxenidas. It was resolved to make an attack by land on Notium,[2] a town close to

---

[1] Livy, xxxvii. 24, 9: Aliquam diu secuti sunt: postquam terrae appropinquasat Hannibal, veriti ne includerentur vento in hostium ora, ad Eudamum recepti hepterem captam aegre Phaselidem pertraxerunt. Cornelius Nepos, *Hannibal*, 8.

[2] Livy, xxxvii. 26, 5. Notium was the port of Colophon. See Weissenborn's note to Livy.

Ephesus, which had taken the Roman side in the hope that the Romans, hearing of the danger of their allies, would sail from Samos to Notium to protect the place, and that they could be compelled to accept battle.

Æmilius, the Roman admiral, had long been tired of remaining inactive at Samos, and would have been glad to sail to the Hellespont, where a great crisis was expected; but the Rhodian admiral, Eudamus, who, after the battle of Sida, had again joined the Roman fleet with the Rhodian squadron, persuaded him to remain, so that he might protect Notium, and at the same time keep the hostile fleet in check. This led to a second encounter with the Syrian fleet near the promontory of Myonnesus, not far from Corycus, where in the former battle Polyxenidas had been defeated.

Æmilius had obtained provisions for his fleet in the island of Chios, and then sailed to the little town of Teos, to take in a supply of wine. On this occasion the Roman crews behaved in a very disorderly manner, and a great portion of them had gone on land. The whole fleet had entered the port of Teos, the entrance of which was so narrow that only one ship could pass through at a time. The attention of Æmilius having been directed to this circumstance by the Rhodian Eudamus, he ordered the fleet to be stationed in the open roadstead before the town. This proved a fortunate precaution. Polyxenidas, learning the movements of the Romans, had stood out to sea, hoping to surprise their fleet in the narrow port, and thus to repeat the operation which had been successful against the Rhodians at Samos. He had approached unperceived the small island of Macris, near the promontory of Myonnesus, when the alarm was given in the Roman fleet, and the crews were in the greatest haste and confusion called back from the land, and had only just time to get on board their ships. This time the Syrians were superior to the allies in numbers, having eighty-nine against fifty-eight Roman and twenty-two Rhodian vessels. But the Roman vessels were better manned, and the

Battle of Myonnesus.

Rhodian were constructed for greater speed than the Syrian ships. In addition to this, the Rhodians had adopted a new mode of attack, which terrified and disordered their enemies. On both sides of their bows they had fastened long horizontal poles, at the ends of which were attached pans with burning pitch. With these fire-ships they boldly advanced on the enemy, and threw their line of battle into confusion.[1] A complete and brilliant victory was the result. Though Ephesus was very near, and the wind was favourable to the defeated Syrians, scarcely half of their ships regained the port; thirteen were taken, twenty-nine were sunk or burnt. The loss of the allies was insignificant. Only two Rhodian vessels were sunk and one Rhodian ship was taken.[2]

Effect of the victory of Myonnesus.

The victory of Myonnesus, the fourth naval battle in the course of the year, can rank with the great battles which the Romans fought in the first war with the Carthaginians. It not only put an end to the hostilities by sea, but had a decided influence also on the progress of the war by land. Antiochus was so stunned by the news, that he lost all confidence and self-possession. He at once raised the siege of Notium,[3] and (what was of far more importance) withdrew the garrison and the whole body of inhabitants from Lysimachia, thus giving up the defence of the Chersonesus and of the Hellespont. The order was given and executed with such inconsiderate haste, that no measures were taken to remove, or at least to destroy, the magazines collected in Lysimachia. This town, therefore, which had been restored and colonised by Antiochus with great pains, instead of delaying the march

---

[1] Livy, xxxvii. 30, 3: Id tum maximum momentum ad victoriam fuit.

[2] Livy, xxxvii. 26–30. It is curious to notice the manner in which this Rhodian vessel was lost. Livy describes it in the following words: Rhodia una capta memorabili casu. Nam cum rostro percussisset Sidoniam navem, ancora, ictu ipso excussa e nave sua, uncodente, velut manu ferrea iniecta, adligavit alterius proram, inde tumultu iniecto cum, divellere se ab hoste cupientes, inhiberent Rhodii, tractum ancorale et implicitum remis latus alterum detersit: debilitatam ea ipsa, quae icta cohaeserat, navis cepit. Compare Appian, *Syr.* 27.

[3] Livy, xxxvii. 21. Instead of Notium we often find the name of Colophon, without any distinction being made between the two.

of the Romans, and of detaining them in the inhospitable region of Thrace till the approach of winter, supplied the Roman army with ample provisions and furnished good shelter, so that the troops could recover themselves from their fatigues before they crossed into Asia with the aid of the fleet, which was now at their disposal.[1]

Immediately after the battle of Myonnesus Æmilius had despatched a squadron of thirty vessels to facilitate the passage of the Hellespont. With the rest of his fleet he sailed to Phocæa, in order to punish this town for its defection to Antiochus.[2] The Phocæans offered a brave resistance; but when they were left without the prospect of support from Antiochus they were at last compelled to accept the terms of capitulation offered by Æmilius. They were promised that they should suffer no violence, and that they should resume their former position as allies of the Roman people.[3] But on this occasion it was shown again that Roman generals were unable to control their soldiers when their object was to keep them from plundering. In defiance of the express orders of Æmilius, the troops broke open the houses and ransacked them, just as if the town had been taken by storm.[4] How they were accustomed to act on such occasions has been reported in detail by Polybius.[5] In the first rage and excitement the soldiers spared no living creature, cutting to pieces without distinction men, women and children, nay even animals. These horrors have been discreetly veiled by Polybius. He passes them over in silence, contenting himself by saying that the prætor endeavoured to save at least the lives of the Phocæans from the rage of the soldiers. They were allowed to retain their freedom and their ransacked town, in which Æmilius took up his winter quarters.

During these proceedings Antiochus remained inactive at Sardes. He lost all hope and courage when he saw

---

[1] Livy, xxxvii. 30. [2] See p. 140.
[3] Livy, xxxvii. 32, 11: Pacti ne quid hostile paterentur, etc.
[4] Compare what happened at the taking of Myttistratum in the first Punic war. Vol. ii. p. 61 f. [5] Polybius, x. 15, 1. See vol. ii. p. 354.

BOOK V.
192–189 B.C.
peace negotiations.

one plan after another miscarry. Prusias, too, the king of Bithynia, declared in favour of the Romans,[1] who then leisurely effected the passage of the Hellespont, and stood now on Asiatic ground. Antiochus again thought of concluding peace. So erroneous was his notion of the policy and character of the Romans, that he flattered himself he could induce them to advance no further if he declared his readiness to accept the conditions which they had offered at the beginning of the war. He sent as his agent Heraclides of Byzantium into the Roman camp on the Hellespont, offering to recognise the independence of the three cities, Smyrna, Lampsacus, and Alexandria Troas, and, if it should be desired, also of the other cities in Asia Minor which had taken the part of Rome. He, moreover, undertook to pay one half of the expenses of the war, and to resign those Thracian cities which he had just been compelled to evacuate. He had great confidence, it seems, in the influence of the powerful Publius Scipio, whose gratitude and friendship he was bent on gaining. Heraclides had a special commission to him of a private and very delicate nature. It appears that a son of Scipio's had been made prisoner in the early part of the war.[2] Antiochus had treated him very kindly, and now promised his father to send him back without a ransom, if in return Scipio would assist him in his negotiations for peace. It appears that even money was promised, as if Scipio could lower himself so much as to accept bribes from an enemy of the republic. Scipio thanked the king

---

[1] Polybius, xxi. 9; Livy, xxxvii. 25.

[2] Polybius, xxi. 12, 3. According to Livy (xxxvii. 31, 5), there was a second version of the story, according to which young Scipio was not taken prisoner at the beginning of the war, but near the end of it: 'Postquam transitum in Asiam est, cum turma Fregellana missum exploratum ad regia castra, effuso obviam equitatu, cum reciperet sese, in eo tumultu delapsum ex equo, cum duobus equitibus obpressum, ita ad regem deductum esse.' It is hardly necessary to say that this circumstantial account is altogether fictitious. Polybius could not be in error with regard to an event which so nearly concerned the family of the Scipios. And, moreover, it seems that the camp of the king was, previous to the battle of Magnesia, never so near the Roman army, that the collision referred to could have taken place. Compare Valer. Maxim. iii. 5, 2.

for the release of his son, and as if to return the kindness advised him at once to make peace on the conditions which would be offered to him.¹ These conditions, of course, could be no longer the same as those which had been proposed when the legions were still on their march to the Hellespont. Scipio asked for the payment of the whole of the war expenses, and for the surrender of all countries in Asia Minor this side the Taurus range.

Such were the terms of peace which Heraclides brought back to Sardes. The king was of opinion that worse terms could not be accepted even in case of a total defeat, and therefore resolved to try once more the fortune of war. Having neglected to oppose the Romans in Thrace, and having allowed them to pass the Hellespont without opposition, and to concentrate their forces in Asia Minor, where the kingdom of Pergamum was a basis for their further operations, he ought to have tried to draw them into the interior of the country, to tire them out with long marches, and to expose them to the difficulties of a prolonged campaign in a country drained of its resources. But he was so confused and bewildered that he adopted precisely that plan which was most favourable to his enemies. He took up his position in a strongly fortified camp behind the river Phrygius, near Magnesia, on the slope of Mount Sipylus, with the intention of making a final stand against the further advance of the Romans.²

The Roman army, as we have seen, had reached the Hellespont without opposition, and had crossed it without difficulty. The consul then allowed his troops some time of repose, during which the army was joined by all those who had not been able to keep up on the march. As it happened to be the time for the festival of the Salians, Publius Scipio, who belonged to the fraternity of the Salian priests, remained behind; for the sacred law required that no priest should leave the place where he

¹ Polybius, xxi. 12, 11; Livy, xxxvii. 36, 8.   ² Livy, xxxvii. 37.

might happen to be during the festive period of thirty days. Having rejoined the army on the Asiatic side of the straits, Scipio, as we have related above, conferred with Heraclides, the king's minister, about terms of peace. Immediately after this he was taken ill, and was obliged to remain at Elæa, the port of Pergamum, to wait for his recovery. To this place Antiochus, according to his promise, sent him his son, and received as a return gift the advice not to accept battle before Publius Scipio should again be with the army.[1] What the meaning of this advice may have been is somewhat doubtful. Antiochus, it appears, could not interpret it in any other way than as a promise that Scipio would prevent a battle from resulting in the entire defeat of the Syrian army. But how could a Roman citizen make such a promise to an enemy? or even hint at the probability of it? Or is it possible that Scipio, knowing the incapacity of his brother, tried by this means to put off the decisive battle in order to destroy the hostile army the more surely, as soon as his health would permit him to conduct the operations himself? In the former case, we should have to accuse the greatest Roman general of a crime of which the worst man in his army was incapable. In the latter case, he appears liable to the charge of discreditable double-dealing and overreaching an enemy who, with regard to himself, at least, had been open and generous. If such perfidious conduct was at that time looked upon as a legitimate stratagem, the individual citizen who might avail himself of it cannot be blamed severely, whatever we may be inclined to think of the public feeling, and the general conscientiousness of a nation that sanctioned it.

After having crossed the Hellespont the Roman army had entered upon ground which to every Roman was, to some extent, sacred, as the original home from which Æneas had started to settle in the plain of Latium. The seed which

---

[1] Livy, xxxvii. 37, 7: Renuntiate gratias regi me agere, referre aliam gratiam nunc non posse, quam ut suadeam, ne ante in aciem descendat, quam in castra me redisse audierit.

had been sown on the banks of the Tiber had grown to such a prodigious and goodly tree, that its extended branches cast a shadow even on the old site of Ilium. For the first time an army of Romans was drawn up in the plains of the Scamander, where the mythical ancestors of their race had fought with Achilles. We should like to know whether Scipio was under the spell of that enthusiasm which many years before had prompted Alexander the Great to celebrate funeral rites in this place, in honour of the ancient heroes. We cannot believe it; for in spite of the official recognition in Rome of the legend of Æneas, and in spite of the growing popularity of the heroic poetry of Greece, the Italians had not enough of the true spirit of poetry to feel real enthusiasm for the grand conceptions of the Homeric age. The Ilians, an insignificant community, living near the spot where the Ilium of old had stood and boasting of belonging to the race of the ancient Trojans, welcomed with delight their mighty descendants, and the Romans, it is said, were pleased to recognise their relationship. The consul went up to the citadel of the town, and offered sacrifices to Athênê, the protecting goddess, but if we may judge from the style of Livy's narrative, the whole affair was a mere empty formality, in which neither the heart nor the imagination of the persons concerned was engaged.[1]

From Troas the Roman army marched to the immediate vicinity of Pergamum. During the absence of Publius Scipio, who lay ill at Elæa, his brother Lucius had for his military adviser Cneius Domitius, apparently an able and experienced officer. Winter was approaching. It was desirable that the Romans should make use of what remained of the favourable season to deal, if possible, a vigorous blow, and thus to prevent the prolongation of the campaign into another year. Antiochus, by concentrating the whole of his force on one point, had made it possible for the Romans to fight a decisive battle. Domitius, therefore,

[1] Livy, xxxvii. 37.

without delay, marched straight upon the Syrian position, crossed the small river Phrygius, which joins the Hermus not far from Magnesia, and encamped close to the enemy. For some time Antiochus declined to accept battle, but fluctuating as usual between two decisions, he at last made up his mind to fight, when Domitius was approaching nearer and nearer, and challenged him to come out of his entrenchments. Thus the memorable battle of Magnesia on Mount Sipylus was brought about late in the autumn of 190 B.C., a battle which was to decide the fate of the Syrian empire, as the battles of Zama and of Cynoscephalæ had decided the fate of Carthage and Macedonia.

The Roman army numbered about thirty thousand men, and was made up of four legions, with a few thousand Achæan, Macedonian, and Pergamenian auxiliaries. Besides these there were Cretan, Illyrian, and Thracian mercenaries, and sixteen Libyan elephants, which, however, were not employed in the battle, as they seemed unfit to be matched against the larger and more spirited Indian elephants, of which Antiochus mustered fifty-four.[1] The Syrian army, as we are informed by Livy, numbered seventy thousand men, of whom not less than twelve thousand were horse.[2] The élite of the infantry composed the phalanx, sixteen thousand men strong, to which Antiochus, to make it irresistible, had given double its usual depth. It consisted of ten solid squares, each fifty men in rank, and thirty-two men in file, resembling so many living walls. In thus condensing his heavy armed infantry, Antiochus made the same mistake which the Romans had committed at Cannæ. He contracted his front and massed his best troops so as to form an unwieldy body, unable to come to the assistance of the light troops, and liable to be outflanked and attacked in the rear, in case the light troops should be first defeated. By the side and in front of the

---

[1] Livy, xxxvii. 39.
[2] According to Florus, i. 23, the army of Antiochus consisted of three hundred thousand men on foot, and of as many mounted on horses or chariots. This is an example which shows how exaggerations grow in course of time.

phalanx Antiochus drew up a heterogeneous mass of his various Asiatic contingents and several bodies of mercenaries, Gallic and Cappadocian infantry, heavy armed horsemen, archers on foot and on horseback, slingers, various kinds of light armed troops, and his body-guard, distinguished by their silver shields. On both flanks were stationed the elephants, and in front of the whole line were chariots with scythes projecting, and Arabs mounted on dromedaries, armed with bows and arrows and with swords of enormous length. The motley armaments of this host were surpassed by the variety of nations of which it consisted. It reminds us of those times when the kings of Persia led all the nations of their vast empire, each in its own peculiar dress and arms, against the Greeks and Macedonians, trusting to numbers alone. And, indeed, the various Græco-Macedonian kingdoms and more particularly the kingdom of Syria under the Seleucidæ, had relapsed into the condition of the old despotic empires of Asia. It was again a contest between the effeminate East and the vigorous and rising countries of the West; and again the torpid mass succumbed to youthful strength.

How the Romans gained the battle of Magnesia, we do not know with any degree of certainty. The description which Livy and Appian [1] have preserved from the lost narrative of Polybius will barely allow us to sketch some vague outlines. It appears that the Syrian army was seized by a panic on the left wing, when the useless chariots armed with scythes were attacked by Pergamenian archers, thrown into confusion, and in their disorderly flight broke through the ranks drawn up behind them. The various bodies of the cowardly Syrians, Phrygians, Lydians, Carians, Cilicians, Pisidians, Pamphylians, Elymeans, Cyrtians, and numerous other tribes, were broken up into a confused mass and driven upon the phalanx, which alone kept its ground. But this, too, was obliged to retreat when the Syrian elephants tore up its ranks.

[1] Livy, xxxvii. 37-44; Appian, *Syr.* 31-36.

While thus the left wing and the centre of the Syrians were forced back, without having offered any serious resistance, Antiochus, who commanded the right wing, had succeeded with his body-guard, aided by Cretans and Dahians, in routing a cavalry division of the Romans, which was drawn up between the Roman left wing and the river Phrygius. He actually advanced as far as the Roman camp. But here he was stopped by the cohorts which defended the camp, and upon the arrival of other Roman troops he was compelled to retreat. He now beheld the whole of his army in full flight, closely pursued by the victorious enemy. Giving up all hopes of further resistance, he rode off straight to Sardes. After a feeble attempt to defend their camp, the routed Syrians were enclosed on all sides, and destroyed like game at a battue. It is said that fifty thousand foot soldiers and three thousand horsemen were on that day killed, or rather slaughtered; for they cannot have offered any resistance, as in the whole battle the Pergamenians lost only twenty-five men and the Romans barely more than three hundred. The overthrow of the great king of Asia was effected at even a smaller cost than the defeat of Philip at Cynoscephalæ, and it was far more complete.[1] The victory was decided by the very first onset of the allied troops, before the Roman legions had time to advance to the attack, and it was gained in the absence of that man who, as the conqueror of Hannibal, had the reputation of being the best general of Rome. Publius Cornelius Scipio was obliged to leave the glory of the victory to his incapable brother, or rather to his brother's adviser, Cneius Domitius. But perhaps we shall not err

---

[1] The statement that fifty-three thousand men were slain in the battle may be greatly exaggerated. That it cannot be considered as accurate is evident from the expression of Appian (*Syr.* 36): εἰκάζοντο ἀπολέσθαι περὶ πεντακισμυρίους· οὐ γὰρ εὐμαρὲς ἦν ἀριθμῆσαι διὰ τὸ πλῆθος. It is difficult for us to understand how so many men could be put to death without the aid of firearms by a comparatively small number. The battle of Cannæ, which exhibits some striking analogies with that of Magnesia, presents the same difficulty in the prodigious number of slain Romans. But the ancient historians seem not to have felt at a loss to account for such numbers. It appears that they were not even struck by them.

in supposing that the plan of the campaign was his work, and that he displayed no less enterprise and ability in this Asiatic expedition than on his expedition to New Carthage and Africa.

By the battle of Magnesia the war was not only decided, but brought to an end. The impression produced by the sudden and total defeat of the king was such that it entirely destroyed his prestige in the eyes of the Asiatic nations accustomed to adore power and to cringe to power alone.[1] The star of the successors of Alexander the Great paled in proportion as that of Rome rose to the ascendant. One town after another surrendered to the victors, and implored them for mercy; among them Thyatira, Tralles, the two Magnesias, one on the Sipylus, the other on the Mæander, and even Sardes, the capital of the satrapy of Asia Minor.[2] Polyxenidas, the admiral of the Syrian fleet, did not think himself any longer safe in the port of Ephesus. He sailed to Patara in Lycia, but, for fear of the Rhodians, abandoned his ships, and with his crews continued his flight to Syria by land.[3] The allied forces by land and by sea advanced without opposition, and the Roman headquarters were soon after the battle removed to Sardes, where Publius Scipio, who had meanwhile recovered from his sickness, rejoined the army.

To the same place Antiochus soon after sent messengers to ask in the most humble terms for peace at any price. The Roman answer had been determined upon beforehand. Scipio did not ask for more than he had stipulated for in the last negotiations which had taken place before the battle of Magnesia was fought. Antiochus had no alternative left but to accept as the basis for a treaty of

---

[1] Appian, *Syr.* 37: πολύ τε σφίσιν ἦν τὸ ἔπος ἐν τοῖς λόγοις ‘ἦν βασιλεὺς Ἀντίοχος ὁ Μέγας.’

[2] Livy, xxxvii. 44 f.

[3] This strange proceeding is an instance of the regular practice of navigation in antiquity. The sailing courses were invariably fixed. It seems never to have occurred to Polyxenidas that he might sail right across the sea, without hugging the coast, and thus easily avoid the Rhodian fleet, which stopped the way.

BOOK V.
192–189 B.C.
Political congress in Rome for the settlement of the affairs of the East.

peace the terms which the Romans proposed. All hostilities were consequently suspended at once. The winter had by this time set in. Whilst the Roman army went into winter quarters at Ephesus, Tralles, and Magnesia on the Mæander, ambassadors were sent to Rome by Antiochus, Eumenes, the Rhodians, and almost all the cities of Asia Minor, each endeavouring to obtain the best possible terms from the men who had in their hands the power of settling the affairs of the Eastern world.[1] It must have been a most curious spectacle for the citizens of Rome to see their Forum and the steps and the interior of the senate-house crowded with foreign ambassadors, who were eager to obtain, not only from the magistrates and senators, but from every one of the people, kind words and promises of protection, and who most probably were not slow in trying the persuasion of words, and things more powerful than words, to which Roman pride was no longer inaccessible. Where such momentous questions were decided as the liberties and rights of many wealthy towns, the enlargement of the territory of such states as Pergamum and Rhodes, and the payment of thousands of talents, we may easily imagine that the indirect influence of money made itself felt. All acts of direct bribery are necessarily kept most carefully secret, and are consequently not easily noticed by the historian; but if one single case can be proved, we may infer that under circumstances like the present, it was not the only one. We know that Lucius Scipio himself was some years afterwards accused of having embezzled large sums of money. Whether he was guilty or not, is a question which we are unable to decide. But even if his innocence had been clearly proved, we must infer from the fact of the accusation alone that his contemporaries did not look upon an act of bribery and corruption

---

[1] Polybius, xxii. 1, 2: σχεδὸν γὰρ ἅπαντες οἱ κατὰ τὴν Ἀσίαν εὐθέως μετὰ τὸ γενέσθαι τὴν μάχην ἔπεμπον πρεσβευτὰς εἰς τὴν Ῥώμην διὰ τὸ πᾶσι τότε καὶ πάσας ὑπὲρ τοῦ μέλλοντος ἐλπίδας ἐν τῇ συγκλήτῳ κεῖσθαι. According to Livy, xxxvii. 45, 21, all these embassies were despatched to Rome in the winter (190–189 B.C.); according to xxxvii. 52, 1, and Polybius l. c., they did not arrive in Rome before the spring.

as something unheard of and impossible. It is well known how accessible the Romans were to bribes not a very long time after. The state of things which induced Jugurtha to declare that the whole of Rome was venal provided a purchaser could be found, was surely not the result of a sudden change in the public morality of the people. If all the Romans had been as upright and honest as Cato, they might have resisted the temptations to which they were now exposed. But we know that men like Cato were rare exceptions, and it is difficult to imagine stronger temptations than those offered on this occasion, when large and wealthy states were vying with each other to secure the favour of the leading men of Rome.

The position which Rome occupied with regard to her clients is sufficiently characterised by the humble and almost abject tone in which the latter thought proper to address the all-powerful senate. This tone is pervaded by the spirit of Oriental slavery and adulation, which must, on the whole, have been faithfully represented by the Roman annalists, although, perhaps, these writers, who saw in it a glorification of Rome, were inclined not to abate but to exaggerate it.[1]

Eumenes, the sovereign of the small kingdom of Pergamum, had played in Asia the part which Hiero had taken in the Sicilian war, and Masinissa in the latter period of the war with Hannibal. He had been staunch and faithful to Rome, and had contributed not a little to the defeat, first, of Philip of Macedonia, and then to that of the king of Syria. Now the time was come in which he could expect his reward. The republic of Rhodes was in a similar position. Having rendered equally important

[1] The greatest perfection in this style of servile adulation was attained by Masinissa after the defeat of Perseus. See Livy, xlv. 13. Livy frequently attributes similar self-abasement and servility to the Italian nations during their wars with Rome in the earlier ages of the republic. He could have no authentic evidence of the transactions he relates, but took the style and substance from the history of the times which we are now engaged on. It appears from this that the Roman historians were flattered by such a style of servility, which in modern times would only move disgust.

services, it looked forward now to a full compensation. But the interests of these two states were to some extent conflicting. Apart from the enlargement of territory which both wished for, and which Rome had it in her power to grant them to their full satisfaction out of the immense territory conquered in the war, they had special wishes of an opposite tendency with regard to the Greek states of Asia Minor, which were now released from the Syrian dominion. Eumenes hoped to obtain these cities for himself: Rhodes, on the other hand, looked upon their independence as a barrier against the extension of monarchical government in Asia, and as a condition for the development of her trade.

Senatorial commission to decide disputed claims.

The Roman senate was obliged to decide between two allies of equal importance and deserts. They could not satisfy one without offending the other, and yet a decision was absolutely necessary. The Roman republic, which had claimed to be the protector and deliverer of the Greeks, could not for very shame rescue a town like Miletus from the dominion of Antiochus in order to hand it over to Eumenes. It would have been still less honourable to curtail the independence of those which, like Smyrna and Lampsacus, had boldly and successfully resisted all the attacks of the king. No towns could possibly be made to suffer degradation or punishment by being incorporated in the Pergamenian kingdom, unless they had been guilty of treason or had taken the part of Antiochus during the war. These views were recognised in principle by the senate, and a commission of ten members was sent out to examine in detail the claims of every town, and to decide their fate accordingly. Eumenes, though sorely disappointed, was obliged to submit to this decision; nor had he in truth cause to complain, for he rose suddenly from the precarious position of a fortunate adventurer and a petty potentate to that of the most powerful prince of Asia Minor, and he became the rival of the king of Syria himself.

Settlement of the

The decisions made by the ten ambassadors, in compliance with the order of the senate, for the final settlement of the conditions of peace, and for the regulation of the affairs of Asia, were substantially the following.¹ The first and most essential of all was the limitation of the kingdom of Syria to that part of Asia which lay beyond the Taurus range. In drawing the boundary line, however, the Roman commissioners seemed to have been so ignorant of the geographical features of Asia, or else so careless, that a dispute could afterwards arise, whether Pamphylia was to be considered as on this side or on the further side of the boundary, and as appertaining to the kingdom of Antiochus or of Eumenes, a question settled ultimately in favour of the latter. Some of the territorial arrangements, it is true, were more nominal than real; for in some cases the king of Syria did not give up what he actually possessed, but what he had only claimed, and had never been able fully to incorporate with his kingdom. Nevertheless, the loss was considerable enough to degrade Syria for ever from the rank of the first great power in Asia, and to weaken it so effectually that, as we shall soon see, the son of Antiochus 'the Great' was obliged to humble himself like a reprimanded menial before the raised stick of a Roman ambassador. Nor was Antiochus allowed to retain without limitation the sovereignty of those countries which remained to him. He was obliged to give up his elephants of war, to reduce his fleet to the number of ten ships, and to promise not to allow his armed vessels to sail further west than Calycadnus, in Cilicia, nor to attack any one of the Greek islands. In addition to these permanent reductions of his former power, he had to submit to the payment of a war indemnity, which even the wealthy country of Syria felt to be a heavy burden. He had to pay to the Romans the sum of fifteen thousand talents (between three and four million pounds), part to be furnished at once, part in annual payments during twelve years to come, and a further sum of five hundred talents to Eumenes. To insure the execution of these terms,

CHAP. II.

192–189 B.C.

affairs of Asia.

¹ Polybius, xxii. 26; Livy, xxxviii. 38.

Antiochus gave twenty hostages, and promised, moreover, to give up Hannibal and four other enemies of the Roman people who had served him, 'provided it were in his power to do so.' This last clause, which made it possible to evade the most humiliating and disgraceful concession, was, as we would fain believe, inserted into the treaty of peace at the instigation of Publius Cornelius Scipio, who may have thought it beneath his dignity to play the part of executioner of his great opponent. He ceded this part to no less a man than Flamininus, the 'liberator' of Greece, who devoted himself to it a few years later with the utmost zeal.

The vast territories which Antiochus had lost through his presumptuous policy, were made use of by the Roman commissioners chiefly to enlarge the Pergamenian kingdom. Eumenes obtained, first, the Syrian possessions on the Thracian Chersonesus; and, secondly, all the country of Asia Minor as far east as the river Halys, and as far south as the Taurus, with the exception of the Greek cities, which were to remain free, of the possessions of Prusias of Bithynia, of a few districts belonging to the Galatians, and of the territories of Rhodes in Lycia and Caria. By this aggrandisement the Pergamenian kingdom was enabled to protect the Roman interests on the one side against Syria, and on the other against Macedonia. Care was taken, however, that the king of Pergamum should not easily become so independent as to forget that he was a client of Rome. For, besides the great neighbouring kingdoms of Macedonia and Syria, Rome allowed the continuance of several smaller states in Asia, such as Bithynia, Cappadocia, greater and lesser Armenia, and even the robber state of the Galatians; and apart from this, the continued independence of the flourishing commercial towns of the Greeks in every direction was calculated to restrain the ambition, and to control the liberty of action, of the Pergamenian kings.

In the regulation of these affairs the senatorial commission had a task which required time and patience.

Until every town and every state should have received its due, the treaty of peace could not be ratified, nor the Roman army withdrawn from Asia. In the course of the winter 190–189 B.C., that army was even reinforced by twelve thousand six hundred men, one-third of whom were Roman citizens and two-thirds Italian allies.¹ At the same time supplies of corn were sent to the east from Sicily and Sardinia. Nor was the Roman fleet recalled.

Thus it happened that in the year 189 B.C. considerable military forces were stationed on the east side of the Ægean Sea without any definite occupation. But the new commanders, who started from Rome in the year 189 B.C., were at no loss to find employment for their troops. The prætor Fabius Labeo, who took the command of the fleet, sailed with it to Crete, where the independent townships were, as usual, at war with each other. Fabius, though he had not the shadow of a pretext for interfering in these quarrels, ordered the Cretans in the name of the Roman republic to lay down their arms, and to deliver up to him all the Romans who in the previous wars had been made prisoners, and had been sold as slaves in the island. The Cretans paid little attention to this request. The town of Gortyna alone sent up a number of Roman prisoners.² Fabius did not think proper to enforce his demands with the means at his disposal. He sailed back to Ephesus without having drawn the sword, but, nevertheless, had the face to ask, and the good luck to obtain from the senate, the honours of a triumph for this bloodless expedition to Crete.³

The consul Manlius Vulso, who commanded the land army, was not content to remain inactive any more than his colleague. He, too, hoped to return from Asia with just claims to a triumph, and to obtain not only glory and honour, but also the material advantages which a distribution or appropriation of rich spoils procured for

---

¹ Livy, xxxvii. 50.
² According to Valerius Antias, who however deserves little credit, the total number of Romans who were set at liberty in the island was four thousand. Livy, xxxvii. 60, 5. ³ Livy, xxxvii. 60.

BOOK V.
192-189 B.C.

a victorious general. The war in Asia, it is true, was ended, but a pretext for hostilities might easily be found, if he thought it necessary to take so much trouble. He knew that the Galatians had supplied the army of Antiochus with mercenaries, or at least had allowed him to engage mercenaries in their country. This was evidently a sufficient reason for making war upon them, although neither the senate nor the Roman people had given any instructions for it. At a great distance from Rome a magistrate invested with the *imperium* was *de facto* in possession of dictatorial power, and able to act without reference to the wishes of the home government. The senate possessed no means of interfering with his proceedings. If, after the termination of his year of office, he had a chance of justifying his actions, or could boast of military success, he ran no risk whatever in employing as he pleased the military forces of the republic. This abuse of official power had first become apparent during the second Punic war in Spain, where the Scipios had acted as if they were independent sovereigns. It became more and more general in consequence of the extension of the Roman dominions, and of the increasing distances of the theatres of war from Rome, which made it impossible for the central government to control the actions of their generals. It was favoured, moreover, by the continual succession of annual magistrates which prevented the systematic carrying out of a preconceived plan, and suggested to every man placed at the head of the armies to think more of the furtherance of his own interests than of the welfare of the republic.

Expedition against the Galatians.

We need not follow step by step the expedition of Manlius through Asia Minor, for its character can be described in a few words. It was simply a plundering razzia of the commonest sort, and would have been as worthy of the Gauls as it was unworthy of a Roman army. Before Manlius reached that country in the interior of Asia Minor where the Galatians dwelt he laid under contributions, without distinction, a number of native tribes through whose country he passed. Those communities which did not readily submit to pay the contributions imposed were unsparingly plundered. From several places the inhabitants fled into the mountains, and left to the mercy of the invaders what they could not carry with them.—The proceedings of Manlius are characterised by the manner in which he managed to extort a hundred talents from one of the petty native chiefs called Moagetes. On the approach of the Roman army, this chief had endeavoured to conciliate the consul by sending him a golden crown, had appeared before him in the attitude of a suppliant, had implored him to spare his country, and had offered a sum of five-and-twenty talents as a ransom for himself and his people. Manlius overwhelmed him with abuse, and threatened to treat him as an enemy if he did not pay five hundred talents within three days. After a great deal of haggling, it was agreed that he should pay one hundred talents and a supply of corn for the army.

Laden with booty, the Romans at last reached the country of the Galatians, which was the northern part of Central Asia Minor. The Galatians were at this time divided into three tribes. Since their immigration, nearly a century before, they had made themselves conspicuous by their bravery in the armies of the different Asiatic princes, but still more by their adventurous plundering expeditions. Even the great king of Syria had not thought it beneath his dignity to pay them a tribute.[1] Attalus the First, of Pergamum, was the only one who had offered them a successful resistance, and after several years of warfare had driven them back to the river Halys, where they now occupied permanent settlements, and gradually began to apply themselves to peaceful occupations. But their youth continued to serve as mercenaries, and a considerable number of them had fought in the army of Antiochus in the battle of Magnesia. This furnished Manlius with a pretext for attacking them; but his real motive, as we

[1] Livy, xxxviii. 16, 13.

have already hinted, was different. It was generally believed that the Galatians had accumulated great wealth in their country, the proceeds of their numerous plundering expeditions. This it was which allured Manlius. He might think, moreover, that he was especially called upon to make war upon the Gauls, for a Manlius had, in times of old, saved the Capitol, when Gallic warriors had scaled it by night, and another Manlius, surnamed Torquatus, had overcome a Gallic giant in single combat. The king of Pergamum, too, was deeply interested in the punishment of the Galatians, for they were still troublesome neighbours. But a true Roman politician, like Flamininus, would, for this very reason, have been inclined to spare them, as a counterpoise to the enlarged power of the Pergamenian kingdom. The consul Manlius appears to have acted from personal motives in deciding upon the expedition. He paid no attention to the entreaties of the Galatians, who tried to pacify him;[1] nor did he find much difficulty, with his greatly superior force, in overcoming the resistance which the barbarians at last offered, more from despair than from any fair prospect of success.

The Tolistobogians were attacked first. They had retired, with their families and property, into the mountain range of Olympus, and had there entrenched themselves. They were defeated with very little trouble.[2] Many thousands of them were made prisoners, especially women and children, and the camp in which they had heaped up their treasures was plundered.[3] The Tektosagians suffered the same fate. The third tribe, called the Trokmians, fled beyond the river Halys, whither the Roman general did not pursue them. As winter was

---

[1] This appears from the negotiations carried on by the chief Eposognatus. See Livy, xxxviii. 18.

[2] This time Valerius Antias yields the palm of exaggeration to his competitor Claudius. He is satisfied with eight thousand Galatians slain in battle, whilst Claudius raises the number to forty thousand. Livy, xxxviii. 23, 8.

[3] Livy, xxxviii. 27, 7: Praeda tanta fuit, quantam avidissima rapiendi gens, cum cis montem Taurum omnia armis per multos annos tenuisset, coacervare potuit.

approaching, Manlius led back his army, laden with spoil, to take up his winter quarters in the countries near the coast. Meanwhile, the peace negotiations between the Roman ambassadors and Antiochus had been brought to an end, and the complicated affairs of the East had been settled in the manner already described.[1] Nothing was left for Manlius but the formal ratification of the treaty by mutual oaths. This business being finished, he received from the towns, which he had secured against Galatian invasions, acknowledgments of gratitude, which took the shape, not of empty declarations and votes of thanks, but of heavy golden crowns.

At length the Roman army evacuated Asia. Instead of returning to Italy by sea,[2] Manlius marched along the coast of Thrace to Macedonia and Greece. On this march the army was exposed to the attacks of warlike barbarian tribes. It was impossible for the Romans to march in a compact body. They were encumbered with booty, which prolonged their straggling lines, and at the same time attracted the barbarians. They suffered greatly, and lost a large portion of the booty before they reached the friendly country of Macedonia. In spite of this ignominious termination of the campaign, Manlius demanded and obtained a triumph upon his arrival in Rome. There was, indeed, in the senate a strong opposition to the granting of this triumph. The more honourable among the senators pointed to the dangers to which the state would be exposed if generals were allowed to undertake wars without the sanction of the home government, and if, instead of being punished for such presumption, they were even rewarded. The warning voices were not heeded; but not many years passed before the republic had to suffer from that overweening power of the nobility which had grown with the growth of the Roman dominion.

[1] See p. 160.
[2] Compare what has been said p. 138, on the preference given to the land route.

The End of the Ætolian War.

New rising of the Ætolians.

When, in the spring of 190 B.C., Lucius Scipio granted the Ætolians a six months' truce, in order to be disengaged for the march into Asia, public attention in Rome had watched him with impatience, though not with great anxiety, for since the battle of Thermopylæ, Antiochus had ceased to be feared.[1] Nevertheless, great excitement ensued at Rome when the false news was spread that the two Scipios had been treacherously taken prisoners, that thereupon the Roman camp had been stormed, and the whole army annihilated, that the Ætolians had again taken up arms, and were collecting troops in Macedonia, Dardania, and Thrace.[2] The news of the brilliant victory at Magnesia, arriving soon after, completely calmed the public mind with respect to the Asiatic war. On the other hand, it turned out that there was some truth in the rumour concerning the rising of the Ætolians, and that the war with these obstinate mountaineers, which was dragging on for such a length of time, was not yet brought to an end. The Ætolians had indeed again taken up arms, either because they really hoped for or believed in a defeat of the Romans in Asia, or because the demands of unconditional submission made again by the senate drove them to despair.[3] They invaded Athamania and the neighbouring territories which Philip had conquered during the war and had hoped to unite with Macedonia. The inhabitants had rebelled against the Macedonian governors and garrisons,

---

[1] Livy, xxxvii. 51, 8.

[2] This report was indeed unfounded and absurd. But this is no reason why we should refuse to credit the story, and call it the invention of Valerius Antias (See Nissen, *Untersuchungen über die Quellen des Livius*, p. 197) The history of recent wars has abundantly shown that very absurd and unfounded reports have found credence for a time. Without going back so far as the battle of Waterloo, we need only remember the Tartar report of the capture of Sebastopol in 1854, and the wild transports of delight into which Paris was thrown, at least for a couple of hours, in August, 1870, when a report was spread of a great victory at Wörth, which turned out to be a great defeat.

[3] Livy, xxxvii. 49.

and thus with their aid the Ætolians and king Amynander, who had returned from exile, succeeded in taking one town after another, and defeating Philip, who approached with a force of six thousand men. The army stationed in Ætolia under Cornelius Mammula[1] watched these proceedings without making an effort to prevent them. We cannot help suspecting that the Romans looked without displeasure on the expulsion of Philip from Athamania by the Ætolians. They were thereby saved the trouble of taking from him countries which they had not intended him to retain, but which, for decency's sake, they had been obliged to leave to him after he had cleared them of the common enemy.[2] The Ætolians now grew bolder. They took possession of the districts of Amphilochia and Dolopia, and defended them successfully against the Macedonians. But at length the time had come when Rome was forced to settle accounts with them, after the war had twice been interrupted by truces on account of the far more important operations against Antiochus. For now the news arrived of the victory at Magnesia. Rome was at full liberty to arrange the affairs of Greece at her leisure and her pleasure. Marcus Fulvius Nobilior, the consul of the year 189 B.C., the colleague of Caius Manlius Vulso, who had been sent to Asia, landed with reinforcements in Apollonia;[3] and now began the third and last period of the war with this bold defiant people, which, in its tenacious struggle against overwhelming numbers, deserves our respect if not our admiration.

The same desperate courage with which the Ætolians had defended Heraclea, Lamia, Naupactus and Larissa,

---

[1] Livy, xxxvii. 2, 7, and 48, 5.

[2] It seems clear, from the scanty information left to us, that after the conclusion of peace Philip did not recover the frontier districts between Ætolia and Macedonia — that is, Athamania, Amphilochia, Aperantia, and Dolopia, or at any rate, that he obtained only a very small portion of them. Compare Hertzberg, *Geschichte Griechenlands*, i. p. 136, Anm. 82.

[3] This Fulvius Nobilior was accompanied by the poet Ennius, for which he was rated by Cato. See Cicero, *Tuscul.* i. 2: Obiecit (Cato) ut probrum M. Nobiliori, quod is in provinciam poetas duxisset. Duxerat autem consul ille in Ætoliam, ut scimus, Ennium.

BOOK V.
192–189 B.C.

Siege of Ambracia.

was now shown by them again in the defence of their last stronghold, Ambracia, which Fulvius attacked in union with the Epirots, whilst on every side the enemies of Ætolia availed themselves of the opportunity for ravaging their country. The frontier districts in the north were invaded by Perseus, the son of Philip; those in the west by the Acarnanians, whilst an Illyrian and Achaean fleet appeared in the south, and devastated the coast.[1] Everywhere the Ætolians fought with a degree of courage such as the natives of the highlands on the eastern side of the Adriatic have ever shown. The defenders of Ambracia were indeed worthy forerunners of the heroes of Missolonghi. Ambracia, which had become an important and flourishing town at the time of king Pyrrhus,[2] had been separated from Epirus since the first war between the Romans and Macedonia, and had become a member of the Ætolian confederation.[3] The inhabitants, supported by an Ætolian garrison, now opposed to the vigorous attack of the Romans and Epirots a still more vigorous resistance. When one part of the walls fell under the force of the battering-rams, a fresh barricade appeared behind it, and the work of destruction had to be continued without much prospect of better success. Ætolian reinforcements succeeded in penetrating into the town through the lines of circumvallation, and in a sally of the defenders some of the Roman siege-works were destroyed. The mode of attack was therefore altered. The Romans attempted to enter the town by underground passages. As soon as the besieged perceived this by the accumulated earth, they dug a passage behind the wall, parallel with it, and there listened to the strokes of the enemy's picks, in order to find the spot towards which the Romans were directing their tunnel.[4] They then worked in this direction, and thus the enemies met under ground, and the struggle

---

[1] Livy, xxxviii. 7. [2] Vol. i. p. 506.
[3] Polybius, xxii. 9, 2; Appian, *Maced*. 2.
[4] Herodotus describes the same manœuvre where he relates the siege of Barca by the Persians in the year 510 B.C. Herodotus, iv. 200.

raged in the dark. At length the Ætolians drove the Romans from the tunnel by pushing in a cask filled with feathers, and lighting the feathers, so that the whole place was filled with suffocating smoke. The accurate description of this extraordinary apparatus given by Polybius is of considerable interest for the history of ancient warfare, and throws a favourable light upon the inventive skill of the Ætolians.[1]

Yet however heroically the Ambracians continued the contest, their efforts were in vain; for the Ætolian confederacy at length gave up the hope of being able to resist the enemies who were advancing on all sides, and leaving Ambracia to its fate, they began to negotiate for peace with the consul. Through the mediation of king Amynander of Athamania, who had now made his submission to Rome, a capitulation was concluded. The Ætolian garrison was allowed to withdraw from the town, and the inhabitants were spared; but the numerous masterpieces of Greek sculpture and painting with which the town had been adorned since the times of Pyrrhus, were all transported to Rome.[2]

At the same time the preliminaries of a peace between Rome and the Ætolians were settled with the help of the Rhodian and Athenian ambassadors, and through the intercession of Caius Valerius, the step-brother of the consul Fulvius, and son of that Marcus Valerius Laevinus who, twenty-two years before, had concluded the first alliance between Rome and Ætolia. The conditions of the peace, which were afterwards more accurately defined in Rome, were more favourable to the Ætolians than was to be expected after their complete subjection, and in the irritation which the Romans felt at their conduct before the war, and at the obstinacy with which they had carried it on.

Peace with the Ætolians.

---

[1] Polybius, xxii. 11.

[2] Polybius, xxii. 13, 9; Livy. xxxviii. 9, 6–9. The passage referring to the works of art (chap. 9, 13) is worth transcribing: Signa aenea marmoreaque et tabulae pictae, quibus ornatior Ambracia, quia regia ibi Pyrrhi fuerat, quam ceterae regionis eius urbes erant, sublata omnia avectaque.

The Romans did not even insist on their former demands, and took off one-half of the war contribution. It is true that the Ætolian state was obliged to have the same friends and the same enemies as Rome, i.e. it was made a vassal state of Rome, as Macedonia, Achaia, the remaining Grecian states, Pergamum, Rhodes, Carthage, and Numidia were already in fact, if not in name. With the exception, however, of the right of peace and war, it retained in a somewhat restricted area all the attributes of an independent state. It was arranged that all the towns which the Ætolian confederation had lost since the beginning of the war were to remain separated from it,[1] especially the island of Cephallenia, which the Romans meant to keep for themselves, and which, after an obstinate resistance, they reduced.[2] On the other hand, the Ætolians were probably allowed to keep the frontier districts towards Macedonia, which they had just reconquered from Philip, and it appears certain that Amynander regained possession of Athamania.[3] Of course these concessions were not made from motives of clemency and forbearance to the obstinate Ætolians, but for the same reasons that formerly operated in the case of Nabis.[4] It was jealousy at the increasing power of Macedonia which determined the Romans to spare the Ætolians; for Philip had lately shown a high degree of energy and ambition. The policy of Rome was directed towards limiting as much as possible Achaia and Macedonia, the two Grecian states which had been employed as auxiliaries in the late war with Antiochus.[5] In order to gain this end, they showed a moderation which the Ætolians had not deserved by their conduct, and which they themselves had not expected.[6]

---

[1] Livy, xxxviii. 11, with Wissenborn's note, and Nissen, *Untersuchungen über die Quellen des Livius*, p. 203.   [2] Livy, xxxviii. 28.

[3] Hertzberg, *Geschichte Griechenlands*, i. p. 136.   [4] Above, p. 75 f.

[5] The Romans were no more anxious to see Greece powerful than in our own time France wished to see Italy rise to the position of a great European power. The liberators in both cases forfeited a great deal of the gratitude of the liberated states because they showed too clearly that they had been actuated by their own interest rather than by generosity.

[6] Polybius, xxii. 13, 8: ἦν ἅπαντα αὐτοῖς παρὰ τὴν προσδοκίαν.

Troubles in the Peloponnesus.

The union of the whole of the Peloponnesus in the Achaean league, the long-wished-for object of the best patriots and the last hope of a degenerate race, was at length accomplished. Messenia, Elis and Sparta had become members of the league, and a new and better time might now begin, if the Greeks of the Peloponnesus could make up their minds to sacrifice the spirit of petty local patriotism and city-autonomy, the besetting sin of their race, and to submit to a greater and more comprehensive political union. Fate, which had been so prodigal to the Greeks of eminent men, was again propitious to them, and had given them in Philopœmen a leader worthy to rank as a statesman, and still more as a general, with the heroes of past ages. But it was soon apparent that even the experience of long years of trouble was unable to control their intertribal animosity, and that the Greeks had not yet learnt to raise the majesty of a national life above the selfishness of factions and local attachments. The Romans have been charged with having caused the decline and fall of the Greeks, and grave accusations have been brought against them on this ground. It is true the Romans did not honestly wish for the national regeneration of Greece; on the contrary, they fomented internal strife and widened existing divisions. They believed that a powerful Greece was not compatible with the interest of their own state. But, to be candid, we can hardly venture seriously to blame the Roman statesmen for acting according to a policy which has been adhered to from their time to our own, and which, to name but one instance, France has always followed with respect to Italy and Germany. On the other hand, it is evident that even if the Romans had not interfered, the Greeks would never have been able to recover in the second century before our era the ground that they had lost during the three hundred years which preceded it. Considering their incapability for

CHAP. II.

192-189 B.C.

The condition of Greece.

forming a national state, it would undoubtedly have been the best thing for them, if they had all been included in the Macedonian empire, and that result would probably have been achieved if Macedonia had remained what it was under Philip II. But the ill-cemented empire of Alexander, comprising both Greeks and Barbarians, even if it had lasted, was not favourable to a separate and national organization of the Greeks. Afterwards, in the period of the successors of Alexander the Great, the tragedy of Hellenic discord was repeated on a larger scale, and Greece was implicated in distant wars without putting an end to internal dissensions. If the second Macedonian kingdom had been qualified by its organization, or by the character of its rulers to inspire confidence, the energetic Philip V. would have been able to solve the problem, and to found a Græco-Macedonian state. But he failed through his own tyranny and boundless ambition, and himself gave a pretext to the Romans for interfering in Greek affairs. In this state of things emancipation from foreign influence was out of the question, and the best, or at least the wisest friends of the Grecian cause, were those who without hesitation recognized Rome as their protecting power, and who sought to gain in union with Rome at least a moderate degree of local independence, to preserve their honour and dignity, to obtain the great blessing of internal peace, with a prospect of material development as a compensation for the loss of complete freedom and political power. This union with Rome was prevented by the want of moderation shown by the extreme parties, and by the relentless spirit with which the Romans, abusing their superior power, finally drove the ill-treated and maddened Greeks to a hopeless resistance.

The light in which the Romans regarded the freedom and independence which Flamininus had announced with so much pomp in the year 196 B.C., was soon shown in an unmistakeable manner. The senate constituted itself a supreme court of appeal for hearing and judging the innumerable disputes which constantly sprung up among neighbours and parties in every one of the small Grecian states.¹ As soon as a difference arose, the contending parties hastened to bring their case before this august assembly, and there to court the intercession of the most influential men. It would certainly have been a great blessing to poor tortured Greece if the Romans had possessed the sense and the desire to allow an impartial judgment to supersede the decisions of rude force, however humiliating it might have been for the Greeks to have to apply to a foreign court of justice. The Romans, however, lacked not only insight into the complicated legal questions submitted to them, but also the wish to let justice prevail without regard to political considerations. Nor could it be otherwise. Even Flamininus, whom generous historians have credited with the noblest intentions in the liberation of Greece, had thought proper, as early as 196 B.C., to censure the Achaeans for having ventured to attack the Messenians without awaiting the result of his arbitration. He ordered them to disband their army, and though he incorporated Messenia in the Achaean league, he encouraged the Messenians to apply directly to him upon any disputed point.² It is clear that under such circumstances, in a country undermined by party strife, the peaceable settlement of old disputes was out of the question. The old national spirit of discord had spread too far among the Greeks to allow a new growth like that of the Achaean league to take root and prosper.

The settlement of the affairs of Sparta, and its annexation to the Achaean league, had been brought about forcibly, and therefore were not likely to remain long undisturbed.

Seeds of discord at Sparta.

---

¹ The Roman senate did not look upon this as a troublesome burden (as Mommsen, *Röm. Gesch.* i. 738, has supposed), but as an agreeable occupation. Polybius, xxv. 1, 4: ἐξ οὗ ('Ρωμαῖοι) καταφανεῖς ἅπασιν ἐγενήθησαν ὅτι τοσοῦτον ἀπέχουσι τοῦ τὰ μὴ λίαν ἀναγκαῖα τῶν ἐκτὸς πραγμάτων ἀποτρίβεσθαι καὶ παρορᾶν, ὡς τοὐναντίον καὶ δυσχεραίνουσιν ἐπὶ τῷ μὴ πάντων τὴν ἀναφορὰν ἐφ᾽ ἑαυτοὺς γίγνεσθαι καὶ πάντα πράττεσθαι μετὰ τῆς αὐτῶν γνώμης. We may safely trust this statement of Polybius, who, if he had been inclined to misrepresent facts, would certainly have suppressed everything distasteful to his patrons.

² Livy, xxxvi. 31, 9. Above, p. 129.

The old citizens, whom Nabis had plundered and expelled, had not been reinstated by Flamininus after the overthrow of the tyrant. They had only obtained the permission to settle as 'free Lacedæmonians' in the townships around Sparta, and these townships had been made independent. The exiles were not satisfied. They hoped for an opportunity of regaining the full enjoyment of their lost rights, and they surrounded Sparta almost like a hostile army, eagerly awaiting an opportunity of returning to their old homes. The new citizens, whom Machanidas and Nabis had recruited from aliens, Periœci, emancipated helots and mercenaries, felt the danger of their position and the weakness of the commonwealth, which, being deprived of the surrounding districts and cut off from the sea, was but a shadow of the warlike Sparta of old. It seemed as if Roman diplomacy had by its tender treatment of Nabis, and by the half-measure with regard to the return of the exiles, purposely scattered the seeds of new dissensions. As we have already seen,[1] Nabis had attempted to overthrow by force the new order of things introduced by Flamininus. He had failed, and perished in the attempt. Now would have been the time to get rid of at least the worst among the partisans of the tyrant, and to reinstate the old citizens in their former rights. But this was again omitted, though the Romans had always given the exiles hope of restitution, and had profited by their aid in the war against the usurpers. After the battle of Thermopylæ, 191 B.C., Acilius Glabrio had at length wished to reinstate the Spartan exiles; but Philopœmen had for good reasons wished to arrange this matter through the Achaean league without Roman interference. In this he had succeeded;[2] but still his measure cannot have been sweeping. At any rate, the exiles were not allowed to return to the town of Sparta itself.[3] The dissensions continued, and passions became more and more heated. In 189 B.C., after the close of the Ætolian war, the disputes broke out anew,

---

[1] Above, p. 99. [2] Plutarch, *Philop*. 17: αὐτὸς κατήγαγε τοὺς φυγάδας.
[3] Livy, xxxvii. 31.

and led to a lamentable incident, which exhibits in the most striking light the hopelessness of the state of Greece, and shows how effectively all parties co-operated to further the ends of Rome.

Disturbances at Sparta

The inhabitants of Sparta, unable to bear the idea of being for ever cut off from the sea, tried to help themselves, and disregarding all the arrangements and settlements made by the Romans, suddenly attempted to seize the small seaport of Las, on the Lacedæmonian coast; but they were repulsed by the free Laconians settled in the neighbourhood. This breach of the peace caused the Achaean league to interfere, and Philopœmen demanded the surrender of those who were guilty of the attack on Las. The Spartans, incensed at this demand, executed thirty men whom they accused of conspiracy with the Achaeans, and declared that they no longer acknowledged themselves members of the league. At the same time they sent messengers to the consul Marcus Fulvius, who was still in Cephallenia, begging him to come to Lacedæmon, and to receive the town formally into Roman protection. We see here how the mere possibility of foreign interference fostered internal quarrels.

put down by the Achaeans.

The Achaeans held firm by their good right, and unanimously declared war against Sparta. The consul came into the Peloponnesus, gave an audience to both parties in Elis, and without interfering himself persuaded them to break off their military operations, and to refer the matter to the arbitration of the Roman senate.[1] Thus, this question also came to be discussed in Rome. A party of the Achaeans, headed by Philopœmen and Lycortas, warmly insisted on maintaining the federal rights, and repudiated all Roman interference in the internal affairs of the Peloponnesus, whilst another party, headed by Diophanes, yielded to the actual predominance of the Romans, and was prepared to leave the decision in this matter to them. That this party judged more wisely than the other is evident from the mere fact that the negotiations were

[1] See p. 175, note 1.

carried on in Rome. A clear decision in favour of one or the other of the two parties would no doubt have been the best for both. But unfortunately the senate's decision was so ambiguous, that the Achaeans considered themselves justified in punishing the Spartan breach of peace as they thought fit, and further in restoring order in a most summary manner. And here it was seen how easily even the best of the Greeks allowed themselves to be carried away by the passion of revenge and cruelty, as if they had meant to show that they did not possess the self-control necessary for the enjoyment of freedom. Philopœmen marched to Sparta with a federal army, in which there was also a number of Spartan exiles, men whom the wrongs, the sufferings, the poverty of many sad years had made reckless, and who hoped now at length to enjoy the sweets of revenge, and to recover their lost privileges and possessions. The Spartans felt that they were unable to resist; and when Philopœmen demanded the surrender of the guilty, they sent eighty men into the Achaean camp, upon the understanding that they should be punished only after a regular trial and a formal judicial sentence. But these unfortunate men had hardly arrived in the Achaean camp, when the Spartan exiles fell upon them and murdered seventeen out of their number. With difficulty Philopœmen succeeded in preventing a general massacre. But those who were thus spared only gained a short time of grace. On the next day they were all summarily tried without being heard in their defence, were all sentenced to death, and instantly executed.[1] Philopœmen then entered Sparta, levelled the walls, and expelled all the foreign mercenaries and liberated slaves, who formed the great majority of the new citizens. By the decision of a federal council of the Achaeans assembled in Tegea, the exiles were now formally reinstated in their rights; and thus the whole social revolution and all the settlements of property of the last twenty years were overthrown with one stroke. These resolutions were carried out with extreme severity.

[1] Livy, xxxviii. 33, and xxxix. 36; Plutarch, *Philop.* 16.

The expelled citizens were not allowed to remain anywhere within the Peloponnesus; those who were caught were sold as slaves, and from the proceeds of their sale a colonnade (stoa) in Megalopolis, which had formerly been destroyed by the Spartans, was rebuilt.[1]

Thus all traces of the usurpation were removed, and liberated Sparta, in which the laws of Lycurgus[2] were now formally abolished, again took its place as a member of the Achaean league. Success seemed to justify Philopœmen's bold uncompromising proceeding; for the Romans raised no objection to the accomplished fact, which seemed to prove that healthy self-reliance and bold resolve inspired more respect in Rome than unconditional obedience.

But it was too soon manifest that Sparta could no more under the new government than under the previous kings and tyrants submit to be merely a member of a Greek confederation; for the oligarchs who had been reinstated by the Achaeans soon forgot their gratitude, and worked with the utmost zeal to get rid of the hateful connexion with the Achaean league.

In Rome all complaints of contending Greek factions were received with open ears.[3] The senate was a standing court of law for deciding all internal quarrels in Greece. Upon the remonstrance of some Spartans two years later (187 B.C.)[4] the senate immediately expressed their disapproval of the harsh proceedings of the Achaeans, and Philopœmen was obliged to justify or to excuse himself in

---

[1] Livy, xxxviii. 34; Plutarch, *Philop.* 16.

[2] By the laws of Lycurgus, nothing is probably meant here but the peculiar gymnastic education of the Spartan youth. The political and social institutions of Sparta, which generally pass under the name of Lycurgus, had been abolished long before this time. Compare Pausanias, vii, 8, 5: τά τε οὖν τείχη τῆς Σπάρτης οἱ Ἀχαιοὶ καθεῖλον καὶ τὰ ἐς μελέτην τοῖς ἐφήβοις ἐκ τῶν Λυκούργου νόμων καταλύσαντες κτλ.

[3] See p. 175, note 1.

[4] Polybius, xxiii. 1, 1. It is significant that these Spartan malcontents who went to Rome to complain of the Achaeans were of opinion that the power and influence of Rome were diminished by the proceedings of Philopœmen (νομίσαντες ὑπὸ τοῦ Φιλοποίμενος ἅμα τὴν δύναμιν καὶ τὴν προστασίαν καταλελῦσθαι τὴν Ῥωμαίων). It seems a legitimate inference that these complaints did not arise originally in Sparta, but in Rome.

Rome by a special messenger. The Romans, after their fashion, prolonged the dispute by commissioning an embassy, which about the same time had to negotiate with Philip, to examine more closely into the dispute between the Spartans and Achaeans. In the following year (186) this commission held its sittings in Argos, under the presidency of the violent and imperious Caecilius Metellus. Metellus disapproved of the proceedings of the Achaeans, and called upon them to undo what had been done;[1] but he found that they took their stand on their formal right, and even refused to convoke an extraordinary federal congress to please the ambassadors of mighty Rome. This led to a greater coolness between the unequal allies, a coolness which encouraged the enemies of the Achaeans to continue their agitation. Areus and Alcibiades, two of the exiles brought back to Sparta by Philopoemen, men from whom he was justified in expecting gratitude rather than enmity, went to Rome and complained loudly that Sparta was obliged to obey the Achaean laws and authorities. No wonder that such perpetual intrigues irritated the Achaeans. By the rules of the league no single state had the right of direct communication with Rome.[2] This salutary and most necessary law, without which the independence of the Achaean league would have been reduced to a shadow, had been more than once violated by the malcontents in Sparta. The Romans, who should have refused to listen to direct complaints, had on the contrary encouraged them,[3] and had thus prolonged and embittered the internal disputes. The Achaeans considered themselves justified in punishing this breach of the established law; and though they knew that they would exasperate the Romans, they plucked up courage to summon the two intriguers, Areus and Alcibiades, before a court of law, and, as they did not appear, to condemn them to death in their absence. At the same time they again sent ambassadors to Rome[4] to justify their course of action. But they were

---

[1] Polybius, xxiii. 10.　　[2] Pausanias, vii. 9, 4.
[3] Compare Polybius, xxv. 1, 4.　　[4] Polybius, xxiii. 11.

obliged to submit to a great humiliation. The senate, not only received and listened to the Spartan deputies, but also allowed them to depart with another Roman embassy for Greece, in order to appear personally, under Roman protection, as complainants before the Achaean authorities, who of course could only regard and treat them as condemned criminals. With such haughty scorn the Romans humbled their allies in their own eyes. The result was that patriotic Achaeans, whose prudence or fear bore down their pride, gave up all hope of saving their independent position, and bowed their heads in despair under the inevitable destiny of their country. It was of no avail that Lycortas, who was then captain of the Achaean league, boldly addressed the Roman ambassador, Appius Claudius, in a manly speech, and proved to him that the Achaeans had but acted as they were by law entitled to act. To the proud Romans it may have appeared simply the act of overbearing self-delusion, and perhaps mere arrogance on the part of a vain-glorious Greek to struggle against the interference of Rome in the internal affairs of Greece, and to remind their masters that Greece had been solemnly declared free, and that the Romans had as little right to criticise the punishment of the rebellious Spartans as the Greeks would have had to blame the treatment of Capua by Rome in the Hannibalic war. But even if the Achaeans recognised Rome as umpire, they, as the tried old friends of Rome, might have expected to be treated at least as favourably as the Spartans, who had always been enemies. They had fought by the side of the Romans against Philip, against the Ætolians, against Antiochus, and against these same Spartans; and it was to keep up the order of things established by Rome and Achaia, and attacked by the Spartans, that Philopœmen had interfered. Moreover, the worst atrocity, the murder of the seventeen Spartans, had been committed by the Spartan exiles themselves, who now, with unparalleled effrontery, accused the Achaeans of severity. In strict law no objection could be taken to the proceeding of the Achaeans, and Appius Claudius could only silence Lycortas by appealing to the will and power of Rome, and by advising the Achaeans to submit in peace, lest they might soon have to yield to force.¹ This peremptory command could not of course be resisted. The Achaeans submitted with murmurs; but they refused to lend their hand for the cancelling of their own resolutions and sentences. They left it to the Romans to make what arrangements they thought proper. Appius Claudius thereupon first caused the sentence of death against Areus and Alcibiades to be annulled; then (184 B.C.) fresh discussions took place before the senate, and finally, a new Roman commission arranged matters so that, though Sparta remained a member of the Achaean league, her walls and her own laws were restored to her, and she was exempted from the penal jurisdiction of the confederacy. The difficult question of disputed titles to land and houses in Sparta remained unsolved, and with it was preserved the seed of new dissensions.²

When Philopœmen subdued the Spartan revolt and punished the leaders of the riot, he expelled, as we have seen, a number of the new citizens received by the tyrants, Machanidas and Nabis. These new citizens appealed to Rome, like the other parties which then wrangled with each other in Sparta, and Rome took up their cause also. The Roman commission, which had carried out the recent settlement of Spartan affairs, had decided in favour of the return of these exiles; but the resistance of the Achaeans, who justly regarded those whom they had expelled as their worst enemies, had prevented the resolution from being carried out.³ The Romans, who might easily have enforced this decision if they had wished, were not displeased to see this wound left open and festering. In the unfulfilled wishes of this party they possessed a weapon which

---

¹ Livy, xxxix. 37, 19: Tum Appius suadere se magnopere Achaeis dixit, ut dum liceret voluntate sua facere, gratiam inirent, ne mox inviti et coacti facerent.
² See p. 178.
³ Polybius, xxiv. 4. The Achaean ambassadors who, being urged by the Roman commissioners, had consented to this decision, had acted without being authorized, and they were probably censured for going beyond their powers.

they could at any time make use of against the Achaeans. At length, in the year 179 B.C., they gave orders for the return of these exiles, after their consistent policy had ruined the party of Philopœmen and Lycortas in Achaia, and had placed at the head of the government men like Callicrates, who had proved themselves willing servants of their Roman masters.

The Messenians were not less reluctant members of the Achaean league than the Spartans. In this reluctance they they were supported by the well-founded conviction that Rome was not pleased to see their union with the league continue. For Flamininus himself had urged them to apply to him if they should have grounds for any complaint.[1] Flamininus accordingly was the man selected as special patron by the leader of the Messenian malcontents, the disreputable Dinocrates, a man, who though possessing eminent qualifications as a soldier and a politician, contributed greatly by his dissolute life to attach a bad reputation to the name of Greek statesmen among the Romans,[2] but who, nevertheless, enjoyed great influence with the honourable Flamininus. In Messenia, as elsewhere, the everlasting disputes between the aristocracy and democracy were mixed up in the engrossing question of the day. The friends of Rome, that is to say, the opponents of the Achaean league, were supported by the aristocratic party, which always sided with Rome, and was favoured by her in return. As early as the year 189 B.C. an insurrection had been attempted by this party, but had been put down by Philopœmen.[3] Now, when in consequence of the Spartan dissensions, the coolness between Rome and the Achaeans had visibly increased, the Messenians thought that their time had come, and with the approval and help of Flami-

[1] Livy, xxxvi. 31, 8. Above, p. 175.
[2] Dinocrates is the man selected by Mommsen (*Röm. Geschichte*, i. 758) as a sample by which to judge the character of Achaean politicians. This alone suffices to show how unfair Mommsen is to the Achaeans, in order to justify the policy of Rome. Compare C. Peter, *Studien über Röm. Geschichte*, p. 169 ff.
[3] Polybius, xxiii. 10, 5. Hertzberg, *Geschichte Griechenlands*, i. p. 163

ninus,[1] they openly seceded from the Achaean league. Their undertaking was at first favoured by success. Philopœmen, in the hope of suppressing the revolt by prompt action, hastened to Messenia with insufficient forces. After an unfortunate battle, he fell into the hands of the enemy, who immediately put to death the venerable statesman, now in his seventy-first year, by making him drink poison.

The death of Philopœmen, who was not only the soul of the Achaean league, but also the most eminent man in the whole of Greece, would certainly have decided the issue of the war if the Achaeans had not fortunately found an able successor to Philopœmen in the brave Lycortas, the father of the historian Polybius. They carried on the war with Messenia with vigour, and at the same time invoked the assistance of the Romans, who were bound in justice, and by special treaty, to maintain the existing order, which they had only themselves helped to establish. But the Romans had consented to the extension of the Achaean league over the whole of the Peloponnesus much against their will, and under the pressure of events, at a time when they thought that they could hardly dispense with the help of the Achaeans. Now even men like Flamininus had so far forgotten their pretended sympathy with the Greeks, that they secretly and publicly favoured the dissensions in the Peloponnesus. The senate accordingly not only refused to grant the aid asked for by the Achaeans, or even to forbid the exportation of arms, but openly declared to the Achaean ambassadors that they would look on with indifference if even Sparta, Argos, and Corinth seceded from the league.[2] This was, as Polybius justly observes, nothing less than an invitation to those states to break up the confederation, and was calculated to discourage even the bravest Achaeans. Nevertheless, Lycortas did not despair. He continued the war with perseverance, and at length, with the help of the Messenian democrats, succeeded in overpowering the rebels, and in forcing them to surrender their capital.

[1] Polybius, xxiv. 5, 14 ; Plutarch, *Flamin.* 17.   [2] Polybius, xxiv. 10.

Thus, in spite of the insidious policy of the Romans, the courage and firmness of the Achaeans had reduced the rebellious members of the league, and had, to a certain degree, restored order in the Peloponnesus. The Romans thought proper to raise no difficulties; and the Greek patriots had now a fair prospect of establishing their independence on the basis which they had thus secured. That these hopes were wrecked was principally the fault of the Greeks themselves; but we shall see how the perfidious policy of the Romans was busy stirring up the evil passions of the Greeks, which they might have restrained, and that they thus hastened the ruin of that freedom which they prided themselves on having given to the Greeks out of pure magnanimity.

CHAPTER III.

THE THIRD MACEDONIAN WAR, 171–168 B.C.

BOOK V.
───
171–168 B.C.

THE war with Antiochus of Syria was decided in the two campaigns of 191 and 190 B.C. The final peace was concluded in the year 188, after the Asiatic affairs had been kept in suspense and uncertainty for more than a whole year on the plea of settling details. The Syrian kingdom was so weakened by the unhappy issue of the war that whole provinces separated themselves from it, and maintained their independence as free states. The payment of the war indemnity caused embarrassment even in a country reputed to possess enormous wealth. Antiochus used desperate means to procure money, and when he attempted to plunder a temple of Baal, in the land of the Elymæans, he was slain by the fanatical natives.[1]

Hannibal's death.

The further history of the Syrian kingdom concerns us only in so far as it bears on the history of Rome. We are still less concerned in the personal adventures of Antiochus, and can therefore pass them over with a word. But our full and genuine sympathy is excited by the fate of another man, a man who, for many years, had so commanded the foreground of the historical stage that we beheld everywhere his mighty form. Even after Hannibal had left Italy, and when he was banished from his country, we could not entirely lose sight of him. We saw how faithfully he endeavoured to discharge the duty of his life, even with almost exhausted strength, and when no longer borne up by the enthusiasm of his countrymen. We saw that

[1] Strabo, xvi. 1, 18; Justin, xxii. 2.

the Romans had not forgotten him, and demanded his extradition of Antiochus as a condition of peace.¹ He avoided the fate which then awaited him by escaping² to Crete, where, however, the treasures which he carried with him proved as dangerous to him as the enmity of the Romans. He deceived the cupidity of the Cretans, and escaped to Asia Minor, where he at length found a refuge with Prusias, king of Bithynia. This king happened just then to be involved in a war with his neighbour, Eumenes of Pergamum, and being hard pressed, was anxious to avail himself of the genius of the great general. Once more, but in a very limited field, Hannibal fought against the hereditary enemy of his native town. This time he was not even in the service of a great power like Syria; and his enemies were but the satellites of the Romans. He succeeded in gaining some advantages for Prusias; but the progress of the war in which Philip of Macedonia, as an old enemy of Eumenes, had also taken a part, was arrested through the interference of the Romans. And now the great Carthaginian approached the end of his career. Titus Quinctius Flamininus, the victor of Cynoscephalae, the 'liberator' of Greece, the leading man in Greek politics at Rome, appeared as ambassador in Asia Minor, to settle the quarrel of Eumenes and Prusias. Openly, or under cover of diplomatic forms, whether of his own free will or commissioned by the senate, he demanded from Prusias the surrender of Hannibal. The dubious light which surrounds this affair seems to indicate that Rome was ashamed to continue the war against a single man, and thereby to express an undignified fear of the old exile.³ Whatever may have been the detail of these disgraceful transactions, so much is undoubtedly true, that Prusias by betraying Hannibal obeyed the orders of the

---

¹ Above, p. 162.

² Justin, xxxii. 4: Namque Hannibal, cum ab Antiocho Romani inter ceteras conditiones pacis deditionem eius deposcerent, admonitus a rege, in fugam versus, Cretam defertur.

³ Livy, xxxix. 51; Plutarch, *Flamin.* 20 and 21 extr.; Cornel. Nepos, *Hannibal.* 13; Justin, xxii. 4; Zonaras, ix. 21.

Roman ambassador, and that the latter, if not strictly commissioned, carried out, at least, the most eager wishes of his countrymen. He had the satisfaction of being able to report to the senate that Hannibal had killed himself by poison, in order to escape extradition; and this news at length (183 B.C.) delivered the ruling nation from the terrifying phantom which had pursued and haunted it for twenty years, ever since the day of Zama.[1]

Unsettled state of affairs.

The anxiety with which Rome looked upon Hannibal, even after the great victory of Magnesia, was to some extent justified by the unsettled and unsatisfactory state of things which followed the last treaties, and which gave no security for the duration of peace. The Romans, it is true, were principally to blame, as they never ceased to offend not only their former enemies but also their most faithful allies, and to torment them with chicaneries, prompted by mere jealousy and ill-will. If even the Achaeans, as we have seen, had occasion to complain of unjust treatment, the policy which the senate observed towards the king of Macedonia bore the stamp of premeditated, systematic enmity, calculated to drive to despair a rival who was but partially humbled, and to ruin him completely. This policy, which we shall find practised against the Carthaginians with still greater indignity and heartlessness, could not fail to produce the desired effect, and led in a few years to the overthrow of the kingdom of Macedonia.

Ungenerous policy towards Macedonia.

We have seen with what zeal and energy Philip co-operated in the war against the Ætolians and Antiochus. His motives for taking such an active share might have been a matter of indifference to the Romans; his services in the cause of Rome were not less valuable because he was principally bent upon his own profit, and upon increasing his own power. But this was precisely what Rome disapproved of on principle, and she could consent to it only

---

[1] On the date of the death of Hannibal, Philopœmen, and Scipio, see Nissen, *Untersuchungen über die Quellen des Livius*, p. 231; Mommsen, *Hermes*, i. p. 199, ff.

with a perfidious reserve under the pressure of war. Philip had been encouraged by Acilius Glabrio to act against the Ætolians, by the prospect of being able to annex to his kingdom the Ætolian towns taken in Thessaly and elsewhere.[1] When, after the war, he was going to make good his claims, complaints against him, directly encouraged by the Romans,[2] were sent in from all sides to Rome, and he saw himself forced to defend himself like a culprit before the senate against a whole crowd of accusers. A Roman commission was sent to Thessaly in the year 186 B.C., to examine into this dispute. They held a court of enquiry in Tempe, and having examined the various claims, formally delivered their sentence to this effect: that Philip had no right to those towns which had, against their will, come into the power of the Ætolians, from whom he had taken them. They declared that he must withdraw his garrisons from the places unjustly occupied, and be satisfied with the ancient boundaries of Macedonia. At a second meeting in Thessalonica this harsh decree was extended to the towns on the Thracian coast, which had been taken from Antiochus, especially to Ænos and Maronea, and this unjust decision was rendered still more unpalatable by an order making over these towns to king Eumenes of Pergamum, who was thus installed as a next-door neighbour, to watch and control king Philip in the Roman interest.[3] Philip was stung with anger when he learnt the unfavourable decision, and unable to contain his feelings he unwisely gave vent to them by saying, 'The evening of all days has not yet come.' The Romans could see that the king was goaded into rage, and they were anxious that his blood should remain hot. They insisted that Philip should obey the command of the senate, and withdraw his garrisons from the Thracian and Thessalian towns.[4] He had now to decide whether he would quietly submit or defy the senate, and run the risk of an open breach. He chose the former course; but being unable to

---

[1] Above, p. 131.
[2] Livy, xxxix. 25 and 26.
[3] Polybius, xxiii. 6.
[4] Livy, xxxix. 33.

vent his passion on the Romans, he cooled it, in a manner as cowardly as it was treacherous and cruel, by revenging himself on one of these towns, which had not occasioned the quarrel and was innocent of his humiliation. He caused a troop of Thracian mercenaries to enter the town of Maronea, and to massacre the inhabitants. He then declared to the Romans that the butchery had taken place in consequence of an internal quarrel of the inhabitants, and that he was perfectly innocent. When Cassander, his officer, who had carried out this bloody order, was, on that account, summoned to Rome for examination, he caused him to be poisoned on the way.

Charges brought against Philip.

A man who was capable of such deeds can hardly excite our compassion, when we see him ill-treated in his turn. Yet with the Romans it was not the feeling of injured justice, but their cool, consistent policy, which induced them to pursue a system of annoyance and torture. Philip, feeling uneasy, and being unprepared to risk a breach, sent his son Demetrius, who was a favourite at Rome, to justify his proceedings before the senate. At the same time deputations, and even private persons without any public commission, flocked from all parts to the same high tribunal, with the most petty complaints, which were all listened to by the senate with great patience for three days running.[1] Not only were questions of disputed boundaries discussed, but Philip was also accused of having carried off cattle, and even men, of having refused justice, and of having decided unfairly in private disputes. Whoever felt himself injured by him calculated on finding in Rome an ear open to his complaints. But the deepest impression was apparently made by the ambassadors of king Eumenes, for they reported not only that Philip had given assistance

---

[1] Polybius, xxiv. 3 and 9. Livy, xxxix. 46, 6: Priusquam consules in provincias proficiscerentur legationes transmarinas in senatum introduxerunt; nec unquam ante tantum regionis eius hominum Romae fuerat. Nam ex quo fama per gentes, quae Macedoniam accolunt, vulgata est, crimina querimoniasque de Philippo non negligenter ab Romanis audiri, multis operae pretium fuisse queri, pro se quaeque civitates gentesque singuli etiam privati Romam aut ad spem levandae iniuriae aut ad deflendae solatium venerunt.

to Prusias of Bithynia in his recent war with Pergamum,[1] but also that he had not yet withdrawn his garrisons from the Thracian towns. The decision of the senate was, as might have been expected from the beginning, extremely harsh and provoking. Philip's son Demetrius was, it is true, treated with ostentatious kindness, and was given to understand that for his sake the strict demands of justice would not be enforced. Nevertheless, no material modification was made in the final decision, and an embassy was sent to Macedonia, and commissioned to declare that the patience of the senate would be exhausted unless its orders were immediately executed.[2]

Philip submitted to what could not be helped, though with inward resentment,[3] and with the firm resolution to prepare for the day of revenge. He was now more and more bent upon strengthening the Macedonian monarchy and forming a powerful army. He had already raised the taxes and import duties in order to improve his finances; had worked his gold mines profitably, and had endeavoured to increase the population by laws regarding the rearing of children, and by drawing colonists from Thrace.[4] Into this country he now made several expeditions, by which he gained the double object of training his army and of securing the frontier from the barbarians. In such proceedings he had not to apprehend any interference on the part of the Romans. For the protection of Greece from her northern neighbours was the special duty of the king of Macedonia; and the Romans themselves, on

CHAP. III.
171–168 B.C.

Philip's preparations for war.

---

[1] Above, p. 187.
[2] Polybius, xxiv. 3, 3 : ἡ σύγκλητος ἔδωκεν ἀπόκρισιν διότι τῶν ἐπὶ Θράκης τόπων ἐὰν μὴ καταλάβωσιν οἱ πρεσβευταὶ πάντα διῳκημένα κατὰ τὴν τῆς συγκλήτου γνώμην καὶ πάσας τὰς πόλεις εἰς τὴν Εὐμένους πίστιν ἐγκεχειρισμένας, οὐκ ἔτι δυνήσεται φέρειν οὐδὲ καρτερεῖν παρακρουομένη περὶ τούτων·
[3] Polybius, xxiv. 6.
[4] Livy, xxxix. 24. The most curious part of these administrative measures is that which refers to the increase of the population. Ut vero (says Livy) antiquam multitudinem hominum quæ belli cladibus amissa erat, restitueret non subolem tantum stirpis parabat cogendis omnibus procreare atque educare liberos, sed Thracum etiam magnam multitudinem in Macedoniam traduxerat. It is not clear how, nor probable that, any laws could enforce more than the rearing of children.

a former occasion, when the Ætolians demanded the destruction of the Macedonian monarchy, had insisted that its preservation was necessary for the security of Greece.[1] Nevertheless, when Philip's extraordinary activity came to be noticed in Rome, it roused suspicion. It was asserted that he wished to excite the Thracian barbarians to an invasion of Italy,[2] to repeat in the eastern Alps the famous exploit of Hannibal. It is hard to decide whether these suspicions arose from the imperfect knowledge which the Romans had of Thrace and Illyria, and thus from unintentional exaggeration, or from malevolent fiction. Perhaps even Philip had no correct idea of the difficulties which made such a plan impracticable. He is reported to have undertaken an expedition to Mount Hæmus, which was supposed to lie so near to the Adriatic, and at the same time to the Euxine and the Danube, that one could see these three waters at the same time from the summit.[3] As the Romans, just about this time (181 B.C.), were founding the colony of Aquileia in the north-east of Italy, it is, indeed, possible that they regarded an invasion on this side as by no means improbable;[4] for they remembered that Hannibal had been withheld neither by the Pyrenees nor by the Alps, nor by the many warlike tribes that lived between and on these mountains. But Philip was no Hannibal. The expedition to Italy was, at the utmost, one of his idle schemes, and, as on a former occasion, he shrank back when the first difficulties presented themselves. He accomplished little in Thrace, and returned home without having gained his object. The only profit which he had from his expedition was, that he was enabled to transplant a Thracian tribe from the in-

---

[1] Above, p. 61.   [2] Livy, xxxi. 35, 4.

[3] Livy, xl. 21. According to Strabo (vii. 5, 1), Polybius shared these views, which confirm what we have said (vol. ii. p. 172) of the great ignorance of the ancients in geographical knowledge. Pomponius Mela (II. 2) expresses the same opinion, though Livy ridicules it.

[4] A confirmation of this is the mad attempt of Cassius Longinus, consul of 171 B.C., who tried to march from Italy by land to Macedonia through Istria and Illyria. Livy, xliii. 1.

terior to the coast, and in exchange to settle in the interior all those Greeks of the coast who had excited his suspicion. According to his wont he carried out this cruel measure unscrupulously. With curses, imprecations, and tears, the exiled inhabitants quitted the homes that had become dear to them, to wander into the wilds of Thrace. Philip remained unmoved, and made use of the opportunity to get rid of the innocent children whose fathers he had previously murdered.[1]

CHAP. III.
171–168 B.C.

The curses which untold victims heaped upon the head of the heartless tyrant seemed directed not to a deaf fate, but to an avenging deity. He was destined to feel this in his own house and family. Perseus, his eldest son, born in unequal marriage, suspected the younger son, Demetrius, of claiming, on account of his birth, a nearer right to the throne, and of intending to assert this right with the help of the Romans. It is difficult to decide how far this suspicion was well founded; at any rate the Romans encouraged it by ostentatiously favouring Demetrius, and by pretending that for his sake they treated Macedonia more leniently. Besides the official favours which the senate conferred on Demetrius during his stay in Rome, several nobles received him into their special intimacy. It was principally Flamininus who, if we may trust Polybius,[2] encouraged Demetrius in his opposition, and who thus chiefly caused his tragic death.

Murder of Demetrius.

---

[1] Livy (xl. 4) describes in his masterly manner the tragic end of the wife and family of Poris, who preferred a voluntary death to the indignities and cruelties awaiting them.

[2] Polybius, xxiv. 3, 5; Πρὸς μέντοι γε τὴν καθόλου τῆς οἰκίας (sc. τοῦ Φιλίππου) ἀτυχίαν οὐ μικρὰ συνέβη τὴν εἰς τὴν Ῥώμην τοῦ νεανίσκου πρεσβείαν συμβάλλεσθαι· Ἥ τε γὰρ σύγκλητος ἀπερεισαμένη τὴν χάριν ἐπὶ τὸν Δημήτριον ἐμετεώρισε μὲν τὸ μειράκιον, ἐλύπησε δὲ καὶ τὸν Περσέα καὶ τὸν Φίλιππον ἰσχυρῶς τῷ δοκεῖν μὴ δι᾽ αὐτοὺς ἀλλὰ διὰ Δημήτριον τυγχάνειν τῆς παρὰ Ῥωμαίων φιλανθρωπίας. Ὁ δὲ Τίτος (i.e., Flamininus) ἐκκαλεσάμενος τὸ μειράκιον καὶ προβιβάσας εἰς λόγους ἀπορρήτους οὐκ ὀλίγα συνεβάλετο πρὸς τὴν αὐτὴν ὑπόθεσιν· τόν τε γὰρ νεανίσκον ἐψυχαγώγησεν, ὡς αὐτίκα μάλα συγκατασκευασάντων αὐτῷ Ῥωμαίων τὴν βασιλείαν, κ.τ.λ. This highly instructive passage gives a clear insight into the iniquitous practices of the Roman statesmen, especially of Flamininus, who is so much extolled for his generous and uninterested policy. But, as we have seen above, he was always actuated by the material interests of Rome, and next to these,

BOOK V.
171–168 B.C.

As soon as it became known that the Romans openly preferred Demetrius, a Roman party was formed, or at least strengthened, in Macedonia, and the opposition between the two princes of the royal house spread over the whole country. The national party inclined more and more to Perseus, who had been inspired by his father with hatred of the Romans just as Hannibal had been by Hamilcar Barkas. In the eyes of Philip, he seemed alone qualified to maintain the independence of Macedonia, and, if it should become necessary, to defend it by a war with Rome. The result of these conflicts was that Philip also began to suspect Demetrius, and that in the end he sacrificed his son to his politics.[1] A forged letter, supposed to have been written by Flamininus to Philip, and referring to the alleged plans of Demetrius, is said to have brought about the crisis. The prince was poisoned at a banquet by order of his own father, and, to avoid public attention, and especially to take from the deed the appearance of hostility to Rome, it was done half secretly in a retired spot (182 B.C.).[2] Thus Roman policy played a fatal part, not only in the relations of State to State, and in the disputes of political factions, but even in the family circle, and sought out its victims with a stern resolve at the hospitable hearth where a befriended stranger was sacrificed, and in the paternal home where it ensnared an inexperienced youth. It is no proof of the boasted generosity of the Romans in their political dealings that such a leading man as Flamininus, the 'friend of the Greeks,' should have been the agent whose footsteps we can trace by the body of the aged Hannibal, and by that of the youthful Demetrius. At any

by motives of vanity. The time in which he stood forth as the great statesman and general, the time of the war with Macedonia, of the battle of Cynoscephalæ, of the peace with Philip, and the liberation of Greece, was now past. He had no longer a public office; but he looked upon the management of the Græco-Macedonian affairs as his own special department, and assumed public authority though he was in a private station, and had really no more to say than any other Roman senator. Compare p. 175.

[1] Livy, xl. 5 15 and 20–24. [2] Livy, xl. 24.

rate, a dark shadow is cast upon the Roman politicians, although the responsibility for the disgraceful deed must be borne by the perpetrators themselves. It is chiefly King Philip of Macedonia who was guilty of the crime, and at the same time he is the man who contributed more than any one of his contemporaries to the downfall of Macedonia. Not his incapacity, but his evil passions were the cause that the last chance of the regeneration of Greece came to nothing. Now all his schemes collapsed: all the innumerable murders and crimes which he had committed, without remorse, had only borne this bitter fruit—that he saw himself openly confronted by external war and internal division, and that in his despair he was tempted to dip his hands in the blood of his own son. With a broken heart and a darkened spirit he sank into his grave three years later, leaving to his son Perseus a task hopeless even for a man of far greater powers.

Yet Perseus was a prince endowed with no mean qualifications for his difficult position. He was tall, strong, and dignified in his personal appearance, and free from those coarse vices which had caused the ruin of his father. He restrained his passions and was moderate in the enjoyment of life and in the exercise of his royal power.[1] Having grown up to manhood in a period of gloom and danger, he had gone through a school of bitter experience, and had been fully impressed with the military and political supremacy of the Romans. He could hardly hope to free himself completely from the unequal alliance which bound him to Rome, still less to regain for Macedonia its old ascendency. Nevertheless he did not intend to act the part of a humble dependent, and to fawn upon the Roman senate like a Masinissa or a Eumenes. He felt that only by her own independent strength could Macedonia resist the encroachments of Rome; and he was, therefore, like his

---

[1] Polybius, xxvi. 5. The charge brought against him, that he murdered his wife with his own hand, and other similar charges, which Livy (xlii. 5, 4) mentions as rumours (*fama est*) cannot be looked upon as satisfactorily established.

father, intent on increasing her national wealth and on renewing the ties which bound her to the kindred States of Greece. He proclaimed an amnesty for all political offences committed during his father's reign, remitted the debts of those who had fled on account of insolvency, and endeavoured to obtain favour with the Greeks, especially with the Achaeans, who, under the influence of the Roman party, had broken off all intercourse with Macedonia. By his marriage with Laodice, daughter of King Seleucus IV., the son and successor of Antiochus, and by the union of his sister with Prusias, king of Bithynia, he tried to gain friends, if not allies, with whose help he might, to a certain extent, keep in check his most troublesome neighbour, Eumenes of Pergamum. Nor did he shrink from boldness in action. He reduced the insurgent Dolopians by force of arms in a very short time, and then, before returning home through Thessaly, he went at the head of an imposing army to Delphi on the pretext of consulting the oracle, but in truth to show the Greeks that Macedonia was still an independent and a powerful State.[1] With the help of his friend Kotys, king of the Odrysians, he conquered the Thracian chief Abrupolis, who, relying on the patronage of the Romans, had ventured to extend his invasions and devastations as far as Amphipolis. According to their usual policy, the Romans had kept up a friendship with this so-called ally in the immediate vicinity of the rival State in order to have, at any time, a pretext for settling disputes among the neighbours. They watched with a jealous eye every step of the young king, in order, if occasion offered, to overwhelm him with complaints which might furnish the cause for a "just and pious" war. Thus they took umbrage, and regarded it as an intentional act of hostility towards Italy, when the Bastarnians, a people on the northern bank of the Danube, attacked the Thracian Dardanians on the borders of Macedonia. They charged

[1] Livy, xl. 22.

Perseus with having been in league with the Bastarnians, and having intended, like his father, to persuade them to invade Italy when the Dardanians should be conquered.[1]

Such pretended fears were clearly and confessedly imaginary. Yet the Romans were justified in treating the matter as serious, since, in the public opinion of Greece, a complete revolution had gradually taken place, and Perseus was becoming more popular from day to day; while, on the other hand, Eumenes, the friend of Rome and the Romans themselves, were regarded more and more as the enemies of the country.[2] The frivolous Greeks had been completely sobered down since, twenty years before, after the defeat of Philip, they had hailed the Roman 'liberators' with unbounded enthusiasm. They cast wistful looks towards that same Macedonia from which they had then been liberated, and they hoped to regain, with the help of Perseus, their national independence, which had now, indeed, become an empty name. According to their custom, they showed their impatience by a childish and useless defiance of Rome and the friends of Rome. Eumenes especially incurred their displeasure. At the time of the prevailing enthusiasm for Rome and her allies innumerable monuments and altars had been erected to him, and festivals instituted in his honour. It was on these that the universal hatred now vented itself. Everywhere the former resolutions were repealed, the monuments destroyed, the festivals abolished. In vain had Eumenes attempted, in a somewhat clumsy manner, to form a party for himself among the Achaeans. His offer to hand over to them a large sum of money in order to pay from the interest the chief magistrates of the league had been scornfully rejected, although the Roman party at that time preponderated in the Peloponnesus, and had succeeded in preventing a friendly understanding with Perseus. For the Greek States had become so dis-

[1] Livy, xli. 19.
[2] Livy, xlii. 5 and 14; Appian, *Maced.* 9, Tauchnitz; 11, Bekker.

198 ROMAN HISTORY.

BOOK V.
171–168 B.C.

ordered and helpless, and wavered so much between the proud feeling of nationality and comtemptible fear, that whilst they showed the pride of outraged honour and insulted the allies of Rome, they remained nevertheless in piteous subjection to Rome herself, while the cankerworm of political dissolution was eating into their vitals.

Frightful condition of Greece.

The condition of various parts of Greece at this time was perfectly frightful. The accumulation of private debts gave rise to constant civil wars,[1] for it had long been the custom to expect a remedy for social disorders from political revolutions, and especially from a spoliation of the wealthier classes, just as in our own days those who call themselves the working classes endeavour, by the war against capital, to bring about general well-being. The primeval habit of the Greeks of living by robbery rather than by labour had cropped up again through the ruins of national wealth. The Ætolians, it is said, had always shown a disposition for this kind of life; but as long as they could levy contributions on their neighbours, they could pass for belligerents, and enjoyed a certain amount of respectability; now, however, they were restrained within their own boundaries, and, as they could not make up their minds to get their living by agriculture, they had no choice but to attack and prey upon each other.[2] Even among the frequent horrors of party strife in Greece, the bloody massacre of Hypata is noticeable for its hideousness.[3] Eighty exiles from this town had been induced to return by the promise of pardon and reconciliation. They were solemnly received and conducted into the town; but they had no sooner entered the gates than they were treacherously attacked and murdered. Such a deed as this was, of course, followed by a counter-blow from the opposite party, and thus the nation drifted helplessly to

---

[1] Livy, xlii. 5.

[2] Polybius, xxx. 14, 1: Οἱ Αἰτωλοὶ τὸν βίον ἀπὸ λῃστείας καὶ τῆς τοιαύτης παρανομίας εἰώθεισαν ἔχειν· Καὶ ἕως μὲν ἐξῆν τοὺς Ἕλληνας φέρειν καὶ λεηλατεῖν, ἐκ τούτων ἐπορίζοντο τοὺς βίους πᾶσαν γῆν ἡγούμενοι πολεμίαν.

[3] Livy, xli. 25.

destruction; for similar disorders prevailed everywhere throughout the unhappy country.

Under these circumstances it was no less an historical necessity than a boon for the Greek nation that Rome considered the time come to put an end to the untenable state of partial independence in which it was then placed. Several events occurred which showed that Rome was preparing to act very soon. King Eumenes of Pergamum had undertaken to bring formal charges against Perseus, and to call upon the Romans to interfere. In the year 172 B.C. he made his appearance in Rome,[1] bringing with him a detailed list of all the violations of peace of which he accused Perseus. In this list all the public acts of Perseus, without exception, were enumerated, and interpreted as preparations for a war with Rome. All that Perseus had done or left undone in order to increase the national wealth and power of his country, to chastise the insurgent Dolopians, to repel the invasions of the Thracians from his own borders or from friendly cities like Byzantium, all his endeavours to make himself popular in Greece, even his moral conduct, his moderation and self-control, were represented as schemes against the suzerainty of Rome.[2] There was, indeed, no real breach of peace or violation of contract that Eumenes could prove against Perseus. The transgressions which he named in no way affected the Romans, who were already aware of them, and who, far from censuring Perseus, had even approved them by remaining on friendly terms with Perseus, and by renewing the treaties. It appears, therefore, that in their negotiations, which were carried on with strict secrecy, Eumenes and the senate occupied themselves, not so much with seeking a motive or a pretext for a war with Perseus, as

CHAP. III.

171–168 B.C.

Eumenes in Rome as accuser of Perseus.

---

[1] Livy, xlii. 6, 3: Eumenes rex commentarium ferens secum, quod de apparatibus belli omnia inquirens fecerat, Romam venit. Compare also Livy, xlii. 11–13; Appian, *Macedon.* 9, Tauchnitz; 11, Bekker.

[2] Appian, *Macedon.* l c.: ἔγκλημα δ' ἐποίει καὶ τὴν ἐπιμέλειαν αὐτοῦ καὶ τὸ νηφάλιον τῆς διαίτης ὄντος οὕτω νέου. Appian concludes by saying: ζήλου δὲ καὶ φθόνου καὶ δέους μᾶλλον ἢ ἐγκλημάτων οὐδὲν ὁ Εὐμένης ἀπολιπὼν ἐκέλευσε τὴν σύγκλητον ὑφορᾶσθαι νέον ἐχθρὸν εὐδοκιμοῦντα καὶ γειτονεύοντα.

with planning the measures which in case of a war they should respectively adopt. At any rate, the war was now decided upon, and nothing but the consideration that the time was inopportune kept the senate from declaring it at once. Harpalus, the Macedonian ambassador, who had in vain asked for permission to defend his master in the presence of Eumenes, was perfectly convinced of this, and summoned courage to say that, if Rome was resolved upon war, it was useless for him to refute unfounded accusations, and that in this case his master would boldly wield the sword forced into his hand, trusting to the god of war and to the uncertain issue of battles. Some few members of the senate, feeling the undignified position of Rome, accused Eumenes of conjuring up a great war from fear and jealousy;[1] but they remained in the minority, and the answer which was given to Harpalus compelled him to tell his master that the rupture with Rome was inevitable. The ambassadors of Rhodes, who were at that time in Rome to complain of Eumenes, and were therefore looked upon as friends of Perseus, received an ungracious reply. Apart from this the Rhodians were in ill favour with the Romans, because they had with great ostentation lent their fleet to escort the bride of Perseus from Syria to Macedonia. The period of friendship was over for them, as well as for Achaia and Macedonia. They had soon to feel that Rome would not suffer even so harmless a state as Rhodes to exist beside her in complete independence, or even in commercial prosperity.

Alleged attempt to murder Eumenes.

Eumenes gained his object in Rome. The war with Macedonia was decided upon.[2] Loaded with honours and marks of favour, he quitted Rome to return to his own kingdom.[3] On his way through the Corinthian gulf he landed in Cirrha, in order to go from that port to Delphi, to offer a sacrifice at the shrine of Apollo. On the road to this place an attempt, so it was said, was

---

[1] Appian, *Macedon.* l. c.
[2] Livy, xlii. 19, 3; bello etsi non indicto, tamen iam decreto.
[3] Diodorus, xxx. p. 129, Tauchnitz; xxix. 31, Dindorf.

made to murder him. At a spot where an old wall lined the road, four assassins, who, being hired by Perseus, were watching for the King of Pergamum, threw stones at him, and hit him so dangerously that he fell down and was nearly killed. While the king's companions were busied in attending to him, the miscreants escaped. Eumenes, badly wounded, was conveyed back to Cirrha, and thence to Ægina, where he remained until he recovered.

How much truth there may be in this strange tale, it is difficult for us to determine, as we have only one-sided reports from Roman sources. But, even without any evidence from the party of the accused, we cannot help suspecting that the whole affair was a prearranged farce, planned for the purpose of finding some plausible complaint of an odious character against Perseus. It is by no means likely that, if Perseus had really wished to get rid of his enemy, he would have caused him to be attacked by four men with stones, even supposing that he were so silly as to think that the death of Eumenes would make the slightest difference in the state of his affairs. With fair assurance we may put down the charge of intended murder as an invention, resembling the charges of the wolf against the lamb. Of the same nature is the far more impudent charge against Perseus, which was founded upon the information of Rammius, a native of Brundusium. This man reported that Perseus had offered him bribes to poison the Roman ambassadors on their passage through Brundusium.[1] It is not easy to determine whether the Roman senate really thought Perseus capable of such silliness, or whether they only pretended to do so. To the unprejudiced inquirer accusations of this kind are a proof that real and well-founded grievances were wanting, and that the Roman government, having decided upon war, was obliged to have recourse to the most frivolous pretexts.[2]

---

[1] Livy, xlii. 17. According to another statement it was the intention of Perseus to poison the whole senate.

[2] An illustration from recent events is perhaps not out of place. When the French government in 1870 was prepared for war with Germany, a pretext was

Book V.

171–168 B.C.

Dispute between the senate and the consul Popillius Lænas.

War being determined upon after the visit of Eumenes to Rome, it remained to fix the time for commencing hostilities, and to take the preliminary steps. But it was not thought necessary to be in any hurry in the matter. The Romans had no need to apprehend a sudden attack on the part of the King of Macedonia, even if they credited him with the bold resolution of undertaking an aggressive war. It was inconvenient to begin the war in the year 172 B.C., because this year was almost completely taken up with a dispute between the senate and the consuls, which, to a certain extent, paralysed the foreign policy of the republic.

Marcus Popillius Lænas, one of the consuls of 173 B.C., had attacked the Statellates, a friendly tribe of Ligurians, without orders, cause, or justification; he had slain several thousands of them, had destroyed their town, and sold the remainder of the tribe into slavery.[1] This wanton act, which was as cruel as it was injudicious, was strongly disapproved by the senate. A resolution was passed that the consul Popillius should redeem from slavery the Ligurians whom he had sold, that he should restore their property and their arms, and not leave the province till this order should be executed.[2] In this resolution the senate had exceeded its powers, for the administrative authority which it practically exercised was in strict law unconstitutional. The senate was only entitled to advise and not to command, and it exercised the functions of government only

---

found in the Hohenzollern candidature for the Spanish throne. When this candidature was formally withdrawn, the story was invented that a gratuitous insult had been offered by the Prussian government to the French nation.

[1] Livy, xlii. 7.

[2] How necessary it was for the senate to interfere in this case, and to repress the tendency of the Roman magistrates to violent and arbitrary measures, is shown by the fact that a few years earlier (in 187 B.C.) a similar outrage had been committed. The prætor, Marcus Furius, had without any justification fallen upon the Cenomanians in the midst of peace, and had disarmed them. Upon the complaints of the Cenomanians the senate commissioned the consul Marcus Æmilius Lepidus to inquire into and decide the case, disregarding the loud protests of the prætor. The consul ordered the prætor to restore their arms to the Cenomanians and to leave the province. Livy, xxxix. 3.

in so far as the magistrates voluntarily submitted to its authority, or were inclined to moderation by the prospect of having to answer for their acts after their year of office. The senate had no means of enforcing the submission of a consul except by the appointment of a dictator,[1] and this could not be done unless the other consul was ready to lend his aid. If this means failed, the senate might call upon a tribune of the people, who by virtue of his inviolability could resist the execution of any magisterial order.[2] But it was very doubtful whether the tribune's inviolability, or any tribunicial order, was entitled to respect beyond the limits of the city, as the military imperium of the consul was unrestrained in the field. M. Popillius knew the extent of his power, and not only refused to carry into execution the decision of the senate, but actually went to Rome in person, assembled the senate in the temple of Bellona outside the town, and censured the senators in an angry and violent tone, because, instead of honouring a victorious general by solemn thanksgivings, they had in a certain manner accused and dishonoured him before the enemies of the republic. He imposed a fine on the prætor Aulus Atilius, who had moved the resolution of the senate, and demanded that the resolution should be rescinded, and that thanks should be offered to the gods for his exploits. But in spite of the defiant attitude of the consul, the senate was immovable, and as neither yielded, the quarrel remained unsettled. The consuls for the following year (172 B.C.) were Publius Ælius Ligur and Caius Popillius Lænas, the brother of Marcus. Owing to this relationship, the dispute of the preceding year was carried on with almost equal violence in that which followed. C. Popillius gave the senate to understand that he would oppose any resolution condemnatory of his brother's proceedings similar to that which had been passed in the

---

[1] Livy, xxx. 24, 1-3.
[2] Such a case had occurred in the course of the Hannibalic war (vol. ii., p. 428), but the action of the tribunes had not become necessary on that occasion.

previous year. The senate refused to yield, and when the question arose whether the command in the impending war with Perseus should be given to one of the consuls, a resolution was passed that both consuls should be sent to Liguria, and that nothing should be decided about Macedonia until the resolution of the preceding year should be executed.

From this postponement of the Macedonian war, which resulted exclusively from internal conflicts, we see that the war did not in the least depend upon the designs and preparations of Perseus, and that it is unjust to cast the responsibility of it on him. The Roman senate, in the feeling of utter security from an attack on the part of Perseus, could even venture to prevent the consuls raising new legions, or bringing the old legions to their full complement. The consuls in their turn refused to co-operate in any measure of internal administration.[1] The Roman republic, on the eve of a great war, was suddenly paralysed. Its condition may be compared to that of a constitutional state of our own time, in which the supplies for a war already determined upon are suddenly refused by the representatives of the people. To make matters worse, the senate was now informed by the obstinate M. Popillius that upon his return to his province he had defeated the Statellates a second time, killing sixteen thousand of them, and that thereupon the other Ligurian tribes had taken up arms. Two of the tribunes of the people now placed themselves at the disposal of the senate. They threatened to impose a fine upon the consuls unless they forthwith started for Liguria, to take the command from M. Popillius, who could not be punished until he should be divested of the imperium. They moreover brought a motion before the people for the nomination of a special judge by the senate, to punish the ex-consul if, before a fixed date, he should not have restored the enslaved Statellates to liberty. This measure at last suc-

---

[1] Livy, xlii. 10.

ceeded. The consuls started for their province. M. Popillius gave up his command, but did not venture to make his appearance in Rome until, by a new motion of the tribunes, a term was fixed after the expiration of which the trial should take place in his absence. Now at last he submitted; but, probably through the influence of his family and his friends, his trial was suspended till the praetor C. Licinius, who was to conduct it, had quitted office. The accusation was finally dropped;[1] but the enslaved Ligurians were set free again, and land was assigned to them on the north side of the Padus. Measures were moreover taken to pacify the warlike mountaineers, and to prevent the outbreak of new hostilities.[2]

In the year 172 B.C. the incident just stated did not allow of a vigorous foreign policy. If the political instinct and moderation of the Romans had not generally prevailed over the obstinacy and perversity of individual statesmen, the republic would long have been distracted by such internal conflicts between the senate and the ill-organised executive. But we may see in the history of Rome, as elsewhere, that the spirit of a nation can accomplish great things, in spite of an imperfect constitution, whereas the best-drawn form of government not animated by such a spirit is only a source of misery.

The clemency, or rather the justice, which caused the senate to condemn the insane cruelty of M. Popillius in Liguria was, no doubt, prompted, at least in part, by the political calculation that, with the prospect of a serious war in the east of the Adriatic, it would be desirable to preserve peace in the Italian peninsula. The same considerations determined the Roman policy when (172 B.C.) the Carthaginians sent ambassadors to complain of the encroachments of Masinissa. It did not appear advisable just at this time, when every ally acquired additional value, and every new quarrel was to be avoided, to exasperate the Carthaginians, who, though weakened and deeply

[1] Livy, xl. 22, 8: Rogatio de Liguribus arte fallaci elusa est.
[2] Livy, xlii. 22 and 26.

humbled, were still a power not to be despised. Masinissa was therefore advised to restrain his greed, and keep within the boundaries marked out to him. Rome was not only counting upon neutrality, but upon the active aid of both Carthage and Numidia, in the impending war.[1]

The beginning of the war was now fixed for the year 171 B.C. Some preparations had been made for it in the course of the year 172 B.C. A fleet of fifty vessels had been collected at Brundusium, and an army of about eighteen thousand men kept in readiness at that place.[2] At the same time Roman diplomacy had been at work. It was of the greatest importance to isolate Perseus as much as possible, and this task was rendered difficult by the great popularity which he enjoyed in Greece. But when the gravity of their situation became apparent to the Greeks, they lost courage and submitted to the hateful necessity. The same submission was shown also by the larger Asiatic states. At least they kept aloof from all connexion with Perseus, who could boast only of one true and valuable ally, the Thracian chief Kotys, whilst Gentius, the king of Illyria, could not make up his mind to encounter the hostility of Rome till after the war had begun.[3] The situation of Macedonia was far less favourable now than it was at the beginning of the second war. At that time a considerable part of Greece was subject to king Philip directly or indirectly. The chief fortresses of the country were in his hands, and he had friends and allies in Bœotia, Locris, and even in the Peloponnesus. The Romans, on the other side, had at that time hardly any allies in Greece, except the Ætolians and Athamanians. The Achaean league was neutral. Above all, Macedonia had not yet been conquered, and the spell of the Macedonian phalanx was yet unbroken. Since then the Roman legions had over-

---

[1] Livy, xlii. 23, 24.   [2] Livy, xlii. 27.
[3] Livy, xlii. 29, 30. It is reported of Kotys (Polybius, xxvii. 8) that he was distinguished by his personal appearance and his warlike virtues, and moreover, that he was anything but a Thracian in character (κατὰ τὴν ψυχὴν πάντα μᾶλλον ἢ Θρᾷξ), being moderate in his pleasures, gentle in disposition, and of a liberal mind.

thrown this phalanx in Europe and Asia, had confined the king of Syria within the Taurus chain, had shut up Macedonia within its old boundaries, had crushed the brave Ætolians, and had reduced the whole of Greece to actual dependence in everything but form and name. How could Perseus hope to stop the triumphal progress of the Roman armies? Surely he must have been not deluded but mad, if he had voluntarily engaged in a conflict with a power so formidable.[1]

The consular elections of the year 171 B.C. were fixed for an earlier period than usual, that no time might be lost for the projected campaign. The consuls of the year, Publius Licinius Crassus and Caius Cassius Longinus, entered upon their office with more than the customary solemnities and celebrations of sacrifices and lectisternia. The haruspices announced happy omens and prophesied victory, triumph, and the extension of the Roman dominion.[2] To the 'highest and best Jupiter' games to last ten days had already been promised, if the republic should remain unshaken for ten years.[3] Now at length the time had come for the senate to ask the people for the formal vote sanctioning the undertaking of the war. This vote was given by the centuries without the slightest delay or hesitation, and nobody seems to have anticipated the possibility of a refusal. The senate controlled the foreign policy so completely that, so long as the nobility were agreed among themselves, no such opposition on the part of the people as that which had shown itself at the beginning of the second Macedonian war was possible.[4] The almost uninterrupted wars in Spain, Corsica, Liguria, and Gallia

---

[1] The narrative of the Roman historians is from the beginning distorted by their wish to represent the war as a just and good war. They did not hesitate for this purpose to suggest false motives, and to invent false statements. A striking instance of this is the narrative (Livy, xlii. 25) of the alleged negotiations between Perseus and the Roman ambassadors. Compare Nissen, *Forschungen über die Quellen des Livius*, p. 126.

[2] Livy, xlii. 30.

[3] Livy, xlii. 28, 8: si res publica decem annos in eodem statu fuisset.

[4] See p. 18.

naturally had the effect of causing war to be looked upon with much indifference. It was impossible for the people to judge whether it was prudent or necessary to commence hostilities with one or another of the tribes dwelling on the Iberus or in the valleys of the Apennines. They had to leave the decision to the senate, and the senate frequently had to leave it to the generals. It was due only to the great importance which the Macedonian kingdom still occupied in the imagination of the Romans, that the present war was solemnly introduced with religious ceremonies and the strict observance of constitutional forms. For this reason also a formal cause had to be assigned for the war. As such, it was alleged that Perseus had made war upon the allies of Rome, and was preparing for a war with Rome herself.[1]

As soon as this resolution was passed, preparations were vigorously made. Veteran volunteers were selected in preference to new conscripts.[2] Military service in the East, the home of Græco-Asiatic civilisation, was much preferred to fighting with the poor and rude inhabitants of Northern Italy, Spain, and Corsica, where the Roman soldiers had to expect privations, difficulties, and dangers without end, but could hope for little booty. The same preference for Oriental warfare was shared in a still higher degree by the generals. Each of the consuls aspired to the command, and their dispute was settled only by the decision of the senate that they should draw lots. Thus the command was obtained by Publius Licinius Crassus, an avaricious, domineering man, unfit for so important a post. Five years before (in 176 B.C.), when he was prætor, he had been ordered out to Spain, which for very good reasons was an unpopular province at that time. He had on that occasion pleaded that he could not leave Rome on account

---

[1] Livy, xlii. 30, 10: Quod sociis populi Romani arma intulisset, agros vastasset urbesque occupasset, quodque belli parandi adversus populum Romanum concilia inisset, arma, milites, classem eius rei causa comparasset.

[2] On the exceptional election of the legionary tribunes by the generals instead of the usual election by the comitia. See vol. i. p. 445.

of some religious duties which absolutely required his services, and on taking a solemn oath in the public assembly that he had stated the truth, he was excused.[1] On no account would he now give up the chance of commanding in Macedonia. For, like every Roman, he reckoned upon an easy and rapid victory as the inevitable result, and he hoped to win valuable spoils. So thorough indeed were the preparations that failure seemed to be impossible. Of the eighteen thousand men who had been despatched to Macedonia, some had already landed in Apollonia, others yet lingered in Brundusium. Apart from these forces, two newly levied legions of veterans and a corresponding number of allies were destined for the campaign, besides two thousand Ligurians, and a reinforcement of Cretan archers and Numidian cavalry and elephants, altogether an army of more than fifty thousand men. In addition to these must be reckoned the crews of the fleet, and the expected auxiliaries of the Greek and Asiatic allies, especially the Achaeans and Pergamenians.

Such a force as this must have appeared to Perseus quite overwhelming. In spite of all his efforts he had not succeeded in collecting more than thirty thousand foot and five thousand horse;[2] and a great part of this force consisted of mercenaries who were not to be depended upon.

---

[1] Livy, xli. 15, 9. It was natural that in 171 B.C. his colleague Cassius should point to this precedent, and argue that if Crassus could not leave Rome on account of religious duties five years before, he could not do so now. (Livy, xlii. 32, 1). 'Cassius sine sorte se Macedoniam optaturum dicebat, nec posse collegam salvo iure iurando secum sortiri: praetorem enim cum, ne in provinciam iret, in contione iurasse, se stato loco statisque diebus sacrificia habere quae absente se recte fieri non possent; quae non magis consule, quam praetore absente recte fieri posse.' However, his objection was overruled by the senate.

[2] Livy, xlii. 12. Perhaps even these numbers are exaggerated. For they are taken from the charges brought against Perseus by Eumenes, when he did everything to urge the Romans to a war with Macedonia (above, p. 199). The more formidable he represented the military strength of Perseus, the more effect he hoped to produce. Moreover, it is not customary for the war chroniclers of any nation to understate the strength of hostile armies and to overstate their own. It may, therefore, be doubted whether the army of Perseus was really as strong as stated by Livy. There is, on the other hand, nothing to induce us to believe that the numbers given for the Roman forces are exaggerated. Nissen (*Untersuchungen*. p. 248) is of different opinion.

BOOK V.
171-168 B.C.

He could hope for no help from Greece, for the sympathy felt for him in many places by the national and democratic party was counteracted by the pressure brought upon his friends by Rome, or neutralised by the machinations of local magistrates, who favoured the Roman interests. He, therefore, still clung to the hope that by yielding and by humbling himself he might preserve peace. He actually sent one more embassy to Rome,[1] when war had already been formally resolved upon by the people, and when the Roman force was partly in process of formation, and partly on the march to Macedonia. He offered to comply with the demands of the senate, and to redress all the grievances of which any Roman allies might complain, provided only the Romans would withdraw their troops. Instead of a reply the Romans commanded the ambassadors to leave Italy within eleven days, and to announce to their master that the consul Licinius would soon be in Macedonia at the head of an army. If Perseus was ready to give satisfaction, he should apply to him.

Perseus isolated and outwitted.

In spite of this arrogant language, which seemed inspired by the consciousness of superior power, the Romans were by no means so far advanced in their preparations as at once to begin the war on a large scale. Only a few thousand men were actually in Greece;[2] the great bulk of the army was not yet fully organized or hardly on its march to Brundusium. A few agents had arrived in Greece for the purpose of securing the co-operation of the Greek states in the impending struggle.[3] Their object was everywhere to strengthen the Roman partisans, to place them in power, and to obtain auxiliaries from them. This was no difficult task. The Achaean league had long been under the direction of the Roman party, at the head of which was Callicrates. They immediately placed at the disposal of the Romans one thousand men, with which force, before

---

[1] Livy, xlii. 36. The exact time when the popular vote was taken in Rome which sanctioned the war (Livy, xlii. 30, 10) cannot be ascertained satisfactorily. It is possible that Perseus had no knowledge of it when he sent this embassy.   [2] Livy, xlii. 36, 8.   [3] Livy, xlii. 37, 38.

the Roman troops could arrive, Chalcis was occupied and secured. The Epirots, although secretly inclined to favour Macedonia, submitted to the Romans, and sent four hundred men as an auxiliary force. In Ætolia, Lyciscus, a zealous adherent of Rome, was appointed commander of the troops of the league. Acarnania and Thessaly also joined Rome. Whilst Roman diplomacy, in anticipation of the Roman arms, was thus isolating Perseus, this prince was induced, by a masterstroke of cunning, to remain inactive, although he was fully armed and prepared to commence hostilities, and the Romans had not yet appeared on the scene of action.[1] Seeing the storm approach, in fear and trembling, and still hoping, in his unaccountable delusion, to be able to arrest it, Perseus had written to the Roman ambassadors before their departure from Corcyra, and had asked them to state to him their reasons for occupying Greek towns with Roman troops.[2] This letter had remained unanswered. When, a short time after, Quintus Marcius Philippus, one of the Roman ambassadors, came to northern Thessaly, Perseus sent to him to inquire whether he would not consent to negotiations. Nothing could have been more welcome to Marcius, as he desired to gain time on some pretext or other. Availing himself, therefore, of the friendly relations between his family and the royal house of Macedonia, he came forward in the guise of a kind and ready mediator, listened to the excuses of Perseus with feigned interest, and advised him to make another attempt in Rome for the peaceable settlement of the dispute, although he knew quite well that there was not the least chance of success.[3] Perseus was caught in

[1] Livy, xlii. 43, 3: Nihil enim satis paratum ad bellum in præsentia habebant Romani, non exercitum, non ducem, cum Perseus, ni spes vana pacis occœcasset consilia, omnia præparata atque instructa haberet et suo maxime tempore atque alieno hostibus incipere bellum posset.

[2] The Roman annalists were ashamed of these perfidious transactions, and tried by a disingenuous and false narrative to save the national honour. See Nissen, *Untersuchungen über die Quellen des Livius*, p. 101.

[3] Livy, xlii. 38-43. On this occasion Livy makes Marcius repeat the charges brought against Perseus by the Roman people. It is not worth while to examine them in detail, as, in truth, they were only pretexts for the war,

BOOK V.
171-168 B.C.

the snare; he agreed to conclude a truce, and he sent one more embassy to Rome. In Rome, it is true, the perfidious cunning of which Marcius boasted, as if he had achieved a great success, met with some disapproval in the senate[1] on the part of men who considered it contrary to Roman dignity and honour, but the majority approved the proceeding, and, according an audience to the Macedonian ambassadors only for the sake of form, ordered them to leave Italy immediately. The same order was extended to all Macedonians residing in Italy, and all therefore were expelled from the territory of the republic with their families within thirty days.[2]

Armistice concluded.

During this time the Romans continued the movement of their troops, while their envoys in Greece, in the islands, and in Asia, actively promoted the scheme of a combined attack upon Perseus, though the latter, honourably observing the conditions of the truce, had not availed himself of his present superiority to obtain any military advantage.[3] The Bœotians, irresolute and wavering between the two parties, were urged to an unconditional union with Rome,

and not the real cause. In so far, moreover, as they were based on the alleged violation of the treaty of peace concluded with king Philip, we are not in a position to examine them, as the conditions of that peace are not known with sufficient accuracy (see p. 66, note). Perseus on this occasion did not admit that the peace had been violated by him, and he pointed out the fact that the Romans had made no complaints and raised no protests at the time when he did those acts which they now called a breach of the treaty of peace. He showed that by continuing their friendly relations to him they had indirectly approved of his proceedings, and that the good understanding between them had remained uninterrupted, until Eumenes for his own interest had been active to bring about a rupture.

[1] Livy, xlii. 47, 1: Marcius et Atilius Romam cum venissent, legationem in Capitolio ita renunciarunt, ut nulla re magis gloriarentur quam decepto per indutias et spem pacis rege; adeo enim apparatibus belli fuisse instructum, ipsis nulla parata re, ut omnia opportuna loca præoccupari ante ab eo potuerint, quam exercitus in Græciam traiceretur; spatio autem indutiarum sumpto secum venturum illum nihilo paratiorem, Romanos omnibus instructiores rebus coepturos bellum.

[2] Appian, Maced. ix. 5; Polybius, xxvii. 7. Livy (xlii. 48) is not honest enough to mention the expulsion of the Macedonian subjects from Italy. No doubt he was ashamed of a measure of such mean and paltry hostility, a measure which the French were not ashamed to repeat as late as 1870.

[3] Polybius, xxvii. 5; Livy, xlii. 46, 10.

and all but the two insignificant places of Haliartus and Coronea were induced to join. The chiefs of the opposite faction were expelled; Achaean troops were raised to garrison Chalcis; Larissa was occupied, and the important republic of Rhodes, which was strongly suspected of inclining to Perseus, was prevailed upon to arm a fleet of forty ships to be placed at the disposal of Rome.[1]

The Romans did not think it necessary to issue a formal declaration of war, such as had been hitherto usual. It seemed much simpler to assume that Rome was attacked, and compelled to defend herself. The consul, Licinius Crassus, left Rome with the usual pomp, after a solemn sacrifice, to join the army in Brundusium, whence he crossed with it to Apollonia in order to commence the campaign.

After what has been related, it seems hardly necessary to add that the war with Perseus was, in the full sense of the word, an iniquitous war of aggression.[2] All that the Romans alleged of the warlike intentions and preparations of Perseus is either distorted truth or deliberate falsehood. The more carefully we trace in detail the dishonourable course of Roman policy, the more we are filled with indignation and disgust. It is true we discover nothing of novelty in their present proceedings. We only recognise in more distinct outlines the motives which had actuated the policy of Rome from the very beginning. Throughout the confused and vague traditions which rather conceal than exhibit the wars with the Latins, Etruscans, and Samnites, we can trace the same greed and the same grasping ambition, joined with the same contempt of justice and equity.

---

[1] Polybius, xxvii. 3; Livy, xlii. 45.

[2] This will become more evident in the sequel. As Livy himself admits, Perseus was at any time ready to make peace, and for three years this peaceful disposition was not forced upon him by military reverses, for the advantage was, on the whole, on his side. Compare Livy, xliv. 25: Eumenes cernebat et Persea iam inde ab initio belli omni modo spem pacis tentasse et in dies magis . . . . nihil nequo agere aliud nequo cogitare. Polybius, xxix. 1, d: Θεωρῶν γὰρ Εὐμένης δυσπαθοῦντα καὶ συγκλειόμενον τὸν Περσέα πανταχόθεν καὶ πᾶν τι ἐπιδεχόμενον χάριν τοῦ τὸν πόλεμον ἀπολύσασθαι καὶ διαπεμπόμενον ὑπὲρ τούτων πρὸς τοὺς στρατηγοὺς καθ' ἕκαστον ἔτος.

BOOK V.
171–168 B.C.

It is absurd to talk of ancient Roman moderation and honesty. The men of the old time, as far as we can judge, differed from their successors only as being ruder and more violent. It is of great importance in the history of Rome to recognise the unity of the Roman character, which has remained unchanged from the oldest periods downwards, and, such as it appears in the legends of prehistoric ages, passed over from the republic to the empire, and from imperial Rome to the despotism of the popes over the minds of men. It is not wonderful that the Roman character should have remained unchanged for centuries; for the character of a nation is almost as durable and unalterable as the climate and the nature of the country which a nation inhabits; but in the fact that the single town of Rome stamped upon the entire population of Italy her own hard type, that even after the admixture of Latins, Sabellians, Etruscans, and Greeks, that which was specifically Roman alone retained predominance over the rest, we have a proof of vigour and tenacity which helps much to show us how Rome achieved the sovereignty over the whole world.

Weakness of Macedonia and Perseus.

While the race of Roman statesmen and warriors in the second century before our era retained the doctrines, traditions, and qualities of the men who fought in the Samnite wars, and now, in the consciousness of exuberant vigour, advanced from conquest to conquest with reckless vehemence and greed, the kingdom of Philip and Alexander, on the other hand, had lost the spirit which had raised it from a state of semi-barbarism, and made the Macedonian chief lord of all Greece and of a great portion of Asia. The ancient race of Macedonian heroes was extinct. The decrepid nation could not boast a single man comparable even to the inferior captains of Alexander's armies. The Macedonian phalanx was no longer what it had been. It had lost the belief in its own invincibility since it had ingloriously broken down on the fields of Cynoscephalæ and Magnesia. Perseus himself, though a brave and experienced soldier, had in him no vestige of a warlike spirit, neither boldness of invention nor self-confidence. From the very beginning he gave himself up for lost, and did not venture, even after some unexpected success, to follow up the road to victory. With a faint heart he drew the sword, not daring to throw away the scabbard. Even in the last moment, when the Romans were already approaching, the question was debated in his council of war, whether unconditional submission or a desperate resistance was to be preferred, and only when no other course was left open to him did Perseus determine to make that choice which was demanded no less by his honour than by necessity.

The army which, after untiring efforts, he had at last collected was such as no Macedonian king had ever led into the field since the great Alexander had set out for the conquest of Asia. It numbered forty-three thousand men, among whom were twenty-one thousand heavy-armed soldiers, forming the phalanx, and four thousand excellent horsemen; the rest were light-armed troops, some of them Thracians, the others mercenaries from all the Greek states, especially Crete, the home of warlike adventurers. His supply of arms, provisions, and money was amply sufficient for several years. He had been collecting and amassing these appliances in the hope of never being compelled to make use of them. When the pressure came, he could not make up his mind to take boldly the offensive, but awaited the attack. Perhaps he was frightened by the recollection of his father's defeat at Cynoscephalae, or he thought he would have a better chance if he drew the enemy into his own country. If he had invaded Greece as soon as his preparations were made, he would have gained a considerable start over his opponents. He could have obtained possession of many fortified towns, and probably have secured some which were still wavering between the two belligerents. But he allowed the consul, Licinius Crassus, to march unmolested through the difficult mountain region of Epirus and Athamania to Gomphi, in western Thessaly, and thence to Larissa, which, as we have seen, had been occupied by the Romans during the armistice.¹ At the same time, the Roman fleet of forty ships and ten thousand naval troops, commanded by Marcus Lucretius, appeared at Chalcis, and was joined there by five thousand Pergamenians under Eumenes, fifteen hundred Achaeans, besides Ætolians, Thessalians, and other Greek allies. If we suppose, therefore, that the consul, Licinius, had left a part of his troops on his line of march, the Roman force was still much greater than that which Perseus could oppose to it.²

Pass of Tempe fortified by Perseus.

The road from Thessaly to Macedonia passes through the narrow gorge of Tempe, where the river Peneus has made for itself a deep bed between the overhanging rocks of Olympus and the woody slopes of Mount Ossa.³ The chain of the Cambunian mountains, extending westward from Olympus, forms a natural boundary between the two countries, which can only be crossed by difficult mountain roads. Thus it happened that the pass of Tempe was, from time immemorial, the only practicable road from north to south, just as further southwards was the pass of Thermopylæ. Perseus, being on the defensive, was obliged to hold this pass. He therefore marched into Thessaly, across the mountains to the west of Olympus, and took by surprise several small places, among which was Gonnos, at the southern extremity of the vale of Tempe. He now fortified the pass by a triple wall and ditch, and took up his position in the neighbourhood at Sycurium, on the slope of Mount Ossa, to await the Roman army.

---

¹ Livy, xlii. 55. Above p. 213.

² Nothing is more difficult than to ascertain the exact number of troops engaged in any military operation; for the falsification of figures is the easiest of all lies, and requires no imaginative power. Besides, even where there is no intention to deceive others, self-deception in counting or estimating numbers is too frequent not to be pardonable. In cases, therefore, where we have no contemporary reports before us, it would be unwise to speak of the strength of contending armies with any degree of assurance.

³ See Bursian, *Geographie Griechenlands*, i. p. 58.

The consul, having been joined in Thessaly by Eumenes and the auxiliary troops from Greece, lay encamped near Larissa, to the east of the river Peneus. His inactivity encouraged the enemy. The Macedonians plundered the surrounding country with impunity, and approached nearer and nearer to the Roman camp. At length Perseus ventured to take the offensive. It was his intention to draw the Romans out of their camp, and to defeat them in the plain with his superior cavalry. After some unimportant skirmishes, the Macedonian horsemen and light-armed troops came so near to the Roman camp, that the consul could no longer avoid marching out to meet them. The battle was fought at the foot of the hill Callicinus, east of the Peneus, between Larissa and Lycurion, immediately outside the Roman camp.[1] The Roman cavalry forming the right wing was attacked with great vehemence by the Thracians, and beaten back with great loss. In like manner the left wing was repulsed, consisting of the cavalry of the Greek allies. Only the four hundred Thessalian horsemen, who had been kept in reserve on the extreme left, stood their ground, and covered the retreat of the defeated army. Fortunately, the fortified camp was near to receive the fugitives; and this is probably the reason why the Macedonian phalanx, which now appeared on the scene of action, did not take part in the battle. It was little suited, on account of its unwieldiness, to storm a Roman camp. Perseus therefore forbade the continuance of the contest. He was satisfied with having inflicted on the Romans a loss of from two to three thousand men killed or taken prisoners, and with having, by this first success, produced a favourable impression upon his own army, and more especially upon the Greek states. He even ventured to hope that the Romans would already despair of success, and be ready to end the war. So little did he know the Romans, or so thoroughly had his love of peace blinded him, that immediately after

[1] Livy, xlii. 58 ff.

the victory he proposed to the consul to settle the dispute by the renewal of the old treaties.[1] He declared himself ready to confirm the alliance which his father Philip had concluded with Rome, and he was even prepared to pay a war indemnity, such as had been imposed upon Philip, if only the Romans would conclude peace. But the consul, who had acknowledged his defeat by crossing in the same night to the left bank of the Peneus, replied with truly Roman firmness, that he would listen to proposals of peace only if Perseus submitted unconditionally. He gave the same reply when the pusillanimous victor offered to pay a larger tribute. Thus ended these premature negotiations, and the war was accordingly resumed.

Combat of Phalanna.

Licinius soon afterwards received a reinforcement of two thousand Numidians and twenty-two elephants, under Misagenes, a son of Masinissa. Both armies marched about in unhappy Thessaly, apparently without a fixed plan, engaged principally in collecting the ripe corn for their own support. At Phalanna they met once more, and here again fortune was unpropitious to the Romans. They lost six hundred prisoners and one thousand waggons laden with corn. A body of eight hundred men, who had retired upon a hill, were in great danger of being cut to pieces, but were at length rescued from their precarious position by the advance of the legions.[2]

Perseus, continuing his defensive operations, soon afterwards crossed the mountains into Macedonia before the summer was past, apparently apprehending no further attack on the part of the Romans. The consul Licinius made another attempt to take the fortified town of Gonnos, and thus to open the pass of Tempe. Failing in this, he continued his plundering expeditions in several parts of

---

[1] Polybius, xxvii. 8; Livy, xlii. 62.

[2] It appears that the deliverance of this corps from their imminent danger was worked up by some Roman annalists into a great feat of arms, and sufficed to stamp the battle of Phalanna as a decisive victory over the Macedonians (Livy, xlii. 66, 9). Livy himself has sense enough not to credit these statements, which spoke of eight thousand enemies killed and two thousand eight hundred prisoners, besides a great number of military trophies.

Thessaly without achieving either glory or military success, and finally took up his winter quarters in Thessaly and Bœotia.

Whilst the main armies were confronting each other in Thessaly, and were in vain attempting to bring matters to a decisive issue, the war was raging most fearfully in Bœotia. The towns of Haliartus and Coronea had, as we have seen,[1] remained true to their alliance with Macedonia, when the other Bœotian towns had, after more or less reluctance, submitted to the demands of Rome. It was now resolved to punish Haliartus for its presumption. Before the arrival of the Roman fleet at Chalcis, the Roman legate Publius Lentulus besieged Haliartus with a troop of Bœotians favourable to Rome.[2] We can easily imagine how eager the contending factions were to attack and mutilate one another under the protectorate of their foreign allies, and that the zeal of the victors was stimulated by the prospect of material gain. But the Romans were not inclined to concede to their allies the profit which resulted from the plundering of a conquered town.[3] When, therefore, Marcus Lucretius had arrived at Chalcis, he ordered the over-hasty Lentulus to retire from Haliartus; in other words, to leave the spoil untouched. He then marched to the town with ten thousand men from the fleet, and two thousand Pergamenians, and was met there by his brother Caius Lucretius, who, in the capacity of prætor, commanded the fleet. A number of ships sent by faithful allies from Carthage, Heraclea, Chalcedon, Samos, and Rhodes, were graciously dismissed because 'their services were not required.' The vultures, gathered around the carcase, were scared away in order that the eagles alone might gorge upon it. Haliartus was now surrounded by the Roman forces, and was taken, after a brave resistance. The entire population was either slain

---

[1] See p. 213.
[2] Livy. xlii. 56.
[3] Nothing shows more clearly in what light military booty appeared to the Greeks than the word ὠφέλεια, with which they designated it.

or sold into slavery, the town plundered and razed to the ground.

The treatment of Haliartus was harsh, yet, according to the laws of war then prevailing, it could not be condemned; for Haliartus had been taken by storm. But a similar justification did not apply in the case of Thebes, Coronea, and Chalcis. Thebes was handed over to the vengeance of the Roman party, who sold their enemies into slavery. Coronea, after surrendering, shared the same fate. Chalcis, however, an allied and friendly town, was treated unmercifully, as if it had committed some unpardonable offence. It was not only plundered by the savage naval troops who were quartered in the houses of the citizens, but the very temples were despoiled of their treasures of art, free citizens were ill-treated and sold as slaves, women and children were disgraced.[1] Everywhere the lowest passions were allowed to riot, and the vilest appetites were gratified without stint. With some of his plundered pictures the prætor Caius Lucretius, on his return home, adorned a temple of Æsculapius at Antium, and with the proceeds obtained by selling the rest he built an aqueduct at the same place, regardless of the complaints of some honourable tribunes, who accused him before the Roman people of cruelty and rapacity.[2] Such were the means by which the Roman nobles acquired princely wealth. Was it to be wondered at that the aristocracy sought for one war after another, and that republican simplicity became more and more a dream? Only forty years after the time which we have reached the Gracchi sought in vain to stem the current of corruption which swept on irresistibly.

In order to clear himself from the charge of incompetence, the consul Licinius was mean enough to attribute the loss of the combat of Callicinus to his Greek allies, and especially to the Ætolian cavalry.[3] Though of all human vices cowardice was the one from

[1] Livy, xliii. 7.   [2] Livy, xliii. 4.
[3] Livy, xlii. 60.

THE THIRD MACEDONIAN WAR.

which the Ætolians were farthest removed, the Romans did not hesitate to charge them with it. They felt, no doubt, some satisfaction in punishing them now for boasting so long and so persistently of having contributed most to the victory of Cynoscephalæ. At the same time, the reproach of cowardice and treachery served as a convenient instrument for removing from Ætolia all who were still opposed to Rome. Several eminent men, who were troublesome to the Roman partisan Lyciscus, were sent to Rome to clear themselves from the charge of having caused the bad conduct of the Ætolian cavalry.[1] This proceeding was as violent and arbitrary as it was impolitic, for the Macedonian victory had brought about a sudden change in the minds of the Greeks. The spirit of patriotism, which had been kept down only by the fear of Roman invincibility,[2] burst forth everywhere. The outrages, extortions, and robberies committed by the Roman officials and soldiers, heaped fuel upon these flames. In Epirus an open insurrection broke out, excited chiefly by the wretched Charops, who had been brought up in Rome, and now sought by means of Roman protection to obtain influence and power. By calumniating the leaders of the national party he succeeded in driving them into open revolt. Almost all the tribes of Epirus now rebelled, with the single exception of the Thesprotians. The country between Italy and Macedonia, which was of the greatest importance to the Romans for the conduct of their operations, they were now compelled to regard as hostile, and Ambracia had to be occupied by a garrison of two thousand men.[3]

Such were the results obtained in the first year of the war by the contemptible strategy of incompetent commanders, and by the cupidity and cruelty of all the Roman

---

[1] Polybius, xxvii. 13, xxviii. 4.
[2] Polybius, xxvii. 7, a, 1: τῆς κατὰ τὴν ἱππομαχίαν φήμης μετὰ τὴν νίκην τῶν Μακεδόνων εἰς τὴν Ἑλλάδα διαγγελθείσης ἐξέλαμψε καθαπερεὶ πῦρ ἡ τῶν πολλῶν πρὸς τὸν Περσέα διάθεσις, τὸν πρὸ τοῦ χρόνον ἐπικρυπτομένων τῶν πλείστων.   [3] Livy, xlii. 67, 9.

222   ROMAN HISTORY.

BOOK V.
171–168 B.C.

officers and soldiers.¹ Many Romans, indeed, enriched themselves; but the reputation of the republic was deeply shaken; and had the Greeks had a national leader such as fortune had so often given them in time of need, had Perseus possessed the warlike virtues even of his father or his great-uncle Antigonus, it is probable that the independence of Greece might have been prolonged, for the benefit even of the Romans, whom the vices of prosperity were already hurrying towards national ruin.

Campaign of 170 B.C.

The year 170 B.C. brought new, but not better, commanders for the Roman army and fleet. The consul Aulus Hostilius Mancinus, proved as incapable as his predecessor, and Lucius Hortensius, who succeeded to the command of the fleet, was perhaps a few shades more greedy and more violent than Lucretius, but not in the least more able as a soldier. The latter, before returning with his plunder to his villa near Antium, had allowed himself to be surprised at Oreos by the hostile fleet, and had lost four quinqueremes and a whole transport fleet with provisions.² To supply the troops with food was a very difficult task, as the exhausted land was unable to furnish what was wanted. It was therefore necessary in the wars with Philip, Antiochus, and the Ætolians, and now in the war with Perseus, to send out large quantities of corn from Sicily, Sardinia, and Africa.³ If such a convoy was delayed or destroyed the operations in the field could easily be paralysed, and it is therefore not unlikely that the inactivity of the army up to this time was owing to some stoppage in the supply of provisions.⁴ On the other hand,

---

¹ Zonaras, ix. 22: ἐν τῷ πρὸς Περσέα πολέμῳ (οἱ Ῥωμαῖοι) πολλὰ καὶ μεγάλα ἠτύχησαν καὶ πολλαχόθι ἐπόνησε τὰ αὐτῶν.

² Plutarch, Æmil. Paul. 9.

³ Corn from Africa, Livy, xliii. 6, 11. Even Athens was required to send supplies of corn. Livy, xliii. 6, 2.

⁴ The fruitless marches and countermarches of the Roman army in Thessaly seems to have been caused chiefly by the want of provisions. This is shown by Livy, xlii. 64, 2: Cum audisset Perseus Romanos circa ex agris demessum frumentum convehere, etc. Ibid. 7: Demessis circa segetibus Romani ad Crannona, intactum agrum, castra movent. Ibid. chap. 65, 2: Ibi cum ex transfuga cognosset rex sine ullo armato præsidio passim vagantes per agros

the soldiers were compelled, by the scantiness of supplies, to get what they wanted wherever they could find it, and thus many an act of cruelty may be explained or excused.[1] Hortensius, probably for the purpose of replenishing his stores, which were reduced by the fault of his predecessor, sailed along the coast to levy contributions from the different maritime cities, and among others from Abdera in Thrace, from which he demanded one hundred thousand denarii and fifty thousand modii of wheat. The Abderites, instead of sending forthwith what had been demanded, asked for a short delay, during which they sent to the consul, and even to Rome, to ask for some reduction. Before an answer came back, Hortensius caused the town to be occupied, the chief men to be executed, and the remainder to be sold as slaves.[2] Perhaps by such a process he succeeded in obtaining the necessary supplies from other towns, which would rather be plundered than utterly destroyed. But some towns, like Emathia, Amphipolis, Maronea, and Ænus, were courageous enough, and strong enough, to shut their gates, and to resist the outrageous rapacity of the Romans.[3]

About the operations of the consul Hostilius Mancinus during the year 170 B.C. hardly anything is known. It appears that he made two fruitless attempts to penetrate into Macedonia, but that, repulsed by Perseus, he spent the remainder of the year in Thessaly without venturing on any further enterprise, occupied only with establishing in the army a certain degree of order and discipline.[4] Perseus had nothing more to apprehend on this side, and

Romanos metere, etc. Appian, *Maced.* 11 : τὸ δὲ λοιπὸν τοῦ θέρους ἀμφότεροι περὶ σιτολογίαν ἐγίγνοντο. See p. 141, note 2.

[1] Indirectly it was the fault of the senate if the troops behaved ill. For whenever they did not receive their pay and clothing in proper time they were tempted or compelled to help themselves. Livy, xliv. 20, 6.
[2] Livy, xliii. 4.
[3] Livy, xliii. 7.
[4] Plutarch, *Æmil. Paul.* 9. Livy, xliv. 1, 5 : Castra eo tempore A. Hostilius in Thessalia circa Palaepharsalum habebat, sicut nulla re bellica memorabili gesta, ita ad cunctam militarem disciplinam ab effusa licentia formato milite.

BOOK V.
171–168 B.C.
Gentius of Scodra.

was for some time engaged in Thrace and Illyria.¹ The Romans also seemed to have been induced by the revolt of the Epirots to devote their attention chiefly to Illyria. Gentius, king of Scodra, the successor of Pleuratus, who had long been on good terms with Rome, was the friend and ally of the Roman people. This friendship had its drawbacks. It prevented Gentius from enjoying full freedom of action, and restrained him in his practice of piracy, without which the Illyrians fancied that they could not exist. Hence arose complaints and disputes,² and there seemed to be good foundation for the news which the Issæans (the Greek colonists on the island of Issa) carried to Rome in the year 172 B.C., that Gentius was in secret correspondence with Perseus.³ Yet Gentius did not dare to oppose Rome openly, and could for the time still be counted as a Roman ally. When, therefore, in the beginning of the war, Lucius Decimius had been sent to him to ask for his aid against Macedonia,⁴ he placed at the disposal of the Romans a fleet of fifty-four Illyrian galleys.⁵

A Roman army of about twenty thousand men, commanded by Cneus Licinius, was destined for Illyria,⁶ and a part of it marched through Dassaretia towards the Macedonian frontier. From thence they expected to be able to penetrate into Macedonia with less difficulty than by way of the strongly defended Thessalian passes. The same road had been attempted in the war with Philip; but the difficulties of supplying the armies with provisions were so great that the consul Sulpicius Galba found himself compelled to retire to the coast.⁷ An enterprising general might, nevertheless, think that the mistakes of the first expedition could be avoided. Accordingly, the consul Caius Cassius, the colleague of Licinius, formed an adventurous plan, founded upon the calculation that Macedonia could

---

¹ Plutarch, Æmil. Paul. 9: ὡς δὴ τοὺς Ῥωμαίους ὑπερορᾶν καὶ σχολάζων.
² Livy, xl. 42.   ³ Livy, xlii. 26.
⁴ Livy, xlii. 37.   ⁵ Livy, xlii. 48, 8.
⁶ Livy, xlii. 27. The five thousand three hundred men mentioned in chap. 36 were probably the advanced corps of this army.   ⁷ Above p. 32.

be invaded from the north-west. Disappointed in his hope of receiving the command in Macedonia, and having obtained by lot Cisalpine Gaul for his province, he, in total ignorance of the natural features of the country and of the distances, had formed the idea of gaining his object by marching round the Adriatic, and reaching Macedonia through Illyria. The fact that the designation 'Illyria' extended, very indefinitely, to the northern extremity of the Adriatic, may have caused him to fancy that when in the land of the Gauls, or in Istria, he would not be very far from the possessions of the Illyrian king Gentius. He had set out on this expedition without the authority or even the knowledge of the senate. It was by mere chance that the senate received the news of this wild undertaking, and in the greatest haste they sent messengers to Cassius to order him to return immediately.[1]

If it was the intention of the Romans to invade Macedonia by way of Illyria in the year 170 B.C., their efforts must either have been very feeble, or else they must have been hindered by the insurrection of the Epirots, or by the doubtful attitude of Gentius of Scodra. Anyhow, what they did undertake had no good result. Appius Claudius Cento, a legate who commanded an army of four thousand Romans and eight thousand Illyrians, attempted to take by surprise Uscana, a mountain fortress on the Macedonian frontier, but was repulsed, and lost on his retreat the greater part of his troops.[2] This news caused great dissatisfaction in Rome, and induced the senate to send a special commission to Greece to investigate the matter. By this means they ascertained what, it appears, the generals purposely kept secret,[3] namely, that matters were not proceeding favourably at all, that Perseus had successfully maintained his position during the summer, and had even reduced several towns, that the Roman allies had lost courage, and, above all, that the army of the consul was diminished

Appius Claudius in Illyria.

---

[1] Livy, xliii. 1.   [2] Livy, xliii. 9, 10.
[3] The news of the disaster at Uscana had reached Rome by chance through a soldier on furlough. Livy, xliii. 11.

VOL. III.   Q

by the absence of a large number of soldiers on leave without any justifiable cause.

It was probably about this time that the senate was assailed by embassies from the ill-used Greek towns, among which that of Chalcis especially produced a great impression. They saw that matters could no longer be carried on in this way, and that the insatiable greed, cruelty, and tyranny of the Roman magistrates not only disgraced the honour of the republic, but also endangered the success of the campaign. If the senate could not, by a formal resolution, bestow military ability on the leaders of the army, they could, at any rate, restrain the abuse of official power; or, at least, they could express their displeasure if they were not entitled to act as a superior administrative authority, and to issue direct orders. It was therefore resolved that in future no commander should levy contributions, or require any services to be rendered to him by the allies of the Roman people, without special authorisation from the senate.[1] The Greeks, who had been ill-treated, were promised redress; the commanders were requested to act with moderation. For the losses which had been suffered compensation was made, or at least promised. One of the guilty, the ex-prætor Caius Lucretius, was accused by two tribunes, and condemned by the popular assembly to pay a considerable fine.[2]

Thus, when the second year of the war had passed, the Romans had rather lost than gained ground. Not one Roman soldier had as yet entered Macedonia; but many had fallen, or had been taken prisoners. Some of the Greek allies were exasperated by ill-treatment, others had become estranged and discouraged, a few were in open rebellion. But the plainest proof of the unfavourable state of affairs was that the cautious, and even timid, Perseus advanced from the defensive to the offensive. Even during the summer of 170 B.C. he had held the wretched consul Hostilius Mancinus in such contempt that he left

---

[1] Polybius, xxviii. 14, 2.   [2] Livy, xliii. 7, 8.

him stationed in Thessaly, and marched northwards to attack the Thracians and Dardanians, who had probably been instigated by the Romans to invade Macedonia whilst the Macedonian army was engaged in the south of the kingdom. In conjunction with his brave ally, Kotys, king of the Odrysians, Perseus defeated the Thracians, and then turned westward, where, in the meantime, the Epirots had declared against Rome,[1] while Gentius of Scodra still remained neutral, in expectation of events. It appears that in the winter of 170–169 B.C. the Romans had taken possession of the town of Uscana in Illyria, from which Appius Claudius had been at first repulsed with great loss in the course of the year.[2] Perseus now forced the town to surrender, and took the Roman garrison of four thousand men prisoners; but he refrained, perhaps out of pity, perhaps out of policy,[3] from selling them into slavery, as the laws of warfare permitted. Then he marched about Illyria, regardless of the severity of the weather, conquering towns, and carrying away with him the Roman garrisons.

After such successes, Perseus commenced negotiations with Gentius, who now mustered courage to declare himself the enemy of Rome. Then he marched southwards into Ætolia, where he expected that a faction in Stratus, now the most important town of the Ætolians, was prepared to make common cause with him. With a part of his army he undertook a most difficult march over snow-covered mountains and swollen rivers, to within a short distance of Stratus, hoping that the town would be betrayed into his hands. But he discovered that a detachment of Romans, warned by the opposite party, had come

---

[1] See p. 221.

[2] See p. 225. We are not informed how the Romans obtained possession of Uscana. It is necessary to suppose that they did take it, as otherwise there would be a contradiction between Livy, xliii. 10, and chap. 18. It is not likely that the two narratives are only two versions of the same fact, as Nissen suggests (*Untersuchungen*, p. 60).

[3] The latter is more probable, as Perseus sold those who were not Romans. Livy, xliii. 19, 1 and 6.

in haste from Ambracia, and had anticipated him in occupying the town. This spirited expedition therefore failed. Ætolia was too well garrisoned by the enemy for Perseus to remain there;[1] he was forced to return into his own kingdom, after an expedition on the whole successful and creditable to him.

The Roman commanders, Appius Claudius and Lucius Cœlius, tried in vain, after his departure, to regain the lost towns. They marched to and fro, without a definite plan, in the wild mountain regions; but the only result was that they lost a great number of men in killed and prisoners. After the complete failure of his military operations, Appius Claudius dismissed his Greek auxiliaries to their respective homes, sent his Italian soldiers into winter quarters in the neighbourhood of Dyrrhachium, and returned himself to Rome, in order, as Livy reports, to perform some sacrifice.[2] Thus ended the Roman campaign of the year 170 B.C. in Illyria, not only without the slightest military advantage, but even with confessed losses, incurred in a manner at once deplorable and dishonourable to the Roman arms.

Q. Marcius Philippus.

The chief command in the East for the year 169 B.C., the third year of the war, was allotted to the consul Quintus Marcius Philippus, the same who, two years previously as ambassador, had outwitted Perseus, and persuaded him to remain inactive.[3] If he had on that occasion proved a keen and crafty diplomatist, he had, on the other hand, played hitherto but a sorry part as a general. During his first consulship, in the year 186 B.C., he had allowed himself to be surprised by the Ligurians in a narrow valley, and to be so completely beaten, that his army fled disgracefully, leaving behind several thousands dead, and many standards.[4] This defeat did not prevent his re-election to the consulship for the year 169 B.C.,

---

[1] Livy, xliii. 22, 10 : Hostium (*i.e.*, Romanorum) haud procul inde hiberna erant.
[2] Livy, xliii. 23, 6 : Ipse Romam sacrificii causa rediit.
[3] See p. 211.   [4] Livy, xxxix. 20.

and when he, with Cneus Servilius Cæpio, had obtained the votes of the centuries for the year 169, he also received by lot the command in Macedonia, although after the unsatisfactory result of two campaigns, the progress of the war was beginning to be regarded with a certain amount of impatience if not anxiety. The unexpected audacity of Perseus during the winter had given rise to the opinion that he would now continue the offensive, and penetrate into Thessaly.[1] The Romans, therefore, made extensive preparations,[2] and, besides sending supplementary troops to Macedonia, formed four legions of reserve. Even in the previous year the consul Hostilius Mancinus had endeavoured to limit the practice of giving leave of absence too liberally to the troops in the field.[3] The Greek allies, especially the Achaeans, offered to exert themselves to the utmost, and to muster an auxiliary force of five thousand men, while king Eumenes, and even Prusias of Bithynia, who had, until now, looked on inactively, sent ships for the reinforcement of the Roman fleet. Marcius was in a position to make a vigorous attack, and perhaps he hoped thus to anticipate the designs of Perseus. He conceived the bold design of crossing the mountains by an extremely difficult pass parallel with that of Tempe, and of penetrating into Macedonia along the coast with the co-operation of the Roman fleet.[4] The fact that this plan succeeded in the main, in spite of the evident incapacity both of Marcius Philippus and of Marcius Figulus, the commander of the fleet, who was absent at the decisive moment, is one of the many proofs that courage is, after all, the first and foremost virtue of a soldier.

Perseus, with his main force, was now at the south-

---

[1] Polybius, xxviii. 10, 1.   [2] Livy, xliii. 12.
[3] Livy, xliv. 1, 5. However, to judge from Livy, xliii. 11 and 14, the condition of the Roman army under Hostilius Mancinus seems not to have been at all satisfactory with respect to the abuses in question. Whatever improvement took place must have been delayed to the latter part of his administration, or it was very slight.   [4] Livy, xliv. 2, 2.

eastern extremity of Macedonia, between the pass of Tempe and the fortress of Dion, which lay ten miles further north, in a part where the mountains again run down eastward to the sea, and thus form another line of defence. The pass of Tempe was strongly occupied in four successive places, from Gonnos in the south as far as the narrowest part of the valley.[1] Besides this Perseus had taken the precaution of placing in two localities, where the mountains could be crossed, strong detachments under Hippias and Asclepiodotus. It was upon the possible negligence of these troops that Marcius founded his plan. After a difficult march an advanced guard of light-armed troops reached the heights, where Hippias and his men, feeling perfectly secure, were easily surprised. The main force followed, and had, it appears, to contend more with the difficult nature of the ground than with the enemy. The elephants, especially, caused great trouble. Circumstances had so changed, that the Romans, who had formerly encountered these animals in the armies of their enemies, were now the only nation that employed them in war. It almost seems as if a kind of superstition attached itself to them; for, according to all reports, they must more often have been the cause of inconvenience, and even of accidents, than of military success; and yet the Romans, after their victories over the Carthaginians, Macedonians, and Syrians, always tried to prevent their enemies from using elephants of war, and had themselves learnt to use them.[2] After unspeakable exertions, which Polybius describes as an eye-witness, Marcius reached the plain, which is bounded on the east by the sea, and on the west by the semicircular range of Olympus. He had avoided, by a flank march, the pass of Tempe; but it seemed as if he had got into a trap set on

---

[1] Livy, xliv. 6, 10: Hic locus suapte natura infestus per quatuor distantia loca praesidiis regiis fuit insessus: unum in primo aditu ad Gonnum erat, alterum in Condylo, castello inexpugnabili, tertium circa Lapathunta, quem Characa appellant, quartum viae ipsi, qua et media et augustissima vallis est, impositum, quam vel decem armatis tueri facile est. [2] See p. 66.

purpose, from which it was impossible to escape. A retreat by the same route by which he had come was out of the question, on account of the physical obstacles, and, if attempted, it might have been prevented by a handful of men. In the vale of Tempe the fourfold Macedonian posts were still stationed, while, in the pass of Dion, in front of him, was the Macedonian main force; to the east was the sea, but not a trace of the Roman fleet, which was to bring supplies and to co-operate, was visible. If Perseus had but possessed the military instinct of a mere barbarian, shown seventeen years before by the Ligurians in their war with Marcius, the Roman army would have been lost. But Perseus was so disconcerted by the audacity of Marcius, that he at once gave up everything for lost. He issued orders that the troops left behind should evacuate the pass of Tempe, and he even retreated from the strong position near Dion, removing, with the greatest haste, the most valuable treasures in the town, and taking even the inhabitants away with him. His fear was so great that he ordered his crown treasures at Pella to be thrown into the sea, and the naval establishments at Thessalonica to be set on fire.

Such abject cowardice cannot be reconciled with the previous conduct of Perseus, which, if not heroic, had at any rate not been contemptible, and we are inclined to believe that the facts were not precisely what our informants tell us. Perhaps Perseus doubted the fidelity of the troops who were charged with the defence of the passes. We know that there were traitors among the servants of the king, for Livy relates that one Onesimus, formerly one of his friends and councillors, went over to the Romans, and was rewarded by them for his services.[1] Hippias, however, who ought to have defended the pass by which the Romans passed, seems to have been guilty only of negligence and not of treason.[2] On the other

[1] Livy, xliv. 16.
[2] At least Perseus afterwards, though he blamed his conduct, did not treat him as a traitor. Polybius, xxviii. 9, a.

hand, we are almost inclined to doubt that the garrison in the pass of Tempe really retreated in compliance with the orders of Perseus; for in this case they would surely have destroyed the magazines of provisions, and not have allowed them to fall into the hands of the Romans; and the garrison of Heracleum, a small town, north of the pass, would have received the same orders to withdraw, whereas we are informed that it offered a stout resistance. Moreover, the retreat of the Macedonian troops northwards, through the narrow plain occupied by the Romans, would have been extremely difficult. We venture, therefore, to surmise that the despair of Perseus was not mere pusillanimity, but the result, at least in part, of treason, and that he did not voluntarily give up his position in the pass of Tempe.[1] But we cannot decide this point with any certainty, as all our reports are derived from Roman sources, and as unfortunately even Polybius, the most trustworthy witness, regarded Perseus with evident disfavour and partiality.[2]

---

[1] Perhaps the Onesimus mentioned in the text as a traitor was the man who commanded the troops in the pass and surrendered the position to the Romans. It is not likely that the Romans would have rewarded him, as they did, with a house and estate at Tarentum (Livy, xliv. 16, 4), if he had not rendered most valuable services. What these services were Livy does not relate, and his silence may be suspected as intentional.

[2] Livy. xliv. 2, 12, says that Perseus, after occupying the mountain passes, took up a position at Dium with the remainder of his troops, and then continued riding about with some light horsemen from one position to another, visiting Dium, Heracleum, and Phila in turns, i.e., the whole ground between the two passes. Livy blames this conduct, and calls it torpidity of mind and lack of resources. But it is difficult to see what Perseus could have done better than by repeated personal inspection to keep his soldiers to their duty, and to see that no precaution was omitted. Diodorus (xxx. 10, *Dindorf*) is still more in error than Livy if he is of opinion that the whole Roman army, after it had crossed the mountains, might have been frightened to surrender merely by a war-cry and the blast of trumpets (κραυγῆς γὰρ μόνον ἦν χρεία καὶ σάλπιγγος εἰς τὸ τὴν στρατιὰν τῶν πολεμίων λαβεῖν αἰχμάλωτον περικεκλεισμένην ἐν κρημνοῖς καὶ φάραγξι δυσεξιτήτοις). This is indeed sheer nonsense, and can hardly have been borrowed from Polybius without considerable modifications. But Polybius is, no doubt, the principal source from which the censure of Livy and Diodorus is derived. He was present in the army of Marcius and witnessed all that passed, and he was fond of laying down the law in military questions. How unjust he was to Perseus is clear from a short passage

The consul Marcius Philippus was at first far from congratulating himself on his successful march across the mountains. He saw with terror the danger of his situation, and only the retreat of the Macedonian troops assured him that his bold plan had succeeded. He now took up the position at Dium which had been abandoned by Perseus, and thence he penetrated further to the northward unmolested. But he was compelled to retreat by lack of provisions. He anxiously watched the sea, where he expected the Roman fleet to arrive. At length it came in sight and anchored; but the commander, Marcius Figulus, had left behind on the coast of Magnesia the ships laden with stores. The Romans would now have perished from hunger, even without any attack on the part of the enemy, had not the tidings happily arrived that the pass of Tempe was occupied by Spurius Lucretius. On receiving this news Marcius again marched back in that direction, in order to feed his soldiers with the provisions there captured in the Macedonian magazines.[1]

Meanwhile Perseus had recovered from his fright. His premature order to burn the naval establishments at Thessalonica had not been executed by his more prudent servant; the crown treasures which had been thrown into the sea he now caused to be fished up by divers.[2] In

---

(xxviii. 9, a), where he says that Perseus blamed Hippias for not having defended the pass, and adds that it is easier to blame others than to do what is right oneself. This is a very superficial remark, indeed a truism very surprising in a man like Polybius, and it is an indication of the personal spite he had for Perseus. Perhaps it was the ill-will between Perseus and the Achaean league that gave Polybius this dislike of Perseus; perhaps his subserviency to his Roman friends swayed his judgment. At any rate, Polybius was too much personally interested in the events which he relates to be quite unbiassed, and his portrait of Perseus has unfortunately remained the only one which has been preserved in history. We are therefore justified and bound to examine whether the admitted conduct of Perseus justifies the conclusions which his enemies have drawn from it.

[1] Livy, xliv. 7, 8.
[2] Here again a story is told which looks very much like a false and malicious libel. According to Livy (xliv. 10) and Appian (*Maced.* 14), Perseus felt ashamed of his pusillanimity, and, in order to suppress all knowledge of it, gave

BOOK V.
171–168 B.C.

order to regain what he had lost by his mistake in giving up his position at Dium, he followed the retreating consul and took up the same ground once more. He naturally found the place plundered and much damaged; but he restored the fortifications, and proceeded further south to the banks of the Elpeus.[1] This river, though almost dry in the summer, had a wide, irregular bed, with high banks, and might be used as a natural line of defence. Perseus erected a fortified camp on the northern bank of the river, and remained in it the rest of the summer; whilst Marcius contented himself with reducing the small fortress of Heracleum, north of the pass of Tempe, the only one which still held out, and sent a detachment to Thessaly, which made vain attempts to take the little town of Meliboea. Marcius seemed to have given up the plan of storming the Macedonian position at Dium, or of marching round it. The result of the third year of the war remained limited, therefore, to the taking of the pass of Tempe, which, it is true, as the gate of Macedonia, was of the greatest importance.

Operations of the fleet.

The Roman fleet accomplished far less than the army. On the whole, it is again clearly perceptible that naval operations were not carried on with the same spirit and on the same scale as in the first war with Carthage, and that even since the Syrian war they had become more and more feeble. At the time of his rupture with Rome, Perseus had no fleet at all. The Romans, therefore, had to apprehend no interference in their movements, and the fleet might easily and effectually have supported the endeavours of the army to penetrate into Macedonia. The mountain ranges protected Macedonia only from an

---

orders for the secret murder of Nicias and the divers who fetched up the treasures from the bottom of the sea, as also of Andronicus, to whom he owed the preservation of the naval arsenal. To ascribe to Perseus conduct so outrageous and so foolish we ought to have witnesses beyond all suspicion of partiality.

[1] Livy, xliv. 8, 5. The name of the river is not quite certain. It varies in the MSS., and is called Enipeus by Polybius, xxix. 3, 4. It is the river now called Vythos.

enemy advancing by land, and it was of no avail to defend mountain passes, if armies could be conveyed beyond them on board a fleet. But instead of acting in common with the army, the commanders of the fleet seem to have confined themselves to the far more lucrative task of plundering, and they refused the reinforcements which were offered them by their Greek allies, because for this purpose they did not need them.[1] We have already spoken of the infamous and systematic plundering of Lucretius and Hortensius. At length, in the third year of the war, it was decided that army and fleet should co-operate according to a fixed plan. But the prætor Marcius Figulus, who was to have supported his kinsman, the consul Marcius Philippus, in his invasion of Macedonia, was foolish enough to leave behind, on the coast of Magnesia, the ships laden with provisions, and appeared north of the pass of Tempe with his armed vessels alone.[2] This blunder forced the consul to retire, and to give up the strong position already occupied at Dium. It would even have placed the Roman army in the greatest danger of perishing from hunger, had not the surrender of the fortresses and stores in the pass of Tempe suddenly changed the aspect of affairs, and relieved the consul for the present.

The prætor now undertook an expedition to the coast of Macedonia for the purpose of plundering; but was repulsed at Thessalonica, Ænea, and Antigonea, and, being reinforced by Eumenes with twenty ships, and by Prusias with five Bithynian vessels, he laid regular siege to Cassandrea, a town built by Cassander on the site of ancient Potidea. This attack, undertaken with considerable vigour, failed, nevertheless, when Perseus succeeded in throwing into the town a reinforcement from Thessalonica. The siege had to be raised with great loss. After an equally fruitless attack upon Torone, Marcius and Eumenes sailed back to the Pagasæan gulf, where the

CHAP. III.

171–168 B.C.

---

[1] See p. 219.   [2] See p. 233.

BOOK V.
171-168 B.C.

Macedonians still had possession of the strong town of Demetrias. The Romans hoped to carry the place by assault; but they found the garrison prepared, and when Perseus succeeded in sending a reinforcement of two thousand men into the town, they were obliged to retire from the place without having accomplished their object.

The allies now parted. Eumenes returned to Asia, and the prætor sent his ships to winter at Sciathus and Eubœa. Thus the fleet had in this year accomplished not more than in the two previous campaigns. Not one of its plans had succeeded; everywhere it had been repulsed with loss; and the expedition could only have one result, namely, that of raising the courage and self-confidence of Perseus, and, on the other hand, of arousing among the allies of Rome a doubt of her invincibility, and a general discontent with the rapacious barbarians.

Attempt to form a coalition against Rome.

After three years of unsuccessful warfare the authority of Rome had indeed greatly suffered, and here and there, among the eastern states, the desire was awakened to make use of the opportunity for gaining a more independent position with respect to Rome. If Macedonia unaided was strong enough to carry on the war for three years, not only without loss but even with credit and varied success, it was surely possible that by a tolerably vigorous policy on the part of the eastern states the advance of the Roman power might be checked at last, and that a kind of balance of power might be established between the Greek and the Italian world. On the strength of this calculation Perseus founded his plan; but, in spite of all his successes and favourable prospects, he indulged no hopes of destroying or even of conquering the Roman power, an object in which even Hannibal had failed. He would have been satisfied if he could have put an end to the war, and placed his relations to Rome on a footing more favourable and dignified. He therefore commenced negotiations with the kings of Pergamum, Syria, and Bithynia,[1] and with

---

[1] Livy, xliv. 14, 5.

the Rhodians—negotiations which were to be kept strictly secret, for fear of the Roman power, until they should have been completed. Unhappily, by the preceding events, he had been so much estranged from Eumenes, that an agreement for the interests of both parties could hardly be made. Above all, there was wanting on the one side all confidence in the honesty of the other. Moreover, Eumenes, not satisfied with a reconciliation with Perseus, in which he was so much interested, tried to make it the occasion for a profitable bargain. He demanded from Perseus five hundred talents for simple neutrality, and fifteen thousand for his mediation in the conclusion of peace.[1] Perseus rejected the first offer, explaining that it was dishonourable to him, and far more so to Eumenes. For the mediation of peace, however, he was willing to pay the sum required, and proposed placing it in the great national sanctuary at Samothrace, until the results should be secured to him; meanwhile, both kings were to send hostages to Cnossus, in Crete, as a security for the execution of the treaty. Eumenes was not satisfied with this suggestion, because Samothrace lay within the dominions of Perseus, whom he believed capable of deceiving him, and of pocketing the price after having gained his object. So paltry was the distrust, and so mean the spirit of overreaching which marked the negotiations of two princes who ought to have made every effort and every sacrifice in order to oppose haughty Rome with combined forces. The apportionment of the degree of blame due to each is a matter with which we need not concern ourselves; but one thing is evident, that it is unjust to make Perseus alone responsible for the failure of the plan, and especially to name his avarice as the cause of it.[2] It is quite natural that Perseus should require security from Eumenes for carrying out his part of the engagement; nor could he be

CHAP. III.
171–168 B.C.

Negotiations of Perseus with Eumenes.

---

[1] Polybius, xxix. 1, 6 ff.; Livy, xliv. 25.
[2] Polybius, xxix. 1, c: τοῦ μὲν (Eumenes) πανουργοτάτου δοκοῦντος εἶναι, τοῦ δὲ (Perseus) φιλαργυροτάτου γελοίαν συνέβη γίνεσθαι τήνδε τὴν μάχην αὐτῶν.

BOOK V.
171–168 B.C.

expected to run the risk of losing unnecessarily the money which he so much needed for carrying on the war.[1]

The negotiations between Perseus and Eumenes are said to have been begun during the maritime expedition of the summer (169 B.C.), in which Eumenes took part with twenty ships, and which ended so ingloriously. They were continued in the following winter after the return of Eumenes to Asia, secretly, of course, and under cover of discussions for the exchange of prisoners. The Romans, it appears, conceived suspicions, but they had no evidence in hand, and it is probable that they purposely avoided forcing the king of Pergamum openly to join the enemy, especially as it was not unknown to them that some other states were inclined to desert them.

Continued neutrality of Syria.

The most powerful of these states was Syria. King Seleucus (187–176 B.C.) had conscientiously kept the peace concluded with Rome by his father, Antiochus; but his disputes with Egypt, occasioned by the possession of Cœle-Syria, might easily give rise to a new rupture with

---

[1] It is not difficult to see that the account of the negotiations between Perseus and Eumenes is not entirely to be trusted. Mommsen (*Röm. Gesch.* 1, 782) brings forward some weighty reasons to discredit them. It is clear that Eumenes would hardly, for the paltry consideration of a few hundred talents, have run the risk of losing the friendship of Rome, to which he owed so much. It was he who had chiefly fomented the war; and if such a plan as is ascribed to him succeeded, he would have lost all the advantages which he had expected from it. On the other hand, if the plan did not succeed, he was necessarily implicated in the ruin of Perseus. Moreover, he could not be sure that Perseus, who was his deadly enemy, did not carry on the negotiations merely for the purpose of showing him up to the Romans as a traitor. Nevertheless, it seems to be a stretch of scepticism to declare the whole story fictitious, a 'fable,' or a 'canard,' as Mommsen says. Nobody will venture to deny that Polybius was competent to form an opinion of the probability of the negotiations; and he had no doubt of their reality. He blames Perseus for hesitating to accept the terms proposed by Eumenes, whom he would have been able thus to get into his power. In fact it does not seem at all improbable that Eumenes wished to act as mediator between Perseus and Rome. The reasons alleged by Mommsen apply only to the plan imputed to Eumenes, of entertaining schemes directly hostile to Rome. They do not bear upon his plan of mediation. We are therefore inclined to think that there is a foundation of truth in the report. We do not think that otherwise Polybius would have spoken of the negotiations with so much seriousness, although of course not even he could have an accurate knowledge of them, for the very reason that they were secret.

Rome, which had always assumed the character of patron of Egypt. Perseus, hoping to profit by this coolness between Syria and Rome, sent a message to Antiochia, to call the attention of Antiochus Epiphanes, the successor of Seleucus, to the common interests which ought to unite the eastern states in resisting the aggressive policy of Rome.[1] But Antiochus was either too indolent to rouse himself to so decided a course of action, or else he hoped more easily to carry out his Egyptian policy, to which he attached greater importance, while the Romans were engaged in a war with Perseus, just as his father, Antiochus the Great, had done during the second Macedonian war. In short, he remained neutral, an act of weakness for which he was made to suffer only too soon.

The proposals of Perseus were more readily received by the small republic of Rhodes. The Rhodians, at the end of the Syrian war, had not met with that attention and those rewards to which they considered themselves entitled. Their interests had, in many respects, been sacrificed to those of the king of Pergamum. The aristocratic party in Rhodes, which was favourable to Rome, was thus discredited, and their opponents, the democrats, who upheld the national cause, gained ground. A feeling hostile to Rome sprang up, and was fostered by all that was left of the old Hellenic spirit of independence. Perseus became more and more popular in Rhodes. Upon his marriage with Laodice, the daughter of king Seleucus Philopator of Syria, they had escorted his bride to Macedonia with the whole of their fleet, and had by that act caused great displeasure in Rome.[2] Now, after the war with Macedonia had broken out, their commerce had suffered frequent interruptions. They justly feared that it would suffer more and more under the vexatious and illiberal mercantile policy of Rome. Yet they had been careful not to take a part

---

[1] Polybius, xxix. 3, 9: μὴ παρορᾶν τὸν καιρὸν μηδ' ὑπολαμβάνειν πρὸς αὐτὸν μόνον (i.e., Perseus) ἀνήκειν τὴν ὑπερηφάνειαν καὶ τὴν βαρύτητα τῶν Ῥωμαίων· σαφῶς δὲ γινώσκειν, ὡς ἐὰν μὴ καὶ νῦν αὐτὸς συνεπιλαμβάνηται, μάλιστα μὲν διαλύων τὸν πόλεμον, εἰ δὲ μή, βοηθῶν ταχέως, πεῖραν λήψεται τῆς αὐτῆς ἑαυτῷ τύχης. [2] See p. 200.

hostile to Rome, or even to give cause of suspicion, and at the beginning of the war they had placed a well-appointed fleet of forty ships at her disposal.¹ Nevertheless, the Romans did not trust the Rhodians. Eumenes, their neighbour and rival, had his spies among them, and took care that every unguarded word which might drop from a public orator in the market-place should at once be reported to the senate. Perhaps this was the reason why the Rhodian fleet was not called upon by the Romans to co-operate. It may have been mistrusted, perhaps also it was not absolutely wanted. The Rhodians, made uncomfortable by the apparent alienation of the Romans, resolved to send ambassadors in the spring of the year 169 B.C. to assure the senate of their fidelity. The embassy was graciously received, as far as appearances went, and obtained, among other marks of favour, the permission to export corn from Sicily.² At the same time Rhodian ambassadors were sent to Greece to the consul Marcius Philippus. The latter, who was fond of crooked ways, took aside one of the ambassadors, and succeeded in convincing him that Rome would welcome a mediation on the part of Rhodes for the purpose of restoring peace. Polybius does not venture to decide whether Marcius, discouraged by the slow progress of the war, was really inclined for an amicable arrangement, or whether he was endeavouring, with perfidious cunning, to entice the Rhodians to a step which he knew would cause the greatest exasperation in Rome.³ Yet Polybius is disposed to accept the latter alternative; and as he knew Marcius personally, and was at that time present with him in the camp, he surely was able to judge correctly.

Thus the Rhodians were misled, and the Roman consul himself contributed not a little to make the anti-Roman policy prevail in Rhodes; for his desire to put an end to the war by the mediation of the Rhodians was naturally looked upon as a proof of timidity and weakness. In the

¹ Livy, xlii. 45.   ² Polybius, xxviii. 14.   ³ Polybius, xxviii. 15.

conflict of factions which at Rhodes, as in every other Greek democracy, determined the policy of the state more by sentiment than by judgment, those men now predominated who had always been zealous for the cause of Hellenic independence, and in their enthusiasm they took no heed of the signs of the times. There were men all over Greece, whose thoughts were full of the heroic deeds of their forefathers, who were inspired with patriotism by the names of Marathon and Salamis, and who failed to see the vast gulf which separated those times from their own. If any Greek community could do so, the Rhodians had a right to think themselves worthy of their ancestors; and indeed against the Persians the Greek sword would still have proved as sharp as ever. But an enemy was now to be encountered of a different temper; and it would have been wiser, though perhaps less dignified, to take into account the altered circumstances than to be guided by patriotic feelings alone.

The treacherous overtures of the consul Marcius Philippus were followed in the course of the year 169 B.C. by reports of the warlike operations, which, especially so far as they regarded the fleet, were far from realising the expectations of the Romans, but which raised once more the wildest hopes of the patriotic party in Greece. Then, in the following winter, ambassadors came to Rhodes from Perseus, and from king Gentius. They brought the news of an alliance formed by the two kings, and invited the Rhodians to join. This seemed the right moment to the hot-headed leaders of the national party. On their advice it was now resolved to send embassies to Rome and Macedonia, to ask the belligerents to put an end to the war, and at the same time to declare that Rhodes would range itself against those who refused to make peace.[1] We shall soon see what lamentable consequences this rash step entailed upon Rhodes.

---

[1] Perhaps we are justified in raising the question whether the last clause in this declaration, at least the offensive tone in which it is worded, is not part of the unjust charges brought forward at a later period by the Romans against

Gallic mercenaries refused by Perseus.

While Perseus was hoping for the support of the Hellenic states in Asia, offers of immediate military assistance came to him from a very different quarter. A horde of twenty thousand Gauls, who had crossed the Danube, and were approaching the frontier of Macedonia, offered to serve as mercenaries. If Perseus had at that time been hard pressed, or in want of troops, he would probably have accepted the offer without hesitation; but his army was strong enough, and twenty thousand Gauls were a force hard to manage, should they take into their heads to mutiny under some pretext or other, as was by no means unusual with Gallic mercenaries. Perseus was willing to take into his pay five thousand of them. These he fancied he could employ and keep in order. But, as the chief of the Gauls would not agree to a division of his forces, the negotiations came to an end, and the Gauls marched back to their own country.[1]

Alliance of Gentius with Perseus.

Perseus thought that he could the more easily dispense with these untrustworthy hordes, because, about this time, the treaty with the Illyrian king, Gentius, had at length been concluded. Gentius had demanded three hundred talents as the price of his participation in the war with Rome, and had received a small amount in advance. Perseus promised to send the remainder, but he was in no hurry to do so, until Gentius should have openly declared war against Rome. When Gentius had done this by seizing two Roman ambassadors, Perseus felt convinced

Rhodes. At any rate, the charges remind us of those which were raised against the Tarentines in 320 B.C. (Livy, ix. 14), and which were without any foundation. See vol. i., p. 487.

[1] The reasons of Perseus for rejecting the services of the Gauls are stated by Livy (xliv. 26, 12): Institit de perfidia et feritate Gallorum disserere, multorum iam ante cladibus experta; periculosum esse tantam multitudinem in Macedoniam accipere, ne graviores eos socios habeant quam hostes Romanos; quinque milia equitum satis esse, quibus et uti ad bellum possent, et quorum multitudinem ipsi non timeant. It would appear that these reasons ought to be conclusive. Nevertheless, Perseus has been universally charged not only with shortsightedness, but simply with avarice. Livy calls him 'pecuniae quam regni melior custos.' We can see no ground for this malicious charge in the king's conduct on the present occasion.

that his aid was secured to him in any case. He therefore kept back the rest of the stipulated sum, as if, to use Livy's expression, he were intent upon keeping undiminished the spoil which the Romans would find after his defeat.[1] If this report be true, Perseus acted not only dishonourably but also unwisely, for, in withholding the reward from a man who only worked for the sake of it, he could not but expect to find in him an unwilling, and therefore a useless servant. It is, however, not impossible that this story, too, belongs to the list of slanders of which the Romans were so liberal towards their enemies.

The prospects of Perseus had never been brighter than during the winter of 169–168 B.C. Everywhere negotiations were being carried on satisfactorily, even where they had not yet, as in Illyria, arrived at the desired conclusion. The Roman army, and still more the fleet, were in a condition which obliged them to remain inactive. The consul Marcius Philippus, in his winter quarters, was intent chiefly upon providing for the efficiency of his army, by procuring corn, clothes, and horses.[2] The force in Illyria, commanded by Appius Claudius, was in a deplorable condition. After his abortive operations[3] in the year 170 B.C., he had been obliged to remain inactive. An attempt to summon to his aid five thousand Achaeans had failed, because the consul Marcius Philippus, probably out of jealousy and envy, had advised the Achaeans to pay no attention to the requests of Appius. It was indeed a delicate question which now presented itself to the Achaeans, for the wily Marcius had given them no written order, and matters had already come to such a pass, that no allied state ventured to refuse compliance with the demands of any Roman commander without trembling for its safety. But, on the other hand, Appius Claudius could show no senatorial authorisation for his request, and only a short time previously the senate had formally told the Greeks

---

[1] Livy, xliv. 27, 12: Velut nihil aliud agens, quam ut quanta maxima posset praeda ex se victo Romanis reservaretur.
[2] Livy, xliv. 16.   [3] See p. 225.

to attend to no demands of any general issued without a written order from the senate.[1] The five thousand men had therefore not been sent, and Appius Claudius found himself in so wretched a state that if he did not now receive other reinforcements he would be obliged to evacuate the country with the rest of his troops.[2]

The fleet was in a worse plight still. The crews had dwindled away, partly by disastrous battles, partly by disease, partly by desertion, while those who remained were suffering from insufficiency of clothing, and complaining of arrears of pay.[3] While the Roman fleet was thus paralysed, the small Macedonian galleys issuing from Thessalonica made the whole sea unsafe, attacked the transports intended for the army, and interrupted the communication. A total change had taken place. In the beginning of the war Perseus had had no ships, and the Romans, feeling their superiority, had declined the assistance offered them by their allies. Now the new fleet of the Macedonians commanded the sea, and the Roman vessels lay useless on the shore.[4] No wonder if the Greeks, especially the Rhodians, began to lose faith in the Romans, and to believe that in the end the Macedonian arms would prevail. However, if they really thought so, they had a very mistaken notion of the Roman power. The ill success which the Roman arms had hitherto met with, was due only to the incapacity of the generals and to the false economy of the senate. A happy choice at the next consular election, and the earnest desire on the part of the government to furnish the necessary means, sufficed to make good the mistakes hitherto committed, and to bear down all resistance. The senate and the people had at length roused themselves, and resolved to complete the work which they had begun.

The consuls of the year 168 B.C. were Caius Licinius Crassus and Lucius Æmilius Paullus, the son of the consul of the same name, who had been killed at Cannæ.[5] The

---

[1] See p. 226.   [2] Livy, xliv. 20, 5.   [3] Livy, xliv. 20, 6.
[4] Livy, xliv. 28; Appian, *Maced.* 16, 2, extr. Tauchnitz; 18, Bekker.
[5] Vol. ii., p. 237.

command in Macedonia was conferred upon the latter in the usual way by casting lots.¹ Æmilius had acquired some reputation as a general. When proconsul in Spain (190 B.C.), he had suffered a considerable reverse, and, after losing six thousand men, had been repulsed by the Lusitanians. But in the following year he had redeemed his loss by defeating the Lusitanians in a great battle. After his first consulship, in the year 182 B.C., he had as proconsul compelled the Ligurians to renounce their habits of piracy, and had been rewarded by a triumph for his military exploits. But he had not succeeded in being reelected until, in the third year of the war with Perseus, the poor results attained by the previous commanders caused public attention to be directed towards him as a more able soldier. His honesty perhaps was still more in his favour; for it was known that he had not enriched himself in his public offices, as was then the custom with most men. He was, however, anything but a democrat, and was closely connected with the ruling families. His eldest son had passed by adoption into the family of the Fabii, and his second son, who afterwards destroyed Carthage and Numantia, was adopted under the name of Scipio Æmilianus by a son of the victor of Zama. After having divorced his first wife, a lady of the ancient and noble family of the Papirii, Æmilius Paullus married a second time, and had four children, two daughters and two sons, who were still very young when their father, a sexagenarian, but hale and strong, entered upon his second consulship (168 B.C.). Love of his children seems to have been a prominent feature in the character of this man, of

¹ This is the statement of Livy, xliv. 17, 7: Designatos extemplo sortiri placuit provincias, ut cum, utri Macedonia consuli cuique praetori classis evenisset, sciretur, iam inde cogitarent pararentque, quae bello usui forent . . . . . 10, consulum Æmilio Macedonia, Licinio Italia evenit. According to Plutarch (*Æmilius Paul.* 10), it was not by casting lots, but by a resolution of the people, that Æmilius Paullus obtained the command in Macedonia. This statement is evidently derived from some family panegyric. There is no reason to doubt Livy's accuracy. Plutarch's account is, moreover, at variance with the usual practice. For whenever a province was not awarded by casting lots, it was the senate and not the people that decided who should have it.

whom, unfortunately, in spite of Plutarch's long biography, in reality we know so little. He employed all his leisure time in superintending their education, and conducted it in the spirit of the age, causing his sons to be instructed by Greek masters in the language and literature of Greece, and in mental as well as bodily accomplishments.[1] We shall see how the day of his triumph over Perseus and the last years of his life were clouded by the death of his two youngest and most beloved children, and how he bore this misfortune with Roman fortitude.

The wars with the barbarous tribes in Spain and Liguria were not a good school for the Roman generals, as is plainly shown by the incapacity of those who commanded in Macedonia. If, therefore, as is reported,[2] something extraordinary was expected of Æmilius Paullus, it must have been his character, apart from his former exploits, that inspired the Romans with confidence. At the same time, care was taken that he should have the means of accomplishing the task entrusted to him. Armaments were made which recall to our minds the time of the Hannibalic war.[3] About eighty thousand infantry and more than four thousand cavalry were levied. The remainder of the troops in Illyria and Macedonia could not amount to less than twenty-five thousand. Thus the republic had far above one hundred thousand men in arms, without counting the

---

[1] Plutarch, *Æmil. Paul.* 6.

[2] Livy, xliv. 22, 17: Traditum memoriæ est maiore quam solita frequentia prosequentium consulem celebratum ac prope certa spe ominatos esse homines e Macedonico bello maturumque reditum cum egregio triumpho consulis ture. Plutarch, *Æmil. Paul.* 10. Plutarch's biography bears in many places the stamp of a family laudation, and is probably based upon family traditions and chronicles of the Æmilian, Cornelian, and Fabian houses. Such documents must be read with a fair amount of scepticism. For instance, Plutarch relates in the chapter quoted above that Æmilius Paullus at first refused the honour of the consulship, and only yielded to the entreaties of the people. We cannot trust that means. It is a repetition of the laudations heaped *ad nauseam* on Quintus Fabius Maximus, who was five times consul in the time of the Punic wars, and repeatedly had to be persuaded to accept the honour (vol. i. p. 2). The truth is, these men would not have been Romans if they had not strained every nerve to obtain the coveted honour as often as possible.

[3] xliv. 21.

forces scattered over Spain, Sardinia, Corsica, and Sicily. Of this overpowering force, fourteen thousand infantry, twelve hundred horse, five thousand marines, besides the remainder of the old troops still fit for use, forming together with the auxiliaries an army which at the very least must have amounted to fifty thousand infantry and two thousand horse, were destined for Macedonia. Twenty thousand four hundred infantry and fourteen hundred horse were sent to Illyria, where the Roman troops had suffered even more than in Macedonia, and where the alliance of Gentius with Perseus had created new enemies. The army in that country must thus have been raised at the very least to thirty thousand infantry and two thousand horse. With such forces the Romans might begin the fourth campaign with a fair prospect of a speedy victory.

The first blow was dealt against king Gentius. The Illyrian pirate vessels were quickly swept off the sea by the Roman fleet, and the praetor Anicius who now relieved Appius Claudius in the command, marched straight upon Scodra, the capital of the country. Gentius had actually courage enough to march out and meet the Romans in the field, but he was immediately driven back into the town. Although he had suffered but a slight loss, and might have stood his ground for a long time in the fortified town, yet he at once lost courage and asked for a truce, and afterwards, when the expected reinforcements did not arrive, for peace.[1] He was obliged to surrender unconditionally, and was carried off as a prisoner to adorn the triumphal entry of the victor. In Rome the news of this first victory of the new campaign arrived before it was known that operations had begun in earnest.

The sudden collapse of Gentius was, from a military point of view, no great loss to Perseus, for up to this time the Illyrian chief had been of no service to him. But it was a bad omen, and could not but lessen the confidence

[1] Livy, xliv. 31.

BOOK V.
171-168 B.C.

Rhodian mediation.

of all those who wished success to the Macedonian arms, or who were more or less inclined to join Perseus. Events, which had hitherto marched so slowly, now followed each other in rapid succession. The aspect of affairs changed so suddenly, that the plans and calculations which the Rhodians had only just made for an armed intervention proved very soon to be most unseasonable.

We have seen[1] that the consul Marcius Philippus had in the preceding year invited the Rhodians to try to bring about a peace between Rome and Macedonia, and that thereby the Macedonian party in Rhodes had become more influential, especially as at the same time the alliance between Perseus and Gentius became known there. The Rhodians had, in pursuance of this plan, resolved to send an embassy to Rome, to declare that they wished to see peace restored, and that they would eventually declare against the side that insisted on continuing the strife. At the same time they had sent messengers to the theatre of war to demand the cessation of hostilities. The former embassy was not received by the senate until after the battle of Pydna; and the Rhodians, finding themselves forestalled by events, tried to represent the original object of their mission as dictated by friendship for the Romans, and now congratulated them on their victory. The ambassadors who had been sent to Macedonia reached the camp of the consul Æmilius Paullus just as the latter, having arrived with reinforcements, had newly organised the army and introduced a stricter discipline. They received the answer that they should wait a fortnight. By that time Æmilius hoped to be no longer obliged to consult their wishes; nor had he made a mistake in his calculations.

Perseus still held his strongly fortified position on the Elpeus, south of Dium.[2] Æmilius was posted immediately in front of it. Octavius, the commander of the fleet, was prepared to co-operate, and to support the front attack by

[1] P. 219.   [2] P. 234.

a diversion in the rear of the Macedonian line. But, after due consideration, Æmilius preferred to engross the attention of Perseus by making a feigned attack in front, while at the same time he attempted a flank march—a plan which had so often been adopted, and had always succeeded. He sent a strong detachment, in which his eldest son, Fabius Maximus,[1] was serving, under the command of Scipio Nasica, across the pass of Pythium, which was indeed occupied by the enemy, but was taken at once without difficulty.[2] Thus Perseus was a second time by a simple flank march driven out of an impregnable position, and he had no alternative but to retreat further north. He took up a new position at Pydna. Æmilius at once followed him, and was joined by the detachment under Scipio Nasica. When he had come up with the Macedonian army south of Pydna, in the immediate vicinity of the sea, his subordinate officers, and especially Scipio Nasica, urged him to commence the attack at once. But he first ordered his troops to encamp, and to rest from their fatiguing march. In the night of the 21st of June, 168 B.C., an eclipse of the moon took place, which the military tribune Sulpicius Gallus is reported to have calculated beforehand, and to have announced to the soldiers as impending, so that this natural phenomenon produced no consternation in the Roman camp, whereas in that of the Macedonians it was unexpected, and consequently filled the soldiers with superstitious fear.[3] Even on the

CHAP. III.

171-168 B.C.

Battle of Pydna.

---

[1] A Fabius by adoption. See p. 245.

[2] According to Polybius (quoted by Plutarch, *Æmil. Paul.* 16), the Macedonians were surprised in their sleep. But Scipio Nasica, who himself wrote an account of the campaign, boasts of having had a hard fight with the enemy on the height of the pass, and of having cut down a Thracian with his own hand. We have not a moment's doubt that the statement of Polybius is correct, and that of Scipio Nasica a fiction, the more impudent as its object was not the glorification of the writer's country, house, or ancestors, but of himself. We have here a good illustration of the vainglorious spirit and of the utter disregard of historical truth which prevailed in the Roman nobility. See Nissen, *Untersuchungen über die Quellen des Livius*, pp. 181, 267.

[3] Livy, xliv. 37; Plin. *Hist. Nat.* ii. 12, 53; Frontin, *Strateg.* i. 12, 8. This statement cannot fail to startle us. It is the first time that the Romans are represented as enlightened and cultivated by scientific observations,

next day Æmilius did not wish to give battle, when, towards evening, the advanced troops on both sides, who were watering their horses, came into collision, and a general engagement was presently the result. Thus, as at Cynoscephalæ, the decisive battle was brought about without the intention of the two commanders,[1] and, as at Cynoscephalæ, the victory was decided partly by the courage of the Roman soldiers, partly by the Roman order of battle, which, owing to the manipular tactics, was more easily moved than the unwieldy phalanx. Wherever in the Macedonian line of battle a gap was formed, which was inevitable in marching over uneven ground, the Romans forced their way in and broke the ranks asunder. Incapable of offering resistance in a hand-to-hand struggle, the phalangites fell by thousands, helpless as sheep, under

---

whereas the Macedonians, who, after all, had Greek science at their command, are described as ignorant barbarians. We are therefore inclined to prefer a statement communicated by Cicero (*Republ.* i. 15, 23), to the effect that Sulpicius Galba enlightened the Roman soldiers on the nature of the phenomenon *after it had occurred*, and thus removed their alarm. This account of the story agrees with Valerius Maximus (viii. 11, 1), Justin (xxxiii. 1, 7), and Plutarch (*Æmil. Paul.* 17), who all say that the Romans, according to their custom (ὥσπερ ἐστὶ νενομισμένον, Plut. l. c. Comp. Livy, xxvi. 5, 9), tried to revive the waning light of the moon by the clashing of brass vessels and by holding up burning torches towards the sky. Men who tried to get over their alarm by such antics surely were not very enlightened, and could hardly have been looking forward to the phenomenon as to a natural event of no moment. It is not probable that even the Thracian barbarians in the Macedonian camp were more frightened than, according to the last-quoted authorities, the Romans themselves. Unfortunately we have not the full account of Polybius. From the short fragment (xxix. 6, 8) preserved it would appear that the Romans endeavoured to persuade themselves that the eclipse foreboded the downfall of Perseus. This, of course, proves that they saw in it a special sign sent by the gods, just as the vulgar of our own time are inclined to do in the case of striking natural events equally regulated by physical laws. But, curiously enough, Polybius adds that the construction which the Romans put upon the phenomenon—viz., that it meant the downfall of Perseus—inspired them with courage, and had upon the Macedonians the opposite effect (καὶ τοῦτο τοὺς μὲν Ῥωμαίους εὐθαρσεστέρους ἐποίησε, τοὺς δὲ Μακεδόνας ἐταπείνωσε ταῖς ψυχαῖς). How this was possible may be hard to show. No doubt the men in both armies were frightened. Of Roman soldiers this is reported often enough in subsequent times; for instance, in the reign of Tiberius (Tacitus, *Annal.* i. 28). Æmilius tried to pacify the vulgar fears by offering up to the moon a sacrifice of eleven calves, and on the following day one to Hercules of twenty-one (Plutarch, l. c.).   [1] See p. 45.

the thrusts of the short Roman swords. It is reported that twenty thousand were killed and eleven thousand taken prisoners. The Macedonian cavalry exhibited the utmost cowardice. It appears to have taken no serious part in the battle, but rode off from the field, first to Pydna, and thence immediately further north. On the other hand, all parts of the Roman army co-operated to produce the most brilliant result. The elephants advanced steadily, and helped to bring about the decision, and even the naval troops came in boats from their ships, and cut down all the fugitives they could overtake.[1] The Macedonian phalanx had fought its last great battle. On Macedonian ground it succumbed in a bloody struggle to the Roman legion, and in its fall it brought down with it the Macedonian monarchy. It was the excellent tactics of the legions, and not the strategic talent of the worthy Æmilius Paullus, that decided the victory—a victory which, like the other great decisive battles in the East, was gained with a surprisingly small sacrifice of blood, for on the Roman side hardly more than one hundred men were killed. Whilst in the struggles with the barbarous tribes of Spain, Gaul, and Liguria, thousands of Roman soldiers were butchered in nameless battles without profit and without glory for the Roman state, the great civilised countries of the successors of Alexander succumbed to the first powerful blow, almost without being able to give a blow in return. But in the East the war was carried on, not by the nations, but by the rulers; besides, civilisation, usually stronger than barbarism, had here become paralysed and enervated during the long period which had estranged the Greek people from their ideals, and had caused them to degenerate in misery and suffering, in unceasing wars of truculent warrior kings, and the desperate struggles of the rich with the poor.

We have contradictory reports of the conduct of King Perseus during the fatal battle.[2] Whilst Polybius unhesi-

---

[1] Livy, xliv. 41, f.; Polybius, xxix. 6; Plutarch, Æmil. Paul. 15, ff.; Zonaras, ix. 23.

[2] Livy, xliv. 42; Plutarch, Æmil. Paul. 19: In all that relates to Perseus

tatingly accuses him of cowardice, relating that he rode off in the beginning of the battle, under the pretext of offering up a sacrifice to Hercules at Pella, a certain Posidonius, the author of a biography of Perseus, tells us that on the previous day he was injured in the thigh by a kick from a horse, that, nevertheless, in spite of the pain, and against the entreaties of his friends, he mounted a baggage horse unarmed, and remained on the battle-field until he was grazed by a spear. As Perseus had, as yet, never exhibited a want of personal courage, the Roman report sounds strange. We are involuntarily reminded of the systematic slandering of Hannibal, and of the meanness which always prompted the Romans to speak ill of their enemies. The authority of Posidonius may be slight, but yet he was in a better position than a Roman writer to know how Perseus behaved in the battle. At any rate, it is not improbable that the chance kick of a horse may have paralysed the spirit and energy of Perseus on the very day which decided his fate.[1]

We cannot, without compassion, watch the fugitive king of Macedonia stealing along byways to the woods, accompanied by a few faithful followers,[2] trying to escape unrecognised, for he already began to fear that he might fall by the dagger of a traitor. Since the memorable flight of the last Persian king from the battle-field of Arbela, the world had witnessed no such event, nor such a fall

---

we must suspect the impartiality of Polybius (see above, p. 232, note 2). Besides, his authority is naturally diminished where he has to relate events in which his patrons Æmilius Paullus and Scipio Æmilianus were actors.

[1] Polybius reported, according to Plutarch (l. c.), that Perseus rode off the field in the very beginning of the battle, under the pretext mentioned in the text. Now if we bear in mind that the battle commenced only towards evening, and was not expected that day by either commander, we can easily believe that Perseus in the morning went to Pydna for the alleged purpose. In the afternoon the battle unexpectedly commenced. In about one hour it was decided. It is therefore possible that Perseus returned only in time to witness the defeat. If this was the real course of events, it was easy for a witness ill-disposed towards Perseus to twist it into the story reported by Polybius.

[2] Three, and none of them native Macedonians. Livy, xliv. 43, 6: "tantum cum eo fugæ comites, Evander Cretensis, Neo Bœotius et ... Ætolus."

from so great a height. If we recollect that, in spite of the partiality of hostile historians, all our sources agree in praising not only the manly, handsome, and noble appearance of the king, but also his clemency, humanity, and moderation, and that in reality they can reproach him with nothing but disinclination to part with his treasures;[1] if we are, moreover, convinced that the war was entirely provoked by the Romans, this compassion is heightened to sympathy such as only great and noble men suffering from undeserved adversity can inspire. Hunted by his pursuers, forsaken by his best friends, the fugitive hastened on without pausing. His magnificent cavalry was scattered in all directions: only about five hundred Cretan mercenaries remained with him, and these remained not from self-sacrificing fidelity, but because they counted upon grasping some of the treasures which he might possibly take with him. Not one of his higher officers remained in his company. Hippias, Midon, and Pantauchus hastened to submit to the approaching consul. All the large towns in the country, among them Pella, the ancient capital, with its impregnable castle, Beroea, and Thessalonica, surrendered within two days. Nowhere was there a pause in the flight, or a shadow of resistance. The Macedonian nation bowed its neck under the Roman yoke. The suffering caused by so many wars, and the oppression of foreign mercenaries, had made the people indifferent to the dignity and pride of independence, and had left them only a longing for peace.

One example will show the total collapse of the Macedonian monarchy.[2] In the strongly fortified and important

---

[1] It is true that Perseus has also been accused of cruelty. The murder of his brother (p. 194) and of his wife (p. 195, note) is laid to his charge. The former of these crimes, even if not perpetrated by himself, was most probably perpetrated with his knowledge and approbation. But we know too little of the detail of that family tragedy to decide which of all the persons concerned is to be made chiefly responsible. The account of the murder of his wife is probably a mere fiction, as also that of his servants Euctus and Eulæus (Plutarch. *Æmil. Paul.* 23), and lastly that of Evander, his most faithful servant. Livy, xlv. 5.   [2] Livy, xliv. 44.

town of Amphipolis there was still a garrison of two thousand Thracians, under a captain called Diodorus. Upon the news of the defeat at Pydna the peaceable inhabitants began to fear not so much the Romans as their own protectors, the Thracian mercenaries. Diodorus, by a stratagem, induced the Thracians to leave the town, pretending that there was a rich booty to be made outside, whereupon the inhabitants immediately shut the gates. Perseus reached Amphipolis on the third day after the battle. He had now crossed the Strymon, and hoped that the Romans would leave him time to negotiate. But his own subjects entreated him to leave them. They feared that his presence might force them to offer resistance to the Romans, whereas their only thought was submission. Perseus yielded to their entreaties. He left fifty talents to the faithful Cretans to loot, and embarked with the rest of his treasures, amounting, as reported, to two thousand talents, for the island of Samothrace.[1]

Æmilius Paullus had at once comprehended the full importance of his victory at Pydna, and resolved to turn it to account, not for the purpose of enriching himself and his friends, but for the advantage of the Roman republic. He protected the inhabitants from being plundered and ill-used by his soldiers,[2] a proceeding by which he doubtless hastened the rapid subjection of the country, but at the same time made himself unpopular in his own army. Towards the conquered king he assumed all the dignity and pride of victorious Rome. The resolution had been formed at Rome from the beginning to put an end to the Macedonian monarchy. When, therefore, Perseus sent a letter, in which he, as 'king of Macedonia,' sent his greeting to the Roman consul, Æmilius returned it unanswered. This humiliation made it clear to Perseus that he was not only conquered but also dethroned. A second letter to the consul was signed only with his name, without the

---

[1] Livy, xliv. 45.
[2] xliv. 46. The town of Pydna, which assumed an attitude of resistance the only one given over to the soldiers to plunder. Livy, xliv. 45, 6.

title which he had forfeited. But the negotiations led to no result, because Æmilius insisted on unconditional surrender, and Perseus desperately clung to vain hopes.¹ The uncertainty was not of long duration. The prætor Cneus Octavius approached with the Roman fleet, and took up his position off the island. Perseus seems to have hoped for some little time that the sanctity of the temple of Samothrace, so highly revered throughout Greece, would protect him from violence. At length, however, he resolved to make his escape to Thrace. A ship was held in readiness by the Cretan Oroandes in a solitary part of the coast, and was laden towards evening with necessaries, and as much money as could be secretly conveyed into it. In the dead of night the king, with his wife and his children, stole away through a back door of the house at which he lodged, crossed the garden, climbed over a wall, and reached the sea. There the fugitives wandered to and fro on the shore, seeking the ship in vain. The faithless Cretan had sailed away at nightfall with the treasures, leaving the king to his fate, and to despair. Perseus, with his eldest son, remained for some time in hiding; but when all his pages had given themselves up to the Roman consul, to whom also his younger children had been handed over by their tutor, he at length surrendered at discretion to the prætor Octavius.² He was immediately taken on board a ship, conducted to Amphipolis, and thence to the camp of Æmilius.

Never before had a Roman consul had in his power so noble a prisoner. There was a great temptation to be haughty and overbearing. But it appears that Æmilius was

---

¹ Livy, xlv. 4.

² Livy, xlv. 5, 6; Plutarch, *Emil. Paul.* 26. Our sources, though varying a little in detail, agree in the main points. But the story of the murder of the Cretan Evander is too silly to deserve credit, or even serious attention, unless we suppose that Perseus was downright mad. It is said that, in order to clear himself from the crime of having attempted the life of Eumenes through this same Evander (see p. 200), he now caused the most devoted of his servants to be put to death, at a time when he was trembling for his own life and liberty. Comp. p. 253, note 1.

too noble-minded to ill-use his unfortunate enemy after his fall, and too wise to exult in his victory. It is true, he spoke harshly to him, and reproached him with his hostile disposition towards Rome, as not only wrong but foolish; but he extended his hand to him, raised him up when he was about to fall on his knees, and offered him a seat before the council of war assembled in the tent; he also ceased questioning him when he saw that Perseus remained silent to all inquiries. Then he turned to his friends, reminded them of the uncertainty of all human greatness, and admonished them to be moderate and humble in good fortune.[1]

The capture of Perseus brought the war to a final close. It was not to be expected that the Macedonians, who even before this event had surrendered rapidly and completely to the conquerors, would, when they were left to themselves, resume hostilities. After a short campaign, Æmilius could safely dismiss his troops into winter quarters at Amphipolis and the neighbouring towns, and await the instructions which the senate would issue with regard to affairs in Macedonia.

This important question now occupied the minds of the leading Roman politicians. Two roads were open to them. Macedonia, now completely conquered, might be converted into a Roman province like Sicily, Sardinia with Corsica, and the two divisions of Spain, or it might be kept politically dependent upon Rome, and free only in name. The senate resolved to pursue the latter course, not from moderation or satisfied ambition, but in the well-founded conviction that the large extent of territory

---

[1] This is the account given by Livy (xlv. 8) and Dio Cassius (Fragm. 75 vol 76. 2, Tauchnitz; 66, 4. 6, Dindorf). On the other hand, Plutarch (*Æmil. Paul* 26) tells us that Æmilius overwhelmed Perseus with contemptuous ... on account of his want of dignity and manliness in his misfortunes. We ... well of Æmilius Paullus to hold him capable of such heartlessness ... He was, we think, one of the few Romans who could be generous ... foe. We therefore prefer Livy's account to that of Plutarch, ... incline I to think, was derived from Nasica (see above, p. 249, n. 2) ... writer unable to rise above the average level of his country- ... and moral refinement.

already acquired was too heavy a superstructure for the foundation on which the republican government was established. It was clearly perceptible that the development in the form of government had not kept pace with the extension of the boundaries. The Roman magistrates, who were to represent the authority of the republic in foreign parts, had already begun to disregard this authority to an alarming extent. The Roman nobles showed more and more an inclination to act independently, and this inclination was justified and supported by the fact that it was impossible for commanders far from the centre of the Roman power, the seat of the actual sovereignty, to be implicitly guided by orders and instructions. A Manlius, who carried on a war with the Galatians on his own responsibility, a Cassius, who, contrary to distinct orders, left his province to march into Illyria and to take part in a war which had been entrusted to his colleague; a Lucretius and a Hortensius, who forgot their duties in eagerness for plunder and rapine—men who, like the brother of the great Scipio, did not return from the field with pure hands, might well serve as a warning to Cato and other honest patriots who were anxious to preserve the spirit of the old republican institutions. As these men, however, could not conceive a plan of reform which would have burst the narrow circle of the ancient town institutions, which would have widened the limits of the old citizenship, and restrained the abuses of office, they attempted to check, at least for a while, the downward course with which the state was hurrying to its fall. Perhaps they felt that their attempt was vain. The momentum of the enormous force set in motion was too great to be stopped or turned into another direction by any man or any party. The attempt which was made ended in a temporary arrangement, altogether unavailing and unsatisfactory to Rome, and ruinous to Macedonia, the country more directly concerned.

The senate resolved that Macedonia should be free.[1]

[1] Livy, xlv. 17.

BOOK V.
171-168 B.C.

Congress at Amphipolis.

How this freedom was to be understood and realised was left to the decision of a committee of ten men selected from the senate, who were despatched to Greece in order to arrange matters on the spot, under the direction of Æmilius Paullus. In Amphipolis a great congress was held. Deputies from all the Macedonian towns appeared before the Roman proconsul and his ten coadjutors to hear what had been decided with regard to their destiny. It is hardly probable that the word liberty, so often misapplied, now produced an effect similar to that which had been called forth at the Isthmian games when Flamininus first pronounced it.[1] The Greeks in the meantime had learnt what was meant by freedom granted by the Romans. The abolition of royalty, which, according to tradition, had been the foundation of liberty in Rome, could not be regarded as a beneficial change by a nation which from time immemorial had been accustomed to a monarchical constitution, and had never wished for any other. But if liberty was to mean independence from other states, especially Rome, the Macedonians knew only too well that it was a mere illusion and a sham.

Settlement of Macedonia.

This was soon made clear to everyone by the demand that Macedonia was from this time forward to pay an annual tribute to the Roman state, only half, it is true, of what had formerly been paid to the native kings, but still a tribute to a foreign state, which alone was to have the disposal of it. In return for this tribute paid to her as the protecting power, Rome undertook to guarantee Macedonia from all foreign enemies, and thus, by relieving the Macedonians from the duty of military service, or rather by taking away from them the right of carrying arms, degraded them in their own estimation. Only in the districts bordering upon the northern barbarians armed posts were to guard the frontier. The brave and warlike Macedonians, who by their habits, customs, and past history, had come to regard the profession of arms as their

---

[1] See p. 68.

chief occupation, a people who had brought the Greek tactics to the highest perfection, and had conquered the whole Eastern world with their phalanx, were condemned, like the Lydians after the fall of Crœsus, to devote themselves only to the arts of peace.

But in the very practice of these arts, and in the enjoyment of tranquil life, the strength of the Macedonian people was paralysed by the insidious policy of their conquerors. The country was divided into four parts, each of which was to govern itself as an independent republic, entirely distinct and separate from the other three. The four divisions were deprived of the connubium and commercium among one another, i.e. no one was allowed to own landed property in more than one division, or to conclude a legitimate marriage with anyone belonging to another division.[1] In addition to this, the commerce of the country was restricted by laws affecting the export and import of merchandise. One of the restrictions which the Romans found it necessary to impose shows plainly the difficulty involved in their new conquest, although they had abstained as yet from converting the land into a regular province. They resolved that the gold and silver mines of Macedonia should not be worked any more, and that the royal domains should not be let. This regulation, which was tantamount to the destruction of national wealth, was dictated by administrative impotence. The military and civil officers in the Roman provinces, and the tax-collectors had by this time attained such power that they inspired more and more alarm to the home authorities, and threatened entirely to escape from their control. The Romans, therefore, chose rather to part with a copious source of revenue than to give the tax-collectors a new sphere for their operations, which had long been abused, to the injury of the public interests and for the oppression of the subjects. On the other hand, they could not make up their minds to allow the Macedonians the profit of the working

---

[1] Livy, xlv. 29, 10: Pronunciavit deinde neque connubium neque commercium agrorum ædificiorumque inter se placere cuiquam extra fines regionis suae esse.

of these valuable domains, because they looked upon their poverty as a security for their obedience.¹

In order to insure the permanence of these new regulations in Macedonia, the Romans conceived a plan which in excessive harshness surpassed everything that Roman policy had as yet invented. All the men who had ever served the king of Macedonia in any important public capacity, as military and naval officers, as civil servants, or as his councillors and friends, in short, all who by their position and capacities had to be regarded as the natural leaders of the people, were transported to Italy, together with their grown-up sons.² Nothing remained but the inert mass of the meaner classes, and these were thrown back into the condition of mere peasants, from which, since the time of their great kings, they had risen almost to equality in education and culture with the Hellenes.

Such was the liberty which Rome granted to the Macedonians, in order, as Livy pompously explains, that it might be clear to all nations that the Romans did not enslave the free, but liberated the enslaved.³ As time showed, the new liberty was so unbearable, that after twenty years of vexation and oppression the Macedonians were driven to despair, and ventured to take up arms once more in a hopeless contest.

Illyria was treated like Macedonia. This country also received its 'liberty' as a gift. It was divided into three cantons, which, like the four divisions in Macedonia, were allowed a certain amount of independence in the manage-

---

¹ Livy, xlv. 18, 3: Metalli quoque Macedonici, quod ingens vectigal erat, locationes praediorumque rusticorum tolli placebat : eam neque sine publicano exerceri posse, et ubi publicanus esset, ibi aut ius publicum vanum aut libertatem sociis nullam esse ; ne ipsos quidem Macedonas exercere posse ; ubi in ea praeda administrantibus esset.

Livy, xlv. 32.

² Livy, xlv. 18, 1: Omnium primum liberos esse placebat Macedonas atque Illyrios, ut omnibus gentibus appareret, arma populi Romani non liberis servitutem, contra servientibus libertatem afferre, ut et in libertate gentes quae essent in eam sibi perpetuoque sub tutela esse, et quae sub regibus viverent, et in tempus mitiores eos iustioresque respectu populi Romani habere eos, et si quando bellum cum populo Romano regibus fuisset suis, exitum victoriam Romanis allaturum, sibi libertatem.

ment of their internal affairs. Some few towns, which during the war had taken the part of the Romans, were rewarded with immunity from taxation.¹ The others were obliged to pay as a tribute to Rome one-half of the sum hitherto paid in taxes.

Kotys, the Thracian ally of Perseus, escaped unscathed, because it seemed not worth while to carry the war into Thrace; the Romans even sent him back his son, who had been taken prisoner with the children of Perseus, and thus he was laid under a special obligation to keep the peace.²

The fall of the Macedonian monarchy was not less fatal to the Greek states than to the Macedonians themselves. Everywhere, as we know, there were Roman parties which, under the protection of the great foreign power, had seized the direction of affairs, and endeavoured to oppress their opponents who inclined more or less to Perseus. Every trace of political principle and of patriotism had long disappeared from the minds of these people. They were not even honest fanatics, but common ruffians who sought to obtain wealth and power for themselves, and for this object stopped short neither of violence nor cunning, treason nor murder.

In Achaea it was Callicrates who undertook to perform the dirty work for the Romans, in Epirus the infamous Charops, in Acarnania Chremes, in Ætolia Lyciscus, in Bœotia Mnasippus, and every one of these men had a host of supporters and partisans ready to commit the most atrocious crimes. The signal for these was given by the Ætolian Lyciscus. He called together to a meeting five hundred and fifty of the richest and most eminent of his countrymen, and caused them all to be massacred by Roman soldiers, commanded by one Aulus Baebius, under the pretext that they had favoured the party of Perseus. Lyciscus and his companions then seized the property of their murdered victims, and of a great number of others who had escaped from the same fate by flight.³ This atrocity

---

¹ Livy, xlv. 26.   ² Polybius, xxx. 12.
³ Livy, xlv. 28, 6. It affords some satisfaction to learn (Livy, xlv. 34, 2) that

was actually countenanced by Æmilius Paullus, who was himself anything but cruel, because he thought it served the interests of Rome. In Amphipolis, where, on the occasion of settling the affairs of Macedonia, the Roman partisans assembled from all parts of Greece, further measures were concerted for the extermination of the Hellenic party. All those men who had had any transactions with Perseus, or who were only suspected were sentenced to transportation to Italy. The whole of Greece was in this manner to be cleared of all the opponents of the Roman partisans, and these partisans were left unchecked in the possession of political power. They were at the same time rewarded for their fidelity, and encouraged to future services by being allowed to divide among themselves the property of their proscribed opponents.

In most of the Greek states these cruel measures were not without an appearance of justification; for in Bœotia, Ætolia, and Acarnania, there had been numerous enemies of the Romans, some of whom were convicted of their guilt by their open acts, others by letters which were found among the papers of Perseus. But with the Achaeans the case was different. They had wisely avoided having any dealings with Perseus. After their disputes with Sparta and Messenia, which had almost involved the Achaean league in a war with Rome,[1] a period of comparative quiet had succeeded, and the national party had given way to that of the friends of Rome headed by Callicrates.[2] This man proved in every respect a ready tool of the Roman policy. As matters stood, it is true, the Achaeans had no choice but to submit to the dictates of Rome, and to waive those rights which formerly belonged to them as independent allies. As soon, therefore, as it became evident that there would be a rupture between Rome and Macedonia, the Achaean league unequivocally took the Roman side, and rejected all advances, and the

---

... was afterwards punished by Æmilius Paullus for the readiness ... allowed Roman soldiers to play the butchers.

[1] 175, ff. [2] See p. 183.

most tempting offers which Perseus made to gain their friendship. Thus far the Roman partisans at the head of the federal government succeeded in their policy, and they were of course backed by direct pressure put upon the league by Rome. But after all it was not possible entirely to suppress among the mass of the people, especially the democratic party, the sympathies which were entertained for Perseus in all parts of Greece. The national patriots were not bold enough to act upon these sympathies resolutely and openly; but they could not be restrained from making at least a demonstration which, though hostile to Rome, was of no practical effect. They carried a decree[1] to deprive Eumenes, the Roman partisan, of the honours and distinctions with which he had been loaded in the form of statues, inscriptions, and festal celebrations. Having in this paltry and somewhat childish manner made an indirect demonstration against Rome, the league nevertheless took the Roman side when the war with Perseus broke out, and were even eager to send forthwith one thousand men to garrison Chalcis,[2] and fifteen hundred men to join the army of the consul Licinius. It is not quite clear from the evidence, whether after the despatch of these auxiliaries some disagreement took place between the Roman generals and the Achaeans, or whether, in consequence of the wretched strategy of the Romans, and the first victories of Perseus, the ardour of the Achaeans cooled down. At any rate, it seems certain that their auxiliary corps was sent back by the Romans or withdrawn, and that from this time the Achaeans occupied a reserved and neutral position. This, however, did not last long. When in the third year of the war the consul Marcius Philippus had taken the command,[3] the Achaeans found it in their interest to prove their continued loyalty to Rome by a formal resolution that the whole of their military force, consisting of five thousand men, should be placed at the disposal of the Romans. At the same time the decree was repealed which

---

[1] This was probably done as early as 175 B.C.
[2] Livy, xlii. 44, 7. [3] See p. 228.

deprived Eumenes of his honours.[1] The historian Polybius, who, like his father, Lycortas, was among the leaders of the national party, distinctly recognised the necessity of changing the policy hitherto pursued. He had been elected hipparchus, or second officer of the league, for the year 169 B.C., and undertook himself an embassy to the consul Marcius for the purpose of offering him the contingent of the Achaeans. It happened just to be the time when Marcius had undertaken his bold expedition into Macedonia, across the range of Mount Olympus, an expedition which, contrary to all expectations, succeeded.[2] Polybius delivered himself of his commission when Marcius, after having crossed the mountains, had already entered Macedonia. The offer was declined, and at the same time, as we have seen, Marcius authorised the Achaeans to refuse the auxiliaries which Claudius, the Roman praetor commanding in Illyria, had asked of them. We have seen how dangerous it was for Roman allies to refuse such a request of a Roman general.[3] It seemed almost as if the directions given by Marcius to the Achaeans were as insidious as the advice which about the same time he gave to the Rhodians, and which caused them such distress.[4] Yet the Achaeans, as we have seen, knew how to extricate themselves out of the difficulty. They declined the request of Claudius, taking their stand on the instructions of the senate, that without a written order from that body no Roman officer should call upon the allies for any assistance.[5] Nevertheless, they did not feel quite comfortable in this matter. They knew that they were suspected of secret sympathies with Perseus, and they wished to clear themselves of this suspicion. They resolved to do this in an indirect way by sending a portion of their army as an auxiliary force to the king of Egypt, who just then happened to be at war with Syria. By thus supporting a friend of the Roman republic, they showed clearly that they did not wish to reserve their troops with a view hostile to Rome, in case the Macedonian

[1] P. 263. [2] P. 230. [3] P. 243.
[4] P. 240. [5] P. 243.

war should present an opportunity. But at the instigation of Callicrates, the resolution of sending the troops to Egypt was postponed, and as shortly afterwards Marcius disapproved of it, it was not carried into execution at all.[1]

Shortly afterwards the decisive blow was struck at Pydna. This put an end to the uncertainty of the position in which the Achaeans were placed. Equality of rights with Rome was now out of the question. It was a settled resolve in Rome to establish Roman supremacy beyond dispute in Achaia, as well as in the whole of Greece. But as in the papers of King Perseus nothing was found which could incriminate the league or individual Achaeans, a pretext was wanting to chastise them. Nevertheless, Callicrates was sent with two Roman plenipotentiaries, Caius Claudius and Cneus Domitius, from Amphipolis to the Peloponnesus, in order to institute an inquiry against the adherents of the king of Macedonia.[2] Accusations were not wanting, and a pretext was soon found for a measure which had been from the first intended, namely, that of removing all suspicious personages to Italy. When one of these men indignantly refuted the accusation, and declared that he was ready to prove his innocence before any Roman tribunal, he and all who thought like him were taken at their word, and the resolution was passed that all the accused Achaeans should plead their case in Italy. The Roman partisans had ample scope now to clear the field of all their opponents. They knew well the men who were in their way, and they eagerly and skilfully drew up the lists of proscription. More than one thousand of the noblest and best Achaeans were selected for punishment. Every man who was conspicuous by his authority, patriotism, wealth, or birth, was taken away from his home and his occupation, in order to justify his political acts before foreign judges. Thus the unhappy country was deprived of its best citizens,

[1] Polybius, xxix. 8, 9.   [2] Polybius, xxx. 7, 5; Pausanias, vii. 10.

and treated as Macedonia had been treated before. The Achaeans were punished, because, as allies of the Roman republic, they had presumed to claim a certain degree of independence, and because there were men among them who could submit only with disgust and reluctance to the brutal word of command of the Roman magistrates and the perfidious policy of the senate.[1] Among the exiled leaders of the national party was the historian Polybius, who afterwards undertook the sad task of relating the downfall of his country, which he himself had witnessed, and who was able, through his personal influence with the victors, to soften in some measure the deplorable fate of his countrymen. We shall see, in the course of this history, how the personal adventures of the thousand transported Achaeans were connected with the final catastrophe which befell Greece.

The same violent measures which the Romans adopted to secure the dominion of their adherents in Macedonia and Achaia was also applied in other parts of Greece. The most notable opponents of the Roman supremacy in Ætolia, Acarnania, Epirus, and Bœotia were sent to Italy, and detained there for an indefinite time.[2] Some few, who were more especially obnoxious, even suffered death,[3] as, for instance, the Bœotian Neon, one of the few faithful friends who had not forsaken Perseus in his flight.[4] Thus the Romans thought that they had cleared the whole country of every hostile element, and that they had permanently established obedience to their commands.

It was not Greece proper alone that felt the disastrous effects of the battle which had raised Rome to uncontested supremacy over the whole Grecian world. The commotion caused by it extended to Asia, and threatened to

---

[1] Livius, vii. 10.
[2] Polybius. xxx. 6, ff.; Livy, xlv. 31; Justin. xxxiii. 2.
[3] Livy, xlv. 31, 15: Duo securi percussi viri insignes, Andronicus Andronici ... quod patrem secutus arma contra populum Romanum tulisset,
Neon ... s. quo auctore societatem cum Perse iunxerant.
[4] p. 252, note 2.

overthrow more particularly the republic of Rhodes. We have seen [1] that, in consequence of the first miscarriages of the Roman generals, that party gained strength in Rhodes which endeavoured to rescue the island from Roman tutelage, and that Perseus and Gentius addressed themselves to Rhodes for military aid. We have seen, moreover, that the Rhodians were induced by the crafty consul Marcius to act as mediators between the belligerents. This step was looked upon as an unpardonable crime after the victory at Pydna. The Rhodian ambassadors, who had been delayed in Rome for some time, and were admitted to an audience by the senate only when the news of the victory had arrived, received now a harsh, threatening, and yet indistinct answer.[2] They were charged with having offered their mediation not, as they said, in a spirit of benevolence for Rome and the Grecian states, but in the interest of Perseus. Much would the Rhodians have given to undo what they had been tempted to do. They trembled at the mere thought of having incurred the displeasure of the powerful republic, and not only asked forgiveness in a humble and undignified manner, but also attempted to throw the guilt upon a few individual citizens, by punishing, without delay, the chiefs of the anti-Roman party. They eagerly anticipated the measures which the Romans had taken in Macedonia, Achaia, and the rest of Greece, by banishing all the leading men of the national party. We are presented with a fearful picture of the omnipotence of the Roman state, already established in the whole of the ancient world, when we read how a man proscribed by Rome could find no place of refuge in all the countries round the Mediterranean, and had only the alternative of choosing a voluntary death or of being delivered up to his executioners.[3] On the news of the battle of Pydna, Polyaratus, the head of the national party at Rhodes, had fled to Egypt, and had

Fate of Polyaratus.

---

[1] P. 239, f.   [2] P. 248.
[3] Compare Livy, xlv. 35, 2: Nam ii quoque non solum praesentes exciti erant, sed etiam si qui apud reges esse dicebantur, literis arcessiti sunt.

sought the protection of King Ptolemy. When the Romans demanded his extradition, Ptolemy was so far afraid of violating the law of hospitality, that he did not deliver up the fugitive directly to them; but not daring to keep and protect him, he extricated himself from the difficulty by ordering him to be sent back to Rhodes. Polyaratus, knowing full well what fate awaited him at Rome, escaped on the way, and sought a refuge at the public hearth of the town of Phaselis. The people of this town, perplexed and fearing the revenge of Rome, endeavoured to rid themselves of the fugitive, and begged the Rhodians to fetch him. The latter called upon the Egyptian captain, who was commissioned to deliver him up, to perform his duty. Polyaratus, shunned and cast out like a leper, escaped a second time, and sought protection in the Rhodian town of Caunus. But here also he could not remain. The Caunians pressed him to deliver them from his presence, which threatened them with danger, and the unhappy man fled further to the independent Phrygian town of Cibyra, the ruler of which, Pancrates, had long been his friend, and lay under obligations to him. But even here, in the heart of Asia Minor, the strong and dreaded arm of the Roman republic made itself felt. Pancrates applied to Rhodes, and at the same time to Æmilius Paullus, to ask what he should do. An order from the proconsul, directed both to Pancrates and to the Rhodian republic, left them no alternative. The wretched man was transported first to Rhodes and then to Rome. Under such circumstances, it would have been better for Polyaratus to act as Polybius advised all those to act who were placed in a similar position. He tells them not to expose their weakness before the world, but to follow the example of the high-spirited Molossians, Antinous, Theodotus, and Cephalus, and voluntarily to put an end to their lives.[1] The world had, indeed, become a huge prison, from which an outlaw could escape only through the gate of death.

[1] Polybius, xxx. 9.

Whilst the Rhodians, by expelling the leaders of the national party, endeavoured to regain the favour of Rome; while they assured the Romans by a new embassy of their undiminished loyalty, and perhaps indulged in the vain hope that their fault had been expiated and forgiven, the dreadful news arrived in the island that a formal proposal had been made in Rome to declare war against Rhodes.[1] There were men in Rome who were not ashamed, under some paltry pretext, to treat an old, deserving ally as an enemy, or to overthrow an almost defenceless state from motives of the meanest rapacity and cupidity. The prætor Manius Juventius Thalna acted as spokesman for these men, who, however, to the honour of Rome, did not as yet command a majority in the senate. Without, therefore, asking for the approval of the senate, the prætor made known his intention to bring in a motion before the popular assembly to declare war against Rhodes, and to give the command in it to one of the magistrates of the current year (167 B.C.). He probably hoped to obtain this command himself, and after an easy victory to enrich himself and a Roman army with the spoils which that small but wealthy island promised. But he had overrated his power. The Rhodian ambassadors in Rome, who, on meeting with an ungracious reception, had put on mourning,[2] and entreated the most influential men with prayers and tears for protection, found in old Cato a powerful advocate of their cause. Cato, who was a narrow-minded but an honest man, protested against a scheme which would dishonour the Roman name. He opposed it still more, perhaps, because he feared that a mere war of plunder with Rhodes would give the Roman nobles an opportunity to increase their individual and family power, which was already menacing the foundations of the Roman republic. A fragment from the speech which Cato delivered on this occasion is the first really genuine sample of ancient Roman eloquence and honesty which has been preserved

[1] Polybius. xxx. 4, 4; Livy, xlv. 21.   [2] Livy, xlv. 20.

to us. It is highly creditable to the speaker, both on account of its style and on account of the policy it recommends;[1] but it would produce a more agreeable impression upon us if we could forget that the same man who spoke so warmly for the oppressed Rhodians, lost no opportunity of inflaming to a war of extermination the hatred and jealousy which was felt in Rome for the humbled and ill-used Carthaginians. As the motion of Juventius had not found favour with the majority of the senate, and was supported only by a few men, it fell to the ground, two of the tribunes of the people having moreover declared their intention to stop it by their formal intercession. The Rhodian ambassadors felt relieved.[2] The storm which threatened their town had passed over it without breaking. Whatever might come now, the Rhodians had reason to congratulate themselves, and to render thanks to the Romans as their deliverers.

The ambassadors who brought this good news to Rhodes returned to Rome with a golden wreath, as an emblem of homage to the protecting power,[3] and continued their endeavours to ward off the anger of the powerful men. Up to this time Rhodes had been on terms of intimate friendship with Rome, but had not formally entered into an alliance. It had preserved full freedom of action, as became an independent people.[4] But recent events showed

---

[1] Livy only mentions it (xlv. 25, 2): Plurimum causam eorum adiuvit M. Porcius Cato, qui asper ingenio tum lenem mitemque senatorem egit. Non inseram simulacrum viri copiosi, quae dixerit referendo; ipsius oratio scripta extat, Originum quinto libro inclusa. A fragment is quoted by Gellius, Noct. Att. vii. 3, 14–17. It is the longest preserved passage from any of Cato's numerous speeches, and highly characteristic of his oratory.

[2] The extreme terror through which they had passed is described as follows Polybius, xxx. 5, 5: τότε δὲ παντάπασι ἔξω τοῦ φρονεῖν γενόμενοι διὰ τὸν περὶ τῆς πατρίδος κίνδυνον, εἰς τοιαύτην ἦλθον διάθεσιν, ὥστε καὶ φαιὰ βαλεῖν ἱμάτια, κ.τ.λ. According to Livius, xlv. 20, they had done this even before.

[3] Livy, xlv. 25, 7: Itaque extemplo coronam viginti milium aureorum decreverunt. Polybius, xxx. 5, 4: στέφανον ἀπὸ μυρίων χρυσῶν. The difference of the sum (twenty thousand in Livy, ten thousand in Polybius) is a real error, but fortunately immaterial for characterising the event.

[4] Polybius (xxx. 5, 8) describes somewhat fully this independent policy: βούλεσθαι Ῥοδίους μηδένα τῶν ἐν ὑπεροχαῖς καὶ δυναστείαις ἀπελπίζειν τὴν ἐξ αὐτῶν

how dangerous such a position was under the present circumstances. The Rhodians were convinced that it would be better for them to give up their full independence, and that in the character of Roman allies they would be protected from the danger of complete annihilation. They therefore commissioned one of their ambassadors, Theaetetus, their admiral (nauarchus), to ask as a favour to be received into the Roman alliance. The free state voluntarily surrendered its independence, in order to insure its continued existence. Rome, after a delay of a couple of years, accepted the offer with apparent reluctance,[1] but not without first placing the Rhodians in a position of such weakness that their submission and their permanent obedience seemed guaranteed. By a decree of the senate, those territories in Lycia and Caria, which the Rhodians had received as a reward for their services in the war with Antiochus, were declared to be free. They were only allowed to retain their ancient possessions on the continent of Asia Minor (the district called Peraea), with the exception of Caunus and Stratonicea, which two towns, on hearing of the distress of Rhodes, had rebelled, and placed themselves under Roman protection.[2] Thus the island of Rhodes lost its most valuable dependencies.[3] But the

ἐπικουρίαν καὶ συμμαχίαν οὐκ ἐβούλοντο συνδυάζειν οὐδὲ προκαταλαμβάνειν σφᾶς αὐτοὺς ὅρκοις καὶ συνθήκαις, ἀλλ' ἀκέραιοι διαμένοντες κερδαίνειν τὰς ἐξ ἑκάστων ἐλπίδας. Compare Livy, xlv. 25, 9: Nam ita per tot annos in amicitia fuerant, ut sociali foedere secum Romanis non illigarent, ob nullam aliam causam quam ne spem regibus absciderent auxilii sui, si cui opus esset, neu sibi ipsis fructus ex benignitate et fortuna eorum percipiendi.

[1] It is highly probable that the apparent zeal with which the Rhodians sought the formal alliance of Rome was not genuine, but forced upon them by the conviction that Rome desired it. For the advantage of it was, in truth, more imaginary than real. When Philip of Macedonia had concluded peace with Rome, he too had, to comply with the desire of the senate, become a Roman ally. But this relation proved no security from Roman aggression, as Perseus found out to his cost. This could be no secret to the Rhodians, and therefore they could not of their own accord be over zealous to enter into that state of subjection which passed by the honourable name of alliance. They were compelled to accept it, and even to petition for it, as soon as they discovered that it was the wish of Rome.

[2] Polybius, xxx. 19, xxxi. 1 and 7.

[3] It would appear from the speech of Astymedes, the Rhodian ambassador

BOOK V.
171–168 B.C.

Humiliation of Eumenes of Pergamum.

decree of the senate that the island of Delos should be a free port was probably a more serious blow to the prosperity of Rhodes.[1] By this decree Delos was made the chief centre of commerce in the Eastern seas, and the harbour dues of Rhodes were reduced to a sixth of their former amount.[2] Even indirectly Roman policy tried to injure the Rhodians by supporting the Cretan pirates who annoyed the Rhodian commerce. Nevertheless, the thrifty people of Rhodes, though in more humble circumstances, continued for the time to enjoy a fair amount of prosperity.

If the Romans, in order to reap the fruits of their victory over Perseus, thought it necessary to crush in the various Greek states the party hostile to them, and in so doing to weaken and paralyse these states, their proceeding was indeed harsh; but from their point of view it was intelligible and justifiable. For in Achaia, Ætolia, and Rhodes, the state of parties was so unsettled before and during the war, that a sudden reaction in favour of the Macedonians, which had actually taken place in Epirus, might be expected anywhere. But it was not so in the kingdom of Pergamum. Here there were no republican parties with divided sympathies. The ruling house of Attalus alone determined the policy of the state, and this house was faithful to Rome. King Eumenes himself had urged the Romans to make war upon Perseus.[3] He had not ceased to set spies, to denounce his enemies, and to excite the Romans against him, until war was declared.

(Polybius, xxxi. 7, 12), that Rhodes derived an annual revenue of one hundred and twenty talents from Caunus and Stratonicea. It is impossible to suppress the suspicion that this is a huge exaggeration.

[1] Polybius, xxxi. 7, 10.

According to Polybius (xxx. 7, 12), they fell from a million of drachmae to one hundred and fifty thousand. But we ought to bear in mind that this statement, like that of the revenue derived from Caunus and Stratonicea (p. 271, note 3), is derived from a speech which the Rhodian ambassador delivered in Rome, with the object of moving compassion. It is therefore not worthy of full credit. Besides, it is difficult to see how, at the time when the speech was made (165 B.C.), the establishment of the free port of Delos, less than two years before, could have produced such a great effect.

p. 199

His personal appearance in Rome (172 B.C.) had brought about the decision of the senate. During the war, Pergamenian auxiliaries, under Attalus and Athenæus, the brothers of the king, accompanied the Roman armies, and Pergamenian ships took part in the operations of the Roman fleet, which turned out so inglorious and unsuccessful.[1] It is therefore surprising that the news was spread, in the third year of the war, that Eumenes had entered upon negotiations with Perseus, the object of which was nothing less than to give up the alliance with Rome, or eventually to mediate between the belligerents for the restoration of peace.[2] As these negotiations were carried on secretly, and came to no result, it is hard to decide how far the statements regarding them are trustworthy, and whether, indeed, Eumenes entertained any treacherous intentions.[3] The latter supposition is in the highest degree improbable, and, considering the relation in which Eumenes stood to Perseus and to the Romans, it seems almost impossible. We can only surmise that for some time he entertained the idea of attempting by his mediation to put an end to the war, which, by its unexpectedly long duration, must have been very burdensome to him as well as to all other Eastern states. Even king Prusias of Bithynia made an attempt in the same direction,[4] little thinking that the Romans would be displeased. Prusias was of so little importance that his fault might be overlooked. Not so the king of Pergamum, who, since the overthrow of Macedonia, was the only prince able to claim the right of carrying out an independent policy. He was therefore made to suffer for having entertained the mere hope of being able to deal with Rome as an equal. One breath of suspicion blighted the recollection of all

---

[1] See p. 244.   [2] See p. 237.

[3] Diodorus relates (xxxi. 7. 2, Dindorf) that documents were found to prove that Eumenes had planned an alliance with Perseus against Rome. This statement is not confirmed by any other evidence. Polybius does not refer to it, and indirectly contradicts it. Probably the only authority for it is some annalist who tried to justify the proceeding of Rome, and did not scruple to invent the facts for his indictment.   [4] Livy, xliv. 14, 6.

BOOK V.
171-168 B.C.

the devoted services which he had rendered in the war with Antiochus, and then in that with Perseus. In the exaggerated or altogether fictitious charges which Livy has borrowed from the Roman annalists, we hear only the echo of the complaints which were at that time loudly brought against Eumenes in the Roman camp or in Rome itself. It was said that he had suddenly and without cause called away his auxiliaries and his ships.[1] A pretext was evidently wanted for lowering the petted and somewhat spoiled ally to his former level of unconditional dependence.

Roman intrigues to cause dissension in the family of the Attalidæ.

The method adopted to reach this end is one of the worst specimens of the craftiness of Roman policy. After the victory of Rome and her allies over Macedonia, when Attalus, the brother of Eumenes, and commander of the Pergamenian auxiliaries, arrived in Rome in the crowd of congratulating and petitioning ambassadors from all states, several eminent men among the Roman nobility took him into their confidence, trying to set him against his brother,[2] and thus to sow the seeds of discord in the royal family of Pergamum. They gave him to understand that he was personally in great favour at Rome, and might obtain anything for himself, but that his brother Eumenes had forfeited the Roman friendship. A partition of the kingdom would have been desirable for the Romans. It was not difficult to find a pretext for rewarding Attalus and for resenting the intrigues of Eumenes. But the family of the Attalidæ presented a rare example of mutual affection and fidelity. Instead of conspiring against and betraying each other, as was so common in the Græco-Macedonian dynasties, the members of this family had always aided and supported one

---

[1] Livy, xliv. 13, 12 ; 20, 7.

[2] This is the report of Polybius (xxx. 1): γιγνομένης τῆς ἀπαντήσεως ὑπὲρ τὴν προσδοκίαν μετέωρος ἐγενήθη ταῖς ἐλπίσιν οὐκ εἰδὼς τὴν ἀληθινὴν αἰτίαν τῆς ἀποδοχῆς. Livy (xlv. 19) tries to produce the impression that Attalus, when he came to Rome, had already entertained ambitious views. He says: Suberat et secreta spes honorum præmiorumque ab senatu, quæ vix salva pietate ei contingere poterant.

another, and this was one of the most efficacious means by which they, in a short time, established and extended their dominion. It was not so easy to excite enmity between Attalus and Eumenes as it had been on a former occasion between Perseus and Demetrius.[1] Attalus, it is related, was almost tempted by the delusive proposals made to him, and was, for a moment, doubtful what to do; but he listened to the advice of his true friend, the physician Stratius, whom his brother had sent after him to Rome.[2] Besides, it was not hard to see that, apart from all natural feelings, policy commanded him to remain faithful to his brother; for as the latter was old and still childless, Attalus had the surest prospect of succeeding him on the throne, and he had actually begun to take an active part in the government.—Attalus showed much sense in escaping from his critical position. For the moment he gave no direct refusal to the insidious offers. He only asked for himself the two Thracian towns of Ænos and Maronea, as an earnest of what he was to have afterwards. Having obtained an encouraging reply, he left Rome without letting the Romans suspect that their perfidious design had failed. When they afterwards discovered this, their feigned partiality for him turned to anger, and they unceremoniously deprived him of the promised towns by declaring them free.[3]

Besides his chief commission of congratulation to the Romans, Attalus had been charged with another, which was to complain of an inroad of the Galatians into Pergamenian territory, and to ask for Roman help against them. In consequence of this request Roman ambassadors were sent to Asia Minor to remonstrate with the Galatians. We should fancy that these barbarians, who had already felt the heavy arm of the Romans, would without hesitation comply with the demands of the ambassadors; but, as the Romans gave out, they were only

---

[1] See p. 193, f.   [2] Polybius, xxx. 2, 1.
[3] The Romans nevertheless did not give up the scheme altogether, as appears from Polybius, xxxii. 5, 5.

the more exasperated, and continued their devastating inroads.[1] It is no injustice to these ambassadors to infer, and it is even hinted by Polybius, that they did in reality instigate the Galatians whilst they pretended to pacify them.

Eumenes began to perceive that his relations to Rome were no longer what they had been. Feeling that he must make an effort to regain the position which he had occupied before the war, he resolved, notwithstanding the bad state of his health, to undertake, in the winter of 167-166 B.C., the long journey to Italy, in order to try what effect he could produce in Rome by his personal appearance. But he met with a mortification which he could not have expected. When he had landed in Brundusium, a quæstor appeared before him, and informed him that a resolution had been passed in the senate forbidding foreign princes to come to Rome. He was therefore asked to state if he had any request to make to the senate, otherwise he must leave Italy without delay.[2] Eumenes saw that the old times were gone, that he was no longer wanted as an ally, and that he was contemptuously pushed aside. Declaring that he had no request to make of the senate, he left Italy to return to his own kingdom. He had but a short time to live; but it was long enough for him to see that he had now arrived at the stage which Philip of Macedonia had occupied after the defeat of Antiochus. Roman ambassadors went backwards and forwards, undermining the ground upon which he stood. It became known to everybody that he had fallen into disgrace. His subjects and his neighbours were formally called upon to prefer complaints against

---

[1] Livy says (xlv. 34, 13): P. Licinius cum regulo Gallorum est locutus
retulitque ferociorem eum deprecando factum. He then continues very
[...]ly ut mirum videri possit, inter tam opulentos reges Antiochum Ptole-
[...] tantum legatorum Romanorum verba valuisse, ut extemplo pacem
[...] apud Gallos nullius momenti fuisse. Polybius, who was either more
[...] more sensible or both tells us (xxx. 38): οἷς (the ambassadors)
[...]μεν ἔδωκαν ἐντολὰς εἰπεῖν οὐ ῥᾴδιον, στοχάζεσθαι δ' ἐκ τῶν μετὰ ταῦτα συμ-
[...]ων οὐ δυσχερές. [2] Polybius, xxx. 17.

him. The arrogant Caius Sulpicius Gallus, sent by the Roman senate, invited the malcontents to Sardes, and here, in the second city of the Pergamenian kingdom, he established his tribunal in the public gymnasium for the trial of the king, and listened for ten days with apparent satisfaction to the abuse and the complaints which were brought forward from all sides against Eumenes.[1] Though the Romans did not allow these proceedings to have any further result, but remained satisfied for the present with having humiliated an old friend, they nevertheless gained their object. Only by submitting unreservedly to Rome could Eumenes escape the fate of his former rivals, to whose ruin he had unwisely contributed. He died 159 B.C., leaving behind him[2] a son of tender age, for whom his brother Attalus, deservedly called Philadelphus, conducted the regency for twenty-one years. The kingdom of Pergamum preserved its seeming independence a little longer, until, in the time of the Gracchi, it suddenly, and without any painful death-struggle, passed over into the condition of a Roman province.

The ungenerous treatment of Eumenes by the Romans is the more striking if we compare it with that of the contemptible Prusias. This potentate was among those who, immediately after the Roman victory over Perseus, hastened to offer their congratulations to the senate, and on this occasion he exceeded the most servile flattery that had ever been witnessed in Rome. Appearing in the costume of a freedman, his shorn head covered with a hat, he humbly asked leave to bring an offering of thanks to the gods of the Roman people, his deliverers. When he was introduced into the senate, he bowed down to the ground according to the custom of Asiatic courtiers, and greeted the senators as 'the gods of his salvation.' So undignified was the manner in which he implored them to bestow their favour on him and on his son Nicomedes

Servility of Prusias.

---

[1] Polybius, xxxi. 10.   [2] Polybius, xxxii. 23.

whom he had brought with him, and to grant him a slight increase of territory, that Polybius felt too much disgust fully to report the scene. This writer gathers up the full significance of what passed in a single sentence. "Because Prusias appeared so utterly contemptible he received a favourable reply."[1] So much had the Roman nation by this time degenerated that they adopted the despotic principles of eastern rulers, and in their dealings with other states measured their benevolence according to the servility of their submission. It is easy to comprehend that the spectacle of such abject behaviour as that of Prusias must have had a demoralising effect upon the nation destined for universal dominion. If Roman magistrates became despots, and the spirit of republican equality vanished more and more, no inconsiderable part of the result was due to these wretched princes, who vied with one another in self-abasement and slavish flattery.

The effects of the Roman victory were felt not only by those Hellenic states which had been directly involved in the war with Perseus. Antiochus Epiphanes, the king of the distant Syria, had hoped meanwhile to carry out quietly his designs upon Egypt; but he was now reached by the hand of Rome. Cœlesyria was once more the bone of contention between Syria and Egypt. Antiochus defended it so successfully against an attack on the part of his rival, that after a victory at Pelusium he could penetrate into Egypt. Having here taken prisoner the young king Ptolemæus Philometor, his nephew, he entertained the idea of conquering the whole country; but the national pride of the Egyptians was now at length roused. In Alexandria, Euergetes, the younger brother of Ptolemæus Philometor, afterwards ironically called Physcon (pot-bellied), was proclaimed king, and Antiochus, after an ineffectual siege, was obliged to return to Syria. He left Ptolemæus, whom he had now taken under his

---

[1] Polybius, xxx. 16, 7: φανεὶς δὲ τελέως εὐκαταφρόνητος ἀπόκρισιν ἔλαβε δι' αὐτὸ τοῦτο φιλάνθρωπον.

protection, in Egypt to fight against the pretender. The two brothers, however, understanding what their interest demanded, came to an agreement, and opposed their combined forces to the claims of Antiochus, who kept possession of Pelusium and conquered Cyprus. At the same time they applied to Rome for protection.

Antiochus now invaded Egypt a second time, and had advanced as far as Alexandria, when he was met by a Roman embassy sent by the senate to arrange a peace between the two rival states. The chief of the embassy was C. Popillius Lænas,[1] a man eminently qualified by his harsh, imperious temper to enforce obedience to a Roman word of command. In this mission the Romans did not think it necessary to act as cautiously and tenderly as their Greek allies, whose attempts at mediation they had so cruelly resented. They had indeed tried already to settle the quarrel; but as long as the war with Macedonia lasted, Antiochus had not listened to their remonstrances.[2] Popillius Lænas was determined that this time the voice of Rome should not be slighted. Meeting the king of Syria a few miles from Alexandria, he handed him the letter of the senate without any previous greeting, and asked him to read it. It contained a request that he should leave Egypt at once and make peace. The king replied evasively that he would consider the matter. Popillius then drew with his staff a circle in the sand round the king, saying, 'Before you step out of this circle tell me what answer I shall bear to the senate.'[3] 'I shall do what the senate requires of me,' replied Antiochus, after some hesitation, and not until then did Popillius offer his hand to the king as a friend and ally of the Roman people. Having thus performed his task, he sailed to Cyprus, and ordered the Syrian fleet to with-

---

[1] As consul, 172 B.C., he had for a time defied the authority of the senate in the interest of his brother Marcus, consul of 173 B.C., whose conflict with the senate is related above, p. 202, ff.   [2] Polybius, xxix. 10.
[3] Polybius, xxix. 11; Livy, xlv. 12; Cicero, *Philipp.* viii. 8; Valer. Maxim. vi. 4, 3.

BOOK V.
171-168 B.C.

Results of the battle of Pydna.

draw. Antiochus evacuated Pelusium, and returned to his own states. It was evident that the battle of Pydna had had its effect even upon the far east. The Roman republic had, without a formal recognition, acquired sovereign rights over Syria and Egypt.

The great importance of this battle has now been noticed in its effect upon Macedonia, Illyria, Greece, Rhodes, the Pergamenian kingdom, Syria, and Egypt. It was so decisive that we can date from this time the establishment of the Roman dominion over the world.[1] As a mere battle, it cannot be reckoned among the great military achievements of the Romans or any other nation; but the more remote causes which led to it are, as it were, manifested in its results. It was gained not by the military genius of the Roman general, nor in consequence of an exceptional effort with an excessive sacrifice. On the contrary, it was fought by a single consular army and a general of average capacity; and the victory was gained not by any display of genius, but by common military routine. The result was due to the Roman institutions, not to extraordinary events or extraordinary men. What chances had the world in those days in struggling against a nation which, even when it sent out men as incompetent as Licinius, Hostilius, Lucretius, or Hortensius, found itself at the worst only interrupted for a short time in its victorious course, and could look on calmly until a more able general or some fortunate accident brought the hostile armies under the sword of the legions? The barbarous tribes in the north and west, who were too ignorant to appreciate the relative proportion of strength, and too poor to have much to forfeit besides their bare lives, could alone venture to defy the Roman legions for some years longer; and in thus acting these

---

[1] Polybius, xxxii. 11. 6. Speaking of the deterioration of public morality consequent upon the war with Perseus, Polybius says: συνέβη δὲ τὴν παροῦσαν ἄγνοιαν οἷον ἐκλάμψαι κατὰ τοὺς νῦν λεγομένους καιρούς, πρῶτον μὲν διὰ τὸ, καταλυθείσης τῆς ἐν Μακεδονίᾳ βασιλείας, δοκεῖν ἀδήριτον αὐτοῖς ὑπάρχειν τὴν περὶ τῶν ὅλων ἐξουσίαν.

tribes relied partly on their courage, and still more perhaps on the difficulties which their countries presented for the march of armies. The wars that still continued in civilised countries were nothing but the final death-struggle of despairing nations.

Æmilius Paullus would not have been a member of the Roman nobility if he had not taken to himself the greater part of the credit of this glorious victory, and if he had not conducted himself from this time forward as a general justly entitled to triumph. There was very little left to do after the battle of Pydna that could be called military work. A few towns in Thessaly had still to be conquered, or rather to be plundered; for serious resistance was out of the question.[1] There were also a few penal sentences to be executed, for instance, on the town of Antissa, in the island of Lesbos, which was charged with having harboured and supported the Macedonian fleet during the war. This place was destroyed, and the inhabitants were removed to Methymna.[2] The dreadful punishment which was inflicted on Epirus before the return of the Roman army to Italy was perhaps not yet resolved upon.[3] The consul had leisure to enjoy a journey through Greece until the ten plenipotentiaries of the senate should arrive to settle with him the affairs of Macedonia. Æmilius showed an unfeigned admiration for Greek antiquity by visiting with his son Scipio, and with Athenæus, a brother of king Eumenes, all those places which were sacred in the mythology and religion of the Greeks or memorable in their history, such as Delphi, Aulis, Athens, Corinth, Sicyon, Argos, Epidaurus, Lacedæmon, Megalopolis, and Olympia.[4] Everywhere he offered up sacrifices in that spirit of toleration which marked the religion of the Greek and Roman world, and which, recognising under

---

[1] The towns of Æginium and Agassæ evidently offered no resistance (Livy, xlv. 27), but perhaps Meliboea did. On the destruction of the walls of Demetrias, see Diodorus. xxxi. 8, 6, Dindorf.   [2] Livy, xlv. 31, 14.
[3] Below, p. 283.   [4] Livy, xlv. 27.

BOOK V.
171–168 B.C.

Congress of Amphipolis.

numerous names and shapes embodiments of the same deity,[1] allowed every nation, and even every man, the right of worshipping this deity in his own fashion. At Olympia he was struck by the masterpiece of Phidias, which brought the great Zeus visibly before him. The Olympian Jupiter was honoured by him with such sacrifices as if he had been the high and mighty protector of the Roman Capitol itself. At Delphi Æmilius found the pedestal on which statues of Perseus were to have been placed.[2] We regret to hear that he was mean enough to order that his own should be erected in the place of those of his conquered enemy.

On his return to Amphipolis he conducted the long and important discussions of the senatorial delegates regarding the new settlement of Macedonia and of the whole of Greece.[3] Ambassadors had arrived from all parts of the Grecian world in Europe and Asia, from Africa and all the innumerable islands in the eastern seas. The smallest community had some request to make of the powerful Roman imperator, or to implore pardon and mercy; the most powerful states were eager to make professions of loyalty. Before this large assemblage Æmilius celebrated at great expense magnificent games, such as it was customary to exhibit at the regular national festivals in Olympia or on the isthmus of Corinth. The Roman general was proud of being able to arrange a festival as skilfully as the Greeks in accordance with approved rules. But it did not occur to him to exhibit any contest, game, or sport of national Italian growth. He showed the Greeks no fighting gladiators, but collected athletes and racehorses from all parts of the Hellenic world, and issued invitations in all directions.[4] There was a certain significance in the fact that while the first liberator of Greece, Flamininus, proclaimed the success of his mission at the regular Isthmian festival, the present

---

[1] Livy, xlii. 3, 9, contrasts this feeling with the notions of those who acted 'tanquam non idem ubique dii immortales essent.'
[2] Polybius, xxx. 14; Livy, xlv. 27.   [3] See p. 256.
[4] Livy, xlv. 32, 8.

conqueror of Macedonia did not bind himself to ancient times or places, but assembled the Greeks in the country recently subjected, and thus made it clear that they had left their old orbits, and would henceforth have to move as satellites round a new sun. A huge pile of captured arms was erected, and lighted by Æmilius himself, as if it were intended to show that the funeral games of Græco-Macedonian independence should be finished by an act emblematic of the burning of the body.

In the autumn of the year 167 B.C. the Roman army began its homeward march. Æmilius was anxious to preserve undiminished the valuable booty, consisting of money and works of art, in order to show it to his countrymen on the day of his triumph, and then deliver it into the state treasury. The Roman soldiers, exasperated at being deprived of it, received a promise of compensation. Epirus lay on their way. A portion, at least, of Epirus had joined Perseus, and was now to undergo its deserved punishment. It was in vain that after the Roman victory the leaders of the hostile party had been deserted by their followers, and had died by a voluntary death. It was in vain that all the towns had surrendered to Lucius Anicius, who entered the country from Illyria. Paramount considerations required that Epirus should be visited by a punishment justified by the terrible usages of the ancient world. Every Roman soldier was here to receive the extra pay to which he considered himself entitled, and which had been withheld in Macedonia. The senate sent an order to Æmilius that he was to deliver up the whole country to plunder,[1] an order which was executed in cold blood. As the leaders of the Macedonian party had been sent from Epirus to Italy, and Charops, the Roman partisan, was *de facto* the ruler of the country, the Epirots hoped to be spared further sufferings. They were soon undeceived. Æmilius marched into the country with his legions, summoned the heads of the towns and villages

[1] Livy, xlv. 34.

to his presence, ordered them to set apart from their property all the gold and silver, and sent troops with them, as if the intention had been merely to receive the treasures. Then, on one and the same day, the Roman soldiers fell upon all the towns throughout Epirus,[1] and plundered them completely. About one hundred and fifty thousand people were then made slaves, and seventy towns sacked and destroyed. Never yet had Rome annihilated a whole nation so systematically and so cruelly; and this was done not to execute a penal sentence, but to satisfy the rapacity and greed of Roman soldiers, which, after all, as was shown by later experience, was insatiable.[2]

News of the battle of Pydna brought to Rome.

Four days after the battle of Pydna the news of a great victory was spread in Rome.[3] The joy was great. But on investigating the matter it was found to be merely an empty rumour. So much the greater was the delight when nine days later Quintus Fabius, Lucius Lentulus, and Quintus Metellus, the messengers despatched by Æmilius with the news of the victory, sent a man in advance before them with the authentic report and details of the battle, and when soon after they themselves made their solemn entry. The people were in almost as boundless an excitement as they had been when, in their great distress at the time of the Hannibalic war, the long succession of evil tidings was at last interrupted by the news of a glorious victory over Hasdrubal on the river Metaurus. Again, as at that time, the crowd poured forth to meet the messengers of victory, and almost blocked their way to the forum and to the senate-house. There was indeed no

---

[1] It appears from Strabo, vii. 7, 3, that of all the Epirots the Molossians suffered most.   [2] Plutarch, *Æmil. Paull.* 29.

[3] Livy, xlv. 1: Quarto post die quam cum rege est pugnatum, cum in ludi fierent, murmur repente populi tota spectacula pervasit, pugnatum in Macedonia et devictum regem esse; dein fremitus increvit; postremo clamor … que velut certo nuntio victoriæ allato est exortus. According to Cicero (*de Natura Deorum*, ii. 2) it was the divine twins Castor and Pollux who … the news just as they had done after the battle of the lake Regillus … They appeared to a certain Publius Vatinius by night-time, … on the road from Reate to Rome, and told him that on that day … had been made prisoner. Compare Valerius Max. i. 8, 1.

comparison between the present state of the republic and its circumstances in the second Punic war. Actual danger, distress, and trouble were never felt during the struggle with the Macedonian king. But yet the people impatiently looked forward to peace, and one of the first measures which the senate took was to stop all further preparations for war, and to dismiss the reserves. A festival of public thanksgiving, lasting for five days, showed the satisfaction which the senate felt in the successful end of the war.[1]

These feelings had time to cool before the final return of Æmilius Paullus, which was delayed for a whole year by the settlement of affairs in Macedonia. But even then the reception of Æmilius in Rome was brilliant. He arrived with all the pomp of a general celebrating his triumph. Sailing on a monster ship, with sixteen tiers of oars, the state barge of Perseus, richly decorated with arms, purple sails and streamers, he ascended the Tiber as far as the town, watched by the dense crowds of spectators that lined both banks. Soon afterwards Octavius, the commander of the fleet, and Anicius, the conqueror of Gentius, also arrived in Rome. The senate decreed the honours of a triumph to each of the three. In the whole town, and in the surrounding country, were already accumulated the booty and the prisoners destined to adorn these triumphal processions.

But, after all, the man who had personally the first claim to be rewarded by his country, the man who had served Rome most honestly, faithfully, and successfully in a great and decisive war, was almost deprived of an honour which had been repeatedly accorded to men of mean capacity on the strength of very doubtful victories over contemptible barbarians. This danger Æmilius Paullus incurred because he was distinguished by a virtue rare among Roman politicians of his day. If he had allowed his soldiers and subaltern officers to steal and

[1] Livy, xlv. 2, 12.

plunder to their hearts' content, no one would have opposed his claims to a triumph. But he had saved as much as possible of the Macedonian booty for the state treasury. The proceeds of the plundering of Epirus, which the soldiers were to receive as their only compensation, amounted to four hundred denarii for every horseman and two hundred for every foot soldier.[1] The troops were dissatisfied. They considered themselves curtailed of their rewards, and resolved to make their general suffer for it. Servius Sulpicius Gallus, who had served as military tribune in Macedonia, urged in the comitia tributa that the proposal, which the senate had approved, of granting Æmilius Paullus the 'imperium' within the town during the days of his triumph should be rejected. With the help of the soldiers, who crowded to the voting-place in the Capitol, he almost succeeded in preventing the triumph of Æmilius by a resolution of the people. The friends of the general, with great difficulty, secured a decision in favour of the triumph. Thus Rome was almost deprived of a day of national rejoicing and of a triumphal show more brilliant than any that had, up to this time, been exhibited. The contemptible opposition made to the well-earned honours of one of the best men in Rome revealed a weakness in the military organization which would have had a most pernicious effect, had not the enemies of Rome suffered from greater evils. This weakness was caused by the fact that political dissensions were not confined to the senate or the market-place, but extended to the camp. As the same men were on one day leaders of political parties at Rome, and on another officers of different rank and station in the army, the bonds of discipline were naturally loosened. The divisions among the leaders spread to the mass of common soldiers, who inclined to one side or to the other from such considerations as can be expected to influence the rank and

---

[1] Livy, xlv. 34, 5. The numbers given by Plutarch (*Æmil. Paull.* 29) are different. It is impossible, and not very material, to ascertain the exact number.

file of an army. Every Roman general had therefore to expect to find among his troops a certain amount of ill-will and opposition; but if, in addition to this, he ventured, like Æmilius Paullus, to set his face, on principle, against their disorderly habits and insatiable greed,[1] if he kept strict discipline, and if, especially in money matters, he had an eye to the public interests, his popularity in the army was in a precarious state. It is a proof of unusual honesty in Æmilius Paullus that he did not stoop to act as a military demagogue, although, like every noble Roman, he eagerly aspired to distinction, and especially to his triumph, the highest of all honours. Fortunately he obtained it in full measure, in spite of the undignified jealousy of base and envious detractors.—But he could not escape the jealousy of the gods, which, according to the notions of antiquity, he had drawn upon himself by an excess of good fortune. He was visited by a harder fate than the vanquished and imprisoned king. Perseus had at least the consolation that, in his deep fall, his children were spared to him. But the house of Æmilius was a house of mourning while all Rome cheered and applauded him. Five days before it he lost the third of his four sons, a lad of fourteen, and three days after the festival the youngest, a boy of twelve, was carried off.[2] Thus his home was desolate, for his two remaining sons had already been adopted by the families of the Scipios and Fabii.

We must pause for one moment to contemplate the spectacle of the triumph which ended this memorable war. Rome had long been accustomed to magnificent sights of this kind. The conquerors of Tarentum and Carthage, of Philip and Antiochus, had exhibited before the Roman people the greatness of their exploits in brilliant shows. But the past was entirely eclipsed by the magnificence of the procession which brought home to the Romans the fact that the empire of Alexander the Great was com-

---

[1] This had been done by Æmilius Paullus in Macedonia. Plutarch, *Æmil. Paull.* 13. [2] *Ibid.* 35.

pletely overthrown. The festival lasted three days. On the first day two hundred and fifty wagons, containing the paintings and statues taken in the war, were driven through the streets and exhibited to the people. On the second day were seen wagons with trophies consisting of piles of the finest and most precious arms. Then followed a procession of three thousand men carrying the captured silver (two thousand two hundred and fifty talents); after these the silver vessels, drinking horns, bowls, and goblets. The third day was the most magnificent of the whole festival. A string of animals decorated for sacrifice was followed by the bearers of the captured gold and golden vessels, the heirlooms of the dynasty of Macedonia. Then came the royal chariot of Perseus, with his arms and his diadem; behind it walked his children, led by their attendants and tutors. They were too young to comprehend the full extent of their misfortunes, yet it was a sight that melted even the hard hearts of the Romans to pity. Next came Perseus himself in unkingly garb, bowed down and completely broken in spirit. He had begged and entreated to be spared this humiliation; but even the gentle Æmilius gave him, as is reported, the reproachful answer, 'It lay, and it still lies, in your power to deliver yourself.' But the king of Macedonia had not the courage for self-murder, and paid dearly for the last few years of a miserable life which far surpassed death in bitterness. His friends and higher servants, who had been taken prisoners in the war, and now walked behind their master, had tears and prayers only for him, and almost forgot their own fate in contemplation of his overwhelming misfortune. Four hundred golden crowns, the offerings of Greek communities, were carried behind the prisoners; then came the general himself on his chariot, dressed in the garb and decked with the insignia of Jupiter Capitolinus, with a laurel branch in his hand. The whole army also was adorned with laurels, and marched in warlike order behind their chief, singing songs of victory, mingled with occasional sallies of satire directed against him.¹ A solemn sacrifice in the Capitol concluded the festival.

The triumph of Æmilius was followed at short intervals by the triumphs of the pro-prætor Cn. Octavius and the pro-prætor L. Anicius, who had conquered Gentius. Octavius, who, with his fleet, had in reality accomplished nothing, could produce neither prisoners nor booty, and his triumph only served as a foil for that of Æmilius Paullus. Anicius, it is true, also brought home a captured king. But Gentius was of too little importance to bear comparison with Perseus.² The fame of Æmilius Paullus could only be increased by the fact that the men who had conducted the secondary operations under him also enjoyed the honours of a triumph.

Æmilius Paullus was indeed not only the first citizen of the state,³ but the model of a Roman of the best time. Without possessing eminent qualities as a statesman or as a soldier, he was nevertheless capable of doing his duty creditably in every capacity. He was a man of average abilities, and free from the vices of excessive party spirit, cupidity, and ambition. He was not, like his contemporary Cato, a one-sided worshipper of everything old; but he was conservative in the best sense of the word, anxious to preserve old institutions, but at the same time

CHAP. III.
171-168 B.C.

Character of Æmilius Paullus.

---

¹ This was not an exception on the present occasion, and no proof of special discontent on the part of the soldiers, but a practice common on occasion of a triumphal procession; a license in which the soldiers felt a kind of satisfaction on their release from military control.

² Polybius, xxx. 13, gives an amusing description of the musical entertainment which Anicius provided for his countrymen on the occasion of his triumph. Having sent for the greatest performers from Greece, and having erected a stage in the Circus, he ordered the musicians and chorus singers to produce a musical contest which, according to his notion, was to consist not in harmoniously playing together, but in playing different parts against each other. This resulted in an awful confusion, and changed the musical contest into a muscular contest of the musicians and dancers, to the boundless delight of the enlightened spectators: 10. ὡς δὲ καὶ περιζωσάμενός τις τῶν χορευτῶν ἐκ τοῦ χοροῦ στραφεὶς ἦρε τὰς χεῖρας ἀπὸ πυγμῆς πρὸς τὸν ἐπιφερόμενον αὐλητήν, τότ' ἤδη κρότος ἐξαίσιος ἐγένετο. καὶ κραυγὴ τῶν θεωμένων, κ.τ.λ. Polybius ends by saying: ἄλεκτον ἦν τὸ συμβαῖνον. Περὶ δὲ τῶν τραγῳδῶν ἐὰν ἐπιβάλωμαι λέγειν, δόξω τισὶ διαχλευάζειν. ³ Cicero, Brut. 15.

VOL. III. U

BOOK V.
171-168 B.C.

to improve them. Although adhering to the true Roman virtues, unselfish fidelity to his country, rigorous discipline in the field, temperance and moderation, he did not exclude from his mind the Hellenic culture which at that time had begun to exert its powerful influence. On the contrary, he strove to make his own countrymen more and more familiar with it. It would have been fortunate for Rome if succeeding statesmen had taken him for a model. But with the fall of the Macedonian kingdom the Roman republic had obtained undisputed dominion over the civilised world, and this dominion could not be exercised by simple citizens, who, as the laws of republican government demanded, alternately ruled and obeyed. In the conquered countries Rome educated the men for whom the modest home of republican liberty became too small, who were anxious to be masters also in Rome, and who finally were obliged to submit to one who proved stronger than the rest.

CHAPTER IV.

THE FALL OF MACEDONIA AND GREECE, 148–146 B.C.

It would have been better for the Macedonian nation if the Romans, immediately after the overthrow of the monarchy, had converted the country into a Roman province. The unnatural division of Macedonia into four separate parts, and the restrictions put upon free commercial intercourse, stood in the way of a rapid recovery from the calamities of war which the people had suffered while the form of a republican constitution, forced upon them and called 'liberty', in contrast to their old monarchical government, was of no value to a nation not accustomed to republican institutions. The result was that disputes and civil wars immediately broke out in the unhappy country.[1] If our records were not so extremely meagre (the narrative of Livy breaks off at the forty-fifth book, and the fragments of Polybius become more and more scanty), we should probably hear of more than one act of atrocity like that of a certain Damasippus who caused the whole legislative assembly of a community to be massacred.[2] Perhaps a revolt would have taken place immediately after the fall of Perseus, if the country had not been too much exhausted and deprived of its natural leaders by the banishment of all influential men.[3] But at length, nineteen years after the battle of Pydna, the Macedonians unexpectedly found a chief who led them once more, and for the last time, to a desperate struggle

---

[1] Polybius, xxxi. 12, 12: συνέβαινε γὰρ τοὺς Μακεδόνας ἀήθεις ὄντας δημοκρατικῆς καὶ συνεδριακῆς πολιτείας στασιάζειν πρὸς αὑτούς.

[2] Polybius, xxxi. 25, 2.   [3] See p. 260.

against the Roman legions, and forced the Romans to put an end for evermore to that shadow of independence which was more ruinous than subjection.

Perseus, having borne the disgrace of public exhibition in his conqueror's triumph, was thrown into a close subterraneous dungeon with a number of common criminals, and would have perished of starvation in the midst of foulness and filth, had not his fellow-prisoners, showing more feeling than the Roman gaolers, spared him some scraps of their scanty food. When the unhappy man had been kept for seven days in this condition, Æmilius Paullus and some of the more humane among the Roman nobles obtained for him from the senate the permission to breathe the fresh air of heaven and to see the light of day. He was allowed to spend the remainder of his life in the small Marsian town of Alba, on the lake Fucinus, always, it is said, looking forward to the day which would place him once more on the throne of Macedonia.[1] His eldest son Philip soon followed him to the grave. The younger outlived him, and afterwards served the magistrates in Alba as town-clerk; he is also reported to have distinguished himself as a turner and carver.

Some months after Philip, the son of Perseus, had died in Alba at the age of eighteen, the surprising news arrived from Macedonia that this same Philip had appeared on the banks of the Strymon at the head of an army of Thracians, intending to take possession of the Macedonian throne, the heritage of his father.[2] He had defeated the Macedonian militia, crossed the river Strymon, and then gained another victory which gave him access to the interior of the country. At first the Romans would not believe these reports. They recalled to mind a mean adventurer, the son of a fuller in Adramyttium, who had a short time previously given himself out for a natural son of Perseus, and had been delivered up to Rome by Demetrius of Syria. This adventurer, Andriscus by name,

---

[1] Diodorus, xxxi. 9, Dindorf. [2] Polybius, xxxvii. 1, d.

had hardly been thought worthy of notice, and had been so badly guarded that he succeeded in escaping from Italy.[1] Once more entering upon the scene of action under the name of Philip, he had, as reports ran, in a short time obtained possession of Macedonia, where adherents joined him from all sides. But the Romans would not yet look upon the matter as serious. They thought it sufficient to send Publius Scipio Nasica to Macedonia, without troops, to re-establish order by the mere authority of the Roman name. When Nasica arrived in Greece, he found a state of affairs that could not be controlled by peaceable means. It was necessary to support the commands of the Roman senate by force of arms. He, therefore, collected troops in Greece, especially in Achaia; and with these he succeeded in driving the pseudo-Philip out of Thessaly, into which country he had already penetrated. Soon afterwards the prætor Publius Juventius Thalna arrived with a Roman legion[2] and entered Macedonia. But the despised opponent now showed himself not quite unworthy of the honour to which he had boldly aspired. He defeated the Romans in a pitched battle, killing the prætor and a great part of the army. The Macedonian revolt was assuming the proportions of a war just at a time when Carthage was beginning to defend herself desperately in order to preserve her existence as a state, and when Roman arms in Spain were baffled by an unexpected vigour on the part of the native races. There was plenty of fuel accumulated in all parts of Greece; if this should catch fire, it was possible that a time might come like that of the Hannibalic war, when Rome was threatened by Africa, Spain, and Macedonia at once.

At this conjuncture the Romans had the good fortune to select the prætor Quintus Cæcilius Metellus to take the command (148 B.C.), and to send him with a consular army to Greece. He was supported along the coast by the fleet of King Attalus II. of Pergamum, who was glad of an

[1] Livy, Epit. 49; Zonaras, ix. 28.   [2] Florus, i. 30.

opportunity of serving the Romans, and thus proving his loyal attachment. Andriscus, after a successful cavalry engagement, divided his army, in order to invade Thessaly with a part of it in the prætor's rear. This was the cause of his ruin. The two corps, thus weakened, were defeated one after another. Metellus pursued the adventurer in his flight to Thrace, and after another victory obtained his extradition by the Thracian king Byzes.[1] Within a year the war was ended. Macedonia was converted into a Roman province, and from this time forward lost its position in history as an independent state. It was enlarged as far as the Adriatic, so as to include the harbours of Apollonia and Dyrrhachium. The unlucky division into four separate districts was abolished, and the different communities were allowed to preserve their own local self-government; but all sovereign rights passed over to the Roman republic, and were exercised by an annually changing governor. The defence of the northern frontier was now in the hands of the Romans, the country paying for it the moderate tax of one hundred talents. These conditions were, no doubt, favourable for the social and economic condition of the impoverished country. The preservation of internal peace was a compensation for the loss of the powerful position which Macedonia had held for more than two centuries. If the Romans had known how to protect their subjects from the cupidity of their own officials and capitalists, as well as from foreign enemies, the loss of independence would, under the prevailing circumstances, have been an unqualified gain for Macedonia.

We must notice one more and final struggle of the expiring national feeling in Macedonia. In the year 142 B.C., six years after the overthrow of the false Philip,

---

[1] Zonaras, ix. 28. Zonaras, moreover, relates that a new pretender under the name of Alexander was also defeated by Metellus. This seems to be an error. Zonaras no doubt thought of the insurrection which took place six years later, and which was crushed by the quæstor Tremellius, according to Livy *Epit.* 53, and Eutropius, iv. 7. See below, p. 294.

another pretended son of Perseus made his appearance and attempted to upset the firmly-rooted Roman dominion. However, the quæstor Tremellius soon put an end to the insurrection, and henceforward we hear of no further attempts to restore the monarchy of Philip and Alexander the Great. It was, and remained, absorbed in the new empire of Rome.

For the Hellenic nation too, the same fatal end had by this time come. Although they had degenerated and fallen from the high position to which they had been raised by their intellect, by their wonderful genius in art and literature, by their great achievements in policy and war, by their national virtues and even their passions, they, nevertheless, continue to engage our attention and our sympathy in an immeasurably higher degree than the nations whose early history we do not know or cannot trace back so far as that of the Hellenes. The Greeks, it is true, rushed blindly and madly into the last struggle, and fought in a manner unworthy of their past history; still we cannot deny them our sympathies, for it was the detestable policy of the Roman senate which, creating in Greece a state of things worse than political death, had produced that exasperation which finally turned into rage and madness.

We have seen that after the victory over Perseus all the Greek states, without distinction, were treated by the Romans as open or secret enemies.[1] When the natural leaders and advisers of the people had been carried off to Italy, the intimidated and impoverished remnant was handed over to the tender mercies of the creatures of Rome, who were now lords and masters in the country, without rivals or opponents. The outrages committed by Lyciscus in Ætolia, by Mnasippus in Bœotia, and by others, but especially by the infamous Charops in Epirus,[2] were so great that the Romans themselves could not countenance them, though they were ostensibly committed in the

[1] P. 261, ff. [2] P. 261.

interest of Roman supremacy. It was a system of the most shameless robbery, aided by exile and murder, either without all forms of justice or under such forms as were a mockery of it.[1] When at last the worst of these tyrants had, one after another, sunk into the grave, the tormented countries were allowed a short time of peace; but decay and ruin were visible everywhere, just as if a devastating storm had passed over them. The impoverished people sank into a new and terrible barbarism. The primæval state of man seemed to have returned, in which everybody's hand was raised against his neighbour. Sheer hunger drove the miserable wretches to despair and violence. Whole populations became bands of robbers. It was no longer the despised Ætolians alone who lived by plunder. Other nations, such as the Thebans, nay, the highly cultivated Athenians themselves, were not ashamed to do the same.

Athens had, indeed, suffered greatly during the war, partly from the contributions imposed upon it by the Roman armies and fleets, partly from the stagnation of commerce. In order to indemnify the city, and at the same time to honour the principal seat of Greek science and art, the Romans had bestowed upon it the territory around the ruined town of Haliartus and also the islands of Delos and Lemnos. Nevertheless, the Athenians found themselves in such distress, that they undertook an expedition (156 B.C.) against the town of Oropus, which was subject to them, merely for the purpose of plundering it.[2] Nothing shows in more striking colours the utter wretchedness and degeneracy of the Greeks, at this time, than the consequences resulting from this expedition. The Oropians, of course, complained at Rome of the wrong they had suffered at the hand of Athens. The town of Sicyon was designated by the Romans to act as arbitrator, and con-

---

[1] Polybius, xxx. 14, 7; xxxii. 20 and 24; Diodorus, xxxi. 31. Dindorf.
[2] Pausanias, vii. 11, 4: 'Αθηναίων δὲ ὁ δῆμος ἀνάγκῃ πλέον ἢ ἑκουσίως διαρπάσουσιν Ὠρωπὸν ὑπήκοόν σφισιν οὖσαν· πενίας γὰρ ἐς τὸ ἔσχατον 'Αθηναῖοι τηνικαῦτα ἧκον, ὅτι ὑπὸ Μακεδόνων πολέμῳ πιεσθέντες μάλιστα 'Ελλήνων.

demned Athens to pay to the Oropians a compensation of five hundred talents, a sum which the impoverished city was utterly unable to raise, and which was, moreover, quite out of proportion to the plunder gained in Oropus. The Athenians, in their trouble, applied to Rome for a reduction of the fine. For this purpose they employed the eloquence of the most eminent philosophers, selecting as their spokesman the academician Carneades, the stoic Diogenes, and the peripatetic Critolaus. These men, appearing as ambassadors at Rome, produced so great an impression among the numerous admirers of the Greek language and literature, that old Cato began to fear for the preservation of the ancestral morals, and urged the senate to dismiss the dangerous visitors as quickly as possible. The Roman senate enjoyed the rare pleasure of hearing philosophy and eloquence combined, begging for the remission of a fine which the town of the Muses and Graces, the home of Sophocles, Phidias, and Plato, had incurred by an outrageous act of robbery.[1]

The senate reduced the fine to one hundred talents. But the Athenians had neither the inclination nor the means to pay even this sum. They agreed upon some sort of compromise with the Oropians and placed a garrison in the town, whereupon the dispute seemed to subside and some years passed in peace.[2] But at length the Oropians, wishing to rid themselves of the Athenian garrison, applied to the Achaean league, and, in order to

---

[1] Pausanias, vii. 11; Cicero, *De Orat.* ii. 37. For the benefit of those senators who did not understand Greek, the speeches of the ambassadors were translated by the senator Caius Acilius. Plutarch, *Cato Maior*, 22; Gellius, vii. 14.

[2] Pausanias (vii. 11), to whom we owe the details of this curious transaction, adds that the Oropians gave hostages to the Athenians. This is not quite clear. The Athenians had from the beginning been in the wrong, and had been compelled by the arbitrators and by the Roman senate to make a compensation to the people of Oropus. How came it that now the injured town was made to give hostages to Athens and to receive an Athenian garrison, as if it had given rise to the quarrel? It seems that our informant does not give us the whole story. Perhaps the Athenians had some legal ground for their harsh treatment of Oropus, such as a refusal of obedience, or a refusal to pay taxes.

BOOK V.
148-146 B.C.

insure the aid which they needed, bribed the chief magistrate of the league, the Spartan Menalcidas, with the sum of ten talents; whereupon the Athenians plundered Oropus once more and then withdrew their garrison. Menalcidas, with his troops, arrived too late to save the Oropians from this second spoliation. He nevertheless extorted from them the ten talents for which he had bargained. He had promised to pay to Callicrates one half of this sum for lending him his assistance; but he preferred keeping the whole for himself. Callicrates actually threatened to bring an action for the recovery of the money; Menalcidas sought to screen himself from the charge by applying to Diæus, whom he first propitiated with a bribe. This contemptible quarrel about money grew into a dispute between Sparta and the Achaean league, and caused the Romans to interfere and to sweep away the last remnant of freedom.[1]

Achaia after the war.

After the war with Perseus the expulsion of all the best citizens had, as we have seen, placed the Achaean league in the power of the party which, headed by Callicrates, followed only one principle in their policy, that of showing themselves obedient to Rome in all things. The Romans, having thus full security for their obedience, had allowed the Achaeans to preserve nominally their independence and to call themselves the allies of Rome. The constitution and territory of the league remained what they had been. It included the whole of Peloponnesus, with some towns like Pleuron in Ætolia and Heraclea on Mount Œta. Our records are very meagre regarding the events of the years immediately following the victory at Pydna. It appears that the Peloponnesus was thoroughly exhausted, and that, in consequence, there was a dearth of events. One feeling predominated among the Achaean people for many years, a longing for the return of the exiles. We can easily realise how painfully the sudden removal of one thousand prominent men must

[1] Pausanias, vii. 11, 7, f.

have been felt, if we imagine the occurrence of a similar calamity in a country like Switzerland or Belgium. Nay, would not even a great European power be paralysed for years if so many, or half as many, of its leading citizens suddenly disappeared from the scene of public life?[1]

In addition to their sorrow for the exiles, the Achaeans had the feeling of having suffered an injustice; and this feeling was augmented and aggravated by the consciousness of their impotence to revenge themselves on the authors of their misfortune. Callicrates and his adherents tried in vain to moderate the exasperation of their countrymen, or at least to impose silence. He would have had to banish the whole people if he wished to protect himself from hearing even the boys in the street call him a traitor.[2] By degrees the Achaeans took courage, not indeed to entertain thoughts of resistance, but to proffer a humble request. They carried the resolution in their federal congress, that an embassy should be sent to Rome for the purpose of imploring the senate graciously to let the exiles be tried in a court of law, so that those at least might return home against whom there was no cause of complaint. The Romans pretended to be astonished at this modest request. As the exiles had been condemned by the Achaeans themselves, it was not for the senate, they said, to try them again.[3] A second embassy (164 B.C.) sought to confute this assertion, and entreated the senate,

Return of the exiles delayed.

---

[1] If such a thing could be possible, let anyone imagine what would be the condition of England if of a sudden all the Liberal or all the Conservative statesmen were swept away from the two Houses of Parliament during or after a great national crisis. The banishment of Stein from the councils of the king of Prussia at the dictation of Napoleon I. has justly been looked upon as the brutal outrage of an irresistible conqueror; but what was that compared with cutting through the vital nerves and sinews of a nation! Has Italy even now recovered the loss of Cavour?

[2] Polybius, xxx. 20. f.: ἐθάρρει δὲ καὶ τὰ παιδάρια κατὰ τὰς ὁδοὺς ἐκ τῶν διδασκαλείων ἐπανάγοντα κατὰ πρόσωπον αὐτοὺς (Callicrates and Andronidas) προδότας ἀποκαλεῖν.

[3] Polybius, xxxi. 18, 2: ὅτι θαυμάζουσι πῶς ὑπὲρ ὧν αὐτοὶ κεκρίκασι περὶ τούτων αὐτοὺς παρακαλοῦσι κρίνειν.

if they had no time themselves, at least to allow the Achaean league to appoint judges; but the senate replied that they did not consider it advantageous either for Rome or for the Greek states that the exiles should return home.¹

This answer deprived the unhappy men of the last chance of returning to their country, and showed that the measure was a mere act of violence without even the appearance of justice. Nevertheless, the Achaeans did not cease repeating their request from time to time (from 160 to 155 B.C.), until at length, in the year 150 B.C., through the influence of Polybius, Cato was induced to intercede on their behalf, and persuaded the senate to waste no more time in debating "whether a few decrepit old men should die in Italy or in their own country." He did this not from sympathy or from magnanimity, but because he was indifferent as to the fate of the exiles and tired of the everlasting petitions.² Of the whole number who had been transported seventeen years before, about seven hundred had already died. Disease, grief, and weariness of life had hastened the silent work of time.³ The executioner had also lent his aid; for every attempt at flight had been punished with death. Only one of the exiles had met with a cheerful lot and had almost found a second home in Italy. The learned historian and statesman Polybius had been enthusiastically received as friend and teacher by the two youthful sons of Æmilius Paullus. While the other exiles were scattered about in the country towns of Italy, he had obtained permission to remain in Rome, and had gained great influence, which, with a noble zeal, he always employed to alleviate the hard fate of his countrymen; and now, after he had contributed in great part to the decree of the senate for the return of the exiles, he endeavoured to obtain for them an additional favour. He asked Cato to lend his help, that they might have their lost honours and possessions

¹ Polybius, xxxi. 8, 9. ² Polybius, xxxv. 6; Plutarch, *Cato Mai.* 9.
³ Zonaras, ix. 31.

restored to them. But in this request Polybius found that he had gone too far, and he was obliged to put up with Cato's scornful reply, that Ulysses might as well have returned to the cave of Polyphemus to fetch the hat and belt he had left behind.

The exiles, on their return, found the Peloponnesus in a woful plight. The revolutions following each other in rapid succession had caused a general feeling of insecurity in political as well as social institutions and property. Since Agis and Cleomenes had endeavoured seriously to realise the socialistic theories of the Athenian philosophers, and to restore what they supposed to be the Lycurgean division of property; since the tyrants Machanidas and Nabis had recklessly confiscated and again given away land and houses, had annulled debts, emancipated slaves, and received into the state new citizens in great numbers, a deeply-rooted enmity had everywhere sprung up between the rich and the poor, interfering with the property of all and acting injuriously upon the political life of the people. In spite of the support which the aristocracy found in the protection of Rome, democratic views continued to spread among the people; they became from day to day more extravagant, and adopted more and more the form of socialism. Owing to the practice of using mercenaries in war, a great part of the population of the Peloponnesus had become unsettled and averse to peaceful life. Large tracts of land lay waste. The population decreased with alarming rapidity, not only in consequence of the devastating wars (though these left visible traces in some parts),[1] but much more through the uncertainty of property and the difficulty of gaining the means of living. This prevented the natural increase of population, it diminished the number of marriages, and, worse than that, prompted the cruel and unnatural practice of exposing children to death.[2] A large family of children weighed so heavily on the shoulders even of the rich, that they preferred

---

[1] Pausanias, vii. 18, 5; Polybius, xl. 3, 4.   [2] Polybius, xxxvii. 4, 6.

BOOK V.
148–146 B.C.

getting rid of their offspring to educating them. Probably the practice of pæderasty, the most disgraceful taint in the moral life of the Hellenes, had by this time also begun to produce marked effects, the just chastisement of unnatural sensuality. We must not forget that to all these evils was added slavery, which to ancient thinkers did not appear to be any great evil, merely because it was not a peculiar and exceptional institution, but which, being common to all nations, and equally affecting the whole social and political life of antiquity, prevented everywhere a free development of true humanity.

Political unfitness of the returned exiles.

Such was the condition in which the exiles, on their return in the year 150 B.C., found every part of Greece; and unfortunately they had not the power to apply a remedy. They had become estranged from their native country by long absence, and could not make allowance for the altered state of affairs. One feeling pervaded them all, inextinguishable hatred of Rome. This hatred was accepted as a substitute for talent, and recommended them to the people for public offices. If there had been able men among them, the revolution might have been advantageous to the Achaean league; but the best of them had died in Italy, and Polybius, who was almost the only one of eminent capacities, saw soon after his arrival that the Peloponnesus was not a place where he could do much good, and he, therefore, returned voluntarily to Italy. The difficulty in the state of affairs was increased by disputes concerning the property of the exiles which had been confiscated by their opponents and was now claimed back.[1] It would indeed have been better, as succeeding events showed, if the perpetrated wrong had never been redressed, and if the exiles had remained in Italy. The severed limbs could not be joined again to the body without destroying it. In a commonwealth, as in every living organism, nature begins to repair an injury from the moment it is inflicted; it creates a new state of things

[1] Zonaras, ix. 31.

which cannot, when it has had time to grow and become consolidated, be disturbed without danger even by the most careful restoration.

Immediately after his return to Peloponnesus, Diæus was appointed chief magistrate of the Achaean league for the year 149 B.C. Blinded by his hatred for Rome, this violent and moreover dishonest man[1] seized the first opportunity for rekindling the old disputes with Sparta about the boundaries and the authority of the league. He thus compelled the Spartans again to apply to Rome for protection, a proceeding which increased the antipathy of the Achaeans and made them think that prompt action against Sparta was at the same time a demonstration against Rome. Having got somewhat into discredit by his dishonourable bargain with Menalcidas,[2] Diæus was now eager to avail himself of an opportunity for engaging the attention of his countrymen in another direction, and for showing that he was indeed a true patriot. The Spartans submitted, not thinking themselves a match for their enemies; and while they banished seventy-four of their most prominent citizens marked out as especially obnoxious to the Achaean league, they also sent immediately to Rome, according to the now established custom, to ask for aid. The Achaeans were forced to do the same, and thus the humiliating spectacle was again witnessed of hostile Greek ambassadors wrangling with one another before the Roman senate, to obtain justice from the goodwill and favour of the foreign power.[3] The senate, as on a former occasion,[4] gave no clear or decisive answer. After some vague and general phrases,

New rupture between Achaia and Sparta.

---

[1] That he was dishonest cannot be doubted. Yet Polybius (xxxviii. 2, 8) seems to be too much under the influence of personal hostility when he says of Diæus and Critolaus: οὗτοι δὲ ἦσαν ἐξ ἑκάστης πόλεως κατ' ἐκλογὴν οἱ χείριστοι καὶ τοῖς θεοῖς ἐχθροὶ καὶ λοιμῶν αἴτιοι.

[2] See p. 298.

[3] Pausanias, vii. 12, 8: Δίαιος δ' ἐς ἀντιλογίαν Μεναλκίδᾳ καταστὰς ἐπὶ τῆς βουλῆς πολλὰ μὲν εἶπε, τὰ δὲ ἤκουσε οὐ σὺν κόσμῳ.

[4] Compare p. 178. The same double-dealing was practised with regard to Carthage. See below, chapter 5, and Livy, xxxiv. 62.

they promised to send an embassy to Greece to settle the dispute on the spot. Thus they gained time, and could hope that the difficulties in Macedonia, Africa, and Spain, which were just then looking very serious, would be removed by the time the Greek question would have to be finally decided. The Spartan and Achaean ambassadors returned to the Peloponnesus, both sides bringing home the news that the senate had decided in their favour.[1] The natural result was a continuation of the quarrel with more embittered passions. The Achaeans, being the stronger, resolved to force the Spartans to submission. They hoped that the Romans, as on a former occasion, would not protest against an accomplished fact; and just at this time the war in Macedonia, which occupied the attention of Rome, seemed to furnish an opportunity for gaining their object. In spite of a protest from Metellus, who was commanding in Macedonia, Damocritus, the general of the league, invaded Laconia in the year 148 B.C., defeated the Spartans, and inflicted on them a loss of one thousand men. He neglected, however, to make use of his victory and to take the defenceless town of Sparta. We do not know whether in thus acting he was intimidated by Metellus. At any rate, his successor Diæus, it is reported,[2] was warned by the Roman generals, who, meanwhile, had been victorious in Macedonia, not to continue the war against Sparta. He was told to await the decision of the senate, which, at length, in the year 147 B.C., sent into the Peloponnesus the embassy announced long before to settle the dispute between Sparta and the Achaeans. There could scarcely be any doubt even among the Achaeans themselves what the decision would be. The Romans had always been inclined to defend the independence of Sparta and to oppose the extension of the Achaean league. But hitherto the wars with Syria, Ætolia, and Macedonia had made it necessary for them to treat the Achaeans with some degree of consideration,

---

[1] Pausanias, vii. 12.   [2] Pausanias, vii. 13, 5.

THE FALL OF MACEDONIA AND GREECE.

and even favour. The Romans, though vexed and angry, had, on a former occasion, been compelled to sanction the extension of the league over the whole of Peloponnesus,[1] and even to allow some towns in other parts of Greece to be received into it. But after the defeat of Perseus the true sentiments of Rome with regard to Achaia came to light. The league was so weakened by Rome that it was quite helpless. In the year 163 B.C., the town of Pleuron was separated from it, and other towns were invited to secede, though, it would seem, without result.[2] But, in the war against the pretender Philip, Rome once more needed the aid of Achaean troops, and had, therefore, waited until the final end of this war enabled her to treat the Achaeans with that brutal overbearing and disdain which henceforth she had no inducement to disguise. The Roman ambassador, Aurelius Orestes, appeared in Corinth, in the year 147 B.C., to notify a decree of the senate to the chiefs of the league there assembled.[3] This decree declared that Sparta and Corinth, as well as Argos, Orchomenus, and Heraclea, could not with propriety remain in the league, because the citizens in these towns were not of the same race as the Achaeans. The Achaeans had not expected such a crushing blow. The severance of such important towns as Corinth and Argos would be virtually a sentence of death for the league. What was the object of possessing towns like Dyme and Aegium, if Corinth, then the richest and most flourishing town in Greece, were taken from it? The popular feeling revolted against this humiliation and disgrace. The Achaeans asked themselves by what act they had deserved such hostile treatment. What had they done to injure Rome? Had they ever taken up arms

CHAP. IV.
148–146 B.C.

Roman decree to break up the Achaean league.

---

[1] See pp. 173, ff. 184. [2] Pausanias, vii. 11.

[3] In judging of the policy of Rome with regard to the Achaean league, we must not be entirely guided by Polybius, who, as the client of the noblest house in Rome, was not free to say all that he thought, and was perhaps not quite unbiassed in his judgment. To give one instance, we think that the facts themselves contradict what he says, xxxviii. 1, 6, namely, that the demands of the Romans had been a mere threat, and that in reality they had no intention to break up the league. See Hertzberg, *Geschichte Griechenlands*, i. p. 253, n. 49a.

BOOK V.
148–146 B.C.

Outburst at Corinth against Rome.

against her, or endangered her safety, or even so much as her interests or welfare? On the contrary, it was to them that the Romans, to a great extent, owed the advantages which they had gained in the east. Now their reward was a heartless sentence of annihilation. We cannot be surprised that their anger was exasperated into fierce rage. Without waiting till the Roman ambassadors had finished speaking, the chiefs of the league rushed into the street, called together the people, and imparted to them the message from the senate. The passions of the Greeks, so easily roused, were suddenly fired to a pitch of ungovernable hatred against the Spartans, who were regarded as the authors of the Roman decree. All the Spartans who chanced to be in Corinth at the time, all who from their name or dress appeared to be Spartans, were attacked, ill-used, and thrown into prison, some of them even killed. The mob pursued the detested strangers as far as the house where the Roman ambassador lodged, so far forgetting their fear of the powerful republic that they even mocked and insulted the ambassador himself.[1] This was the protest pronounced by Corinth against the senatorial decree which invited and permitted it to secede from the league. Neither did the other towns, with the exception of the distant Heraclea, show any inclination to fall in with the wishes of Rome. If the Romans had counted upon finding a desire among the confederates to break up their league and to assert the independence of the several members, they were mistaken. The best proof of the utility and popularity of the league was this, that even on the invitation of Rome, now as well as in the year 163 B.C.,[2] all the Peloponnesian members refused to secede.[3] In fact, the league could not be dissolved by a mere decree of the Roman senate. It was necessary to employ the force

---

[1] Pausanias, vii. 14.   [2] See p. 305; Pausanias, vii. 11.

[3] It may even appear doubtful if Sparta directly insisted upon secession from the league. If that had been the case, no further discussions would have been possible between Sparta and the league, such as actually took place soon after at Tegea. Polybius, xxxviii. 3, 2 and 5. See below, p. 307.

THE FALL OF MACEDONIA AND GREECE.

of Roman arms. But this was what the Romans were just at that time not inclined to do. They preferred waiting for a more favourable moment. The senate, disregarding the exaggerated reports[1] which Aurelius brought home of the insults offered to him and to the Roman Republic in Corinth, sent a second embassy to the Peloponnesus, under Sextus Julius Cæsar, for the purpose of appeasing and soothing the Greeks. They seem not to have insisted on the execution of the decree which separated Corinth and the other towns from the league. This design was given up for the present, to be resumed later at a more convenient time. The proceedings at Corinth and the insult to the Roman ambassadors were hardly mentioned. Sextus Julius in a conciliatory speech endeavoured, above all, to settle the dispute between the league and Sparta, and in the meantime to bring about an armistice. A conference of the chief magistrates of the league and the Spartans was appointed to take place at Tegea under the presidency of the Roman ambassador, and it seemed possible, if both sides were inclined for a reconciliation, to prevent the threatened outbreak. On the other hand the Achaeans, by an embassy to Rome, sought to excuse themselves for insulting the Roman ambassadors at Corinth.

But, at this momentous crisis in the history of the Greek nation, a man appeared on the scene who blasted all hopes entertained by the better class of patriots. For the year 146 B.C., Critolaus had been appointed captain of the Achaean league, a demagogue of the worst sort, as incapable as he was passionate. He deluded himself and the blind multitude with vain hopes and false fancies, and knew how to gain the applause of the ignorant by empty phrases which please the populace, and thus to obtain their approval of his mad freaks. He seemed per-

Critolaus captain of the Achaean league.

---

[1] Exaggerated reports of this kind are very natural. Compare vol. i. p. 496. According to most writers, L. Postumius, who went as ambassador to Tarentum in 282 B.C., was only insulted by the Tarentine mob. According to Livy, he was actually beaten.

suaded that Rome acted at present with much apparent moderation, only because she was in great distress on account of the Spanish and Carthaginian wars. There was some truth in this opinion; but instead of keeping in mind the relative strength of Achaeans and Romans, and instead of using the favourable state of affairs for a reasonable arrangement which would, at least, have secured to Achaia a fair amount of national independence, and would have warded off the horrors of a conflict, Critolaus stood upon his dignity, assumed a haughty and defiant air, excited the populace, and finally left the Romans no alternative but to draw the sword.

Agitation against Rome.

Critolaus even succeeded in rendering the negotiations at Tegea abortive.[1] He kept the Romans and Spartans waiting for him a long time, and finally refused to agree to their proposals. He asserted that he had no full powers, and that it would be necessary to await the general meeting of the Achaean league, which would take place in six months. Meanwhile, therefore, both agreement and truce were out of the question. He evidently hoped, before the end of six months, to confront the Romans with an accomplished fact. The Roman ambassadors at once indignantly left the Peloponnesus. Critolaus, on the other hand, employed every means of exciting the nation to war. He travelled to all the towns of the league, assembled public meetings, preached hatred of Rome, and secured the support of the lowest class of people by a decree stopping the recovery of debts during the continuance of the war. He also looked about for allies, and offers actually came from Thebes and Chalcis. But, on the whole, Greece showed no inclination to join the mad democrat in a struggle against mighty Rome.

Meeting of the Achaeans at Corinth.

Metellus had now brought the war in Macedonia to an end, and sent ambassadors (in the spring of 146 B.C.) warning Critolaus to abstain from further measures against Sparta. The regular spring meeting of the Achaean

---

[1] Polybius, xxxviii. 3.

league happened just to be assembled in Corinth, and this time it was more numerously attended than usual. But the greater portion of the assembly consisted of the lower people, the workmen and artisans of the great trading and manufacturing town of Corinth, over whom Critolaus had complete power, and whom he made use of for intimidating the more quiet and sensible men. When the Romans urged the league to yield to the request of the senate, and to allow Sparta, as well as the other towns named in the decree, to secede from the league, a storm of indignation broke out, similar to that of the preceding year when Aurelius had first made the same demand. The Romans were hissed and forced to leave the assembly. But Critolaus made grand speeches of the sort so congenial to the Greeks. They were willing, he said, to serve the Romans as their friends, but not as their masters. If the Greeks were men, they would easily find allies; but if they were women they would be certain to find those who would lord it over them. He hinted that he was not trusting blindly to fortune, but that he could reckon upon the help of kings and confederate republics. Critolaus violently suppressed the opposition of the more prudent members of the executive council by calling in armed men and defiantly challenging his opponents to touch even the hem of his garment. He called them traitors to the common cause, and invited the national assembly to put an end to further hesitation by declaring war against the Spartans, and to invest himself with unlimited military power. His advice was followed. The Roman ambassadors hastily left the town, and Critolaus collected the armed forces of the league for the last struggle which was fought by independent Greece.[1]

The war was formally declared only against Sparta and not against Rome. But that it would, in fact, have to be waged with the latter power could not be doubtful even to those who had tried to deceive themselves. Sparta

[1] Polybius, xxxviii. 4, 5.

BOOK V.
148-146 B.C.

had already been completely defeated and humiliated in the preceding year. From that quarter no attack was to be apprehended. Critolaus, therefore, marched northwards with his troops, with the intention of reducing first the town of Heraclea, near Mount Œta, which had seceded from the league on the invitation of the Romans, but probably also with a view of giving battle to Metellus, who was stationed in Macedonia, and of engaging the northern Greeks in the war.

The great difference between the boasts of Critolaus and his performances now became evident. He received no material aid except from Thebes and Chalcis; Heraclea was defended so bravely that he could not take the town; and when the news arrived that the Roman army was approaching, he gave up in all haste his favourable position at Thermopylæ, and retreated into Locris.

Battle of Scarphea.

But he was overtaken and completely beaten at Scarphea on the Malian gulf. Many thousands were slain or taken prisoners. Critolaus himself was among the former; at least he disappeared in the battle, and no one could say what became of him. The Romans vigorously pushed the pursuit of the defeated army; in Phocis they annihilated the contingent of the town of Patræ, and, at Chæronea in Bœotia, a select body of Arcadians who had not arrived till after the battle.

After such misfortunes a continued resistance seemed, and was in fact, nothing less than madness. Metellus, anxious to bring the war to a close before his appointed successor, the consul Lucius Mummius, should relieve him, requested the Achaeans to accept the conditions of the senate. He was probably willing to treat the conquered enemies with clemency, if we may judge by the indulgence shown to Thebes, which had surrendered to him, and where he had punished only Phæneas, the captain (Bœotarch) of the Bœotian confederacy, who had dragged the town into the war. The Achaeans might now, without discredit, have bowed to superior force. They had done what was in their power. Their former position towards Rome was already forfeited, and further resistance could only bring upon them unspeakable miseries. But, as their ill luck would have it, the management of the league once more fell into the hands of a desperate fanatic, who was determined, without any prospect of success, to continue the struggle to the last. After the death of Critolaus his predecessor Diæus took the command provisionally, according to the constitutional practice of the league, and was then formally elected. He at once prepared for further resistance, and unfortunately Metellus gave him time to do so. Diæus mustered up all men capable of bearing arms, filled the gaps in the army with freedmen, and forced the rich to pay heavy contributions, and even the women to give up their trinkets. By the most atrocious terrorism he overcame the advocates of peace, headed by an inferior general named Sosicrates, together with those members of the aristocratic party who had formerly supported Roman interests under the lead of Callicrates. These men probably began to negotiate with Metellus in the absence of the dictator. All sensible men longed for the end of a war in which they saw no hope of success. Metellus was disposed to offer the most favourable conditions. But Diæus and the rabble frustrated all peaceful measures. The negotiators were branded as traitors. Sosicrates was tortured to death.[1] The others escaped by bribing Diæus, who, in spite of his fanaticism, was avaricious and mean enough to take money from his political opponents in the very crisis and death-struggle of his country. Thus all opposition was silenced, and the deluded people were led to ruin by a madman.[2]

Meanwhile Lucius Mummius, the consul for that year, 146 B.C., had arrived in Greece with a consular army, and had sent back Metellus and his troops to Macedonia. Mummius was not a great general, nor was he distinguished in any other way, but he was not a bad man. On the con-

---

[1] Polybius, xl. 4, 5.
[2] Polybius, xl. 3, 9: κατὰ δὲ τοὺς νῦν λεγομένους καιροὺς ἠτύχησαν ἀτυχίαν ὁμολογουμένην διὰ τὴν τῶν προεστώτων ἀβουλίαν καὶ διὰ τὴν ἰδίαν ἄνοιαν.

trary, he was honest and good-natured, though somewhat dull and ignorant. We do not know by what merits he had risen from a low station to the consular dignity, and had thus become what was technically called 'a new man' (*homo novus*). It was to chance that he was indebted for the command in Greece, as he had drawn lots with his colleague to decide the distribution of provinces. It signified little, however, whether he possessed great military ability or not. The war was already virtually ended. The demoralised and hastily mustered army of the Achaeans consisted of twelve thousand slaves turned into soldiers. It was confronted by a picked Roman army of two double legions and a powerful cavalry of three thousand five hundred men, besides Cretan archers and other auxiliaries. Even before the arrival of Mummius, as soon as Metellus approached from Bœotia, a division of four thousand Achaeans, who had occupied Megara, retreated to the isthmus to join the main force. The two armies now confronted each other, not far from Corinth. An advanced guard of the Romans suffered itself to be surprised, and was driven back to the main body with considerable loss. The courage of the Greeks rose. They already began to think themselves equal at least to the ten thousand who, at Marathon, had driven the countless host of barbarians back to the sea.[1] They advanced, and succeeded in forcing Mummius to give battle. The fate of Greece was decided in the autumn, 146 B.C., near a town on the isthmus, called Leucopetra, which is not mentioned on any other occasion. The Achaean horse was scattered by the first attack of the far stronger Roman cavalry. The infantry resisted the legions for some time until it was attacked in flank and routed. Then the whole defeated army broke up. The majority of the men hastened

---

[1] Justin (xxxii. 2) relates that women and children from Corinth followed the army to witness the destruction of the Romans, and that carriages, to be loaded with the expected booty, accompanied the troops. This story is really too discreditable to the Greeks. Justin's testimony hardly warrants our accepting it.

back at once to their homes. Diaeus seems to have made no attempt to occupy Corinth with the remainder of his troops and to defend this fortified town, a course which would have made the Greek death-struggle similar to that of Carthage, or which might, perhaps, have been followed by favourable conditions of peace. He fled straight to his native town of Megalopolis, killed his wife, and poisoned himself, leaving his countrymen to their fate. Corinth was deserted not only by her defenders, but by almost the whole population. The gates remained open, so that Mummius, fearing that the enemy were in ambush, hesitated for two days before he entered the town, just as in the old time the Gauls had hesitated before the walls of Rome. He then made his entry, and treated Corinth like a town taken by storm. The few remaining inhabitants were killed, the women and children reserved to be sold as slaves; the town was systematically plundered. Thus far Corinth shared the fate of Capua, Syracuse, and Tarentum, and, as we might think, more than expiated the crime which she had committed by insulting the Roman ambassadors. But the Romans thought differently. The senate had resolved to demolish the finest and richest town in Greece, to sweep it from the face of the earth, and to leave the site a desert like those of her former rivals, Alba Longa, Veii, and Carthage. By an express order from Rome the deserted town was set on fire and burnt to the ground, the walls were pulled down, the spot was cursed, and the land was declared to be the property of the Roman people.[1]

In the long list of destroyed towns which mark the course of Greek history by columns of smoke and fire, the devastation of Corinth occupies a foremost place. The flames which consumed Miletus and Athens were the signal for the great rising of the people, the dawn of a magnificent day of Greek splendour: after the fall of Corinth came the long, dark night. Corinth, it

[1] *Liv. Epitome*, 52; Florus, i. 32.

is true, rose once more from her ashes, when one hundred years later Julius Cæsar founded the new Julian Corinth on the site which had been condemned by the priest to lie waste for ever; but it was no longer the Corinth of former days. The new plantation could strike but feeble roots in the soil covered with ruins. The legions of Mummius had thoroughly performed their task. Roman rapacity left nothing behind that recalled the ancient splendour of the Isthmian town. What could not be carried off was destroyed, and many things were thrown away or spoiled through ignorance. When Polybius arrived and saw the ruins, almost before they had ceased to smoke, he found common soldiers playing at dice on the paintings of the most celebrated masters. It is well known how conscientiously the honest Mummius endeavoured to see that nothing was lost which was worth transporting to Italy. An anecdote is reported by Velleius,[1] that he advised those who undertook the transport to take the greatest care, adding that every lost work of art would have to be replaced by another of equal value. But not the whole of the art treasures found their way to Italy. Some were bestowed upon Pergamum, others sent to adorn various sanctuaries in Greece.

Acts of punishment.

This terrible catastrophe was surely not wanted to overawe by sheer terror any further resistance on the part of the Achaeans. All Greece bent under the iron rod of her masters. The towns which had borne arms against Rome were deprived of their walls;[2] among them was Thebes, though Metellus apparently had accorded a pardon to this city.[3] Chalcis was punished with peculiar severity.[4] The chiefs of the popular party paid the penalty of their lives.[5] Even those inhabitants of Corinth who had fled before the approach of the Romans were sold into slavery with the emancipated slaves who had fought in the army.

---

[1] Velleius, i. 15. [2] Pausanias, vii. 16, 9. [3] Polybius, xl. 11, 5.
[4] According to Livy (*Epitome*, 52) both Thebes and Chalcis were destroyed. This seems, however, incorrect. See Hertzberg, *Geschichte Griechenlands*, i. 277
[5] Polybius, xl. 9, 3; Zonaras, ix. 31.

Nothing remained to the Greeks but the mournful consolation that the death-struggle for freedom had been sudden and short, and that it had not, as in the case of Carthage, involved the whole people in one ruin.[1]

After severe punishments had been inflicted on the most guilty, the conquerors were in a mood to show mercy to the rest, and they allowed themselves to be guided herein especially by the advice of Polybius. It was due to his influence that, among other soothing measures, the statues of Achaeus, the mythical ancestor of their race, and those of Aratus and Philopœmen which were already on their way to Rome, were brought back. But the most signal benefit which he conferred upon his countrymen was this, that he obtained permission to regulate the new form of government to be set up in the different communities. After a long series of violent convulsions and revolutions, Polybius established a new order of things, and thus to some extent mitigated the calamity which he had not been able to avert.

The consul Mummius was not by nature one of those hardhearted wretches who take a personal delight in the agonies of victims delivered over to them for execution. He was not a man like Fulvius in the Hannibalic war,[2] who by his promptness in butchering the conquered Capuans prevented the chance of their being pardoned by the senate. Having carried out his orders for inflicting punishment, he gave full scope to the better promptings of his heart, gaining thereby respect and even gratitude among the Greeks themselves. But no intercession could save the conquered from being disarmed, for by no other means was it possible to prevent internal warfare. Nor could they be spared the payment of an annual tribute to Rome as a recognition of their subjection to the Roman commonwealth.[3] The confiscations of land, however, were not

---

[1] Polybius, xl. 5, 12: ἅπαντες δὲ τότε παροιμίαν ταύτην διὰ στόματος εἶχον Εἰ μὴ ταχέως ἀπολώμεθα οὐκ ἂν ἐσώθημεν. Compare Plutarch, *Themistocl.* 29; Zonaras, ix. 31.   [2] Vol. ii. p. 341.
[3] Pausanias, vii. 16, 9: καὶ φόρος ἐτάχθη τῇ Ἑλλάδι. This is, it is true,

BOOK V.
148-146 B.C.

Roman settlement of Greece.

made on a very large scale. They were limited to the territory of Corinth and some tracts in Bœotia and Eubœa, probably parts of the land belonging to Thebes and Chalcis.[1] These became public domains of the Roman state. The local government remained in the hands of the respective communities. Nothing was changed in the existing customs, institutions, and laws. No governors were sent from Rome to force upon the conquered Greeks foreign laws with the help of Italian garrisons. After some time[2] the law was also withdrawn which forbade the acquisition of landed property in more than one community; even the various confederations were re-established. The Achaeans[3] continued to elect their annual Strategos, the Bœotians their Bœotarch and other magistrates. In addition to this, some few towns enjoyed special privileges, such as immunity from paying tribute; for it seemed reasonable that Athens, Sparta, and the other towns which had taken no part in the war, or had even favoured the Romans, should be rewarded rather than punished. But yet such special exemptions and privileges made little difference in the actual subjection of the whole of Greece under the sovereignty of Rome. The Roman governor of the province of Macedonia was charged with the supervision and control of the Greek communities. It was not till the time of Augustus that Greece became a separate province under the name of Achaia.[4] Until then it en-

direct testimony, and might be considered conclusive. But Pausanias is unsupported by other evidence, and his authority is not weighty enough to bear down certain objections to a general liability of paying tribute. See Hertzberg, *Geschichte Griechenl.* i. 281, note, and Kuhn, *Städtische Verfassung*, ii. n. 208.

[1] Cicero, *Leg. Agrar.* i. 2, 5, ii. 19, 51; *De Natura Deorum*, iii. 19, 49; Böckh, *Corpus Inscript.* iii. n. 5879; Mommsen, *Corp. Inser. Latin. Antiquiss.* p. 110, n. 203, 6; Hertzberg, *Gesch. Griechenl.* i. 283, n.

[2] Pausanias, vii. 16, 10: ἔτεσιν οὐ πολλοῖς ὕστερον.

[3] Argos and Orchomenos, it seems, remained members of the league.

[4] It was formerly the prevailing opinion that Greece, under the name of Achaia, was organised as a Roman province immediately after the fall of Corinth. C. F. Hermann first showed in the congress of German philologists at Basel in 1847 (*Verhandlungen*, p. 32 ff.) that there was no province of Achaia at any time previous to the battle of Actium, and he maintained that until that period Greece was not a direct dependency of Rome. This gave rise

joyed a kind of exceptional position, not unlike that which the American territories occupy before their reception into the Union. The several communities retained complete self-government, but the full sovereignty, i. e. the right of peace and war, was taken away from them, and for the military protection which Rome guaranteed them, they paid an annual tribute.

After all that they had of late years gone through, this condition, which at least secured internal peace, might be regarded by the Greeks as a great improvement. If for the present Achaeans and Spartans could no longer make war upon one another in quarrels about wretched frontier villages like Belmina; if they were prevented from laying waste corn-fields, burning houses, killing thousands of people or carrying them away as slaves, they might perhaps miss the excitement which had almost become necessary to their existence. But, if they were so minded, they could find ample compensation in the safety of their property and the chance of enjoying it peaceably. The rich especially were released from the danger of socialistic confiscations, which had been a constant weapon in the hands of demagogues and tyrants. Rome took care that the terrorism exercised by the proletarians should come to an end. Everywhere democracy was restrained within proper barriers, and the poorest class excluded from a share in the government. It was the beginning of a new era, and the Greece of old disappeared from the historical stage. The sovereign states in which the most excitable of all peoples had struggled for centuries in endless contests subsided, from thorough exhaustion, into the sleepy monotony of provincial towns. Material well-being was destroyed for a long time. The country was depopu-

CHAP. IV.
148–146 B.C.

Changed condition of Greece.

to a long and lively controversy, the phases of which are registered by Hertzberg in his *Geschichte Griechenlands* (i. p. 284, n.). See also Mommsen, *Röm. Gesch.* ii. 48, n. As Mommsen remarks, the dispute is, in the main, one of words. Greece was practically subject and tributary, and placed under the governor of Macedonia, though in outward forms she preserved still many attributes of a free allied state, and was not reduced into the form of a Roman province before the time of Augustus.

lated and impoverished, the energy of the people was paralysed. Yet these were the effects of past misfortunes, not the result of the present state of affairs. Greece needed only time and rest to recover by degrees. But before this recovery could take place, the Mithridatic war broke out in the time of Sulla, and again threw the country into a state of complete exhaustion, from which, even in the time of the emperors, it only partially recovered.

Causes of the downfall of Greece.

If we consider the causes which led to the loss of Hellenic independence, we must allow that the Greeks themselves were primarily answerable for it. Their besetting sin was abuse of power and disregard for the rights of others. The Spartans, instead of receiving the conquered Peloponnesians as members into their community, reduced them to the condition of helots, and thus condemned themselves to political stagnation and to the rough camp life of a nation of warriors, ever threatened by internal revolt and mutiny. They thus deprived themselves of the means of establishing a legitimate dominion over their neighbours. The Athenians also, though in a milder form, but essentially in the same spirit, abused the power which their enterprise, their courage, and favourable circumstances had placed in their hands. Being unable to conciliate neighbouring communities by equal rights and just government, and thus to make them part of themselves, the Greeks knew only one way of profiting by their military achievements—that of weakening, taxing, enslaving, or even annihilating their conquered enemies. Hence every individual Greek state was, by the necessity of its position, compelled to fight desperately for its independence, and to oppose every attempt at forming a national state of larger dimensions. Greek cities had a choice only between independence and utter ruin. Animated by this feeling, they opposed the most obstinate resistance to the dominion of the Macedonian kings, which was by no means as oppressive as that of other Greeks, and now they pushed the desperate struggle with Rome to a point where it ceased to be rational and heroic.

But though the Greeks were unable to overcome their attachment to small independent communities, to bind together in one state the whole strength of their race, and to defend their liberty, and though they were thus the authors of their own misfortunes, yet we cannot help tracing to the perfidy of Roman policy the immediate cause of the catastrophe. If there is one thing certain and indisputable in the whole history of antiquity, it is this—that the Romans, ever since they set foot in Greece, strove steadily and systematically to undermine and to destroy the independence of the Greek people. Instead of establishing peace, they scattered the seeds of discord. With masterly skill they availed themselves of the Greek passions to keep the people in a continual ferment, and they drove them at length to a desperate resistance by heartless ill-usage, such as had never been experienced by any proud nation.[1]

---

[1] The view laid down in the text differs *in toto* from that of Mommsen in his *History of Rome*. Whereas Mommsen has only words of abuse and contempt for the Greeks, he tries to justify the insidious policy of the Romans, and even gives the latter credit for sympathies with the nation which they trod under foot.

CHAPTER V.

THE THIRD WAR WITH CARTHAGE, 149–146 B.C.

BOOK V.
149–146 B.C.

The wars by which Rome obtained the dominion over the countries east of the Mediterranean did not last for more than two generations. During the greater part of this period Rome was at peace with Carthage.

Roman feelings towards Carthage.

But the struggle between the rival republics, which had occupied an equal period and had strained the combatants to the utmost of their resources, could not be looked upon as finally determined by the conclusion of peace in 201 B.C. It had been carried on, first, to settle the question of pre-eminence, and finally to secure bare existence. Fear and hatred had worked so deep into the minds of the Romans, that they could not with indifference suffer Carthage to exist by their side as an independent, flourishing, and powerful state. In the long war Carthage had, it is true, become thoroughly weakened and could no longer be formidable to Rome. But memory and imagination often impress men quite as much as real facts. Conquered and humbled Carthage was still to the Romans the same state which with its armies had overrun and harassed Italy for fifteen long years, and which, after the defeat of the first war, had so rapidly recovered its former power. Who could foresee and venture to assert that this same Carthage was for ever fallen from her high rank, that she now belonged to the class of second-rate powers, that she could never resume the struggle, never seek an opportunity for attacking Rome in conjunction with other enemies? Was not the man still living who had sworn eternal enmity to Rome, and who in his fertile mind possessed incalculable resources? Nor was Hannibal alive merely; he was even guiding the policy of Carthage. No one could believe that he would so guide it as to preserve a lasting peace with Rome. It was to be expected that he would be continually on the watch to discover an unprotected part where he might give the hated rival a mortal blow.

With such feelings and convictions the Romans had concluded the peace of 201 B.C., and had watched over the carrying out of its conditions. By this peace Carthage was bound hand and foot, and was placed under the surveillance of Masinissa, the most effective instrument that Roman policy ever made use of to further her interests. It was stipulated in the peace 'that the Carthaginians should give up to this Numidian prince all the land and the towns that had ever belonged to him or to any of his predecessors.' It was further required 'that Carthage should not wage war with any allies of Rome.' These two conditions of peace became in the hands of Masinissa and the senate an instrument with which they could at pleasure annoy, harass, worry, and torture to death their cowed and exhausted enemy. To this power was added a will which knew nothing of magnanimity, pity, or shame, and, moreover, a glowing hatred which could not be extinguished until Carthage sank into a heap of ruins.

The time from the peace of 201 B.C. to the breaking out of the war of extermination in 149 B.C. was filled with uninterrupted attacks of Masinissa against the integrity of the Carthaginian possessions. In his attempts at spoliation he felt that he was justified by the favour of his friends in Rome, and he was actually urged to make them, whilst on the other side the Carthaginians were precluded by the conditions of peace from offering any direct resistance, and compelled to appeal to the arbitration of Rome. The parts of the Carthaginian dominion most coveted by Masinissa were the so-called Emporia, the rich and fertile districts on the coast of the lesser Syrtis. He maintained that the Carthaginians had un-

BOOK V.
149–146 B.C.

justly conquered this district from his predecessors, and that he was therefore entitled to reunite it with his kingdom. In truth, there was in the whole of Africa not a square foot of land, with the single exception of the site of Carthage itself, which the original Phœnician colonists had not acquired by force; and if Masinissa acted upon the principle now laid down, he was entitled to claim the whole of the Carthaginian territory.[1] He had, indeed, not only the right but the power to do so. As an ally of Rome, he was safe from the arms of Carthage, and therefore he did not hesitate at once to invade the territories which he coveted, and to occupy the open country and the unfortified towns.[2] The Carthaginians complained in Rome (193 B.C.). The Romans had not even the shadow of a substantial charge against Carthage. On the contrary, they were obliged to acknowledge that since the peace Carthage had acted loyally. When in Italian Gaul a leader of the name of Hamilcar, left behind by the army of Mago, had continued the war at the head of a troop of Gauls, he had, at the request of Rome, been not only disowned by Carthage, but even proscribed.[3] Carthage had voluntarily sent large supplies of corn to Rome and Greece,[4] to support the Romans in the war with Philip. After Hannibal's flight from Carthage, the reforms which he had made[5] were probably abolished, and the aristocratic party, which was inclined to be on friendly terms with Rome, regained power. There was

---

[1] His ambassadors declared in Rome (Livy, xxxiv. 62; 11): Si quis veram originem iuris exigere vellet, quem proprium agrum Carthaginiensium in Africa esse? Advenis quantum secto bovis tergo amplecti loci potuerint, tantum ad urbem communiendam precario datum; quidquid Bursam, sedem suam, excesserint, vi atque iniuria partum habere.

[2] Polybius, xxxii. 2, 3.   [3] Livy, xxxi. 11 and 19.

[4] Livy, xxxi. 19. Altogether four hundred thousand modii of grain. The Carthaginians did not send troops like Masinissa, who aided Rome with elephants and Numidian cavalry, because Rome, from a feeling of distrust and jealousy, did not wish to furnish them with a pretext or opportunity for reorganizing their military establishment. This accounts for the fact that on the breaking out of hostilities with Masinissa they were altogether unprepared and defenceless. Polybius, xxxii. 2, 3: διὰ τὸ . . . τότε τελέως ἐκτεθηλύνθαι διὰ τὴν πολυχρόνιον εἰρήνην.   [5] See p. 87.

thus clearly no danger that Carthage would violate her neutrality, or be swayed in her policy by the instigations which, it was reported, came from Hannibal.¹ Nevertheless, the Romans could not shake off all fear of Punic schemes of revenge. Even a Scipio degraded himself by adopting that perfidious policy which encouraged the continual disputes between Carthage and Masinissa as a security from Carthaginian machinations. When he arrived in Africa to decide the question relating to the Emporia, he purposely left the matter enveloped in doubt.² Thus we find in Africa the same policy at work with which the Romans, instead of establishing peace among the contending Greek states, encouraged enmity among them. The glowing embers accordingly from time to time burst forth into new flames. We hear of disputes between Carthage and Masinissa in the year 182 B.C.³ Masinissa had taken possession of another strip of land, probably to the west of Carthage, which, as he said, had been taken from his father, Gala, by Syphax, who ceded it to the Carthaginians. Again, the Carthaginians were prevented by the terms of peace from asserting their right. The dispute was referred to Rome. A senatorial deputation went to Africa, and decided that Masinissa should remain in possession of the land until the senate itself had judged the case. What this judgment was, Livy does not tell us. But, in all probability, the possession of the tract in question was assigned to the Numidian king.⁴

---

¹ Livy, xxxiv. 60–62. See p. 93.

² Livy, xxxiv. 62, 16: Missi P. Scipio Africanus et C. Cornelius Cethegus et M. Minucius Rufus audita inspectaque re omnia suspensa neutro inclinatis sententiis reliquere. Id utrum sua sponte fecerint, an quia mandatum ita fuerit, non tam certum est quam videtur tempori aptum fuisse, integro certamine eos reliuqui: nam ni ita esset, unus Scipio vel notitia rei vel auctoritate, ita de utrisque meritus finire nutu disceptationem potuisset. Zonaras, ix. 18: μετέωρον τὴν ἐχθρὰν αὐτῶν κατέλιπεν, ἵν' ἀλλήλοις τε διαφέροιντο καὶ μηδεὶς αὐτῶν διὰ τὴν κρίσιν κατὰ 'Ρωμαίων ὀργίζοιτο.

³ Livy, xl. 17, with Weissenborn's note.

⁴ Livy, xl. 34, 14. See Weissenborn's note. Polybius, xxxii. 2, 5: ἀμφοτέρων δὲ ποιουμένων τὴν ἀναφορὰν ἐπὶ τὴν σύγκλητον ὑπὲρ τῶν ἀμφισβητουμένων καὶ πρεσβευτῶν πολλάκις ἐληλυθότων διὰ ταῦτα παρ' ἑκατέρων ἀεὶ συνέβαινε τοὺς Καρχηδονίους ἐλαττοῦσθαι παρὰ τοῖς 'Ρωμαίοις, οὐ τῷ δικαίῳ

Probably the quarrel about the Emporia was also settled at the same time in favour of Masinissa, so that the Numidian chief obtained this district, and the Carthaginians were besides compelled to pay him a compensation of five hundred talents.[1] The claims of Masinissa were now looked upon as satisfied, and thus peace was apparently established between him and Carthage (181 B.C.).[2]

Continued aggression of Masinissa

We hear nothing more from this time of the quarrels in Africa until the beginning of the new complication between Rome and Macedonia, which led to the war with Perseus. But in the year 174 B.C. Masinissa again brought a complaint against the Carthaginians. A Roman embassy had gone to Africa chiefly, it seems, for the purpose of ascertaining the sentiments and the designs of Carthage.[3] Masinissa did all that was in his power to calumniate the Carthaginians before these ambassadors, and to draw upon them the suspicion of having carried on negotiations with Perseus. Probably he hoped thus to obtain permission from the Romans quietly to pursue his course of action, which consisted in advancing systematically, and conquering one strip of Carthaginian territory after another. Two years later (172 B.C.) his plans had been so far carried out that he had again taken more than seventy towns and castles by force of arms. The Carthaginians, in the greatest distress, begged and

---

ἀλλὰ τῷ πεπεῖσθαι τοὺς κρίνοντας συμφέρειν σφίσι τὴν τοιαύτην κρίσιν. We cannot read this honest, outspoken statement of Polybius without feeling the greatest admiration and respect for an historian who wrote under the very shadow of the Roman eagles. Whatever declamations the Romans may have indulged in with regard to the dishonesty and mendacity of the Greeks, not one of their historians before Tacitus felt the least compunction in twisting, colouring, and concealing facts, whenever they thought that the character of Rome could suffer from them. At the same time we find in the words of Polybius a confirmation of the view of Roman policy which we have taken throughout. See above, p. 318.

[1] Polybius, xxxii. 2, 8.

[2] Livy, xl. 34, 14: Pacem Carthaginiensibus populus Romanus non ab eo non sed ab rege etiam Masinissa praestitit. Appian, viii. 37, speaks of a peace of fifty years. Here the number must be a clerical error.

[3] Livy, xli. 22.

implored the senate to settle once for all the boundary line between their territory and that of the king of Numidia, or else to allow them to take up arms in this just war. 'It would be better,' they said, 'to live as slaves of the Romans than to possess a liberty exposed to the insolence of Masinissa. Nay, utter ruin was preferable to a condition in which they were dependent upon the grace of so cruel a tormentor.'[1]

Whether because the senate was now displeased with the violence of Masinissa, or because they thought proper to keep him a little within bounds, it was notified to him that he had gone too far. Perhaps he was even compelled to give up his last conquest.[2] This we gather from the fact that, though he sent provisions and auxiliaries at the beginning of the war with Perseus, it is reported that he nevertheless expected greater advantage from a Roman defeat than from a victory; for whilst in the former case he would have supreme power in Africa, in the latter he would still have the Romans over him as lords, and they might again find it in their interest, as on the present occasion, to protect the Carthaginians from his aggression.[3] It was evidently in the interest of the Romans not to drive Carthage to despair when they were entering on the final struggle with Perseus.[4] They were always wise enough at a critical moment not to despise any enemy; and they often succeeded, by skilful policy, in separating their adversaries, and then overcoming them singly.

The Carthaginians, therefore, now gave up the idea of an alliance with Perseus, and hoped by loyally adhering to the treaty with Rome to be protected from their

---

[1] Livy, xlii. 23.

[2] Zonaras, ix. 29: σύμβασίν τινα πρὸς τὸν Μασινίσσαν αὐτοῖς ἔπραξαν (the Romans) καί τινος αὐτοῖς ἀποστῆναι χώρας αὐτὸν ἔπεισαν. But we cannot be quite sure whether this passage refers to the present or to some former quarrel between the two African states.

[3] Livy, xlii. 29. 8: Si penes Romanos victoria esset, suas quoque in eodem statu mansuras res esse, neque ultra quicquam movendum; non enim passuros Romanos vim Carthaginiensibus adferri; si fractæ essent opes Romanorum, quæ tum protegerent Carthaginienses, suam omnem Africam fore.

[4] See p. 205.

encroaching and still insatiable neighbour. They showed their gratitude to Rome by sending cargoes of corn to the Roman armies.[1] For a short time, accordingly, they were allowed to remain in peace. They seemed to be sufficiently humbled and weakened, and might now be treated graciously, whilst their oppressor, Masinissa, like king Eumenes of Pergamum, seemed likely to lose the favour of Rome. He had not, indeed, neglected to give proofs of his fidelity in the war against Perseus. His Numidian horse and his elephants had rendered excellent service in Macedonia; but it appears there was no longer the former intimate friendship between him and Rome, from the sole cause, perhaps, that after the defeat of Perseus he was not as indispensable an ally as he had been before.[2] He seemed to feel this, and sent his congratulations and the assurance of his submission to the senate after the battle of Pydna, through his son Masgaba, in a manner which vied with the servility of Prusias.[3] He declared through his messenger that he considered himself fortunate to have been able to be of service to his benefactors. There was only one thing that he regretted—that they had asked him for his assistance instead of simply commanding it.[4] He knew well that he owed his kingdom to the Romans alone. He considered himself not the owner, but the tenant-at-will. That which the Romans did not require was sufficient for his use.

The Romans by that time knew very well what to think of such extravagant professions of attachment, and in nowise allowed themselves to be misled by them. The senate, therefore, bluntly refused the request of Masinissa to be allowed to come to Rome himself, and sent word to him through his son that this would not be in the interest of the republic. If we could penetrate deeper into the details of the Roman policy of that period, we should probably discover

---

[1] Livy, xliii. 6, 11.   [2] Livy, xlv. 14.   [3] See p. 277.
[4] Livy, xlv. 13, 14: Duas res ei rubori fuisse: unam, quod rogasset cum per legatos senatus, quae ad bellum opus essent, et non imperasset; alteram, quod pecuniam ei pro frumento misisset.

that in those debates two parties were opposed to each other, one of which, in the African affairs as well as in those of Macedonia and Greece, was opposed to the acquisition of new provinces, whereas the other party was eager for fresh conquests and a rapid extension of the Roman dominion. For the present the former party, headed by Scipio Nasica, prevailed. But Rome had from the very beginning so decidedly followed the other course, and so pertinaciously aimed at the formation of a dominion over the whole world, that a short delay in her career was soon made up by accelerated speed. Nothing showed more plainly that this was the destiny of Rome than the fact that no personal influence, not even that of the most eminent men, had the least power of modifying it. The same Cato who, with all his might and with temporary success, had opposed the establishment of a province in Macedonia and the conquest of Rhodes,[1] became, in obedience to this inevitable destiny of Rome, the most zealous advocate for the destruction of Carthage.

It was hard for Carthage to remain on good terms with a neighbour like Masinissa. In spite of the peace concluded under the auspices of Rome, he continued his attacks upon her territory. The fact that he was useful to the Romans in their wars in Spain may have encouraged him in the belief that he could act as he chose. Indeed, a Roman deputation left in his possession what he had recently conquered, and thus he soon advanced fresh claims upon a tract of land containing fifty towns,[2] and forced the unhappy Carthage once more to have recourse to the arbitration of Rome.

The embassy which on this occasion (157 B.C.) was despatched by the senate to inquire into the affairs of Africa, contained among its members the most uncom-

---

[1] See p. 269.
[2] Appian, viii 68: Οὐ πολὺ δ' ὕστερον ὁ Μασσανάσσης ἠμφισβήτει καὶ τῶν λεγομένων μεγάλων πεδίων, ἣν Τύσκαν παραγορεύουσιν. We cannot ascertain where this district was situated. Probably it lay to the west of the river Tusca, which formed the boundary between Zeugitana and Numidia.

promising enemy of the Punic town, Marcus Porcius Cato.[1] The Carthaginians appealed to their just rights, guaranteed by treaty. Masinissa, on the contrary, declared his readiness to accept unconditionally the decision of the Romans, whatever it might be. The Carthaginian appeal to their rights appeared to Cato in the light of presumptuous defiance, and he determined to humble them to the dust. With astonishment and jealous envy he had observed the flourishing condition of their country. The Carthaginians had, by their indefatigable industry, recovered from the distress which the long war with Rome had brought upon them. It seemed that these energetic Punians could not be totally ruined, even by the greatest calamity. Though they had lost their foreign possessions, though they had suffered from the late war and from the unceasing attacks of Masinissa, though they had been deprived of so many rich and productive dependencies, their capital was still a town full of life and wealth. The port was thronged with shipping, and the streets and market-places were crowded with a busy multitude. The country was cultivated like a garden, and signs were everywhere visible of wealth and prosperity. It no longer seemed to be the same Carthage which, thoroughly exhausted by the calamities of war, had asked for peace fifty years before. The narrow mind of Cato was stirred by old recollections of the sufferings caused to Italy by the Hannibalic war, which the younger generation had almost forgotten, because they had not themselves witnessed them as Cato had. He returned to Rome with the firm conviction that Carthage must be swept from the face of the earth, if Rome was to continue to exist.

Cato's views with regard to Carthage.

The conviction of Cato soon became that of the Roman senate, although some eminent men upheld the principle that the maintenance of the Carthaginian state, far from being dangerous to Rome, would, on the contrary, be of real use to her. One thing, above all, was clear to the

---

[1] Appian, viii. 69 ; Plutarch, *Cato Mai.* 26. It is probably the same embassy of which Livy speaks, *Epit.* 47.

Romans—that they should not allow Carthage to be swallowed up by the Numidian kingdom, which would in that case become too powerful a rival. The jealousy existing between the two African states was evidently far more favourable to Roman interests than the sole dominion of one. On the other hand, if Rome, in order to gratify her old animosity or from fear of the new power of Carthage, resolved to crush it, there was no alternative but to take immediate possession of the land, and to make it a Roman province. But the establishment of new provinces was, as the more clear-headed men distinctly perceived, a great danger not only for the preservation of the good old customs, but even for the continuance of republican institutions—in other words, of the existing aristocracy.

These well-founded apprehensions failed to influence the decision of the senate, when even so cautious a statesman as Cato had suffered reason to yield to passion. Cato was at that time perhaps the most influential member of the senate. With his experience, his honours, his high connexion, his acknowledged eloquence and learning, his indefatigable zeal, he succeeded to a certain extent in forcing upon the senate the one idea which occupied his whole mind. It is related that on every occasion he returned to the same subject, and that every one of his many speeches ended with the words, 'Carthage must be destroyed.' He laboured successfully, because he found willing listeners. No passion, we know, is more easily roused than that of hatred, especially when united with lust of gain; and no kind of hatred, with the exception of religious hatred, takes the guise of virtue so readily as that kind of national hatred which likes to call itself patriotism.

Soon after the year 157 B.C., in which Cato was sent as ambassador to Africa, a tacit agreement existed among the chief leaders of Roman diplomacy that the Carthaginian state was to be annihilated.[1] It was

---

[1] Appian, viii. 69: Καὶ ὁ Κάτων μάλιστα ἔλεγεν οὔ ποτε 'Ρωμαίοις βέβαιον οὐδὲ τὴν ἐλευθερίαν ἔσεσθαι πρὶν ἐξελεῖν Καρχηδόνα. Ὦν ἡ βουλὴ πυνθανομένη ἔκρινε τὸν πόλεμον· ἔτι δὲ ἔχρῃζε προφάσεων καὶ τὴν κρίσιν ἀπόρρητον εἶχον.

only the time, the opportunity, and the means which were not yet determined. Nor were the promoters of this policy in the least hurry. They felt that Rome was strong enough to wait quietly till the right hour should come.

Although the war of extermination against Carthage was a settled thing in Rome, the senate nevertheless hesitated to deal the first blow. They thought it better to let loose their devoted servant, the Numidian king Masinissa, upon the doomed town, so that, when their enemy was hunted down, they might easily give him the death-blow. As the Romans had Masinissa entirely in their power, and could urge him on or call him back at pleasure; as, moreover, Carthage had hitherto not taken up arms, even in self-defence, without the permission or sufferance of Rome, we may conclude that the war which now broke out was the result of Roman instigation.

Internal strife at Carthage.

The hostility between Carthage and Masinissa had become permanent, owing to the dishonesty of the Roman umpires. The last dispute between them had not yet been settled. The Roman party in Carthage needed only a hint that Rome would be pleased to see them oppose Masinissa. The democrats were prepared for this at any moment. There were three political parties at Carthage —the aristocratic party, which consisted of partisans of Rome; the democratic or national party; and a Numidian party, the adherents of which were of opinion that, by an alliance with Masinissa, Carthage might free itself from the humiliating dependence on Rome. In an internal struggle this party succumbed and forty of its most influential members were banished. They went to Masinissa, and begged for his mediation. Masinissa sent two of his sons, Gulussa and Micipsa, and demanded of the Carthaginians the recall of the fugitives. As this embassy was not admitted, and was even treated as hostile, war broke out. Masinissa attacked a Carthaginian town (Oroscopa), and

War with Masinissa.

Κάτωνα δ' ἐξ ἐκείνου φασὶν ἐν τῇ βουλῇ συνεχῆ γνώμην λέγειν, Καρχηδόνα μὴ εἶναι.

the Carthaginians, instead of humbly appealing to Rome, as was their wont, took up arms, and sent troops against him. How they came to possess the power to do this, we can gather from some indications contained in our very scanty sources. A Numidian chief, named Ariobarzanes, a grandson of Syphax, probably oppressed in the same manner as the Carthaginians by the rapacious Masinissa, had revolted against him, and placed an army of twenty-five thousand men at the disposal of the Carthaginians. The latter seemed now really in earnest. The Romans took no part in the war, although, at least according to Roman reports, several embassies were sent from Rome to dissuade the Carthaginians from it, and though the Roman messengers with difficulty escaped ill-usage when they demanded that the Carthaginians should disarm and destroy their fleet.[1] With great satisfaction they watched the two African states mutually weakening one another, fully resolved to interfere only in case Masinissa should succumb. But this was in the highest degree unlikely. For half a century Carthage had had no army; how could she, then, carry on a successful war with the well-armed and able Numidian chief? But the Carthaginians—that 'nation of tradesmen'—were not deficient in courage and determination on this as on other occasions. The town had still ample resources left. In all haste an army was formed, and advanced, under the command of a general named Hasdrubal, to meet Masinissa. As soon as hostilities had commenced, it became evident that allies were to be found against the tyrannical Masinissa, even in Numidia, which was continually in a ferment of internal disturbances. Two Numidian chiefs, with six thousand men, joined the Carthaginians. In the year 151 B.C. a battle took place, which lasted from morning till night. P. Scipio, the son of Æmilius Paullus, happened to be in

---

[1] It seems pretty certain that the alleged warnings and injunctions of the Romans, and especially the defiant and insulting reception given to their ambassadors, are altogether fictitious, or very much misrepresented and exaggerated. If not, Rome could not have delayed declaring war at once.

the camp of Masinissa, on a message to ask for elephants to carry on the war in Spain. He had the satisfaction of watching from an elevated spot the two rivals tear each other to pieces, and of seeing the battle take its course precisely as he desired. The victory was on the side of Masinissa, but it was neither easy nor decisive.[1] The Carthaginians, after the battle, endeavoured to obtain peace through the mediation of Rome, and declared their readiness to make great sacrifices; but the negotiations fell to the ground when Masinissa required that his partisans who had been exiled from Carthage should be allowed to return. The war, accordingly, went on, the Romans even then taking no part in it. Old Masinissa, now bordering on his ninetieth year, but still vigorous in body and mind, managed to detain the Carthaginian army in a desert tract of country,[2] and finally to blockade it completely, until at length, weakened by hunger and sickness, the survivors were obliged to surrender at discretion. Hasdrubal obtained permission to return home with the miserable remnant of his army, on agreeing in the name of Carthage to all Masinissa's conditions. But even this disgraceful agreement is said to have been violated by the Numidians. The Carthaginians, having been dismissed under the yoke, exhausted and disarmed, were surprised on their way home by Gulussa, the son of Masinissa, and slain almost to the last man.[3]

Roman interference. Masinissa now thought he had gained his end. Carthage was humbled, and he had but to stretch out his hand in order to extend his dominion over the whole of Africa. But at this moment an order from Rome compelled him

---

[1] Appian, viii. 72.

[2] It seems that he succeeded in this not so much by superiority in the field as by pretending to carry on peace negotiations, in which he was supported by Rome. So much appears to be implied by Appian, viii. 72, extr.: Καὶ παρέμενε (Hasdrubal) πυνθανόμενος ἅμα καὶ Ῥωμαίων ἐπιέναι πρέσβεις ἐς διαλύσεις. Οἱ δ᾽ ἦλθον μὲν· εἴρητο δ᾽ αὐτοῖς, εἰ Μασσανάσσης ἐλασσοῖτο, λῦσαι τὴν διαφορὰν· εἰ δ᾽ ἐπὶ κρείσσόνων εἴη καὶ παροξύναι.

[3] According to Appian, viii. 79, the loss of the Carthaginians amounted on this occasion to fifty thousand men.

to stop. Rome had resolved that Carthage should fall, but not that it should be united with Numidia. The time for her interference had now come, and she pushed aside her old ally without the least scruple.

CHAP. V.
149–146 B.C.

The war which now began between Rome and Carthage was not a war in the true and honourable sense of the word; it was a cruel execution. Carthage, bound hand and foot, exhausted and discouraged, found herself in the grasp of her mortal enemy. For victory she could not hope. Only a fall worthy of her past greatness could be the reward of her last effort of heroism, and this reward she obtained.

After their recent defeat the Carthaginians were indeed in a wretched plight. They knew the Romans well enough to foresee that they would make use of their weakness and helplessness to carry out their long-cherished design of crushing them utterly. They hastened, therefore, to forestall the complaints which, as they well knew, Rome would make as a pretext for war, namely, that, contrary to the terms of the treaty of peace, they had taken up arms against an ally of Rome. They condemned Hasdrubal and Carthalo, the leaders of the war party, to death, and sent ambassadors to Rome to throw the guilt on these men alone, and at the same time to appease the anger of the Romans.[1] They were not mistaken, if they feared the worst. The senate had already decreed a general armament throughout Italy, and, considering the feeling which prevailed in Rome at this time, there could be little doubt against whom these preparations were intended. The Carthaginian ambassadors were not cordially received, and obtained the ambiguous reply that they would have to give Rome satisfaction. A second embassy, which endeavoured to ascertain the meaning of these words, was told that they ought themselves to know it.

Carthaginian endeavours to deprecate the hostility of Rome.

Whilst the Carthaginians indulged in the hope of being able to preserve peace by submission and by material

War decreed.

[1] Appian, viii. 74.

sacrifices, the strongly fortified town of Utica, which was second in wealth and power to Carthage alone, gave up their case for lost. Utica, which in the second Punic war had by a brave resistance so long detained the Roman arms, now surrendered to the Romans, and thus furnished them with a useful basis for their military operations. Even if the war had not been decided upon long before, there was now no reason for further delay. The senate accordingly despatched the two consuls for the year 149 B.C., Manius Manilius and Lucius Marcius Censorinus, to Sicily, with an unusually powerful army of eighty thousand foot and four thousand horse, on a numerous transport fleet and under the escort of fifty quinqueremes, with orders to cross over from Lilybæum to Africa.[1] They had received the secret but peremptory order to allow nothing to deter or stop them until Carthage should be destroyed. The same messenger carried the declaration of war and the news that the fleet had sailed.

An unprejudiced statesman might now have known that every prospect of a peaceable arrangement was lost, and it would have been better, as the result proved, to collect the last forces of the nation with a bold resolution and to obtain by arms those concessions which it was vain to expect from Roman magnanimity. But Carthage felt too much weakened to risk a contest with the oppressor. Another embassy with unlimited powers appeared before the senate, and offered the submission of Carthage.[2] It was well known what this submission (*deditio*, ἐπιτροπή) meant according to the Roman interpretation of international law. It handed over the state unconditionally, as if it were conquered in war, to the discretion

---

[1] If we can trust the numbers given by Appian, viii. 75, the force must have consisted of at least two consular armies of two double legions each, and legions of the exceptional strength of six thousand men. This would constitute a force of forty-eight thousand Romans and Italian socii. Mention is made, moreover, of a great number of volunteers. Among the latter there may have been many non-combatants, who accompanied the army in quest of plunder. It is possible that the marines on board the fleet were also included in the number of eighty thousand. Still the numbers are suspiciously high, especially that of the cavalry (four thousand). [2] Polybius, xxxvi. 1.

of the victor. But there was a custom, as universally recognised as the formal law, that this right should not be exercised by the conquerors to its full extent, and it was in the hope of generous treatment that voluntary submission was resorted to before the final appeal to arms.¹ The senate accepted the submission, and ordered the Carthaginians to send three hundred hostages within thirty days and to obey the further commands of the consuls. Upon these terms they were promised their liberty and independence, their territory and possessions.² Who could suspect what was hidden under the deceptive words, 'to obey the further commands of the consuls'? Some suspicion was aroused by the fact that the Romans had made no definite promise that the town of Carthage should be spared. Fearful forebodings filled the minds of statesmen who would not be deceived by the hope to which conscious weakness clings.³ But the state was too much reduced to muster courage for a defiant resistance. The first step to submission had been taken. In their downward course the Carthaginians could not halt without some cause which would rouse the deepest passions. Therefore, though with a heavy heart, they resolved to send the pledges of their obedience demanded by the Romans.⁴ But it was useless to hope that hereby the tempest would be warded off which was approaching the unhappy town. Although the hostages had been given over to the Roman consuls in Sicily within the prescribed date, the latter nevertheless sailed from Lilybaeum, and landed in the port

---

¹ In the year 173 B.C. the senate had compelled the consul Marcus Popillius Laenas to make such a generous use of his formal right. See p. 202, and Livy, xlii. 8.

² It is of great importance to note here the very words, fortunately preserved by Diodorus (xxxii. 6, *Dindorf*): δίδωσιν αὐτοῖς ἡ σύγκλητος νόμους, χώραν, ἱερά, τάφους, ἐλευθερίαν, ὕπαρξιν, οὐδαμοῦ προστιθεῖσα πόλιν τὴν Καρχηδόνα, παρακρύπτουσα δὲ τὴν ταύτης ἀνήρεσιν.

³ Polybius, xxxvi. 3.

⁴ Polybius, xxxvi. 3, 7. The simple narrative of Polybius is worked up by Appian, viii. 77, into a pathetic scene. Here the mothers of the children sent as hostages hold on by the ropes of the ships; they follow the ships, swimming, tear their hair, and scratch their faces bloody!

BOOK V.
149-146 B.C.

The Carthaginians disarmed.

of Utica, which was now open to them as to allies. Once more Carthaginian deputies appeared to receive further orders from the consuls; and now the Romans accomplished the master-stroke of their treachery—treachery which was in fact more than Punic, for it was truly Roman.[1] The consuls required that the Carthaginians should be disarmed.[2] 'How,' they said, 'could those want arms who were resolved to live in peace, who were protected from their enemies by the strong arm of Rome, and had their liberty, independence, and possessions guaranteed to them?' The distressed suppliants might well hesitate for a long time before giving up their weapons and delivering themselves, without defence, to the mercy of an enemy who knew no such thing as mercy. But the counsels of the timid preponderated, and as yet no one suspected what final demand was still kept in the background. The arms were surrendered, the arsenals and wharves were cleared, and two thousand catapults were taken from the walls.

A long line of wagons conveyed two hundred thousand suits of armour and an immense amount of projectiles of all sorts to the Roman camp. A solemn embassy, accompanied by the chief priests, the most noble citizens and members of the senate, surrendered the arms in the Roman camp, hoping that now at length the anger of the enemy would be appeased, and that they would return with the announcement of peace to the defenceless town.[3] For so many years the Carthaginians had now had intercourse with the Romans, and still they did not know the full extent of Roman perfidy. They were destined to

---

[1] The Roman declaration of 'perfidia plus quam Punica' (Livy, xxi. 4, 9) ill becomes the mouths of men who could plan or approve such an excess of revolting perfidy as that of which the slandered Punians were the victims.

[2] According to Zonaras, ix. 26, the Carthaginians were also required to furnish provisions for the Roman army.

[3] Appian, viii. 80. According to Diodorus, xxxii. 6, 3, *Dindorf*, the Carthaginians, after having delivered up their arms, sent, at the request of the Romans, a special deputation to be informed of the last orders of the Romans, and this deputation consisted of thirty of the first men of the town (τριάκοντα τῶν ἐπιφανεστάτων).

have it made known to them in the agony of death. They were informed that they would have to leave their town and settle ten miles from the sea.¹ The decree of the senate was irrevocable. Carthage must be destroyed. With a cry of anguish the deputies heard this terrible sentence. They threw themselves on the ground in despair and begged for mercy. Even the Romans, it is said, were moved and shed tears of pity. But their resolution was firm, and neither the eloquence nor the lamentations of the condemned victims could change the stern decree of the senate. The Carthaginians were even denied leave to send ambassadors once more to Rome; but one request was granted them. A Roman squadron was sent to the mouth of the harbour of Carthage, that the people might see with their own eyes how hopeless it was to defy the orders of the Roman people. The trembling deputies foresaw that an outburst of passion would meet them on their return, and many of them had not the courage to face their countrymen again. The others succeeded with difficulty in forcing their way through the excited crowd to the senate-house; for their downcast looks sufficiently indicated the nature of their message. When the requirements of the Romans became known, a unanimous feeling shot through the whole Carthaginian people. They would rather die than give up the sacred soil of their country. Without an army, without weapons and ships, without allies, betrayed, deceived, surrounded by a powerful hostile army, reduced to the narrow circuit of their bare walls, they nevertheless resolved to resist, were it only that they might fall with the fall of their town.

No man now living has any idea of the feeling which, in the ancient world, bound individual citizens to the homes of their fathers. Our religion differs from that of the ancients inasmuch as it is limited by no geographical boundaries. Our most ardent patriotism is but a human and not a religious feeling. In antiquity the commonwealth engaged every sentiment, human and divine, of

¹ Appian. viii. 81. Eighty stadia, or rather more than ten English miles.

every individual citizen. The national deity dwelt within the walls of the town and there alone. The dead lay in the soil of their own home, and required uninterrupted funeral rites to secure their peace in the world unseen.[1] These convictions underlay the wonderful and pertinacious attachment with which men in antiquity clung to the very soil on which their body politic was established. A Carthaginian state or a Carthaginian nation, while Carthage lay in ruins, was as inconceivable as a Roman republic separated from the town which was, as it were, the body of the political soul, where not only every temple and every tomb, but every stone was sacred to the protecting gods of the people.[2] Yet Rome might have been abandoned with less detriment to the material welfare of the nation than Carthage. For what would have become of the Carthaginian people transferred to the interior; separated from that element on which they had from time immemorial founded their greatness, their power, and their wealth? With cruel mockery the senate declared that the Carthaginian state was not the town but the people, who could live free and independent away from the sea, as well as near it. The sophistry with which the Romans insisted that they were keeping their first promises, even in destroying the town, would have been met by the Romans themselves with an outburst of indignation, if any foreign power had presumed to try it on them. The Carthaginians had not less patriotism than the Romans, and, in spite of their hopeless situation, they rejected the worthless offer of bare life in exile.

It is no easy task to defend or even to excuse the

---

[1] See Fustel de Coulanges, *La Cité Antique*, liv. i. Cox. *History of Greece*, book i. chap. ii. It is hardly an exaggeration, but it expresses the feelings of the Carthaginians when Hanno is related to have implored the Romans rather to destroy the Carthaginian people than the town, with its sanctuaries and its tombs. Appian, viii. 84 : τὴν μὲν πόλιν ἐᾶτε τὴν οὐδενὸς ὑμῖν αἰτίαν, αὐτοὺς δὲ ἡμᾶς οὓς ἀνοικίζετε, εἰ θέλετε, διαχρήσασθε · οὕτως ἀνθρώποις δόξετε χαλεπαίνειν, οὐχ ἱεροῖς καὶ θεοῖς καὶ τάφοις καὶ πόλει μηδὲν ἀδικούσῃ.

[2] Urbem auspicato inauguratoque conditam habemus ; nullus locus in ea non religionum deorumque est plenus ; sacrificiis solemnibus non dies magis stati quam loca sunt, in quibus fiant. Liv. v. 52.

course of action which Rome pursued with regard to Carthage. The ancient world, it is true, was unacquainted with that modern spirit of chivalrous honour which disdains to gain an advantage over one's enemy by falsehood and deception, by perjury and casuistry. But there were men, even at that time, whose moral sense condemned the treachery with which Rome gradually increased her demands, and after having induced Carthage, first to give hostages, and then to surrender her arms, finally dealt the death-blow to the defenceless town.[1] Modern historians, therefore, may be still more outspoken in condemning, from a moral point of view, the most shameless and fiendish perfidy of which any nation was ever the victim.

CHAP. V.
149–146 B.C.

In the first moment of disappointment, when the Roman demands became known, the fury of the people turned against all those who in any way seemed responsible for the terrible misfortune. The Italians residing in Carthage, the senators who had advised submission, even the deputies who brought the fatal news, were attacked and savagely ill-treated. The crowd rushed like madmen, weeping with rage, through the despoiled arsenals, the empty harbour, and along the walls cleared of all munitions of war. They entered the temples, not to pray, but to mock the protecting gods of the town, and to reproach them with impotence. Whilst the multitude indulged in these useless bursts of passion, the more sensible men thought of means of defence. In order to repel the first attack, they collected stones on the ramparts and provided themselves with such weapons as they could manufacture in

Resolve to defend the town.

---

[1] Again it is Polybius who, in spite of his Roman connexions, had the courage to speak out. He tells us (xxxvii. 1, b. 3) that some people were of opinion that μηδενὸς ἀνηκήστου γεγονότος ἐκ Καρχηδονίων ἀνηκήστως καὶ βαρέως βεβουλεῦσθαι περὶ αὐτῶν πᾶν ἀναδεχομένων καὶ πᾶν ὑπομενόντων ποιήσειν τὸ προσταττόμενον; and again (ibid. 1. c. 2), νῦν δὲ Ῥωμαίους πάντα περὶ τοὺς Καρχηδονίους δι᾽ ἀπάτης καὶ δόλου κεχειρικέναι κατὰ βραχὺ τὸ μὲν προτείνοντας, τὸ δ᾽ ἐπικρυπτομένους, ἕως οὗ παρείλοντο πάσας τὰς ἐλπίδας τοῦ βοηθεῖν αὐτοῖς τοὺς συμμάχους· τοῦτο δὲ μοναρχικῆς πραγματοποιίας οἰκεῖον εἶναι μᾶλλον ἢ πολιτικῆς καὶ Ῥωμαϊκῆς αἱρέσεως καὶ προσεοικὸς ἀσεβήματι καὶ παρασπονδήματι κατὰ τὸν ὀρθὸν λόγον. Though Polybius pretends to report not his own opinion but that of others, the passage is a strong condemnation of the conduct of Rome.

haste. The whole town was turned into a single workshop for arms, where men and women toiled unremittingly day and night. In a large and rich centre of commerce like Carthage there could be no lack of stores of all sorts. Iron, wood, leather, and other materials were of course to be found, and skilful labourers were plentiful.

If, as we are told, the women sacrificed their hair to provide strings for the catapults, this was rather a proof of their zeal than of lack of the materials usually employed. In a short time the most necessary articles were supplied. Every day the factories sent out one hundred shields, three hundred swords, five hundred projectiles, and a number of catapults. The whole people was animated by one sentiment, by courage and enthusiasm to fight to the death. A resolution was passed to set free the slaves and to invite them to take part in the struggle. Hasdrubal, who had been expelled to please the Romans, was recalled. He had, with his own resources, formed an army of twenty thousand men and placed himself with this force at the disposal of his country.[1] He was entrusted with the chief command in the field, whilst another Hasdrubal, though a grandson of Masinissa, was commissioned to conduct the defence of the capital.

Postponement of the siege.

It was of the greatest importance to the Carthaginians to obtain a short respite for the purpose of organizing the defence. They begged that the attack might be postponed for thirty days, alleging that they wished once more to send ambassadors to Rome. The consuls, it is true, refused permission to send this embassy, but from other reasons granted the respite to which the Carthaginians attached so much importance.[2] They could not imagine

---

[1] In the second Punic war a Hasdrubal Gisgo showed the same magnanimity and self-denial. See vol. ii. p. 446.

[2] Mommsen, who has not one word of reproof for the proceedings of the Romans, says (*Röm. Gesch.* ii. 27) of the Carthaginians on this occasion: 'At the same time they tried to deceive the enemy .... in true Phœnician style.' It is not easy to repress a feeling of deep moral indignation, when we thus find the Carthaginians censured for attempting to avail themselves of an artifice commonly employed in war to gain a short respite from the attacks not of honourable enemies but of merciless traitors.

that the disarmed town would after all offer any serious resistance. The passionate excitement of the first moment, they thought, would gradually subside. The Carthaginians would come to their senses, and, seeing the hopelessness of the struggle, would submit to the Roman demands. The consuls therefore allowed some little time to elapse before they started from Utica and advanced to Carthage. When at length they did approach, they found the state of affairs very different from what they had expected. Yet they trusted to be able, without much trouble, to take the town by storm. They assaulted the walls in the west and south; but they soon saw the uselessness of an attack without sufficient preparations. After having been twice repulsed, they were obliged to make up their minds to undertake a siege in due form.

As the events of the last Punic war centre entirely in the siege of Carthage and end with its destruction, the first thing necessary to understand this war is to study the site and the fortifications of that remarkable town. Unfortunately our knowledge of the topography of Carthage is extremely imperfect. Our chief source of information regarding the war is the report of Appian. Appian, it is true, made use of the books of Polybius lost to us; but in abridging and working up the subject he has left much in the dark. The ancients, on the whole, were not skilful in accurate topographical descriptions.[1] It is therefore possible that even Polybius gave no clear picture of Carthage. These deficiencies in our historical record cannot be entirely replaced by the investigations which in our own time have been made on the site of the town. The history of Carthage has always been under the influence of an evil star. All the documents from which we might have learnt what the Carthaginians themselves had to say about themselves and their history were swallowed up in the destruction of their national capital. Not only have the language and

Difficulty of ascertaining the topography of Carthage.

---

[1] Compare vol. ii. p. 172.

the whole literature of the Carthaginians been swept away, but even the mighty edifices which covered the soil have disappeared almost without leaving a trace. What was spared by the destructive fury of Scipio's army furnished the materials, many years later, for a new Roman Carthage; and even this was obliged to make room for a Vandal, and in later times for a Byzantine town, to be at length transformed by the Arabs into a heap of ruins for all times. But even these ruins have, with few exceptions, disappeared. Tunis was built of the stones of ancient Carthage; nay, the Spaniards, the Genoese, and the Pisans carried off the finest blocks of marble as ballast in their ships to build new palaces at home. Thus it has come to pass that hardly a stone of Punic Carthage is to be seen above ground; only deep under the piled-up rubbish of centuries are still buried the foundations of the gigantic structures of the oldest period; but on the spots where in former times stood temples and halls, six-storied houses and high pinnacled towers, the wretched peasants of Tunis now cultivate the arid soil.

More has perhaps been done by nature in the course of centuries than by the hand of man to change the aspect of the place. The channels of watercourses have been altered, the seashore has advanced, harbours have been filled up with sand, hollows and heights made even. How is it possible under such circumstances to obtain a clear picture of ancient Carthage? It is not to be wondered at that modern investigators have arrived at the most varied and perplexing results in trying to identify the several spots. Even the last two writers to whom we are indebted for excavations[1] differ in important points of their conclusions. We must, therefore, be satisfied if we can succeed in ascertaining with partial correctness the main features of the town, and thus, to a certain extent, understand the last desperate struggle of the inhabitants.[2]

---

[1] The late M. Beulé, Minister of Public Instruction under the Republic, and Mr. N. Davis, whose book (*Carthage and her remains*) is no proof of great scholarship. [2] See plan of Carthage, p. 314.

Within the bay which is formed in the northern coast of the African continent by Cape Farina on the west and Cape Bon on the east, a low peninsula extends into the sea between the Gulf of Tunis and that of Sukara. The width of this peninsula does not exceed two miles and a half. At the eastern extremity two groups of hills rise to a height of about four hundred feet. The northern (Jebel Kawi) lies near Cape Camart; the southern, separated from the other by the plain called El Mersa, lies near Cape Cartagena, the most eastern point of the peninsula. Further south a few low hills may be seen scattered about. One of these, about one hundred and eighty-eight feet high, rising between the last-named cape and the Gulf of Tunis, was the site of the Byrsa, or castle of Carthage.[1] The earliest settlement of the Phœnicians, originally confined to the Byrsa, gradually grew into a town, and was fortified by massive walls about thirty feet thick and forty-five feet high, containing in their hollow interior stables for three hundred elephants and four thousand horses, besides buildings for stores and barrack room for twenty-four thousand soldiers (Plan No. 2). But even this gradually-enlarged town became too small for the rapidly-increasing population of the rich ruler of the

CHAP. V.

149-146 B.C.

Site of Carthage.

---

[1] Plan No. 1. Here king Louis Philippe of France caused a chapel to be built in honour of the French king Louis IX., or St. Louis. This hill is the only spot which answers the descriptions given by the ancients of the Byrsa, or castle of Carthage. The Danish captain Falke who published in 1833 a most accurate topographical survey of the whole country (*Recherches sur l'emplacement de Carthage*), has shown this beyond doubt. Of the same opinion is Barth (*Wanderungen durch die Küstenländer des Mittelmeers*, p. 93 f.), and Beulé (*Les fouilles de Byrsa*, published in the *Journal des Savants*, 1859, pp. 498 and 561 ff.) On the other hand, Davis (*Carthage and her remains*, p. 370 ff.) places the Byrsa on a hill in the north-eastern extremity of the town, close to the sea. His arguments have no force whatever. They are sufficiently refuted by the statement of Strabo (xvii. 3, 14), who calls the Byrsa περιοικουμένη, and by the words of Appian (viii. 95), τὰ πρὸς μεσημβρίαν ἐς ἤπειρον, ἔνθα καὶ ἡ Βύρσα ἦν ἐπὶ τοῦ αὐχένος. The last words alone decide the question. The Byrsa was towards the neck of land which connected the peninsula of Carthage with the mainland. It is not very material that the expression πρὸς μεσημβρίαν is not quite correct. For it alters nothing in the fact that the Byrsa was situated not near the sea, but towards the mainland.

seas. By degrees the whole surface of the peninsula, as far as the extreme west, became covered by a suburb (Megara

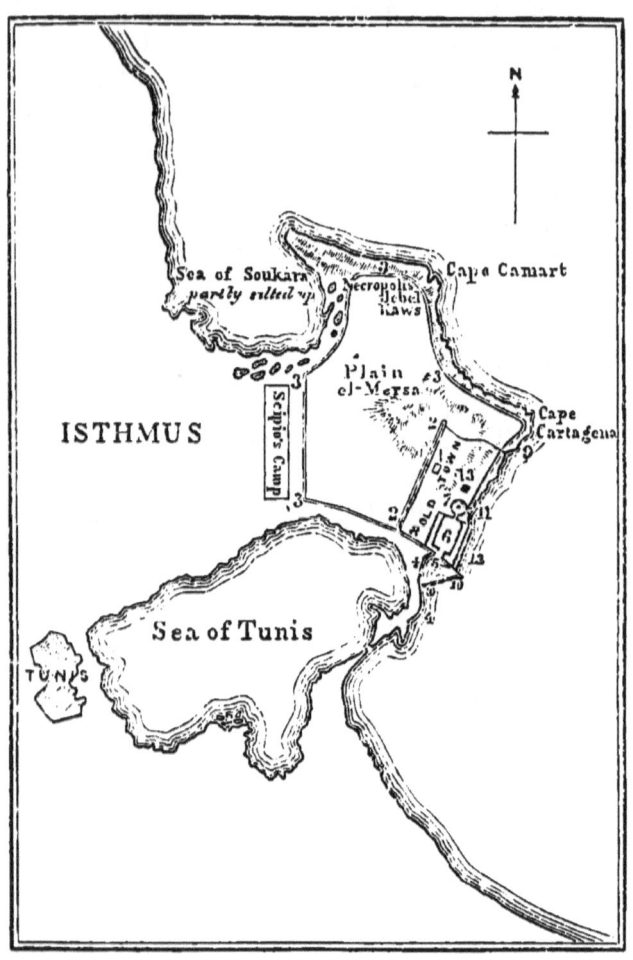

Explanation of Map.—1, Byrsa; 2, Triple interior wall; 3, Outer wall and ditch; 4, Tongue of land; 5, Mouth of ports; 6, Mercantile port; 7, Kothon, war port; 8, Weak part of wall; 9, Place attacked by Mancinus; 10, Dam to block up the mouth of the port; 11, New entrance to war port made during the siege; 12, Outer quay; 13, Market.

or Megalia) filled with houses surrounded by gardens. This suburb was also defended by a wall and ditch,[1] so

---

[1] See Plan No. 3. Appian, viii. 97, 117. At present no traces can be found of this line of fortification; but there can be no doubt that it existed at the time of the siege. It is mentioned by Appian, and distinguished from the 'high walls lying behind,' *i.e.*, from the triple walls of the old town.

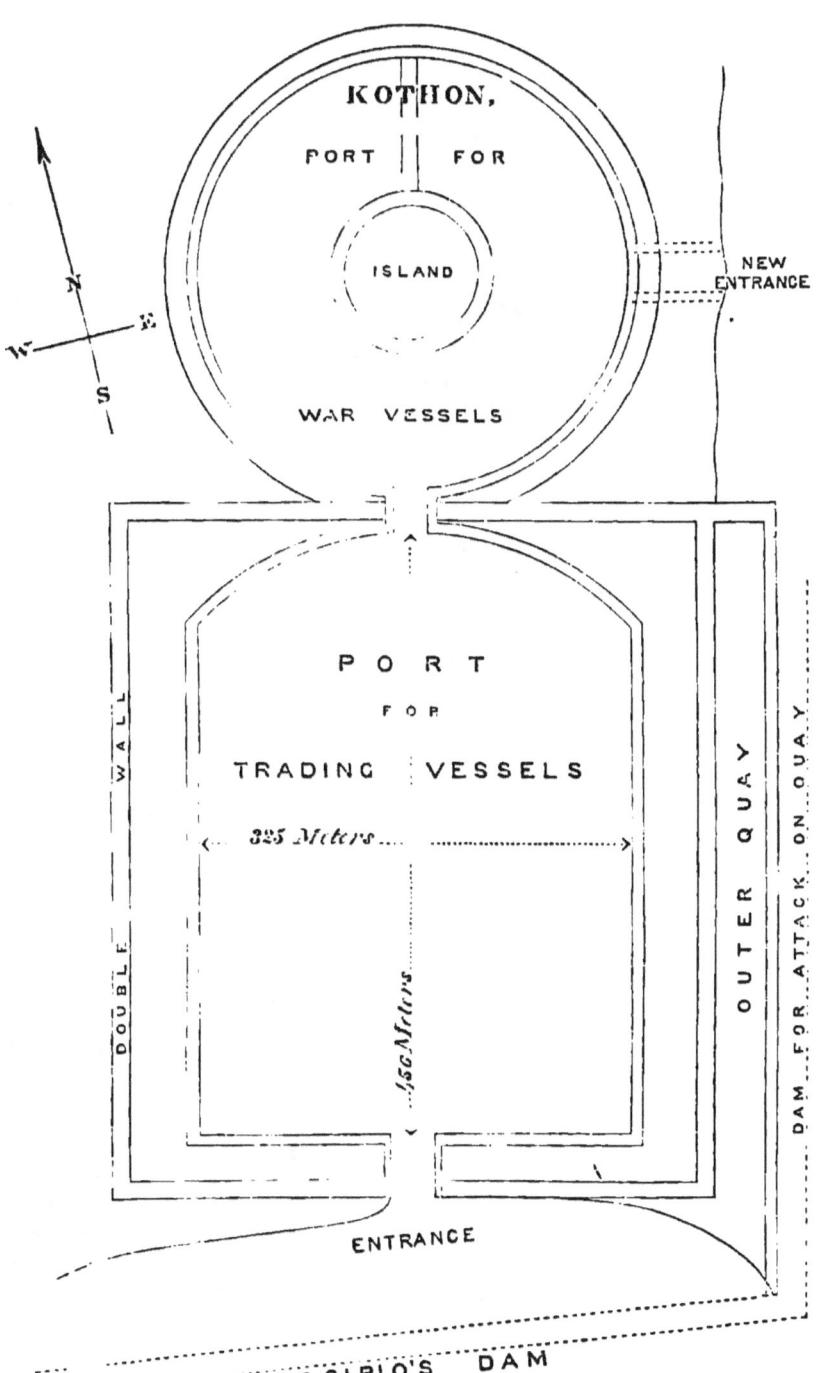

that at the time of the last war the town covered the entire peninsula, or at least its eastern portion.[1]

It seems strange that the Phœnician colonists should have chosen a place for their settlement which did not contain a sufficiently large natural harbour. They were obliged to dig an artificial harbour, if they did not—as is rather more probable—enlarge and improve a natural roadstead which they had found. At the south-eastern end of the peninsula, where it was perfectly flat, was the entrance (No. 5) to an artificial basin (No. 6) of a rectangular shape (456 × 325 metres), the harbour for trading vessels. In the continuation of the axis of this harbour, which ran almost due south and north, was a second circular basin (No. 7) (325 metres in diameter), connected with the outer basin by a short and narrow channel.[2] In the centre lay an island, also of a circular shape (100 metres in diameter), joined to the outer quay by a road on a dam. The round basin was the port for ships of war, called Kothon. On the quay, which surrounded it, were two hundred and twenty sheds for vessels, and all the stores and yards necessary for a large fleet. On the island was the dwelling of the port-governor, from which he could overlook both harbours, and had a view eastward to the open sea.

[1] Appian, viii. 95 f.

[2] All the measurements given in the text are taken from Boulé (*Journal des Savants*, 1860, p. 299). Everybody will be struck by the small dimensions of the port of Carthage. The two basins are, in truth, nothing but two docks. How the rectangular dock could suffice for all the mercantile shipping of Carthage does not easily appear, even if we take into account the small size of the ancient vessels. The port of Liverpool contained in 1860 no less than fourteen docks, among which the Prince's Dock alone is about equal in length to the commercial dock of Carthage. The total length of quay space in Liverpool where ships may load and unload amounts to twenty-two thousand metres. In Carthage it was no more than one thousand six hundred metres. The old port of Marseilles covers, according to Boulé, two hundred and seventy thousand square metres, the commercial port of Carthage only one hundred and forty-eight thousand square metres. Barth (*Küstenländer des Mittelmeers*, p. 88 ff.) and Boulé have tried to account for the smallness of the Carthaginian port. They are of opinion that the lake of Tunis and the gulf itself served as roadsteads, and that a considerable portion of the Carthaginian navy was regularly stationed abroad.

The Kothon was as strongly fortified as the old port of the town. The outer mercantile harbour, however, was defended only by a thinner wall. South of this wall was a flat beach which extended southwards, in the shape of a long narrow ridge of sand (No. 4), and thus formed a barrier between the sea and the large shallow bay of Tunis.

The first attempts to take the town by a *coup-de-main* were made, as has already been observed, on the western and southern sides; westwards on the isthmus which connected Carthage with the continent, and southwards on the narrow tongue of land and on the flat beach which extended between the city wall and the bay of Tunis. When these attempts had failed, Manilius erected a camp to the west of the town, on the isthmus, where he could intercept all communications with the interior. The other consul, Marcius Censorinus, who commanded the fleet, encamped on the narrow tongue of land south-west of the entrance to the harbours, and stationed his fleet in the bay of Tunis. The Romans were now compelled to prepare for a regular siege, and, above all, to collect materials for the engines of attack. On the expeditions which they undertook for this purpose into the interior they encountered the troops which Hasdrubal had collected. On one occasion they met with considerable check from a cavalry leader called Himilco Phameas, one of Hasdrubal's officers. Their task was becoming difficult. They succeeded, however, in completing several engines, and resumed the attack for the third time. Once more repulsed, they began again on a larger scale. Marcius filled up a portion of the shallow bay of Tunis, in order to gain more room for his operations near the walls of the town. Two battering towers were built, of the size of which we can form an idea, when we hear that six thousand men were required to move one of them towards the wall. The wall (No. 8), which was but weak at this part,[1]

[1] Appian, viii. 95: γωνία δ' ἡ παρὰ τὴν γλῶσσαν ἐκ τοῦδε τοῦ τείχους (the triple wall on the west side) ἐπὶ τοὺς λιμένας περιέκαμπτεν, ἀσθενὴς ἦν μόνη καὶ ταπεινὴ καὶ ἠμέλητο ἐξ ἀρχῆς.

Siege of Carthage begun.

was thrown down, and the Romans prepared to storm the breach. During the following night the besieged Carthaginians made a sally, and damaged the engines so much that they became useless. When the Romans, nevertheless, ventured to make an assault, they were driven back with great loss. Nothing was gained. The summer had passsd away without result. The crews of the fleet began to suffer from disease in their unhealthy station in the bay of Tunis. The consul therefore left the stagnant bay with his ships, causing his troops to encamp on the seashore, and his fleet to take up a position close by. The Carthaginians now advanced from the defence to the attack. When the wind was favourable they sent out fire-ships against the Roman fleet; they made a night attack upon the camp of the consul Manilius, on the west side of the town, and were with difficulty driven back. They thus compelled the Romans to fortify strongly not only their naval camp on the shore, but also that of the army on the isthmus, and for the present to give up all thoughts of further attacks upon the town.

Towards the close of the year the consul Marcius Censorinus returned to Rome to conduct the elections for the following year. His colleague, Manilius, left his position before Carthage with ten thousand foot and two thousand horse, and started on an expedition into the interior against Hasdrubal.[1] This expedition, it seems, ended in a series of reverses.[2] The scanty report of Appian gives us no particulars. This historian, drawing his information from Polybius, appears to have made it his chief business to extol Scipio. He continually points out to us how the legions were rescued by the military ability of the young officer from dangerous situations into which they had been brought by the foolhardiness or inexperience of the general. Some truth, no doubt, there must be in these stories; but it is not worth while to scrutinise minutely

---

[1] Appian, viii. 100.
[2] Appian, viii. 105: πολλῶν γεγενημένων πταισμάτων. Ibid. iii.: ἐπῄρτο Ἀσδρούβας τῷ δὶς κρατῆσαι τοῦ Μανιλίου.

these one-sided and imperfect reports. The final result of the campaign is known. It was a complete failure. Neither in the field nor before the walls of Carthage had the Romans in the first year of the war won laurels enough to cover the horrible treachery of their policy, even in the eyes of those for whom military glory leaves all other glory in the shade.

It now became evident that the senate had in the arrogance of power made a great mistake. They had taken too soon the step which had now become a regular practice in Roman diplomacy, and which consisted in casting aside an ally after he had been made use of for a time. Masinissa had brought the Carthaginians to the ground.[1] Rome had reserved to herself the dealing of the deathblow, in order to be able to despoil the fallen victim herself. Masinissa was naturally not a little exasperated at this. He had, however, promised to send auxiliaries as soon as he should hear that they were wanted. Seeing now that the Roman operations did not advance, he asked, as if in scorn, whether his aid was not yet needed. The consuls, offended by the tone in which he addressed them, and distrusting his intentions, replied that they would send word to him in case of necessity. They had not expected that the fallen enemy would rise once more and deal such powerful blows, and they now came to the conviction that they could not well dispense with the Numidians. Accordingly, the young Scipio, who, through his adoptive grandfather, the elder Scipio Africanus, had an hereditary friendship with Masinissa, and had, moreover, made his personal acquaintance on a former occasion,[2] was selected by the senate as the most suitable man to persuade the old ally to enter the field once more for Rome.

Many circumstances tended to make the task of the

CHAP. V.

149 146 B.C.

Death of Masinissa.

Settlement

---

[1] Appian, viii. 94: Μασσανάσσης δὲ ἤχθετο 'Ρωμαίοις καὶ ἔφερε βαρέως ὅτι τὴν Καρχηδονίων δύναμιν αὐτὸς ἐς γόνυ βαλὼν ἄλλους ἑώρα τῷ ἐπιγράμματι αὐτῆς ἐπιτρέχοντάς τε καὶ οὐ κοινώσαντας αὐτῷ πρὶν ἐπελθεῖν, ὡς ἐν τοῖς πάλαι πολέμοις ἐποίουν. [2] See p. 332.

young diplomatist very easy. When he arrived in Numidia, Masinissa had just died, at the age of ninety, and had in his will left to him full power to settle the succession in his kingdom.[1] Here the Romans had precisely what they desired. What in Macedonia, Pergamum, and Syria they had striven to attain by the cunning and the intrigues of the most crafty negotiators, namely, a division of the government among rival princes, they received in Numidia without an effort. Masinissa had left behind a host of sons.[2] Three of these—Micipsa, Gulussa, and Mastanabal—were looked upon as legitimate heirs. The rest, being sons of concubines, were not taken into account. Through the mediation of Rome an agreement was made among the three privileged princes more precarious and dangerous for the order and peace of the country than any that could be imagined. Micipsa, recognised as the first and real successor to the royal dignity, obtained Cirta, the capital, with the royal treasures. The chief command over the army was given to Gulussa, who had already been several times in Rome as ambassador, and, it appears, was most intimate with the Romans. The office of judge fell to the share of Mastanabal. All three were to rule in common. By this means a state of things was created such as, at a later period, existed under Jugurtha—a situation which could not fail to aggravate all the infirmities of a decaying kingdom, while it might be admirably turned to profit by a power like Rome without involving the smallest danger to Roman interests.

When the new arrangement had been made in the kingdom of Masinissa, Numidian cavalry, under Gulussa, at once took part in the war against Carthage. The most

---

[1] It would be well if we could ascertain the truth of this 'full power' delegated to Scipio. The story looks ugly and suspicious. It reminds us of the opportune testament of king Attalus III. of Pergamum, by which the Romans became heirs to the whole kingdom.

[2] Diodorus (xxxii. 16, Dindorf), it is true, speaks only of ten, but Zonaras (ix. 27) mentions πλῆθος υἱέων; and indeed it seems that a man who had had many wives, and when he died, at the age of ninety, left a son of four years behind, must have had a very numerous family.

important event, however, which followed the death of Masinissa was that the able Himilco Phameas was induced by Scipio to join the Romans with two thousand two hundred horse. We do not know whether this desertion was in any way the result of the altered state of affairs in Numidia. But it is possible that the Numidian party in Carthage now grew more determined, and separated itself from the patriotic party, which was resolved to continue the opposition to the last. We cannot otherwise explain the incident that Hasdrubal, the grandson of Masinissa, who commanded in Carthage, and had up to this time performed his duty, was soon afterwards accused of treason, and slain in the senate.

The year 148 B.C. was not more favourable for the Romans than the preceding one. The new consuls, it appears, entirely gave up the siege of Carthage, and confined themselves to occupying the Carthaginian territory, and reducing the towns which still held out. They besieged Clupea by land and sea, but without effect. The whole summer passed away in fruitless attempts to take the town of Hippo Diarrhytus. A sally made by the garrison was vigorously supported by the Carthaginians. The Roman engines were destroyed, and the consuls compelled to beat a disgraceful retreat. The prospects of the Carthaginians brightened. In Numidia a dispute had broken out among the three sons of Masinissa. Whilst Gulussa, in the hope of personal advantage, supported the Romans to the best of his ability, Micipsa and Mastanabal remained very lukewarm in their service, so that the Carthaginians began to hope for the possibility of securing their alliance against Gulussa and the Romans.[1] A body of Numidian horse actually joined them. The constant changes in the Numidian kingdom, where everything depended upon the influence of the man who chanced for the time to be uppermost, seemed to show that a complete revolution might possibly sever altogether the alli-

[1] Appian, viii. 111.

BOOK V.
149-146 B.C.

ance with Rome. Moreover, the war against Pseudo-Philippus had just at this time broken out in Macedonia. With this pretender the Carthaginians entered into negotiations, and encouraged him to persevere in his adventurous course. The brave and enterprising people continued the war with unabated vigour and gained fresh hopes, not altogether unfounded, that they might in the end succeed in saving their country from utter destruction.

What we have repeatedly remarked in the second and third Macedonian wars, and even in earlier periods of Roman history, took place once more in the third war with Carthage. After the Romans had carried on the contest for some time in a lax and inglorious manner, they succeeded at last in crushing their opponents by sheer perseverance, and by the overpowering weight of their military resources. It was not the superior strategic talent of Flamininus or Æmilius Paullus which overthrew the Macedonian kings, but the fact that Rome could continually send new legions of brave soldiers into the field. Thus, again, Carthage was vanquished in the end not by the personal ability of the overrated younger Scipio, but by the means which he had at his disposal, and the perseverance with which he made use of them. It was only by shutting out the town from all communication by land and sea that he at length reduced it.

Scipio Æmilianus elected consul.

Scipio Æmilianus, as we have seen, had served honourably as legate under the consuls Marcius and Manilius in the year 149 B.C.[1] Among the 'flitting shadows' he was,

---

[1] It has been remarked above (p. 348) that in the narrative of Appian, which is borrowed from Polybius, the eulogistic element is clearly apparent, and that the writer seizes every opportunity of extolling the merits of Scipio at the expense of the other Roman generals. We are of course willing to pardon Polybius for the weakness of being somewhat partial to his friend, patron, and pupil. It is not to be expected that he should be over-punctilious in examining the evidence for the facts, with which the family of the Scipios supplied him. But it must be confessed that he has transgressed all bounds of fair and pardonable partiality. He overshoots the mark by representing Scipio on all occasions as the man who restores the fortunes of war, and saves the Roman army from loss or destruction. See Appian, viii. 98, 100, 101, 102, 103 f., 114.

as even the severe Cato admitted, the only man.¹ Besides his military virtues, he also possessed political skill, and had therefore been employed on negotiations with Masinissa. After having arranged affairs in Numidia in the interest of Rome, he returned to the army, and, by his personal influence, induced the Carthaginian cavalry leader, Himilco Phameas,² to desert his post. Accompanied by him, as a tangible proof of his ability, he went to Rome in the second year of the war, intending to ask for the consulship of the following year. He was, indeed, only thirty-seven years old, and therefore, according to law, too young for this office.³ But the rumour, which his friends zealously spread, of his valour and prudence, the influence of his powerful family, and also the promising omen which lay in his name,⁴ induced the people, in spite of his legal disqualification, to elect him for the consulship in 147 B.C., and to give him the command of the war in Africa, without resorting to the customary decision by the drawing of lots. His grandfather, Scipio Africanus, had brought the long and trying war with Hannibal to a victorious end. It might be expected of a Scipio that he would also this time be victorious over Carthage.

Scipio had hardly landed in Utica, in the year 147 B.C., when he heard that Mancinus, the commander of the fleet, was in a most perilous situation. This incapable and vainglorious man was anxious, it appears, before the end of his year of command, to make a bold attempt to obtain for himself the glory of conquering Carthage. He landed on a part of the coast (No. 9), where the hills of Cape Car-

Perilous situation of Mancinus.

---

¹ We should, however, bear in mind that Cato's son married Scipio's sister (Plutarch, *Cato Mai.* 20). No Roman was unprejudiced when speaking of a near relative. Family connexions and family cliques, which are not unknown in other countries and in other ages, were in Rome all-powerful.

² We are not informed if this Himilco was a Carthaginian or a Numidian by birth. His defection points to the latter hypothesis.

³ By the lex Villia annalis of the year 180 B.C. Livy. xl. 14.

⁴ Appian. viii. 109 : θεόληπτος γάρ τις αὐτοῖς ᾔδε ἡ δόξα ἐνέπιπτε Σκιπίωνα μόνον αἱρήσειν Καρχηδόνα.

tajena rise abruptly from the sea, and where the suburb of Carthage, extending in this direction, was but weakly fortified.[1] He gained the undefended height with a few hundred soldiers, and was followed by a number of unarmed men from the ships, who probably looked forward to plundering the town without difficulty. But the Romans soon met with resolute resistance, and found it alike impossible to penetrate further into the town, or to retreat safely to the ships. It was then that they were rescued by the unexpected appearance of the vessels with which Scipio had approached in all haste from Utica.[2] It had been proved once more that Carthage was not to be taken by a *coup-de-main*.

Scipio takes the command.

Scipio sent home the incompetent Mancinus, and took the command of the Roman army in the place of his predecessor, Calpurnius Piso. We are not informed how many troops he brought with him from Italy. The legions had suffered much, and were now reinforced. Besides these reinforcements, Scipio had received permission to

---

[1] Zonaras, ix. 29 : Μαγκῖνος παραπλέων τὴν Καρχηδόνα χωρίον τι τοῦ τείχους αὐτῆς ἐντὸς ὂν Μεγαλία ὀνομαζόμενον καὶ ἐπὶ πέτρας ἀποτόμου καθῆκον πρὸς θάλασσαν πολὺ δὲ τῆς ἄλλης πόλεως ἀπηρτημένον καὶ μηδὲ πολλοὺς φρουροὺς ἔχον ὡς τῇ φύσει ὂν ἐρυμνὸν κατανοήσας, κλίμακας ἐξαπιναίως προσθεὶς ἀπὸ τῶν νεῶν ἐπανέβη. The spot here so accurately described is probably the southern extremity of Cape Cartajena, near Sibi-bu-Said, marked on our map No. 9.

[2] Appian, viii. 111. The report of Zonaras (ix. 29) does not quite agree with that of Appian. He says : ὁ μέντοι Σκιπίων τὰ μὲν Μεγαλία τὸν Μαγκῖνον φρουρεῖν κατέλιπεν. According to this version Mancinus was enabled, by the arrival of Scipio, not to effect his retreat, but to hold the position which he had seized. It may be that for a short time the spot actually remained in the hands of the Romans. But, at any rate, it was not held long, and the foolhardy feat of Mancinus did not lead to the capture of Carthage, nor had it the least effect upon the ulterior operations. Nevertheless Mancinus had the face to assert that he had taken Carthage. He actually caused a picture to be painted, and to be exhibited in the Forum, in which the capture of Carthage was represented, and in which he was the first man to penetrate into the town. This gave great offence to Scipio ; but Mancinus made himself so popular in Rome that he was elected for the consulship in 145 B.C. We have here a most instructive illustration of the boundless audacity with which the Roman nobles falsified facts to gratify their own personal vanity. It reminds us of a similar piece of reckless disregard of truth related, vol. ii. p. 43, of M. Valerius Messala.

invite the allies to give him voluntary aid.¹ But the bad results thus far had been caused not so much by the want of troops as by the incapacity of the generals and the defective discipline of the army. It was in Africa as it had been in Greece. The Roman soldiers thought more of plunder and luxury than of real hard fighting. They had imagined that the rich city of Carthage, having been previously disarmed, would become an easy prey. Numerous volunteers had been attracted by this tempting prospect. An immense number of traders, speculators, sutlers, a motley and disreputable crowd, had followed the army, and undermined its discipline. Like his father in Macedon and his grandfather in Spain, Scipio was obliged to begin by bringing back the degenerate soldiers to their duty, by purifying the camp, and by tightening the reins of command.² This done, he took in hand the operations of the siege with a steady and persistent energy which brought him step by step nearer to his aim.

He resolved to make his first attack by land on the isthmus which connected Carthage with the continent. When the Carthaginians marked his intention, Hasdrubal established himself in a fortified camp on the same side before the walls of the suburb. But Scipio, by making a feigned assault in one part, and thus deceiving Hasdrubal, succeeded, under the guidance of some deserters, in penetrating unperceived into a remote part of the town, in opening a gate, and admitting his troops. It is true, he was now only in the suburb, and in this large space, intersected by hedges and ditches, his army could neither move forward nor effect a lodgment. It also appears that the nature of the ground would not allow him to make an attack upon the inner town from this side.³ He therefore resolved voluntarily to evacuate the suburb.⁴ But he had

---

¹ Appian, viii. 112.   ² Appian. viii. 115.
³ Appian, viii. 117 : τὸ γὰρ χωρίον, τὰ Μέγαρα ἐλαχανεύετο καὶ φυτῶν ὡραίων ἔγεμεν, αἱμασιαῖς τε καὶ ὀριγκοῖς βάτου καὶ ἄλλης ἀκάνθης καὶ ὀχετοῖς βαθέος ὕδατος ποικίλοις τε καὶ σκολιοῖς κατάπλεον ἦν.
⁴ Appian, xviii. 117 : ὁ δὲ Σκιπίων ἔδεισε μὴ ἄβατον καὶ δυσχερὲς ᾖ (τὸ χωρίον) στρατῷ διώκοντι, ἐν ἀγνωσίᾳ μάλιστα διϊόδων καί τις ἐν νυκτὶ ἐνέδρα

effected so much, at least, that Hasdrubal, no longer able to hold his position outside the walls, gave up his camp on the isthmus, and retired into the town.

Scipio followed up his first advantage. He burnt the abandoned camp of Hasdrubal, and then erected a double line of fortifications before the town, right across the isthmus, from shore to shore, within which his troops were safe from a surprise, and cut off all communication between Carthage and the continent. This was the first step towards reducing the town by famine. The population could receive no more supplies by land. It is probable that a large portion of the inhabitants now gave themselves up as prisoners, or fled from the devoted town. The more resolute citizens retired to the old part of Carthage to continue the struggle.[1] If we may trust the scanty words of Appian, a violent quarrel broke out on this occasion between the senate, *i.e.* the aristocratic party, and Hasdrubal, who stood at the head of the fanatical people; several senators were slain in consequence, and Hasdrubal obtained dictatorial power.[2] In order to

---

γένοιτο· ἀνεζεύγνυε δή. This account represents the evacuation of the suburb as a measure of precaution on the part of Scipio, not as a result of any reverse suffered in consequence of an attack from the Carthaginians. It is difficult for us to imagine why a besieging army should first take and then give up again a place in which, as we should fancy, a lodgment could be made close to the inner wall. But the case seems only a repetition of what had happened before (p. 354), when Mancinus had penetrated into the outer town, and was obliged again to retire. At the siege of Syracuse, in the Hannibalic war (214–212 B.C.) Marcellus had gained possession of the suburbs many months before the inner town fell into his hands (vol. ii. p. 305 ff.).

[1] Zonaras, ix. 29: τὴν μὲν ἄλλην πόλιν ἐξέλιπον, ἐς δὲ τὸν Κώθωνα τήν τε Βύρσαν κατέφυγον. The designation Byrsa stands here, as elsewhere, for the whole of the old town. See Appian, viii. 117, 118. If the population of Carthage is stated to have amounted to seven hundred thousand at the beginning of the siege, of which only fifty thousand were left at the time of the capture, it does not follow that six hundred and fifty thousand men perished. A great portion of the inhabitants of the suburbs must have left the place before the final catastrophe.

[2] Appian, viii. 118; Zonaras, ix. 29. There are many points of resemblance between the siege of Carthage and that of Syracuse in the Hannibalic war. One has been pointed out already (p. 355, note 4). Another is this, that there existed two parties in the town, one fanatical and determined to resist to the death, the other inclined to give up the struggle when all hope of victory

make a reconciliation and a peaceable agreement with the Romans quite impossible, Hasdrubal is even said to have resorted to the process of torturing Roman prisoners to death on the walls before the very eyes of the besieging army.

The attack was now directed upon the oldest part of the town,[1] which contained the harbour and the fortress of Byrsa. The defence was continued by a comparatively small portion of the citizens, who replaced by determination what they lacked in natural resources. When it was no longer possible to bring in supplies by land, the remaining population was reduced to importing provisions by sea, and this could only be done under favourable circumstances with a strong wind, which carried the bold sailors and their cargoes past the Roman cruisers. In order to prevent even this, Scipio undertook to construct a colossal barrier in front of the harbour. From the frequently mentioned tongue of land (No. 4) between the bay of Tunis and the open sea, he caused an embankment of stones (No. 10) to be thrown right across the mouth of the harbour (No. 5), a structure which reminds us of the mole which Alexander made from the land to the island town of Tyre. Having at first ridiculed an undertaking which seemed to them vain and hopeless, the Carthaginians next tried to prevent it; but the soldiers, of whom Scipio had an abundance, worked steadily day and night, and at length the embankment reached the opposite side of the entrance to the harbour.

Thus the harbour of Carthage was closed. What the was gone. The fanatics were largely reinforced on both occasions by Roman deserters, who knew perfectly well what fate awaited them in case of surrender, and were determined to sell their lives dearly.

[1] It seems that the vast extent of the suburbs was now entirely given up. Zonaras, ix. 29, says: τὰ τε γὰρ τείχη καρτερὰ ἦν καὶ οἱ ἐντὸς πολλοὶ ὄντες ἰσχυρῶς ἐν ὀλίγῳ χώρῳ ἠμύνοντο. By this 'restricted space' Appian does not mean to designate the citadel alone—the Byrsa, properly speaking—but the whole of the old town. For we know from the further narrative of the siege that not only the Byrsa, but also the fortified port and the quarter lying between the two, were held by the Carthaginians, and were taken after a long and obstinate struggle.

BOOK V.
149–146 B.C.

Romans had repeatedly attempted in vain before Lilybæum in the Sicilian war, now succeeded at Carthage. But while they diligently worked to block up the old entrance to the harbour, the Carthaginians had been busy digging a new one. The rectangular mercantile harbour and the round naval port (Kothon) were separated from the sea on the eastern side only by a narrow strip of land. This strip the Carthaginians now pierced, probably at the part where the circumference of the naval port approached nearest to the sea.[1] Day and night men, women, and children continued to work. At the same time they built a fleet out of old timber, and the work was carried on with such secrecy that the Romans could only ascertain from prisoners that a knocking and hammering was heard in the Kothon, the cause of which was unknown.[2] At length it came to light. When the last strip of earth which separated the sea from the basin of the port had been removed, a fleet of fifty triremes and a number of smaller vessels sailed proudly out into the sea, and by their mere appearance inspired the Romans with astonishment and fear. Had they at once proceeded to the attack, the unprepared Roman ships would have been lost. But after a short trial trip, which was probably necessary for the newly built vessels and their new crews,[3] the Carthaginians returned to the harbour, and not till the third day did they sail forth again to offer battle. The enemy meanwhile had made preparations, and a murderous fight took place, which lasted the whole of one day, without any decisive result. When, towards evening, the Carthaginians returned to their harbour, the smaller vessels stopped up the defective entrance, and

Sea fight.

---

[1] See plan No. 11 Falbe, *Recherches sur l'Emplacement de Carthage*, p. 21, planche 1, No. 50; Beulé, *Journal des Savants*, 1860, p. 363.

[2] This secrecy was possible, because the Kothon was surrounded by a high wall. Appian, viii. 127.

[3] Appian, viii. 122, says that this was done ἐς μόνην ἐπίδειξιν, and Mommsen (*Röm. Gesch.* ii. 35) calls it a 'mere parade' (*Paradezug*). We are inclined to think that both the ancient and the modern writer fail to appreciate the ability of the Carthaginians to judge what was best, and their determination to do it. Men of the temper of the Carthaginians, and in such desperate straits, are not likely to indulge in idle shows.

compelled the larger ones to remain outside.¹ The latter took up their position alongside a quay (No. 12) of considerable breadth, which extended along the outside of the commercial port as far as the south-eastern extremity of the peninsula, very near, therefore, to the old blocked-up entrance to the port.² Here they were at once attacked by the Roman fleet, and fought this, the last naval battle of the Carthaginian people, with a degree of courage worthy the former mistress of the seas. The Romans, however, finally remained victorious, and destroyed some of the Carthaginian ships, which, being hurriedly constructed out of old timber, were probably by no means equal to the Roman vessels. During the night the Carthaginians retired into the harbour, nor did they attempt once more to try the fortune of war by sea.

Scipio now directed his attack against the quay (No. 12), near which the Carthaginian ships had last taken up their position. This quay extended, as we have seen, from the south-eastern extremity of the land along the eastern shore, in a line parallel with the commercial harbour, which it separated from the sea. It had been constructed as a landing-place for the merchant vessels at a time when the harbour became too small for the growing traffic.³ It was not till the outbreak of the last war that the Carthaginians found it necessary to fortify this spot on the sea side by a strong wall, so that the enemy might not be able to make a lodgment upon it.⁴ This was precisely what Scipio intended to do. It appears that he prolonged the dam which closed the old mouth of the harbour in this direction, and thus formed a communication by land with the quay.⁵ Here, therefore, he erected his engines, and

Attack on the dock quay.

¹ Appian, viii. 122, 123.
² Falbe, *Recherches*, p. 17, planche 1, Nos. 44–47.
³ See p. 346, note 2.
⁴ Appian, viii. 123: τὸ χῶμα ... ὃ πρὸ τοῦ τείχους εὐρύχωρον ἐμπόροις ἐς διάθεσιν φορτίων ἐγεγένητο ἐκ πολλοῦ· καὶ παρατείχισμα ἐπ' αὐτοῦ βραχὺ ἐν τῷδε τῷ πολέμῳ ἐπεποίητο, ἵνα μὴ ὡς ἐν εὐρυχώρῳ στρατοπεδεύσειάν ποτε οἱ πολέμιοι.
⁵ This appears from the fact that the Roman soldiers attacked by the Carthaginians in the night fled as far as their camp, and could not be rallied by

BOOK V.
149–146 B.C.

destroyed a portion of the wall. But one night a number of Carthaginians waded and swam through the water, reached the dam, and set the engines on fire. The Roman soldiers were so surprised and alarmed that they fled before the unarmed enemy, nor could they be stopped until they had gained their camp, although Scipio ordered them to be attacked by other troops and driven back.[1] The task had to be begun again. Whilst the Romans erected new siege-works, the Carthaginians restored their wall, and fortified it with wooden towers. At last Scipio succeeded in establishing himself on the quay, but he could neither penetrate further, nor take the walls of the harbour. As the summer was now drawing to a close, and he did not wish to give up the quay which he had conquered with so much difficulty, he fortified it by a wall and ditch, parallel with the wall of the Carthaginian harbour, and left in it for the winter a garrison of four thousand men, which, being the extreme outposts, kept up with the Carthaginians a continued exchange of missiles.[2]

Terms of surrender rejected by Hasdrubal.

The third year of the war was drawing to a close, and yet the heroic town remained defiant and unconquered. It appears to have been about this time[3] that Hasdrubal made a final attempt to arrange terms of peace. He required nothing but that the town and her defenders should be spared; everything else the Carthaginians were prepared to suffer.[4] Gulussa was the mediator, and advised Scipio to yield, because the result was still uncertain, and at the impending consular election it was possible that another consul might be sent from Rome to continue the war. Perhaps the wily Numidian thought in his own mind that the continued existence of Carthage would be more conducive to his safety than the immediate vicinity of a Roman proconsul. But Scipio, with great decision, rejected this advice. He would only agree

Scipio and the cavalry. There must have been, therefore, a direct communication between the quay and the camp.

[1] Appian, viii. 124. [2] Appian, viii. 125.
[3] Zonaras, ix. 30. [4] Polybius, xxxix. 1, 6.

to one thing. Hasdrubal was to be allowed unmolested departure for himself, his wife and children, and ten families nearly related to him. The remaining inhabitants were to surrender at discretion. If Hasdrubal had been the miserable coward that Polybius, strangely enough, pictures him to be, he would surely not have hesitated to agree to these conditions. But he disdained the idea of forsaking his brave compatriots in their last death-struggle, and indignantly rejected the offer.[1]

The Carthaginians had still one spot in their territory from which, in spite of the blockade by land and sea, intrepid sailors from time to time brought them supplies. This spot was Nepheris, a town the position of which we are unfortunately unable to determine on account of the contradictory reports of Appian and Strabo,[2] and which, in spite of its evident importance, is not otherwise known. In this place was stationed an officer of the name of Diogenes, who commanded the army collected and formerly so well conducted by Hasdrubal.[3] Scipio sent a part of his army under Caius Laelius and the Numidian prince Gulussa against Nepheris, and conducted the siege himself from his camp before Carthage. The particulars of this siege are not well known. The town and the camp of Diogenes fell into the hands of the besiegers in the course of the winter, and Appian relates that on this occasion seventy thousand people were slain in their flight, and ten thousand made prisoners, an act in which Gulussa, with his elephants and his Numidian horse, seems to have taken the greatest share.[4]

In truth, no hope remained now for the unhappy town of Carthage. The Romans could wait patiently, as they had once done at the siege of Capua, till hunger had completed their task for them. Although the number of defenders had greatly diminished, a famine broke out so terrible that, if we may believe the reports,[5] some com-

Capture of Nepheris.

Capture of Carthage.

---

[1] Polybius, xxxix. 9 f.; Zonaras, ix. 30.
[2] Appian, viii. 126; Strabo, xvii. 3, 16.   [3] See p. 318.
[4] Appian, viii. 126.   [5] Polybius, xxxix. 2, 12; Zonaras, ix. 30.

mitted suicide, others devoured the dead bodies of their fellow-sufferers, or gave themselves up to the Romans, *i.e.* to slavery. In the beginning of the spring of 146 B.C., when exhaustion, disease, and despair had already weakened the nerves and the spirits of the defenders, Scipio advanced to storm the town. It was no longer necessary to set the battering-rams in motion. The Carthaginians themselves evacuated the commercial harbour which they had defended so long, and consigned it to the flames with all that it contained. In the confusion which ensued, a party of Romans, conducted by Caius Lælius, succeeded unperceived in scaling the wall which surrounded the naval port, and in penetrating thence into the town. The legions first occupied the market-place (No. 13), which was not far off. From this place three narrow streets led to the Byrsa, between houses towering six stories high. Here a bloody street-fight took place, which was the more deplorable because it could have no practical purpose, and was merely the result of rage and exasperation. From house to house the Romans were obliged to force their way, penetrating through the division walls, fighting on the flat roofs, and advancing from one to another on boards and beams. When they had reached the foot of the Byrsa, Scipio caused the conquered part of the town to be set on fire, in order to gain space for the attack upon the last refuge of the defeated enemy. But it was unnecessary to storm it. On the seventh day after the Romans had entered the town,[1] the wretched remnant of the Carthagi-

---

[1] This is Appian's account (viii. 128 ff.). Mommsen (*Röm. Gesch.*, ii. 36), Davis (*Carthage and her Remains*, p. 373), and others make the street-fight, before the Romans reached the Byrsa, last six days. But Appian distinguishes two periods within the six days. The first was that of the fight from house to house. How long it lasted is not stated. But no houses were set on fire until the whole place up to the Byrsa was in the hands of the Romans (ἐνεπίμπρη δ' οὐδὲν οὐδεὶς πω διὰ τοὺς ἐπὶ τῶν τεγῶν ἕως ἐπὶ τὴν Βύρσαν ἧκεν ὁ Σκιπίων, Appian, l.c.). Then Scipio gave orders to set fire to the houses (καὶ τότε τοὺς τρεῖς ὁμοῦ στενωποὺς ἐνεπίμπρη), and to level the ground. How long this process lasted Appian does not say. It may have taken half or more than half of the six days which elapsed between the first assault and the surrender of the fifty thousand Carthaginians. Had the fighting alone lasted six

nian people surrendered. Fifty thousand men, women, and children were let out of the citadel through a gate, and carried off as prisoners. The rest of the garrison, a body of nine hundred Roman deserters, occupied the temple of Æsculapius in the citadel, with the intention of burying themselves under its ruins. Among them, with his wife and children, was Hasdrubal, an involuntary participator, it would seem, in the desperate struggle of those who had devoted themselves to death. He at length succeeded in escaping from the furious band, and surrendered to the victor at discretion. His wife, however, it is said,[1] had a prouder spirit than he. She disdained to outlive her country. From the roof of the burning temple into which the surviving deserters had been driven back, she cursed her husband, whom she saw crouching at the feet of Scipio, as a coward and a traitor, and before his very eyes threw first her two sons and then herself into the flames.

CHAP. V.

149-146 B.C.

The Roman deserters.

The conquered town was now given up to plunder. The booty was immense, even after all the havoc of the war.[2] The gold and silver was reserved for the state treasure of the republic. The works of art, which the Carthaginians, in the time of their power, had carried away from Sicily, were restored to their original owners, as, for instance, the celebrated brazen bull of Phalaris

Destruction of Carthage.

days, there would have remained only one night for the conflagration and the clearing away of the ruins.

[1] We have serious doubts about the truth of this dramatic effect, which would do honour to any stage manager. A woman standing on the roof of a burning temple, and, in the midst of uproar and carnage, haranguing her husband, who is at a safe distance, is a scene passing all bounds of historical probability. What makes it particularly suspicious is the pretty little piece of adulation which the frantic woman has the politeness to address to Scipio: σοὶ μὲν οὐ νέμεσις ἐκ θεῶν ὦ Ῥωμαῖε, ἐπὶ γὰρ πολεμίαν ἐστρατεύσας. Appian, viii. 31. καὶ τῷ στρατηγῷ μεγάλας ἐπανῆγε τὰς χάριτας. Polybius, xxxix. 3, 6. All this is as much a fiction as any scene in a sensational novel. We have no doubt that Hasdrubal and his wife were retained by the Roman deserters against their will. At last Hasdrubal succeeded in escaping from them (λαθὼν ἔφυγε. Appian, viii. 131). It is possible that thereupon his wife and children were murdered before his eyes.

[2] In a temple of the sun the Roman soldiers had, in defiance of all discipline, whilst the battle was still raging, hacked to pieces with their swords a golden statue of the god.

BOOK V.
149-146 B.C.

from Agrigentum. The plundered town was then consigned to the flames. As Scipio watched the ocean of fire, which raged in the streets for seventeen days, he was so impressed with the transitoriness of all that is great, that, foreseeing in his mind's eye the ruin of his own country, he involuntarily pronounced the Homeric words: 'The day will come when sacred Ilium will sink into ashes, with Priam and the people of Priam the strong-sceptred.'[1] By his side stood his friend and teacher, Polybius, who heard and marked these words. Perhaps he had a foreboding that about this same time the glorious city of Corinth, the chief town of his own country, was sinking into ashes.

The plough was drawn over the site of destroyed Carthage, and a solemn curse was pronounced against any one who should ever undertake to build a new town on that spot. Rome was at length delivered from the ever-gnawing fear, from the envy and jealousy which Carthage, even humbled and prostrate, never ceased to inspire. Old Cato had not lived to see the fulfilment of his most ardent desire. He had died at the beginning of the war. But the unbounded joy which the news of the fall of Carthage caused in Rome was a proof that Cato had only given words to what was felt by the majority of the Roman people. A glorious triumph was in store for Scipio, worthy of those which had been celebrated by his father, Æmilius Paullus, over Perseus, and by his grandfather over Carthage. The unparalleled heroism with which the Carthaginians had fought to the last bitter hour had caused the fact to be forgotten that, at the outbreak of the war, they had been defenceless. They had raised themselves to a position all but equal to that of Rome, and had once more inspired the Romans with respect, a respect which unfortunately was expressed only in the joy at Scipio's victory. The Roman nation was not capable of showing respect for a fallen enemy by magnanimity. The

---

[1] Ἔσσεται ἦμαρ, ὅταν ποτ' ὀλώλῃ Ἴλιος ἱρὴ
Καὶ Πρίαμος καὶ λαὸς ἐϋμμελίω Πριάμοιο.

Carthaginian prisoners were partly sold as slaves, but many died in prison from hunger and misery. Only Hasdrubal [1] and a few other eminent men were more merci-

[1] This eminent man shares the fate of the great enemies of the Roman writers, who delighted in reviling their enemies. The one-sided narratives of Romans or partisans of Rome have determined the verdict of general history, and given us caricatures of Perseus, and even of Hannibal. As we have no historians who wrote from the opposite point of view, we must be satisfied to rest our judgment on facts admitted by the Romans themselves. But from such facts we are at liberty to draw our own conclusions as to the character and motives of the men in question. Now, as regards Hasdrubal, we know that he was banished from Carthage to please Rome, because his policy was decidedly national and anti-Roman, that when the war broke out he forgot the wrong he had suffered, and offered his services to his country; that he formed an army, and for two years kept the Romans in check and repeatedly defeated them; that he was the leading spirit in the heroic defence made by Carthage; that he disdained to accept favourable terms for himself alone from which his countrymen should be excluded, and that he did not ask for mercy until all was lost. Polybius (xxxix. 1, 2) represents this man in the most glaring colours as an incapable general; as a pot-bellied glutton, fit to be compared to a fattened bull, as an epicure at a time when his fellow-countrymen were suffering famine, as a bloodthirsty tyrant, a vain fool and boaster, and lastly as a perjured coward, who craved mercy for himself, though he had sworn to perish with his country. There seems to be something of personal rancour in this tirade. Can it be possible that the quarrelsome Greek and Hasdrubal, at some later period, when both lived in Italy, had fallen out with one another? At any rate, our great respect for Polybius as a statesman and historian must not blind us to any human weaknesses which he may have had. Certainly his picture of Hasdrubal is not dictated by the cool spirit of the historian, nor is it consistent with the facts related of him. We cannot impute vulgar vanity or low sensuality to a man who, in the most desperate hour of Carthage, placed himself at the head of her citizens. The man who rejected the offer of personal safety for himself and his family and nearest friends unless it was to be extended to all his countrymen, was surely no mean, selfish coward. A man who, with a band of volunteers, resisted the Roman legions for two years was no despicable general; and it is hardly credible that Scipio would have spared Hasdrubal's life if it were true that he had caused Roman prisoners to be mutilated and tortured to death. He was, on the contrary, generous to an enemy in the field, as is proved by the fact that he gave honourable burial to three Roman military tribunes (Appian, viii. 104). Now, as regards the final catastrophe, we suspect that the real facts were something like this: Hasdrubal continued the defence of Carthage as long as his fellow-citizens were determined to persevere. When the town, with the only exception of the Byrsa, was in the hands of the enemy, when the last fifty thousand Carthaginians had surrendered at discretion, and the fight was continued only by the nine hundred Roman deserters whose lives were forfeited, then even the most patriotic and heroic Carthaginian citizen had done his duty. A voluntary death might indeed have seemed a deliverance from the worst horrors of life, but it could be of no use to Carthage. If, therefore, Hasdrubal escaped from

fully treated, and were not tortured like Perseus. They spent the rest of their days in peace, if they could enjoy peace, with the knowledge that their nation was annihilated, and their native town lay in ruins.

The greater part of the Carthaginian territory was joined to Utica, which now became the capital of the Roman province of Africa. The towns which had remained true to Carthage, like Hippo, Clupea, and others, were punished with loss of land. The germ of Semitic culture, the Phœnician language, art, literature, and religion gave way gradually, though slowly, to Roman influence, and at last quite disappeared. The Numidian kingdom, it seems, was not enlarged. It was left to internal disputes, which rendered it a safe neighbour. Thus peace was established in this quarter for a considerable time.

that desperate band of men devoted to death, who, it seems, wished him to die with them, and if he asked for his life, let those condemn him who can look upon death indifferently. To us he appears, by his deeds, to have deserved the name of the 'last Carthaginian' in the best sense of the word, as a representative of the intensity of strength, endurance, and patriotism, as well as of the versatility of his race.

CHAPTER VI.

THE WARS IN SPAIN UP TO THE FALL OF NUMANTIA, 200–133 B.C.

<small>CHAP. VI.
200–133 B.C.
Geographical condition of political power.</small>

HISTORIANS have long been reluctant to recognise in the history of the world a development according to fixed laws, dependent on external nature. On the one hand a guiding Providence, on the other hand human free will, have been looked upon as altogether independent of laws, and consequently unfathomable. It is true scientific research, which has everywhere endeavoured to investigate the laws which regulate phenomena, has not yet at its command sufficient materials to determine the results which, in spite of occasional deviations, must necessarily ensue from the reciprocal action of nature and man, results which might be looked upon as the intentions of the divine will. But in one respect man is confessedly so completely under the influence of nature that an entirely free course of action is quite out of the question. As every individual is under the influence of space, so every political association, being established in a particular region on the varied surface of the earth, is endowed from the very beginning with more or less capability of expansion, and has no choice as to the direction in which such a capability is to be manifested. We have had to notice earlier in this history[1] how important the central position of Rome was for the establishment of her dominion over Italy. The position of the Italian peninsula, in the centre of the Mediterranean countries, was not less important

---

[1] Vol. ii. p. 462.

BOOK V.
200-133 B.C.

for the foundation of an empire including all these territories. The enemies of Rome, being thus separated, succumbed one by one to the central power. Hence the process of subjugation was continued almost uninterruptedly and equally on all sides when, with the victory over Pyrrhus, Rome had come out from her former isolation. The conclusion of the Hannibalic war hastened this process. We have traced its course in Greece, Illyria, Macedonia, Asia, and Africa. We have now to turn our eyes away from these civilised states to the barbarous countries of Spain and that part of Gaul which lies at the foot of the Alps. After this survey, we shall turn to the inner life of the Roman commonwealth, in order to investigate as far as possible the nature of the forces which produced such tremendous effects, and to study the influence of external power upon the inner national life, an influence which was visible during the whole of this time, weak at first, but gradually increasing until, after violent revolutions, it worked out a new constitution for the Roman world.

Geographical seclusion of Spain.

We see plainly by the position which Spain occupied with regard to Italy, Greece, and the East, during the five centuries previous to our era, how geographical separation keeps nations apart from one another in an age when the means of communication are but feebly developed. Though, from the earliest ages, the rich country in the far West had been the subject of wonderful tales, yet the bold Phœnicians ventured but stealthily and rarely to steer their ships towards it, and to settle here and there on the coast. From Massilia their rivals, the Greeks, did not advance further than Emporiæ, where they were obliged to watch and defend their walls and their single gate day and night against the natives, who had settled all round. No arm of the sea opened access into the compact interior of the peninsula. Lofty mountain ranges rose up steep and wild, separating the fertile strip of low land by the sea from the vast table land of the interior. It was not until the unhappy issue of the first war with Rome that the Carthaginians succeeded in extending their dominion inland from a few fortified settlements on the coast. Had they been able to continue their work of colonisation, and to touch and penetrate the rude natives with their spirit, they would probably have developed in this country forms of civil and political life which might have been of great influence as a new element in the Græco-Roman civilisation of antiquity.

Character of the native Spaniards.

Just as in climate and in the nature of the soil, in her unbroken coast line, her rarely navigable rivers, and the high lands in her interior, with their arid steppes, Spain represented in miniature the peculiarities of the opposite African continent, so the original inhabitants of both countries, whether through affinity of race, or through the influence of similar climate and soil, show similar mental qualities. The original Spanish tribes had the virtues and the vices of barbarians. The multiplicity of small states and almost unceasing wars fostered courage while, especially in the more mountainous parts, they kept the people in poverty. The men were occupied chiefly in warfare for the sake of plunder. Domestic work and agriculture were left to the women.[1] At the same time we meet with a degree of contentment and simplicity of living, a perseverance in fatigues and dangers, which remind us of the hardy inhabitants of the African and Arabian deserts, and contrast strikingly with the Gauls, who were notorious for their fickleness, their gluttony, and their excitability. In spite of all wars and migrations, the character of the European nations has essentially remained what it was in antiquity. We may therefore be justified in

---

[1] Justin, xliv. 2. Appian speaks of the courage of the Spanish men and women, vi. 71 : συμμαχομένων τοῖς ἀνδράσι τῶν γυναικῶν καὶ συναιρομενων καὶ οὔ τινα φωνὴν οὐδ' ἐν ταῖς σφαγαῖς ἀφειοῶν. Ibid. c. 72 : καὶ ἅμα ταῖς γυναιξὶν ὡπλισμέναις ἐμάχοντο καὶ προθύμως ἔθνησκον, οὐκ ἐπιτρεφόμενος αὐτῶν οὐδεὶς οὐδὲ τὰ νῶτα δεικνὺς οὐδὲ φωνὴν ἀφιεὶς κ.τ.λ. It is also characteristic of them that they preferred death to slavery. Appian, vi. 77 : τῶν αἰχμαλώτων οὐδεὶς ὑπέμεινε δουλεύειν· ἀλλ' οἱ μὲν αὐτοὺς, οἱ δὲ τοὺς πριαμένους ἀνῄρουν, οἱ δὲ τὰς ναῦς ἐν τῷ διάπλῳ διετίτρων. Even of the women it is reported, Appian, vi. 72 : χαίρουσαι τῷ θανάτῳ μᾶλλον τῆς αἰχμαλωσίας.

BOOK V.
200-133 B.C.

First Roman possessions in Spain.

recognising in the chivalrous, proud, and frugal Spaniards of our time the true descendants of the old Iberians.[1]

Among the inhabitants of the valleys and plains which slope towards the Mediterranean milder manners and more settled institutions were found than among the tribes of the interior. The Turdetanians, in what is now called Andalusia, exhibited even the beginnings of a national civilisation and literature.[2] The fertility and the delightful climate of this favoured district almost spontaneously produced wealth, and attracted from the highlands hordes of mountaineers eager for plunder. Between these maranders and the foreigners who also collected with the hope of profit and plunder, the inhabitants of the coast districts had no chance of maintaining an independent position. The foreigners assumed the part of protectors of the weak and peaceably disposed against their troublesome neighbours,[3] and as long as this protection did not degenerate into oppression the relation between them was mutually satisfactory and advantageous.[4] The Carthaginian dominion lasted exactly long enough to excite the national aversion to foreigners. Then the Romans interfered as deliverers and allies of the Spaniards, and thus succeeded at the beginning in gaining the sympathies of the natives. The friendly understanding lasted until the Carthaginians were entirely driven out of Spain. But after the humiliation of Carthage the deluded Spaniards began to perceive that they had only exchanged one master for another. The Romans did not dream of giving

---

[1] The appellation Celtiberians indicates that in the north-eastern part of the peninsula there was a mixture of Celts and Iberians. Nevertheless the Iberians must have been the prevailing race, for we find no indications of Celtic characteristics in the people.

[2] Strabo, iii. 1, 6: σοφώτατοι δ' ἐξετάζονται τῶν Ἰβήρων οὗτοι (οἱ Τουρδητανοί) καὶ γραμματικῇ χρῶνται, καὶ τῆς παλαιᾶς μνήμης ἔχουσι συγγράμματα καὶ ποιήματα καὶ νόμους ἐμμέτρους ἑξακισχιλίων ἐπῶν, ὥς φασιν.

[3] Frequent causes of war were furnished by the attacks of the free races of the interior upon those who were allied with the Romans. See Appian, vi. 48, 51, 56, 57, 58; Polybius, xxxv. 2; Livy, xxxiv. 11.

[4] Similar was the position of the Campanians between the Romans, their protectors, and the Samnites, their enemies.

up Spain after they had once set their foot in it. They had, it is true, great difficulty in holding the land, and the immediate advantages won for the republic were scarcely perceptible. But as long as Carthage existed, the Romans feared that she might rise once more to power, as she had done under Hannibal, and therefore they must retain possession of Spain, where Hannibal had collected his forces for the attack upon Italy. The country therefore remained occupied by Roman troops, and was divided into two military districts, the provinces of citerior and ulterior Spain, *i.e.* the east coast, from the Pyrenees to the Xucar, and the south coast as far as the Anas (Guadiana). The boundaries of these districts towards the interior were uncertain, as must always be the case when the conquest of land takes place slowly and gradually. Between the Roman provinces and the peoples of the northern and western parts of the peninsula, who had not yet been attacked or even become known, lived several tribes in the half-free condition of Roman friends and allies, who were ready on every opportunity not only to repel the invasions of the foreign conquerors into their own territory, but even to make inroads into the Roman province, and to support the revolts of tribes already conquered.

It would be very instructive if we could carefully and accurately trace the course which the Romans pursued in the extremely arduous task of conquering Spain. But for this investigation we lack trustworthy materials. The reports which the Roman governors sent home of their achievements and their successes were one and all disfigured by vanity and private interest, and out of these reports Roman annalists, who had the vaguest notions of the geography and political condition of Spain, compiled a history to the honour and glory of the Roman republic, in which, as in a labyrinth, the historian gropes about without comprehending how the separate parts fit into the plan and scheme of the whole.[1] We must not venture

[1] We will give one sample. Cato, who, in his consulship 195 B.C., went to Spain, defeated the natives in a battle at Emporiæ, in which he boasts of

BOOK V.
200-133 B.C.

Distance of Spain.

into this labyrinth for the purpose of compiling a complete narrative in chronological order; but we may attempt to form, from the scattered fragments of trustworthy record, an outline sketch of the wars in Spain, until we arrive at that point where the grand figure of Viriathus and the heroic struggle of the little town of Numantia will rivet our attention.

The first difficulty which presented itself to the success of Roman arms in Spain was the great distance of that country from Rome, and this difficulty was increased by the faintheartedness of the Romans at sea and by their aversion to naval enterprise. Instead of sending their troops straight across the Tyrrhenian sea, they usually let them march by land as far as Pisa or Luna,[1] and then sail along the Ligurian and Gallic coast,[2] until they reached Emporiæ or Tarraco, where they landed and continued their march by land to New Carthage or Gades. This road to Gades was about six times as long as the distance from Brundusium to Thessalonica in Macedonia. The history of the war shows what difficulties were caused by this great distance.

These difficulties were increased by the peculiar organization of the Roman civil and military service, which required annual changes in all the chief offices of state. We have seen how this difficulty was felt even in the Sicilian war.[3] Nor was it otherwise in Macedonia and Syria. It was absolutely necessary to make some changes in the old practice, especially by prolonging the

having slain 'many' enemies. As Livy observes (xxxiv. 15, 9), Cato was not stingy in his own praise. But Valerius Antias was not satisfied with such a vague and modest statement, which Cato himself judged sufficient for his own credit. He therefore related in his annals that forty thousand enemies were killed in that battle. See below, p. 377, note 4.

[1] That is, since the establishment of this fortified port in the year 177 B.C.

[2] According to circumstances, the Roman armies, instead of sailing along the coast, marched round the Ligurian gulf by land, although the road was bad and very unsafe as long as the Ligurians were independent. In the year 189 B.C., for instance, the prætor Lucius Bæbius was attacked on this road; a portion of his suite were killed; he himself escaped with a few companions to Massilia, where he died of his wounds. Livy, xxxvii. 57.

[3] Vol. ii. p. 110 ff.

time of service in the legions, by enlisting more volunteers and veterans, and by employing more auxiliaries and mercenary troops.[1] These deviations from the old Roman practice are strikingly apparent in the Spanish campaigns of the Hannibalic war. At the same time the prolongation of the command in the hands of one man became more frequent. But this last change, which would have had a most salutary effect upon military affairs in general, was not carried out systematically, lest the aristocracy, and even the republic, might suffer from it. The Romans did not wish their Spanish generals to return home with a taste for monarchy, and they preferred to sacrifice the chance of rapid conquests in that country.

The simplest substitute for a standing army for the safety of the Spanish provinces would have been a systematic colonisation of Spain by Italians. By Roman and Latin colonies the old republic had taken firm possession of the Italian peninsula. Nothing could have been more natural than to apply this process to Spain, a country the climate of which was peculiarly favourable for the bodily health of the Italian peasant, and in which no superior culture opposed the spreading of the Latin language. Colonisation was actually begun by Scipio Africanus. He had settled a number of old soldiers in the fertile valley of the Bætis, and had thus founded Italica, the first Italian town beyond the sea.[2] All circumstances strongly recommended the continuation of this course. In the years which followed the first conquest the Roman soldiers had married Spanish women, and the result was a mixed population of Spanish and Italian blood. Such were the people who in the year 171 B.C. founded Carteja as a Latin colony, not far from the Straits of Gibraltar. But here the attempts at a

---

[1] In the year 193 B.C. the prætor C. Flaminius asked for a reinforcement of six thousand five hundred men, which he required to put down an insurrection. But he only obtained permission to enlist soldiers elsewhere but in Italy. He did this in Sicily, Africa, and Spain. Livy, xxxv. 2. Respecting the employment of Numidian elephants in Spain, see p. 332.

[2] Appian, vi. 83. Italica was the birth-place of Trajan and Hadrian.

BOOK V.
200-133 B.C.

Character of the wars in Spain.

systematic colonisation of Spain began and ended. It became necessary, therefore, from the lack of a sufficient supply of native mercenaries and auxiliaries, to supply annually[1] from Italy the troops needed for the harassing campaigns in Spain.[2]

Service in Spain was exceedingly disliked.[3] There were no easy, bloodless victories to be gained here, as in Greece, Macedonia, and Asia Minor, and no rich towns to be plundered. On the contrary, the battles were hard-fought, the fatigues exhausting, and the booty comparatively small. The Roman citizens and the Italian

---

[1] But the troops were nowhere kept so long in service as in Spain. This was the cause of frequent insubordination and even mutiny. In the year 141 B.C. the Spanish legions consisted of men who had served six years in succession. Appian, vi. 78.

[2] We do not possess a complete list of the Italian troops sent out to Spain. The actual strength of the armies is not always stated, as, for instance, that of the army of Cato in the year 195 B.C. Nevertheless we can gather even from the fragmentary accounts of Livy that Spain absorbed a very considerable number of men, and was a great and constant drain on Italy. The following figures will illustrate this fact. In 196 B.C. two legions and eight thousand six hundred allies were sent. Livy, xxxiii. 26. In 193 B.C. sixteen thousand six hundred men. Livy, xxxiv. 56, 8. In 189 B.C. ten thousand two hundred and fifty men. Livy, xxxvii. 50, 11. In 188 B.C. six thousand four hundred men. Livy, xxxviii. 36, 3. In 186 B.C. twenty-four thousand men. Livy, xxxix. 20, 3. In 184 B.C. nine thousand eight hundred men. Livy, xxxix. 38. In 182 B.C. eleven thousand four hundred men. Livy, xl. 1. In 181 B.C. nine thousand five hundred men. Livy, xl. 18. In 180 B.C. thirteen thousand nine hundred and fifty men. Livy, xl. 36, 8. In 174 B.C. eight thousand four hundred and fifty men. Livy, xli. 21. 1. In 173 B.C. three thousand two hundred men. Livy, xlii. 1. In 172 B.C. eight thousand four hundred and fifty men. Livy, xlii. 18, 6. In 169 B.C. ten thousand three hundred men. This list, which cannot be complete, gives for the period from 196 B.C. to 169 B.C. more than one hundred and fifty thousand Roman citizens and Italian allies, of whom we may be sure that a very small portion ever returned to Italy. It was by no means an isolated case, when in 193 B.C. Sextus Digitius handed over to his successor scarcely half the number of troops he had received, and yet he had not fought a single great battle (crebra magis quam digna dictu proelia). Livy, xxxv. 1; ibid. 2. The disastrous wars in Spain were not the only cause of the decrease of population in Italy, but they were not the least.

[3] Livy, xxxix. 38, 8; xl. 35, 36; xlii. 18, 6. In the year 180 B.C. the praetor Q. Fulvius Flaccus reported to Rome that it was absolutely necessary to relieve the troops in Spain: 'Ita enim obstinatos esse milites, ut non ultra retineri posse in provincia viderentur, iniussuque abituri inde essent, si non dimitterentur, aut in perniciosam, si quis impense retineret, seditionem exarsuri.'

peasants were not easily induced to risk their lives in a foreign land to fight against enemies by whom their homes were not threatened, and to do so without any prospect of personal profit, but merely in order to give the members of the ruling houses an opportunity of acquiring honours, triumphs, and riches.[1] Spain, it is true, was not actually poor. Prisoners of war could always be sold as slaves,[2] and in the Spanish mines much silver had been found which was current in the land. But the Roman commanders were mostly intent upon filling their own pockets first; and few were so sensible or so just as Cato, who conducted the war in Spain in 195 B.C., and caused the booty to be distributed as much as possible among the mass of the common soldiers.[3] The result was that war in Spain was more a system of plundering than fair and honest war. Leaders and troops became so savage that they have been surpassed only by the descendants of the Spaniards, who for the sake of plunder hunted down the natives of Mexico and Peru as if they had been wild beasts. The bare acts of violence, the treachery and bloodthirstiness which marked the dealings of the Romans in Spain as they marked the conduct of Spaniards at a later period in America, would be hardly comprehensible, if we were not justified in believing that they regarded the natives as an inferior race to be dealt with wholly according to their good pleasure.

The wars which the Romans carried on in Spain ever since the year 200 B.C. exhibit a succession of battles, surprises, stratagems, victories, and defeats following each

---

[1] Appian, vi. 80 : ὡς γὰρ ἐπὶ δόξαν ἢ κέρδος ἢ θριάμβου φιλοτιμίαν ἐξῄεσάν τινες ἐς τὰς στρατίας, οὐκ ἐπὶ τὸ τῇ πόλει συμφέρον.

[2] See, however, p. 369, note 1.

[3] Plutarch, *Cato Mai.* 10. On the contrary, it is related of Servius Sulpicius Galba by Appian, vi. 60 : τότε δὲ ὁ Γάλβας Λουκούλλου φιλοχρηστότερος ὤν (Lucullus had commenced a war without any authorisation, merely with a view to enrich himself) ὀλίγα μέν τινα τῆς λείας τῇ στρατιᾷ διεδίδου, καὶ ὀλίγα τοῖς φίλοις, τὰ λοιπὰ δὲ ἐσφετερίζετο. It appears from Valerius Max. vi. 4. 2, that the war in Spain was looked upon as a profitable business by the nobility.

other, as it seems, quite capriciously. At one time the country appears quiet and peaceful; at another the fire of insurrection suddenly breaks out and spreads over extensive tracts which had long been thought secure. The Romans were compelled from time to time to make great efforts, and, to a certain extent, to begin anew the task of conquest. Thus in the year 195 B.C. almost the whole country was lost to them.[1] When Cato arrived he was obliged to fight his first battle at Emporiæ, *i.e.* on the extreme north-eastern frontier. The prætor Marcus Helvius, who was at this time returning to Rome from the southern province, needed a body of six thousand men to conduct him safely through the enemies all along the coast line.[2] The losses which the Romans sustained were very serious, as we can ascertain even from the disfigured reports in the Roman annals. In the year 197 B.C. the proconsul Caius Sempronius Tuditanus was defeated in a great battle, in which he himself was killed, with a number of Roman nobles.[3] In the year 194 B.C.—the year after Cato's campaign, which has been so much boasted of and represented as quite successful—the prætor Sextus Digitius fought several bloody battles against insurgent tribes, and lost almost half his troops.[4] In the year 190 B.C. Lucius Æmilius Paullus, who afterwards defeated Perseus, lost six thousand men in the southern province, and barely saved the rest of his army by a dis-

---

[1] The peace with King Philip of Macedonia had just been concluded when, according to Livy, xxxiii. 25, 'quo magis pacem ratam esse in Macedonia vulgo lætarentur, tristis ex Hispania allatus nuntius effecit, vulgatæque literæ, C. Sempronium Tuditanum proconsulem in citeriore Hispania prœlio victum, exercitum eius fusum fugatum, multos illustres viros in acie cecidisse, Tuditanum cum gravi vulnere relatum ex prœlio haud ita multo post expirasse.' Orosius, vi. 20: Sempronius Tuditanus in Hispania citeriore bello oppressus cum omni exercitu Romano interfectus est. A similar disaster is reported of the year 190 B.C. After the great victory at Magnesia, and the triumph of Manius Acilius over the Ætolians, Livy says, xxxvii. 46, 7: Huius triumphi minuit lætitiam nuntius ex Hispania tristis, adversa pugna in Bastetanis ductu L. Æmilii proconsulis cum Lusitanis sex milia de Romano exercitu cecidisse, ceteros paventes intra vallum compulsos ægre castra defendisse et ad modum fugientium magnis itineribus in agrum pacatum reductos.

[2] Livy, xxxiv. 10. [3] See preceding note 1. [4] Livy, xxxv. 1.

orderly retreat.¹ Five years later another battle is mentioned in which two Roman armies were beaten and five thousand men killed. Had not such reverses as these been balanced after a time by victories, Roman dominion in Spain must, of course, soon have come to an end. But historic doubts are nowhere more justified than when Roman generals and annalists talk of their military exploits. In this respect even men like Cato were boastful, and from this model Roman we learn emphatically that modesty and truthfulness are not to be reckoned as specially Roman virtues. Cato boasted, among other things, of having destroyed more towns in Spain than he had spent days there.² Tiberius Sempronius Gracchus, we are told, carried on the war after the same fashion (179–178 B.C.).³ To him three hundred towns had surrendered, and he compelled the Celtiberians to submit to Rome.⁴ Numerous were the battles in which Roman generals slew thousands of enemies, and obtained a right to ovations,

CHAP. VI.

200–133 B.C.

Roman victories.

---

¹ Livy, xxxvii. 46, 7.
² Plutarch, *Cato Mai.* 10. According to Plutarch this was no empty boast, ' if indeed the number of towns taken by Cato amounted to four hundred !' The stratagem by which Cato is reported to have effected this great success is the following. He sent to the various towns messengers, who were timed to present themselves on the same day, and to demand that the walls should be destroyed. Now, as each town thought itself the only one recipient of the order, and feared to incur the vengeance of the Roman general if it disobeyed, they all submitted and pulled down their walls. It is hardly necessary to point out how silly this story is. Cato's messengers, of course, could not destroy the walls of all the towns themselves, and it is not likely that the inhabitants of the various towns were in so violent a hurry to do it that the work of destruction was completed before they had time to hear from their neighbours, and thus to discover the trick. The walls of a town are its shield, and we are informed that the Spaniards were as ready to sacrifice their lives as to part with their arms. See Livy, xxxiv. 17, 6. That Cato did in truth accomplish very little in Spain is proved by the condition of the province after he had returned to Rome. It was far from being cowed or pacified. See Livy, xxxv. 1.
³ Livy, xl. 47–50.
⁴ According to Polybius, quoted by Strabo, iii. 4, 13. Such ridiculous exaggerations moved the scorn of the historian Posidonius, who knew from his own personal inspection that there were not nearly so many towns in all Spain. Polybius, he says, must have reckoned every tower as a separate town, as was customary in triumphal processions. Strabo himself adds significantly: καὶ γὰρ οἱ στρατηγοὶ καὶ οἱ συγγραφεῖς ῥαδίως ἐπὶ τοῦτο φέρονται τὸ ψεῦσμα καλλωπίζοντες τὰς πράξεις.

thanksgivings, or even triumphs. Thus Æmilius Paullus (190 B.C.) repaired his defeat by brilliant victories in which he killed thirty thousand enemies. He then conquered two hundred and fifty towns, and, after the expiration of his year of office, defeated the Lusitanians with an army collected in the greatest haste, killing eighteen thousand of them, and taking over two thousand prisoners, after which he left the province contented and loyal, and returned to celebrate his triumph in Rome.[1] Similar events occurred again in the year 185 B.C.,[2] and still oftener in later years, until it became almost a fixed rule, and the war presented a monotonous and, on the whole, a wearisome picture. The Romans are represented as invariably victorious in the end. In spite of their courage the Spaniards were unable to resist either the martial strength of the Romans or their policy. Internal jealousies made it easy for the Romans, as we have already seen, to set the Spaniards to fight against one another, and the conquest of the whole country would certainly have advanced more rapidly and steadily had not the Roman officials, by their unbounded greed, harshness, and cruelty, almost compelled the natives again and again to rebel. We can form an idea of the proceedings of the Roman magistrates in Spain from the complaints which the Spaniards made in Rome in the year 171 B.C.[3] The senate found themselves at last called upon to appoint officers for the special purpose of investigating complaints. Thus it was that Spain gave the first impulse for the establishment of those judicial commissions which had to try Roman magistrates for extortion (the *Quæstiones repetun-*

---

[1] Livy, xxxvii. 57. Of course Æmilius Paullus must in the end have gained some signal triumph in Spain. But what slender reliance is to be placed on our informants is shown by the fact that Plutarch, who professes to give us a life of Æmilius Paullus, does not say a single word of the reverses which he suffered in Spain, though he speaks in full of his victory.

[2] Livy, xxxix. 30, 42.

[3] Livy, xliii. 2: De magistratuum Romanorum avaritia superbiaque conqu...i nixi genibus ab senatu petierunt, ne se socios fœdius spoliari vexarique qu...n hostes patiantur.

darum), and were designed to protect the provincials from illegal treatment on the part of the governors. The intention of these courts was good, but it was seldom realised. The very first commission was of bad augury for those that followed. Of three accused men one was acquitted by the senatorial judges. The two others escaped condemnation by going into exile—one to Præneste, the other to Tibur. Further complaints of the Spaniards were cut short by the departure of the prætor Canuleius, who left Rome to go into his province. Thus the remaining trials were quashed; in other words, the Spaniards were denied judicial redress, although the most eminent statesmen — such as Scipio Nasica, Æmilius Paullus, and even the severe Cato—had been appointed to act on their behalf. It can have been no great satisfaction to the ill-used Spaniards to learn that their oppressors now no longer dwelt in Rome, but in some pleasant suburban villa in its neighbourhood. The disgraceful denial of justice, of which Rome was guilty in screening her unjust citizens and sacrificing to them her subjects, bore bitter fruits, and had to be expiated by long years of suffering. For the present the senate thought that they had done enough in issuing a decree to the effect that the provincial magistrates were not to be unfair in levying the taxes and extraordinary contributions.[1]

---

[1] Livy, xliii. 2, 12: In futurum consultum ab senatu Hispanis, quod impetrarunt, ne frumenti æstimationem magistratus Romanus haberet, neve cogeret vicesimas vendere Hispanos quanti ipse vellet, et ne præfecti in oppida sua ad pecunias cogendas imponerentur. The meaning of the passage 'ne frumenti . . . haberet' is that the provincial governors should not be allowed to put an arbitrary price on the grain which the Spaniards had to furnish for the governor's establishment (in cellam), and which was generally commuted for money, the governors fixing an exorbitant price. The second part of the passage (neve . . . vellet) refers to the *vicesimæ*, which the Spaniards were not to be compelled to furnish at a price fixed by the governors. These vicesimæ were supplies required for the Roman troops, and their value was deducted from the tribute the provincials had to pay. In this case, therefore, the price was fixed too low in the interest of the Roman treasury or the private purse of the governor. The third part of the senatorial decree (ne præfecti . . . imponerentur) refers to the assessors and collectors, who were in future to be appointed not by the provincial governors, but by the towns themselves. See Weissenborn's note to Livy.

Treaty of Gracchus with Spanish towns.

We do not know whether the regulations which the senate made had any practical effect, and induced the governors to be more reasonable. Perhaps we may infer thus much from the fact that for several years from this time Spain enjoyed a period of comparative peace. This, however, may have been partly the result of a treaty which in the year 178 B.C. had been concluded with a number of towns by Tiberius Sempronius Gracchus, and by which their relations to Rome had been regulated.[1] In these treaties the sovereignty of the Roman republic was recognised, and the Spanish tribes were obliged as Roman allies to supply auxiliaries if necessary, or to pay contributions of war, in return for which Rome undertook their military protection. As long as the Romans contented themselves with the formal recognition of their dominion,[2] and did not make use of their alliance with the Spaniards as a pretext for oppressing them, the natives remained quiet, and their masters were at leisure to regulate the administration of their two Spanish provinces, to establish order in the collection of the revenue, in the working of the mines, and in the administration of justice, and to accustom the natives to Roman modes of life.

The division of the peninsula into Roman provinces and communities, more or less independent, could not be of long duration. The march of conquest could not come to a standstill unless the expansive power of Rome collapsed, for no lasting peace can be maintained at any time between barbarians and a civilised state.[3] One would

---

[1] Appian, vi. 43: πᾶσιν ἔθνεσιν ἔθετο συνθήκας ἀκριβεῖς καθ' ἃς 'Ρωμαίων ἔσονται φίλοι· ὅρκους τε ὤμοσε αὐτοῖς καὶ ἔλαβεν. Livy (xl. 49, 1) relates the same event in a somewhat different way, making Gracchus subdue the Spaniards by force of arms, and thus compelling one hundred and three towns to submit (in jugum accipere). Florus, ii. 17, raises the number to one hundred and fifty, and in Strabo, iii. 4, 13, we read that Polybius had stated the number at three hundred, which must be an error of a transcriber for one hundred and three.

[2] According to Appian, vi. 44, two of the Spanish tribes, the Bellians and Tithians, maintained τῶν φόρων καὶ τῆς ξεναγίας ὑπ' αὐτῶν 'Ρωμαίων ἀφεῖσθαι μετὰ Γράκχον. He adds: δίδωσι δ' ἡ βουλὴ τὰς τοιάσδε δωρεὰς, ἀεὶ προστιθεῖσα κυρίας ἔσεσθαι, μέχρι ἂν αὐτῇ καὶ τῷ δήμῳ δοκῇ.

[3] This is shown by the gradual extension of European power in India, South Africa, and in North America.

imagine that the Spaniards, being the more restless and reckless, would have given the first occasion for new disputes. But it appears that, with the exception of the hordes that lived exclusively by plunder, they had a correct idea of the strength of Rome, and desired nothing more than to live in peace with their powerful neighbour, provided only they were allowed to retain a moderate degree of independence. It was the Romans themselves who first renewed the strife.[1]

After the defeat of Perseus, 168 B.C., and before the outbreak of the third Punic war, 149 B.C., the arms of Rome were not directed against any of the other great civilised states which might be considered as equal or nearly equal to her in power; and thus a suitable opportunity seemed to present itself for continuing the interrupted conquest of Spain, and for acquiring honour and profit for the Roman nobility. The senate and the town populace, in whose hands lay the direction of Roman policy, cared little whether war was or was not advantageous to the Italian peasantry. The interest of Rome alone was taken into account.

Among the cities which had concluded the treaty with Gracchus[2] was the Celtiberian town of Segeda,[3] inhabited by the tribe of the Bellians. This people had resolved to enlarge their city by uniting with it several neighbouring townships belonging to the Tithians, another Celtiberian tribe in the interior of Spain. But in the year 154 B.C., when they were occupied with the building of the new town-wall, an order came from Rome bidding them to desist, and at the same time a demand was made for tribute and for an auxiliary contingent.[4] The Bellians refused to obey these orders, because, according to the

War with the Bellians.

---

[1] Florus, i. 34, 3, makes a confession which, from the pen of a Roman writer, is no less than miraculous: Non temere, si fateri licet, ullius causa belli iniustior.   [2] See p. 380.

[3] The situation of Segeda, like that of many other towns mentioned in the Spanish wars, is entirely unknown. Probably it was somewhere on the table land of Cuenca, not far from the sources of the Tagus and Xucar.

[4] Appian, v. 44.

Disastrous campaign of Fulvius Nobilior.

treaty with Gracchus, they were deprived only of the liberty of building a new town, not of that of enlarging the one which they already inhabited, and because, up to this time, they had paid no tribute and supplied no soldiers.[1] As the Romans insisted upon their demand, the war broke out afresh. The consul Quintus Fulvius Nobilior invaded the territory of Segeda in the year 153 B.C. with a powerful army of thirty thousand men. The inhabitants, with their wives and children, abandoned their incompletely fortified town, and took refuge among the brave Arevakians, whose capital was Numantia (on the upper Douro). When Fulvius pursued them into these mountainous regions, he was unexpectedly attacked and defeated, with a loss of six thousand Roman troops.[2] The seriousness of the Spanish war again became evident on the very first encounter. The defeat was suggestive of the great catastrophes of Caudium and the Allia, and the anniversary of it, the 23rd of August, was reckoned henceforth among the fatal days of the republic, and was carefully avoided by the Roman generals for warlike undertakings. As the Spaniards had lost many men, among them their brave leader Carus, and as Fulvius had received reinforcements, consisting chiefly of Numidian cavalry and elephants, he shortly afterwards advanced and drove the enemy into the town of Numantia. Before this town a second battle was fought, and again the Romans were compelled to abandon the field with almost equal losses. The elephants, which the Spanish tribes now encountered for the first time, inspired, as usual, fear at the first moment; but when one of them was wounded, the rest became wild, and, rushing through the Roman ranks, caused the defeat.[3] The unfortunate Fulvius was worsted

---

[1] See above, page 380, note 2.
[2] Appian, vi. 45, distinctly says Ῥωμαίων τῶν ἐξ ἄστεος. The loss of Spanish auxiliaries would not have been rated very high. The death of six thousand Romans could not, of course, be left unavenged. Accordingly Appian relates that an equal number of enemies, too eager in the pursuit, were slain by the Roman cavalry.
[3] Appian, vi. 46.

a third and even a fourth time;[1] at last the town of Okilis, where he kept his military chest and his supplies, was lost by treason. The winter approached, and caused a great mortality among the exhausted and famished troops. The campaign which Rome, in the consciousness of her power, had undertaken without necessity, ended in a check so disastrous that, had her enemy been a state of equal power, it might have been followed by the most serious consequences. As it was, the defeats of Fulvius' Nobilior had as their result only a new and larger enlistment for a second campaign.

In the year 152 B.C. M. Claudius Marcellus took the field with new troops to the number of eight thousand five hundred men, reconquered the town of Okilis, and, more by wise moderation than by force of arms, induced several tribes to ask for peace. He himself used his influence in Rome on behalf of the Spanish tribes, who demanded nothing but a continuance of friendly relations on the terms of the treaties of Tiberius Gracchus in the year 179 B.C. The negotiations, however, were broken off when the senate insisted on unconditional submission. In fact, Lucius Licinius Lucullus, who was appointed consul for the year 151 B.C., desired a command in which he would have a chance of winning glory and money, and accordingly he made great efforts to prevent a peaceable settlement of the dispute, although, after the late misfortunes, the war in Spain had lost all charm for the Roman soldiers and subaltern officers. Marcellus, nevertheless, carried his point. He came to an agreement with the Arevakians, the Bellians, and the Tithians, according to which they were to pay an indemnity, to give hostages, and to submit to him personally. The tribes who had so recently been victorious could give no more striking proof of their peaceable disposition. They were wise enough, in spite of their military success, not to defy Rome, and they probably obtained from Marcellus the assurance that their

CHAP. VI.

200–133 B.C.

Treaty of Marcellus.

---

[1] Appian, vi. 47.

formal submission should not furnish a pretext for enslaving them, but that, being, as hitherto, Roman allies, they should preserve their independence.

Lusitania in arms.

In thus establishing peace on his own responsibility and against the senatorial decree, Marcellus must have had very strong reasons of his own which could not be appreciated in Rome. The year 153 B.C., which, as we have seen, had brought serious defeats upon the Roman arms in Celtiberian Spain, was disastrous also in the southwest. The Lusitanians on the lower Tagus (whether from their own impulse, or exasperated by the Romans, or tempted by the success of their countrymen in Celtiberia, we cannot say) had taken up arms under a chief called Punicus, had defeated a Roman army under Calpurnius Piso and Manilius, with a loss of six thousand men, and had thereupon invaded the territory of the tribes friendly with Rome.[1] In the following year, whilst Marcellus was stationed in Celtiberia, they defeated the prætor Lucius Mummius, inflicting on him a loss of nine thousand men, took his camp, and sent the trophies captured in it all about Spain, to excite the nations to a general insurrection against the foreign invader. Though Mummius, as we are told, afterwards obtained such advantages[2] that a triumph was accorded to him in Rome, yet matters in Spain remained in a precarious state, and Marcellus probably was right in inducing the warlike Celtiberians by concessions to keep the peace.

Campaign of Lucullus.

But such considerations, it appears, were not regarded by men like the grasping and ambitious Lucullus. In consequence of the last defeats in Spain, this officer had had great difficulty in levying troops in Rome,[3]

---

[1] Appian, vi. 56.

[2] Appian, vi. 57, records a triumph of Mummius. If such a triumph was really celebrated, it proves that the honour was very cheap, even if the statement of Eutropius, iv. 9, should be substantially correct, that L. Mummius in Hispania bene pugnavit, though such faint praise sounds very suspicious.

[3] Livy, *Epit.* xlviii.: L. Licinius Lucullus, A. Postumius Albinus consules quum delectum severe agerent, nec quemquam gratia dimitterent, ab tribunis plebis, qui pro amicis suis vacationem impetrare non poterant, in carcerem conjecti sunt.

and had been obliged, instead of selecting the best men, to enlist troops by lottery;[1] but although the common soldiers, and even the higher officers, so dreaded service in Spain that the requisite number of military tribunes and legates could not be found until young Scipio gave the example by voluntarily offering his services,[2] Lucullus was nevertheless determined to carry on the war in that country.[3] He did not, indeed, venture to violate the treaty concluded by Marcellus, which had probably been sanctioned by the senate; but he at once, and without either provocation or any order from Rome, attacked the peaceable tribe of the Vaccæans beyond the Tagus. When these in their consternation begged for mercy, Lucullus at first demanded hostages, one hundred talents of silver, and a contingent of cavalry. Having obtained this, he insisted that the town of Cauca should receive a Roman garrison. When this order also had been complied with, Lucullus ordered his whole army to march into Cauca, to slay all within it who were capable of bearing arms, and to plunder the place.[4] This act of unparalleled atrocity not only disgraced the Roman name, but roused to desperate resistance a tribe which, in spite of natural courage and martial spirit, had made great sacrifices to preserve the peace. The treacherous and savage lawlessness of Lucullus was but one of very many instances which showed what Rome herself would have to expect from her nobility, if the evil passions of these men should ever have full play in any civil disturbances in Rome. But it was a still worse sign for the Roman republic that such a crime was not punished, or, as far as we know, even censured.

---

[1] Polybius, xxxv. 4. The whole of this chapter, too long for quotation, is exceedingly interesting, and gives a graphic account of the difficulties of the enlistment under the present circumstances. Appian, vi. 49 : ἔδοξεν ἀπὸ κλήρου τότε συναγαγεῖν.

[2] Polybius, xxxv. 4; Livy, Epit. 48. Compare vol. ii. p. 350.

[3] Appian, vi. 51 : Ὁ δὲ Λούκυλλος δόξης τε ἐπιθυμῶν καὶ ἐκ πενίας χρῄζων χρηματισμοῦ, ἐς Οὐακκαίους . . . ἐνέβαλεν . . . οὔτε τινὸς αὐτῷ ψηφίσματος γεγονότος, οὔτε Οὐακκαίων Ῥωμαίοις πεπολεμηκότων.

[4] Appian, vi. 52.

On hearing of the monstrous atrocities committed in Cauca, the inhabitants of the neighbouring country fled into the woods and hills. The town of Intercatia, however, to which Lucullus now laid siege, resisted obstinately.[1] After a time the Roman legions began to suffer from want and sickness in this devastated land, and Lucullus offered favourable terms to the besieged; but how could the barbarians trust a man whose very name was synonymous with breach of faith? Not until young Scipio had pledged his word that the terms should be conscientiously kept, did the Intercatians surrender, giving hostages and supplying ten thousand cloaks and a certain number of cattle. In the hope of obtaining gold and silver from them Lucullus was deceived, for they had none.[2] But hearing of the wealth of the town of Pallantia, he marched across the Durius with a courage and perseverance truly Roman. The season must have been far advanced. The troops were exhausted and the country offered but scanty resources. The enemy surrounded the Roman army, and cut off all supplies. Lucullus was obliged to make up his mind to beat a retreat, which he accomplished, though continually molested by the Spaniards, until he reached his winter quarters in Turdetania, the modern Andalusia.

In the same year, 151 B.C., the prætor, Marcus Atilius Serranus, had carried on the war in the southern province. It appears that he gained some advantages there, and induced all the Lusitanian communities to submit. But he had no sooner marched off to his winter quarters than the Lusitanians, in conjunction with another tribe, known as the Vettonians, set upon him, and kept him closely

---

[1] During the siege of this town Scipio is said to have slain a Spaniard who had challenged him to single combat. Appian, vi. 53; Livy, *Epit.* 48. In an attack upon the town he was the first man upon the wall, and received the decoration of a mural crown, though the attack was in the end repulsed. Valer. Max. iii. 2, 6; Velleius, i. 12. At this time he was sent to Masinissa, in Africa, to ask for reinforcements, especially of elephants. See above, p. 331.

[2] Appian, vi. 51: χρυσόν τε καὶ ἄργυρον Λούκουλλος αἰτῶν (οὗ δὴ χάριν, νομίζων ἄλλην Ἰβηρίαν πολύχρυσον εἶναι καὶ πολυάργυρον, ἐπολέμει) οὐκ ἔλαβεν· οὐ γὰρ εἶχον, οὐδ' ἐν δόξῃ ταῦτ' ἐκεῖνοι Κελτιβήρων τίθενται.

besieged in his camp. From this perilous situation he was rescued by Servius Sulpicius Galba, the prætor designated to succeed him. Galba was a man qualified to vie with Lucullus in all the vices to which Roman provincial governors were addicted.[1] At once resuming the war against the Lusitanians, because, as he alleged, they annoyed Roman allies, he achieved no better success than his worthy colleague. After a defeat[2] which cost him seven thousand men, he hastily retreated, and spent the winter with Lucullus in the southern province.[3] There these two agreed upon joint action for the subjection of the Lusitanians. In the year 150 B.C. Lucullus attacked some bands who were engaged on plundering expeditions, and killed some thousands.[4] Galba traversed the country in another direction, marking his route by devastations. An embassy from the Lusitanians begged for peace, and for a renewal of the treaty which they had concluded with Atilius. Galba pretended to agree to their representations, and promised to settle them on fertile lands, so that they should not have to live by plunder. The simple-minded barbarians believed his words, and a large number came to be conducted to the promised tracts of land. Galba divided them into three groups, persuaded them to lay down their arms, which, as friends of the Romans, they could no longer need, and then caused them to be surrounded and slain by his own troops. Of the whole number only seventeen escaped, but among them there was one who was worth many thousands. This was Viriathus, a man who, although a barbarian and of low descent among barbarians, defied for the next eight years the armies of the proud republic, and thereby secured for himself a position in history among the feared and fearful enemies of Rome, a position almost equal to that of Hannibal and Mithridates.

[1] Appian, vi. 60.
[2] Orosius, iv. 21: Ser. Galba prætor a Lusitanis magno prœlio victus est. Livy, Epit. 48: Ser. Sulpicius Galba male adversus Lusitanos pugnavit.
[3] In a place called Conistorgis, according to Appian, vi. 58.
[4] Appian, vi. 59.

BOOK V.
200–133 B.C.
Trial and acquittal of Galba.

The deed of Servius Sulpicius Galba was one of exceptional blackness, even for an age which had witnessed many acts of cruelty. If the conscience of his contemporaries had not revolted against it, we might not have been justified, perhaps, in making Galba personally responsible. But we should then have to look upon the Roman people as being still on the lowest level of human feeling, and we should find it difficult or impossible to explain how such a people could create a state worthy of being called civilized, and establish their dominion over other nations. Happily the conscience of the Roman people was not yet so blunted as to defy all principles of decency and humanity in its dealings with strangers or even enemies. It still made sometimes a difference between hostile nations and the wild beasts of the forest. Even Cato, who was now eighty-four years old, and who used to sell his slaves when they were aged and infirm in order not to be obliged to support them, thought the treatment of the Lusitanians culpable, and almost with his last breath supported the charge against Galba which the tribune Lucius Scribonius brought before the tribes. The trial which ensued appears to have awakened the most lively interest. Galba himself was among the most famous orators of his time, specially gifted with the power of touching his hearers, a power which, in a popular court of law like that of the Roman tribes, produced a much greater effect than cool logic and a sound knowledge of jurisprudence. He succeeded, it is said, in moving the people to compassion by pointing to his children, who, without him, would perish as forsaken orphans.[1] By such theatrical tricks the Roman people were cajoled in a matter in which they were bound to act as incorruptible judges. They acquitted Galba, and thereby made themselves partakers of his guilt. Galba's crime was from this time forward, if not justified, at least excused and forgiven. But the accusation and trial showed that the feeling of jus-

---

[1] Cicero, *De Orat.* i. 53; *Brutus*, 23.

tice among the Romans condemned the deed; while the acquittal of the confessed malefactor proves that there were considerations under which Roman magistrates regarded themselves as released from all obligations of justice and humanity. Justice was, indeed, made subordinate to the policy of factions and individuals. Such a state of things presented in truth a gloomy prospect, not only for the provinces, but for the whole state. But the acquittal of Galba was still more to be deplored, if it be true, as Appian reports in plain words, that he procured it by bribing the judges.[1]

The punishment which the guilty man escaped had to be borne by thousands of Italian soldiers who were, year after year, led to Spain to be butchered. The war was now indeed a fiery war, as Polybius calls it,[2] and the fire could be quenched only in streams of blood. Viriathus, awakened by misfortune and the pressure of war to the consciousness of his military genius, and soon appreciated[3] by his admiring countrymen, carried on the heroic struggle of the small tribe of Lusitanian barbarians against the gigantic power of Rome. He possessed all the qualities of body and mind needed for conducting an irregular war in the mountains.[4] As wily and deceitful as he was brave, he managed to entice Roman generals into regions where death awaited them, or to surprise them where they thought themselves secure. So blind and clumsy were these men that, one by one, as they succeeded each other in the yearly command, they were caught in the same trap, like animals which learn nothing from the experience of others.

In the year 149 B.C., Viriathus gave the first proof of his qualifications as a commander. With a small troop

---

[1] Appian, vi. 60: καὶ μισούμενος καὶ κατηγορούμενος διέφευγε διὰ τὸν πλοῦτον.

[2] Polybius, xxxv. 1.

[3] Diodorus, xxxiii. 1, 5, Dindorf: συνέβαινε τοὺς Λυσιτανοὺς προθυμότατα συγκινδυνεύειν αὐτῷ τιμῶντας οἱονεί τινα κοινὸν εὐεργέτην καὶ σωτῆρα.

[4] Appian, vi. 72; Dio Cass. fragm. 73 Dindorf, 78 Tauchn.; Diodor. xxxiii. 1, 5; 7, 21a. Dindorf.

of horse he kept in check a Roman army which had almost surrounded the Lusitanians, and covered the retreat so that it was accomplished without loss.¹ He then enticed the Romans by a feigned flight to a place where he lay in ambush, and killed four thousand of them, including their leader, Caius Vetilius.² After this he totally annihilated an army of five thousand men which the Bellians and Tithians, in compliance with their new treaty, had sent in aid of the Romans.³ The years that followed proved equally disastrous to the Romans. Caius Plautius was defeated twice with great loss in 184 B.C.,⁴ and in the next year Claudius Unimanus suffered a still greater reverse.⁵ The captured fasces of the lictors were exhibited, with other trophies, far and wide on the Spanish mountains, and encouraged the stubborn Lusitanians and Celtiberians to continue their resistance. It was just the time when the last wars were being waged with Carthage (149–146 B.C.), Macedonia, and Greece. Naturally the hopes of the expiring nations in the East and in Africa revived when they heard how legion after legion perished in the gorges of the Spanish mountains. But Viriathus was not able to lend them a helping hand, and when they at length succumbed, his fate too seemed decided. Rome had her hands free once more. After a period of several years, during which not consuls, but prætors only, had been sent to Spain, a consul again set out in the year 145 B.C., with two new legions, for the seat of war in the West. This was the eldest son of Æmilius Paullus, who, having been adopted by the Fabian family, bore the name of Quintus Fabius Maximus Æmilianus. He carried on the war against Viriathus for two years; but

---

¹ Appian, vi. 61.   ² Orosius, v. 4.
³ Appian, vi. 63.   ⁴ Appian, vi. 64.
⁵ Orosius, v. 4: Claudius Unimanus cum magno instructu belli contra Viriathum missus, quasi pro abolenda superiore macula turpiorem auxit ipse infamiam. Nam congressus cum Viriatho universas quas secum deduxerat copias maximasque vires Romani exercitus amisit. Viriathus trabeas, fasces ceteraque insignia Romana in montibus suis trophæa præfixit. Flor. ii. 17; Aurel. Victor, 71.

even he was not able to break the resistance of the Lusitanians, or to make any noticeable impression upon Viriathus; acting, however, in his command with Fabian precaution, he succeeded in conquering several towns without suffering any great reverses.[1] It seems likely that some events occurred extremely unfavourable for the Romans which our informants have concealed; for in the following year the Arevakians, Bellians, and Tithians, who had made peace (in the year 150 B.C.), again rebelled, and took part in the war. Thus a new struggle in Celtiberia was added to that in Lusitania, a struggle which was destined to have an ominous sound in Roman ears ever after. It was the war with the small but heroic Numantia, the town of eight thousand fighting men, which for ten years following defied the powerful republic, and fell only after having inflicted on Rome a disgrace similar to that of Caudium. This memorable struggle will occupy our attention later on. For the present we must rapidly trace the progress of the war against Viriathus, which continued without interruption and with little change of military fortune.

Having fought unsuccessfully under a certain Quinctius in the year 143 B.C., the Romans in the following year made greater efforts. The consul Quintus Fabius Maximus Servilianus, who, like the son of Æmilius Paullus, had passed by adoption into the Fabian family, and was therefore in law a brother of Q. Fabius Maximus Æmilianus, was sent to Lusitania with a new consular army and reinforcements, consisting especially of elephants. It seemed, however, that the successes of the bold barbarian chief were only to be the greater in proportion to the strength of the armies which the Romans opposed to him in the field. The new consul allowed himself to be deceived like his predecessors. In his first encounter he drove his enemies before him. At least they retreated, or seemed to retreat. Perhaps it was only a stratagem to lure him

[1] Appian, vi. 65.

on. If so, it succeeded completely; for the Roman general in his eager pursuit fell into an ambush, was defeated with a loss of three thousand men, and disgracefully driven back to his camp, which his discouraged soldiers could only with difficulty defend. But after this disaster the fortune of war suddenly changed. At any rate, the consul managed, in the absence of Viriathus, to surprise several towns and take ten thousand prisoners. Thinking that he could cow the Lusitanians by severity, he caused five hundred of his prisoners to be beheaded, and the rest to be sold as slaves.[1] He spared a chief who surrendered to him, but caused the hands of his warriors to be chopped off.[2] In the next year Fabius tried to follow up his successes, and besieged the town of Erisane. But Viriathus penetrated with a reinforcement into the hard-pressed city, made a sally, drove the Romans from their siege-works, and forced them to retreat into a rock-bound valley, where all escape was impossible. The whole Roman army, including the consul, was in his power. He might now have proceeded, in his turn, to cut off the hands and heads of his enemies. But the barbarian did not abuse the fortune of war.[3] He hoped to obtain peace by showing clemency, and dismissed the Roman army uninjured, after the consul had agreed to an honourable treaty. The treaty was sanctioned in Rome. Viriathus was recognised as a friend of the Roman nation, and the Lusitanians as the independent possessors of their country (141 B.C.).

Thus the war which had been waged for nine years against the Lusitanian Hannibal seemed ended; at any rate peace was concluded. But how could Rome seriously live in peace with such an enemy? Was not their recent

---

[1] Appian, vi. 68.

[2] Orosius, v. 5, characterises this atrocious cruelty in the following words: Fecit facinus ultimis barbaris Scythiae, non dicam Romanae fidei et moderationi execrabile. Quingentis enim principibus eorum quos societate invitatos deditionis iure susceperat, manus praecidit.

[3] Appian, vi. 69: Οὐριάτθυς δ' ἐς τὴν εὐτυχίαν οὐχ ὕβρισεν.

disgrace a thorn in the flesh which must be pulled out?[1] The peace, as Appian reports, did not last even a short time.[2] Quintus Servilius Cæpio, the consul for the following year (140 B.C.), and brother of Fabius Maximus Servilianus, succeeded to the command in the south of Spain. Upon his remonstrance that the treaty was dishonourable for Rome, he received permission from the senate to exasperate Viriathus secretly,[3] then to violate the treaty, and finally to wage war openly. Unfortunately the imperfect reports of our informant do not enable us to obtain a clear insight into this latter period of the great war. It appears that the Romans succeeded in sowing dissension in the camp of Viriathus. He felt that he was no longer strong enough to defy the legions in the open field, and at length found himself compelled to sue for peace. If we may believe a short report of Dio Cassius,[4] he caused his own father-in-law to be murdered, and delivered up to the Romans several other leaders of the revolt, whose hands the consul caused immediately to be chopped off. But when the Romans required him to give up his arms he refused. He remembered the massacres committed by Galba, and preferred to die fighting as a free man to being slaughtered without the means of defence. Roman pride had now descended to a level of disgrace lower than that which would be involved by the acceptance of equal terms of peace. The proconsul was not ashamed to hire murderers to rid himself of the enemy whom he could not overcome in

CHAP. VI.

200–133 B.C.

Murder of Viriathus.

---

[1] It is most characteristic that in the *Epitome* of Livy (*Ep.* 54) the peace with Viriathus is described in the following words: Q. Fabius rebus in Hispania prospere gestis *labem imposuit*, pace cum Viriatho *aquis conditionibus facta*. Diodorus (xxxiii. 1, 4) writes in the same strain. He says that Viriathus Φάβιον εἰς συνθήκας ἐλθεῖν ἀναξίους Ῥωμαίων ἠνάγκασεν. A peace on equal terms was looked upon as disgraceful to Rome. How could such a peace last? nay, how could it have been concluded with the intention that it should last?

[2] Appian, vi. 70: οὐ μὴν ἐπέμεινεν οὐδ' εἰς βραχὺ τὰ συγκείμενα.

[3] Appian, vi. 70: Καιπίων διέβαλλε τὰς συνθήκας καὶ ἐπέστειλε Ῥωμαίοις ἀπεπρεστάτας εἶναι· καὶ ἡ μὲν βουλὴ τὸ μὲν πρῶτον αὐτῷ συνεχώρει κρύφα λυπεῖν τὸν Οὐρίατθον ὅτι δοκιμάσειεν· ὡς δ' αὖθις ἠνώχλει καὶ συνεχῶς ἐπέστελλεν, ἔκρινε λῦσαί τε τὰς σπονδὰς καὶ φανερῶς πολεμεῖν αὖθις Ὑριάτθῳ.

[4] Dio Cass. fragm. 75, Dindorf; fragm. 163. Tauchn.

the field. Among the most intimate friends of Viriathus were some who had come into the Roman camp for the purpose of continuing the negotiations. These were induced by presents and promises to do the deed.[1] There was a vast contrast between the manner of acting in these times and that which had been so often and so loudly extolled in the past, when the Roman people indignantly rejected designs for the murder of their enemies.[2] Viriathus, who was wont to sleep but little, and never slept except in full armour, was yet surprised when asleep in his tent, and stabbed by the traitors. The Roman consul welcomed the murderers in his camp, and sent them to Rome to receive their reward. It is merely an empty boast of a later historian, fond of hollow phrases about the virtues of the ancient Romans, that Servilius Cæpio disdained to avail himself of the services of the murderers, saying that the Romans never sanctioned the murder of a general by his soldiers.[3] The crime of which their national hero had been the victim once more roused the enthusiasm of the Lusitanians. Having given him a magnificent funeral, they elected Tautamus to be his successor, and penetrated into the Roman province, devastating it as they advanced. But it soon appeared that with the death of Viriathus the spirit of the nation had been paralysed. Tautamus was repulsed, pursued, overtaken on the banks of the Bætis, and compelled to surrender at discretion. The Lusitanians were disarmed; but so much land was left to them that they could live by agriculture, and had no temptation to resume their predatory life. The country, it is true, was even then far from being pacified. Roman

---

[1] Appian, vi. 71: Οὐρίατθος δὲ Καιπίωνι περὶ συμβάσεων τοὺς πιστοτάτους αὐτῷ φίλους ἐπέπεμπεν, οἱ διαφθαρέντες ὑπὸ τοῦ Καιπίωνος δώροις τε μεγάλοις καὶ ὑποσχέσεσι πολλαῖς ὑπέστησαν αὐτῷ κτενεῖν τὸν Οὐρίατθον· καὶ ἔκτειναν ὧδε κ.τ.λ. Diodor. xxxiii. 21, Dindorf; Livy, Epit. 54; Valerius Maximus, ix. 6, 1; Velleius Paterculus, ii. 1; Aurel. Victor. 71; Florus, i. 33.

[2] The story of the treacherous physician of Pyrrhus, who offered to poison his master and was sent back by the Romans, is no doubt a fiction, but it shows what virtue the Romans were then fain to be proud of.

[3] Eutropius, iv. 16. The same version of the story, betraying shame of the deed, was adopted by Orosius, v. 4, and Suidas, s. v. Βορίατθος.

generals had repeatedly to fight against armed bands or insurgent communities, as, for instance, Junius Brutus, in the years 138 and 137 B.C.;[1] but the struggles of the expiring people never again assumed the proportions of a war such as that which had been waged by Viriathus. In truth the war was over in the year 139 B.C. It was a war justly called by Velleius sad and disgraceful.[2] It was sad and disgraceful for the Roman arms, but in a far higher degree for Roman morals. It sowed moreover the seeds of the Numantine war, in which both the warlike ability and the moral virtues of the Roman nation appear more deteriorated than even in the war with Viriathus.

In the year 143 B.C., as we have seen,[3] the Celtiberian tribes of the Arevakians, Bellians, and Tithians, who had concluded peace seven years before, were encouraged by the successes of the Lusitanians to take up arms once more. The most important towns belonging to these tribes were Termantia and Numantia, the latter situated on the upper course of the Durius (Duero), in a position strongly fortified by nature and by art. Steep precipices surrounded it on all sides except one, and here the inhabitants had constructed mounds and stockades instead of walls. In this small town the chief interest of the war is concentrated, as is that of the Lusitanians in the person of Viriathus. It was the soul of the resistance which the brave Celtiberians opposed for ten years to the power of Rome; and not until it had fallen could the war be regarded as having come to an end. It must be counted among the wonders of history that so insignificant a town, defended only by eight thousand men and supported by a nation of barbarians small in number, sustained such a glorious struggle against the power which, having defeated Carthage, Macedonia, Greece, and

CHAP. VI.

200–133 B.C.

War with Numantia.

---

[1] Appian, vi. 71; Orosius, v. 5.

[2] Velleius Paterculus, ii. 1: Tristo et contumeliosum bellum in Hispania duce latronum Viriatho secutum est, quod ita varia fortuna gestum est, ut saepius Romanorum gereretur adversa. Sed interemto Viriatho fraude magis quam virtute Servilii Caepionis Numantinum gravius exarsit.

[3] See p. 391.

Syria, now ruled the world without a rival, and had at its command an almost unlimited number of brave and well-disciplined soldiers. The wonder is not explained only by the courage of the Spanish nations, which is above all praise, nor by the distance of the seat of war from Rome, and the difficulties of the ground; but it is to be attributed, in conjunction with all these causes, which certainly were of great moment, to the incapacity of the Roman generals.

As we have but scanty information, we can trace the course of the war only in its mere outlines. During the first two years the command was in the hands of Metellus, who, on account of his victory over the false Philip, bore the name of Macedonicus. He appears to have made no progress towards reducing the two towns of Termantia and Numantia, but to have performed the task of devastating the open country so successfully that the Numantines made an attempt to conclude peace. They declared themselves willing to give hostages and to pay an indemnity. But when they were also required to deliver up their arms, they hesitated. They could not make up their minds to trust themselves to the Romans, of whose treachery they had seen too many proofs, and the war accordingly went on.[1]

Treaty of Pompeius.

Metellus was succeeded in the command, 141 and 140 B.C., by Quintus Pompeius, a 'new man,' that is, not a member of the nobility; a man, therefore, of whom one would expect that great military merit and proofs already given of ability had raised him to so high a position as that of first magistrate in a warlike republic. But it seems he was only a good speaker and lawyer, and had, like Cicero at a later time, acquired influence by these qualities. In this manner he had naturally become the enemy of the old noble families, which regarded the highest offices in the republic as exclusively their property and inheritance.[2]

---

[1] Diodorus, xxxiii. 16, Dindorf.
[2] Of the enmity between Pompeius and the nobility we have some evidence in the story related by Valerius Maximus (ix. 3, 7)—a story which is perhaps a

He could justify his election and his electors only by gaining great triumphs in Spain. Unfortunately he failed most signally and covered himself with disgrace. Neither on Numantia nor on Termantia did he produce the least impression. All his undertakings ended in a series of reverses, in which he lost a great number of men.[1] New troops were sent from Rome to relieve the old soldiers, who had now served six years in Spain. With the reinforcements came a senatorial commission, not, as was generally the case, to organize conquered provinces, but, on the contrary, to investigate the state of affairs and to give advice to the incapable general. When the winter arrived the new troops suffered from cold and other inconveniences in the inhospitable, devastated country, and were exposed, on their foraging expeditions, to the attacks of the indefatigable mountaineers. Pompeius despaired of his ability to subdue the enemy by force of arms. He therefore tried what he could do by persuasion, and found this means far easier. The Numantines, like the Lusitanians, like the Carthaginians, like Perseus and even Hannibal after the victory at Cannæ, like the Samnites in ancient times, were prepared to make great sacrifices in order to obtain peace with Rome, although the course of the war was calculated to inspire them with self-confidence and even defiance. They came to a formal agreement with Pompeius to submit to the Romans, to give hostages, to exchange prisoners of war

little exaggerated—that Metellus, the predecessor of Pompeius, purposely weakened his army by dismissing great numbers of soldiers on furlough, in order to cause inconvenience to Pompeius. The friends of Metellus denied this, as is apparent from Appian, vi. 76. A quarrel arose between the two which was the cause of much bitterness of feeling. For Pompeius tried to account for his reverses in Spain by accusing his predecessor. The same charge was repeated soon after by Mancinus (Appian, vi. 83). In reading of such reckless accusations, which seem almost inconceivable, we are reminded of the old times of the republic, in which, as is related, party spirit ran so high that the plebeians would rather suffer a defeat in the field than fight to gain a triumph for a hated patrician consul.

[1] Appian, vi. 76-78. Orosius, v. 1: Pompeius . . . accepta maxima clade discessit non solum exercitu pæne omni profligato, verum etiam plurimis nobilium, qui eius militiæ aderant, interemtis.

and deserters, and to pay, moreover, thirty talents of silver. Secretly Pompeius promised them that their submission should be only a formal one, that they should preserve their independence, and, what was of the greatest importance to them, their arms.[1] In this manner, perhaps, he thought he could finish the war, even though he had gained no victories. But when, in the year 139 B.C., his successor, the consul Marcus Popillius Lœnas arrived, and the Numantines offered to pay him the remainder of the indemnity, he declared the treaty to be invalid, and the wretched Pompeius saw no other way of escaping from the difficulty than by denying the secret promise which he had made.[2] The result was a dispute between him and the Numantines, which the new commander cut short by ordering both parties to plead their case in Rome. The senate decreed that the war should go on. We do not hear that the duplicity of Pompeius was condemned or even censured.

The war was resumed and carried on with the same result as before. Popillius Laenas, consul of 139 B.C., had no better success than his predecessors. According to Appian,[3]

---

[1] This seems to be the meaning of the somewhat obscure narrative of Appian, vi. 79 : ὁ μὲν (Πομπήϊος) ἐς μὲν τὸ φανερὸν ἐκέλευεν αὐτοὺς Ῥωμαίοις ἐπιτρέπειν· οὐ γὰρ εἰδέναι συνθήκας ἑτέρας Ῥωμαίων ἀξίας· λάθρα δ᾿ ὑπισχνεῖτο, ἃ ἔμελλε ποιήσειν. The secret articles of the treaty were not embodied in the written document; they were personal promises of Pompeius, which he could deny if he thought proper. The denial of Pompeius, however, could not go so far as to affect the whole agreement, for some of the conditions of it had been actually carried out by the Numantines when the question of authenticity arose.

[2] It is clear (see preceding note) that Pompeius could not deny the existence of a treaty. His denial could refer only to the secret articles which he λάθρα ὑπισχνεῖτο (Appian, vi. 79), and which made the whole treaty appear 'unworthy of Rome,' a 'pax ignobilis' (Eutrop. iv. 17), a 'fœdus turpissimum' (Velleius, ii. 1). If the Numantines had submitted unconditionally, the treaty would not have been dishonourable to Rome, and Pompeius would have had no motive to deny it. Afterwards Mancinus declared (Appian, vi. 83; Orosius, v. 4) that the agreement which he concluded with Numantia was similar to that of Pompeius. Now, as the treaty of Mancinus did certainly leave to the Numantines their independence, and was on that account rejected in Rome as 'disgraceful,' it follows that Pompeius made the same concession. But this he could have done only by a secret engagement, since εἰς τὸ φανερὸν ἐκέλευεν αὐτοὺς Ῥωμαίοις ἐπιτρέπειν.   [3] Appian, vi. 79.

he attacked the neighbouring Lusonians, probably while the negotiations with Numantia were still going on in Rome. He accomplished nothing. Livy reports that he was even routed in a pitched battle.¹ His successor (137 B.C.) was the consul Caius Hostilius Mancinus. This man filled to the brim the cup of military disgrace which the Romans were obliged to drain. He allowed himself to be repeatedly beaten by the Numantines.² His troops became so disheartened, that, on the mere report of the approach of the Vaccaeans and Gallaekians, they fled in a dark night from their camp in great disorder, and were surrounded by the Numantines in a place which had many years before (153 B.C.) been a fortified camp of Fulvius Nobilior, but which had since been neglected, and was no longer in a condition in which it could be of any use. Although far superior in numbers to the enemy, they did not dare to fight their way through.³ The unfortunate Mancinus had no alternative but to surrender.

No two events have probably ever occurred so like each other in the smallest detail as the capture of Mancinus before Numantia and the defeat of the legions in the Caudine passes. On this occasion, as on the former, the Roman general was compelled to save his army by a disgraceful treaty, in which he granted the enemy peace and independence. The treaty was rejected by the senate, and no compensation was offered to the Numantines for the advantage they had sacrificed by trusting to Roman integrity. The Numantines, with much chivalry, and appreciating only their own strength and that of their enemies, had waived the right of inflicting upon the Romans the disgrace of passing under the yoke; nevertheless, the national dishonour

---

¹ Livy, *Epit.* 55.
² Appian, vi. 80: Μαγκῖνος ἡττᾶτό τε πολλάκις καὶ τέλος ἀναιρουμένων πολλῶν ἐς τὸ στρατόπεδον ἔφυγεν.
³ The respective numbers of the Romans and Numantines are given by Livy (*Epit.* 56) as thirty thousand and four thousand. But these numbers are either corrupt, or the statement is a great exaggeration. It is absolutely impossible that thirty thousand Romans should have surrendered to a force of only four thousand enemies.

was for the Romans far greater than at the time of the Samnite wars, because the superiority of Rome over Numantia was overwhelming, whilst in the Samnite wars the strength of the belligerents was almost evenly balanced. If, at the former time, the Romans might have excused their treachery by saying that the war with Samnium was a life-and-death struggle, it was on this occasion nothing but Roman imperiousness and Roman pride, mingled with the personal interests of the nobility, that denied to the citizens of Numantia the right of living as free men in the mountains of distant Spain.

Treaty of Mancinus rejected by the Senate.

We may, indeed, be astonished that the Numantines, after they and other Spanish tribes had had such sad experience of Roman faith and honesty, once more entered upon negotiations, when they had it in their power to annihilate a whole Roman army by one blow. It is true they tried to secure the recognition of the treaty by causing it to be sworn to by a number of the higher officers, and especially the quæstor Tiberius Sempronius Gracchus, as well as by the consul Mancinus. But they might perhaps have known that a similar measure had been of no avail to the Samnites, though they moreover had kept six hundred Roman knights as hostages, a precaution which the Numantines neglected. It is strange that no one seems to have thought of detaining the whole army as prisoners until peace should be concluded. Perhaps the frivolous renewal of the war with Viriathus had shown that there could be no prospect of a real and lasting peace, unless the Romans felt themselves overcome by the magnanimity of their enemies; and, indeed, if Numantia had had to negotiate only with the people of Rome, and not with the selfish and shameless nobility, such a calculation would have been correct. The Roman people were not disinclined to make peace, because the Spanish war annually demanded great sacrifices, and brought no profit. But the nobility refused to give their sanction to the treaty concluded by Mancinus with the Numantines; and the conqueror of Carthage especially, who was at this time very powerful, used his influence to oppose the peace. Even the wretched consul Mancinus, with the show of self-denying patriotism, advocated its rejection, knowing full well that he would be delivered up to the Numantines as the guilty person, and equally convinced that, like the Samnites of old, the Numantines would refuse to release the Roman people from all their obligations by punishing a single individual. The quaestor Gracchus in vain advised his countrymen to respect the treaty for which he had pledged his honour. He and the other guarantees were declared not to be responsible. Mancinus alone was given up to the Numantines by the Roman fetialis. Naked, with chained hands, he was brought before the town, and when the Numantines refused to receive him, he remained there a whole day, forsaken and rejected, as it were, by the whole world. Hereupon, the auspices having been consulted, he was again admitted into the Roman camp, and returned to Rome, where, in spite of the objections of some scrupulous casuists, he was permitted to resume his former position as a Roman citizen.

Thus Rome, under the sanction of her most eminent citizen, had renounced the obligation which the head of the republic had taken upon himself in the name of the commonwealth. We see plainly in this, as in so many other dishonourable actions of which the Romans were guilty, that in that age of the world's history outrageous violations of right and justice on the part of the powerful were not restrained or controlled by the verdict of public opinion, or, at any rate, that if such a verdict was muttered, Roman ears were deaf against it.

Immediately after his capitulation, Mancinus had proceeded to Rome to abdicate, and in his stead his colleague, M. Æmilius Lepidus, had taken the chief command in citerior Spain. Whilst in Rome the question was being discussed whether the treaty should be approved of or rejected, military operations were naturally suspended. But Æmilius Lepidus did not like to be idle at the head of an army. Finding some frivolous pretext for making war upon the Vaccæans, he invaded and devastated their country, and laid siege to their capital Pallentia.[1] In vain the senate tried through two envoys to dissuade him from a war which was unnecessary and, under the prevailing circumstances, even unadvisable. The time was long past when new wars were undertaken only after a formal vote of the people; and, indeed, what could the peasants of Latium know about the advisability of a war in a country which they hardly knew by name? Even the orders of the senate were no longer respected by the generals, who were intent above all upon increasing their own fame and profit.[2] Lepidus took no notice of the instructions sent out to him. Having once begun the war, he thought that the dignity of Rome demanded that it should be carried on. The Vaccæans, however, were men of a like stamp with the brave defenders of Numantia. Lepidus suffered an utter defeat. He lost six thousand men, was obliged to abandon his camp with his arms, and even the sick and wounded, and escaped the fate of Mancinus only by a retreat which was much like a flight.[3] If he had been victorious, his disobedience to his instructions would probably have been overlooked. But his defeat was a proof of his guilt. He was recalled, tried, and condemned to pay a fine.[4]

[1] Lucullus had acted in precisely the same way with reference to the same Vaccæans. See p. 385.

[2] Appian, vi. 80. See p. 385, n. 3; and p. 386, n. 2.

[3] Appian, vi. 82; Livy, *Epit.* 56: M. Æmilius Lepidus adversus Vaccæos rem gessit cladenique similem Numantinæ passus est. Orosius, v. 5: Lepidus Vaccæos, innoxiam gentem et supplicem, senatu prohibente, pertinaciter expugnare tentavit. Sed mox accepta clade gravissima improbæ pertinaciæ poenas luit. Sex quippe milia Romanorum *in hoc iniusto bello iustissime cæsa sunt*; reliqui exuti castris, armis etiam perditis evaserunt. Nec minus turpis haec sub Lepido clades quam sub Mancino fuit.

[4] Appian, vi. 83. A mere fine as the punishment for an offence which had caused the death of six thousand Roman citizens, and which contributed to shake still more the general belief of Roman invincibility, which was already much weakened, is surely a striking proof of a lenient administration of justice. But we are more disposed to consider it a proof of the power of the Roman nobility, which would not allow an Æmilius to be punished severely. It appears that the Carthaginians were not so scrupulous when their generals came to be tried for misconduct in the field. It has been the custom to blame

The war with Numantia paused for the next two years, 136 and 135 B.C., although the treaty of peace concluded in 137 B.C. had been rejected. We do not know whether this was the result of the losses which the Romans had sustained, or whether they did not like to resume the war at once. But the interruption shows how entirely the Romans had it in their power to continue the war, or to let it rest, as they chose. They had no reason to fear that the Numantines in their turn would become the aggressive party while they were taking breath and leisurely preparing for the next campaign. For the year 134 B.C. Scipio Æmilianus was chosen consul for the second time, in spite of a law, passed probably seventeen years earlier, which regulated the order of magisterial elections, and altogether prohibited the re-election of a consul.[1] The Romans were heartily sick of the war, and thought that, in the prevailing scarcity of able leaders, the conqueror of Carthage was the only man who could reduce the stubborn little town in Spain. Scipio was permitted, as his grandfather had been,[2] to ask for voluntary aid from the allies.[3] We have no details of this aid; but it is stated that Jugurtha, the grandson of Masinissa, joined him with Numidian archers and elephants. Among the young soldiers who came from Italy in the same army was Caius Marius, and thus the two men met for the first time and as comrades in arms, who were destined at a later period to stand opposed to each other in a most desperate war. By degrees other men also appeared on the scene who took a part in the revolutions of the succeeding period. We have already met with Tiberius Gracchus, and the names of Pompeius, Lepidus, and others cast before them a shadow of that age

the Carthaginians for their severity, and to praise the Romans for their leniency; but the case of Æmilius Lepidus shows that leniency to an incompetent and disobedient public servant is not equivalent with justice.

[1] Livy, Epit. 56; Mommsen, Röm. Staatsrecht, i. 425.
[2] Vol. ii. p. 418.
[3] One innovation is very striking and ominous. Scipio formed a bodyguard for himself out of five hundred of his clients and friends. Appian, vi. 84.

of blood and horrors which awaited the republic in the next generation.

Scipio's first task, when he arrived in Spain, was to accustom the army which he found there, once more to Roman discipline. We have already been compelled to notice how Roman soldiers from time to time lost their ancient military virtues, and gave themselves up to luxury and indolence, so that a strong hand was required to tighten the rein, and to teach them again the qualities of soldiers. As it had been in Macedonia and Africa, so it was now in Spain. The camp was filled with a useless and noxious train, with harlots and soothsayers, with traffickers of every description, who purchased the booty of the soldiers, and supplied them with the objects of enjoyment and luxury. Military duties were performed in a slovenly and careless manner, and cowardice—the most unroman of all vices—began to creep in. Scipio did not dare to lead an undisciplined mob into the field against the brave Numantines until he had again made soldiers of them. He drove the useless rabble out of the camp, and swept away all the superfluous baggage, all the costly utensils for the use of the table, and all the soft couches which had been carried along by the army on innumerable waggons. The soldiers were allowed only a spit for roasting, a copper kettle, and a drinking horn, and were made to sleep not in beds, but upon straw, as their general himself set them the example. All the vehicles which were not absolutely indispensable were sent away, as well as the great number of mules and horses on which it had become customary for the soldiers to ride, for marching on foot had almost been forgotten. Scipio then unmercifully compelled the soldiers to drill from morning till night, to dig trenches and fill them again, to build fortification walls and pull them down again, to make long marches in rank and file, loaded with all their arms and baggage. He always showed to his men a severe and gloomy brow, and was sparing even in legitimate indulgences.[1]

[1] Appian, vi. 85 f.

Among such preparations the summer of 134 B.C. passed away without any serious attack being made upon Numantia. Scipio then advanced to the town, and took up a position before it in two camps, one of which he placed under the command of his brother Fabius Maximus. His operations were similar to those which he had adopted with success at the siege of Carthage. He persisted in declining a battle, though repeatedly challenged by the Numantines. It was too great a risk, he thought, to lead his troops against men who were determined either to conquer or to die. The means to which he trusted were a blockade and the effects of hunger, and, having sixty thousand men at his disposal, he could, in the approved old manner of the Romans, draw a double ditch and a wall ten feet high and eight feet thick round the town, and wait patiently behind it until hunger should have done its work.[1] His lines extended for more than five miles, and, as Numantia lay at the confluence of two rivers, they were intersected by three river-beds. There was also a lake or pond in the line of circumvallation, along the margin of which only a mound and not a wall could be erected. The river Durius, by which the town had hitherto kept up communication with the country, was blocked by Scipio with beams covered with sword-blades and spear-heads, and fastened by ropes so as to float in the river, and prevent the besieged not only from receiving aid, but even from obtaining news from without. Day and night the line of circumvallation was guarded by the besiegers, who relieved one another, and repulsed all attempts of the Numantines to fight their way through. A few bold men, indeed, contrived in a dark night to scale the wall and to slip through the Roman ranks in order to report to their countrymen in the neighbouring

Siege of Numantia.

---

[1] According to Appian, vi. 91, Scipio Æmilianus was the first to adopt the process of circumvallation against enemies who were ready to give battle in the open field, whereas formerly this means was resorted to only in cases where the enemies were determined to keep on the defensive behind their walls.

towns the distress of Numantia, and to ask for help. But in one town only did they find the younger men willing to aid them; and these patriots were soon punished by Scipio, who appeared at the head of a Roman detachment, and caused their hands to be cut off. Numantia was left to her own resources; and when at length hunger began to produce its terrible effects, when the besieged inhabitants were driven to eat the flesh of the dead, and to slaughter the weak and sick, then their stubborn courage gave way, and they surrendered at discretion. But not all of them could be induced to take upon themselves the yoke of slavery. A great number committed suicide. The remainder fell into the hands of the victor, a number of beings whose savage appearance and gloomy look of hatred made them rather objects of fear and horror than of compassion. Scipio selected fifty to adorn his triumph, the rest he sold as slaves. Thereupon he razed the town to the ground. He had no distinct order from the senate to do this, as he had had with regard to Carthage; but he was eager for the honour of being called the destroyer of this town also, which had so long resisted the Roman arms. This honour he obtained. Besides his title of Africanus Minor, the surname of Numantinus also adorned the name of the younger Scipio, the son of Æmilius Paullus.

With the reduction of Numantia in the year 133 B.C., all serious resistance in citerior Spain was finally broken. About the same time the ulterior province was pacified, and the Roman dominion extended as far as the Atlantic Ocean. After the death of Viriathus, in the year 138 B.C., the consul Decimus Junius Brutus had undertaken the command in those parts. This consul conducted a number of Lusitanians, who had served under Viriathus, to the eastern coast of Spain, where he settled them in a colony called Valentia.[1] He appears to have been one of the most able men sent out by the republic about this time to Spain, and he fortunately remained in command for five

---

[1] Livy, Epit. 55.

years. Instead of pursuing the armed bands into the mountain ravines, as his predecessors had so often done to their own destruction, he attacked only the towns, and, by a generous treatment of those who surrendered voluntarily, brought into his power the whole country as far as the Durius, and even beyond it.[1] For the first time the Romans now obtained a footing in the most north-westerly corner of Spain, inhabited by the Gallæci, a people whose name the country has retained to this day.[2] Brutus was less successful after the misfortune of Mancinus before Numantia, for he took part in the unjust and fatal expedition of Æmilius Lepidus against the Vaccæans.[3] Occasionally also some tribes revolted who had submitted reluctantly. But, on the whole, the resistance of the Spanish nation was broken, and when, in the year 132 B.C., Decimus Junius Brutus, surnamed 'Gallæcus,' and P. Cornelius Scipio, surnamed 'Numantinus,' celebrated their triumph, the succeeding governors of citerior and ulterior Spain had no longer to wage war, but merely to keep the people submissive and quiet. The legions had not indeed penetrated into the mountains of Asturia, and there some of the Spanish tribes remained untouched by the Roman yoke up to the time of Augustus. But in the rest of the peninsula the Roman language and customs rapidly gained ground, and before long Italian culture took deep root in the country.

---

[1] Appian, vi. 71 ff.   [2] Livy, *Epit.* 56; Florus, ii. 17, 12; Oros. v. 5.
[3] Appian, vi. 80; see p. 402.

CHAPTER VII.

THE CONQUEST OF NORTHERN ITALY. THE WARS WITH THE GAULS, LIGURIANS, AND ISTRIANS.

BOOK V.
201–133 B.C.

Annalistic method of history not applicable.

IT is not the only defect in all historical writing, that, owing to the imperfect nature of all records, past events can be but imperfectly understood and represented, a defect which we must feel especially with regard to ancient histories. In addition to the incompleteness of the picture, we must remember that the historic scene is usually too vast to be surveyed at one glance. Whilst our eyes are directed towards one part, much escapes us that is going on at a short distance to the right and to the left, and we have not the least idea of what lies behind us. Thus, even that part which we are enabled to study, we fail to understand fully whenever it is influenced, either directly or indirectly, by what happens in another part not exposed to our view. History, therefore, gives us not so much a picture as a panorama, and the impression left on our minds is not complete until we have cast our eyes in every direction, and are able to place simultaneous events side by side, or to judge of their relation to one another. Since, with the enlargement of the empire, Roman history extended to the Hellenic East, to Africa and Spain, we have several times found ourselves called upon to point out the connexion of the events which took place in the various quarters of the world; but this was not possible in detail, for otherwise the thread of the narrative would at every moment have been broken, and the comprehension of every single fact would have been lost. It is impossible for modern writers to adopt the annalistic plan of Livy and Polybius, as our narrative must pass by many incidents which are of less importance to us than to the ancient reader, and it is, therefore, only by gathering together in one continuous narrative all that has reference to each particular country, that we can obtain clear and interesting pictures of the leading events. We shall pursue the same course now in considering the events which took place in Italy itself simultaneously with the wars in Macedonia, Greece, Asia, Africa, and Spain, from the time when the second peace with Carthage was concluded (201 B.C.) up to the complete destruction of the Macedonian kingdom and of Greek independence (146 B.C.) to the annihilation of Carthage (146 B.C.), and to the subjection of the rebellious tribes in Lusitania and Celtiberia (133 B.C.).

The wars with the Gauls and Ligurians settled in Italy resembled, as we might expect, those which the Spanish barbarians waged with so much determination and perseverance. Of these wars also it is impossible to give a continuous account, although we are less troubled with one of the main difficulties that we meet with in Spain. The Roman annalists understood the geography of northern Italy somewhat better than that of Spain. Hence we are enabled to find the dwelling-places of various tribes and the situation of towns mentioned by the narrator, with an accuracy which we cannot carry into the history of the Spanish wars. But we are still obliged to gather our information from the writings of Roman historians, and these are derived from the falsified reports of Roman generals, who almost invariably vaunted their own exploits to the utmost. We must be content, therefore, if we succeed in following the gradual progress of Roman arms in general, and in understanding the character of the warfare on both sides, without attempting to ascertain the particulars which might enliven and diversify the vague and uncertain outlines.

The Hannibalic war had brought the Roman conquest

CHAP. VII.
201–133 B.C.

Our knowledge of the Italian wars.

The Gauls

BOOK V.
201–133 B.C.

during the Hannibalic war.

in northern Italy to a standstill.¹ The extreme Roman outposts on the Po, the fortresses of Placentia and Cremona, were for some time almost completely isolated and exposed to continued attacks, not only of the Gauls, but also of their Carthaginian allies. Mutina, which was intended to secure the communication between these towns and Ariminum could not be fully fortified as a colony.² If the Gallic tribes had had the political instinct of the Romans, they would have made use of the Hannibalic war to weaken Rome permanently. It appears that they were, for the present, content not to be molested, and they enjoyed the short period of quiet which Hannibal's victories secured for them, without steadily supporting him. But immediately after the conclusion of peace between Rome and Carthage they suddenly put forth an unexpected and astonishing degree of vigour which, had it been shown at the right moment, would most probably have given a different issue to the Hannibalic war.

The Gauls continue the war under Hamilcar.

As early as 201 B.C., the consul Publius Ælius Pætus marched at the head of a strong army into the country of the Boians, between the middle course of the Po and the Apennines. This tract of land was naturally the first object of the attack of the Romans, because it lay between the ancient portion of Italy and the line of the Po, and threatened the fortresses Placentia and Cremona in the rear. But the Boians were the most powerful of all the Gallic tribes in Italy, and maintained for a long time a stubborn resistance. They surprised a detachment of the consul's army under Caius Ampius, who commanded the allies, and killed about seven thousand men.³ After so promising a beginning, the Boians, in conjunction with the Insubrians, their kinsmen north of the Po, and even with the Cenomanians, who had at an earlier period been on most friendly terms with the Romans, and several neighbouring Ligurian tribes, made an attack upon the Roman fortresses in their country. A

¹ Vol. ii. p. 135.   ² Vol. ii. p. 167.   ³ Livy, xxxi. 2.

THE CONQUEST OF NORTHERN ITALY.

Carthaginian officer of the name of Hamilcar, who had remained behind from Mago's army,[1] conducted the military operations of the barbarians so successfully that Placentia was taken by them, and only two thousand of the Roman inhabitants escaped. One great triumph was thus obtained, greater than any that even Hannibal had been able to accomplish; and now Hamilcar undertook the siege of Cremona, the sister town of Placentia. We must recollect that in this year (200 B.C.) the war with Philip of Macedonia was undertaken, that the Roman people at first refused to sanction this war,[2] and could only with difficulty be induced to reverse their vote. The loss of a Roman colony was a far more serious matter than the destruction of an army. It signified the ruin of a large number of families, the death or slavery of women and children, the destruction of property, and the annihilation of a town that was, as it were, a daughter and an image of Rome herself. 'It was a matter of great concern to the Roman people,' Livy remarks, even with reference to the Samnite wars, 'that their colonists should be safe.'[3] We can therefore fully understand what impression the conquest of Placentia produced upon Rome. The first thought was naturally to look to the safety of Cremona. This town was relieved by the prætor Lucius Furius Purpureo, who defeated the Gauls, blockading the town.[4]

But when in the ensuing year an army under Cn. Bæbius Tamphilus invaded the country of the Insubrians, it was almost entirely destroyed.[5] It was not possible to secure the colonies against repeated attacks. The discouraged colonists left their homes in great numbers, and fled to

CHAP. VII.
201–133 B.C.

Capture of Placentia.

Reverses of the Romans.

---

[1] See pp. 4, 25, 322.   [2] See p. 18.   [3] Livy, ix. 24.

[4] No Roman family surpassed the Furii in the habit of exaggeration and self-laudation. The victories of the great Camillus were an incentive for the successive chroniclers and orators of that family to boast of victories over the Gauls in particular. The exploits of Lucius Furius Purpureo were therefore dressed out with the glories properly belonging to C. Cornelius Cethegus, consul of 197 B.C. See Livy, xxxi. 21 f. compared with xxxii. 29–31. Nissen, *Quellen des Livius*, p. 139.

[5] Livy, xxxii. 7: Cn. Bæbius Tamphilus . . . prope cum toto exercitu est circumventus, supra sex milia et sexcentos milites amisit.

safer regions. The consul Sextus Ælius Pætus spent almost the whole of the year 198 B.C. in the work of re-organising the colonies,[1] into which the fugitives were compelled to return.

On account of the danger with which the Gauls threatened Rome in the year 197 B.C., the year of the battle of Cynoscephalæ, both consuls were sent to Cisalpine Gaul,[2] where the Insubrians and Cenomanians north of the Po, and the Boians and Ligurians south of the river, had conjointly taken up arms.[3] The consul Caius Cornelius Cethegus gained a great victory over the Insubrians, which turned out the more disastrous to them, as during the battle their allies, the Cenomanians, deserted and joined the Romans.[4] Minucius, the other consul, carried on operations against the Ligurians and Boians, and succeeded in preventing their union with the Insubrians. But he accomplished this only by means of a great sacrifice of men, and as he could not boast of any memorable exploit, the senate refused to accord him a triumph, though that honour was bestowed upon his colleague.[5] Minucius defied the resolution of the

---

[1] Livy, xxxii. 26.

[2] Polybius, xvii. 11, 2 : διὰ τὸν ἀπὸ τῶν Κελτῶν φόβον. It seems that even now the Romans had not quite mastered the old fear with which they looked upon a Gallic war. Vol. i. p. 266, n. ; p. 464.

[3] Livy, xxxii. 29.

[4] Livy, xxxii. 30. In this battle it is reported that Hamilcar was taken prisoner, though according to another account (Livy, xxxi. 21, 18) he was killed some years before (200 B.C.) in a battle with Furius Purpureo. The descriptions of the two battles agree in so many particulars (the number of enemies killed in each being thirty-five thousand men) that they appear to be two versions of the same story.

[5] Livy, xxxiii. 22. On this occasion the tribunes who opposed the triumph of Minucius said : Q. Minucium in Liguribus levia proelia, vix digna dictu, fecisse ; in Gallia magnum numerum militum amisisse; nominabant etiam tribunos militum, T. Juventium, Cn. Ligurium legionis quartæ adversa pugna cum multis aliis viris fortibus, civibus ac sociis, cecidisse; oppidorum paucorum ac vicorum falsas et in tempus simulatas sine ullo pignore deditiones factas esse. Here we get an insight into the tricks with which incompetent mediocrity and impudent vanity tried to obtain triumphal honours. The case of Minucius was by no means isolated, as appears from a law mentioned by Valerius Maximus (ii. 8, 1), which imposed penalties on generals guilty of making false reports of the number of slain enemies and of losses in their own

senate; he declared that he had earned a claim to the honour, and he actually celebrated a triumph on the Alban Mount, following in this matter the precedent of previous consuls, and availing himself of his military imperium, which was unlimited beyond the precincts of the town.

But neither this triumph on the Alban Mount nor the legitimate triumph of the other consul on the Capitol was justified by complete subjection of the enemies. In the following year both consuls were again obliged to march against the Insubrians and Boians, the former of whom inflicted on the consul M. Claudius Marcellus a defeat in which he lost three thousand men,[1] among them officers out of the first families, a Sempronius Gracchus, a Julius Silanus, an Ogulnius, and a Claudius. It is surprising that after so unfavourable a beginning Marcellus was able to penetrate further into the land of the Insubrians, leaving behind him the victorious Boians,[2] and to fight a great battle near Comum, in which he killed forty thousand enemies, according to the reports of Valerius Antias, who, it is true, is utterly untrustworthy. The consul Lucius Furius Purpureo, who in his capacity of praetor four years previously had gained so signal a victory,[3] meanwhile entered the country of the Boians, joined his colleague, and then so effectually defeated the Boians that scarcely one man escaped to carry the news.[4] We cannot

---

armies. An attempt was made to make triumphs less easily obtainable, by a law requiring that no general should be entitled to the honour who had not slain at least five thousand enemies. The only effect of this law was no doubt to multiply lies. Cato, who was indignant when others prided themselves on fictitious exploits, thought proper to write a pamphlet, 'de falsis pugnis.' It is a great pity that this interesting work is lost.

[1] Livy, xxxiii. 36, 4.

[2] Livy, xxx. 36, 8, is at no loss to give an explanation. As the Romans kept within their fortified camp to recover from their terror and their wounds, the Boians lost patience and dispersed into their homes. Whether this is true or not we cannot decide. At any rate it is an explanation based upon the well-known character of the Gauls. The annals of this period are still so contradictory and uncertain that it is doubtful whether the campaign of Marcellus against the Boians preceded or followed that against the Insubrians. See Livy, l.c. [3] See p. 411.

[4] Livy, xxxiii. 37: Ut vix nuntium cladis hosti relinquerent.

BOOK V.
201–133 B.C.

be certain that this battle was one of those fictitious exploits of which Cato speaks;[1] but if such a glorious victory was really and truly gained, it seems strange that Furius obtained no triumph, an honour of which the senate was by no means chary, and which was accorded even to Marcellus for his victory of Comum in spite of his previous defeat. Serious doubt, at any rate, seems justified; for the war continued with undiminished force in the following year (195 B.C.), and occupied the attention of one of the consuls, Lucius Valerius Flaccus, whilst Cato, the other consul, was fighting in Spain. Flaccus defeated the Boians, and in the beginning of the next year, as proconsul, he also routed their allies the Insubrians;[2] but he appears to have succeeded so little in breaking the power of the Gallic tribes that, in the year 194 B.C., both consuls had again to be sent against them, and one of them, Tiberius Sempronius, was so unsuccessful that he could only defend himself with great difficulty in his camp against the attacks of the Boians, and lost five thousand men.[3]

Campaign of Cornelius Merula, consul of 193 B.C.

In this manner the war continued. In the following year (193 B.C.) the consul Cornelius Merula was attacked by the Boians on his march to Mutina, and lost five thousand men. Nevertheless he sent reports of a splendid victory to Rome, and had the face to demand a triumph. He almost succeeded in obtaining it; but the senate was informed of the true state of affairs through a letter sent to Rome[4] by the former consul Marcus Claudius Marcellus, now serving as legate under Merula. In this letter Marcellus said that it was due not to the consul, but to the good fortune of the Roman people and to the courage of the soldiers, that the affair had not ended worse. He

---

[1] See p. 412, n. 5.   [2] Livy, xxxiv. 22, 46.
[3] Livy, xxxiv. 46. The loss of the Gauls is stated to have been eleven thousand. Varia hinc atque illinc nunc fuga nunc victoria fuit. Gallorum tamen ad xi milia, Romanorum v milia sunt occisa. Galli recepere in intima finium sese. The campaign must have been far from satisfactory if the Roman annalist was obliged to own such a considerable loss, and the Roman general did not venture to ask for a triumph.   [4] Livy, xxxv. 6, 9.

added that the consul was responsible for the loss of many men and for the escape of the enemy, who might have been annihilated. Thus Merula was deprived of his triumph, and the senate resolved in the following year (192 B.C.) to send once more both consuls against the stubborn Boians, in order to crush them at length by an overwhelming force.

It seems that the Romans now succeeded in separating the Boians from their Gallic countrymen. The Cenomanians were already won over to the side of Rome. Since the battle of Comum[1] the Insubrians had also remained inactive. Only the Ligurians, of whom we must speak presently, were continually in arms against Rome. But as the strength of the Ligurians depended chiefly upon their wild mountains, they could accomplish little out of their country, and the Boians, left to their own resources, were confronted by the whole force of Rome.

From this time forward the resistance of this once so powerful people grew weaker. In the continuous wars they must have sustained great losses which they could not repair without help from their neighbours. Hence we hear that in the year 192 B.C. many of them surrendered to the Romans, and when, in the following year (191 B.C.), the consul Scipio Nasica attacked them again, and routed them in a great battle, the remainder of the nation also submitted to the conquerors.[2]

Steps were now taken to insure the permanence of Roman dominion over the Boians. Almost half of the country was confiscated for distribution among Roman colonists. The establishment of new colonies was decreed, one of which, Bononia, was founded in the year 189 B.C. Placentia and Cremona, the two oldest frontier fortresses in that part, which, since 218 B.C., had been exposed to so many sieges, and which, having rendered such important services, had suffered most severely, had already been

The Boians exhausted and subdued.

Colonisation of conquered districts.

---

[1] See p. 413. [2] Livy, xxxvi. 38–40.

supplied with new colonists, six thousand families having been sent out to them.¹ This policy was continued. In the year 184 B.C. the colonies of Pisaurum and Potentia were founded in the country south of Ariminum, which had long been secured from enemies; and in the following year the colonies of Mutina and Parma² were established on the straight line which connected Ariminum by Bononia with Placentia. Here M. Æmilius Lepidus had begun in the year 187 B.C. to construct a military highway, called after him the via Æmilia, which conferred upon the whole of this tract the name of Æmilia, a name revived in our own time. In the same year (187 B.C.) C. Flaminius made a road across the Apennines from Arretium to Bononia, a continuation of the via Cassia, which led from Rome to Arretium. Thus a double line of communication was established between Rome and Bononia: one direct line through Etruria by Arretium and Florentia; and a second line, the via Flaminia, through Umbria as far as the Adriatic, and continued, under the name of via Æmilia, to Bononia, and further by Mutina and Parma to Placentia on the Po. From this time forward the latinization of the Gallic parts of North Italy made rapid progress. The country, though fertile,³ had up to this time been but thinly peopled. When peace was re-established it became filled with emigrants from Italy, who introduced Roman laws and institutions and the Latin language.

After the subjection of the Boians the Romans had no more difficulty with the tribes living north of the Po. They were satisfied with compelling them to recognise their authority, without forcing upon them an oppressive provincial government, or taking from them their old institutions. It was more advantageous to entrust them with the defence of the Alpine passes against the northern tribes than to drive them to an alliance with these tribes by demanding tribute or otherwise oppressing them.

---

¹ Livy, xxxvii. 26, 9.   ² Livy, xxxix. 55, 7; comp. xxi. 25, 6.   ³ Polybius, ii. 15.

The only wars of which we still hear in these parts took place on the extreme north-east frontier of the peninsula. Here the Romans founded the colony of Aquileia in 181 B.C.,[1] to protect the Italian frontier and to suppress piracy in the Adriatic. On this occasion a quarrel broke out between the Romans and the Istrians. The consul Manlius Vulso marched from Aquileia, without orders from the senate, along the coast into the land of the Istrians, accompanied by a Roman fleet of war and transport vessels; but, through his foolhardiness and incapacity, he sustained a reverse, disgraceful to the Roman arms, and injurious to the prestige of Rome among the barbarians. The Roman camp near the sea was unexpectedly attacked by the enemy, and the soldiers, instead of preparing for the defence, sought to save themselves by a disorderly flight to their ships. The enemy took possession of the camp, and the news, which accidentally arrived in Rome a short time after, spread a panic unworthy of Rome throughout Italy, and induced the senate to take precautions in all haste, as if the State were in the greatest danger. Fortunately the barbarians allowed themselves to be surprised while revelling and rioting in the conquered camp, and the temporary and inexplicable cowardice of the Roman soldiers was soon forgotten. The war with the Istrians was virtually finished when Caius Claudius Pulcher, the consul for the following year (177 B.C.), appeared with a new army, and secured the safety of Italy in this quarter.

By the side of the Gallic tribes in northern Italy there dwelt at that time the Ligurians on both sides of the Apennines. At an earlier time the Ligurians had been more widely spread; but they had been driven by the Gallic invaders into the mountains which surrounded the gulf named after them the Ligurian. There they lived in freedom and poverty as peasants and shepherds, in a wild and sterile mountain district, and sought to obtain

---

[1] Livy, xl. 34. The establishment of a colony at Aquileia had been resolved upon two years before, in 183 B.C. Livy, xxxix. 55.

BOOK V.
201–133 B.C.

by the sword in the rich neighbouring countries what their own barren land denied them. They were for a long time a dreadful scourge of northern Etruria, and their pirate ships scoured far and wide the western sea. By them the road between Pisæ and Massilia and the voyage along the coast were for a long time rendered dangerous. This was a state of affairs which Rome could not suffer after she had assumed the sovereignty over Etruria. But the Hannibalic war prolonged the independence of the Ligurians, although they seem hardly to have taken any part in it. When, after the peace with Carthage, Rome resumed the interrupted task of reducing northern Italy, the Ligurians found themselves in a similar position to that of the Gauls, and, therefore, frequently fought in conjunction with them. But a close and lasting alliance was out of the question in the case of barbarous tribes. It was not difficult for Rome to isolate her enemies and to attack them singly, especially as they thought only of defence, and generally remained quiet when not attacked—plundering expeditions, of course, being always excepted.

The frequent wars with the Ligurians.

As early as the year 201 B.C., when the wars in northern Italy were breaking out anew, the consul Ælius Pætus succeeded in concluding a treaty with the Ligurian tribe of the Ingaunians.[1] But after the year 197 B.C., Ligurian tribes appear regularly at war with Rome. They invaded the Roman territory, and finally, in the year 193 B.C., devastated the land round Luna, Pisæ, and Placentia.[2] Extraordinary measures to oppose them became necessary. The consul Minucius Thermus had to defend Pisæ against them, but did not venture to give battle, and when he was himself attacked in his camp, could scarcely hold his ground.[3] Nay, he was even in danger of undergoing a disgrace similar to that of the Caudine passes. Shut in as he was by the bold mountaineers in a narrow valley, he escaped only through the courage of a body

---

[1] Livy, xxxi. 2, 11: 'Cum Ingaunis Liguribus foedus icit.'
[2] Livy, xxxiv. 56.   [3] Livy, xxxv. 3.

of Numidian horse, who fought their way through the enemy and forced them to retreat, by devastating the land in their rear.¹ In the following year (192 B.C.) Minucius was more fortunate. He routed the Ligurians in a great battle near Pisae with a loss of nine thousand men, pursued them, and, it is said,² took from them the booty which they had seized in Etruria. It is evident that this victory was, after all, not decisive, because in the following year the Ligurians again attacked the camp of Minucius. This time also he boasted of having gained a great victory, and even claimed a triumph, which, however, he did not obtain.³ In this way year after year passed with almost wearisome uniformity. Repeatedly both consuls were sent against the Ligurians with four legions, i. e. armies of forty thousand men, but were so far from being able to overcome the enemies in their mountains that Pisae and Bononia were several times threatened by them.⁴ The Roman generals had not the talent of forming, everyone for himself, a sensible plan for a campaign; still less, in the continual succession of annual commanders, did the earlier leaders keep in mind the necessities of those who were to follow them, and thus prepare the way for them by their own operations.⁵ Each commander was constrained naturally to begin the work afresh, and thus it happened that it remained so long unfinished. If we consider the small extent of the Ligurian mountain-land, its nearness to the Roman territory and the sea, and then place beside it the immense power of Rome in the second century before our era, we

---

¹ Livy, xxxv. 11.   ² Livy, xxxv. 21.
³ Livy, xxxvii. 46, 1. Compare Gell. xiii. 25, 12.
⁴ Livy, xxxvii. 57; xxxviii. 42; xxxix. 1, 2; xxxix. 20, 32, 38, 45, 56; xl. 1, 16, 25, 27, 38, 41, 43, 53; xli. 12, 13, 15, 18, 19; xlii. 1, 21, 22. *Epitome*, 46; Julius Obsequens, 71. The numerous campaigns to which the above-quoted passages refer represent wars which, in the aggregate, far surpass in magnitude all the wars in Greece and Asia between the peace with Carthage and the destruction of Corinth.
⁵ So far from this, it happened, as we have seen above (p. 396 note 2), that from jealousy or private enmity a commander was tempted to make the work more difficult for his successor.

may justly assert that of all the enemies of Rome, no people, not even the Samnites, opposed to them a more resolute resistance than the Ligurians.

It would be wearisome to follow the reports of the annalists in detail through year after year of Ligurian campaigns. Of the many Roman generals who carried on these wars with more or less success up to the year 166 B.C., we need notice only two, whom we have already met with elsewhere. Of these, one is Quintus Marcius Philippus,[1] who, in the beginning of the war with Perseus (171 B.C.), managed to overreach him in diplomatic skill, and in the third year with reckless courage penetrated into Macedonia by a difficult mountain pass. Conducting a campaign against the Ligurians, in his first consulship, 186 B.C., this same Marcius allowed himself to be enticed into a part where the enemy lay in ambush, and, having lost four thousand men and a number of arms and ensigns, escaped with great difficulty, and dismissed the remainder of his army as soon as he was beyond the reach of the enemy, in order to hide the extent of his reverses. But he could not prevent the people from speaking of the spot where he had been beaten as the Marcian forest (*saltus Marcius*), and thus perpetuating the memory of his disaster.

The second leader is Æmilius Paullus, the much extolled conqueror of Perseus. This man is known to us also from the wars in Spain, where he sustained a great defeat in the year 190 B.C., which he repaired shortly afterwards.[2] He had almost the same bad fortune in Liguria. When, after his first consulship, in the year 181 B.C., he was stationed as pro-consul in Liguria, he was attacked in his camp, it is said, during a truce, and he defended himself bravely, but with great difficulty, for a whole day. He was in danger of being taken prisoner, with his whole army; for neither his colleague, who was near enough, in Pisae, but had no troops at hand, nor

[1] See pp. 211, 228.   [2] See p. 376.

Marcellus, who was stationed in distant Gaul, could come to his rescue; and the hasty preparations which the senate made on receiving the alarming tidings, could not have saved the general from his peril. In this strait, despairing of aid, he made a bold sally, and succeeded in fighting his way through the blockading force.[1]

On this occasion, as in many other similar difficulties, the fault of the general was repaired by the courage of the soldiers. The tribe of the Ingaunians soon after submitted and gave hostages. The Romans, on their side, had recourse to the severe measure of carrying off whole tribes in order to put an end to the war. Four thousand Ligurians were transplanted to Samnium,[2] where public lands were allotted to them. The same thing was done (180 B.C.) with seven thousand more who were transported by sea to Naples, in order to join their countrymen in Samnium.[3] But either these numbers are exaggerated, or the gaps which were made by the transportation of so many men were immediately filled up again by new immigrants. The war, at any rate, continued without any perceptible decrease of violence. The town of Pisæ was so hard-pressed and had lost so many men, that it begged the senate to send out a reinforcement of citizens in the shape of Latin colonists, whom it offered to supply with land.[4] The request was granted, and in

Transference of Ligurians to Southern Italy.

Pisæ reinforced.

---

[1] Livy, xl. 25–28. [2] Livy, xl. 37, 38. [3] Livy, xl. 41.

[4] Livy, xl. 13. In a similar situation, not long before this time, Placentia and Cremona had asked for reinforcements, and six thousand families had been sent out there. In fact, it was a frequent measure thus to strengthen colonies (Livy, xxxii. 2; xxxiii. 24) or allied states (see Voigt, *Das ius Civile und ius gentium der Römer*, p. 348, Anmerkung. 379) at their special request. We are not informed that the reinforcement was actually despatched to Pisæ, but the appointment of a commission of triumvirs is reported, and the names are given by Livy as Q. Fabius Buteo, M. et P. Popillii Lænates, so that it seems safe to infer that they performed the task for which they were selected. Nevertheless, Mommsen is of opinion that the colonists sent from Rome were destined not for Pisæ but for Luna, a place in which it is known that three years later a colony was established (Livy, xli. 13). Mommsen, to get a footing for his conjecture, proposes an alteration in the text of Livy. In the passage, 'Pisanis agrum pollicentibus quo Latina colonia deduceretur,' he substitutes 'Luna' for 'Latina.' We cannot agree to this conjecture. For, in the

the following year (179 B.C.) both consuls were again sent to Liguria. Although after the campaign one of the consuls celebrated a triumph, neither of them accomplished much.¹ In the year 177 B.C. the colony of Luna was founded on the Macra, as an advanced post on the frontier of the hostile country.² But in the same year the Ligurians had still courage and strength enough to undertake an expedition against the Roman colony of Mutina, and even to conquer it. They could not keep possession of the town, and probably did not even intend to do so, but were content with plundering and then devastating it.² Accordingly, the senate thought it advisable in the following year again to send two consuls against them, and to direct the pro-consul Caius Claudius, who commanded in Cisalpine Gaul, to co-operate with them. Thus the Ligurians were completely overpowered, and sustained a great defeat in 176 B.C. Yet, in the year 173 B.C. the senate again resolved to send both consuls against them; but only one of them, Marcus Popillius Laenas, actually went into the province. Of the manner in which he carried on the war something has been said already.⁴ Attacking the Ligurian tribe of the Statellates on the north side of the mountains, although they had as yet taken no part in the wars of their countrymen with Rome, he defeated them, as he asserted, in a great battle,⁵ disarmed them, when they had submitted to him, in the hope of lenient treatment, destroyed their town,

---

first place, the commission of triumvirs for the establishment of the colony of Luna was composed of different men (their names are, P. Aelius, M. Aemilius Lepidus, Cn. Licinius). In the second place, the land for the colonists of Luna was taken from the Ligurians, not presented by the people of Pisae. (See Livy, xli. 13.) It is therefore necessary to keep the reinforcement of Pisae and the colonisation of Luna apart as two distinct events.

¹ Livy, xl. 53 and 57. Livy says of the triumph of Fulvius that it was due 'magis gratiae quam rerum gestarum magnitudini.'

² Livy, xli. 13, 1.   ³ Livy, xli. 16, 18.   ⁴ See p. 202.

⁵ Livy, xlii. 7. This victory was perhaps one of the *pugnae falsae* of which Cato complained (above, p. 354 note), for if Popillius had indeed gained a great battle, it is not likely that the senate would have scrutinised his conduct so closely and would have so severely censured his cruelty.

THE CONQUEST OF NORTHERN ITALY.

and sold them into slavery. The senate disapproved of these acts,[1] and ordered that those Ligurians who had been sold should be set free again. Thereupon a violent quarrel arose between the consul and the senate. Refusing to obey, the former actually continued the war, and sent a message to Rome that he had again defeated the Ligurians, and killed sixteen thousand of them. The consul's brother, Caius Popillius, who succeeded him in the consulship, endeavoured to shield him from the anger of the senate; but he was obliged to give in to the threats of two tribunes, and to repair the injury by redeeming from slavery the ill-used Ligurians, and settling them in the valley of the Po. Marcus Popillius was impeached for misconduct; but his trial was not seriously proceeded with, and he escaped without punishment.[2]

From this time the wars in Liguria gradually ceased. After an interval of several years, in 166 B.C. another war is reported, in which the Ligurians are said to have been entirely defeated.[3] Twelve years later the Romans had penetrated beyond the Maritime Alps, and defended Massilia, which was on friendly terms with them, against the Axybian Ligurians, whose land they assigned to the Massilians.[4] At length in the year 143 B.C., when the war with Numantia began, we find a Roman army in the extreme north-west of Italy at war with the Gallo-Ligurian tribe of the Salassians. This war, which concludes the long succession of Roman conquests in Italy, presents more than ordinary interest, on account of the conduct of Appius Claudius, the commanding consul, which throws a passing light upon the internal state of affairs, and con-

CHAP. VII.

201–133 B.C.

Appius Claudius' war with the Salassians.

---

[1] Livy, xlii. 8 : 'Atrox res visa senatui: Statellates, qui uni ex Ligurum gente non tulissent arma adversus Romanos, tum quoque oppugnatos, non ultro inferentes bellum, deditos in fidem populi Romani omni ultimæ crudelitatis exemplo laceratos ac deletos esse, tot milia capitum innoxiorum, fidem implorantia populi Romani. . . . pessumo exemplo venisse,' etc.

[2] Livy, xlii. 22 : ' Rogatio de Liguribus arte fallaci elusa est.'

[3] Livy, Epit. 46 ; Julius Obsequens, 71.

[4] Polybius, xxxiii. 7 ; Livy, Epit. 47.

firms all that we have in this last period noticed of the imperiousness of the Roman aristocracy, and the impossibility of preventing the approaching revolution.

Appius Claudius was consul in the year 143 B.C., together with Quintus Cæcilius Metellus, the conqueror of Pseudo-Philippus of Macedonia. Inflated with family pride and goaded by the ambition not to be behind his colleague in military reputation, he sought some pretext for war.[1] Italy, which had been allotted to him as his sphere of office (his *provincia*), enjoyed perfect peace. But Claudius was not disconcerted. The Salassians, who happened just then to have a dispute with their neighbours about a stream used for washing gold, applied to him to settle the matter amicably by acting as umpire. Instead of doing this, he attacked them with an armed force, but was completely beaten, and lost no less than ten thousand men. In a second battle he was more fortunate, and killed (as he asserted)[2] five thousand enemies, the number which, according to a law recently passed,[3] gave him a right to ask for a triumph. He accordingly determined to enjoy this honour, whether the senate or people consented or not. Without deigning to apply for leave, he only asked the senate to vote the necessary money. When this was refused he bore the expenses himself, and celebrated a triumph in defiance of all customs and laws. A tribune was about to pull him down from his triumphal chariot; but his daughter, who was a vestal virgin, clung to him and protected him with her sacred person.[4] Thus far had the monarchic, or, rather, the despotic, element in the mixed constitution of the Roman republic gained the preponderance over the aristocratic and democratic element, that an audacious

---

[1] Dio Cassius, fragm. 74 : ὁ Κλαύδιος . . . πρός τε τὸ γένος ὠγκωμένος καὶ τῷ Μετέλλῳ φθονῶν ἔτυχεν ἐν τῇ Ἰταλίᾳ λαχὼν ἄρχειν καὶ πολέμιον οὐδὲν ἀποδιδειγμένον εἶχε· καὶ ἐπιθύμησε πάντως τινὰ ἐπινικίων πρόφασιν λαβεῖν· καὶ Σαλάσσους Γαλάτας μὴ ἐγκαλουμένους τι ἐξεπολέμωσε τοῖς Ῥωμαίοις.

[2] Orosius, v. 4.   [3] See p. 354 note.

[4] Dio Cass. fragm. 74, 2; Cicero, *Pro Cæl.* 11; Valer. Maxim. v. 4, 6; Suetron. *Tiber.* 2.

noble might, at least temporarily, succeed in playing the part of an absolute king without incurring any danger for his present safety. This same Claudius, who so contemptuously trampled upon the republican institutions, became in due time censor, and died as the leader (*princeps*) of the senate.

Chap. VII. 201–133 B.C.

The first conquest which Rome had made beyond Italy after the Sicilian war was in Illyria, which had been compelled to recognise the sovereignty of Rome in two wars, 229 and 219 B.C.[1] This sovereignty was at first disregarded by the Illyrian people and princes as long as they believed themselves powerful enough, but it was changed into a complete dominion after the war with Gentius, the ally of Perseus. Between the Illyrian possessions and Istria dwelt several independent tribes, who, like their neighbours, were addicted to piracy, and, issuing from the narrow channels of a sea full of islands and creeks, were long a scourge of the adjacent country. These lawless practices could be brought to an end only by the subjection of the whole coast. In a war which lasted for two years (156–155 B.C.), the Romans conquered Dalmatia, and thus the whole east coast of the Adriatic, from Epirus to Istria, was in their possession.[2]

Conquest of Illyria and Dalmatia.

The islands of Sardinia and Corsica had been seized immediately after the first war with Carthage, but were not entirely subjected, even at the end of the present period (133 B.C.). In the rugged mountains of the interior the natives preserved their independence, and lost none of their original barbarism. Only the towns and villages on the coast were in the safe possession of the Romans, and even these had to be continually defended by force of arms from the attacks of the mountaineers. From time to time these border hostilities assumed the proportions of wars, and gave the Roman generals opportunities for reports of glorious battles, and for triumphal honours. In the year 179 B.C. a serious revolt broke out in Sardinia, which Tiberius Sempronius Gracchus put down after a war of

Wars in Sardinia and Corsica.

---

[1] Vol. ii. book iv. chaps. 6 & 7.   [2] Livy, *Epit.* 47; Zonaras, ix. 25.

BOOK V.
201–133 B.C.

two years, with a strong consular army of two double legions (twenty-three thousand two hundred men).¹ He celebrated a triumph, and caused a picture to be painted representing his victories, which he placed in the temple of Mater Matuta. In an inscription under this picture Gracchus proclaimed his own glory, and asserted that he had killed or captured over eighty thousand enemies.² Nevertheless, similar wars occurred from time to time, as, for instance, in the years 126, 124, 122, and 115 B.C. The sister island of Corsica was treated in the same way. The resistance of the natives seems to have been still more stubborn, and it was prolonged, in fact, up to the time of the emperors.

The formation of the Roman empire

The extension of the Roman dominion over the chief countries round the Mediterranean resembles, more than the formation of any other great state in the old or new world, a spontaneous and natural growth determined by fixed laws. In the Persian and Macedonian kingdoms, as in those of Alexander's successors, the founder himself was the chief agent. Religious fanaticism made conquerors of the Arabs. The maritime discoveries of the fifteenth century opened a road to splendid conquests in America and India to the enterprising spirit and the cupidity of the European nations. But the peasantry on the Tiber rose to the position of rulers over the surrounding country and the whole of Italy gradually and almost imperceptibly. They then crossed the sea almost simultaneously in all directions, as if urged on by an irresistible impulse, without any extraneous determining cause, even without the guidance of any eminent genius, or the influence of such emotions as religious fanaticism, commercial enterprise,

¹ Livy, xli. 12, 17, 21.

² Livy, xli. 28: 'Eodem anno tabula in æde Matris Matutæ cum indice hoc posita est: Tib. Semproni Gracchi imperio auspicioque legio exercitusque populi Romani Sardiniam subegit; in ea provincia hostium cæsa aut capta octoginta milia; republica felicissime gesta atque liberatis sociis, vectigalibus restitutis exercitum salvum atque incolumem plenissimum præda domum reportavit; iterum triumphans in urbem rediit, cuius rei ergo hanc tabulam Iovi dedit.' Livy adds: 'Sardiniæ insulæ forma erat, atque in ea simulacra pugnarum picta.' Surely this must have been no easy task for a painter. We should be glad to know how he executed it.

or a passion for emigration or colonisation. Their course could be arrested by no obstacle of nature, by no strength of will or mental power that opposed them. They crossed seas and mountains, wrestled victoriously with the genius of Hannibal, with the Macedonian phalanx, and Greek policy, with the unbroken force of savage tribes and their pathless mountains. Their frequent defeats were but pauses, rests on the way, giving time for new attacks and new victories. They advanced as if unconscious of their aim, urged on by an uncontrollable instinct, not encouraged but rather restrained by some far-sighted men, who were free from the passions of the vulgar.

This phenomenon is not sufficiently explained by the circumstance that the Romans were warlike and fond of conquests, and that they were trained to war by the necessity of constantly defending their independence. For every nation of antiquity was in the same position. It was the normal policy of all peoples at that time to allow their neighbours only so much of independence as they could maintain by force of arms. The habit of living in peace with neighbouring nations, which is gradually becoming the rule in modern Europe, was as unknown in antiquity as it is now among the Anglo-Americans and the Red Indians. Only the weak were content to keep securely what they possessed. The right of the stronger, in its widest sense, prevailed among all nations, and was, even among the Greeks, hardly softened by the highest intellectual culture. From this point, therefore, the Romans could advance no further than the Spartans or Carthaginians, the Gauls or Macedonians. There must have been circumstances to facilitate the task which all nations alike had set themselves. One of these circumstances we have already pointed out. It was the central position of Rome in the long and narrow peninsula of Italy. If the city of Rome had been situated in Sicily, or in southern Italy, or on the Po, it could not, like a wedge, have divided the north from the south, and have successively subjected both. In the same way the central position of Italy was, in the decisive crisis of the Hannibalic

CHAP. VII.

201–133 B.C.

facilitated by the geographical position of Rome and Italy,

BOOK V.
201–133 B.C.

and by the submission of the Romans to the government of laws.

and in the succeeding wars, the great obstacle to a combined attack upon Rome by all her enemies.

Still the favourable geographic position was not alone sufficient to raise Rome above Italy, and Roman Italy above all the countries round the Mediterranean. The most important condition of success was that political system and organization which was based upon the national character of the Roman people, and which they applied also to conquered nations. It was the willing submission to the authority of an established government, the sacrifice of the individual will to the national, that made them a nation of warriors, and thus the rulers of the world. Their distinguishing character was logical thought without imagination, consistent action without sentiment. These qualities early laid the foundation of a political constitution, which remained in its principle unchanged for ages. The "government of laws, and not of men,"[1] was more fully realised in Rome than in any other state of the ancient world. It was a blessing also for the subject nations, and because it was felt to be a blessing, the subjects clung to the ruling city, as living members of one body politic. It was not until the abuse of power began to undermine these foundations of Roman greatness, that the republic broke down. But, even then, the empire, under a new system of legitimate order, preserved to the peoples of the world the blessings of peace for centuries.

Hence, to understand the greatness of Rome we must study its inner life, the moral and intellectual forces by which it was moved. On this task we have now to fix our attention. We must endeavour to trace the phases of development through which the people and the State passed after they had established their dominion over Italy.

[1] Livy, ii. 1, 1 : imperia legum potentiora quam hominum.

END OF THE THIRD VOLUME.

A CATALOGUE OF WORKS IN GENERAL LITERATURE & SC...

PUBLISHED BY

MESSRS. LONGMANS, GREEN, & CO.
39 PATERNOSTER ROW, LONDON, E.C.

Classified Index.

AGRICULTURE, HORSES, DOGS, and CATTLE.

Dog (The), by Stonehenge	21
Fitzwygram's Horses and Stables	10
Greyhound (The), by Stonehenge	21
Horses and Roads, by Free-Lance	12
Loudon's Encyclopædia of Agriculture	14
Lloyd's The Science of Agriculture	14
Miles' (W. H.) Works on Horses and Stables	17
Nevile's Farms and Farming	18
——— Horses and Riding	18
Scott's Farm-Valuer	20
Steel's Diseases of the Ox	21
Ville's Artificial Manures	23
Youatt on the Dog	24
——— Horse	24

ANATOMY and PHYSIOLOGY.

Ashby's Notes on Physiology	5
Buckton's Health in the House	7
Cooke's Tablets of Anatomy and Physiology	8
Gray's Anatomy, Descriptive and Surgical	11
Macalister's Vertebrate Animals	15
Owen's Comparative Anatomy and Physiology	18
Quain's Elements of Anatomy	20
Smith's Operative Surgery on the Dead Body	21

ASTRONOMY.

Ball's Elements of Astronomy	22
Herschel's Outlines of Astronomy	12
'Knowledge' Library (The)	20
Proctor's (R. A.) Works	19
Nelson's The Moon	18
Webb's Celestial Objects for Common Telescopes	23

BIOGRAPHY, REMINISCENCES, LETTERS, &c.

Bacon's Life and Works	5
Bagehot's Biographical Studies	5
Bray's Phases of Opinion	7
Carlyle's (T.) Life, by James A. Froude	7
——— Reminiscences	7
——— (Mrs.) Letters and Memorials	7
Cates' Dictionary of General Biography	7
Cox's Lives of Greek Statesmen	8
D'Eon de Beaumont's Life, by Telfer	8
Fox (C. J.), Early History of, by G. O. Trevelyan	10
Grimston's (Hon. R.) Life, by Gale	11
Hamilton's (Sir W. R.) Life, by R. P. Graves	11
Havelock's Memoirs, by J. C. Marshman	11
Macaulay's Life and Letters, by G. O. Trevelyan	15
Malmesbury's Memoirs	16
Maunder's Biographical Treasury	16
Mendelssohn's Letters	17
Mill (James), a Biography, by A. Bain	6
Mill (John Stuart), a Criticism, by A. Bain	6
Mill's (J. S.) Autobiography	18
Mozley's Reminiscences of Oriel College, &c.	18
——— Towns, Villages, &c.	18
Müller's (Max) Biographical Essays	18
Newman's Apologia pro Vitâ Suâ	18
Pasolini's Memoir	18
Pasteur's Life and Labours	18
Shakespeare's Life, by J. O. Halliwell-Phillipps	21
Southey's Correspondence with Caroline Bowles	21
Stephen's Ecclesiastical Biography	21
Wellington's Life, by G. R. Gleig	23

BOTANY and GARDENING.

Allen's Flowers and their Pedigrees	4
De Caisne & Le Maout's Botany	8
Lindley's Treasury of Botany	14

BOTANY and GARDENING—continued.

Loudon's Encyclopædia of Gardening	14
——— Encyclopædia of Plants	14
Rivers' Orchard-House	20
——— Rose Amateur's Guide	20
Thomé's Botany	22

CHEMISTRY.

Armstrong's Organic Chemistry	22
Kolbe's Inorganic Chemistry	13
Miller's Elements of Chemistry	17
——— Inorganic Chemistry	17
Payen's Industrial Chemistry	18
Thorpe & Muir's Qualitative Analysis	22
——— 's Quantitative Analysis	22
Tilden's Chemical Philosophy	22
Watts' Dictionary of Chemistry	23

CLASSICAL LANGUAGES, LITERATURE, and ANTIQUITIES.

Aristophanes' The Acharnians, translated	5
Aristotle's Works	5
Becker's Charicles	6
——— Gallus	6
Cicero's Correspondence, by Tyrrell	7
Homer's Iliad, translated by Cayley	12
——— ——— Green	12
Hort's The New Pantheon	12
Mahaffy's Classical Greek Literature	16
Perry's Greek and Roman Sculpture	19
Plato's Parmenides, by Maguire	19
Rich's Dictionary of Antiquities	20
Simcox's History of Latin Literature	21
Sophocles' Works	21
Virgil's Æneid, translated by Conington	8
——— Poems	8
——— Works, with Notes by Kennedy	23
Witt's Myths of Hellas	24
——— The Trojan War	24
——— The Wanderings of Ulysses	24

COOKERY, DOMESTIC ECONOMY, &c.

Acton's Modern Cookery	4
Buckton's Food and Home Cookery	7
Reeve's Cookery and Housekeeping	20

ENCYCLOPÆDIAS, DICTIONARIES, and BOOKS of REFERENCE.

Ayre's Bible Treasury	5
Blackley's German Dictionary	6
Brande's Dict. of Science, Literature, and Art	6
Cabinet Lawyer (The)	7
Cates' Dictionary of Biography	7
Contanseau's French Dictionaries	8
Cresy's Encyclopædia of Civil Engineering	8
Gwilt's Encyclopædia of Architecture	11
Johnston's General Dictionary of Geography	13
Latham's English Dictionaries	14
Lindley & Moore's Treasury of Botany	14
Longman's German Dictionary	14
Loudon's Encyclopædia of Agriculture	14
——— ——— Gardening	14
——— ——— Plants	14
M'Culloch's Dictionary of Commerce	16
Maunder's Treasuries	16
Quain's Dictionary of Medicine	20
Rich's Dictionary of Antiquities	20
Roget's English Thesaurus	20
Ure's Dictionary of Arts, Manufactures, &c.	23
White's Latin Dictionaries	23
Willich's Popular Tables	24
Yonge's English-Greek Dictionary	24

ENGINEERING, MECHANICS, MANUFACTURES, &c.

Anderson's Strength of Materials	22
Barry & Bramwell's Railways, &c	6
———'s Railway Appliances	22
Black's Treatise on Brewing	6
Bourne's Works on the Steam Engine	6
Cresy's Encyclopædia of Civil Engineering	8
Culley's Handbook of Practical Telegraphy	8
Edwards' Our Seamarks	9
Fairbairn's Mills and Millwork	10
——— Useful Information for Engineers	10
Goodeve's Elements of Mechanism	11
——— Principles of Mechanics	11
Gore's Electro-Metallurgy	22
Gwilt's Encyclopædia of Architecture	11
Mitchell's Practical Assaying	17
Northcott's Lathes and Turning	18
Piesse's Art of Perfumery	19
Preece & Sivewright's Telegraphy	22
Sennett's Marine Steam Engine	21
Shelley's Workshop Appliances	22
Swinton's Electric Lighting	22
Unwin's Machine Design	22
Ure's Dictionary of Arts, Manufactures, & Mines	23

ENGLISH LANGUAGE and LITERATURE.

Arnold's English Poetry and Prose	5
——— Manual of English Literature	5
Latham's English Dictionaries	14
——— Handbook of English Language	14
Roget's English Thesaurus	20
Whately's English Synonyms	23

HISTORY, POLITICS, HISTORICAL MEMOIRS, and CRITICISM.

Abbey & Overton's Eng. Church in 18th Century	4
Amos' Fifty Years of the English Constitution	4
——— Primer of the English Constitution	4
Arnold's Lectures on Modern History	5
Beaconsfield's Selected Speeches	6
Boultbee's History of the Church of England	6
Bramston & Leroy's Historic Winchester	6
Buckle's History of Civilisation	7
Chesney's Waterloo Lectures	7
Cox's General History of Greece	8
——— Lives of Greek Statesmen	8
Creighton's History of the Papacy	8
De Witt's (John) Life, by Pontalis	8
De Tocqueville's Democracy in America	8
Doyle's The English in America	9
Epochs of Ancient History	9
——— Modern History	9
Freeman's Historical Geography of Europe	10
Froude's History of England	10
——— Short Studies	10
——— The English in Ireland	10
Gardiner's History of England, 1603-42	10
——— Outline of English History	11
Grant's University of Edinburgh	11
Greville's Journal	11
Hickson's Ireland in the 17th Century	12
Lecky's History of England	14
——— European Morals	14
——— Rationalism in Europe	14
——— Leaders of Public Opinion in Ireland	14
Lewes' History of Philosophy	14
Longman's (W.) Lectures on History of England	14
——— Life and Times of Edward III.	14
——— *(F. W.)* Frederick the Great	14
Macaulay's Complete Works	15
——— Critical and Historical Essays	15
——— History of England	15
——— Speeches	15
Maunder's Historical Treasury	16
Maxwell's Don John of Austria	16
May's Constitutional Hist. of Eng. 1760-1870	16
——— Democracy in Europe	16
Merivale's Fall of the Roman Republic	17
——— General History of Rome	17
——— Romans under the Empire	17
——— The Roman Triumvirates	17
Rawlinson's Seventh Great Oriental Monarchy	20
Seebohm's The Oxford Reformers	20
——— The Protestant Revolution	20

HISTORY, POLITICS, HISTORICAL MEMOIRS and CRITICISM—*cont.*

Short's History of the Church of England	21
Smith's Carthage and the Carthaginians	21
Taylor's History of India	22
Walpole's History of England, 1815-41	23
Wylie's England under Henry IV.	24

ILLUSTRATED BOOKS and BOOKS on ART.

Dresser's Japan; its Architecture, &c.	9
Eastlake's Five Great Painters	9
——— Hints on Household Taste	9
——— Notes on Foreign Picture Galleries	9
Jameson's (Mrs.) Works	13
Lang's (A.) Princess Nobody, illus. by R. Doyle	14
Macaulay's (Lord) Lays, illustrated by Scharf	15
——— illustrated by Weguelin	15
Moore's Irish Melodies, illustrated by Maclise	18
——— Lalla Rookh, illustrated by Tenniel	18
New Testament (The), illustrated	18
Perry's Greek and Roman Sculpture	19

MEDICINE and SURGERY.

Bull's Hints to Mothers	7
——— Maternal Management of Children	7
Coats' Manual of Pathology	7
Dickinson On Renal and Urinary Affections	9
Erichsen's Concussion of the Spine	10
——— Science and Art of Surgery	10
Garrod's Materia Medica	10
——— Treatise on Gout	10
Hawara's Orthopaedic Surgery	12
Hewitt's Diseases of Women	12
——— Mechanic. System of Uterine Pathology	12
Holmes' System of Surgery	12
Husband's Questions in Anatomy	12
Jones' The Health of the Senses	13
Little's In-Knee Distortion	14
Liveing's Works on Skin Diseases	14
Longmore's Gunshot Injuries	14
Mackenzie's Use of the Laryngoscope	15
Macnamara's Diseases of Himalayan Districts	16
Morehead's Disease in India	18
Murchison's Continued Fevers of Great Britain	18
——— Diseases of the Liver	18
Paget's Clinical Lectures and Essays	18
——— Lectures on Surgical Pathology	18
Pereira's Materia Medica	18
Quain's Dictionary of Medicine	20
Richardson's The Asclepiad	20
Salter's Dental Pathology and Surgery	20
Smith's Handbook for Midwives	21
Thomson's Conspectus, by Birkett	22
Watson's Principles and Practice of Physic	23
West's Diseases of Infancy and Childhood	23

MENTAL and POLITICAL PHILOSOPHY, FINANCE, &c.

Abbott's Elements of Logic	4
Amos' Science of Jurisprudence	4
Aristotle's Works	5
Bacon's Essays, with Notes, by Abbott	5
——— by Hunter	5
——— by Whately	5
——— Letters, Life, and Occasional Works	5
——— Promus of Formularies	5
——— Works	5
Bagehot's Economic Studies	5
Bain's (Prof.) Philosophical Works	6
De Tocqueville's Democracy in America	8
Dowell's History of Taxes	9
Hume's Philosophical Works	13
Jefferies' The Story of My Heart	13
Justinian's Institutes, by T. Sandars	13
Kant's Critique of Practical Reason	13
Lang's Custom and Myth	13
Lewis' Authority in Matters of Opinion	14
Lubbock's Origin of Civilisation	14
Macleod's (H. D.) Works	16
Mill's (James) Phenomena of the Human Mind	17
Mill's (J. S.) Logic, Killick's Handbook to	13
——— Works	17
Miller's Social Economy	17
Monck's Introduction to Logic	18
Morell's Handbook of Logic	17
Seebohm's English Village Community	20

MENTAL and POLITICAL PHILOSOPHY, FINANCE, &c.—continued.

Sully's Outlines of Psychology	22
Swinburne's Picture Logic	22
Thompson's A System of Psychology	22
Thomson's Laws of Thought	22
Twiss on the Rights and Duties of Nations	22
Webb's The Veil of Isis	23
Whately's Elements of Logic	23
—— Elements of Rhetoric	23
Wylie's Labour, Leisure, and Luxury	24
Zeller's Works on Greek Philosophy	24

MISCELLANEOUS WORKS.

Arnold's (Dr.) Miscellaneous Works	5
A. K. H. B., Essays and Contributions of	4
Bagehot's Literary Studies	5
Beaconsfield Birthday Book (The)	6
Beaconsfield's Wit and Wisdom	6
Evans' Bronze Implements of Great Britain	10
Farrar's Language and Languages	10
French's Drink in England	10
Hassell's Adulteration of Food	12
Johnson's Patentee's Manual	13
Longman's Magazine	14
Macaulay's (Lord) Works, Selections from	15
Müller's (Max) Works	18
Peel's A Highland Gathering	19
Smith's (Sydney) Wit and Wisdom	21

NATURAL HISTORY (POPULAR).

Dixon's Rural Bird Life	9
Hartwig's (Dr. G.) Works	11
Maunder's Treasury of Natural History	16
Stanley's Familiar History of Birds	21
Wood's (Rev. J. G.) Works	24

POETICAL WORKS.

Bailey's Festus	5
Dante's Divine Comedy, translated by Minchin	8
Goethe's Faust, translated by Birds	11
—— translated by Webb	11
—— with Notes by Selss	11
Homer's Iliad, translated by Cayley	12
—— translated by Green	12
Ingelow's Poetical Works	13
Macaulay's (Lord) Lays of Ancient Rome	15
Macdonald's A Book of Strife	15
Pennell's 'From Grave to Gay'	19
Reader's Voices from Flower-Land	20
Shakespeare, Bowdler's Family Edition	21
—— Hamlet, by George Macdonald	15
Southey's Poetical Works	21
Stevenson's Child's Garden of Poems	21
Virgil's Æneid, translated by Conington	23
—— Poems, translated by Conington	23

SPORTS and PASTIMES.

Dead Shot (The), by Marksman	8
Francis' Book on Angling	10
Jefferies' Red Deer	13
Longman's Chess Openings	14
Pole's The Modern Game of Whist	19
Ronalds' Fly-Fisher's Entomology	20
Verney's Chess Eccentricities	23
Walker's The Correct Card	23
Wilcocks' The Sea-Fisherman	24

SCIENTIFIC WORKS (General).

Arnott's Elements of Physics	5
Bauerman's Descriptive Mineralogy	22
—— Systematic Mineralogy	22
Brande's Dictionary of Science &c.	6
Ganot's Natural Philosophy	10
—— Physics	10
Grove's Correlation of Physical Forces	11
Haughton's Lectures on Physical Geography	11
Helmholtz Scientific Lectures	12
—— On the Sensation of Tone	12
Hullah's History of Modern Music	12
—— Transition Period of Musical History	12
Keller's Lake Dwellings of Switzerland	13
Kerl's Treatise on Metallurgy	13
'Knowledge' Library (The)	20
Lloyd's Treatise on Magnetism	14
Macfarren's Lectures on Harmony	15
Maunder's Scientific Treasury	16
Proctor's (R. A.) Works	19
Rutley's The Study of Rocks	22

SCIENTIFIC WORKS (General).

Smith's Air and Rain	
Text-books of Science	
Tyndall's (Prof.) Works	

THEOLOGY and RELIGION.

Arnold's (Dr.) Sermons	5
Ayre's Treasury of Bible Knowledge	5
Boultbee's Commentary on the 39 Articles	6
Browne's Exposition of the 39 Articles	7
Calvert's Wife's Manual	7
Colenso's Pentateuch and Book of Joshua	7
Conder's Handbook to the Bible	7
Conybeare and Howson's St. Paul	8
Davidson's Introduction to the New Testament	8
Dewes' Life and Letters of St. Paul	9
Edersheim's Jesus the Messiah	9
—— Warburton Lectures	9
Ellicott's Commentary on St. Paul's Epistles	9
—— Lectures on the Life of Our Lord	9
Ewald's Antiquities of Israel	10
—— History of Israel	10
Hobart's Medical Language of St. Luke	12
Hopkins' Christ the Consoler	12
Jukes' (Rev. A.) Works	13
Kalisch's Bible Studies	13
—— Commentary on the Old Testament	13
Lyra Germanica	15
Macdonald's Unspoken Sermons (second series)	15
Manning's Temporal Mission of the Holy Ghost	16
Martineau's Endeavours after the Christian Life	16
—— Hours of Thought	16
Monsell's Spiritual Songs	18
Müller's (Max) Origin and Growth of Religion	18
—— Science of Religion	18
Paley's Christian Evidences, &c., by Potts	18
Psalms (The) of David, translated by Seymour	21
Rogers' Defence of the Eclipse of Faith	20
—— The Eclipse of Faith	20
Sewell's Night Lessons from Scripture	21
—— Passing Thoughts on Religion	21
—— Preparation for Holy Communion	21
Smith's Shipwreck of St. Paul	21
Supernatural Religion	22
Taylor's (Jeremy) Entire Works	22

TRAVELS, ADVENTURES, GUIDE BOOKS, &c.

Aldridge's Ranch Notes	4
Alpine Club (The) Map of Switzerland	4
Baker's Eight Years in Ceylon	5
—— Rifle and Hound in Ceylon	5
Ball's Alpine Guide	4
Brassey's (Lady) Works	7
Crawford's Across the Pampas and the Andes	8
Dent's Above the Snow Line	8
Freeman's United States	10
Hassall's San Remo	12
Howitt's Visits to Remarkable Places	12
Johnston's Dictionary of Geography	13
Maritime Alps (The)	16
Maunder's Treasury of Geography	16
Melville's In the Lena Delta	16
Miller's Wintering in the Riviera	17
Three in Norway	22

WORKS of FICTION.

Anstey's The Black Poodle, &c.	5
Antinous, by George Taylor	5
Atelier du Lys (The)	17
Atherstone Priory	17
Beaconsfield's (Lord) Novels and Tales	6
Burgomaster's Family (The)	17
Elsa and her Vulture	17
Harte's (Bret) In the Carquinez Woods	17
—— On the Frontier	12
In the Olden Time	13
Mademoiselle Mori	17
Modern Novelist's Library (The)	17
Oliphant's (Mrs.) In Trust	17
—— Madam	18
Payn's Thicker than Water	17
Sewell's (Miss) Stories and Tales	21
Six Sisters of the Valleys (The)	17
Sturgis' My Friends and I	22
Trollope's (Anthony) Barchester Towers	17
—— The Warden	17
Unawares	17
Whyte-Melville's (Major) Novels	17

A CATALOGUE

OF

WORKS IN GENERAL LITERATURE & SCIENCE

PUBLISHED BY

Messrs. Longmans, Green & Co.

39 PATERNOSTER ROW, LONDON, E.C.

ABBEY and OVERTON.—*THE ENGLISH CHURCH IN THE EIGHTEENTH CENTURY.* By the Rev. C. J. ABBEY and the Rev. J. H. OVERTON. 2 vols. 8vo. 36s.

ABBOTT. — *THE ELEMENTS OF LOGIC.* By T. K. ABBOTT, B.D. 12mo. 2s. 6d. sewed, or 3s. cloth.

ACTON. — *MODERN COOKERY FOR PRIVATE FAMILIES,* reduced to a System of Easy Practice in a Series of carefully tested Receipts. By ELIZA ACTON. With upwards of 150 Woodcuts. Fcp. 8vo. 4s. 6d.

A. K. H. B.—*THE ESSAYS AND CONTRIBUTIONS OF A. K. H. B.*—Uniform Cabinet Editions in crown 8vo.

Autumn Holidays, 3s. 6d.
Changed Aspects of Unchanged Truths, 3s. 6d.
Commonplace Philosopher, 3s. 6d.
Counsel and Comfort, 3s. 6d.
Critical Essays, 3s. 6d.
Graver Thoughts of a Country Parson. Three Series, 3s. 6d. each.
Landscapes, Churches, and Moralities, 3s. 6d.
Leisure Hours in Town, 3s. 6d.
Lessons of Middle Age, 3s. 6d.
Our Little Life. Two Series, 3s. 6d. each.
Present Day Thoughts, 3s. 6d.
Recreations of a Country Parson. Three Series, 3s. 6d. each.
Seaside Musings, 3s. 6d.
Sunday Afternoons, 3s. 6d.

ALDRIDGE. -- *RANCH NOTES IN KANSAS, COLORADO, THE INDIAN TERRITORY AND NORTHERN TEXAS.* By REGINALD ALDRIDGE. Crown 8vo. with 4 Illustrations engraved on Wood by G. Pearson, 5s.

ALLEN.—*FLOWERS AND THEIR PEDIGREES.* By GRANT ALLEN. With 50 Illustrations engraved on Wood. Crown 8vo. 7s. 6d.

ALPINE CLUB (The).—*GUIDES AND MAPS.*

THE ALPINE GUIDE. By JOHN BALL, M.R.I.A. Post 8vo. with Maps and other Illustrations :—

THE EASTERN ALPS, 10s. 6d.

CENTRAL ALPS, including all the Oberland District, 7s. 6d.

WESTERN ALPS, including Mont Blanc, Monte Rosa, Zermatt, &c. 6s. 6d.

THE ALPINE CLUB MAP OF SWITZERLAND, on the Scale of Four Miles to an Inch. Edited by R. C. NICHOLS, F.R.G.S. 4 Sheets in Portfolio, 42s. coloured, or 34s. uncoloured.

ENLARGED ALPINE CLUB MAP OF THE SWISS AND ITALIAN ALPS, on the Scale of Three English Statute Miles to One Inch, in 8 Sheets, price 1s. 6d. each.

ON ALPINE TRAVELLING AND THE GEOLOGY OF THE ALPS. Price 1s. Either of the Three Volumes or Parts of the 'Alpine Guide' may be had with this Introduction prefixed, 1s. extra.

AMOS.—*WORKS BY SHELDON AMOS, M.A.*

A PRIMER OF THE ENGLISH CONSTITUTION AND GOVERNMENT. Crown 8vo. 6s.

A SYSTEMATIC VIEW OF THE SCIENCE OF JURISPRUDENCE. 8vo. 18s.

FIFTY YEARS OF THE ENGLISH CONSTITUTION, 1830-1880. Crown 8vo. 10s. 6d.

ANSTEY.—*The Black Poodle*, and other Stories. By F. ANSTEY, Author of 'Vice Versâ.' With Frontispiece by G. Du Maurier and Initial Letters by the Author. Crown 8vo. 6s.

ANTINOUS.—An Historical Romance of the Roman Empire. By GEORGE TAYLOR (Professor HAUSRATH). Translated from the German by J. D. M. Crown 8vo. 6s.

ARISTOPHANES. — *The Acharnians of Aristophanes.* Translated into English Verse by ROBERT YELVERTON TYRRELL, M.A. Dublin. Crown 8vo. 2s. 6d.

ARISTOTLE.—*The Works of.*
The Politics, G. Bekker's Greek Text of Books I. III. IV. (VII.) with an English Translation by W. E. BOLLAND, M.A.; and short Introductory Essays by A. LANG, M.A. Crown 8vo. 7s. 6d.
The Ethics; Greek Text, illustrated with Essays and Notes. By Sir ALEXANDER GRANT, Bart. M.A. LL.D. 2 vols. 8vo. 32s.
The Nicomachean Ethics, Newly Translated into English. By ROBERT WILLIAMS, Barrister-at-Law. Crown 8vo. 7s. 6d.

ARNOLD. — *Works by Thomas Arnold, D.D. Late Head-master of Rugby School.*
Introductory Lectures on Modern History, delivered in 1841 and 1842. 8vo. 7s. 6d.
Sermons Preached Mostly in the Chapel of Rugby School. 6 vols. crown 8vo. 30s. or separately, 5s. each.
Miscellaneous Works. 8vo. 7s. 6d.

ARNOLD. — *Works by Thomas Arnold, M.A.*
A Manual of English Literature, Historical and Critical. By THOMAS ARNOLD, M.A. Crown 8vo. 7s. 6d.
English Poetry and Prose: a Collection of Illustrative Passages from the Writings of English Authors, from the Anglo-Saxon Period to the Present Time. Crown 8vo. 6s.

ARNOTT.—*The Elements of Physics or Natural Philosophy.* By NEIL ARNOTT, M.D. Edited by A. BAIN, LL.D. and A. S. TAYLOR, M.D. F.R.S. Woodcuts. Crown 8vo. 12s. 6d.

ASHBY. — *Notes on Physiology for the Use of Students Preparing for Examination.* With 120 Woodcuts. By HENRY ASHBY, M.D. Lond., Physician to the General Hospital for Sick Children, Manchester. Fcp. 8vo. 5s.

AYRE. –*The Treasury of Bible Knowledge;* being a Dictionary of the Books, Persons, Places, Events, and other matters of which mention is made in Holy Scripture. By the Rev. J. AYRE, M.A. With 5 Maps, 15 Plates, and 300 Woodcuts. Fcp. 8vo. 6s.

BACON.—*The Works and Life of.*
Complete Works. Collected and Edited by R. L. ELLIS, M.A. J. SPEDDING, M.A. and D. D. HEATH. 7 vols. 8vo. £3. 13s. 6d.
Letters and Life, including all his Occasional Works. Collected and Edited, with a Commentary, by J. SPEDDING. 7 vols. 8vo. £4. 4s.
The Essays; with Annotations. By RICHARD WHATELY, D.D., sometime Archbishop of Dublin. 8vo. 10s. 6d.
The Essays; with Introduction, Notes, and Index. By E. A. ABBOTT, D.D. 2 vols. fcp. 8vo. price 6s. The Text and Index only, without Introduction and Notes, in 1 vol. fcp. 8vo. price 2s. 6d.
The Essays; with Critical and Illustrative Notes, and other Aids for Students. By the Rev. JOHN HUNTER, M.A. Crown 8vo. 3s. 6d.
The Promus of Formularies and Elegancies, illustrated by Passages from SHAKESPEARE. By Mrs. H. POTT. Preface by E. A. ABBOTT, D.D. 8vo. 16s.

BAGEHOT. — *Works by Walter Bagehot, M.A.*
Biographical Studies. 8vo. 12s.
Economic Studies. 8vo. 10s. 6d.
Literary Studies. 2 vols. 8vo. Portrait. 28s.

BAILEY. — *Festus, a Poem.* By PHILIP JAMES BAILEY. Crown 8vo. 12s. 6d.

BAKER.—*Works by Sir Samuel W. Baker, M.A.*
Eight Years in Ceylon. Crown 8vo. Woodcuts. 5s.
The Rifle and the Hound in Ceylon. Crown 8vo. Woodcuts. 5s.

BAIN. — *Works by Alexander Bain, LL.D.*

Mental and Moral Science; a Compendium of Psychology and Ethics. Crown 8vo. 10s. 6d.

The Senses and the Intellect. 8vo. 15s.

The Emotions and the Will. 8vo. 15s.

Practical Essays. Crown 8vo. 4s. 6d.

Logic, Deductive and Inductive. Part I. *Deduction*, 4s. Part II. *Induction*, 6s. 6d.

James Mill; a Biography. Crown 8vo. 5s.

John Stuart Mill; a Criticism, with Personal Recollections. Crown 8vo. 2s. 6d.

BARRY & BRAMWELL. — *Railways and Locomotives:* a Series of Lectures delivered at the School of Military Engineering, Chatham. *Railways*, by J. W. Barry, M. Inst. C.E. *Locomotives*, by Sir F. J. Bramwell, F.R.S., M. Inst. C.E. With 228 Wood Engravings. 8vo. 21s.

BEACONSFIELD. — *Works by the Earl of Beaconsfield, K.G.*

Novels and Tales. The Cabinet Edition. 11 vols. Crown 8vo. 6s. each.

Endymion.

Lothair.	Henrietta Temple.
Coningsby.	Contarini Fleming, &c.
Sybil.	Alroy, Ixion, &c.
Tancred.	The Young Duke, &c.
Venetia.	Vivian Grey, &c.

Novels and Tales. The Hughenden Edition. With 2 Portraits and 11 Vignettes. 11 vols. Crown 8vo. 42s.

Novels and Tales. Modern Novelist's Library Edition, complete in 11 vols. Crown 8vo. 22s. boards, or 27s. 6d. cloth.

Selected Speeches. With Introduction and Notes, by T. E. Kebbel, M.A. 2 vols. 8vo. Portrait, 32s.

The Wit and Wisdom of Benjamin Disraeli, Earl of Beaconsfield. Crown 8vo. 3s. 6d.

The Beaconsfield Birthday-Book: Selected from the Writings and Speeches of the Right Hon. the Earl of Beaconsfield, K.G. With 2 Portraits and 11 Views of Hughenden Manor and its Surroundings. 18mo. 2s. 6d. cloth, gilt; 4s. 6d. bound.

BECKER. — *Works by Professor Becker, translated from the German by the Rev. F. Metcalf.*

Gallus; or, Roman Scenes in the Time of Augustus. Post 8vo. 7s. 6d.

Charicles; or, Illustrations of the Private Life of the Ancient Greeks. Post 8vo. 7s. 6d.

BLACK. — *Practical Treatise on Brewing;* with Formulæ for Public Brewers and Instructions for Private Families. By W. Black. 8vo. 10s. 6d.

BLACKLEY & FRIEDLÄNDER. — *A Practical Dictionary of the German and English Languages:* containing New Words in General Use not found in other Dictionaries. By the Rev. W. L. Blackley, M.A. and C. M. Friedländer, Ph.D. Post 8vo. 3s. 6d.

BOULTBEE. — *Works by the Rev. T. P. Boultbee, LL.D.*

A Commentary on the 39 Articles, forming an introduction to the Theology of the Church of England. Crown 8vo. 6s.

A History of the Church of England; Pre-Reformation Period. 8vo. 15s.

BOURNE. — *Works by John Bourne, C.E.*

A Treatise on the Steam Engine, in its application to Mines, Mills, Steam Navigation, Railways, and Agriculture. With 37 Plates and 546 Woodcuts. 4to. 42s.

Catechism of the Steam Engine, in its various Applications to Mines, Mills, Steam Navigation, Railways, and Agriculture. With 89 Woodcuts. Crown 8vo. 7s. 6d.

Handbook of the Steam Engine; a Key to the Author's Catechism of the Steam Engine. With 67 Woodcuts. Fcp. 8vo. 9s.

Recent Improvements in the Steam Engine. With 124 Woodcuts. Fcp. 8vo. 6s.

Examples of Steam and Gas Engines of the most recent Approved Types. With 54 Plates and 356 Woodcuts. 4to. 70s.

BRAMSTON & LEROY. — *Historic Winchester;* England's First Capital. By A. R. Bramston and A. C. Leroy. Cr. 8vo. 6s.

BRANDE'S *Dictionary of Science, Literature, and Art.* Re-edited by the Rev. Sir G. W. Cox, Bart., M.A. 3 vols. medium 8vo. 63s.

BRASSEY. — *Works by Lady Brassey.*

A Voyage in the 'Sunbeam,' our Home on the Ocean for Eleven Months. By Lady Brassey. With Map and 65 Wood Engravings. Library Edition, 8vo. 21s. Cabinet Edition, crown 8vo. 7s. 6d. School Edition, fcp. 2s. Popular Edition, 4to. 6d.

Sunshine and Storm in the East; or, Cruises to Cyprus and Constantinople. With 2 Maps and 114 Illustrations engraved on Wood. Library Edition, 8vo. 21s. Cabinet Edition, cr. 8vo. 7s. 6d.

In the Trades, the Tropics, and the 'Roaring Forties'; or, Fourteen Thousand Miles in the *Sunbeam* in 1883. By Lady Brassey. With 292 Illustrations engraved on Wood from drawings by R. T. Pritchett, and Eight Maps and Charts. Edition de Luxe, imperial 8vo. £3. 13s. 6d. Library Edition, 8vo. 21s.

BRAY.—*Phases of Opinion and Experience during a Long Life:* an Autobiography. By Charles Bray, Author of 'The Philosophy of Necessity' &c. Crown 8vo. 3s. 6d.

BROWNE.—*An Exposition of the 39 Articles,* Historical and Doctrinal. By E. H. Browne, D.D., Bishop of Winchester. 8vo. 16s.

BUCKLE.—*History of Civilisation in England and France, Spain and Scotland.* By Henry Thomas Buckle. 3 vols. crown 8vo. 24s.

BUCKTON.— *Works by Mrs. C. M. Buckton.*

Food and Home Cookery; a Course of Instruction in Practical Cookery and Cleaning. With 11 Woodcuts. Crown 8vo. 2s. 6d.

Health in the House: Twenty-five Lectures on Elementary Physiology. With 41 Woodcuts and Diagrams. Crown 8vo. 2s.

BULL.— *Works by Thomas Bull, M.D.*

Hints to Mothers on the Management of their Health during the Period of Pregnancy and in the Lying-in Room. Fcp. 8vo. 1s. 6d.

The Maternal Management of Children in Health and Disease. Fcp. 8vo. 1s. 6d.

CABINET LAWYER, The; a Popular Digest of the Laws of England, Civil, Criminal, and Constitutional. Fcp. 8vo. 9s.

CALVERT.—*The Wife's Manual;* or Prayers, Thoughts, and Songs on Several Occasions of a Matron's Life. By the late W. Calvert, Minor Canon of St. Paul's. Printed and ornamented in the style of *Queen Elizabeth's Prayer Book.* Crown 8vo. 6s.

CARLYLE. — *Thomas and Jane Welsh Carlyle.*

Thomas Carlyle, a History of the first Forty Years of his Life, 1795-1835. By J. A. Froude, M.A. With 2 Portraits and 4 Illustrations, 2 vols. 8vo. 32s.

Thomas Carlyle, a History of his Life in London: from 1834 to his death in 1881. By James A. Froude, M.A. with Portrait engraved on steel. 2 vols. 8vo. 32s.

Reminiscences. By Thomas Carlyle. Edited by J. A. Froude, M.A. 2 vols. crown 8vo. 18s.

Letters and Memorials of Jane Welsh Carlyle. Prepared for publication by Thomas Carlyle, and edited by J. A. Froude, M.A. 3 vols. 8vo. 36s.

CATES. — *A Dictionary of General Biography.* Fourth Edition, with Supplement brought down to the end of 1884. By W. L. R. Cates. 8vo. 28s. cloth; 35s. half-bound russia. The Supplement, 1881-4, 2s. 6d.

CHESNEY.— *Waterloo Lectures;* a Study of the Campaign of 1815. By Col. C. C. Chesney, R.E. 8vo. 10s. 6d.

CICERO.—*The Correspondence of Cicero:* a revised Text, with Notes and Prolegomena.—Vol. I., The Letters to the end of Cicero's Exile. By Robert Y. Tyrrell, M.A., Fellow of Trinity College, Dublin, 12s.

COATS.—*A Manual of Pathology.* By Joseph Coats, M.D. Pathologist to the Western Infirmary and the Sick Children's Hospital, Glasgow; formerly Pathologist to the Royal Infirmary, and President of the Pathological and Clinical Society of Glasgow. With 339 Illustrations engraved on Wood. 8vo. 31s. 6d.

COLENSO.—*The Pentateuch and Book of Joshua Critically Examined.* By J. W. Colenso, D.D., late Bishop of Natal. Crown 8vo. 6s.

CONDER.—*A Handbook to the Bible,* or Guide to the Study of the Holy Scriptures derived from Ancient Monuments and Modern Exploration. By F. R. Conder, and Lieut. C. R. Conder, R.E. Post 8vo. 7s. 6d.

CONINGTON. — WORKS BY JOHN CONINGTON, M.A.
  THE ÆNEID OF VIRGIL. Translated into English Verse. Crown 8vo. 9s.
  THE POEMS OF VIRGIL. Translated into English Prose. Crown 8vo. 9s.

CONTANSEAU. — WORKS BY PROFESSOR LÉON CONTANSEAU.
  A PRACTICAL DICTIONARY OF THE FRENCH AND ENGLISH LANGUAGES. Post 8vo. 3s. 6d.
  A POCKET DICTIONARY OF THE FRENCH AND ENGLISH LANGUAGES; being a careful Abridgment of the Author's 'Practical French and English Dictionary.' Square 18mo. 1s. 6d.

CONYBEARE & HOWSON. — THE LIFE AND EPISTLES OF ST. PAUL. By the Rev. W. J. CONYBEARE, M.A., and the Very Rev. J. S. HOWSON, D.D. Dean of Chester.
  Library Edition, with all the Original Illustrations, Maps, Landscapes on Steel, Woodcuts, &c. 2 vols. 4to. 42s.
  Intermediate Edition, with a Selection of Maps, Plates, and Wood-cuts. 2 vols. square crown 8vo. 21s.
  Student's Edition, revised and condensed, with 46 Illustrations and Maps. 1 vol. crown 8vo. 7s. 6d.

COOKE. — TABLETS OF ANATOMY AND PHYSIOLOGY. By THOMAS COOKE, F.R.C.S. Being a Synopsis of Demonstrations given in the Westminster Hospital Medical School, A.D. 1871-1875. Anatomy, complete, Second Edition, 4to. 15s. Physiology, complete, Second Edition, 4to. 10s.
  *** These TABLETS may still be had in separate Fasciculi as originally published.

COX. — WORKS BY THE REV. SIR G. W. COX, BART., M.A.
  A GENERAL HISTORY OF GREECE: from the Earliest Period to the Death of Alexander the Great; with a Sketch of the Subsequent History to the Present Time. With 11 Maps and Plans. Crown 8vo. 7s. 6d.
  LIVES OF GREEK STATESMEN. SOLON-THEMISTOCLES. Fcp. 8vo. 2s. 6d.

CRAWFORD. — ACROSS THE PAMPAS AND THE ANDES. By ROBERT CRAWFORD, M.A. With Map and 7 Illustrations. Crown 8vo. 7s. 6d.

CREIGHTON. — HISTORY OF THE PAPACY DURING THE REFORMATION. By the Rev. M. CREIGHTON, M.A. Vols. I. and II. 8vo. 32s.

CRESY. — ENCYCLOPÆDIA OF CIVIL ENGINEERING, Historical, Theoretical, and Practical. By EDWARD CRESY. With above 3,000 Woodcuts, 8vo. 25s.

CULLEY. — HANDBOOK OF PRACTICAL TELEGRAPHY. By R. S. CULLEY, M. Inst. C.E. Plates and Woodcuts. 8vo. 16s.

DANTE. — THE DIVINE COMEDY OF DANTE ALIGHIERI. Translated verse for verse from the Original into Terza Rima. By JAMES INNES MINCHIN. Crown 8vo. 15s.

DAVIDSON. — AN INTRODUCTION TO THE STUDY OF THE NEW TESTAMENT, Critical, Exegetical, and Theological. By the Rev. S. DAVIDSON, D.D. LL.D. Revised Edition. 2 vols. 8vo. 30s.

DEAD SHOT, The, OR SPORTSMAN'S COMPLETE GUIDE; a Treatise on the Use of the Gun, with Lessons in the Art of Shooting Game of all kinds, and Wild-Fowl, also Pigeon-Shooting, and Dog-Breaking. By MARKSMAN. With 13 Illustrations. Crown 8vo. 10s. 6d.

DECAISNE & LE MAOUT. — A GENERAL SYSTEM OF BOTANY. Translated from the French of E. LE MAOUT, M.D., and J. DECAISNE, by Lady HOOKER; with Additions by Sir J. D. HOOKER, C.B. F.R.S. Imp. 8vo. with 5,500 Woodcuts, 31s. 6d.

DENT. — ABOVE THE SNOW LINE: Mountaineering Sketches between 1870 and 1880. By CLINTON DENT, Vice-President of the Alpine Club. With Two Engravings by Edward Whymper and an Illustration by Percy Macquoid. Crown 8vo. 7s. 6d.

D'EON DE BEAUMONT. — THE STRANGE CAREER OF THE CHEVALIER D'EON DE BEAUMONT, Minister Plenipotentiary from France to Great Britain in 1763. By Captain J. BUCHAN TELFER, R.N. F.S.A. F.R.G.S. With 3 Portraits. 8vo. 12s.

DE TOCQUEVILLE. — DEMOCRACY IN AMERICA. By ALEXIS DE TOCQUEVILLE. Translated by H. REEVE. 2 vols. crown 8vo. 16s.

DE WITT. — THE LIFE OF JOHN DE WITT, GRAND PENSIONARY OF HOLLAND; or, Twenty Years of a Parliamentary Republic in the 17th Century. By M. ANTONIN LEFÈVRE PONTALIS. Translated from the French by S. E. and A. STEPHENSON. 2 vols. 8vo.

DEWES.—THE LIFE AND LETTERS OF ST. PAUL. By ALFRED DEWES, M.A. LL.D. D.D. Vicar of St. Augustine's, Pendlebury. With 4 Maps. 8vo. 7s. 6d.

DICKINSON. — ON RENAL AND URINARY AFFECTIONS. By W. HOWSHIP DICKINSON, M.D. Cantab. F.R.C.P. &c. With 12 Plates and 122 Woodcuts. 3 vols. 8vo. £3. 4s. 6d.

*** The Three Parts may be had separately: PART I.—Diabetes, 10s. 6d. sewed, 12s. cloth. PART II. Albuminuria, 20s. sewed, 21s. cloth. PART III.—Miscellaneous Affections of the Kidneys and Urine, 30s. sewed, 31s. 6d. cloth.

DIXON.—RURAL BIRD LIFE; Essays on Ornithology, with Instructions for Preserving Objects relating to that Science. By CHARLES DIXON. With 45 Woodcuts. Crown 8vo. 5s.

DOWELL.—A HISTORY OF TAXATION AND TAXES IN ENGLAND, FROM THE EARLIEST TIMES TO THE PRESENT DAY. By STEPHEN DOWELL, Assistant Solicitor of Inland Revenue. 4 vols. 8vo. 48s.

DOYLE.—THE ENGLISH IN AMERICA: Virginia, Maryland, and the Carolinas. By J. A. DOYLE, Fellow of All Souls' College, Oxford. 8vo. Map, 18s.

DRESSER.—JAPAN; ITS ARCHITECTURE, ART, AND ART MANUFACTURES. By CHRISTOPHER DRESSER, Ph.D. F.L.S. &c. With 202 Graphic Illustrations engraved on Wood for the most part by Native Artists in Japan, the rest by G. Pearson, after Photographs and Drawings made on the spot. Square crown 8vo. 31s. 6d.

EASTLAKE.—FIVE GREAT PAINTERS; Essays on Leonardo da Vinci, Michael Angelo, Titian, Raphael, Albert Dürer. By LADY EASTLAKE. 2 vols. Crown 8vo. 16s.

EASTLAKE.—WORKS BY C. L. EASTLAKE, F.R.S. B.A.

HINTS ON HOUSEHOLD TASTE IN FURNITURE, UPHOLSTERY, &c. With 100 Illustrations. Square crown 8vo. 14s.

NOTES ON FOREIGN PICTURE GALLERIES. Crown 8vo.

The Louvre Gallery, Paris, with 114 Illustrations, 7s. 6d.

The Brera Gallery, Milan, with 55 Illustrations, 5s.

The Old Pinakothek, Munich, with 107 Illustrations, 7s. 6d.

EDERSHEIM.—WORKS BY THE REV. ALFRED EDERSHEIM, D.D.

THE LIFE AND TIMES OF JESUS THE MESSIAH. 2 vols. 8vo. 42s.

PROPHECY AND HISTORY IN RELATION TO THE MESSIAH: the Warburton Lectures, delivered at Lincoln's Inn Chapel, 1880-1884. 8vo. 12s.
[Nearly ready.

EDWARDS. —OUR SEAMARKS. By E. PRICE EDWARDS. With numerous Illustrations of Lighthouses, &c. engraved on Wood by G. H. Ford. Crown 8vo. 8s. 6d.

ELLICOTT. — WORKS BY C. J. ELLICOTT, D.D., Bishop of Gloucester and Bristol.

A CRITICAL AND GRAMMATICAL COMMENTARY ON ST. PAUL'S EPISTLES. 8vo. Galatians, 8s. 6d. Ephesians, 8s. 6d. Pastoral Epistles, 10s. 6d. Philippians, Colossians, and Philemon, 10s. 6d. Thessalonians, 7s. 6d. I. Corinthians
[Nearly ready.

HISTORICAL LECTURES ON THE LIFE OF OUR LORD JESUS CHRIST. 8vo. 12s.

EPOCHS OF ANCIENT HISTORY.
Edited by the Rev. Sir G. W. COX, Bart. M.A. and C. SANKEY, M.A.
Beesly's Gracchi, Marius and Sulla, 2s. 6d.
Capes's Age of the Antonines, 2s. 6d.
—— Early Roman Empire, 2s. 6d.
Cox's Athenian Empire, 2s. 6d.
—— Greeks and Persians, 2s. 6d.
Curteis's Macedonian Empire, 2s. 6d.
Ihne's Rome to its Capture by the Gauls, 2s. 6d.
Merivale's Roman Triumvirates, 2s. 6d.
Sankey's Spartan and Theban Supremacies, 2s. 6d.
Smith's Rome and Carthage, 2s. 6d.

EPOCHS OF MODERN HISTORY.
Edited by C. COLBECK, M.A.
Church's Beginning of the Middle Ages, 2s. 6d.
Cox's Crusades, 2s. 6d.
Creighton's Age of Elizabeth, 2s. 6d.
Gairdner's Lancaster and York, 2s. 6d.
Gardiner's Puritan Revolution, 2s. 6d.
—————— Thirty Years' War, 2s. 6d.
—————— (Mrs.) French Revolution, 2s. 6d.
Hale's Fall of the Stuarts, 2s. 6d.
Johnson's Normans in Europe, 2s. 6d.
Longman's Frederick the Great, 2s. 6d.
Ludlow's War of American Independence, 2s. 6d.
M'Carthy's Epoch of Reform, 1830-1850, 2s. 6d.
Morris's Age of Anne, 2s. 6d.
Seebohm's Protestant Revolution, 2s. 6d.
Stubbs' Early Plantagenets, 2s. 6d.
Warburton's Edward III. 2s. 6d.

ERICHSEN.—*Works by John Eric Erichsen, F.R.S.*

The Science and Art of Surgery: Being a Treatise on Surgical Injuries, Diseases, and Operations. Illustrated by Engravings on Wood. 2 vols 8vo. 42s.; or bound in half-russia, 60s.

On Concussion of the Spine, Nervous Shocks, and other Obscure Injuries of the Nervous System in their Clinical and Medico-Legal Aspects. Crown 8vo. 10s. 6d.

EVANS.—*The Bronze Implements, Arms, and Ornaments of Great Britain and Ireland.* By John Evans, D.C.L. LL.D. F.R.S. With 540 Illustrations. 8vo. 25s.

EWALD.—*Works by Professor Heinrich Ewald, of Göttingen.*

The Antiquities of Israel. Translated from the German by H. S. Solly, M.A. 8vo. 12s. 6d.

The History of Israel. Translated from the German. Vols. I.–V. 8vo. 63s. Vol. VI. *Christ and his Times*, 8vo. 16s. Vol. VII. *The Apostolic Age*, 8vo. 21s.

FAIRBAIRN.—*Works by Sir W. Fairbairn, Bart, C.E.*

A Treatise on Mills and Millwork, with 18 Plates and 333 Woodcuts. 1 vol. 8vo. 25s.

Useful Information for Engineers. With many Plates and Woodcuts. 3 vols. crown 8vo. 31s. 6d.

FARRAR.—*Language and Languages.* A Revised Edition of *Chapters on Language and Families of Speech.* By F. W Farrar, D.D. Crown 8vo. 6s.

FITZWYGRAM. — *Horses and Stables.* By Major-General Sir F. Fitzwygram, Bart. With 39 pages of Illustrations. 8vo. 10s. 6d.

FOX.—*The Early History of Charles James Fox.* By the Right Hon. G. O. Trevelyan, M.P. Library Edition, 8vo. 18s. Cabinet Edition, cr. 8vo. 6s.

FRANCIS.—*A Book on Angling*; or, Treatise on the Art of Fishing in every branch; including full Illustrated Lists of Salmon Flies. By Francis Francis. Post 8vo. Portrait and Plates, 15s.

FREEMAN.—*Works by E. A. Freeman, D.C.L.*

The Historical Geography of Europe. With 65 Maps. 2 vols. 8vo. 31s. 6d.

Some Impressions of the United States. Crown 8vo. 6s.

FRENCH. — *Nineteen Centuries of Drink in England,* a History. By Richard Valpy French, D.C.L. LL.D. F.S.A.; Author of 'The History of Toasting' &c. Crown 8vo. 10s. 6d.

FROUDE.—*Works by James A. Froude, M.A.*

The History of England, from the Fall of Wolsey to the Defeat of the Spanish Armada. Cabinet Edition, 12 vols. cr. 8vo. £3. 12s. Popular Edition, 12 vols. cr. 8vo. £2. 2s.

Short Studies on Great Subjects. 4 vols. crown 8vo. 24s.

The English in Ireland in the Eighteenth Century. 3 vols. crown 8vo. 18s.

Thomas Carlyle, a History of the first Forty Years of his Life, 1795 to 1835. 2 vols. 8vo. 32s.

Thomas Carlyle, a History of His Life in London from 1834 to his death in 1881. By James A. Froude, M.A. with Portrait engraved on steel. 2 vols. 8vo. 32s.

GANOT.—*Works by Professor Ganot.* Translated by E. Atkinson, Ph.D. F.C.S.

Elementary Treatise on Physics, for the use of Colleges and Schools. With 5 Coloured Plates and 898 Woodcuts. Large crown 8vo. 15s.

Natural Philosophy for General Readers and Young Persons. With 2 Plates and 471 Woodcuts. Crown 8vo. 7s. 6d.

GARDINER.—*Works by Samuel Rawson Gardiner, LL.D.*

History of England, from the Accession of James I. to the Outbreak of the Civil War, 1603-1642. Cabinet Edition, thoroughly revised. 10 vols. crown 8vo. price 6s. each.

Outline of English History, B.C. 55–A.D. 1880. With 96 Woodcuts, fcp. 8vo. 2s. 6d.

*** For Professor Gardiner's other Works, *see* 'Epochs of Modern History,' p. 9.

GARROD. — *Works by Alfred Baring Garrod, M.D. F.R.S.*

A Treatise on Gout and Rheumatic Gout (Rheumatoid Arthritis). With 6 Plates, comprising 21 Figures (14 Coloured), and 27 Illustrations engraved on Wood. 8vo. 21s.

The Essentials of Materia Medica and Therapeutics. Revised and edited, under the supervision of the Author, by E. B. Baxter, M.D. F.R.C.P. Professor of Materia Medica and Therapeutics in King's College, London. Crown 8vo. 12s. 6d.

GOETHE. — *Faust.* Translated by T. E. Webb, LL.D. Reg. Prof. of Laws and Public Orator in the Univ. of Dublin. 8vo. 12s. 6d.

Faust. A New Translation, chiefly in Blank Verse; with a complete Introduction and Copious Notes. By James Adey Birds, B.A. F.G.S. Large crown 8vo. 12s. 6d.

Faust. The German Text, with an English Introduction and Notes for Students. By Albert M. Selss, M.A. Ph.D. Crown 8vo. 5s.

GOODEVE. — *Works by T. M. Goodeve, M.A.*

Principles of Mechanics. With 253 Woodcuts. Crown 8vo. 6s.

The Elements of Mechanism. With 342 Woodcuts. Crown 8vo. 6s.

GRANT. — *Works by Sir Alexander Grant, Bart. LL.D. D.C.L. &c.*

The Story of the University of Edinburgh during its First Three Hundred Years. With numerous Illustrations. 2 vols. 8vo. 36s.

The Ethics of Aristotle. The Greek Text illustrated by Essays and Notes. 2 vols. 8vo. 32s.

GREVILLE. — *Journal of the Reigns of King George IV. and King William IV.* By the late C. C. F. Greville. Edited by H. Reeve, C.B. 3 vols. 8vo. 36s.

GRIMSTON. — *The Hon. Robert Grimston:* a Sketch of his Life. By Frederick Gale. With Portrait. Crown 8vo. 10s. 6d.

GRAY. — *Anatomy, Descriptive and Surgical.* By Henry Gray, F.R.S. late Lecturer on Anatomy at St. George's Hospital. With 557 large Woodcut Illustrations; those in the First Edition after Original Drawings by Dr. Carter, from Dissections made by the Author and Dr. Carter; the additional Drawings in the Second and subsequent Editions by Dr. Westmacott, and other Demonstrators of Anatomy. Re-edited by T. Pickering Pick, Surgeon to St. George's Hospital. Royal 8vo. 30s.

GWILT. — *An Encyclopædia of Architecture,* Historical, Theoretical, and Practical. By Joseph Gwilt, F.S.A. Illustrated with more than 1,100 Engravings on Wood. Revised, with Alterations and Considerable Additions, by Wyatt Papworth. Additionally illustrated with nearly 400 Wood Engravings by O. Jewitt, and nearly 200 other Woodcuts. 8vo. 52s. 6d.

GROVE. — *The Correlation of Physical Forces.* By the Hon. Sir W. R. Grove, F.R.S. &c. 8vo. 15s.

HALLIWELL-PHILLIPPS. — *Outlines of the Life of Shakespeare.* By J. O. Halliwell-Phillipps, F.R.S. 8vo. 7s. 6d.

HAMILTON. — *Life of Sir William R. Hamilton,* Kt. LL.D. D.C.L. M.R.I.A. &c. Including Selections from his Poems, Correspondence, and Miscellaneous Writings. By the Rev. R. P. Graves, M.A. Vol. I. 8vo. 15s.

HARTWIG. — *Works by Dr. G. Hartwig.*

The Sea and its Living Wonders. 8vo. with many Illustrations, 10s. 6d.

The Tropical World. With about 200 Illustrations. 8vo. 10s. 6d.

The Polar World; a Description of Man and Nature in the Arctic and Antarctic Regions of the Globe. Maps, Plates, and Woodcuts. 8vo. 10s. 6d.

The Arctic Regions (extracted from the 'Polar World'). 4to. 6d. sewed.

The Subterranean World. With Maps and Woodcuts. 8vo. 10s. 6d.

The Aerial World; a Popular Account of the Phenomena and Life of the Atmosphere. Map, Plates, Woodcuts. 8vo. 10s. 6d.

HARTE.—*ON THE FRONTIER.* Three Stories. By BRET HARTE. 16mo. 1s.

HASSALL.—*WORKS BY ARTHUR HILL HASSALL, M.D.*

FOOD; its Adulterations and the Methods for their Detection. Illustrated. Crown 8vo. 24s.

SAN REMO, climatically and medically considered. With 30 Illustrations. Crown 8vo. 5s.

HAUGHTON.—*SIX LECTURES ON PHYSICAL GEOGRAPHY,* delivered in 1876, with some Additions. By the Rev. SAMUEL HAUGHTON, F.R.S. M.D. D.C.L. With 23 Diagrams. 8vo. 15s.

HAVELOCK.—*MEMOIRS OF SIR HENRY HAVELOCK, K.C.B.* By JOHN CLARK MARSHMAN. Crown 8vo. 3s. 6d.

HAWARD.—*A TREATISE ON ORTHOPÆDIC SURGERY.* By J. WARRINGTON HAWARD, F.R.C.S. Surgeon to St. George's Hospital. With 30 Illustrations engraved on Wood. 8vo. 12s. 6d.

HELMHOLTZ.—*WORKS BY PROFESSOR HELMHOLTZ.*

POPULAR LECTURES ON SCIENTIFIC SUBJECTS. Translated and edited by EDMUND ATKINSON, Ph.D. F.C.S. With a Preface by Professor TYNDALL, F.R.S. and 68 Woodcuts. 2 vols. Crown 8vo. 15s. or separately, 7s. 6d. each.

ON THE SENSATIONS OF TONE AS A PHYSIOLOGICAL BASIS FOR THE THEORY OF MUSIC. Translated by A. J. ELLIS, F.R.S. Second English Edition. Royal 8vo. 21s.

HERSCHEL.—*OUTLINES OF ASTRONOMY.* By Sir J. F. W. HERSCHEL, Bart. M.A. With Plates and Diagrams. Square crown 8vo. 12s.

HEWITT.—*WORKS BY GRAILY HEWITT, M.D.*

THE DIAGNOSIS AND TREATMENT OF DISEASES OF WOMEN, INCLUDING THE DIAGNOSIS OF PREGNANCY. New Edition, in great part re-written and much enlarged, with 211 Engravings on Wood, of which 79 are new in this Edition. 8vo. 24s.

THE MECHANICAL SYSTEM OF UTERINE PATHOLOGY. With 31 Life-size Illustrations prepared expressly for this Work. Crown 4to. 7s. 6d.

HICKSON.—*IRELAND IN THE SEVENTEENTH CENTURY;* or, The Irish Massacres of 1641-2, their Causes and Results. Illustrated by Extracts from the unpublished State Papers, the unpublished MSS. in the Bodleian Library, Lambeth Library, &c. ; a Selection from the unpublished Depositions relating to the Massacres, and the Reports of the Trials in the High Court of Justice, 1652-4, from the unpublished MSS. By MARY HICKSON. With a Preface by J. A. FROUDE, M.A. 2 vols. 8vo. 28s.

HOBART.—*THE MEDICAL LANGUAGE OF ST. LUKE:* a Proof from Internal Evidence that St. Luke's Gospel and the Acts were written by the same person, and that the writer was a Medical Man. By the Rev. W. K. HOBART, LL.D. 8vo. 16s.

HOLMES.—*A SYSTEM OF SURGERY,* Theoretical and Practical, in Treatises by various Authors. Edited by TIMOTHY HOLMES, M.A. Surgeon to St. George's Hospital ; and J. W. HULKE, F.R.S. Surgeon to the Middlesex Hospital. In 3 Volumes, with Coloured Plates and Illustrations on Wood. 3 vols. royal 8vo. price Four Guineas.

HOMER.—*THE ILIAD OF HOMER,* Homometrically translated by C. B. CAYLEY. 8vo. 12s. 6d.

THE ILIAD OF HOMER. The Greek Text, with a Verse Translation, by W. C. GREEN, M.A. Vol. I. Books I.-XII. Crown 8vo. 6s.

HOPKINS.—*CHRIST THE CONSOLER;* a Book of Comfort for the Sick. By ELLICE HOPKINS. Fcp. 8vo. 2s. 6d.

HORSES AND ROADS; or How to Keep a Horse Sound on His Legs. By FREE-LANCE. Crown 8vo. 6s.

HORT.—*THE NEW PANTHEON,* or an Introduction to the Mythology of the Ancients. By W. J. HORT. 18mo. 2s. 6d.

HOWITT.—*VISITS TO REMARKABLE PLACES,* Old Halls, Battle-Fields, Scenes illustrative of Striking Passages in English History and Poetry. By WILLIAM HOWITT. With 80 Illustrations engraved on Wood. Crown 8vo. 7s. 6d.

HULLAH.—*WORKS BY JOHN HULLAH, LL.D.*

COURSE OF LECTURES ON THE HISTORY OF MODERN MUSIC. 8vo. 8s. 6d.

COURSE OF LECTURES ON THE TRANSITION PERIOD OF MUSICAL HISTORY. 8vo. 10s. 6d.

HUME.—*THE PHILOSOPHICAL WORKS OF DAVID HUME.* Edited by T. H. GREEN, M.A. and the Rev. T. H. GROSE, M.A. 4 vols. 8vo. 56*s*. Or separately, Essays, 2 vols. 28*s*. Treatise on Human Nature. 2 vols. 28*s*.

HUSBAND. — *EXAMINATION QUESTIONS IN ANATOMY, PHYSIOLOGY, BOTANY, MATERIA MEDICA, SURGERY, MEDICINE, MIDWIFERY, AND STATE-MEDICINE.* Arranged by H. A. HUSBAND, M.B. M.C. M.R.C.S. L.S.A. &c. 32mo. 4*s*. 6*d*.

INGELOW.—*POETICAL WORKS OF JEAN INGELOW.* New Edition, reprinted, with Additional Matter, from the 23rd and 6th Editions of the two volumes respectively. With 2 Vignettes. 2 vols. Fcp. 8vo. 12*s*.

IN THE OLDEN TIME.—A Novel. By the Author of 'Mademoiselle Mori.' Crown 8vo. 6*s*.

JAMESON.—*WORKS BY MRS. JAMESON.*
LEGENDS OF THE SAINTS AND MARTYRS. With 19 Etchings and 187 Woodcuts. 2 vols. 31*s*. 6*d*.
LEGENDS OF THE MADONNA, the Virgin Mary as represented in Sacred and Legendary Art. With 27 Etchings and 165 Woodcuts. 1 vol. 21*s*.
LEGENDS OF THE MONASTIC ORDERS. With 11 Etchings and 88 Woodcuts. 1 vol. 21*s*.
HISTORY OF THE SAVIOUR, His Types and Precursors. Completed by Lady EASTLAKE. With 13 Etchings and 281 Woodcuts. 2 vols. 42*s*.

JEFFERIES.—*WORKS BY RICHARD JEFFERIES.*
THE STORY OF MY HEART: My Autobiography. Crown 8vo. 5*s*.
RED DEER. Crown 8vo. 4*s*. 6*d*.

JOHNSON.—*THE PATENTEE'S MANUAL;* a Treatise on the Law and Practice of Letters Patent, for the use of Patentees and Inventors. By J. JOHNSON and J. H. JOHNSON. 8vo. 10*s*. 6*d*.

JOHNSTON.—*A GENERAL DICTIONARY OF GEOGRAPHY,* Descriptive, Physical, Statistical, and Historical; a complete Gazetteer of the World. By KEITH JOHNSTON. Medium 8vo. 42*s*.

JONES. — *THE HEALTH OF THE SENSES: SIGHT, HEARING, VOICE, SMELL AND TASTE, SKIN;* with Hints on Health, Diet, Education, Health Resorts of Europe, &c. By H. MACNAUGHTON JONES, M.D. Crown 8vo. 3*s*. 6*d*.

JUKES.—*WORKS BY THE REV. ANDREW JUKES.*
THE NEW MAN AND THE ETERNAL LIFE. Crown 8vo. 6*s*.
THE TYPES OF GENESIS. Crown 8vo. 7*s*. 6*d*.
THE SECOND DEATH AND THE RESTITUTION OF ALL THINGS. Crown 8vo. 3*s*. 6*d*.
THE MYSTERY OF THE KINGDOM. Crown 8vo. 2*s*. 6*d*.

JUSTINIAN.—*THE INSTITUTES OF JUSTINIAN;* Latin Text, chiefly that of Huschke, with English Introduction, Translation, Notes, and Summary. By THOMAS C. SANDARS, M.A. Barrister-at-Law. 8vo. 18*s*.

KALISCH. — *WORKS BY M. M. KALISCH, M.A.*
BIBLE STUDIES. Part I. The Prophecies of Balaam. 8vo. 10*s*. 6*d*. Part II. The Book of Jonah. 8vo. 10*s*. 6*d*.
COMMENTARY ON THE OLD TESTAMENT; with a New Translation. Vol. I. Genesis, 8vo. 18*s*. or adapted for the General Reader, 12*s*. Vol. II. Exodus, 15*s*. or adapted for the General Reader, 12*s*. Vol. III. Leviticus, Part I. 15*s*. or adapted for the General Reader, 8*s*. Vol. IV. Leviticus, Part II. 15*s*. or adapted for the General Reader, 8*s*.

KANT. — *CRITIQUE OF PRACTICAL REASON,* and other Works on the Theory of Ethics. By EMMANUEL KANT Translated by Thomas Kingsmill Abbott, B.D. With Memoir and Portrait. 8vo. 12*s*. 6*d*.

KELLER.—*THE LAKE DWELLINGS OF SWITZERLAND,* and other Parts of Europe. By Dr. F. KELLER, President of the Antiquarian Association of Zürich. Translated and arranged by JOHN E. LEE, F.S.A. F.G.S. 2 vols. royal 8vo. with 206 Illustrations, 42*s*.

KERL.—*A PRACTICAL TREATISE ON METALLURGY.* By Professor KERL. Adapted from the last German Edition by W. Crookes, F.R.S. &c. and E. Röhrig, Ph.D. 3 vols. 8vo. with 625 Woodcuts, £4. 19*s*.

KILLICK.—*HANDBOOK TO MILL'S SYSTEM OF LOGIC.* By the Rev. A. H. KILLICK, M.A. Crown 8vo. 3*s*. 6*d*.

KOLBE.—*A SHORT TEXT-BOOK OF INORGANIC CHEMISTRY.* By Dr. HERMANN KOLBE. Translated from the German by T. S. HUMPIDGE, Ph.D. With a Coloured Table of Spectra and 66 Illustrations. Crown 8vo. 7*s*. 6*d*.

LANG.—*Works by Andrew Lang, late Fellow of Merton College.*
CUSTOM AND MYTH; Studies of Early Usage and Belief. With 15 Illustrations. Crown 8vo. 7s. 6d.
THE PRINCESS NOBODY: a Tale of Fairyland. After the Drawings by Richard Doyle, printed in colours by Edmund Evans. Post 4to. 5s. boards.

LATHAM.—*Works by Robert G. Latham, M.A. M.D.*
A DICTIONARY OF THE ENGLISH LANGUAGE. Founded on the Dictionary of Dr. JOHNSON. Four vols. 4to. £7.
A DICTIONARY OF THE ENGLISH LANGUAGE. Abridged from Dr. Latham's Edition of Johnson's Dictionary. One Volume. Medium 8vo. 14s.
HANDBOOK OF THE ENGLISH LANGUAGE. Crown 8vo. 6s.

LECKY.—*Works by W. E. H. Lecky.*
HISTORY OF ENGLAND IN THE 18TH CENTURY. 4 vols. 8vo. 1700-1784, £3. 12s.
THE HISTORY OF EUROPEAN MORALS FROM AUGUSTUS TO CHARLEMAGNE. 2 vols. crown 8vo. 16s.
HISTORY OF THE RISE AND INFLUENCE OF THE SPIRIT OF RATIONALISM IN EUROPE. 2 vols. crown 8vo. 16s.
LEADERS OF PUBLIC OPINION IN IRELAND. — Swift, Flood, Grattan, O'Connell. Crown 8vo. 7s. 6d.

LEWES.—THE HISTORY OF PHILOSOPHY, from Thales to Comte. By GEORGE HENRY LEWES. 2 vols. 8vo. 32s.

LEWIS. — ON THE INFLUENCE OF AUTHORITY IN MATTERS OF OPINION. By Sir G. C. LEWIS, Bart. 8vo. 14s.

LINDLEY and MOORE. — THE TREASURY OF BOTANY, or Popular Dictionary of the Vegetable Kingdom. Edited by J. LINDLEY, F.R.S. and T. MOORE, F.L.S. With 274 Woodcuts and 20 Steel Plates. Two Parts, fcp. 8vo. 12s.

LIVEING. — *Works by Robert Liveing, M.A. and M.D. Cantab.*
HANDBOOK ON DISEASES OF THE SKIN. With especial reference to Diagnosis and Treatment. Fcp. 8vo. 5s.
NOTES ON THE TREATMENT OF SKIN DISEASES. 18mo. 3s.
ELEPHANTIASIS GRÆCORUM, OR TRUE LEPROSY. Crown 8vo. 4s. 6d.

LITTLE. – ON IN-KNEE DISTORTION (Genu Valgum) : Its Varieties and Treatment with and without Surgical Operation. By W. J. LITTLE, M.D. Assisted by MUIRHEAD LITTLE, M.R.C.S. With 40 Illustrations. 8vo. 7s. 6d.

LLOYD.—A TREATISE ON MAGNETISM, General and Terrestrial. By H LLOYD, D.D. D.C.L. 8vo. 10s. 6d.

LLOYD.—THE SCIENCE OF AGRICULTURE. By F. J. LLOYD. 8vo. 12s.

LONGMAN.—*Works by William Longman, F.S.A.*
LECTURES ON THE HISTORY OF ENGLAND from the Earliest Times to the Death of King Edward II. Maps and Illustrations. 8vo. 15s.
HISTORY OF THE LIFE AND TIMES OF EDWARD III. With 9 Maps, 8 Plates, and 16 Woodcuts. 2 vols. 8vo. 28s.

LONGMAN.—*Works by Frederick W. Longman, Balliol College, Oxon.*
CHESS OPENINGS. Fcp. 8vo. 2s. 6d.
FREDERICK THE GREAT AND THE SEVEN YEARS' WAR. With 2 Coloured Maps. 8vo. 2s. 6d.
A NEW POCKET DICTIONARY OF THE GERMAN AND ENGLISH LANGUAGES. Square 18mo. 2s. 6d.

LONGMAN'S MAGAZINE. Published Monthly. Price Sixpence. Vols. 1-4, 8vo. price 5s. each.

LONGMORE.—GUNSHOT INJURIES Their History, Characteristic Features Complications, and General Treatment By Surgeon-General T. LONGMORE, C.B F.R.C.S. With 58 Illustrations. 8vo price 31s. 6d.

LOUDON.— *Works by J. C. Loudon F.L.S.*
ENCYCLOPÆDIA OF GARDENING ; the Theory and Practice of Horticulture, Floriculture, Arboriculture, and Landscape Gardening. With 1,000 Woodcuts. 8vo. 21s.
ENCYCLOPÆDIA OF AGRICULTURE ; the Laying-out, Improvement, and Management of Landed Property; the Cultivation and Economy of the Productions of Agriculture. With 1,100 Woodcuts. 8vo. 21s.
ENCYCLOPÆDIA OF PLANTS; the Specific Character, Description, Culture, History, &c. of all Plants found in Great Britain. With 12,000 Woodcuts. 8vo. 42s.

LUBBOCK.—THE ORIGIN OF CIVILIZATION AND THE PRIMITIVE CONDITION OF MAN. By Sir J. LUBBOCK, Bart. M.P. F.R.S. 8vo. Woodcuts, 18s.

LYRA GERMANICA; Hymns Translated from the German by Miss C. WINKWORTH. Fcp. 8vo. 5s.

MACALISTER.—AN INTRODUCTION TO THE SYSTEMATIC ZOOLOGY AND MORPHOLOGY OF VERTEBRATE ANIMALS. By A. MACALISTER, M.D. With 28 Diagrams. 8vo. 10s. 6d.

MACAULAY.— WORKS AND LIFE OF LORD MACAULAY.

HISTORY OF ENGLAND FROM THE ACCESSION OF JAMES THE SECOND:
Student's Edition, 2 vols. crown 8vo. 12s.
People's Edition, 4 vols. crown 8vo. 16s.
Cabinet Edition, 8 vols. post 8vo. 48s.
Library Edition, 5 vols. 8vo. £4.

CRITICAL AND HISTORICAL ESSAYS, with LAYS of ANCIENT ROME, in 1 volume:
Authorised Edition, crown 8vo. 2s. 6d. or 3s. 6d. gilt edges.
Popular Edition, crown 8vo. 2s. 6d.

CRITICAL AND HISTORICAL ESSAYS:
Student's Edition, 1 vol. crown 8vo. 6s.
People's Edition, 2 vols. crown 8vo. 8s.
Cabinet Edition, 4 vols. post 8vo. 24s.
Library Edition, 3 vols. 8vo. 36s.

ESSAYS which may be had separately price 6d. each sewed, 1s. each cloth:
Addison and Walpole.
Frederick the Great.
Croker's Boswell's Johnson.
Hallam's Constitutional History.
Warren Hastings.
The Earl of Chatham (Two Essays).
Ranke and Gladstone.
Milton and Machiavelli.
Lord Bacon.
Lord Clive.
Lord Byron, and The Comic Dramatists of the Restoration.
The Essay on Warren Hastings annotated by S. HALES, 1s. 6d.
The Essay on Lord Clive annotated by H. COURTHOPE-BOWEN, M.A. 2s. 6d.

SPEECHES:
People's Edition, crown 8vo. 3s. 6d.

MISCELLANEOUS WRITINGS
Library Edition, 2 vols. 8vo. Portrait, 21s.
People's Edition, 1 vol. crown 8vo. 4s. 6d.

[*Continued above.*

MACAULAY — WORKS AND LIFE OF LORD MACAULAY —continued.

LAYS OF ANCIENT ROME, &c.
Illustrated by G. Scharf, fcp. 4to. 10s. 6d.
———— Popular Edition, fcp. 4to. 6d. sewed, 1s. cloth.
Illustrated by J. R. Weguelin, crown 8vo. 3s. 6d. cloth extra, gilt edges.
Cabinet Edition, post 8vo. 3s. 6d.
Annotated Edition, fcp. 8vo. 1s. sewed, 1s. 6d. cloth, or 2s. 6d. cloth extra, gilt edges.

SELECTIONS FROM THE WRITINGS OF LORD MACAULAY. Edited, with Occasional Notes, by the Right Hon. G. O. TREVELYAN, M.P. Crown 8vo. 6s.

MISCELLANEOUS WRITINGS AND SPEECHES:
Student's Edition, in ONE VOLUME, crown 8vo. 6s.
Cabinet Edition, including Indian Penal Code, Lays of Ancient Rome, and Miscellaneous Poems, 4 vols. post 8vo. 24s.

THE COMPLETE WORKS OF LORD MACAULAY. Edited by his Sister, Lady TREVELYAN.
Library Edition, with Portrait, 8 vols. demy 8vo. £5. 5s.
Cabinet Edition, 16 vols. post 8vo. £4. 16s.

THE LIFE AND LETTERS OF LORD MACAULAY. By the Right Hon. G. O. TREVELYAN, M.P.
Popular Edition, 1 vol. crown 8vo. 6s.
Cabinet Edition, 2 vols. post 8vo. 12s.
Library Edition, 2 vols. 8vo. with Portrait, 36s.

MACDONALD,— WORKS BY GEORGE MACDONALD, LL.D.

UNSPOKEN SERMONS. Second Series. Crown 8vo. 7s. 6d.

A BOOK OF STRIFE, IN THE FORM OF THE DIARY OF AN OLD SOUL: Poems. 12mo. 6s.

HAMLET. A Study with the Texts of the Folio of 1623. 8vo. 12s.

MACFARREN.—LECTURES ON HARMONY, delivered at the Royal Institution. By Sir G. A. MACFARREN. 8vo. 12s.

MACKENZIE.—ON THE USE OF THE LARYNGOSCOPE IN DISEASES OF THE THROAT; with an Appendix on Rhinoscopy. By MORELL MACKENZIE, M.D. Lond. With 47 Woodcut Illustrations. 8vo. 6s.

MACLEOD.—*WORKS BY HENRY D. MACLEOD, M.A.*

PRINCIPLES OF ECONOMICAL PHILOSOPHY. In 2 vols. Vol. I. 8vo. 15s. Vol. II. PART I. 12s.

THE ELEMENTS OF ECONOMICS. In 2 vols. Vol. I. crown 8vo. 7s. 6d. Vol. II. crown 8vo.

THE ELEMENTS OF BANKING. Crown 8vo. 5s.

THE THEORY AND PRACTICE OF BANKING. Vol. I. 8vo. 12s. Vol. II.

ELEMENTS OF POLITICAL ECONOMY. 8vo. 16s.

ECONOMICS FOR BEGINNERS. 8vo. 2s. 6d.

LECTURES ON CREDIT AND BANKING. 8vo. 5s.

MACNAMARA.—*HIMALAYAN AND SUB-HIMALAYAN DISTRICTS OF BRITISH INDIA*, their Climate, Medical Topography, and Disease Distribution. By F. N. MACNAMARA, M.D. With Map and Fever Chart. 8vo. 21s.

McCULLOCH.—*THE DICTIONARY OF COMMERCE AND COMMERCIAL NAVIGATION* of the late J. R. McCULLOCH, of H.M. Stationery Office. Latest Edition, containing the most recent Statistical Information by A. J. WILSON. 1 vol. medium 8vo. with 11 Maps and 30 Charts, price 63s. cloth, or 70s. strongly half-bound in russia.

MAHAFFY.—*A HISTORY OF CLASSICAL GREEK LITERATURE.* By the Rev. J. P. MAHAFFY, M.A. Crown 8vo. Vol. I. Poets, 7s. 6d. Vol. II. Prose Writers, 7s. 6d.

MALMESBURY.—*MEMOIRS OF AN EX-MINISTER;* an Autobiography. By the Earl of MALMESBURY, G.C.B. Cheap Edition, 1 vol. crown 8vo. 7s. 6d.

MANNING.—*THE TEMPORAL MISSION OF THE HOLY GHOST;* or, Reason and Revelation. By H. E. MANNING, D.D. Cardinal-Archbishop. Crown 8vo. 8s. 6d.

THE MARITIME ALPS AND THEIR SEABOARD. By the Author of 'Vera,' 'Blue Roses,' &c. With 14 Full-page Illustration and 15 Woodcuts in the Text. 8vo. 21s.

MARTINEAU.—*WORKS BY JAMES MARTINEAU, D.D.*

HOURS OF THOUGHT ON SACRED THINGS. Two Volumes of Sermons. 2 vols. crown 8vo. 7s. 6d. each.

ENDEAVOURS AFTER THE CHRISTIAN LIFE. Discourses. Crown 8vo. 7s. 6d.

MAUNDER'S TREASURIES.

BIOGRAPHICAL TREASURY. Reconstructed, revised, and brought down to the year 1882, by W. L. R. CATES. Fcp. 8vo. 6s.

TREASURY OF NATURAL HISTORY; or, Popular Dictionary of Zoology. Fcp. 8vo. with 900 Woodcuts, 6s.

TREASURY OF GEOGRAPHY, Physical, Historical, Descriptive, and Political. With 7 Maps and 16 Plates. Fcp. 8vo. 6s.

HISTORICAL TREASURY: Outlines of Universal History, Separate Histories of all Nations. Revised by the Rev. Sir G. W. COX, Bart. M.A. Fcp. 8vo. 6s.

TREASURY OF KNOWLEDGE AND LIBRARY OF REFERENCE. Comprising an English Dictionary and Grammar, Universal Gazetteer, Classical Dictionary, Chronology, Law Dictionary, &c. Fcp. 8vo. 6s.

SCIENTIFIC AND LITERARY TREASURY: a Popular Encyclopædia of Science, Literature, and Art. Fcp. 8vo. 6s.

MAXWELL.—*DON JOHN OF AUSTRIA;* or, Passages from the History of the Sixteenth Century, 1547-1578. By the late Sir WILLIAM STIRLING MAXWELL, Bart. K.T. With numerous Illustrations engraved on Wood taken from Authentic Contemporary Sources. Library Edition. 2 vols. royal 8vo. 42s.

MAY.—*WORKS BY THE RIGHT HON. SIR THOMAS ERSKINE MAY, K.C.B.*

THE CONSTITUTIONAL HISTORY OF ENGLAND SINCE THE ACCESSION OF GEORGE III. 1760-1870. 3 vols. crown 8vo. 18s.

DEMOCRACY IN EUROPE; a History. 2 vols. 8vo. 32s.

MELVILLE.—*IN THE LENA DELTA:* a Narrative of the Search for LIEUT.-COMMANDER DE LONG and his Companions, followed by an account of the Greely Relief Expedition, and a Proposed Method of reaching the North Pole. By GEORGE W. MELVILLE, Chief Engineer, U.S.N. Edited by MELVILLE PHILIPS. With Maps and Illustrations. 8vo. 14s.

MENDELSSOHN.—*The Letters of Felix Mendelssohn.* Translated by Lady Wallace. 2 vols. crown 8vo. 10s.

MERIVALE.—*Works by the Very Rev. Charles Merivale, D.D. Dean of Ely.*
History of the Romans under the Empire. 8 vols. post 8vo. 48s.
The Fall of the Roman Republic: a Short History of the Last Century of the Commonwealth. 12mo. 7s. 6d.
General History of Rome from B.C. 753 to A.D. 476. Crown 8vo. 7s. 6d.
The Roman Triumvirates. With Maps. Fcp. 8vo. 2s. 6d.

MILES.—*Works by William Miles.*
The Horse's Foot, and How to keep it Sound. Imp. 8vo. 12s. 6d.
Stables and Stable Fittings. Imp. 8vo. with 13 Plates, 15s.
Remarks on Horses' Teeth, addressed to Purchasers. Post 8vo. 1s. 6d.
Plain Treatise on Horse-shoeing. Post 8vo. Woodcuts, 2s. 6d.

MILL.—*Analysis of the Phenomena of the Human Mind.* By James Mill. With Notes, Illustrative and Critical. 2 vols. 8vo. 28s.

MILL.—*Works by John Stuart Mill.*
Principles of Political Economy.
Library Edition, 2 vols. 8vo. 30s.
People's Edition, 1 vol. crown 8vo. 5s.
A System of Logic, Ratiocinative and Inductive.
Library Edition, 2 vols. 8vo. 25s.
People's Edition, crown 8vo. 5s.
On Liberty. Crown 8vo. 1s. 4d.
On Representative Government. Crown 8vo. 2s.
Autobiography, 8vo. 7s. 6d.
Essays on some Unsettled Questions of Political Economy. 8vo. 6s. 6d.
Utilitarianism. 8vo. 5s.
The Subjection of Women. Crown 8vo. 6s.
Examination of Sir William Hamilton's Philosophy. 8vo. 16s.
Dissertations and Discussions. 4 vols. 8vo. £2. 6s. 6d.
Nature, the Utility of Religion, and Theism. Three Essays. 8vo. 10s. 6d.

MILLER.—*Works by W. Allen Miller, M.D. LL.D.*
The Elements of Chemistry, Theoretical and Practical Re-edited, with Additions, by H. Macleod, F.C.S. 3 vols. 8vo.
Part I. Chemical Physics, 16s.
Part II. Inorganic Chemistry, 24s.
Part III. Organic Chemistry, 31s. 6d.
An Introduction to the Study of Inorganic Chemistry. With 71 Woodcuts. Fcp. 8vo. 3s. 6d.

MILLER.—*Readings in Social Economy.* By Mrs. F. Fenwick Miller, Member of the London School Board. Library Edition, crown 8vo. 5s. Cheap Edition for Schools and Beginners, crown 8vo. 2s.

MILLER.—*Wintering in the Riviera;* with Notes of Travel in Italy and France, and Practical Hints to Travellers. By W. Miller. With 12 Illustrations. Post 8vo. 7s. 6d.

MITCHELL.—*A Manual of Practical Assaying.* By John Mitchell, F.C.S. Revised, with the Recent Discoveries incorporated. By W. Crookes, F.R.S. 8vo. Woodcuts, 31s. 6d.

MODERN NOVELIST'S LIBRARY (THE). Price 2s. each boards, or 2s. 6d. each cloth:—
By the Earl of Beaconsfield, K.G.
    Endymion.
  Lothair.   Henrietta Temple.
  Coningsby.   Contarini Fleming, &c.
  Sybil.   Alroy, Ixion, &c.
  Tancred.   The Young Duke, &c.
  Venetia.   Vivian Grey, &c.
By Mrs. Oliphant.
  In Trust.
By James Payn.
  Thicker than Water.
By Bret Harte.
  In the Carquinez Woods.
By Anthony Trollope.
  Barchester Towers.
  The Warden.
By Major Whyte-Melville.
  Digby Grand   Good for Nothing.
  General Bounce. Holmby House.
  Kate Coventry.   The Interpreter.
  The Gladiators. Queen's Maries.
By Various Writers.
  The Atelier du Lys.
  Atherstone Priory.
  The Burgomaster's Family.
  Elsa and her Vulture.
  Mademoiselle Mori.
  The Six Sisters of the Valleys.
  Unawares.

MONCK. — *AN INTRODUCTION TO LOGIC.* By WILLIAM H. STANLEY MONCK, M.A. Prof. of Moral Philos. Univ. of Dublin. Crown 8vo. 5s.

MONSELL. — *SPIRITUAL SONGS FOR THE SUNDAYS AND HOLIDAYS THROUGHOUT THE YEAR.* By J. S. B. MONSELL, LL.D. Fcp. 8vo. 5s. 18mo. 2s.

MOORE. — *THE WORKS OF THOMAS MOORE.*
LALLA ROOKH, TENNIEL'S Edition, with 68 Woodcut Illustrations. Crown 8vo. 10s. 6d.
IRISH MELODIES, MACLISE's Edition, with 161 Steel Plates. Super-royal 8vo. 21s.

MOREHEAD. — *CLINICAL RESEARCHES ON DISEASE IN INDIA.* By CHARLES MOREHEAD, M.D. Surgeon to the Jamsetjee Jeejeebhoy Hospital. 8vo. 21s.

MORELL. — *HANDBOOK OF LOGIC,* adapted especially for the Use of Schools and Teachers. By J. D. MORELL, LL.D. Fcp. 8vo. 2s.

MOZLEY. — *WORKS BY THE REV. THOMAS MOZLEY, M.A.*
REMINISCENCES CHIEFLY OF ORIEL COLLEGE AND THE OXFORD MOVEMENT. 2 vols. crown 8vo. 18s.
REMINISCENCES CHIEFLY OF TOWNS, VILLAGES, AND SCHOOLS. 2 vols. crown 8vo. 18s.

MÜLLER. — *WORKS BY F. MAX MÜLLER, M.A.*
BIOGRAPHICAL ESSAYS. Crown 8vo. 7s. 6d.
SELECTED ESSAYS ON LANGUAGE, MYTHOLOGY AND RELIGION. 2 vols. crown 8vo. 16s.
LECTURES ON THE SCIENCE OF LANGUAGE. 2 vols. crown 8vo. 16s.
INDIA, WHAT CAN IT TEACH US? A Course of Lectures delivered before the University of Cambridge. 8vo. 12s. 6d.
HIBBERT LECTURES ON THE ORIGIN AND GROWTH OF RELIGION, as illustrated by the Religions of India. Crown 8vo. 7s. 6d.
INTRODUCTION TO THE SCIENCE OF RELIGION: Four Lectures delivered at the Royal Institution; with Notes and Illustrations on Vedic Literature, Polynesian Mythology, the Sacred Books of the East, &c. Crown 8vo. 7s. 6d.
A SANSKRIT GRAMMAR FOR BEGINNERS, in Devanagari and Roman Letters throughout. Royal 8vo. 7s. 6d.

MURCHISON. — *WORKS BY CHARLES MURCHISON, M.D. LL.D. F.R.C.S. &c.*
A TREATISE ON THE CONTINUED FEVERS OF GREAT BRITAIN. New Edition, revised by W. CAYLEY, M.D. Physician to the Middlesex Hospital. 8vo. with numerous Illustrations, 25s.
CLINICAL LECTURES ON DISEASES OF THE LIVER, JAUNDICE, AND ABDOMINAL DROPSY. New Edition, revised by T. LAUDER BRUNTON, M.D. 8vo. with numerous Illustrations. 24s.

NEISON. — *THE MOON,* and the Condition and Configurations of its Surface. By E. NEISON, F.R.A.S. With 26 Maps and 5 Plates. Medium 8vo. 31s. 6d.

NEVILE. — *WORKS BY GEORGE NEVILE, M.A.*
HORSES AND RIDING. With 31 Illustrations. Crown 8vo. 6s.
FARMS AND FARMING. With 13 Illustrations. Crown 8vo. 6s.

NEWMAN. — *APOLOGIA PRO VITÂ SUÂ;* being a History of his Religious Opinions by Cardinal NEWMAN. Crown 8vo. 6s.

NEW TESTAMENT (THE) of our Lord and Saviour Jesus Christ. Illustrated with Engravings on Wood after Paintings by the Early Masters chiefly of the Italian School. New and Cheaper Edition. 4to. 21s. cloth extra, or 42s. morocco.

NORTHCOTT. — *LATHES AND TURNING,* Simple, Mechanical, and Ornamental. By W. H. NORTHCOTT. With 338 Illustrations. 8vo. 18s.

OLIPHANT. — *MADAM.* A Novel. By Mrs. OLIPHANT. 3 vols. crown 8vo. 21s.

OWEN. — *THE COMPARATIVE ANATOMY AND PHYSIOLOGY OF THE VERTEBRATE ANIMALS.* By Sir RICHARD OWEN, K.C.B. &c. With 1,472 Woodcuts. 3 vols. 8vo. £3. 13s. 6d.

PAGET. — *WORKS BY SIR JAMES PAGET, BART. F.R.S. D.C.L. &c.*
CLINICAL LECTURES AND ESSAYS. Edited by F. HOWARD MARSH, Assistant-Surgeon to St. Bartholomew's Hospital. 8vo. 15s.
LECTURES ON SURGICAL PATHOLOGY. Delivered at the Royal College of Surgeons of England. Re-edited by the AUTHOR and W. TURNER, M.B. 8vo. with 131 Woodcuts, 21s.

PALEY.—*View of the Evidences of Christianity and Horae Paulinae.* By Archdeacon PALEY. With Notes and an Analysis, and a Selection of Questions. By ROBERT POTTS, M.A. 8vo. 10s. 6d.

PASOLINI.—*Memoir of Count Giuseppe Pasolini, late President of the Senate of Italy.* Compiled by his SON. Translated and Abridged by the DOWAGER-COUNTESS OF DAL-HOUSIE. With Portrait. 8vo. 16s.

PASTEUR.—*Louis Pasteur,* his Life and Labours. By his SON-IN-LAW. Translated from the French by Lady CLAUD HAMILTON. Crown 8vo. 7s. 6d.

PAYEN.—*Industrial Chemistry;* a Manual for Manufacturers and for Colleges or Technical Schools; a Translation of PAYEN's 'Précis de Chimie Industrielle.' Edited by B. H. PAUL. With 698 Woodcuts. Medium 8vo. 42s.

PEEL.—*A Highland Gathering.* By E. LENNOX PEEL. With 31 Illustrations engraved on Wood by E. Whymper from original Drawings by Charles Whymper. Crown 8vo.

PENNELL.—*'From Grave to Gay':* a Volume of Selections from the complete Poems of H. CHOLMONDELEY-PENNELL, Author of 'Puck on Pegasus' &c. Fcp. 8vo. 6s.

PEREIRA.—*Materia Medica and Therapeutics.* By Dr. PEREIRA. Abridged, and adapted for the use of Medical and Pharmaceutical Practitioners and Students. Edited by Professor R. BENTLEY, M.R.C.S. F.L.S. and by Professor T. REDWOOD, Ph.D. F.C.S. With 126 Woodcuts, 8vo. 25s.

PERRY.—*A Popular Introduction to the History of Greek and Roman Sculpture,* designed to Promote the Knowledge and Appreciation of the Remains of Ancient Art. By WALTER C. PERRY. With 268 Illustrations. Square crown 8vo. 31s. 6d.

PIESSE.—*The Art of Perfumery,* and the Methods of Obtaining the Odours of Plants; with Instructions for the Manufacture of Perfumes, &c. By G. W. S. PIESSE, Ph.D. F.C.S. With 96 Woodcuts, square crown 8vo. 21s.

PLATO.—*The Parmenides of Plato;* with Introduction, Analysis, and Notes. By THOMAS MAGUIRE, LL.D. D.Lit. Fellow and Tutor, Trinity College, Dublin. 8vo. 7s. 6d.

POLE.—*The Theory of the Modern Scientific Game of Whist.* By W. POLE, F.R.S. Fcp. 8vo. 2s. 6d.

PROCTOR.—*Works by R. A. Proctor.*

The Sun; Ruler, Light, Fire, and Life of the Planetary System. With Plates and Woodcuts. Crown 8vo. 14s.

The Orbs Around Us; a Series of Essays on the Moon and Planets, Meteors and Comets. With Chart and Diagrams, crown 8vo. 7s. 6d.

Other Worlds than Ours; The Plurality of Worlds Studied under the Light of Recent Scientific Researches. With 14 Illustrations, crown 8vo. 10s. 6d.

The Moon; her Motions, Aspects, Scenery, and Physical Condition. With Plates, Charts, Woodcuts, and Lunar Photographs, crown 8vo. 10s. 6d.

Universe of Stars; Presenting Researches into and New Views respecting the Constitution of the Heavens. With 22 Charts and 22 Diagrams, 8vo. 10s. 6d.

New Star Atlas for the Library, the School, and the Observatory, in 12 Circular Maps (with 2 Index Plates). Crown 8vo. 5s.

Larger Star Atlas for the Library, in 12 Circular Maps, with Introduction and 2 Index Pages. Folio, 15s. or Maps only, 12s. 6d.

Light Science for Leisure Hours; Familiar Essays on Scientific Subjects, Natural Phenomena, &c. 3 vols. crown 8vo. 7s. 6d. each.

Studies of Venus-Transits; an Investigation of the Circumstances of the Transits of Venus in 1874 and 1882. With 7 Diagrams and 10 Plates. 8vo. 5s.

Transits of Venus. A Popular Account of Past and Coming Transits from the First Observed by Horrocks in 1639 to the Transit of 2012. With 20 Lithographic Plates (12 Coloured) and 38 Illustrations engraved on Wood, 8vo. 8s. 6d.

Essays on Astronomy. A Series of Papers on Planets and Meteors, &c. With 10 Plates and 24 Woodcuts, 8vo. 12s.

A Treatise on the Cycloid and on all Forms of Cycloidal Curves, and on the use of Cycloidal Curves in dealing with the Motions of Planets, Comets, &c. &c. With 161 Diagrams. Crown 8vo. 10s. 6d.

Pleasant Ways in Science, with numerous Illustrations. Crown 8vo. 6s.

Myths and Marvels of Astronomy, with numerous Illustrations. Crown 8vo. 6s. [*Continued on next page.*

PROCTOR—*Works by R. A. Proctor*—continued.

THE 'KNOWLEDGE' LIBRARY. Edited by RICHARD A. PROCTOR.

How to Play Whist: with the Laws and Etiquette of Whist; Whist Whittlings, and Forty fully-annotated Games. By 'FIVE OF CLUBS' (R. A. Proctor). Crown 8vo. 5s.

Science Byways. A Series of Familiar Dissertations on Life in Other Worlds. By RICHARD A. PROCTOR. Crown 8vo. 6s.

The Poetry of Astronomy. A Series of Familiar Essays on the Heavenly Bodies. By RICHARD A. PROCTOR. Crown 8vo. 6s.

Nature Studies. Reprinted from *Knowledge.* By GRANT ALLEN, ANDREW WILSON, THOMAS FOSTER, EDWARD CLODD, and RICHARD A. PROCTOR. Crown 8vo. 6s.

Leisure Readings. Reprinted from *Knowledge.* By EDWARD CLODD, ANDREW WILSON, THOMAS FOSTER, A. C. RUNYARD, and RICHARD A. PROCTOR. Crown 8vo. 6s.

The Stars in their Seasons. An Easy Guide to a Knowledge of the Star Groups, in Twelve Large Maps. By RICHARD A. PROCTOR. Imperial 8vo. 5s.

QUAIN'S ELEMENTS of ANATOMY. The Ninth Edition. Re-edited by ALLEN THOMSON, M.D. LL.D. F.R.S.S. L. & E. EDWARD ALBERT SCHÄFER, F.R.S. and GEORGE DANCER THANE. With upwards of 1,000 Illustrations engraved on Wood, of which many are Coloured. 2 vols. 8vo. 18s. each.

QUAIN.—*A Dictionary of Medicine.* Including General Pathology, General Therapeutics, Hygiene, and the Diseases peculiar to Women and Children. By Various Writers. Edited by R. QUAIN, M.D. F.R.S. &c. With 138 Woodcuts. Medium 8vo. 31s. 6d. cloth, or 40s. half-russia; to be had also in 2 vols. 34s. cloth.

RAWLINSON. — *The Seventh Great Oriental Monarchy;* or, a History of the Sassanians. By G. RAWLINSON, M.A. With Map and 95 Illustrations. 8vo. 28s.

READER.—*Voices from Flower-Land,* in Original Couplets. By EMILY E. READER. A Birthday Book and Language of Flowers. 16mo. 2s. 6d. limp cloth; 3s. 6d. roan, gilt edges, or in vegetable vellum, gilt top.

REEVE. — *Cookery and House-keeping;* a Manual of Domestic Economy for Large and Small Families. By Mrs. HENRY REEVE. With 8 Coloured Plates and 37 Woodcuts. Crown 8vo. 7s. 6d.

RICH.—*A Dictionary of Roman and Greek Antiquities.* With 2,000 Woodcuts. By A. RICH, B.A. Crown 8vo. 7s. 6d.

RICHARDSON. — *The Asclepaid:* a Book of Original Research and Observation in the Science, Art, and Literature of Medicine, Preventive and Curative. By BENJAMIN WARD RICHARDSON, M.D. F.R.S. Published Quarterly, price 2s. 6d. Vol. I. 1884. 8vo. 12s. 6d.

RIVERS. — *Works by Thomas Rivers.*

The Orchard-House; or, the Cultivation of Fruit Trees under Glass. Crown 8vo. with 25 Woodcuts, 5s.

The Rose Amateur's Guide. Fcp. 8vo. 4s. 6d.

ROGERS. — *Works by Henry Rogers.*

The Eclipse of Faith; or, a Visit to a Religious Sceptic. Fcp. 8vo. 5s.

Defence of the Eclipse of Faith. Fcp. 8vo. 3s. 6d.

ROGET.—*Thesaurus of English Words and Phrases,* classified and arranged so as to facilitate the expression of Ideas, and assist in Literary Composition. By PETER M. ROGET, M.D. Crown 8vo. 10s. 6d.

RONALDS. — *The Fly-Fisher's Entomology.* By ALFRED RONALDS. With 20 Coloured Plates. 8vo. 14s.

SALTER.—*Dental Pathology and Surgery.* By S. J. A. SALTER, M.B. F.R.S. With 133 Illustrations. 8vo. 18s.

SCOTT.—*The Farm-Valuer.* By JOHN SCOTT. Crown 8vo. 5s.

SEEBOHM.—*Works by Frederick Seebohm.*

The Oxford Reformers—John Colet, Erasmus, and Thomas More, a History of their Fellow-Work. 8vo. 14s.

The English Village Community Examined in its Relations to the Manorial and Tribal Systems, and to the Common or Openfield System of Husbandry. 13 Maps and Plates. 8vo. 16s.

The Era of the Protestant Revolution. With Map. Fcp. 8vo. 2s. 6d.

SENNETT.—*The Marine Steam Engine*; a Treatise for the use of Engineering Students and Officers of the Royal Navy. By RICHARD SENNETT, Chief Engineer, Royal Navy. With 244 Illustrations. 8vo. 21s.

SEWELL.—*Works by ELIZABETH M. SEWELL.*

Stories and Tales. Cabinet Edition, in Eleven Volumes, crown 8vo. 3s. 6d. each, in cloth extra, with gilt edges:—

    Amy Herbert.   Gertrude.
    The Earl's Daughter.
    The Experience of Life.
    A Glimpse of the World.
    Cleve Hall.   Ivors.
    Katharine Ashton.
    Margaret Percival.
    Laneton Parsonage.   Ursula.

Passing Thoughts on Religion. Fcp. 8vo. 3s. 6d.

Preparation for the Holy Communion; the Devotions chiefly from the works of JEREMY TAYLOR. 32mo. 3s.

Night Lessons from Scripture. 32mo. 3s. 6d.

SEYMOUR.—*The Psalms of David*; a new Metrical English Translation of the Hebrew Psalter or Book of Praises. By WILLIAM DIGBY SEYMOUR, Q.C. LL.D. Crown 8vo. 2s. 6d.

SHORT.—*Sketch of the History of the Church of England to the Revolution of* 1688. By T. V. SHORT, D.D. Crown 8vo. 7s. 6d.

SHAKESPEARE.—*Bowdler's Family Shakespeare.* Genuine Edition, in 1 vol. medium 8vo. large type, with 36 Woodcuts, 14s. or in 6 vols. fcp. 8vo. 21s.

Outlines of the Life of Shakespeare. By J. O. HALLIWELL-PHILLIPPS, F.R.S. 8vo. 7s. 6d.

SIMCOX.—*A History of Latin Literature.* By G. A. SIMCOX, M.A. Fellow of Queen's College, Oxford. 2 vols. 8vo. 32s.

SMITH, Rev. SYDNEY.—*The Wit and Wisdom of the Rev. Sydney Smith.* Crown 8vo. 3s. 6d.

SMITH, R. BOSWORTH.—*Carthage and the Carthaginians.* By R. BOSWORTH SMITH, M.A. Maps, Plans, &c. Crown 8vo. 10s. 6d.

SMITH, R. A.—*Air and Rain*; the Beginnings of a Chemical Climatology. By R. A. SMITH, F.R.S. 8vo. 24s.

SMITH, JAMES.—*The Voyage and Shipwreck of St. Paul.* By JAMES SMITH, of Jordanhill. With Dissertations on the Life and Writings of St. Luke, and the Ships and Navigation of the Ancients. With numerous Illustrations. Crown 8vo. 7s. 6d.

SMITH, T.—*A Manual of Operative Surgery on the Dead Body.* By THOMAS SMITH, Surgeon to St. Bartholomew's Hospital. A New Edition, re-edited by W. J. WALSHAM. With 46 Illustrations. 8vo. 12s.

SMITH, H. F.—*The Handbook for Midwives.* By HENRY FLY SMITH, M.B. Oxon. M.R.C.S. late Assistant-Surgeon at the Hospital for Sick Women, Soho Square. With 41 Woodcuts. Crown 8vo. 5s.

SOPHOCLES.—*Sophoclis Tragœdiæ superstites*; recensuit et brevi Annotatione instruxit GULIELMUS LINWOOD, M.A. Ædis Christi apud Oxonienses nuper Alumnus. Editio Quarta, auctior et emendatior. 8vo. 16s.

SOUTHEY.—*The Poetical Works of Robert Southey*, with the Author's last Corrections and Additions. Medium 8vo. with Portrait, 14s.

The Correspondence of Robert Southey with Caroline Bowles. Edited by EDWARD DOWDEN, LL.D. 8vo. Portrait, 14s.

STANLEY.—*A Familiar History of Birds.* By E. STANLEY, D.D. Revised and enlarged, with 160 Woodcuts. Crown 8vo. 6s.

STEEL.—*A Treatise on the Diseases of the Ox*; being a Manual of Bovine Pathology specially adapted for the use of Veterinary Practitioners and Students. By J. H. STEEL, M.R.C.V.S. F.Z.S. With 2 Plates and 116 Woodcuts. 8vo. 15s.

STEPHEN.—*Essays in Ecclesiastical Biography.* By the Right Hon. Sir J. STEPHEN, LL.D. Crown 8vo. 7s. 6d.

STEVENSON.—*The Child's Garden of Poems.* By ROBERT LOUIS STEVENSON. 1 vol. small fcp. 8vo. printed on hand-made paper, 5s.

'STONEHENGE.'—*The Dog in Health and Disease.* By 'STONEHENGE.' With 78 Wood Engravings. Square crown 8vo. 7s. 6d.

The Greyhound. By 'STONEHENGE.' With 25 Portraits of Greyhounds, &c. Square crown 8vo. 15s.

STURGIS.—*My Friends and I.* By JULIAN STURGIS. With Frontispiece. Crown 8vo. 5s.

SULLY.—*Outlines of Psychology*, with Special Reference to the Theory of Education. By JAMES SULLY, M.A. 8vo. 12s. 6d.

SUPERNATURAL RELIGION; an Inquiry into the Reality of Divine Revelation. Complete Edition, thoroughly revised. 3 vols. 8vo. 36s.

SWINBURNE.—*Picture Logic;* an Attempt to Popularise the Science of Reasoning. By A. J. SWINBURNE, B.A. Post 8vo. 5s.

SWINTON.—*The Principles and Practice of Electric Lighting.* By ALAN A. CAMPBELL SWINTON. With 54 Illustrations engraved on Wood Crown 8vo. 5s.

TAYLOR.—*Student's Manual of the History of India*, from the Earliest Period to the Present Time. By Colonel MEADOWS TAYLOR, C.S.I. Crown 8vo. 7s. 6d.

TEXT-BOOKS OF SCIENCE: a Series of Elementary Works on Science, Mechanical and Physical, forming a Series of Text-books of Science, adapted for the use of Students in Public and Science Schools. Fcp. 8vo. fully illustrated with Woodcuts.

Abney's Photography, 3s. 6d.
Anderson's Strength of Materials, 3s. 6d.
Armstrong's Organic Chemistry, 3s. 6d.
Ball's Elements of Astronomy, 6s.
Barry's Railway Appliances, 3s. 6d.
Bauerman's Systematic Mineralogy, 6s.
——— Descriptive Mineralogy, 6s.
Bloxam and Huntington's Metals, 5s.
Glazebrook's Physical Optics, 6s.
Glazebrook and Shaw's Practical Physics, 6s.
Gore's Electro-Metallurgy, 6s.
Griffin's Algebra and Trigonometry, 3s. 6d.
Jenkin's Electricity and Magnetism, 3s. 6d.
Maxwell's Theory of Heat, 3s. 6d.
Merrifield's Technical Arithmetic, 3s. 6d.
Miller's Inorganic Chemistry, 3s. 6d.
Preece and Sivewright's Telegraphy, 5s.
Rutley's Petrology, or Study of Rocks, 4s. 6d.
Shelley's Workshop Appliances, 4s. 6d.
Thomé's Structural and Physiological Botany, 6s.
Thorpe's Quantitative Analysis, 4s. 6d.
Thorpe and Muir's Qualitative Analysis, 3s. 6d.
Tilden's Chemical Philosophy, 3s. 6d. With Answers to Problems, 4s. 6d.
Unwin's Machine Design, 6s.
Watson's Plane and Solid Geometry, 3s. 6d.

TAYLOR.—*The Complete Works of Bishop Jeremy Taylor.* With Life by Bishop Heber. Revised and corrected by the Rev. C. P. EDEN. 10 vols. £5. 5s.

THOMSON.—*An Outline of the Necessary Laws of Thought;* a Treatise on Pure and Applied Logic. By W. THOMSON, D.D. Archbishop of York. Crown 8vo. 6s.

THOMSON'S CONSPECTUS *Adapted to the British Pharmacopœia.* By EDMUND LLOYD BIRKETT, M.D. &c. Latest Edition. 18mo. 6s.

THOMPSON.—*A System of Psychology.* By DANIEL GREENLEAF THOMPSON. 2 vols. 8vo. 36s.

THREE IN NORWAY. By Two of THEM. With a Map and 59 Illustrations on Wood from Sketches by the Authors. Crown 8vo. 6s.

TREVELYAN. — *Works by the Right Hon. G. O. Trevelyan, M.P.*

The Life and Letters of Lord Macaulay. By the Right Hon. G. O. TREVELYAN, M.P.
LIBRARY EDITION, 2 vols. 8vo. 36s.
CABINET EDITION, 2 vols. crown 8vo. 12s.
POPULAR EDITION, 1 vol. crown 8vo. 6s.

The Early History of Charles James Fox. Library Edition, 8vo. 18s. Cabinet Edition, crown 8vo. 6s.

TWISS.—*Works by Sir Travers Twiss.*

The Rights and Duties of Nations, considered as Independent Communities in Time of War. 8vo. 21s.

On the Rights and Duties of Nations in Time of Peace. 8vo. 15s.

TYNDALL.—*Works by John Tyndall, F.R.S. &c.*

Fragments of Science. 2 vols. crown 8vo. 16s.

Heat a Mode of Motion. Crown 8vo. 12s.

Sound. With 264 Woodcuts. Crown 8vo. 10s. 6d.

Essays on the Floating-Matter of the Air in relation to Putrefaction and Infection. With 24 Woodcuts. Crown 8vo. 7s. 6d.

[Continued on next page.

TYNDALL.—*Works by John Tyndall, F.R.S. &c.*—continued.

Lectures on Light, delivered in America in 1872 and 1873. With Portrait, Plate, and Diagrams. Crown 8vo. 7s. 6d.

Lessons in Electricity at the Royal Institution, 1875-76. With 58 Woodcuts. Crown 8vo. 2s. 6d.

Notes of a Course of Seven Lectures on Electrical Phenomena and Theories, delivered at the Royal Institution. Crown 8vo. 1s. sewed, 1s. 6d. cloth.

Notes of a Course of Nine Lectures on Light, delivered at the Royal Institution. Crown 8vo. 1s. sewed, 1s. 6d. cloth.

Faraday as a Discoverer. Fcp. 8vo. 3s. 6d.

URE.—*A Dictionary of Arts, Manufactures, and Mines.* By Dr. URE. Seventh Edition, re-written and enlarged by R. HUNT, F.R.S. With 2,064 Woodcuts. 4 vols. medium 8vo. £7. 7s.

VERNEY.—*Chess Eccentricities.* Including Four-handed Chess, Chess for Three, Six, or Eight Players, Round Chess for Two, Three, or Four Players, and several different ways of Playing Chess for Two Players. By Major GEORGE HOPE VERNEY. Crown 8vo. 10s. 6d.

VILLE.—*On Artificial Manures,* their Chemical Selection and Scientific Application to Agriculture. By GEORGES VILLE. Translated and edited by W. CROOKES, F.R.S. With 31 Plates. 8vo. 21s.

VIRGIL.—*Publi Vergili Maronis Bucolica, Georgica, Æneis;* the Works of VIRGIL, Latin Text, with English Commentary and Index. By B. H. KENNEDY, D.D. Crown 8vo. 10s. 6d.

The Æneid of Virgil. Translated into English Verse. By J. CONINGTON, M.A. Crown 8vo. 9s.

The Poems of Virgil. Translated into English Prose. By JOHN CONINGTON, M.A. Crown 8vo. 9s.

WALKER.—*The Correct Card;* or, How to Play at Whist; a Whist Catechism. By Major A. CAMPBELL-WALKER, F.R.G.S. Fcp. 8vo. 2s. 6d.

WALPOLE.—*History of England from the Conclusion of the Great War in 1815 to the Year 1841.* By SPENCER WALPOLE. 3 vols. 8vo. £2. 14s.

WATSON.—*Lectures on the Principles and Practice of Physic,* delivered at King's College, London, by Sir THOMAS WATSON, Bart. M.D. With Two Plates. 2 vols. 8vo. 36s.

WATTS.—*A Dictionary of Chemistry and the Allied Branches of other Sciences.* Edited by HENRY WATTS, F.R.S. 9 vols. medium 8vo. £15. 2s. 6d.

WEBB.—*Celestial Objects for Common Telescopes.* By the Rev. T. W. WEBB, M.A. Map, Plate, Woodcuts. Crown 8vo. 9s.

WEBB.—*The Veil of Isis:* a Series of Essays on Idealism. By THOMAS W. WEBB, LL.D. 8vo. 10s. 6d.

WELLINGTON.—*Life of the Duke of Wellington.* By the Rev. G. R. GLEIG, M.A. Crown 8vo. Portrait, 6s.

WEST.—*Lectures on the Diseases of Infancy and Childhood.* By CHARLES WEST, M.D. &c. Founder of, and formerly Physician to, the Hospital for Sick Children. 8vo. 18s.

WHATELY.—*English Synonyms.* By E. JANE WHATELY. Edited by her Father, R. WHATELY, D.D. Fcp. 8vo. 3s.

WHATELY.—*Works by R. Whately, D.D.*

Elements of Logic. 8vo. 10s. 6d. Crown 8vo. 4s. 6d.

Elements of Rhetoric. 8vo. 10s. 6d. Crown 8vo. 4s. 6d.

Lessons on Reasoning. Fcp. 8vo. 1s. 6d.

Bacon's Essays, with Annotations. 8vo. 10s. 6d.

WHITE.—*A Concise Latin-English Dictionary,* for the Use of Advanced Scholars and University Students. By the Rev. J. T. WHITE, D.D. Royal 8vo. 12s.

WHITE & RIDDLE.—*A Latin-English Dictionary.* By J. T. WHITE, D.D. Oxon. and J. J. E. RIDDLE, M.A. Oxon. Founded on the larger Dictionary of Freund. Royal 8vo. 21s.

WILCOCKS.—THE SEA FISHERMAN. Comprising the Chief Methods of Hook and Line Fishing in the British and other Seas, and Remarks on Nets, Boats, and Boating. By J. C. WILCOCKS. Profusely Illustrated. New and Cheaper Edition, much enlarged, crown 8vo. 6s.

WILLICH.—POPULAR TABLES for giving Information for ascertaining the value of Lifehold, Leasehold, and Church Property, the Public Funds, &c. By CHARLES M. WILLICH. Edited by MONTAGU MARRIOTT. Crown 8vo. 10s.

WITT.—WORKS BY PROF. WITT, Head Master of the Alstadt Gymnasium, Königsberg. Translated from the German by FRANCES YOUNGHUSBAND.

THE TROJAN WAR. With a Preface by the Rev. W. G. RUTHERFORD, M.A. Head-Master of Westminster School. Crown 8vo. 2s.

MYTHS OF HELLAS; or, Greek Tales. Crown 8vo. 3s. 6d.

THE WANDERINGS OF ULYSSES. Crown 8vo. 3s. 6d.

WOOD.—WORKS BY REV. J. G. WOOD.

HOMES WITHOUT HANDS; a Description of the Habitations of Animals, classed according to the Principle of Construction. With about 140 Vignettes on Wood. 8vo. 10s. 6d.

INSECTS AT HOME; a Popular Account of British Insects, their Structure, Habits, and Transformations. 8vo. Woodcuts, 10s. 6d.

INSECTS ABROAD; a Popular Account of Foreign Insects, their Structure, Habits, and Transformations. 8vo. Woodcuts, 10s. 6d.

BIBLE ANIMALS; a Description of every Living Creature mentioned in the Scriptures. With 112 Vignettes. 8vo. 10s. 6d.

STRANGE DWELLINGS; a Description of the Habitations of Animals, abridged from 'Homes without Hands.' With Frontispiece and 60 Woodcuts. Crown 8vo. 5s. Popular Edition, 4to. 6d.

OUT OF DOORS; a Selection of Original Articles on Practical Natural History. With 6 Illustrations. Crown 8vo. 5s.

[Continued above.

WOOD. — WORKS BY REV. J. WOOD—continued.

COMMON BRITISH INSECTS: BEETLES, MOTHS, AND BUTTERFLIES. Cr. 8vo. with 130 Woodcuts, 3s. 6d.

PETLAND REVISITED. With numerous Illustrations, drawn specially Miss Margery May, engraved on W. by G. Pearson. Crown 8vo. 7s. 6d.

WYLIE.—HISTORY OF ENGLAND UNDER HENRY THE FOURTH. By JAMES HAMILTON WYLIE, M.A. one of H Majesty's Inspectors of Schools. Vol. crown 8vo. 10s. 6d.

WYLIE.—LABOUR, LEISURE, AND LUXURY; a Contribution to Present Practical Political Economy. By ALEXANDER WYLIE, of Glasgow. Crown 8vo. 6s.

YONGE.—THE NEW ENGLISH-GREEK LEXICON, containing all the Greek words used by Writers of good authority. By CHARLES DUKE YONGE, M.A. 4to. 21s.

YOUATT. — WORKS BY WILLIAM YOUATT.

THE HORSE. Revised and enlarged by W. WATSON, M.R.C.V.S. 8vo. Woodcuts, 7s. 6d.

THE DOG. Revised and enlarged. 8vo. Woodcuts. 6s.

ZELLER. — WORKS BY DR. E. ZELLER.

HISTORY OF ECLECTICISM IN GREEK PHILOSOPHY. Translated by SARAH F. ALLEYNE. Crown 8vo. 10s. 6d.

THE STOICS, EPICUREANS, AND SCEPTICS. Translated by the Rev. O. J. REICHEL, M.A. Crown 8vo. 15s.

SOCRATES AND THE SOCRATIC SCHOOLS. Translated by the Rev. O. J. REICHEL, M.A. Crown 8vo. 10s. 6d.

PLATO AND THE OLDER ACADEMY. Translated by S. FRANCES ALLEYNE and ALFRED GOODWIN, B.A. Crown 8vo. 18s.

THE PRE-SOCRATIC SCHOOLS; a History of Greek Philosophy from the Earliest Period to the time of Socrates. Translated by SARAH F. ALLEYNE. 2 vols. crown 8vo. 30s.

www.ingramcontent.com/pod-product-compliance
Lightning Source LLC
Chambersburg PA
CBHW021632020526
44117CB00048B/635